ADVANCES IN DIGITAL ARCHAEOLOGY

sidestonepress

ADVANCES IN DIGITAL ARCHAEOLOGY

Proceedings of the 2023 conference Computer Applications and Quantitative Methods in Archaeology – 50 years of synergy

J.W.H.P. **VERHAGEN**, J. **WAAGEN**, A. **BRANDSEN**, A. **QUEFFELEC**, R.M. **VISSER** & D. **TAELMAN** (EDS)

Published by Sidestone Press, Leiden
www.sidestone.com
E-mail: info @ sidestone.nl
Phone: (+31)(0)71-7370131

Imprint: Sidestone Press Academics
This book was peer-reviewed through PCI Archaeology (https://archaeo.peercommunityin.org/PCIArchaeology).

Peer-reviewed & recommended by PCI Archaeo

Lay-out & cover design: Sidestone Press
Cover image: Louise Tharandt - 3D timeline reconstruction: the changes of the megalithic tomb Düwelsteene; background Rian Adi Setyo, stock.adobe.com

ISBN 978-94-6427-135-5 (softcover)
ISBN 978-94-6427-136-2 (hardcover)
ISBN 978-94-6427-137-9 (PDF e-book)

DOI: 10.59641/d4g5a1b2c3

Contents

Preface

This proceedings volume contains the written contributions that were submitted after being presented at the CAA2023 conference, held from 3-6 April 2023 in Amsterdam. This 50th anniversary conference of CAA was organised in a challenging period, shortly after the COVID-19 pandemic. Initially, we had planned to organise the Amsterdam conference in 2022 to celebrate the exact 50th anniversary of CAA. However, as the CAA2020 conference in Oxford had to be cancelled and rescheduled as CAA2022 in August 2022, the 50th-anniversary conference was postponed by one year. The conference theme chosen for CAA2023 was "50 Years of Synergy", to reflect that the strength of digital archaeology is in how it combines computational approaches and archaeological research questions and has thus pushed the field forward for already half a century.

Covid implied that we had to deal with many uncertainties regarding the availability and affordability of facilities as well as potential travel restrictions, which led to a conference edition that, despite running very smoothly, was also much more complicated to organise than expected. We were therefore very happy to welcome more than 450 participants from 32 countries to the conference, who were able to choose from 339 presentations spread over 42 sessions (Brandsen et al. 2023; Figure 0.1). We want to thank all conference participants, the CAA Executive Steering Committee, the CAA Scientific Committee, and all volunteers who helped during the conference for their support in making the conference a success. Once again, it has been shown that the field of digital and computational archaeology is not only a very exciting one from a scientific perspective but also one that is characterised by a strong sense of community.

For the current proceedings, we have decided to explore a different workflow compared to previous conferences, as the timely publication of CAA Conference Proceedings has proved to be a major obstacle in the recent past. Long review times, a lack of workforce in the organising teams, and the requirement to wait for the last paper to be typeset before a final volume could be published, led to frustration among authors and editors alike about the delays in publication, which in some cases ran into four or five years. In the current academic climate, this is frankly unacceptable. Not only does it hinder the spread of novel research results in the fast-moving field of digital and computational archaeology, but it also has negative repercussions for the careers of individual researchers.

In preparing for the CAA2023 conference, we decided, in consultation with the CAA International Executive Steering Committee, to opt for preprint reviews in collaboration with PCI Archaeology (https://archaeo.peercommunityin.org). Written papers could be uploaded as a preprint on Zenodo in the CAA2023 Community (https://zenodo.org/communities/caa2023), after which they were subjected to Open Peer Review, using the PCI Archaeology review management system. Conference session chairs were appointed as Recommenders, who were tasked with approaching reviewers from the CAA Review College to assess the submitted contributions, ask for revisions where necessary, and provide a recommendation once the preprint had been accepted. Once the recommendation was written, authors could either leave the paper as a preprint on Zenodo, opt for inclusion in the current Proceedings volume free of charge, or find a different outlet, for example,

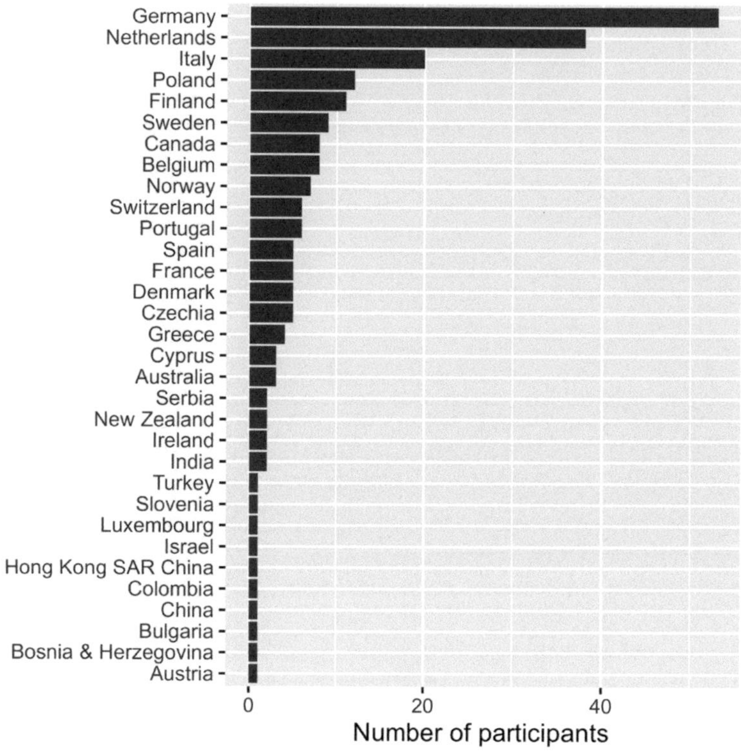

Bar chart of CAA2023 participants per country.

with a PCI-friendly journal such as the Journal for Computer Applications in Archaeology (JCAA; https://journal.caa-international.org), or PCI's own journal (https://www.pci.org/PCI/PCI/Publications/PCI_Journal/PCI_Journal.aspx). In the end, 46 papers were submitted, of which 26 have been included in the current volume and 7 appeared in JCAA (Câmara et al. 2024, Diamanti et al. 2024, Landauer et al. 2025, Lien-Talks 2024, Paukkonnen 2023, Raykovska et al. 2024, Stephan 2024).

As this was the first time we used this procedure, we encountered some teething problems, especially in making it clear to contributors, recommenders and reviewers what was expected of them. Nevertheless, we managed to finalise all the reviewing within a year of the conference and could provide final recommendations shortly afterwards. In this process, we were immensely helped by Alain Queffelec, who – with his experience as founder and manager of PCI Archaeology – was able to keep everything on track and help with any queries of authors and editors alike. We would also like to thank all the reviewers and recommenders for their time and effort in reviewing and recommending the papers.

The papers in this volume are organised alphabetically by first author, listing the session of the CAA2023 conference in which the paper was presented. Not all sessions resulted in submissions. An overview of all sessions and presentations at the conference is still available at https://2023.caaconference.org. Also, a single paper (Chapter 19) is included that was presented at the CAA2022 conference in Oxford, which, due to its modest attendance, did not have enough contributions to warrant its own proceedings.

The editors:
Philip Verhagen
Jitte Waagen
Alex Brandsen
Ronald Visser
Devi Taelman

References

Brandsen, A., P. Hacıgüzeller, L. van der Knaap, D. Taelman, P. Verhagen, R. Visser, and J. Waagen (eds). 2023. *Book of Abstracts. CAA 2023: 50 Years of Synergy*. Zenodo. DOI: 10.5281/ZENODO.7930991

Câmara, A., de Almeida, A. and Oliveira, J. (2024) 'Transforming the CIDOC-CRM Model Into a Megalithic Monument Property Graph', *Journal of Computer Applications in Archaeology*, 7(1), p. 213-224. DOI: 10.5334/jcaa.151

Diamanti, E., Yip, M., Stahl, A. and Ødegård, Ø. (2024) 'Advancing Data Quality of Marine Archaeological Documentation Using Underwater Robotics: From Simulation Environments to Real-World Scenarios', *Journal of Computer Applications in Archaeology*, 7(1), p. 153-169. DOI: 10.5334/jcaa.147

Landauer, J., Maddison, S., Fontana, G. and Posluschny, A.G. (2025) 'Archaeological Site Detection: Latest Results from a Deep Learning Based Europe Wide Hillfort Search', *Journal of Computer Applications in Archaeology*, 8(1), p. 42-58. DOI: 10.5334/jcaa.178

Lien-Talks, A. (2024) 'How FAIR Is Bioarchaeological Data: With a Particular Emphasis on Making Archaeological Science Data Reusable', *Journal of Computer Applications in Archaeology*, 7(1), p. 246-261. DOI: 10.5334/jcaa.154

Paukkonen, N. (2023) 'Towards a Mobile 3D Documentation Solution. Video-Based Photogrammetry and iPhone 12 Pro as Fieldwork Documentation Tools', *Journal of Computer Applications in Archaeology*, 6(1), p. 143-154. DOI: 10.5334/jcaa.135

Raykovska, M., Jones, K., Klecherova, H., Alexandrov, S., Petkov, N., Hristova, T. and Ivanov, G. (2024) 'Implementing Digital Documentation Techniques for Archaeological Artifacts to Develop a Virtual Exhibition: The Necropolis of Baley Collection', *Journal of Computer Applications in Archaeology*, 7(1), p. 202-212. DOI: 10.5334/jcaa.152

Stephan, R. (2024) 'Student Feedback On Archaeogaming: Perspectives from a Classics Classroom', *Journal of Computer Applications in Archaeology*, 7(1), p. 126-133. DOI: 10.5334/jcaa.139

1 Cultural Significance Assessment of Archaeological Sites for Heritage Management

From Text of Spatial Networks of Meanings

Yael Alef
Technion – Israel Institute of Technology
yaelalef@technion.ac.il
ORCID 0000-0003-3278-2644

Yuval Shafriri
EdTec & HeriTech Consultant
yuval.shafriri@gmail.com

Abstract

This study examines the integration of Context-Based Significance Assessment (CBSA) with semantic technologies into digital ARM inventories, as part of the shift from a material-based towards a values-based approach in Archaeological Resource Management (ARM). We uncovered the "context-effect" phenomenon through qualitative analysis of inventory records from 66 ancient synagogues in northern Israel, with the Huqoq Synagogue as a detailed case study. This phenomenon shows how a site's cultural significance is significantly enhanced by its reciprocal relationships with various contextual elements – such as artifacts, narratives, and traditions – which, in turn, gain added value through their interconnections, weaving a spatial network of meaning. Using knowledge graph visualisation, we demonstrate the applications of semantic technologies in representing these contextual elements and their interconnected values. This marks a shift from the traditional inventory as lists of sites to a network of heritage entities. The Huqoq case study provides insights into the broader implications for ARM and the practical challenges of modelling contextual relationships within knowledge graphs. The paper briefly explores the potential of generative AI to address some of these challenges and outlines a research agenda for CBSA integration in ARM inventories. Overall, the study provides insights into the transformative impact of semantic technologies in CBSA and ARM inventories and offers a potential pathway to enhance values-based management decision-making.

Keywords: Archaeological Resource Management (ARM); Heritage Inventory; Semantic Technologies; Knowledge-Graph (KG); Context-effect; Conservation; Ancient synagogues; Israel; Linked Data; Significance Assessment

1.1 Introduction

The shift in Archaeological Resource Management (ARM) from material-based towards a values-based approach has placed the cultural values of sites at the core of decisions regarding their future. Accordingly, the question changed from "How significant is

In *Advances in Digital Archaeology. Proceedings of the 2023 conference Computer Applications and Quantitative Methods in Archaeology – 50 years of synergy*, edited by J.W.H.P. Verhagen, J. Waagen, A. Brandsen, A. Queffelec, R.M. Visser and D. Taelman, 13–30. Leiden: Sidestone Press.

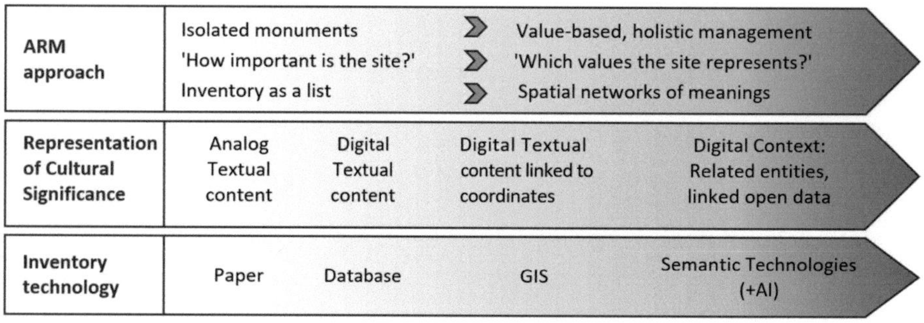

Figure 1.1. Interrelationships of ARM, digital transformation, and CBSA representations.

the site?" to "What values does the site represent, and where do they come from?" (Avrami and Mason 2019). ARM Inventories, which have become widespread in recent years, are a central tool in ARM decision-making concerning research, protection, and conservation of archaeological sites (Hansen and Myers 2024). The idea of significance, which forms the basis for values-based heritage practice, was developed to help decide which sites should be protected and included in these inventories. Yet, "...assessing significance has proven to be one of the most difficult chores facing the conservation archaeologist..." (Schiffer and Gumerman 1977, 240). The result is often either a lack of values-based information or inadequate representation in many current ARM digital inventories.

A usable and accurate inventory is fundamental for effective heritage management, as Sullivan argues (1993). Therefore, given the greater weight of values in ARM, it is important to adapt the inventory knowledge model to enhance understanding and communication of these values. In light of the significance assessment's central role in ARM, exploring how emerging technologies may facilitate both the site assessment and the representation of significance in inventories is worthwhile. Despite the availability of spatial and semantic tools to some extent, there are still no guiding principles to ensure their informed use in cultural evaluation. Thus, the main question is: What are the building blocks of the site values, and how can these be represented with contemporary technologies in ARM inventories?

We will explore this question by laying the background for the shift in ARM inventory, particularly regarding the information requirements for cultural evaluation and its potential implication on ARM practices. Based on this background, an inventory of ancient synagogues in the Galilee is used as a case study. This demonstrates the representation of significance assessment within the ARM inventory. Finally, we will illustrate the findings by analysing a single inventory record: the Huqoq synagogue significance assessment. This will allow us to discuss how contexts can be used as information entities to form the building blocks of site values and support values-based decision-making.

Note that we are not trying to identify or describe the values of the sites or why and by whom they are articulated. Instead, we intend to demonstrate how contemporary technologies can construct and represent this information category. Furthermore, we will argue that technologies capable of implementing context as entities could support the shift in current ARM approaches towards integrated conservation, a more holistic approach, and system thinking.

1.1.1 ARM Inventories, Significance Assessment, and Digital Transformation

The shift from managing isolated monuments to a holistic values-based approach parallels the changing technologies and media. Traditionally, significance assessments were written on paper records lists. With the development of digital technologies, these records transformed into text fields. When Geographic Information Systems came along, these records were connected to geographical coordinates (see Figure 1.1).

Over the past two decades, semantic technologies, including Knowledge Graphs (KGs) stored in Graph Databases and Open Linked Data, have been increasingly recognised for their potential to transform heritage data management (Alam et al. 2022)[1]. These technologies facilitate the digitisation of records and unlock deeper insights through spatial and semantic representations. By allowing the exploration of relationships among heritage entities, they can enhance machine interoperability and contribute to a richer, semantic web of cultural narratives. Examples of these technologies are Wikidata and the CIDOC-CRM (Le Boeuf et al. 2018) ontology, which offer enhanced semantic insights across various domains within cultural heritage and digital humanities. Some current research and implementations also include heritage archives and collections (Alba et al. 2023; Li and Bikakis 2023) and archaeological data management (ARIADNE 2016; Lombardo et al. 2022; McKeague et al. 2020). These technologies support engagement in museums, the documentation of intangible heritage (Diaz-Mendoza et al. 2023), and the enrichment of place-based education (Ruiz-Calleja et al. 2022). They also play a significant role in web cultural heritage media by improving storytelling

1 The Semantic Web Journal, for example, dedicates a special issue each year for cultural heritage.

and the representation of relationships between artifacts, artists, and other heritage objects, as demonstrated in projects like Google Art.[2]

Regarding ARM inventories, integrating semantic technologies with CBSA has the potential to offer valuable insights not only from individual site records but also from extensive datasets. Particularly in the field of cultural evaluation, semantic layers may enable more nuanced representations of site values and support a dynamic, interconnected understanding of heritage beyond traditional cataloguing methods (Li and Bikakis 2023). However, the integration of semantic tools in the ARM domain is still in its early stages, and the shift is not yet complete. Most ARM inventories still resemble their analogue medium and do not exploit current capabilities to compute resource interconnections. This phenomenon is common when transitioning to a new medium, as McLuhan observes in his canonical book Understanding Media (1964). Most digital ARM inventories today still function primarily as enhanced lists of sites, offering improved online accessibility but overlooking the network of relations and meanings that underlie each site's cultural significance. One exceptional example is the Arches Platform, which is also used in this paper. It offers semantic features and a context-oriented approach (Dalgity et al. 2022), which already has some advanced project implementations.[3]

Looking ahead, the potential of using knowledge graphs to refine our approach to significance assessment offers promising yet underexplored avenues. This evolution could transform inventory systems into more effective tools for values-based management (Carlisle et al. 2014). To "understand the medium" of representing CBSA as a knowledge graph, we first need to discuss the role of CBSA information in the ARM inventories.

1.1.2 Significance Assessment in the ARM Knowledge Model

"Managing heritage is about managing values" writes Clark (2014, 70), capturing the essence of the values-based heritage management approach formalised in the Burra Charter (Australia ICOMOS 2013). In heritage practice, "values" are defined as the meanings ascribed to an attribute by individuals, communities, and nation-states (Ireland et al. 2020). As a mechanism for public accountability, categories of values have been developed (Darvill 1995; Fredheim and Khalaf 2016). This research adopts the contemporary distinctions between heritage-intrinsic and societal-instrumental perspectives on values (Avrami and Mason 2019; Wijesuriya et al. 2013). It specifically focuses on the contexts of historical, artistic, and scientific values closely associated with the curatorial perspective. The economic, social, political, and environmental benefits or uses of heritage, known as instrumental values, significantly influence ARM decision-making. However, they are assessed using different methods (Mason 2002) and fall outside the scope of the current study, which relies on data from the conservation survey (Alef 2017; Alef and Rosenblum 2015) and archaeological publications about the sites.

Context-Based Significance Assessment (CBSA): To transform the abstract and, at times, intuitive concept of values into practical application in planning and management, the field of heritage practice developed significance assessment methodologies. Although these methods remain general and unclear, in principle, they employ contextual frameworks, including regional, chronological, and site type, to clarify the significance of archaeological sites (Hardesty and Little 2009; Mathers et al. 2005). This approach is based on the idea that "Heritage sites and objects must be understood in relation to their contexts – in other words, holistically. One cannot fully understand a site without understanding its contexts, which, perforce, extend beyond the site itself both literally and conceptually" (Mason 2002, 14). Thus, Context-Based Significance Assessment (CBSA) aims to place the site within broader historical processes, enabling the perception of broad patterns and how individual resources fit within these patterns. It situates the site within its historical themes and geographical contexts to help explain spatial and cultural interconnections (Briuer and Mathers 1997; Carman 2015). This study applies CBSA as its methodological framework. It focuses on the elements that constitute the intrinsic values in the significance assessment rather than identifying the categories of the sites' values. These elements could be represented in the ARM inventory knowledge model, namely its information needs.

Information For Archaeological Resource Management (In4ARM): ARM inventory that adopts a values-based approach ought to include information necessary to conserve the site's values. This study is part of a larger research project that proposed a conceptual knowledge model for the ARM inventory (Alef 2021). It involved identifying and assessing ARM information needs in different aspects. A total of 6 categories were identified at three levels of knowledge: 1) Data: site identification and administrative data; 2) Assessment: risk, significance, and data quality; 3) Decision-related information regarding research, protection, conservation, and development.

2 See example of a picture and its related artifacts in Google Art: https://bit.ly/gaa-toledo.

3 Examples of Arches implementation include UK Historic Environment Records https://www.archesproject.org/arches-for-hers; The Los Angeles Historic Resource Inventory https://historicplacesla.lacity.org; San Francisco Cultural Heritage https://sfculturalheritage.org.

These categories collectively form the "Information For Archaeological Resource Management" (In4ARM) categorical system.[4] The significance assessment was a major analytical effort, and its results on representation aspects are presented in this paper.

1.1.3 Challenges in Shifting Significance Assessment Representation

ARM inventories converted from paper records to digital systems have led to advancements and inherent challenges. A digital inventory can be a powerful tool for information on the cultural significance of archaeological heritage. However, for it to be effectively used in value-based management, these inventories should provide adequate and accessible data about the site's values. This requires optimising the representation and usability of CBSA within inventories. This optimisation poses a major challenge in bridging the theoretical and practical aspects within CBSA In4ARM.

The Complexity Challenge: CBSA is complicated to incorporate into ARM inventories due to its intricate, multi-layered nature. This data is based on a network of concepts spanning multiple domains. Moreover, the uncertainty and vagueness of archaeological knowledge make the task even more complicated. As mentioned, no established principles exist for using semantic tools, particularly for CBSA data.

The Inherent Representation Issue: ARM inventory records are not the heritage itself and do not represent how people think about places. They inherently disconnect the archaeological sites and artifacts from their historical and cultural context (Sullivan 1993). That detachment can obscure the unique interaction between a place's cultural and physical characteristics (Carman 2015). Thus, as integral components of a broader historic environment, they should not be seen as separate objects. This relates also to the inherent problem in sampling. Recording and conserving only the "best" examples will fail to preserve the sense of place in the cultural landscape. Sullivan (1993, 647) points out that "this pervasive quality of heritage is both more important and more fragile than its component parts".

Operational Challenges: This section highlights the various obstacles in optimising the creation and representation of CBSA. Firstly, the process relies heavily on expert analysis, which is context-specific, time-consuming, and complex, especially when dealing with large volumes of data. Secondly, while semantic technologies can assist in representing CBSA, integrating them presents its own challenges, such as specialised KG and ontologies expertise and complex modelling processes.

In this context, integrating knowledge graphs with generative AI based on Large Language Models (LLMs) could significantly contribute to both challenges, i.e., CBSA production and representation. Pan et al. (2024) propose a roadmap for combining a) the creation and retrieval of semantic insights through LLM-augmented knowledge graphs and b) enhancing the transparency and accuracy of knowledge generation with KG-enhanced LLMs. While this paper does not directly address AI assistance, acknowledging its potential marks a promising research direction in the CBSA domain.

1.1.4 The research case study

Considering the challenges and opportunities presented by semantic tools, the following sections explore the information characteristics of CBSA through a case study of the Huqoq synagogue. This case study draws from a broader study of 66 ancient synagogues surveyed between 2013 and 2018 as part of the Synagogue Conservation Project (Alef 2017; Alef and Rosenblum 2015). The survey's data was analysed in the research on information for ARM (Alef 2021). Although synagogues from Late Antiquity highlight Israeli archaeology, the survey revealed that while some sites have been developed for tourism, many others remain neglected. This project led to the creation of the first GIS-based ARM inventory by the Israel Antiquities Authority, revealing considerable data gaps and shortcomings in meeting ARM information requirements.

The analysis aimed to understand the information requirements by identifying contextual features related to significance assessments. The Huqoq Synagogue site record was used as a case study to illustrate the CBSA information elements. Our objective was to demonstrate how the significance of even a single site is interconnected with other sites and various types of heritage assets. This interconnectedness requires a network of relations to fully represent the meaning of these sites. The paper addresses the use of knowledge graphs in CBSA to represent the contexts of site values as separate information entities within the inventory.

1.2 Methodology

The methodology of this paper is grounded in analysing the significance assessment information category as part of the broader In4ARM categorial system mentioned above. The study aims to identify key information elements of current significance assessment methods to be formally incorporated into the digital ARM inventories' knowledge model. Using a qualitative research framework to analyse texts of various sites' significance assessments, we defined the building blocks of site values that can be formalised into the inventory data model.

4 The abbreviation In4ARM was introduced in research on the Information Needs of Archaeological Sites Evaluation for Cultural Heritage Management Inventory (Alef 2021).

1.2.1 Research field: Analysis of 66 Galilean Synagogue Records

The research comprises 66 survey records of synagogues from Late Antiquity in northern Israel (see Figure 1.2). By the first century CE, the synagogue institution had already assumed an important role in Jewish life, serving social and cultural functions. Its significance grew after the Romans' destruction of the Temple in Jerusalem in 70 CE in response to the Jews' Great Revolt. Subsequently, the synagogue offered a radical alternative to Temple rituals, becoming a central place for worship and gathering of the local community. In the aftermath of the revolt, the Jewish population concentrated in Galilee, where synagogues were built as the principal public buildings in villages and towns. Like other public buildings of that era in the Roman–Greco world, they were lavishly decorated with architectural features and mosaics (Levine 2000).

The largest concentration of synagogue buildings in ancient Palestine is preserved in the Galilee region. In 2000, Galilee's ancient synagogues were added to UNESCO's tentative list for their universal value (*Early Synagogues in the Galilee – UNESCO World Heritage Centre* 2000). However, this recognition does not reflect the management status of the sites. Of the 66 sites, 18 have not been excavated, resulting in limited information about them. As a result, these sites are often at risk of inappropriate use due to lack of awareness. Three sites were undergoing excavation at the time of the survey. Among the 45 sites that have been excavated, 16 have been conserved and developed for visitors, 13 are partially managed, 13 remain unmanaged and neglected, and three have been destroyed (Alef 2019). The surveyed synagogues form a well-defined regional typology of high cultural value and historical, archaeological, and geographic characteristics.[5] As a cultural theme, they provide a variety of contexts and values, making this field particularly suitable for In4ARM analysis.

1.2.2 Analysis Framework

To analyse the In4ARM significance assessment category, the research field, encompassing 66 sites, was systematically classified. We used a criterion of management status in relation to the excavation status, which generated six types of sites (Alef 2019). Representative sites from each type were then selected to serve as samples for detailed analysis. Subsequently, a three-step analytical approach was devised to evaluate the significance of different information elements in the assessment's records as follows:

- *Cultural Assessment:* Cultural assessment records were formulated for eight key sites.[6] Following the CBSA approach, the assessment involved identifying the cultural elements and context, such as typological, structural, and geographical context; historical information referring to figures, events, and processes related to the site or its context; cultural themes related to stories, artistic themes depicted in artifacts, traditions, and practices. These were contextualised to explain why these elements are significant in relation to the synagogue theme, demonstrating how the broader context amplifies their significance. Finally, each site was compared to similar sites to highlight its uniqueness or representativeness, considering the integrity of the remains and criteria such as rarity, workmanship, and artistic quality.
- *Qualitative analysis to identify In4ARM information characteristics:* Manual content analysis (Schreier 2012) was conducted to identify the themes and key information elements from the eight significance assessment records. The analysis was conducted without software or complex coding within an intuitive coding framework (ibid., 174).
- *Refining*: This step entailed an iterative process in which the assessment text was broken down into information elements based on the resource's values (see Figure 1.3 and for the detailed Huqoq analysis, see Table 1.1).
- *Refining the significance assessment category within In4ARM*: Finally, we refined the key information elements prevalent across all the analysed records to establish a comprehensive profile for the significance assessment category within In4ARM (see Table 1.1).

We will now discuss these findings regarding the representation of significance assessment within the ARM inventory, using the Huqoq example to illustrate our points.

1.2.3 Representing the CBSA: Graph Visualisation Approach

Initially, our research did not incorporate semantic technologies. However, following the insights from the analysis, we further investigated the challenges and opportunities associated with representing the CBSA through a knowledge graph. To facilitate this, we utilised the Arches platform, which leverages a graph database architecture optimised for documenting and managing cultural heritage data. We modelled Huqoq's significant assessment information elements with Arches, representing them as entities and their relationships. This approach enabled us to visualise the key elements in a simplified knowledge graph. The following "Case Study" section will

5 The survey excluded over 90 sites where only architectural fragments of synagogues were found, but no in situ structures were located.

6 See raw data of eight site records in the Zenodo repository of the CAA2023 Conference Proceedings: doi.org/10.5281/zenodo.10954078.

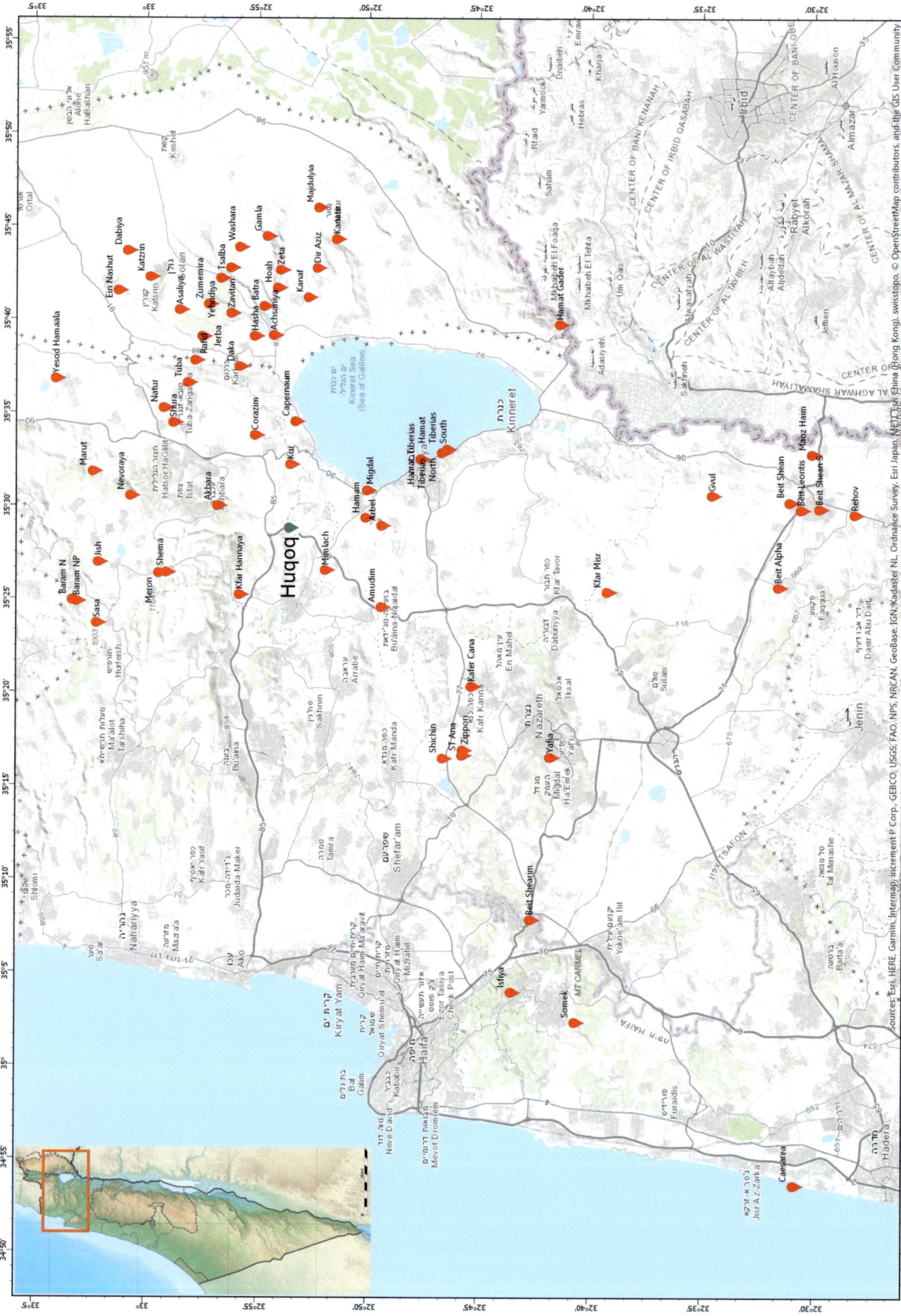

Figure 1.2. Map of northern Israel and the 66 ancient synagogue sites included in the research.

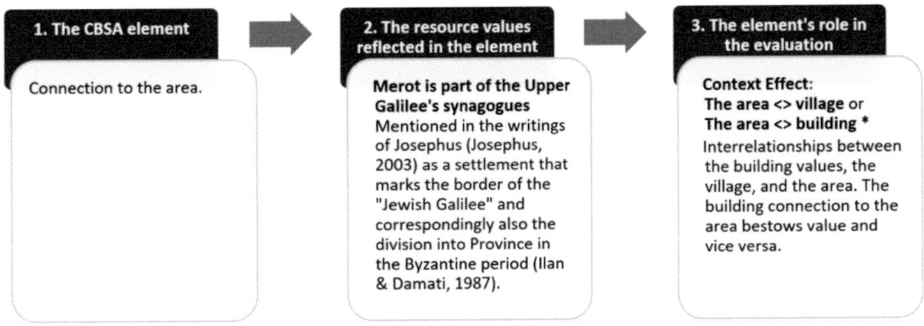

Figure 1.3. Analysis steps of regional context and village context in the Merot significance assessment. The <> symbol indicates a reciprocal relationship where entities bestow value on one another.

describe the initial research insights and further investigate the knowledge graph.

1.3 Huqoq Case Study: Interconnectedness as the Medium and the Message

This section summarises the main findings related to the information elements in the significance assessment text and their representation. The Huqoq Synagogue record will serve to demonstrate the analysis process. Then, we will show how simplified knowledge graphs can represent the elements identified in the analysis. The key information characteristics found in the Huqoq record were dominant in all other records studied; therefore, they can be considered representative.

The primary finding from the qualitative analysis is that the building blocks of the site values are the context entities within significance assessment texts. These context entities are the key information elements of the site's significance assessment. These contexts bestow value upon various aspects of a site, which in turn redefines the significance of these contexts themselves. We call this reciprocal process the Context-Effect phenomenon, which we will explain further below. This finding highlights the importance of integrating contextual details into the ARM inventory by representing each context as a distinct entity in the data model rather than mere text blocks.

1.3.1 The building blocks of the site values

Types of resource contexts: The analysis identifies three primary context domains: structural-spatial, thematic, and documentary, each contributing to the resource's significance. The structural-spatial contexts encompass tangible elements like the area, cultural landscape, villages, towns, structures, and artifacts. Thematic contexts cover the type and use of archaeological resources, such as Galilean synagogues. The documentary context enhances a resource's value through narratives, traditions, and historical evidence. These contexts are not merely abstract categories but are treated as distinct entities within the data model, each playing a role in constructing the overall value of the resource and its contexts. These could be seen as a suggested conceptual "context effect ontology".

The Context-Effect Phenomenon: The term "context effect" is adopted from cognitive psychology and marketing, yet it proves relevant in the cultural heritage evaluation domain. This phenomenon was observed in all eight significance assessment records. In our analysis, the context effect is reflected in the reciprocal relationship between a resource's value and its context's significance. This study examines the intrinsic values of a site, typically determined by various contexts: archaeological, geographical, cultural, and historical. It is important to distinguish between these different contexts, as the "Context-Effect Phenomenon" refers to the interplay between a resource's overall significance and these varied contexts rather than being limited to its archaeological context alone. For instance, the importance of an ancient synagogue serving its community can only be fully understood within the context of the village where it was situated. Similarly, the village's significance is connected to the discoveries made within the synagogue. These contexts are dynamic, evolving with new findings related to the site or associated resources. Treating contexts as distinct entities significantly enhances our ability to assess the overall inventory and the contextual value of resources. This interplay between a resource and its contextual elements, the "Context-Effect Phenomenon", emerges as a key insight in our study.

We will illustrate the context-effect phenomenon using Huqoq synagogue site record. The text below is an updated summary of an in-depth cultural significance assessment conducted by the author as part of the planning for the Huqoq Archaeological Park (Alef and Kisilevitz 2018).

1.3.2 The significance assessment of the Huqoq synagogue

"Recent excavations of the Byzantine synagogue in Huqoq, 5 kilometres north of the Sea of Galilee, revealed a well-preserved ensemble of extraordinary mosaic floors with a unique wealth of narratives (Magness et al. 2023). A large public building structure, which may most likely be a synagogue from the beginning of the

The CBSA element	The resource values reflected in the element	The element's role in the evaluation
Structural-Spatial Contexts: Area	Huqoq is in the North of the Sea of Galilee Vicinity to ancient Jewish villages, including Mimlah, Vadi Hamam, and Capernaum (Ilan 1991). Associations of the area with the gospels and early Christianity. Vicinity to the Arbel, an area associated with Jewish eschatological traditions in Late Antiquity (Jerusalem Talmud, Berakhot).	Context Effect: Area<>Building The building narratives enrich and bestow value upon the area's intercultural character and vice versa.
Village ruins	**The Huqoq installations** are evidence of the village economy and its agricultural life.	**Context Effect: Village<>Building** The installation sheds light on the synagogue's daily life and vice versa.
Artifacts	**A mosaic assemblage** displays an extraordinary collection of mythological motifs, daily life scenes, and Bible scenes, including the Samson mosaic, which is related to the one in the Vadi Hamam synagogue.	Context Effect: Artifact<>Building The mosaics are valuable partly because they are a synagogue floor, which contributes to the synagogue's unique intercultural character.
The synagogues as a thematic context: Typology	**Galilean synagogues:** During the Byzantine period, Galilee was home to thriving Jewish communities, as evidenced by the high concentration of synagogues. These synagogues are a testament to these communities' rich culture, art, and architecture.	Context Effect: Typology<>Building The building as part of a regional typology contributes to the typology and vice versa
Documentary Context: Historical Evidence, Narratives, and Traditions	Talmud commentary on Reish Lakish in Huqoq and the mustard seed (Jerusalem Talmud, Shevi'it) The biblical narratives of Samson	Landscape as Narrative, Narrative as Landscape in collective memory. Reflects Jewish Eschatological traditions

Table 1.1. Analysis of the Huqoq Significance Assessment: Unveiling the Context Effect.

Spatial-structural concept			
Huqoq	Site/Synagogue	Contains | Bestows value	Huqoq Installation, Huqoq Synagogue, Samson Mosaic
Vadi Hamam	Site/Synagogue	Contains | Bestows value	Samson Mosaic, Samson
Capernaum	Site/Synagogue	Associated	Jesus
Horvat Mimlah	Site/Synagogue	Associated	Eschatological traditions, Jesus
Huqoq Installation	Element/Artifact	Mentioned in| Bestows value	Mustard gathering, Talmud
Samson Mosaic, Huqoq Synagogue	Element/Artifact	Depicts	Samson (In the gates of Gaza)
Samson Mosaic, Vadi Hamam	Element/Artifact	Depicts	Samson (Fighting the Philistines)
Documentary concept			
Mustard seed parable, gospel	Narrative	Narrated by	Jesus
Mustard gathering, Talmud	Narrative	Mentions | Bestows value	Huqoq Installation
Eschatological traditions	Narrative	Mentions | Bestows value	Horvat Mimlah, Samson, Jesus
Samson	Figure (person)	Depicted in | Bestows value	Samson Mosaic, Vadi Hamam Synagogue
Jesus	Figure (person)	Associated | Bestows value	Capernaum
Synagogues as a Thematic Context			
Galilean Synagogues	Typology	Features found in | bestows value	Vadi Hamam, Horvat Mimlah, Huqoq, Capernaum

Table 1.2. Simplified KG of Huqoq Significance Assessment: Relationships between contextual entities in the text.

Middle Ages, was uncovered above it. If so, it is one of the few known from this period in Israel. The excavation is ongoing, but this is already one of Israel's largest, most impressive, and surprising synagogue sites. The mosaics are the highlight of the site. They present an unusual and rich set of mythological motifs alongside scenes from the Bible and everyday life. Those depict biblical scenes, including Noah's Ark, Moses' parting of the Red Sea, Jonah being swallowed by the fish, and the Biblical hero Samson, also depicted on a nearby mosaic in the Vadi Hamam synagogue (Leibner 2023). It also describes an extra-biblical tradition revealed for the first time in an ancient synagogue. The collection of mosaics expresses the local eschatological traditions that developed in Tiberias and the Arbel, with a combination of influences from the Greco-Roman and Byzantine worlds. This assemblage is a remarkable example of the cultural interrelationships in the

Jewish realm at a time when the Christian Church was established in the North of the Sea of Galilee. It reflects the diversity of thought, belief, and worship among the ancient Jewish communities in the Galilee and sheds new light on the history of Jewish art in the Byzantine period.

"The Huqoq Jewish village is part of a thousand-year-old succession of settlements from the Bronze Age through the Byzantine period, the Middle Ages, until the destruction of the Muslim village of Yaquq in 1948. Many references in historical sources also provide evidence of the significance of the place. One is about Reish Lakish, who was in Huqoq and saw them gathering mustard (Jerusalem Talmud, Shevi'it), which relates to unique installations found on the site that could have been used in the mustard industry (Tepper et al. 2000). Associations to mustard around Capernaum also relate to Jesus's parable of the mustard seed in the Gospel (Mark 4: 30-32, NIV). Other traditions of pilgrims to Habakkuk's tomb continue to this day. The remains from the various periods, including mikveh (ritual bath), quarries, and tombs, were preserved in the village as an enclave of a typical Mediterranean cultural landscape" (Alef and Kisilevitz 2018).

Based on the significance assessment text, Table 1.1 illustrates how context effects emerge when analysing CBSA information elements in the text. The context elements are grouped according to structural-spatial, thematic, and documentary contexts. The next column describes the resource values reflected in the element. The last column analyses the element's role in the evaluation and how the context effect emerges.

1.3.3 Knowledge Graph for Huqoq CBSA

To represent the site's significance in the digital inventory, we can model the elements from Table 1.2 as information entities. In the simplified example below, we constructed a knowledge graph to represent the contexts, relationships, and entities. This graph is a conceptual illustration rather than a definitive knowledge graph or data model. Although this simplified graph is not part of the qualitative analysis, it demonstrates the potential of modelling the significance assessment by integrating it into a broader "network of meanings". This method could enhance our understanding of Huqoq's significance and role in the cultural landscape.

The graph features selected entities associated with the mustard installation and the Samson mosaic. These two elements alone reveal a complex network of meanings that may not be immediately evident from the text alone. Table 1.2 below breaks down the assessment and the context effects we previously described, mapping them to

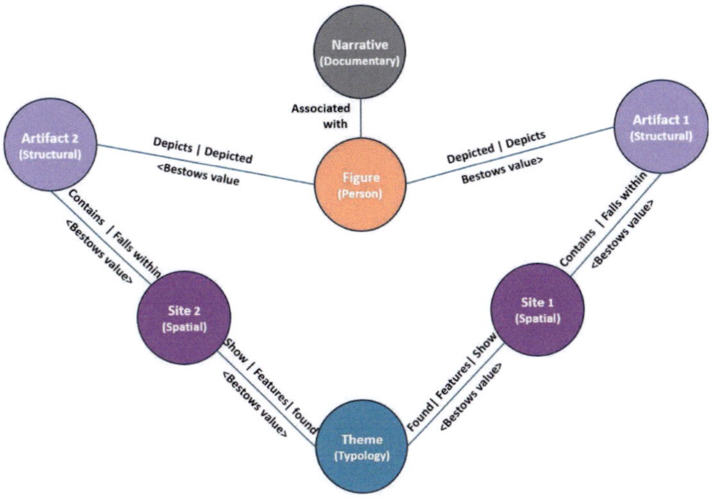

Figure 1.4. Conceptual Model of the KG for Huqoq Significance Assessment (detailed in Table 1.2).

relationships between entities in the knowledge graph. An important insight from this modelling experiment is the predicate of "bestow value" as a distinct relationship within the CBSA knowledge graph, which can be used and reused through semantic searches and queries.

1.3.4 Visualising the context effect in the Huqoq case study

While tables effectively categorise and describe, they fail to depict the complex interconnections among significant contexts treated as entities within the inventory data models. The graph visualisations below are included to clarify these entities and their relationships. Our concept model featured several resource models – sites, related artifacts, narratives, and historical figures – which reflect some significant contexts that emerged from the textual analysis. This simplified model describes the entities' interrelations and contextual interplay (see Figure 1.4).

In this model, artifacts from two different sites of the same typology illustrate a narrative related to a historical figure. Each site indirectly confers value upon the other through these shared narratives and artifacts, enriching the collective heritage narrative. Targeted semantic queries within a knowledge graph can reveal this intricate network of interconnected values and relationships.

The text block below presents a conceptual query of the knowledge graph shown in Table 1.2, along with its result. Using the data presented in Table 1.2 and the visual scheme depicted in Figure 1.4, we prompted ChatGPT-4 to generate an example query. This demonstrates the capability of generative AI to extract knowledge in our domain, which we will discuss further later.

We chose the Arches platform for its no-code design to explore the potential of knowledge graphs further. This platform simplifies the modelling and the visual representation of relationships between key contextual

```
CONCEPTUAL PSEUDO-QUERY: Uncovering Interconnected Significance through 'Bestows Value'

1. START with a list of Sites in the ARM inventory.
2. FOR EACH Site, DO:
   a. FIND all direct 'Bestows Value' relationships with Artifacts or Narratives.
   b. FOR EACH Artifact and Narrative directly related to the Site, DO:
      i. IDENTIFY other Sites where the same Artifact or Narrative also 'Bestows Value'.
3. COUNT the total number of unique direct and indirect 'Bestows Value' relationships for each Site.
4. OUTPUT Sites alongside their counts of interconnected significance, reflecting both direct and indirect
contributions to and from the cultural heritage network.

GOAL:
This process aims to map out the network of significance around each site,
 highlighting how direct and indirect connections via 'Bestows Value'
relationships enrich our understanding of each site's role and value within the broader cultural heritage context.

EXAMPLE:
- Site: "Huqoq Synagogue"
  - Direct 'Bestows Value' Connections: 3 (e.g., "Mosaic of Samson")
  - Indirect 'Bestows Value' Connections through Shared Artifacts/Narratives: 5
    (e.g., connections via "Samson Mosaic" shared with "Vadi Hamam")
- Total Interconnected Significance: 8

This approach facilitates a comprehensive view of the interconnected significance of sites
 within ARM inventories, emphasizing the rich, multi-layered context that contributes
  to the cultural value of each site.
```

Figure 1.5. A conceptual query example of the knowledge graph.

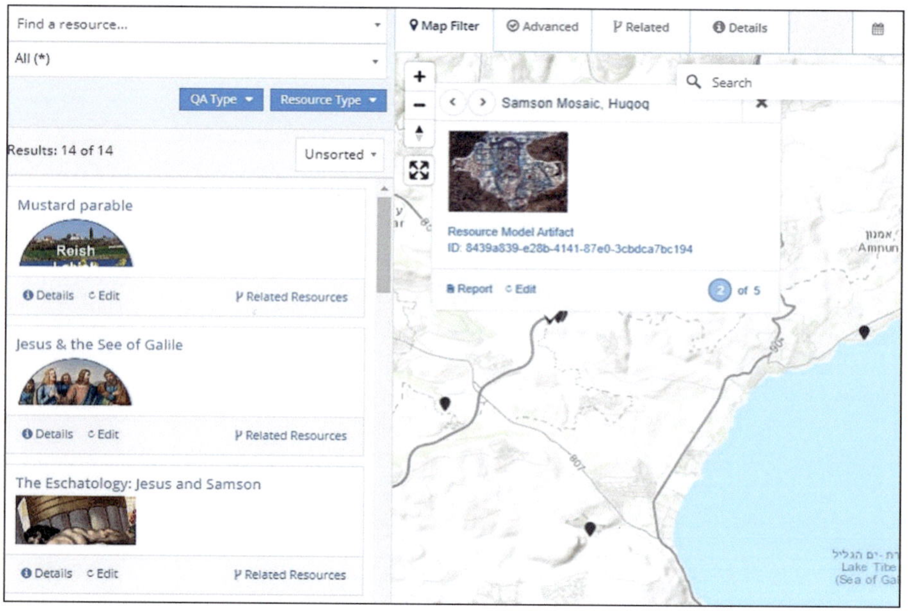

Figure 1.6. Resource Models as presented in Arches Platform UI.

entities. Huqoq's significant assessment information elements are represented as "resource models" for selected entity types (e.g., Site, Artifact, Figure) and as "resource instances" (e.g., Huqoq, Samsom Mosaic, Samson). As a simplified KG, Our Arches resource models consist only of the instance name, associated instances, and spatial data (in cases of spatial-structural entities (see Figure 1.6).

However, while the platform allows for the visual representation of entities and their connections, its map interface does not show the relational connections between spatial entities. Consequently, the graph visualisations and spatial representations are presented as separate components in Figures 1.7-1.10. The "network of meanings" generated represents a fraction of the potential for linking various cultural contexts. Yet, it still aids in enhancing

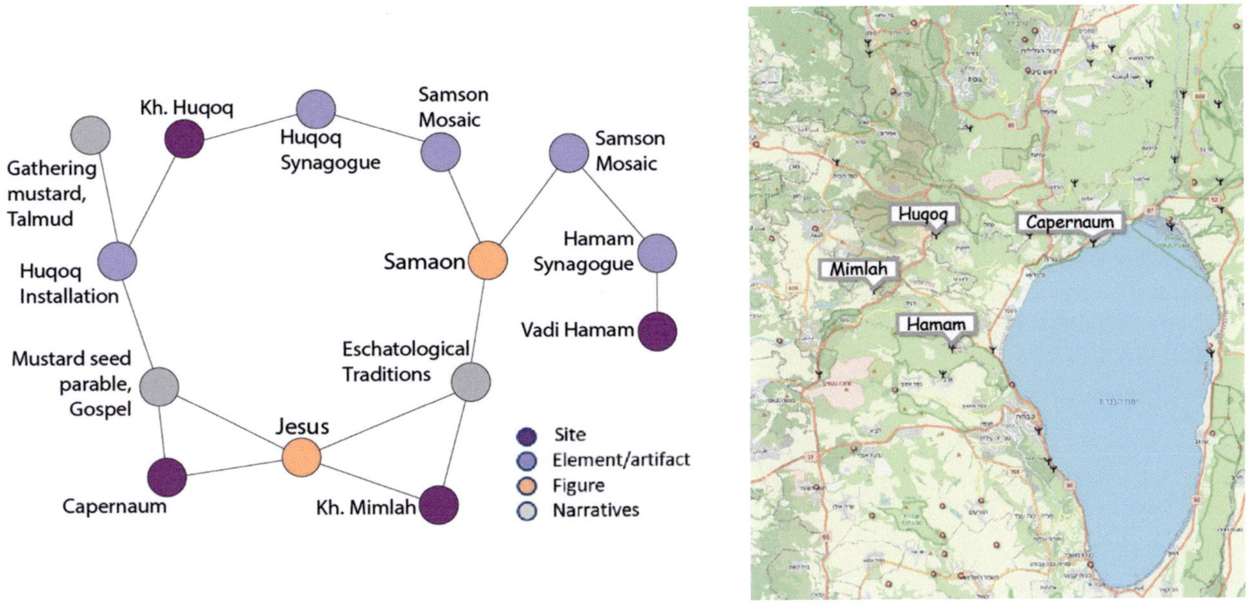

Figure 1.7. Regional context effect: Huqoq <> synagogues cluster. Located north of the Sea of Galilee, the Huqoq Synagogue is part of a regional cluster that includes Capernaum, Horvat Mimlah, and Vadi Hamam. This positions Huqoq within a distinct regional typology that reflects the distribution of the Jewish communities following the destruction of the Temple in 70 CE. Thus, "area context" and "typological context" emerge as meaningful entities, illustrating the synagogue's value within this broader historical and geographical framework.

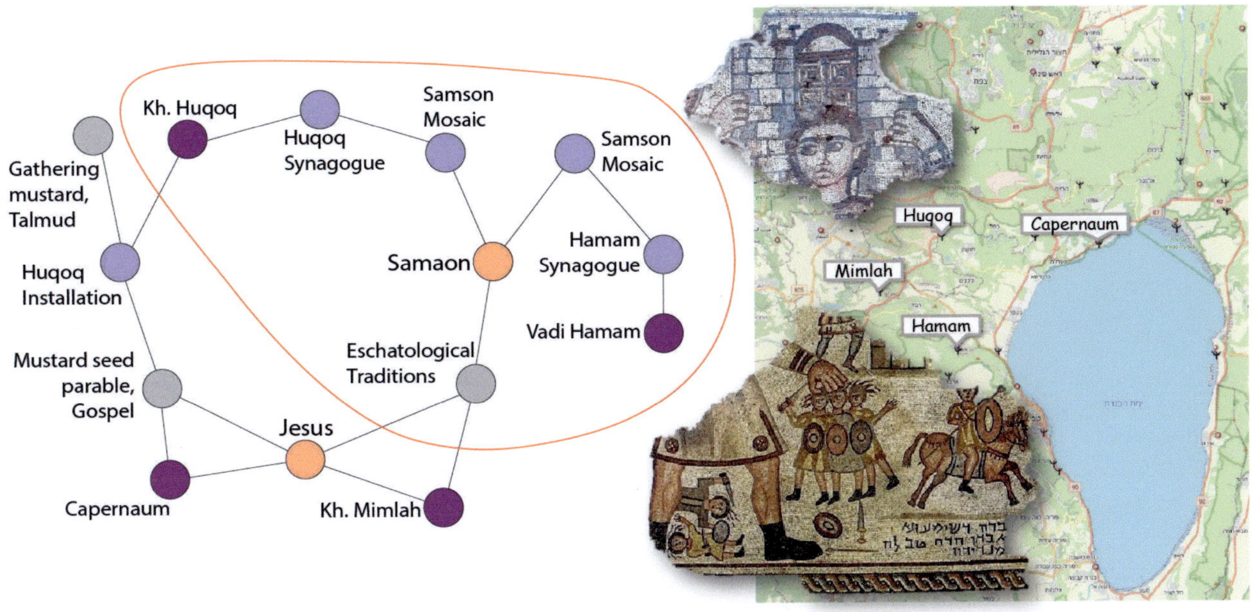

Figure 1.8. Mosaics' context effect: Huqoq <> Vadi Hamam. Rare Samson mosaic scenes discovered in the Huqoq and Vadi Hamam synagogues are linked to Jewish eschatological traditions that position Samson in the Arbel area. Thus, the Huqoq Samson mosaic enhances the value of Vadi Hamam's and vice versa, contributing to a biblical artistic theme. This allows the "narrative context" to be identified as another essential information entity in the data model.

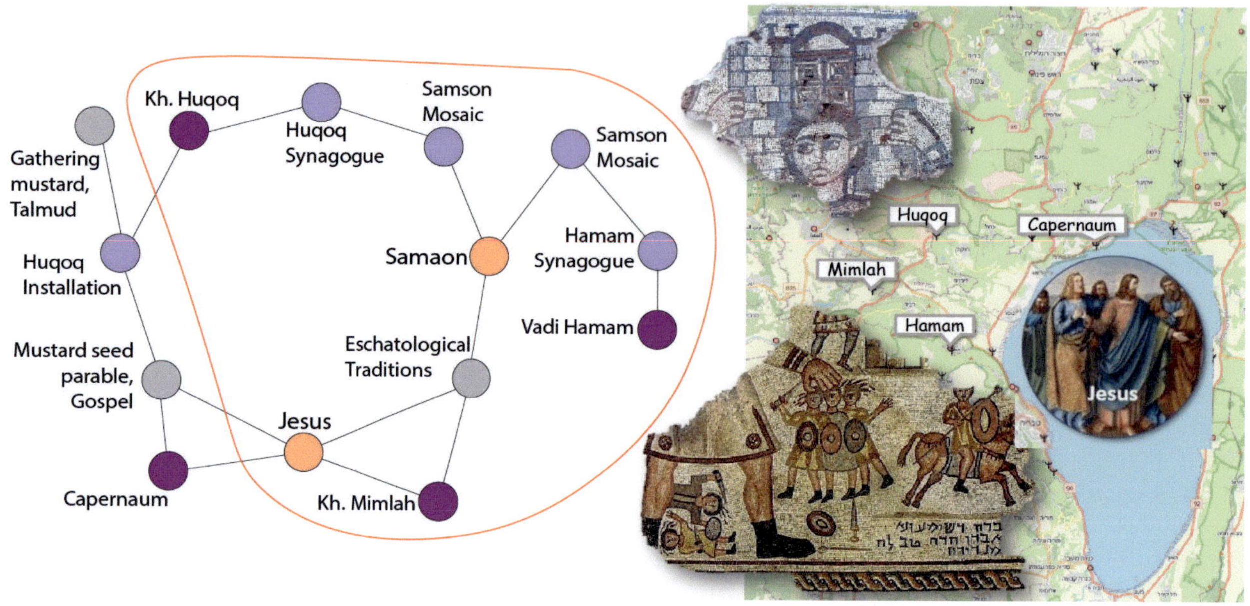

Figure 1.9. Huqoq <> Eschatological traditions. This region is also associated with Christian eschatology, exemplified by the Acts of Pilate, which recount Jesus' resurrection on Mt. Mimlah, home to the Horvat Mimlah synagogue. We have noted that the Samson mosaics in Huqoq and Vadi Hamam contribute to the area's significance. In turn, the area's connections to Jewish and Christian eschatological traditions and the interrelationships between Christian and Jewish communities offer a new understanding of the Huqoq synagogue.

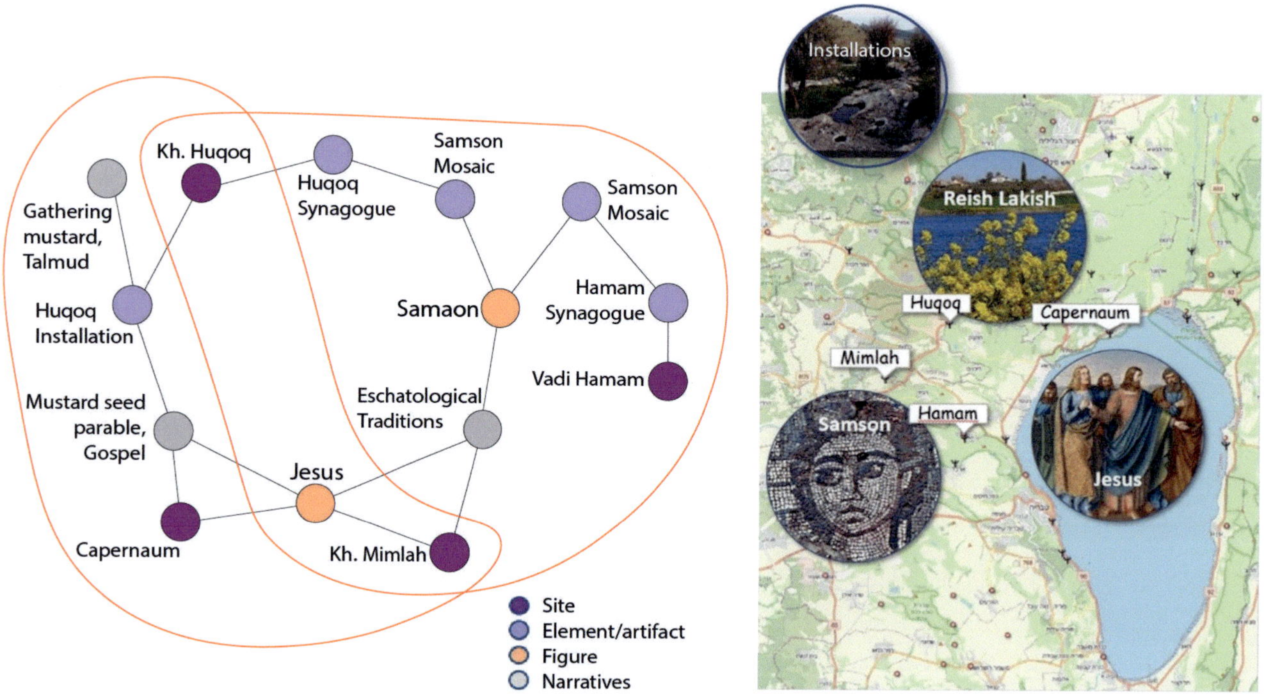

Figure 1.10. Huqoq <> installations. Another example demonstrates the development of a spatial network of meanings, where the "Village ruin context" links the Huqoq Synagogue to Huqoq's installations, interpreted as part of the mustard oil industry (Tepper 2000). These installations are associated with the Talmud's story of sage Reish Lakish who was in Huqoq and saw them gathering mustard seeds (Jerusalem Talmud, Shevi'it, 9, 25, 71). Furthermore, this context is enriched by the mustard seed parable found in the gospels (Mark 4: 30-32, NIV), adding another layer of contextual depth.

our understanding of the interconnections between resources, highlighting how each entity contributes to a broader collective narrative. The context entities we identified in Huqoq, such as eschatological traditions, impart significance to Huqoq, and at the same time, Huqoq shapes the character of the north of the Sea of Galilee. It points out how even a site like Huqoq Synagogue cannot be fully appreciated or understood in isolation despite its significant inherent qualities – such as architectural or artistic elements like mosaics. At the regional level, the early Christian and Jewish communities' interrelationships are not merely a lens of context through which to assess culture but the building blocks of the places' cultural identity. Figures 1.7-1.10 showcase the Arches graph visualisation. Our manual demarcation in Figures 1.8-1.10 clarifies the interconnections of the synagogue thematic contexts, underlining their role in the inventories' network of meaning. The regional typology theme of the synagogue in this example is described briefly in the methodology section. The network scheme is the standard representation of related entities in the Arches platform.

1.3.5 Huqoq CBSA application to the interpretation and presentation plan

The Huqoq Synagogue's conservation and presentation planning began soon after its excavation. Its planning principles reflect an understanding of its broad contexts. The plan involves conserving and presenting the synagogue structure and its mosaic floors in situ, integrating them as part of the village with all its cultural layers. This approach ensures that the shelter will protect the synagogue and its mosaics while allowing views of the surroundings without isolating them from their context, as is often the case with such shelters. Walking paths are planned around the hill, showcasing the village and the Huqoq installations. Lookouts along these paths will point towards visible sites in the area, including Vadi Hamam, the Sea of Galilee, and Horvat Mimlah to the east. Though not excavated or known to the public, Horvat Mimlah is an important context to the Huqoq story and should be managed accordingly. Signage and other museological tools will help convey Huqoq's message of cultural interconnectedness.

1.4 Discussion

The Huqoq synagogue holds a unique cultural significance that reflects the spatial network built by resources and contexts. This enhances its cultural meanings and contributes to the broader cultural identity of the area around the Northern Sea of Galilee, highlighting the interconnectedness between different cultures and communities. A knowledge graph is an effective way to convey this message. The emergence of values from contexts emphasises the need for semantic representation in the CBSA across ARM inventories. This is a valuable consideration in the shift of inventories as an effective tool for values-based ARM. To provide broader insights, we will widen our discussion to consider implications beyond our single-site case study.

1.4.1 Representing Context-Effect in the Knowledge Model

Despite variation in values and conditions, the context-effect phenomenon is evident across all analysed sites. This led us to propose contexts as distinct entities in the ARM inventory. CBSA's representation reveals various context elements, such as structural components like artifacts and architecture, and thematic contexts, such as types, uses, narratives, traditions, and historical evidence. For example, Samson mosaics in Huqoq and Vadi Hamam intertwine deeply with the eschatological traditions of the Sea of Galilee area. Visualising and analysing this complex interplay can improve our understanding of a site's cultural significance and contextual value.

The reciprocal "context-effect" enhances the value of each interconnected entity. This understanding suggests the need for a more integrated approach to managing assets. The conservation plan proposes using this method to make Huqoq an anchor heritage asset that enhances related sites such as Vadi Hamam, Arbel, and Horvat Mimlah, as well as the artistic themes and traditions of the Northern Sea of Galilee area.

Defining the "bestows value" relationship in the knowledge graph suggests that entities can be related not only by relationships like "contains" or "depicts", but also by their ability to influence the perceived value of another heritage asset. This introduces an interpretive layer in the knowledge graph where certain entities are acknowledged for their potential to enhance or change the value of an asset.

1.4.2 Implications: Contexts as Entities in ARM Inventory – from list to network of meaning

CBSA's incorporation of semantic tools could support ARM's evolution from a site-centric approach to a more holistic one. This shift means the inventory could become a network of entities instead of just a list of sites. Representing contextual entities could lead to a more informed discussion on conservation priorities and enable a multidimensional perspective on conservation strategies. Additionally, this approach could promote ethical considerations in data management, including transparency, inclusivity, accountability, and dynamic updating, especially in the context of cultural heritage. A dynamic system of relationships and meanings based on interconnected values suggests that the assets included are not ranked as a "standalone" asset but are part of a broader cultural landscape. This shift raises several ethical, conceptual, and practical implications, which are outlined below:

Clarity, Validity, and Values-Based Knowledge Discovery:
Extracting a list of significantly related entities, such as from Huqoq's graph (see figures 1.7-1.10), simplifies comprehension compared to interpreting from significance synthesis text. Representing contexts explicitly as entities in the inventory could enhance evaluation clarity, aids in peer review and validation, and increases the data's reliability and inclusiveness.

Developing a CBSA knowledge graph enables semantic search, querying, and the exploration of new meanings, offering functionalities beyond traditional relational databases.

Dynamic representation:
ARM is continually influenced by new archaeological discoveries and interpretations. Following such discoveries, introducing a new entity into the network can subtly alter the entire "network of meanings", thereby enhancing the value of existing entities like site records without necessitating direct updates to each. This approach highlights the advantages of network representations, where the "context effect" of integrating new entities could enrich the values of others.

Expanding Inclusivity and Diversity in ARM Practices:
Inclusion: Recognising sites as context entities enables re-evaluating insignificant sites in a broader network (Ireland et al. 2020). Previously overlooked sites, such as Horvat Mimlah and other unexcavated sites, are often ignored due to limited data. This perspective challenges the conventional ARM focus on well-documented resources by addressing Carver's concern (1996) about the undiscovered sites that treasure the more significant part of the knowledge about past human activity. Broadening the evaluation network helps reduce biases towards data-rich sites. It emphasises the importance of integrating significant but unmanaged resources like Horvat Mimlah into the spatial network of values.

Multiple interpretations:
A knowledge graph permits multiple contexts that could offer varied and conflicting interpretations to coexist. This approach could help reduce the inherent bias in inventories by representing a diversity of periods and cultures. Moreover, treating themes as dynamic entities within the system allows for the introduction of new themes that are responsive to cultural sensitivities, thereby capturing the diversity of societal voices. This feature complements the previous points, representing various sites and interpretations in the inventory.

Broadened scope and bridging the gap:
The ARM inventory CBSA data model could pay particular attention to the diversity of the contexts. That includes diverse types of assets in the historical landscape, encompassing not only archaeological sites but also associated artifacts and historic and intangible heritage. These contribute to the comprehensive understanding of the environment's values as a whole. Representing The "context effect" is especially effective in bridging the divide between sites and their external artifact collections by promoting the preservation of both artifacts and sites.

Educational and Community Aspects:
The medium of knowledge graphs and proper CBSA site information convey the message of cultural interconnectedness as an educational goal. This can support place-based activities and transform both sites and their contextual entities into what Turkle (2011) calls "Objects To Think With".

1.4.3 Meeting the CBSA representation challenges

In the example of Huqoq, we have highlighted how the KG representation of CBSA matches the current ARM approaches. With semantic tools such as GraphDB, neo4j[7], or the Arches Platform, we can treat these contexts as related information entities and discover their meaningful connections. However, as discussed in the introduction, capturing the nuanced connections across multiple sites is challenging conceptually and practically. It requires expert input and time. Expanding datasets can lead to information overload. Therefore, the challenge is to look for innovative ways to use and reuse this data for decision-making, especially for integrating site values into management strategies. Outlined below are some significant challenges within the CBSA domain:

Multi-Site Network Integration Complexity:
Establishing a network for multiple sites poses a practical challenge. Even modelling a single site's complete contextual elements can create an extensive network, let alone with connections to other sites. This limitation impedes our understanding of the site's complex value and interdependencies with other resources. More feasible solutions are required to create, represent, and gain insights from CBSA.

Integrated Spatial Relationships:
Archaeological sites are integral to a broader historical landscape. Considering our visualisation examples, integrating maps, and automating the demarcation and visualisation of spatial relationships, emphasise the need for sophisticated representations, such as using Geo-KG

7 GraphDB (https://graphdb.ontotext.com) is used by archaeological research infrastructures such as the ARIADNE project. Another example is the (Neo4J https://neo4j.com) used in various cultural heritage research projects, described by Li and Bikakis (2023).

(Wang et al. 2019). This shift could potentially increase the interpretive value of this vast spatial network.[8]

Limitations of Arches:
Arches is well-suited software for managing cultural heritage and inventory. It uses a graph database approach and has strong data modelling capabilities. However, there are some limitations to its search functionality. Even though the geolocation of entities in Arches is possible, no filter is available for map search results by related entities. It cannot perform semantic searches or SPARQL queries and does not offer advanced analytics tools such as neo4j. As a result, Arches is primarily used for generating visualisations or reports and is not ideal for conducting in-depth network analysis.[9]

1.4.4 Generative AI as an Assistant to CBSA

Although not directly demonstrated in the case study, exploring the emerging generative AI capabilities holds much promise for future ARM research (Bickler 2021). Thus, it is essential to investigate how the CBSA field can benefit from generative AI, mainly when extracting knowledge from data sets and individual site records. This approach might help navigate the complexities of CBSA and semantic technologies and integrate them into broader management strategies without overwhelming the CBSA production process. Following Pan et al. (2024), CBSA KG can be produced with AI assistance (KG-Enhanced LLM), while KG can enhance the accuracy and transparency of the generative AI process (LLM-Enhanced KG).[10] Assisting CBSA and integrating complex site contexts could be explored through several functions.

Automating Knowledge Extraction:
This simplifies knowledge extraction from various formats, including unstructured data, to enhance understanding of values and their contexts.

Assisting in Constructing Knowledge Graphs:
Enables more visual and interactive exploration of the connections between sites, artifacts, narratives, and other entities.

Assisting in Customising Data Models:
Provides flexibility in data representation to better reflect the unique aspects of each heritage site's contexts.

Enabling Natural Language Queries:
Allows stakeholders to query the database in natural language, facilitating intuitive access to specific semantic information from the inventory.

1.4.5 Limitations of Scope – Data modelling and instrumental values

This study aims to identify key building blocks and focuses on intrinsic contexts based on archaeological publications and the conservation survey. This approach has two main limitations:

Data modelling:
Our KG model is simplified as we did not perform detailed data modelling. This requires extensive collaboration and careful examination of the data's use and reuse.

Scope of Values and Contexts:
Expanding the context-effect phenomenon to include instrumental values and contexts is worth exploring. If our conceptual model is proven valid and adaptable, further research could explore broader societal aspects. Although other methods may assess these aspects, they are undoubtedly crucial in the ARM practice.

1.5 Conclusion

> *"Heritage conservation is best understood as a sociocultural activity, not simply a technical practice"* (Mason 2002, 5).

1.5.1 Transformation in Cultural Significance Assessment Representation

The paper explores the changes in evaluating cultural significance, explicitly focusing on representation in the ARM inventories. It emphasises the importance of context and the potential of semantic technologies for significance assessment. The study examines the incorporation of CBSA in ARM inventories from a transformative perspective. It entails creating a conceptual knowledge model for site contexts as entities in the inventory and considering the "context effect" between assets, as illustrated in the case study of Huqoq's ancient Synagogue. The study demonstrates how semantic technologies can help represent and comprehend the meanings and values of a site within its geographical, cultural, and historical environment. By adopting this approach, we can move beyond mere textual descriptions of values as "content" and instead centre on "context", the relationships between places, objects, and people, both tangible and intangible.

This shift can also promote a change in ARM policies regarding what is assessed and which archaeological resources to include in the inventory, including "the

---

8 The Valencian design archive project mentions an example of such features (Alba et al. 2023).

9 Arches API allows external queries but requires technical skills of developing query interfaces. Adding built-in network and semantic analysis features can enhance Arches' impact on heritage management.

10 The query pseudo-code demonstrated in Figure 1.5, exemplifies this capability in a nutshell.

management of the unknown" and sites that otherwise would not be protected.

1.5.2 Future Research – Methods for Integrating CBSA in ARM Inventories

A few basic questions emerge regarding the future of significance assessment representation:

Evolution of Significance Assessment Methods in ARM:
How can significance assessment methods be developed with informed use of emerging technologies and representation media?

CBSA Data Modelling for ARM:
What information and use-case requirements are needed for the practical and informed application of CBSA and KG in ARM Inventories? One way to address this might be establishing archaeological thematic frameworks, like the historical and societal ones developed for the HPLA inventory.

Technological Considerations:
What tools, semantic, AI, or otherwise, can be used to create and present CBSA data for optimal decision-making?

As this is an area of ongoing research, further investigation is required, specifically on the potential of AI in this research agenda. Generative AI could offer a new perspective, particularly for improving efficiency and accuracy in extracting values and comprehending context roles from extensive datasets and individual site records. This sets the foundation for a deeper understanding of site values and their presentation as spatial networks of meanings.

1.5.3 Final note

"A spatial network of meaning" is more than a medium, it is a cultural value.

The case of Huqoq's CBSA serves as an example of how a knowledge graph can effectively convey cultural interconnectedness. This aligns with the very core values of the Huqoq synagogue, as reflected in its artifacts and other broader contexts. At the same time, the medium itself promotes inclusion, diversity, and a dynamic multicultural character. By employing it, we can effectively support management needs and convey complex and relevant cultural messages like interconnectedness.

Cultural values are shaped and reshaped by interactions with technology. Therefore, it is essential to understand the message behind the technological medium we choose. It is, therefore, important to remember that cultural evaluation is inherently a human activity. Technology, especially AI, should not be expected to replace human judgment. Relying on a strictly automated process for cultural evaluation would strip it of its meaning. In that sense, the inventory is a cultural formation shaped by curatorial selections. The cultural assets and contexts we select are more than just building blocks of heritage values; they reflect our continuously evolving culture.

Acknowledgements

The authors would like to thank David Myers and colleagues at the Getty Conservation Institute for generously providing information and engaging in numerous discussions that enriched our understanding of the subject. We also extend our gratitude to the reviewers of the article for their valuable comments.

Funding

This paper incorporates additional insights gained during the author's participation in the Getty Scholar Program in Fall 2023. The participation in the CAA 2023 "50 Years of Synergy" conference in Amsterdam was supported by the Israel Antiquities Authority Fund for Scientific Relations.

Conflict of interest disclosure

The authors declare that they comply with the PCI rule of having no financial conflicts of interest in relation to the content of the article.

Data, Scripts, Code, and Supplementary Information Availability

The raw data of eight site records used in this study is available as a Word file: DOI:10.5281/zenodo.8309992.

Peer review

This article has been reviewed and recommended by PCI Archaeology.

Taylor, James S. 2024. "How Semantic Technologies and Spatial Networks Can Enhance Archaeological Resource Management." *Peer Community in Archaeology* 100411. DOI:10.24072/pci.archaeo.100411.

References

Alam, Mehwish, Victor De Boer, Enrico Daga, Marieke Van Erp, Eero Hyvönen, and Albert Meroño-Peñuela. 2022. "Editorial of the Special Issue on Cultural Heritage and Semantic Web." *Semantic Web* 14 (2): 155–58. DOI:10.3233/SW-223187.

Alba, Ester, Mar Gaitán, Arabella León, Javier Sevilla, Álvaro Solbes, and Vicente Pla. 2023. "Technological Tools for the Conservation and Dissemination of Valencian Design Archives." *Heritage* 6 (9): 6066–96. DOI:10.3390/heritage6090319.

Alef, Yael. 2017. "Towards an Inventory for Archaeological Heritage Management in Israel." In *The International Archives of the Photogrammetry, Remote Sensing and Spatial Information Sciences* XLII–2: 21–25. DOI:10.5194/isprs-archives-XLII-2-W5-21-2017.

Alef, Yael. 2019. "Classification of Archaeological Sites for Heritage Management Inventory: The Case of the Ancient Synagogues in the Galilee." In *ISPRS Annals of the Photogrammetry, Remote Sensing and Spatial Information Sciences* 4: 17–24. DOI:10.5194/isprs-annals-IV-2-W6-17-2019.

Alef, Yael. 2021. "Information Needs of Archaeological Sites Evaluation for Cultural Heritage Management Inventory: The Case of the Ancient Synagogues in Northern Israel." PhD diss., Tel Aviv: Bar Ilan University.

Alef, Yael, and Shua Kisilevitz. 2018. *Huqoq: Master Plan Conservation Annex.* Not published.

Alef, Yael, and Amit Rosenblum. 2015. *Saving the Synagogues in the Galilee: Conservation from a Regional Perspective.* Jerusalem: Israel Antiquities Authority. https://www.iaa-conservation.org.il/Projects_Item_eng.asp?subject_id=10&site_id=72&id=162.

ARIADNE. 2016. *ARIADNE Data Integration Case Study.* Cardiff: University of South Wales Hypermedia Research Group. http://ariadne-lod.isti.cnr.it/description.html.

Australia ICOMOS. 2013. *The Burra Charter: The Australia ICOMOS Charter for Places of Cultural Significance.* Burwood: Austrialia ICOMOS.

Avrami, Erica, and Randall Mason. 2019. "Mapping the Issue of Values." In *Values in Heritage Management: Emerging Approaches and Research Directions*, edited by Erica Avrami, Susan Macdonald, Randall Mason, and David Myers, 9–33. Los Angeles: The Getty Conservation Institute.

Boeuf, Patrick Le, Martin Doerr, Christian Emil Ore, and Stephen Stead (eds). 2018. *Definition of the CIDOC Conceptual Reference Model. Version 6.2.3.* ICOM/CIDOC CRM Special Interest Group.

Briuer, Fredrick L., and Clay Mathers. 1997. *Trends, and Patterns in Cultural Resource Significance: An Historical Perspective and Annotated Bibliography.* Vicksburg: US Army Corps of Engineers Waterways Experiment Station.

Carlisle, Philip, Ioannis Avramides, Alison Dalgity, and David Myers. 2014. "The Arches Heritage Inventory and Management System: A Standards-Based Approach to the Management of Cultural Heritage Information." In *CIDOC Conference: Access and Understanding–Networking in the Digital Era, Dresden, Germany, 6–11 September*. Dresden: ICOM.

Carman, John. 2015. *Archaeological Resource Management*. Cambridge: Cambridge University Press. DOI:10.1017/CBO9781139020473.

Carver, Martin. 1996. "On Archaeological Value." *Antiquity* 70 (267): 45–56. DOI:10.1017/S0003598X00082879.

Clark, Kate. 2014. "Values-Based Heritage Management and the Heritage Lottery Fund in the UK." *APT Bulletin: The Journal of Preservation Technology* 453 (2): 65–71.

Dalgity, Alison, David Myers, and Cathrine Scmidt Patterson. 2022. "The Arches Platform: Bridging Heritage Pasts and Data-Rich Futures." *Conservation Perspective: The GCI Newsletter* Fall 2022: 10–12.

Darvill, Timothy. 1995. "Value Systems in Archaeology." In *Managing Archaeology*, edited by M.A. Cooper, J. Carman, A. Firth, and D. Wheatley, 40–50. London: Routledge.

Diaz-Mendoza, María Antonia, Emiro De-La-Hoz-Franco, Jorge Eliecer Gómez Gómez, and Raúl Ramírez-Velarde. 2023. "An Ontological Model for the Representation of Vallenato as Cultural Heritage in a Context-Aware System." *Heritage* 6 (8): 5648–71. DOI:10.3390/heritage6080297.

Fredheim, L. Harald, and Maal Khalaf. 2016. "The Significance of Values: Heritage Value Typologies Re-Examined The Significance of Values: Heritage Value Typologies Re-Examined." *International Journal of Heritage Studies* 22 (6): 466–81. DOI:10.1080/13527258.2016.1171247.

Hardesty, Donald L., and Barbara J. Little. 2009. *Assessing Site Significance : A Guide for Archaeologists and Historians, 2nd Ed.* Walnut Creek: Altamira Press.

Ilan, Zvi. 1991. *Ancient Synagogues in Israel (Hebrew).* Tel Aviv: משרד הבטחון.

Ireland, Tracy, Steve Brown, and John Schofield. 2020. "Situating (in)Significance." *International Journal of Heritage Studies* 26 (9): 826–44. DOI:10.1080/13527258.2020.1755882.

Leibner, Uzi. 2023. "The Synagogue at Khirbet Wadi Ḥamam." In *Ancient Synagogues Revealed: 1981-2022*, edited by Lee I. Levine, Zeev Weiss, and Uzi Leibner, 66–77. Jerusalem: Israel Exploration Society.

Levine, Lee I. 2000. *The Ancient Synagogue: The First Thousand Years*. New Haven: Yale University Press.

Li, Jiayu, and Antonis Bikakis. 2023. "Towards a Semantics-Based Recommendation System for

Cultural Heritage Collections." *Applied Sciences* 13 (15): 8907. DOI:10.3390/app13158907.
Lombardo, Vincenzo, Tugce Karatas, Monica Gulmini, Laura Guidorzi, and Debora Angelici. 2022. "Transdisciplinary Approach to Archaeological Investigations in a Semantic Web Perspective." *Semantic Web* 14 (2): 361–83. DOI:10.3233/SW-223016.
Magness, Jodi, Shua Kisilevitz, Matthew Grey, Karen Britt, and Ra'anan Boustan. 2023. "The Ḥuqoq Synagogue Excavations: Report on the 2011–2018 Seasons." In *Ancient Synagogues Revealed: 1981-2022*, edited by Lee I. Levine, Zeev Weiss, and Uzi Leibner, 48–65. Jerusalem: Israel Exploration Society.
Mason, Randall. 2002. "Assessing Values in Conservation Planning: Methodological Issues and Choices." In *Assessing the Values of Cultural Heritage*, edited by Marta de la Torre, 5–30. Los Angeles: The Getty Conservation Institute. DOI:10.2979/aft.2003.50.2.66.
Mathers, Clay, Timothy Darvill, and Barbara J. Little. 2005. "Introduction: Archaeological Value in a World Context." In *Heritage of Value, Archaeology of Renown: Reshaping Archaeological Assessment and Significance*, edited by Clay Mathers, Timothy Darvill, and Barbara Little, 1–20. Gainesville: University Press of Florida.
McKeague, Peter, Anthony Corns, Åsa Larsson, Anne Moreau, Axel Posluschny, Koen Van Daele, and Tim Evans. 2020. "One Archaeology: A Manifesto for the Systematic and Effective Use of Mapped Data from Archaeological Fieldwork and Research." *Information* 11 (4): 222. DOI:10.3390/INFO11040222.
McLuhan, Marshall. 1964. *Understanding Media: The Extensions of Man*. New York: McGraw-Hill.
Myers, David, and Janet Hansen. 2024. *Inventories and Surveys for Heritage Management: Lessons for the Digital Age*. Los Angeles: The Getty Conservation Institute.
Pan, Shirui., Linhao Luo, Yufei Wang, Chen Chen, Jiapu Wang, and Xindong Wu. 2024. "Unifying Large Language Models and Knowledge Graphs: A Roadmap." *IEEE Transactions on Knowledge and Data Engineering* 36 (7): 3580–99. DOI:10.1109/TKDE.2024.335210.
Ruiz-Calleja, Adolfo, Pablo García-Zarza, Guillermo Vega-Gorgojo, Miguel L. Bote-Lorenzo, Eduardo Gómez-Sánchez, Juan I. Asensio-Pérez, Sergio Serrano-Iglesias, and Alejandra Martínez-Monés. 2022. "Casual Learn: A Linked Data-Based Mobile Application for Learning about Local Cultural Heritage." *Semantic Web* 14 (2): 181–95. DOI:10.3233/SW-212907.
Schiffer, Michael B., and George J. Gumerman. 1977. "Assessing Significance." In *Conservation Archaeology: A Guide for Cultural Resource Management Studies*, edited by Michael B. Schiffer and George J. Gumerman, 239–47. New York: Academic Press.
Schreier, Margrit. 2012. *Qualitative Content Analysis in Practice*. London: Sage Publications Ltd.
Sullivan, Sharon. 1993. "Conservation Policy Delivery." In *Cultural Heritage in Asia and the Pacific, Conservation and Policy: Proceedings of a Symposium Held in Honolulu, Hawaii, September 8–13, 1991, Organized by the U.S. Committee of the International Council on Monuments and Sites for the U.S. Information Age*, edited by Margaret G. H. MacLean, 16–26. Marina del Rey: The Getty Conservation Institute. DOI:10.1080/19455224.2014.960693.
Tepper, Yotam, Gil Derin, and Yigal Tepper. 2000. *Nahal Amud Area: Chapters on the Local Settlement* (in Hebrew). Tel Aviv: Habbikutz Hameuchad.
UNESCO. 2000. *World Heritage Centre – Tentative Lists: Early Synagogues in the Galilee*. http://whc.unesco.org/en/tentativelists/1470.
Wijesuriya, Gamini, Jane Thompson, and Christopher Young. 2013. *Managing Cultural World Heritage*. Paris: UNESCO.

2 Body Mapping the Digital

Visually representing the impact of technology on archaeological practice

Leila H. Araar
Department of Archaeology
The University of York
leilaharaar@gmail.com
ORCID 0000-0001-7014-9300

Colleen Morgan
Department of Archaeology
The University of York
ORCID 0000-0001-6907-5535

Louise Fowler
Museum of London
Archaeology
ORCID 0000-0002-4262-0967

Abstract

This paper uses a participatory, art-based methodology to understand how digital and analogue tools impact individuals' experiences and perceptions of archaeological recording. Body mapping involves the creation of life-sized drawings and narratives representing individuals' lived experiences, perceptions, and meanings within their social context. Based on data gathered during a series of focus groups, this paper explores body mapping as a visual research method in understanding the lived experiences of archaeologists with respect to changes brought about by digital technology.

While still ongoing, this research aims to encourage archaeologists to consider their evolving relationships with technology. Preliminary studies suggest that there are significant pedagogical, cognitive, and professional implications to consider when replacing analogue with digital approaches in archaeological recording.

Keywords: Archaeological methods; Analogue recording; Digital Archaeology; Embodiment; Body mapping; Art-based research

2.1 Introduction

Recording during archaeological fieldwork has developed from relatively rudimentary diaries and notes during antiquarian excavations to more routinised pro forma recording, a procedure developed in part in the United Kingdom as a response to large, urban excavations. With the advent of digital technologies, archaeology has adopted a range of technological solutions to address archaeological recording. Digital systems have been embedded within post-excavation processes for many years, with most finds and environmental recording work now born digital. Recent years have seen the pace of the so-called "digital turn" accelerate, as mobile computing has expedited the full digitalization of archaeological workflows (Costopoulos 2016). A growing number of projects are choosing fully paperless recording, with tablets replacing context sheets while hand drawings are exchanged for digital drawings or replaced by 3D based methods altogether. With the promise of accuracy and speed, as well as gaining novel ways of viewing archaeological evidence, a celebratory dialogue has developed around these technological advancements emphasising the efficiencies that digital tools have brought (Roosevelt et al. 2015; Berggren et al. 2015; Taylor et al. 2018).

In *Advances in Digital Archaeology. Proceedings of the 2023 conference Computer Applications and Quantitative Methods in Archaeology – 50 years of synergy*, edited by J.W.H.P. Verhagen, J. Waagen, A. Brandsen, A. Queffelec, R.M. Visser and D. Taelman, 31–44. Leiden: Sidestone Press.

While digital recording technologies have frequently been hailed for their benefits, rarely do these novel approaches bring critical methodological reflection on fieldwork practices (Perry and Taylor 2018). Concerns have been raised regarding the focus on speed and efficiency within digital archaeology and the impact of these technologies on training, analysis, and data preservation (Caraher 2016; Kersel 2016; Morgan and Wright 2018; Morgan et al. 2021; Perry 2018). Digital systems often mirror paper-based systems without considering how these novel datasets contribute differently to the analysis and dissemination of the archaeological record. As a result, the adoption of technology in archaeology has frequently pushed pre-existing frameworks and exacerbated issues present in archaeological field practice. While archaeological excavations have become increasingly efficient over the years, there have been concerns that this trend towards speed may compromise our understanding of the site. Traditional archaeological methods require archaeologists to spend more time in the field, carefully excavating each layer, drawing and recording their findings. Their digital counterparts, designed for speed, often result in fieldworkers engaging less intimately with the site during the recording process (Morgan et al. 2021).

Digital recording has been introduced in archaeological fieldwork, and while there have been studies regarding their proposed utility in increased speed, fidelity, and even reflexivity (Sapirstein 2020; Roosevelt et al. 2015; Berggren et al. 2015; Taylor et al. 2018, amongst others), there has been little examination of the impact of digital recording in the commercial sector. There are many questions raised by the mass adoption of digital archaeological recording techniques, including: "How do digital recording strategies impact the documentation and interpretation of archaeological remains in the field? How does the transition to digital recording impact the experience of fieldworkers? Do digital technologies facilitate or impede recording workflows in the field?"

To gain insight into these problems and knowledge production in archaeology as a whole, this paper uses a creative, art-based methodology in order to empower archaeologists to consider the changing relationships between mind, body and practice brought about by digital technologies. Research incorporating alternative forms of knowledge have demonstrated the potential of visual methods in qualitative research (Letsiou 2017). In recent years, body mapping has gained increasing recognition within research communities as an art-based approach that extends beyond the limitations of words in conveying the complexities of embodied experiences (Skop 2016). With data gathered during a series of focus groups, this paper explores body mapping as a visual research method in understanding the experiences of archaeologists in regard to changes brought about by digital technologies.

This research complements existing research (e.g., Morgan et al. 2021) in understanding the cognitive and physical impacts of digital recording in the context of archaeological fieldwork. It represents preliminary investigations derived from a wider AHRC CDP funded project, co-supervised by the Department of Archaeology at the University of York and the Museum of London Archaeology (MOLA), which investigates the impact of digital methods on the documentation, interpretation, publication, and dissemination of archaeological knowledge. This research will provide the background to understanding digital recording in terms of the long tradition of archaeological craft at MOLA, with particular attention to the process of archaeological knowledge production, the role of fieldworkers, and the changes brought about by digital recording technologies in archaeological fieldwork.

2.2 Body Mapping

Body mapping is an established form of art-based research that examines the way in which participants interpret, give meaning to and make sense of their experiences within their social context. As a participatory research method, body mapping focuses on constructing a narrative through creative, reflexive and emotive means, viewing the body as a space of inquiry. Rooted in feminist theories of embodiment and multiplicity of experience, body mapping is a visual and visceral approach that seeks to communicate complicated lived experiences in a way that goes beyond the scope of language (Haraway 1988; Moss and Dyck 2003; Jokela-Pansini 2021). It employs visual storytelling to illustrate social, political and economic processes of an individual's lived experience through the creation of life-sized drawings (body maps) as part of a reflective and creative process and has been employed by a range of disciplines for both therapeutic and research purposes (Gastaldo et al. 2012).

The approach originated in Jamaica as an art therapy approach to investigate female sexuality (MacCormack and Draper 1987) and was subsequently developed (seemingly independently from the previous study) to explore the personal and political dimensions of HIV/AIDS (MacGregor 2009). An initial facilitation guide was developed by South African artist, Jane Solomon (2002), and used as an international training tool. Using this guide, the approach was further developed by clinical psychologists as a therapeutic way to record stories (Morgan 2003). The technique was later adapted for research as a way to encourage participant reflection through a narrative process (Gastaldo et al. 2012). Body mapping has since developed as a research method used to explore a range of topics, including health related issues (Skop 2016), sexuality and gender, psychological trauma (Santen 2014, 2015), experiences of discrimination (Gastaldo et al. 2012), urban planning (Sweet and Ortiz Escalante 2015), and workplace risks (Keith and Brophy 2004; for a full review see de Jager et al. 2016).

The body mapping process varies depending on its application and purpose and can last anywhere from a few hours to several days. The researcher begins by introducing body mapping as an approach, its process and its application in the study, ensuring participants are informed about how the resulting data will be used. Once consent has been obtained, participants are asked to trace their body outline on large paper before commencing a series of reflective exercises. The process is facilitated and guided by the researcher, who encourages participants to consider symbols, colours, feelings, and environment as they reflect on their embodied experiences (Gastaldo et al. 2012). Participants are encouraged to portray their experiences in the manner which makes sense to them without restriction to a singular mode of communication.

Through this creative approach, participants are empowered to consider their experience beyond the boundaries of language, allowing for the representation of sensory, physical, and emotional dimensions of experience. The body mapping process draws participants' attention to their bodies and embodied experience, encouraging awareness and reflection. It offers participants an empowering means to communicate ideas, experiences, and meanings in the way they would like it told. As a result, the process has the potential to engage and enable its participants to communicate creatively through a deeper, more reflexive process. Body Mapping challenges ideas that the social world can be explored using solely language and aims to represent otherwise intangible and difficult dimensions of experience (Baerg 2003). As such, body mapping is a holistic approach which examines the interplay of individuals' mind, body, and social context, gaining access to their perceptions, meanings, and the explanatory models they bring into an encounter. In this way, the process of body mapping moves beyond Cartesian dualism by bringing together participants' minds, bodies, feelings, thoughts, experiences, and social interactions (Skop 2016). Crucially, when participants are provided with the extended process of body mapping, they can identify insights that may not arise in conventional interview approaches. The approach lends itself to alternate story telling while providing the capacity for eliciting feeling states among participants, creating an atmosphere conducive towards introspection, reflection and the organisation of emotions and meanings. These elements made body mapping a compelling research methodology to address the questions central to this research.

2.2.1 Exploratory Workshops

This study uses body mapping to capture rich, multi-dimensional information on the impact of digital recording on the embodied experiences of archaeologists to understand the cognitive and physical impacts of digital recording in the context of archaeological fieldwork.

2.2.1.1 Pilot Study

An initial pilot study was conducted amongst the three named researchers and a volunteer archaeologist. We tested the method on a small scale, with the aim to evaluate

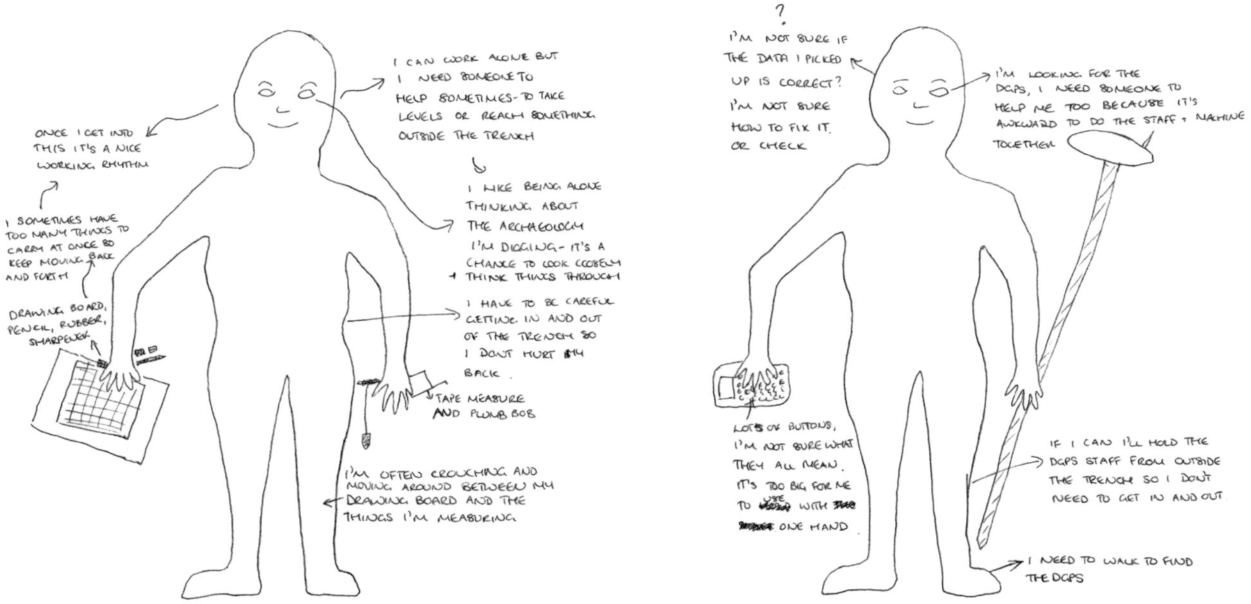

Figure 2.1. Examples of exploratory body maps from the pilot study, exploring analogue recording (left) compared to digital approaches (right).

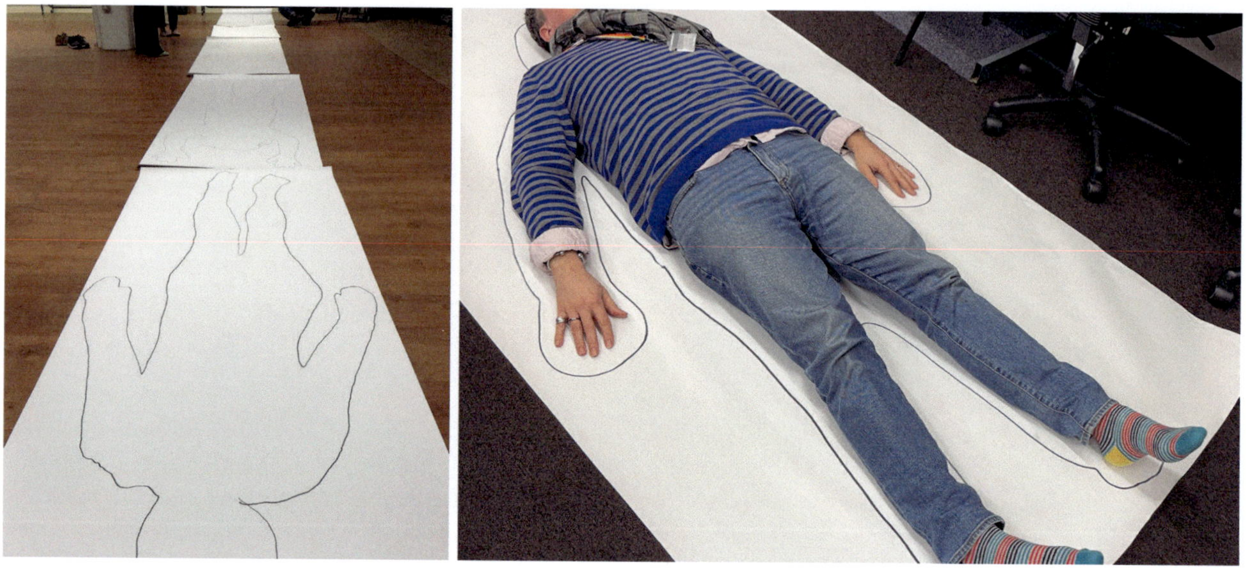

Figure 2.2. Body tracing in progress. Left: Rolled out paper roll with participant bodies traced. Right: Participant laying on large paper as their body is traced.

Amount of Experience	Number of Participants
0 - 1 year	4
1 - 3 years	4
7+ years	10

Table 2.1. Length of participant involvement in archaeological fieldwork.

its potential in exploring the transition from analogue to digital recording. The experiment took place after a day of excavation at the Hili-16 Archaeological Excavations in the United Arab Emirates (UAE), so the experience was fresh in our minds. Using an A4 piece of paper, participants drew a body outline and illustrated the impact of analogue recording on their experience in the field. The exercise was then replicated using another sheet of paper, but focused on the impact of digital recording, resulting in two separate body maps (Figure 2.1).

Participants took turns sharing their narratives, using the body maps to reflect first on their experience recording with analogue tools, then digital. Even at this scale, body mapping showed promise in exploring individuals' experience of this transition, highlighting key themes for exploration. It became clear that issues surrounding engagement, movement, interactivity, agency, and collaboration were at the centre of tensions between analogue and digital recording.

2.2.1.2 Focus Groups

Following the initial pilot study, two further exploratory focus groups were conducted in order to explore body mapping at its full scale. The initial focus group was held in the Digital Archaeology and Heritage Lab at Kings Manor (University of York). Our call for participants, shared among postgraduate students and staff at the University of York, resulted in the recruitment of eight participants with varying fieldwork experience in both research projects and commercial excavations.

The second study took place at MOLA offices in London and focused on the lived experience of commercial archaeologists. The call for participants, shared with both the field and survey teams at MOLA led to the participation of six archaeologists with varying levels of experience in fieldwork (Table 2.1), project management and geomatics. As colleagues and co-workers, this group of participants were much more familiar with each other resulting in a relaxed environment.

These sessions began with an introduction to the study, body mapping as a method, and a breakdown of the session. As some of the participants had not been in the field for some time, we used photographs from our recent fieldwork in the UAE as memory aids, but otherwise did not define what constituted analogue or digital recording.

Large meter wide paper rolls were then spread out onto the floors and art materials provided to participants, including pens, paint, markers, brushes, and sponges. As an initial exercise, participants were asked to consider their practice and choose a posture to be traced for their body map. The exercise demanded a degree of vulnerability for participants, as they laid down on the floor and trusted another individual to trace the outline of their body (Figure 2.2). However, the size and personal nature of the exercise also allowed for

Figure 2.3. Participants engaged in the body mapping process, visually translating their experience of analogue and digital recording onto their body maps.

greater commitment and investment throughout the process inviting deeper reflection.

Once all participants had had their body traced, they were shown slides relating to each recording type (analogue/digital), with accompanying prompts. Participants were asked to reflect on their use of analogue and digital recording respectively and communicate, by putting to paper in different colours/mediums, elements of their experience documenting using each approach (Figure 2.3).

The resulting body maps were then used as a reference, as participants shared their narratives with the group, eventually provoking group wide discussion on the challenges of each approach (Figure 2.4). It was evident for both groups that the provided time frame was just short of sufficient and perhaps three hours, as opposed to two, would have been better suited for this adaptation and scale of the body mapping process.

2.3 Analysis and Results

The dataset for this study includes participants' narratives, the body maps, and any researcher notes made during the session. Sessions were recorded and analysis began by reviewing the audio and photographing the body maps. The sessions' verbal recordings were transcribed, cleaned and uploaded into the qualitative data management software program NVivo 12, which was used to code and analyse the transcripts.

The study adopted an inductive approach which involved reviewing the transcripts multiple times and generating initial codes line-by-line. These codes were further refined to develop axial codes through the systematic organisation of data into wider categories and subcategories. The organisation of data ultimately facilitated the identification of thematic codes which aimed to provide a comprehensive understanding of participants' experiences (Braun and Clarke 2006).

2.3.1 Thinking about the Body

The body maps created by the participants depicted a range of responses and when describing their experiences with analogue and digital recording, several themes emerged consistently. Due to the nature of the research approach, participants' attention was drawn to their bodies, encouraging the characterisation of experience in physical and sensory terms: how they were moving in relation to the archaeology and other fieldworkers; the posture they adopted; what their hands were doing; what they were looking at; what they could smell; where an experience was felt on the body. For example, one participant illustrated the visceral, gut feeling they associated with analogue recording, *"I don't know where my guts are...but I feel that when you do, um, analogue, you also involve your feelings more"* (Figure 2.5).

In addition to its instinctive nature, it was clear that analogue recording required greater physical load. Many emphasised various areas of physical pain (back, knee, hand, elbow).

> *"It's more labour intensive to do like analogue because I just think of all the bending down, standing up, bending down, squatting in the trenches trying to get your drawings in and measurements and how long you're stood in a position to draw something."*

Surprisingly, despite the added physical labour and chance of injury, participants still expressed a preference for analogue recording, finding it *"easier to engage"*. One participant described that as *"there were sort of negatives to [analogue] in terms of the pain and possible personal risk, but I also did really enjoy it because I felt a connection to what we were doing."*

When comparing analogue and digital recording approaches, participants identified differences in proximity

Figure 2.4. Participants standing in front of their body maps as they reflect on and describe visual elements (colours, symbols, lines, shapes) representing their experience of analogue and digital recording.

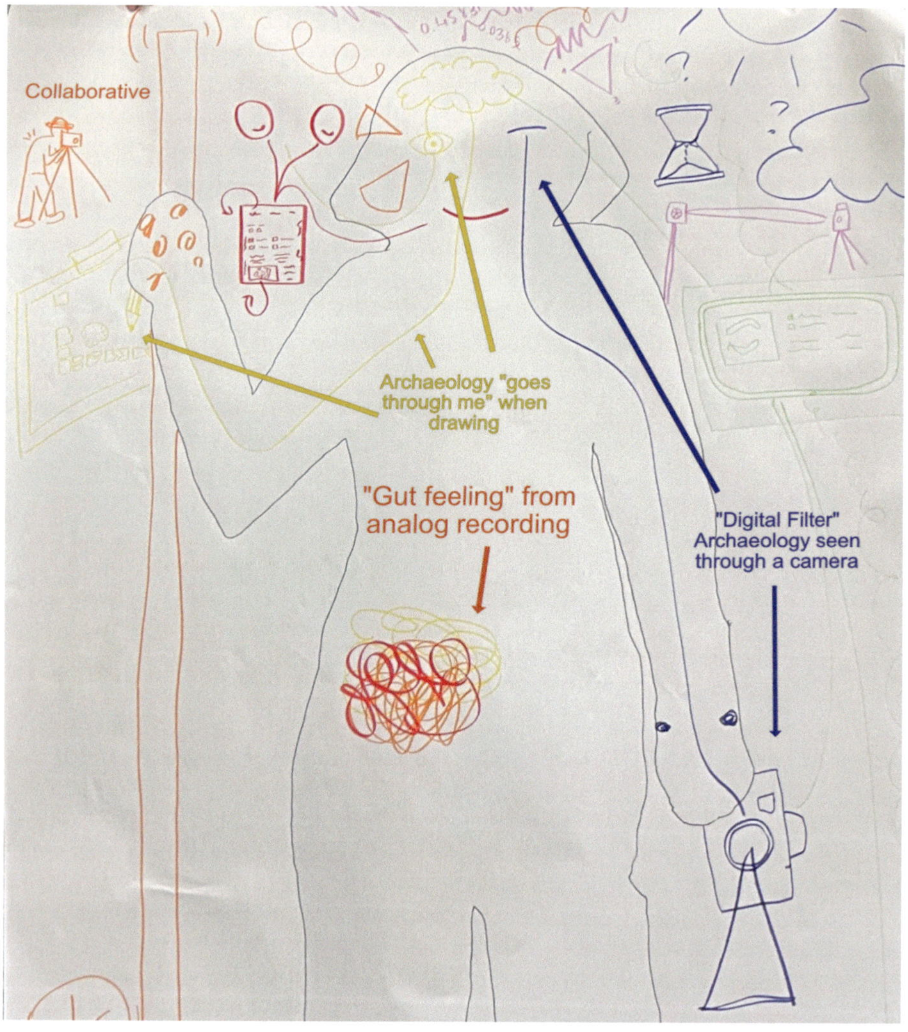

Figure 2.5. An example of a body map created by a study participant. Analogue recording is illustrated in warm colours (yellow, orange, red), while cool colours (blue, purple, green) are used for digital recording.

and interactivity. In reference to digital approaches, one participant pointed out the greater distance when recording:

> *"I'm usually standing up with photogrammetry compared to when I'm drawing, um, which is usually quite up close to the archaeology."*

Participants noted that the greater level of interactivity involved when using analogue recording facilitated a deeper engagement between the recorded material and their own cognitive processes, whilst digital approaches shifted the interaction towards a screen (Figure 2.6):

> *"You've got the dirt falling from the hands as well, sort of like the archaeology is at your fingertips. It's right there. It's, it's engaged with you. As opposed the hand over there. It's more of the circuit. Your hands are used for the digital, the moving of screens rather than anything else."*

The act of manually engaging in the recording process requires an individual to closely observe, explore and interpret the archaeological objects or features, facilitating mental head space. It allowed individuals to *"see things better"*, making it *"easier to understand the archaeology."*

This active involvement promoted heightened cognitive engagement, allowing individuals to make connections, identify patterns and develop a more nuanced understanding of the recorded material.

Of particular interest were themes surrounding movement and embodiment:

> *"the top half of my body is where I think about when I'm doing analogue recording...cause I'm like using my hip to lean things...my legs just don't seem to come into it. It's all about this part of my body."*

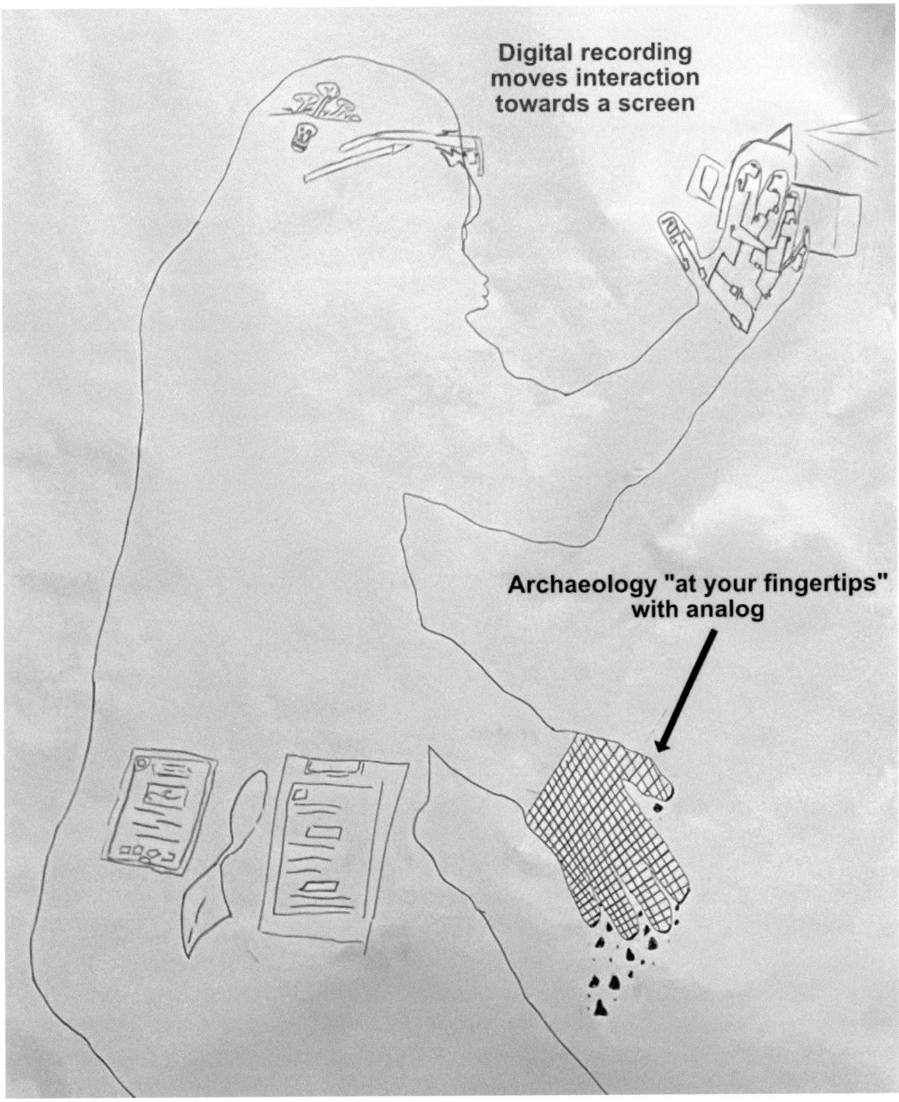

Figure 2.6. Body map example showing comparison in interactivity when using analogue (black) recording as opposed to digital (purple) recording.

One participant intentionally engaged less in creative aspects of the process, relying on a couple of symbols to convey how little they were aware of their body when recording digitally:

> *"when I'm thinking about digital... I think about my legs a lot more because I'm aware that I'm moving and that I need to not step on things but the rest of my body kind of disappears. I don't think about it."*

In general, depictions describing the impact of digital recording were less likely to feature embodied aspects of experience.

2.3.2 Tangibility, Adaptivity and Agency

It was clear that many participants preferred analogue recording, considering it more comfortable and familiar. One participant characterised analogue recording as "*second nature*" while associating the change brought by digital methods as a discomfort, requiring increased mental effort: "*I can't just do it off the top of my head...which is mentally draining.*"

This discomfort was shared by various other participants, particularly those with significant field experience. Yet, amongst those with under three years' experience in archaeological fieldwork, three participants expressed that having been trained in both from the start of their career, they felt equally comfortable using either recording system or believed their applicability was dependent on the needs of each project:

> *"I don't feel like my interpretations change, whether I'm doing digital or paperwork just because I am digitally like coherent and comfortable enough with it."*

One participant expressed that they trusted each approach differently; analogue recording involved tangible engagement. The archaeologists must intentionally execute each component of the recording process.

> *"I'm physically doing each element and putting it to paper and so I'm trusting it because I'm physically seeing myself do it."*

On the other hand, digital recording methods offered increased accuracy and reduced the likelihood of human error, but its data only existed digitally:

> *"You're just pressing a button, you're typing some stuff in and it kind of, you know, disappears for the moment."*

The ethereal nature of digital data was similarly noted by another participant:

> *"The archaeology only exists in your head digitally, it's all virtual. It's not at your fingertips anymore...the information still exists, but it exists absent from those other tools."*

Furthermore, it was communicated that when using digital approaches, the recorder's sense of agency and control diminishes, specifically in circumstances where recorders must rely on specialists:

> *"Then kind of similar to what was discussed about having to be reliant...sometimes with tech like you have to rely on somebody else because you may not fully understand it."*

Several participants also highlighted the inflexibility of digital data entry when discussing adaptability in the field. Paper records are "*easily adaptable to changing situations. So, if someone happens to accidentally machine out something, you can really quickly record something on a bit of permatrace in any way that you need to.*"

Whereas with digital methods "*you can't actually just adapt the system, you have to use it as it is. You can't without a lot of effort...you can't change it for something off the hoof or on the fly.*" (Figure 2.7). Using paper recording, archaeologists can make real-time adjustments to their recording, adding or refining details as necessary. This interactive process empowered them to actively shape and refine their understanding of the archaeology being recorded.

However, the added effort needed to make changes to digital data often resulted in these changes being dismissed or forgotten all together:

> *"If it's been drowned out and buried by 200 other entries, you're very likely going to forget that that was even a thing."*

Another participant agreed:

> *"Mentally, you're gonna go, oh, I need to make a note to change that. But then by the time you get through everything, you just forget."*

Many participants remarked on the depth of information captured through by-hand drawing that was lost when replaced by digital planning, which could be done "*from a distance*" and only captured "*an outline and not all the details of the feature*".

Furthermore, in reference to the interpretative power of by-hand drawing, one participant described a loss in understanding:

> *"I think there might be a certain loss with digital recording, to do with the drawing because sometimes when you're drawing in the field, you're interpreting as you draw."*

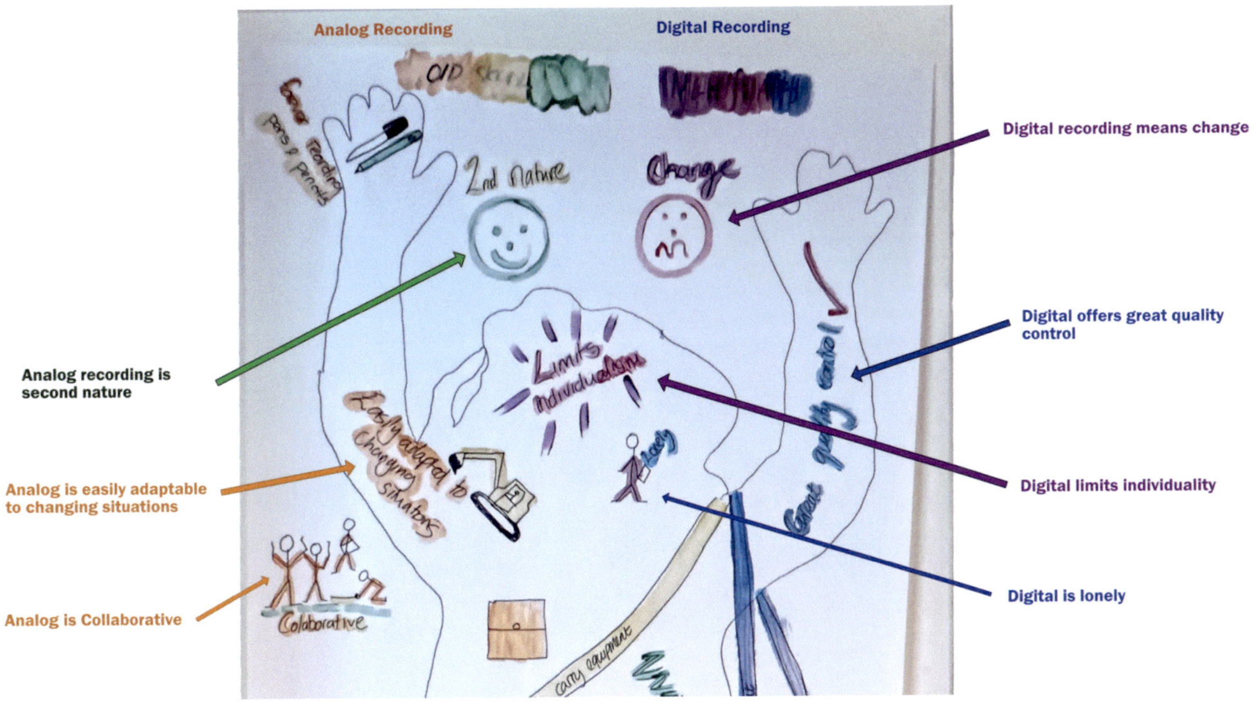

Figure 2.7. An example of a participant body map showing various themes related to their experience of analogue (left) and digital (right) recording.

Figure 2.8. Participant body map illustrating on-site collaboration and feedback which occur using analogue tools.

Figure 2.9. Participant standing next to their body map imitating the traced body posture on their map.

2.3.3 Feedback and Connection

Analogue recording was characterised as facilitating collaborative data collection and on-site interaction among team members (Figure 2.8). Several members of the team can take part in the recording process simultaneously, fostering the dynamic exchange of ideas, cross-checking of data, and collaborative decision-making during fieldwork:

> *"So old school, from my perspective, I think it's way more collaborative. I think you have to talk to people, you have to get people to hold like the end of the tape, then...you have to go and get their piece of permatrace off them, you have to go and look at their context sheets."*

Digital recording, on the other hand, was described to enhance feedback through the ease of data sharing between the field and the lab, promoting remote collaboration, efficient information exchange, and synchronised updates.

2.4 Reflection and Discussion

This study provides valuable insights into the physical and cognitive impact of recording approaches on the lived experiences of archaeologists. During data collection and analysis, it was clear that visual and art-based methods facilitated a deep reflection among participants and evoked richer information than verbal interviews. The body mapping process took longer than a verbal interview, encouraging participants to linger longer, reflecting more deeply on the research topic as a result (see narrative therapy practise "loitering with intent"; White and Epston 1990; White 2007).

The up-close and personal nature of the exercise encouraged participants to consider bodily and sensory dimensions of experience in ways they might not have done otherwise (Figure 2.9). According to one participant in particular, the scale and interactive nature of the body map encouraged deeper reflection on the use of their body during the recording process:

> *"I feel like I stepped out of myself... if you had just said like, tell me what parts of your body you used, rather than like, show me on a drawing. I would never have considered so many different parts of my body... Like what does this limb actually... how is it useful in archaeological recording?"*

Fieldworkers have frequently been described as having "*no voice*" in literature (Lucas 2002). However, this approach shifts the dynamics of the interview process, putting the narrative power in the hands of the archaeologists. In this way, participants have authority and play an active role during the research process, making decisions on how to represent their own experiences in a personal manner.

Consistently noted in the results of this study is the perception among participants that analogue and digital recording techniques both provide value, in different ways, for the documentation and interpretation of archaeological remains. It was clear that participants believed that the two approaches were not comparable, offering different levels of interaction, engagement, and cognition during the recording process.

The perceived gains brought by digital technologies were undeniable and included increased speed, ease of access, and the ability to examine features from new perspectives. In line with Taylor et al. (2018) observations on the benefits of digital access in the field, participants in this study, in particular those working in the commercial sector, highlighted an enthusiasm for access to lab and specialists' data. However, while many argued in favour of digital systems, they still found issues with the replacement of analogue drawing with digital alternatives. Morgan et al.'s (2021, 625) conclusions that "*drawing is both essential to archaeological recording and of great pedagogical importance*" is very much echoed in the results of this study. The unique role of by-hand drawing played in archaeological recording was shared by all participants in this study, who also expressed deep frustration with the impending nature of digital drawing software.

2.5 Conclusions

The application of body mapping in this study has proven a useful tool in encouraging participants to consider bodily and sensory dimensions of experience when using analogue and digital recording approaches in the field. In this approach, participants were encouraged to pay attention to their embodied experiences, promoting reflection on the interplay of the mind, body, and environment in the process of archaeological recording. Using this holistic approach, this study was able to highlight the role of embodied cognition and enactive knowledge in archaeological recording. The findings indicated a clear appreciation for the tangible and sensory aspects of analogue recording, which fostered a deeper connection with the archaeological material and contributed to a sense of ownership and control over the recorded data. Digital recording, however, offered advantages in terms of data capture, efficiency, feedback and data sharing, enabling remote collaboration and information exchange. The study underscores the importance of recognizing the value of both approaches and adopting a balanced approach that leverages the strengths of analogue and digital methods to enhance archaeological documentation and interpretation. Future work on this research will further refine the research methods and recommend holistic solutions that address the problems and opportunities of digital and analogue recording in archaeology.

Funding

This research was funded by the Arts and Humanities Research Council (AHRC) Collaborative Doctoral Partnership (CDP).

Conflicts of interest disclosure

To the best of the authors knowledge, there were no conflict of interests present in the undertaking of this research.

Peer review

This article has been reviewed and recommended by PCI Archaeology.

Dell'Unto, N. 2023. "Understanding archaeological documentation through a participatory, arts-based approach." *Peer Community in Archaeology* 100345. DOI:10.24072/pci.archaeo.100345.

References

Baerg, Susan. 2007. "'Sometimes There Just Aren't Any Words': Using Expressive Therapy With Adolescents Living With Cancer." *Canadian Journal of Counselling and Psychotherapy* 37 (1): 65–74.

Berggren, Åsa, Nicolo Dell'Unto, Maurizio Forte, Scott Haddow, Ian Hodder, Justine Issavi, Nicola Lercari, Camilla Mazzucato, Allison Mickel, and James S. Taylor. 2015. "Revisiting Reflexive Archaeology at Çatalhöyük: Integrating Digital and 3D Technologies at the Trowel's Edge." *Antiquity* 89 (344): 433–48. DOI:10.15184/aqy.2014.43.

Braun, Virginia, and Victoria Clarke. 2006. "Using Thematic Analysis in Psychology." *Qualitative Research in Psychology* 3 (2): 77–101.

Caraher, William. 2016. "4.1 Slow Archaeology: Technology, Efficiency, and Archaeological Work." In *Mobilizing the Past: The Potential of Digital Archaeology*, edited by Erin Walcek Averette, Jody Michael Gordon, and Derek B. Counts, 421–41. Grand Forks: The Digital Press at The University of North Dakota. DOI:10.17613/M6ZG8P.

Costopoulos, Andre. 2016. "Digital Archeology Is Here (and Has Been for a While)." *Frontiers in Digital Humanities* 3 (4). DOI:10.3389/fdigh.2016.00004.

Gastaldo, Denise, Lilian Magalhães, Christine Carrasco, and Charity Davy. 2012. "Body-Map Stroytelling as Research: Methodological Considerations for Telling the Stories of Undocumented Workers through Body Mapping." http://www.migrationhealth.ca/undocumented-workers-ontario/body-mapping.

Haraway, Donna. 1988. "Situated Knowledges: The Science Question in Feminism and the Privilege of Partial Perspective." *Feminist Studies: FS* 14 (3): 575–99. DOI:10.2307/3178066.

Jager, Adèle de, Anna Tewson, Bryn Ludlow, and Katherine Boydell. 2016. "Embodied Ways of Storying the Self: A Systematic Review of Body-Mapping." *Forum Qualitative Sozialforschung / Forum: Qualitative Social Research* 17 (2). DOI:10.17169/fqs-17.2.2526.

Jokela-Pansini, Maaret. 2021. "Body Mapping as a Feminist Visual Method." In *Raum Und Bild - Strategien Visueller Raumbezogener Forschung*, edited by Raphaela Kogler and Jeannine Wintzer, 69–82. Berlin: Springer. DOI:10.1007/978-3-662-61965-0_6.

Keith, Margaret M., and James T. Brophy. 2004. "Participatory Mapping of Occupational Hazards and Disease among Asbestos-Exposed Workers from a Foundry and Insulation Complex in Canada." *International Journal of Occupational and Environmental Health* 10 (2): 144–53. DOI:10.1179/oeh.2004.10.2.144.

Kersel, Morag M. 2016. "5.1 Response: Living a Semi-Digital Kinda Life." In *Mobilizing the Past: The Potential of Digital Archaeology*, edited by Erin Walcek Averette, Jody Michael Gordon, and Derek B. Counts, 475–92. Grand Forks: The Digital Press at The University of North Dakota. DOI:10.31356/dpb008.

Letsiou, Maria. 2017. "Mapping Experience Through Art-Based Research." *Research in Arts and Education* 2017 (1): 122–35. DOI:10.54916/rae.118852.

Lucas, Gavin. 2002. *Critical Approaches to Fieldwork: Contemporary and Historical Archaeological Practice*. London: Routledge. DOI:10.4324/9780203132258.

MacCormack, Carol, and Alizon Draper. 1987. "Social and Cognitive Aspects of Female Sexuality in Jamaica." In *The Cultural Construction of Sexuality*, edited by Patricia Caplan, 143–65. London: Tavistock Publications.

MacGregor, Hayley N. 2009. "Mapping the Body: Tracing the Personal and the Political Dimensions of HIV/AIDS in Khayelitsha, South Africa." *Anthropology & Medicine* 16 (1): 85–95. DOI:10.1080/13648470802426326.

Morgan, Colleen, Helen Petrie, Holly Wright, and James Stuart Taylor. 2021. "Drawing and Knowledge Construction in Archaeology: The Aide Mémoire Project." *Journal of Field Archaeology* 46 (8): 614–28. DOI:10.1080/00934690.2021.1985304.

Morgan, Colleen, and Holly Wright. 2018. "Pencils and Pixels: Drawing and Digital Media in Archaeological Field Recording." *Journal of Field Archaeology* 43 (2): 136–51. DOI:10.1080/00934690.2018.1428488.

Morgan, Jonathan, and Bambanani Women's Group. 2003. *Long Life: Positive HIV Stories*. Cape Town: Double Storey Books.

Moss, Pamela, and Isabel Dyck. 2003. "Embodying Social Geography." In *Handbook of Cultural Geography*, edited by Kay Anderson, 58-73. London: SAGE Publications. DOI:10.4135/9781848608252.

Perry, Sara. 2018. "Why Are Heritage Interpreters Voiceless at the Trowel's Edge? A Plea for Rewriting the Archaeological Workflow." *Advances in Archaeological Practice : A Journal of the Society of American Archeaology* 6 (3): 212–27. DOI:10.1017/aap.2018.21.

Perry, Sara, and James Taylor. 2018. "Theorising the Digital: A Call to Action for the Archaeological Community." In *Oceans of Data: Proceedings of the 44th Conference on Computer Applications and Quantitative Methods in Archaeology*, edited by Mieko Matsumoto and Espen Uleberg, 11–22. Oxford: Archaeopress.

Roosevelt, Christopher H., Peter Cobb, Emanuel Moss, Brandon R. Olson, and Sinan Ünlüsoy. 2015. "Excavation Is Destruction Digitization: Advances in Archaeological Practice." *Journal of Field Archaeology* 40 (3): 325–46. DOI:10.1179/2042458215Y.0000000004.

Santen, Bart. 2014. "Into the Fear-Factory: Connecting with the Traumatic Core." *Person-Centered*

& Experiential Psychotherapies 13 (2): 75–93. DOI:10.1080/14779757.2013.871574.

Santen, Bart. 2015. "Treating Dissociation in Traumatized Children with Body Maps." *Creative Interventions with Traumatized Children., 2nd Ed.*, edited by C. A. Malchiodi, 126–49. New York: The Guilford Press.

Sapirstein, Philip. 2020. "Human versus Computer Vision in Archaeological Recording." *Studies in Digital Heritage* 4 (2): 134–59. DOI:10.14434/sdh.v4i2.31520.

Skop, Michelle. 2016. "The Art of Body Mapping: A Methodological Guide for Social Work Researchers." *Aotearoa New Zealand Social Work* 28 (4): 29–43. DOI:10.11157/anzswj-vol28iss4id295

Solomon, Jane. 2002. "Living with 'X': A Body Mapping Journey in the Time of HIV and AIDS. Facilitator's Guide." Johannesburg: Regional Psychosocial Support Initiative (REPSSI). https://asksource.info/resources/living-x-a-body-mapping-journey-time-hiv-and-aidsfacilitators-guide.

Sweet, Elizabeth L., and Sara Ortiz Escalante. 2015. "Bringing Bodies into Planning: Visceral Methods, Fear and Gender Violence." *Urban Studies* 52 (10): 1826–45. DOI:10.1177/0042098014541157.

Taylor, James, Justine Issavi, Åsa Berggren, Dominik Lukas, Camilla Mazzucato, Burcu Tung, Nicoló Dell'Unto, and University of York. 2018. "'The Rise of the Machine': The Impact of Digital Tablet Recording in the Field at Çatalhöyük." *Internet Archaeology* 47. DOI:10.11141/ia.47.1.

White, Michael, and David Epston. 1990. *Narrative Means To Therapeutic Ends*. New York: Norton.

White, Michael. 2007. *Maps of Narrative Practice*. New York: Norton.

3 Survey Planning, Allocation, Costing and Evaluation (SPACE) Project

Developing a Tool to Help Archaeologists Conduct More Effective Surveys

Edward B. Banning
University of Toronto
ted.banning@utoronto.ca
ORCID 0000-0002-4281-7639

Steven Edwards
Nova Scotia Community College
steven.edwards@nscc.ca
ORCID 0009-0004-4485-278X

Isaac Ullah
San Diego State University
iullah@sdsu.edu
ORCID 0000-0002-3533-9421

Abstract
Designing an effective archaeological survey can be complicated and confidence that a survey was effective requires post-survey evaluation. The goal of SPACE is to develop software to facilitate survey designers' decisions and partially automate some of the tools for this that depend on mathematical models so that archaeologists can conduct surveys that accomplish their goals and evaluate their results more easily. We aim for SPACE to be a modular and accessible web-based platform for survey planning and quality assurance, with a "front end" that has a non-threatening, question-and-answer format. Its several interacting modules will ultimately include ones for evaluating visibility, estimating sweep widths and coverage, costing, determining sample sizes, transect and test-pit intervals, allocating effort optimally for stratified samples and predictive surveys, and quality assurance. In this paper, we focus on the module for estimating fieldwalkers' sweep widths on the basis of "calibrations" on fields seeded with artifacts, while also reviewing the overall structure of the project. Sweep widths are critical for estimating coverage, evaluating survey effectiveness and quality, and planning transect intervals.

Keywords: Archaeological Survey; Quality Assurance; Planning; Sweep Width; Calibration; Automation

3.1 Introduction
As archaeologists have known for decades, there is an array of search and statistical theory that could immensely benefit the design, implementation and evaluation of archaeological survey (e.g., Almagro-Gorbea et al. 2002; Banning 2002; Cochran 1977; Kintigh 1988; Koopman 1980; McManamon 1981; Plog et al. 1978; Schiffer et al. 1978; Shott 1987; 1989; Stone 1975; Wobst 1983). Despite this awareness, archaeologists have generally not taken advantage of these capabilities, perhaps because they think they are too difficult, make too little difference, or require math. The goal of the project that is the focus of this paper is to make these proven methods available to archaeologists in an easy-to-use tool that they can apply in their own work without having statistical or mathematical expertise.

In *Advances in Digital Archaeology. Proceedings of the 2023 conference Computer Applications and Quantitative Methods in Archaeology – 50 years of synergy*, edited by J.W.H.P. Verhagen, J. Waagen, A. Brandsen, A. Queffelec, R.M. Visser and D. Taelman, 45–54. Leiden: Sidestone Press.

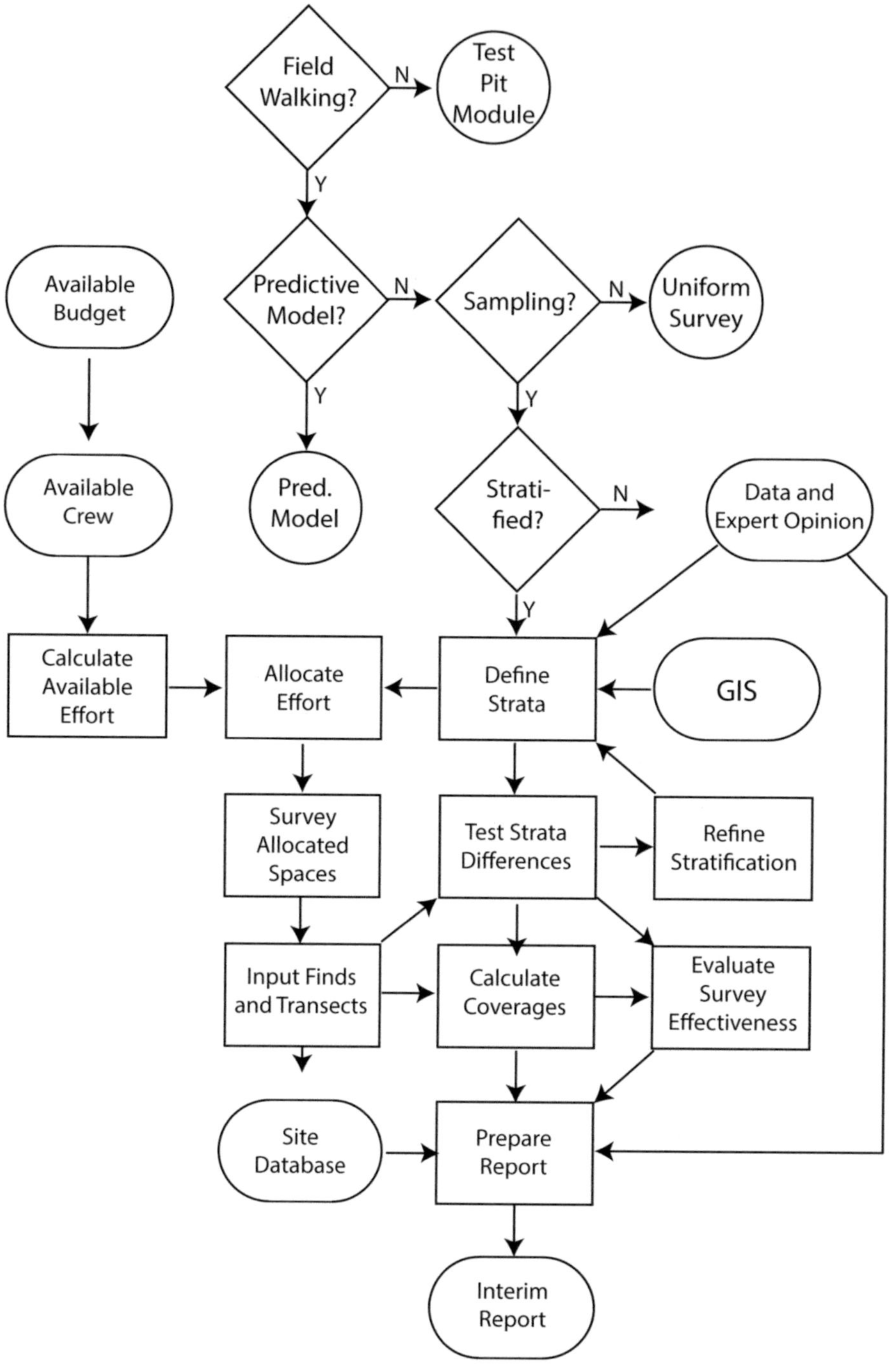

Figure 3.1. Flow chart for designing a stratified cluster sample for a fieldwalking survey. It has inputs from a GIS and a budget, an allocation process that may be proportionate or disproportionate and, for disproportionate sampling, options to minimize relative error on estimates of key parameters or to minimize cost for a fixed, acceptable error.

We believe that such a software platform will allow survey planners to design more effective surveys rather than just copying conventional designs in "cookie-cutter" fashion. Specifically, it would allow them to accomplish several goals: improve the quality of surveys with respect to their main objectives, make more effective use of typically limited resources, and improve accountability by making it easier to assess the thoroughness of survey, the statistical adequacy of samples and, more generally, the extent to which the survey has achieved its goals.

3.2 Our Proposed Solution

Our proposal to fill this gap is to develop a modular, accessible, and simple web-based platform for survey planning and quality assurance, with a "front end" that has a non-threatening, question-and-answer format and avoids a programming-like structure or display of off-putting equations.

The aim of the Survey Planning, Allocation, Costing and Evaluation (SPACE) Project is to create this online platform whose interacting modules will:

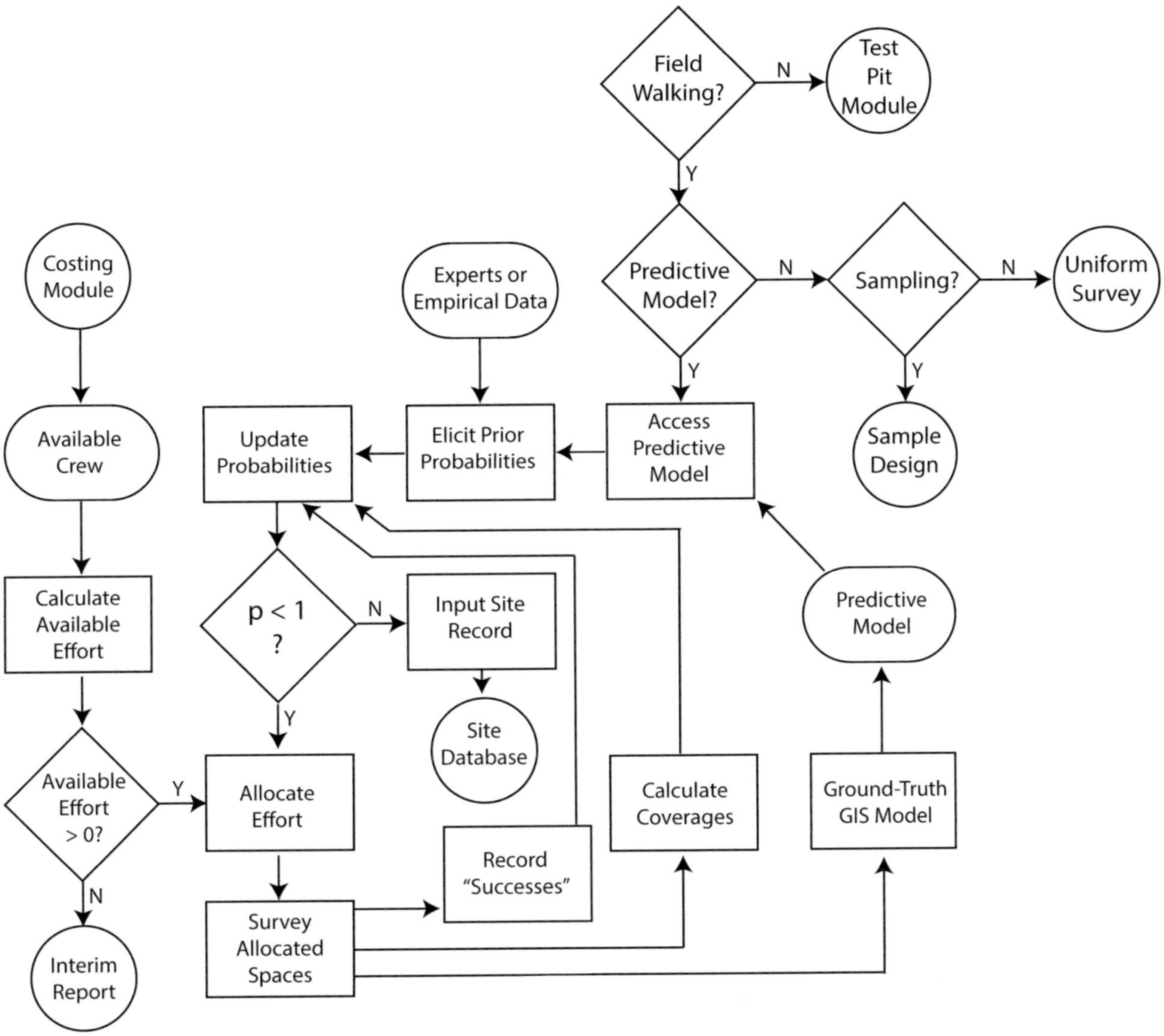

Figure 3.2. Flow chart for an archaeological survey by fieldwalking that employs a predictive model and optimal allocation. The allocation requires inputs from experts or empirical data, or both, data from the GIS model on the sizes of spaces and coverage to date, information on resources available, and updated information on field conditions and site or artifact detections as survey progresses. The design and implementation is too complex to be easily accomplished "on the fly", but most of the processes are relatively easy to automate.

- Help budget resources effectively (Costing module)
- Assist decision-making about the spacing of transects, cores, or shovel tests (Sweep Width module)
- Define strata and allocate effort optimally in disproportionate stratified cluster samples (Allocation module)
- Determine adequate sample sizes (Sample Size module)
- Allocate effort in surveys guided by predictive models (Allocation module)
- Provide more empirical estimates of visibility (Visibility module)
- And estimate survey coverage as a quality indicator (Coverage module)

To accomplish these goals, we need to identify the decisions that survey planners must make and the information inputs they need to make these decisions. For example, a Flow Diagram for some of the decisions, inputs and outputs involved in designing a stratified cluster sample for a fieldwalking survey (Figure 3.1) has inputs from a GIS and a budget, an allocation process that may be proportionate or disproportionate and, for disproportionate sampling, options to minimize relative error on estimates of key parameters or to minimize cost for a fixed, acceptable error. It also includes a process for post-survey testing the strata to ensure that they have been effective at partitioning variability in the population.

3.3 Applications, or "Why do This?"

We hope that the SPACE modules will assist archaeologists in a number of ways. For those conducting academic surveys, they will help them achieve objectives within their typically restrictive budgets and allow greater confidence in survey results.

In the heritage industry, we would expect the Sweep Width and related modules to be especially useful for surveys that "clear" a space for development by allowing greater confidence that they have not missed significant cultural resources. Once development has begun, it can be extremely costly to mitigate unanticipated sites that surveys failed to detect (Campana 2017, 4; Schiffer 1987, 353).

In another example (Figure 3.2), the Flow Diagram for allocating survey effort guided by a predictive model has processes based on classical Bayesian search allocation (Banning 2002; Koopman 1980; Stone 1975). This tool, originally developed to search for U-boats during the Second World War, has been the basis of search-and-rescue for decades, but has rarely seen use in archaeology (Hitchings et al. 2016). Archaeologists' failure to take note of this method may be due to the inaccurate perception that it is too computationally complex. Automating the mathematics, however, should make this useful method much more accessible to archaeologists.

The product we are developing includes several distinct modules, most of which are currently at the conceptual stage. In addition, most of these currently emphasize fieldwalking, but one is explicitly for subsurface survey. In this paper, we focus on the only module for which we have a working prototype, the Sweep Width module.

3.4 Sweep-Width Module

The purpose of this module is to help survey planners estimate sweep widths for fieldwalking in varying conditions (Banning et al. 2011, 2017; Milwid 2016). Sweep width (*W*) is the most general summary of all the factors that contribute to the probability that surveyors will find targets, whether sites or artifacts, and concerns the relationship between range (the perpendicular distance from the surveyor's path to the target) and the probability that the surveyor will detect the target.

The data for the Sweep Width Module come from mock surveys, what we call "calibration runs", over fields that are ideally devoid of artifacts except for ones we have seeded in known locations at varying ranges from the surveyor's path. The reason for such mock surveys is that it is the only way of which we are aware to evaluate the actual effectiveness of survey teams at detecting artifacts. Resurvey, for example, is not sufficient for this because it is likely that both the original and the resurvey team missed some of them. The calibration field can be prepared with an actual grid marked by strings (Banning et al. 2006; 2011), but we have found that the artificiality of such a setup outweighs the greater precision of artifact placement that the strings allow. More recently, we have used invisible grids, marked only by a tape along the centre line and markers for major divisions, such as 25 m or 50 m to help surveyors track their progress along a walking transect (Banning et al. 2017). Surveyors scan the area left and right of the tape as they walk but have to estimate the range to each artifact they see to their left or right. They are not allowed to wander off the path to investigate it.

Each surveyor makes multiple calibration runs on a particular calibration field that has been selected as typical of some real survey conditions, and accumulates data on tablets, including time of day, a photo of the field, and the type and estimated range of artifacts to the left or right of the path. We have used a custom data collection form in the Filemaker Go app, but other mobile data collection apps, such as ODK Collect, Qfield, or ArcGIS Collector[1], could equally fulfil this function. The digital data collection form also records surveyors' average speed from the tablets' built-in GPS. The full method for conducting calibration runs is explained in a supplementary document archived and accessible through Zenodo (Banning 2024). A direct permalink to this document is provided in the Materials and Methods section, below.

Once the calibration data are collected, they are uploaded to the Sweep Width module as .csv files. The module plots the reported detections by artifact type. Because surveyors vary in their estimates of distance, these plots show considerable spread in the range (Figure 3.3). To account for errors in estimating distances, the module currently uses a simplistic approach whereby an error tolerance is given to a hypothetical detection that is proportional to the estimated distance from the transect (we expect surveyors to estimate short distances more accurately than long ones).

This tolerance represents the radius of a circle around the detection. If a seeded artifact is found to be within the error tolerance for a given estimate, it is deemed a positive detection. Future updates to the model will adapt more sophisticated approaches to accounting for errors in distance estimation, including algorithms based on psychology research on distance perception (Li et al. 2011; Loomis and Philbeck 2008; Ooi and He 2007) to create ellipses around the known locations of artifacts. Once the positive and negative detections (or "false positives") have been counted, the module can use those data to display some general statistics, such as false-target rates, but the

1 FileMaker Go: https://apps.apple.com/us/app/claris-filemaker-go-19/id1484857908; ODK Collect: https://play.google.com/store/apps/details?id=org.odk.collect.android&hl=en_CA&gl=US&pli=1; Qfield: https://qfield.org; ArcGIS: https://doc.arcgis.com/en/collector-classic/ (all accessed February 19, 2024).

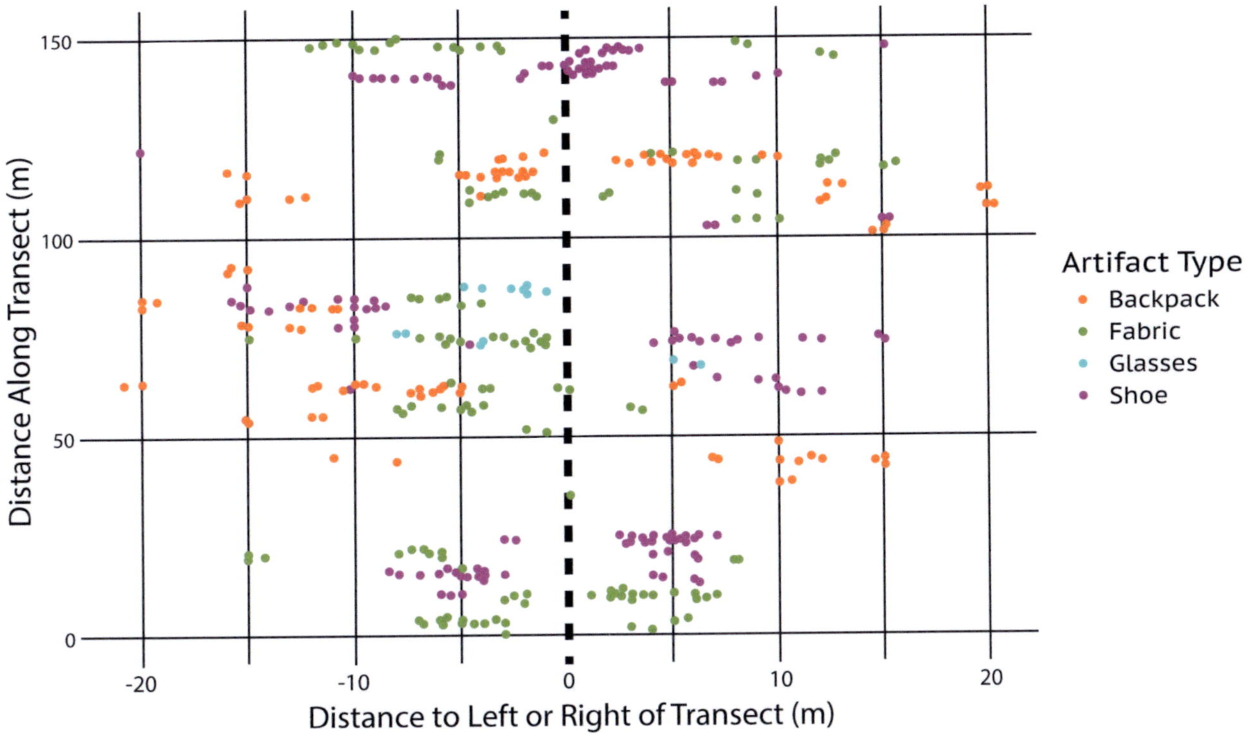

Figure 3.3. View of the reported detections for a set of calibration runs on a field seeded with artifacts relevant to a forensic search (backpacks, fabric pieces, eyeglasses, shoes). Note the considerable spread in range, due to surveyors' inaccurate estimates of distance.

more important role of the positive detections is to calculate detection functions and sweep widths.

Of the competing models for the relationship between detection probability and range away from the surveyor's path (Figure 3.4), in our applications to both archaeological and forensic types of artifacts, we have found the exponential function most realistic. Sweep width (*W*) is the swath, centred on the survey path, within which surveyors detect the same number of targets as they would have detected under the definite-detection model. Under definite detection, surveyors find 100% of targets within the sweep width and none at all outside it, which is not a realistic scenario.

Under the exponential model, surveyors find just as many artifacts outside the sweep width as they fail to detect inside it, so these cancel out (the shaded areas in Figure 3.4c, Figure 3.5).

The Sweep Width Module uses the calibration data – either for single artifact types or for all of them combined – to calculate the detection probabilities for each artifact type at different ranges and then fits an exponential detection function:

Here, *p(r)* is the probability of detecting a target at range *r*, and *b* is the probability of detection right on the surveyor's path. The variable *k* in this function summarizes all the factors that contribute to detectability, including visibility in the field being surveyed, average surveyor speed, obtrusiveness and clustering of the target artifacts, and others. Sweep width is then just the area under the detection function; because probability is unitless, this area yields a result in m.

The value of *k*, and therefore of *W*, varies by artifact type, visibility and other aspects of field conditions. Determining it with calibration surveys allows us to account for these factors simultaneously. Ideally, such calibrations should occur regularly over the course of a survey and in calibration fields that vary in their characteristics but mimic the conditions in spaces that will be the subject of "real" survey.

We have tested this process on surveys in Jordan and Cyprus with mock surveys on field types that include olive groves, ploughed fields, pastures, and harvested fields with stubble, and then applied the results to estimating coverages for actual surveys. In addition, we used sweep widths estimated in this way, multiplied by the total amount of effort we would expect a survey team to make in a day (total m walked) to allocate that effort near-optimally with Bayesian methods that we discuss elsewhere (Figure 3.6; Hitchings et al. 2016; Stewart et al. 2016). For example, in a region for which we estimated a sweep width of only 0.5 m, and an available effort of 5000 m, the coverage we would distribute among a set of survey spaces would be 2500 m^2.

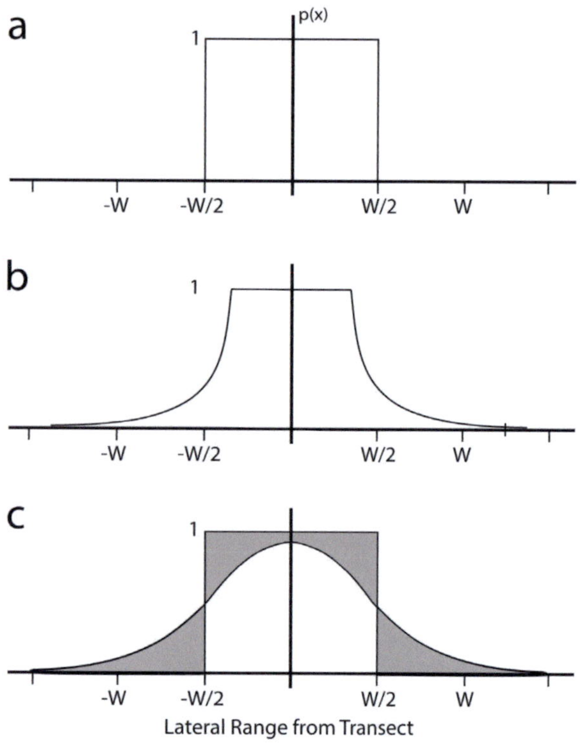

Figure 3.4. Three competing models for the relationship between detection probability (y-axis) and range from the transect centre-line: (a) definite detection, (b) inverse-cube detection, whereby detection probability declines with the cube of the range, and (c) exponential detection with sweep width (*W*), the grey area above the curve is equal to the grey area in the tails.

SPACE's Sweep Width Module automates the calculations once the calibration data are available, and we can update the estimates of Sweep Width as additional calibrations are complete.

Once sufficient data are available to provide sweep widths for the artifact types and conditions to be expected in a survey, we can use these either to provide a basis for selecting effective transect spacings or, after a more standard survey is complete, to allow accurate estimates of the probability that the survey has missed "targets" of a given size and density. In Jordan and Cyprus, we used the resulting sweep widths to distribute survey effort with Bayesian allocation (Hitchings et al. 2016; Stewart et al. 2016).

Because *k* varies by artifact type, survey planners must decide which value they want to use for planning purposes. If they want to be conservative, and minimize the risk of missing targets, they might use the smallest sweep width among the ones the module calculates. If they want to be more cost-conscious, they might elect to use the sweep width for the most important artifact type even if it is relatively large, or an intermediary one for all artifact types combined. Whatever choice they make, SPACE would fully

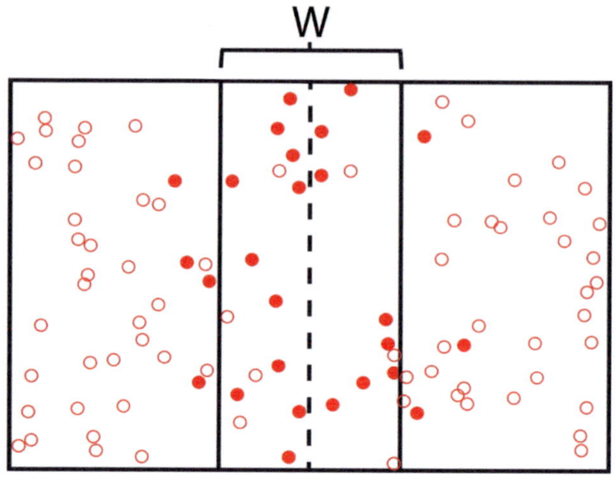

Figure 3.5. A visualization of sweep width in plan view. Note that the number of detected artifacts (red dots) outside W is equal to the number of undetected artifacts (white dots) within W (after Banning et al. 2011).

inform survey planners of the potential impacts of that choice in terms of the risk of missed detections or error in density estimates.

Ideally, projects would carry out their own calibrations to account for the specific conditions, including personnel, that are unique to those projects. However, we anticipate that some projects experience barriers to doing this. Consequently, we hope to make an online version of SPACE available that would allow users to access sweep width data from other projects operating with similar conditions. This will require creating a large database of anonymized, open-access data that past users have made available for different combinations of terrain, vegetation, and artifact types. We recognize that archaeologists may be reluctant to conduct calibration surveys, whether for their own use or as contributions to such a database. However, the costs are not prohibitive. In our survey in Jordan, for example, we devoted only six calibration sessions, each about three hours long, in which surveyors in turns made multiple passes along the survey path. This provided sufficient data to yield sweep widths.

The results of the Sweep Width module provide critical inputs to some of the other modules, still under development. For example, coverage is just the product of sweep width and the total length of all survey transects, determined in a GIS, while dividing coverage by the total area of the survey region provides a basic summary of how thorough a survey has been. Sweep width is also a key consideration for allocating effort, whether that is simply deciding on transect spacings, allocating coverage to each stratum in a stratified sample, or estimating posterior probabilities that undiscovered sites remain in certain spaces in a predictive model. Even approximate estimates of sweep width allow surveyors to use transect spacings that assure a minimum coverage of surveyed spaces or,

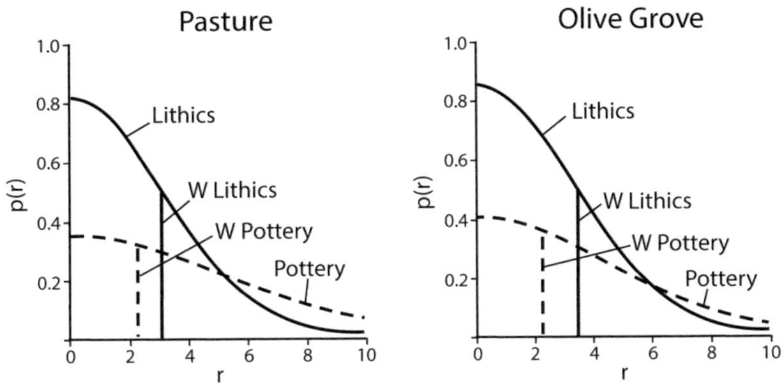

Figure 3.6. Example of some detection functions with range (in m) for lithic flakes (solid curves) and a variety of pottery (dashed curves) as determined from results on two different calibration fields, a pasture (a), and a ploughed olive grove (b), in northern Jordan (after Banning et al. 2017).

for surveys that follow fixed, regulated transect spacings, allow them to estimate artifact densities in survey patches or the probability, and therefore the risk, that the survey could have missed artifact scatters.

Our working prototype of the Sweep Width Module is written in the open-source scripting language R, and makes use of some common data-analysis packages (dplyr, ggplot2; Wickham 2016; Wickham et al. 2023). The prototype leverages the RMarkdown language and R Notebooks to create an intuitive graphical user interface, and can run on any operating system with a working R installation running in RStudio. Users currently enter their own data or use the provided sample datasets of synthetic calibration and test data. The module runs interactively by executing each successive code chunk, and outputs simple graphical plots of the calculated detection functions, as well as summary statistics such as effective sweep widths.

We plan to improve the usability and accessibility of this module before making it more broadly available, but its current code, written as an R notebook, is available on GitHub and archived with Zenodo (Edwards 2024). While the R Notebook format is accessible to anyone with basic familiarity with R and Python coding environments, especially those with experience in Jupyter Notebooks, our goal is to adapt the current version of the module into a Shiny App that can be deployed in a browser. This should increase the overall accessibility of the module, making it usable by archaeologists with no prior knowledge of R, R Notebooks, or RStudio.

3.5 Expandability, Open Source, and Open Access

We consider it desirable to add modules to accommodate other aspects of survey design and management that our current plan does not include, and would like to have users actively participate in building a database of visibility and sweep width information that would improve estimates of sweep widths and survey coverage.

Whether or not we can anticipate what future modules may be useful, it is important to construct the software in such a way that it will not be difficult to accommodate them. Further, creating the software with open-source tools such as Python and R, and hosting the code in accessible repositories such as GitHub, or by hosting interactive webapps, ensures equitable long-term access to the tools beyond the core team that initially created them (Marwick 2016; Marwick et al. 2017). Further, using accessible platforms such as GitHub facilitates central management of the project while still encouraging community-wide co-development through “branch-and-fork” dispersed collaboration.

3.6 Conclusions

Many methods are already available to facilitate the efficient design, implementation and evaluation of archaeological surveys, but most archaeologists do not avail themselves of these tools because of the perception that they are difficult, “academic”, or of limited importance in an environment where simply following standard practices or regulations is considered sufficient. While standardization of practice has some attractions (Carver et al. 2015) – including simplicity and facilitating inter-survey comparisons – standardized surveys can also be inefficient, more costly than necessary to achieve their objectives, or vulnerable to the risk of missing significant archaeological resources that could lead to unanticipated mitigation costs or construction delays. The modules we are developing in our SPACE project will, we hope, counteract the negative perceptions and help archaeologists reap the benefits of proven methods, which include controlling the costs of surveys that still accomplish their main goal of finding the archaeological traces that we are committed to document and protect.

Acknowledgements

The SPACE Project originated at the University of Toronto but has partners at San Diego State University, and the Centre of Geographic Sciences at Nova Scotia Community College. Besides the co-authors, participants in the project include Alicia Hawkins, Philip Hitchings, Diana Sharpe, and Sarah T. Stewart. We thank Yaron Milwid for creating an early version of the sweep-width module code and the many students and the members of the field crews of the Wadi Quseiba and Tremithos Neolithic Survey projects who participated in survey experiments and sweep width calibration runs in the field.

Funding

Funding for this research was provided by the Social Sciences and Humanities Research Council of Canada, grant number 435-2020-0500.

Conflict of Interest Disclosure

The authors declare that they comply with the PCI rule of having no financial conflicts of interest in relation to the content of the article.

Data, Scripts, Code, and Supplementary Information Availability

The R code and sample data for the sweep width module are publicly available online via Zenodo at the following persistent URL: https://zenodo.org/records/10798638, and can be cited using the DOI: 10.5281/zenodo.10798638.

Materials and Methods

The methods used to set up the calibrations and execute the calibration runs can be found on Zenodo at the following persistent URL: https://zenodo.org/records/10801966, and can be cited using the DOI: 10.5281/zenodo.10801965.

Peer review

This article has been reviewed and recommended by PCI Archaeology.

Waagen, J. 2024. "A new tool to increase the robustness of archaeological field survey". *Peer Community in Archaeology* 100351. DOI: 10.24072/pci.archaeo.100351.

References

Almagro-Gorbea, Martin, Pablo Alonso, José Enrique Benito, Ana M. Martín, and José Luis Valencia. 2002. "Statistical Quality Control in Archaeological Survey." *Archaeological Prospection* 9: 45–53.

Banning, Edward B. 2002. *Archaeological Survey*. New York: Kluwer Academic/Plenum Publishing.

Banning, Edward B. 2020. "Sampled to Death? The Rise and Fall of Probability Sampling in Archaeology." *American Antiquity* 86: 43–60.

Banning, Edward B. 2024. "Materials and Methods for Setting Up and Executing Calibration Runs for Sweep-Width Estimation." DOI: 10.5281/zenodo.10801966.

Banning, Edward B., Alicia L. Hawkins, and Sarah T. Stewart. 2006. "Detection Functions for Archaeological Survey." *American Antiquity* 71: 723–42.

Banning, Edward B., Alicia L. Hawkins, and Sarah T. Stewart. 2011. "Sweep Widths and the Detection of Artifacts in Archaeological Survey." *Journal of Archaeological Science* 38: 3447–58. DOI: 10.1016/j.jas.2011.08.007.

Banning, Edward B., Alicia L. Hawkins, Sarah T. Stewart, Philip Hitchings, and Steven Edwards. 2017. "Quality Assurance in Archaeological Survey." *Journal of Archaeological Method and Theory* 24: 466–88. DOI: 10.1007/s10816-016-9274-2.

Brython Development Team. 2022. *Brython*. https://brython.info/

Campana, Stefano. 2017. "Towards Mapping the Archaeological Continuum. New Perspectives and Current Limitations in Planning Led Archaeology in Italy." *Archéologies Numériques* 17. DOI: 10.21494/ISTE.OP.2017.0176.

Carver, Martin, Bisserka Gaydarska, and Sandra Montón-Subías. 2015. "Preface." In *Field Archaeology from Around the World: Ideas and Approaches*, edited by Martin Carver, Bisserka Gaydarska, and Sandra Montón-Subías, vii–viii. Cham: Springer International Publishing.

Cochran, William G. 1977. *Sampling Techniques, 3rd Ed.* New York: John Wiley & Sons.

Edwards, Steven. 2024. *Automating Sweep Widths for Archaeological Surveys (v1.0.0)* [Computer software]. Zenodo. DOI: 10.5281/zenodo.10798638.

Hitchings, Philip M. N., Peter Bikoulis, Steven Edwards, and Edward B. Banning. 2016. "Predict and Confirm: Bayesian Survey and Excavation at Three Candidate Sites for Late Neolithic Occupation in Wadi Quseiba, Jordan." In *CAA 2015 Keep the Revolution Going: Proceedings of the 43rd Annual Conference on Computer Applications and Quantitative Methods in Archaeology*, edited by Stefano Campana, Roberto Scopigno, and Gabriella Carpentiero, 605–11. Oxford: Archaeopress.

Kintigh, Keith. 1988. "The Effectiveness of Subsurface Testing: A Simulation Approach." *American Antiquity* 53: 686–707. DOI: 10.2307/281113.

Koopman, Bernard O. 1980. *Search and Screening: General Principles with Historical Applications*. New York: Pergamon Press.

Li, Zhi, John Phillips, and Frank. H. Durgin. 2011. "The Underestimation of Egocentric Distance: Evidence from Frontal Matching Tasks." *Attention, Perception, & Psychophysics* 73 (7): 2205–17.

Loomis, Jack M., and John W. Philbeck. 2008. "Measuring Spatial Perception with Spatial Updating and Action." In *Embodiment, Ego-space, and Action*, edited by Roberta L. Klatzky, Brian MacWhinney, and Marlene Behrman, 1–43. New York: Psychology Press.

Marwick, Ben. 2016. "Computational Reproducibility in Archaeological Research: Basic Principles and a Case Study of Their Implementation." *Journal of Archaeological Method and Theory* 24: 424–50. DOI:10.1007/s10816-015-9272-9.

Marwick, Ben, Jade d'Alpoim Guedes, C. Michael Barton, Lynsey A. Bates, Michael Baxter, Andrew Bevan, Elizabeth A. Bollwerk, R. Kyle Bocinsky, Tom Brughmans, Alison K. Carter, Cyler Conrad, Daniel A. Contreras, Stefano Costa, Enrico R. Crema, Adrianne Daggett, Benjamin Davies, B. Lee Drake, Thomas S. Dye, Phoebe France, Richard Fullager, Domenico Giusti, Shawn Graham, Matthew D. Harris, John Hawks, Sebastian Heath, Damien Huffer, Eric C. Kansa, Sarah Whitcher Kansa, Mark E. Madsen, Jennifer Melcher, Joan Negre, Fraser D. Neiman, Rachel Opitz, David C. Orton, Paulina Przystupa, Maria Raviele, Julien Riel-Salvatore, Philip Riris, Iza Romanowska, Jolene Smith, Néhémie Strupler, Isaac I. Ullah, Hannah G. Van Vlack, Nathaniel VanValkenberg, Ethan C. Watrall, Chris Webster, Joshua Wells, Judith Winters, and Colin D. Wren. 2017. "Open Science in Archaeology." *SAA Archaeological Record* 17(4): 8–14.

McManamon, Francis P. 1981. "Probability Sampling and Archaeological Survey in the Northeast: An Estimation Approach." In *Foundations of Northeast Archaeology*, edited by Dean Snow, 195–227. New York: Academic Press.

Milwid, Yaron. 2016. "Automated Calculation of Sweep Width for Archaeological Purposes." Honors diss., Engineering Science, University of Toronto.

Ooi, Teng Leng, and Zijiang J. He. 2007. "A Distance Judgment Function Based on Space Perception Mechanisms: Revisiting Gilinsky's (1951) Equation." *Psychological Review* 114 (2): 441–54. DOI:10.1037/0033-295x.114.2.441.

Plog, Steven, Fred Plog, and W. Wait. 1978. "Decision Making in Modern Surveys." *Advances in Archaeological Method and Theory* 1: 384–421. DOI:10.1016/B978-0-12-624180-8.50017-2.

Schiffer, Michael B. 1987. *Formation Processes of the Archaeological Record*. Albuquerque: University of New Mexico Press.

Schiffer, Michael B., Alan P. Sullivan, and Timothy C. Klinger. 1978. "The Design of Archaeological Surveys." *World Archaeology* 10: 1–28.

Shott, Michael L. 1987. "Feature Discovery and the Sampling Requirements of Archaeological Evaluations." *Journal of Field Archaeology* 14: 359–71. DOI:10.1179/jfa.1987.14.3.359.

Shott, Michael L. 1989. "Shovel-Test Sampling in Archaeological Survey: Comments on Nance and Ball, and Lightfoot." *American Antiquity* 54: 396–404. DOI:10.2307/281714.

Stewart, Sarah T., Edward B. Banning, Steven Edwards, and Peter Bikoulis. 2016. "Predicting Survey Coverage Through Calibration: Sweep Widths and Survey in Cyprus and Jordan." In *CAA 2015 Keep the Revolution Going: Proceedings of the 43rd Annual Conference on Computer Applications and Quantitative Methods in Archaeology*, edited by Stefano Campana, Roberto Scopigno, and Gabriella Carpentiero, 612–21. Oxford: Archaeopress.

Stone, Lawrence D. 1975. *Theory of Optimal Search*. New York: Academic Press.

Wickham, Hadley 2016. *ggplot2: Elegant Graphics for Data Analysis*. New York: Springer-Verlag. https://ggplot2.tidyverse.org.

Wickham, Hadley, Romain François, Lionel Henry, Kirill Müller, and Davis Vaughan. 2023. "dplyr: A Grammar of Data Manipulation. R package version 1.1.4." https://github.com/tidyverse/dplyr, https://dplyr.tidyverse.org.

Wobst, Martin H. 1983. "We Can't See the Forest for the Trees: Sampling and the Shapes of Archaeological Distributions." In *Archaeological Hammers and Theories*, edited by James A. Moore and Arthur S. Keene, 37–85. New York: Academic Press.

4 Visual encoding of a 3D virtual reconstruction's scientific justification

Feedback from a proof-of-concept research

Jean-Yves Blaise
UPR 2002 CNRS MAP, Marseille,
jean-yves.blaise@map.cnrs.fr,
ORCID 0000-0001-5479-7527

Iwona Dudek
UPR 2002 CNRS MAP, Marseille

Laurent Bergerot
UPR 2002 CNRS MAP, Marseille

Gaël Simon
UMR CNRS/Université de
Tours 7324 CITERES-LAT, Tours

Abstract

Over the last decades, 3D virtual reconstructions have become a classical means to communicate analysts' visions concerning past stages of development of an edifice or a site. However, they often remain a one-shot output, neither reusable, nor expressing visually the diversity of the evidence behind the reconstruction. A 3D virtual reconstruction – obtained by means of a synchronic or diachronic study – is a hypothesis, but also a technical work, and ultimately confronts researchers with the challenge of finding a compromise between interpretation and assertion, even within the graphical encoding of a 3D model.

This research is based on a methodological proposal: introducing ***justification matrices*** that allow to associate indicators to the components of a 3D virtual reconstruction that formalise an assessment of plausibility in a synthetic way. These matrices allow to assign to individual 3D objects or to groups of objects a quantitative evaluation of their plausibility by combining four criteria: shape, dimensions, existence, and position.

The experiment led to the creation of a proof-of-concept prototype allowing a user to interact in real time with the graphic appearance of each object, represented in a 3D reconstruction, according to the values of its justification matrix. The approach is applied to four phases of the evolution of Marmoutier abbey's hostelry (corresponding to four synchronous states – 12th, 13th, 15th and 18th centuries), and re-uses 3D virtual reconstructions produced several years ago for communication. The paper positions and discusses the three families of issues the research intersects (knowledge modelling, visual encoding and 3D content reuse), presents the case study, details the services offered by the prototype and assesses lessons learned and limitations. The experiment should be seen as an attempt to reason about heritage data sets by drawing on practices from the InfoVis (information visualisation) field and is thought of as a call to design and discuss in the scientific community new ways of visualising architectural data, information, and pieces of knowledge.

Keywords: Plausibility; Uncertainty; 3D virtual reconstructions; Information Visualization; HMI; 3D content reuse

In *Advances in Digital Archaeology. Proceedings of the 2023 conference Computer Applications and Quantitative Methods in Archaeology – 50 years of synergy*, edited by J.W.H.P. Verhagen, J. Waagen, A. Brandsen, A. Queffelec, R.M. Visser and D. Taelman, 55–70. Leiden: Sidestone Press.

4.1 Introduction

A 3D virtual reconstruction is the result of experts' analyses aiming to propose a plausible spatial arrangement for a building that has changed over time. It is before all the result of an interpretation of available data and information underpinned by "knowledge" (explicit, tacit, ...). Each 3D reconstruction – obtained by means of a synchronic or diachronic study – is a hypothesis.

But a 3D virtual reconstruction is also a technical work, through which assertive geometrical forms must be chosen in order to represent that spatial arrangement, even if uncertainties were spotted during the interpretation step. Ultimately, from the knowledge and information visualisation standpoint, a 3D virtual reconstruction confronts researchers with the challenge of finding a compromise between interpretation and assertion, even within the graphical encoding of a 3D model (if the model aims to serve analytical purposes).

This research is based on a methodological proposal: introducing *justification matrices* that allow to associate "indicators" to the components of a 3D virtual reconstruction that formalise an assessment of plausibility in a synthetic way. In other words, these matrices deliver information on the scientific justification of a given spatial arrangement.

The experiment led to the creation of a proof-of-concept prototype allowing a user to interact in real time with the graphic appearance of each object, represented in a 3D reconstruction, according to the values of its justification matrix. The approach is applied to four phases of the evolution of Marmoutier abbey's hostelry (corresponding to four synchronous states – 12th, 13th, 15th and 18th centuries), and re-uses 3D virtual reconstructions produced several years ago (for communication purposes) by the team of archaeologists involved in this experiment.

Several system querying modalities have been experimented with in order to better circumscribe the services that such a prototype can offer. The prototype is based on a combination of classical and open technologies for the web (RDBMS, JS/CSS/HTML interface, 3D JavaScript library Three.js). It is already operational and available online with free access.

The paper first positions and discusses the three families of issues this research intersects (knowledge modelling, visual encoding and 3D content reuse), and then presents the case study the prototype is applied to before detailing the ways users can interact with the data thanks to the abovementioned prototype. A discussion, an assessment of the research's limitations, and conclusions are provided in the last section.

4.2 Research background and methods

The need to differentiate, in a 3D model, between attested and assumed elements is not new, far from it. This methodological challenge was already there before the digital era and is behind Jean-Claude Gardin's approach (Dallas 2015), which we will discuss later. For the past 30 years (see Messemer 2016), the issue has been regularly discussed in the scientific literature and in various scientific communities (architecture, history, archaeology, ...) both in the form of recommendations and of feedback (Alkhoven 1993; Sylaiou and Patias 2004; Pfeiffer et al. 2013; Morandi and Tremari 2017).

We have been part of this movement for about twenty years, with reports of experiments centred on 3D modelling and graphic encoding per se or in the form of online 3D information systems, at different scales, scanning different technological solutions (Blaise and Dudek 2002; 2005; 2008). These experiments have led to a collection of "rules of conduct" inspired by practices in the InfoVis (Information Visualisation) field, now used as a teaching tool (Blaise and Dudek 2006). The issue remains topical even if it tends to become more marginal under the double effect of an overwhelming presence of 3D data acquisition experiments in the literature, and following on this question the emergence of the still rather vague concept of "digital twin" – most often viewed as an avatar of the real thing, of an attested thing (and thus an unworkable concept when talking about 3D virtual reconstructions and plausibility).

We have chosen to reinvestigate the issue in the context of a wider research programme[1] focusing on methodological aspects such as reproducibility[2], traceability of research workflows, and this along with archaeology colleagues. There are three main reasons for this new attempt:

- new technological setups (3D js libraries, Collada 3D file format, etc.),
- a pre-existing set of 3D models, sort-of dead branch, needing repurposing, and acting as a test bench,
- finally, the idea that repurposability and interpretability are coming forward as a major part of the research agenda in heritage studies at large.

In view of these elements, the result we present should be understood basically as a proof-of-concept experiment, a way to question ourselves on *why not (re)dig a bit further into the question of what a 3D model can say, and be used for?* The experiment is described below by distinguishing three complementary aspects: the knowledge representation problem, the visual encoding choices, and finally the technical approach to the re-use of pre-existing 3D models.

1 See the MEMORIA IS platform: http://memoria-dev.gamsau.archi.fr/is/enter.php.

2 An acute question today, and one that obviously needs to be addressed in view of the effort involved in producing 3D reconstructions and the heavy risk of seeing this effort lost very quickly (whether on the technical level – obsolescence of the tools, or on the cognitive level – failure to perpetuate the reasoning mechanisms).

4.3 The knowledge modelling issue

What exactly is *uncertain* when an expert proposes a 3D virtual reconstruction? How to account for the uncertainties associated with a 3D virtual reconstruction in a formal and shareable way, conducive to a comparison within a study case, or between case studies? And what exactly are these uncertainties about? Architectural forms? Their spatial arrangement? Their very existence? Can this notion of uncertainty be formalized in any way other than by an accompanying discourse? On this question, the scientific literature proposes numerous methodological reference points, often discipline-centered, leading to a formalization of uncertainty factors (e.g., Skeels et al. 2010; Zuk and Carpendale 2007; Thomson et al. 2005). In addition, from an archaeological standpoint, how can we exploit the notion of argumentation, present for example in J.C Gardin's logicism (Dallas 2015), to make the choices made by an analyst more readable within 3D models?

Uncertainty is in fact a sort of catchword covering a vast number of situations. Analysing different types of uncertainties (and their consequences in terms of decision making) is indeed a research issue by itself, and one that goes far beyond the scope of this paper (see on this issue Blaise and Dudek 2020).

Our contribution introduces a formal model, *justification matrices*, addressing the specific issue of handling *uncertainty* in the task of proposing a 3D virtual reconstruction. We therefore rather use the word *plausibility*, denoting a particular occurrence of *uncertainty*. Justification matrices deliver information on the reason for a proposal present in the 3D model, a proposal that is concretised by given 3D shapes in given positions within the model. It allows to assign to individual 3D objects or groups of objects a quantitative evaluation of their plausibility by combining four criteria: shape, dimensions, existence, and position. This formalisation embodies the vision of one analyst and could potentially allow the materialisation of differences between analyses. It does not constitute an argumentation as such, but it reveals the result of an argumentation. The argumentation itself can naturally be associated with the object as paradata – but this is another discussion, falling outside of the scope of our contribution.

Our approach is a methodological questioning that complements the work done by the CITERES-LAT team on digital architectural models (LAT stands for Archeology and Territories Laboratory). This team of archaeologists published a final volume of the research on the abbey in

Figure 4.1. Top: plausibility of an individual architectural element (angle buttress). Bottom: plausibility of a group constituted of walls, bays and a covering.

Marmoutier and used that opportunity to model in 3D four synchronic states of this building (12th, 13th, 15th and 18th centuries). Emeline Marot and Elisabeth Lorans (LAT) worked with Nicolas Nony (a computer graphics designer) to create these four models. The reconstructions of the various elements appearing on the models were based on arguments of analogical, symmetrical and functional order. Many graphic documents were used. While these choices were partly explained in the graphic and textual documentation accompanying the file of the models, nothing allowed to take into account the reliability of these reconstructions in the model itself, and thereby to explain the passage between what is observed and what is returned in reconstruction models. The case of the hostelry and its four models appeared to us as an appropriate case study to try and fill this gap.

By starting to work on these objects produced by other researchers and with an objective of valorisation, we quickly asked ourselves the question of multiple or at least different uncertainties depending on the architectural objects questioned. Indeed, according to the available evidence we can be certain of the existence of an object without knowing its location, its shape and its dimensions. For example, it may be a fragment of a staircase, the location, shape or dimensions of which are unknown. In other cases, we are certain of the existence of an object, for example a buttress whose foundations we were able to observe by excavation attesting its location, but its shape and dimensions are not fully known. Thus, it appeared relevant to question the plausibility of each object according to four criteria: its existence, its position, its shape and its dimensions.

It also seemed interesting to question the plausibility not just of an object but of a group constituted on the basis of associations of functional, structural and/or rhythmic order (for example all the bays of the first synchronic state; Figure 4.1).

Indeed, the uncertainties applied to each object are not necessarily the same as the ones applied to the whole, the whole is not always the sum of the parts! To account for these different situations, we have proposed to synthesize this information in the form of a matrix presenting four plausibility criteria (form, dimensions, existence and position) with four values, ranging from 1 (highest plausibility) to 3 (least plausible proposal); the value 4 is used to indicate elements for which the plausibility analysis remains to be conducted (Figure 4.2).

4.3 The visual encoding issue

A 3D virtual reconstruction is in essence a visual product, in which graphic components are combined. What graphic vocabulary should be proposed, what interaction modalities in the 3D model should be implemented so that the subjective choices behind a hypothesized reconstruction are legible? How can comparisons between the different components of a 3D model (from the point of view of their relative plausibility) be facilitated? Bertin's graphic semiology (Bertin 2010) has spread well beyond its original discipline geography, and particularly in the field of information visualisation (InfoVis). However, it is hard to say if there is an equivalent methodological reference point in the field of 3D heritage-related modelling. In that area of interest, after decades of research, practices still tend to privilege realism over semantic encoding, and representations often primarily serve visual communication objectives. At the end of the day, 3D virtual reconstructions often do not really provide services (in terms of scientific added value) that are commensurate to the effort made.

In the proof-of-concept prototype we present, once a plausibility evaluation – here formalised as *justification*

Plausibility criterions	1 : "Attested"	2 : "Likely"	3 : "Possible"	4 : "Unassesed"
Existence	Presence of the element on the model attested because it still fully or partially elevated in reality	Presence on the model considered as likely on the basis of symmetry patterns, composition arguments, etc.	Presence of the element possible but not grounded on actual remains or documents	Plausibility still unassessed
Position	Position of the element in the model attested because it is still fully or partially elevated in reality	Position on the model considered as likely on the basis of symmetry patterns, composition arguments, etc.	Position of the element on the model possible but not grounded on actual remains or documents	Plausibility still unassessed
Shape	All the information needed to propose a given 3D shape is available.	Only partial information about the shape of an element is available.	The shape proposed is an expert's vision, not grounded on evidence	Plausibility still unassessed
Dimensions	All dimensions of the element or a large majority are known	Some of the dimensions of the element are known	No dimensions are grounded on evidence	Plausibility still unassessed

Figure 4.2. Verbalisation of the justification matrices' values, showing also value *4* "unassessed" added at implementation time – elements for which the plausibility analysis remains to be conducted.

matrices – is done, the time comes when this evaluation has to be encoded visually, some would say *mapped* visually. Representing uncertainties using visual means is not a new issue or practice: for instance, Joseph Priestley's *A chart of Biography* is a classic timeline from 1765 that positions the lives of more than two thousand famous men in time, using tiny lines running from left to right (Rosenberg and Grafton 2010). When the dates of birth or death of these famous men are ill-known, the otherwise continuous line turns dash-dotted, thereby intuitively transferring a sense of uncertainty.

A large number of solutions have been tried out before and since the digital age, often in relation to time-oriented data with for instance planning lines visualisation, chronograph formalism and many others described in Aigner et al. (2011). Cartographers, geographers and historians have also faced the issue of how to distribute an objectivised representation in space – a 2D map – of items of which the exact position is not clearly assessed. Depending on the nature of the type of uncertainty to handle solutions can range from the use of glyphs conveying the uncertainty information, through colours or shapes (see for instance Reimer 2010) to clouds of 2D points, polygons or other shapes that localise a *likeliness* area, an area in which the item is supposed to be localised, but that does not exactly match the geometry and position of the item (Davies 1997).

Visual mapping is a task that has been somewhat rationalised both in cartography and in information visualisation by Jacques Bertin's (2010) graphic semiology, and as part of it his identification of a finite vocabulary of graphic variables. Although written before the digital age in the context of 2D paper-based graphic outputs, his "methodological frame" can still act as a reference model helping to explain visual encoding strategies.

The prototype we have implemented exploits five graphic variables: position, orientation, size, shape and colour. The first four variables are endowed with conveying information about the architectural elements: 3D components distributed somewhere in the 3D space. The plausibility information is conveyed by the fifth variable: colour. Depending on the interaction mode chosen by the user one or several colours are used to represent the plausibility evaluation visually in the 3D space. As will be shown in section Results a more abstract, InfoVis-inspired solution has also been developed that uses the same set of graphic variables. This solution consists of a sort of visual metaphor (Kienreich 2006), used independently of the 3D space.

Obviously, our choice of using colour (and only colour) to visually convey the plausibility analysis can be debated. Other solutions that go beyond Bertin's original framework, based on specificities of digital platforms (such as interactive texture mapping or translucency), have been tried out but they have not been considered convincing. Translucency, typically, is not easy to handle since shapes tend to get harder to apprehend visually and what is gained in terms of visual differences between the known and the ill-known can be lost in terms of global understanding of the 3D layout/structure.

Our strategy has been to privilege simplicity – as defined by J. Maeda (Maeda 2006; Schuller 2009) – as a means to minimise the learning curve and augment the acceptability of the prototype. The graphic encoding is a simple bichromatic scale, allowing a natural ordering of values, with the grey used to convey lacking information. We acknowledge that a thorough and robust evaluation of alternative visual encodings remains to be done: a potential perspective for this work.

4.4 3D model re-use

How can we re-use 3D content for other purposes, in our case 3D virtual reconstructions created primarily for scientific mediation and in a technological context that is obsolete today? This sub-issue can be seen primarily as a purely practical matter concerning technology. But it can also be seen as part of a broad societal movement towards more sustainability and economy of means, a movement that affects the field of scientific research as well.

This is not a new issue, however, and the emergence of many XML-based formats where the information is detached from the application contexts is proof of this. But developing good practices today does not necessarily provide practical solutions concerning the reuse of existing 3D content. The interface that we present has been developed to work online thanks to the open source Three.js library and exploits a systematic repurposing of the original 3D models.

The original data we have are based on four polygonal mesh models corresponding to four synchronous states – 12th, 13th, 15th and 18th centuries – in the evolution of the abbey's hostelry, and available today in the form of OBJ-format saves (Figure 4.3).

Each of these four models was first divided into meaningful architectural elements (a wall, a door, a buttress, an alignment of windows, etc.), to which justification matrices were associated (one matrix per element, single object or group of objects). This work was carried out using the Blender software in editing mode, and consisted of separating and, if necessary, closing each element of the model. Choices had to be made during this step such as the suppression of the internal parts of the models (vaults) insofar as the experiment concerned only the external envelope of the building.

Each element was thus given its own geometry, exported in Collada (.dae) format, and corresponding to a justification matrix described in a relational database. The link between the 3D data and the matrices is made dynamically by exploiting correspondence tables (the identifier of an element in the database is used to name the corresponding Collada 3D file). In order to optimise the use of these models in a browser, each state (each synchronous 3D model) is loaded dynamically: only one 3D model is loaded at a time, while the others are removed from memory as they are loaded, a possibility offered by the Collada loader of the Three.js library.

The interface allows the selection of elements directly in 3D using the raycasting method – a native function of three.js – which has been adapted to our needs, in particular for the first interaction mode (see Results section) which required this direct selection of elements by clicking in the interface.

Finally, the interface allows to display or hide the ground and offers a dimensional grid that the user can move along the horizontal or vertical axis using the keyboard. In addition, symbols with dimensions and orientation (in accordance with archaeological standards) allow the dimensioning and orientation of the model.

The method developed has the merit of demonstrating both the feasibility of the 3D models reuse scenario that we had imagined, thus reversing the usual process of research to valorisation, and the rather generic character of this type of web3D interface, reusable with few modifications for other architectural sites. It should not be forgotten that the time needed to segment and partly redraw the 3D models is a constraint, even a limitation, but only a relative limitation compared to the time needed to build the original models (a few days versus several weeks per model).

4.5 The case study: Marmoutier's abbey hostelry

The prototype re-uses the 3D virtual reconstructions of four phases in the evolution of the Marmoutier abbey hostelry, a site that has been thoroughly studied for years by a team of archaeologists, the UMR 7324 CITERES-LAT. The name of Marmoutier is inextricably linked to that of Martin, bishop of Tours from 371 to 397. In fact, during his episcopate he chose this place for his retreat and attracted disciples who gave rise to the first or second monastic community of the West. After several centuries of development, this great Benedictine monastery became one of the most important in France. This establishment lasted until the French Revolution, which led to the destruction of most of the buildings in the early 19th century.

Archaeological research has been conducted since 2004 under the direction of Elisabeth Lorans of the Archeology and Territories Laboratory (University of Tours, National Center for Scientific Research). These investigations concerned both the spatial organization of the monastery and the architecture of its various buildings, and the uses of

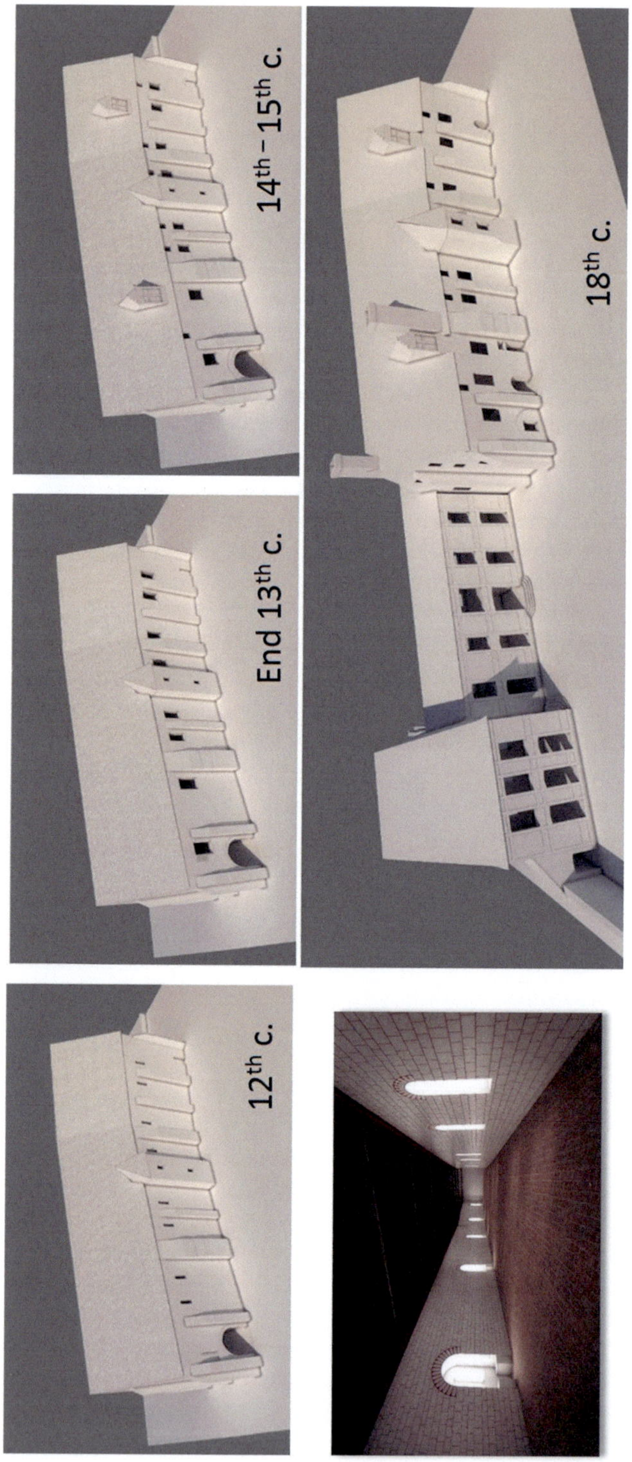

Figure 4.3. The original data: four polygonal mesh models and (bottom left) an illustration of the primary purpose of these models by the LAT team: communication for the general public (including texture mappings) (UMR CNRS/Université de Tours 7324 CITERES-LAT).

the land that preceded and followed the fifteen centuries of monastic life. The research employed a global approach to the site and its environment based on combining all possible sources at different scales of time and space: archaeological data, written sources, which have existed since the end of the 4th century, and iconographic sources, available since the 17th century. One of the buildings partially spared by the revolutionaries is the monastic hostelry which had the function of welcoming distinguished guests visiting the monastery (Figure 4.4).

The hostelry was installed near the main entrance in order not to interfere with monastic life. A text from the Middle Ages indicates that it was built during the abbotship of Hervé de Villepreux (1179-1189).

Today only 20m of the hostelry's length are preserved, but it originally measured 55m, a length known before the excavation from 18th century plans (Figure 4.5). A study of the archaeology of the building was conducted on elevations (façades) while the destroyed part was completely excavated from 2006 to 2017.

Several synchronic architectural states of the building were defined:

State 1

This building originally had two levels. A vaulted passage located at the western end of the building allowed circulation between the part accessible to lay people, to the north, and the rest of the monastery, reserved for the community and its dependents. This passage was opened by large pointed arches still visible on the façade.

The rest of the ground floor, also vaulted, was used for storage and may have been used as a refectory. The floor, used for lodging, was covered directly by the frame and was lit with bays to the north and south. It had access to latrines installed in a turret.

State 2

At the end of the thirteenth or the beginning of the fourteenth century, the vault of the ground floor was probably remodelled, the bays of the south façade were enlarged and the whole decoration was redone in false white joints on a yellow background.

State 3

In the fifteenth century, the function of hostelry seems to have been abandoned for that of residence of the Grand Prior, one of the main dignitaries of the abbey. This change in assignment required a significant redesign of the building. The available space was increased as the upper level was divided into three. The latrine turret was turned into a staircase to serve these new floors and bays were pierced to illuminate them. The ground floor was used by craftsmen (forge).

State 4

In the eighteenth century, the building underwent a new transformation when the interior ground level was raised. The old doors and windows were thus blocked and the vaults partially destroyed before the deposit of nearly a m of earth on the entire surface of the ground floor and the installation of a paved floor still preserved to the west of the building. New doors were created at this level, still visible today. A new wing was built against the north facade of the building. At this time, the vaulted passage, losing its function, was transformed into a living room.

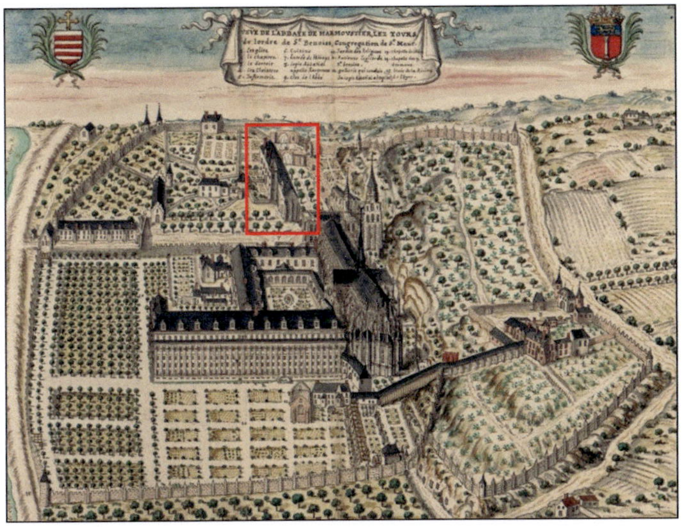

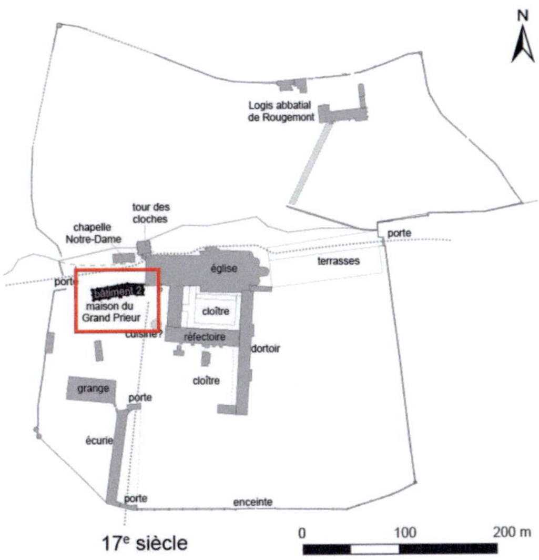

Figure 4.4. Overall views of the monastery, showing (outlined in red) the position of the hostelry within the site. Left: the monastery before the destruction of the 19th century. Elevated view from Marmoutier abbey from the east, 1699, Gaignières Collection (BNF VA 407 (1) FT 4-H-183734). Right: Reconstructed plan of the monastery in the 17th century (UMR CNRS/Université de Tours 7324 CITERES-LAT).

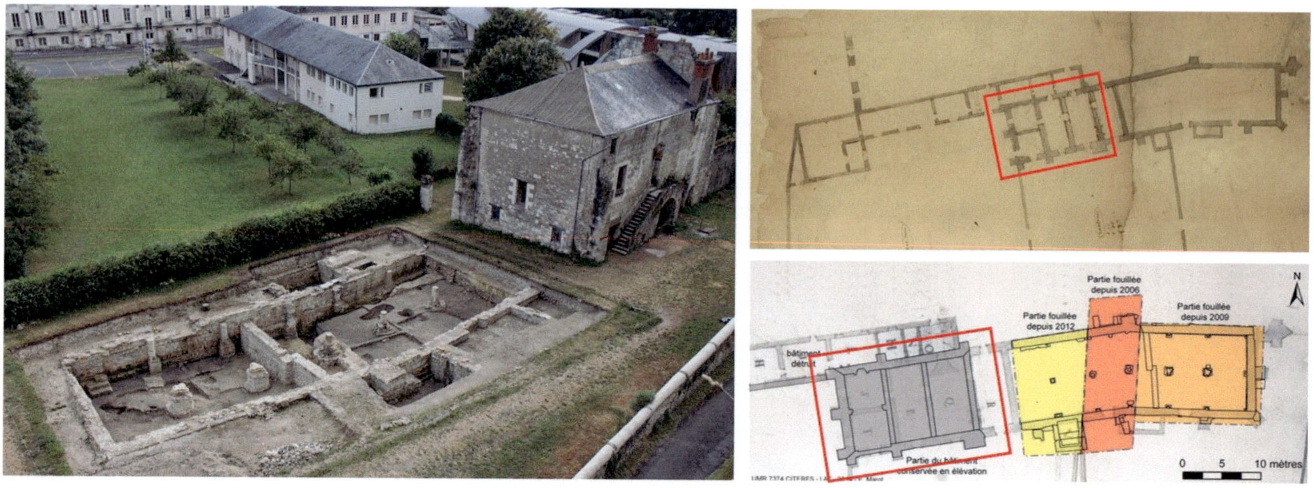

Figure 4.5. Left, a view of the hostelry today showing the part preserved above ground and the excavated elements (the picture shows the north façade). Right, plans of the hostelry, with preserved parts outlined in red (UMR CNRS/Université de Tours 7324 CITERES-LAT).

Figure 4.6. *Interaction mode 1*, illustrated on the first synchronic state (13th century). The justification matrix corresponding to the angle buttress highlighted in orange in the 3D scene is displayed in the right part of the interface. The existence and location of this element are fairly well established (remains exist, value 1 for the two first lines of the matrix). Its shape and size are less certain (value 2 for the two last lines of the matrix means likely, but not attested). Two URLs exist for this element that the user can exploit to retrieve more information.

State 5
This building does not seem to have been used for a long time, since the Revolution, which took place shortly after, led to its destruction (no virtual reconstruction was produced for this state). All that remains today are its south wall and the western end, in the street. Similarly, the eastern two-thirds of building 2 were levelled in the early 19th century, with the western end used as a dwelling and agricultural dependency in the 19th and 20th centuries. However, the walls of the submerged part were kept in the basement, which allowed, thanks to archaeological research, to reconstruct the chronology of the occupation of this area.

4.6 Results: the online prototype

The basic service expected from our prototype is fairly simple: allow users to interact (through basic clicks on shapes) with architectural elements in the 3D scene to retrieve information about their plausibility. Naturally, once each architectural element is associated with a justification matrix (concretely here inside an RDBMS), other services can be introduced that will build on the same data set. The prototype proposes three interaction modes exploiting the 3D virtual reconstructions, illustrated in the sub-sections below. In addition, the prototype also introduces an InfoVis-inspired overlay. In this case the focus is put on information patterns at an abstract level: the prototype enables comparing collection of justification matrices corresponding to the various synchronic phases or architectural elements.

4.6.1 Interaction modes in the 3D environment

For all three interaction modes building on the 3D environment, users first select one of the reconstructions, corresponding to one of the four synchronic phases of development of the hostelry that the LAT team has modelled. Users will then be empowered with three different means to analyse the plausibility of the reconstructions' components.

Mode 1: visualising the matrix corresponding to one architectural element
The first interaction mode is extremely simple: users select an architectural element in the 3D space and as a result the element's justification matrix is displayed on the right of the interface (Figure 4.6). When relevant, links to associated URLs are also available, that can be used to get more detailed archaeological information thanks to online content made available by the LAT team (the ArSol database factsheet, or the online complete archaeological publication, covering not only the architecture but also the burial area, craftworks, etc.).

Mode 2: visualising elements corresponding to one matrix
In this mode the user selects a matrix (four values) by choosing values for each plausibility criterion (Figure 4.7). Once this is done, all architectural elements documented with a matrix that corresponds to the selected values are highlighted in orange. In other words, this mode allows users to explore the information set starting this time from a selection of plausibility criteria (one value per plausibility criterion) in the matrix, rather than from the 3D scene itself.

Mode 3: visualising all plausibility values for one criterion across all architectural elements
The third mode corresponds to a filtering of the plausibility evaluation. A user selects a row of the matrix (the "existence" or "shape" criterion for example) and all the architectural components in the 3D model are recoloured according to their plausibility evaluation for this specific criterion (Figure 4.8).

4.6.2 The *information visualisation* layer

The three interaction modes presented here focus on the use of a 3D environment that allows a user to interact with one architectural element, or one matrix, and one synchronic state *at a time*. But what if the user wants to observe, for instance, the plausibility pattern of buttresses in comparison to the one of openings, or differences between synchronic states? As a solution we have implemented a more abstract overlay, building on the concept of "cumulative matrices". Cumulative matrices are based on the same visual formalism as the one used elsewhere in the interface: a grid in which each row corresponds to a plausibility criterion (existence, location, aashape, and dimension), and each column corresponds to a plausibility value (attested, likely, possible, unassessed). The visualisation shows in an abstract way values for *collections* of elements, either promoting chronological comparisons across the four synchronic states, or comparisons based on architectural types. The size of the coloured circles is proportional to the frequency of occurrence of a [criterion, value] pair: the larger the radius of the coloured circles, the more frequently a pair appears (Figure 4.9).

The top part of the graphic is used to compare values of matrices corresponding to the four synchronic states (values of the matrices of all the architectural elements for a state are cumulated).

The bottom part of Figure 4.9 is used for *one-to-one* comparisons of plausibility patterns corresponding to various architectural types (vaults, arches, doors, buttresses, etc.). The graphic is composed of four visual matrices, two per architectural type. For each architectural type the two matrices correspond to two alternative readings of the plausibility information:

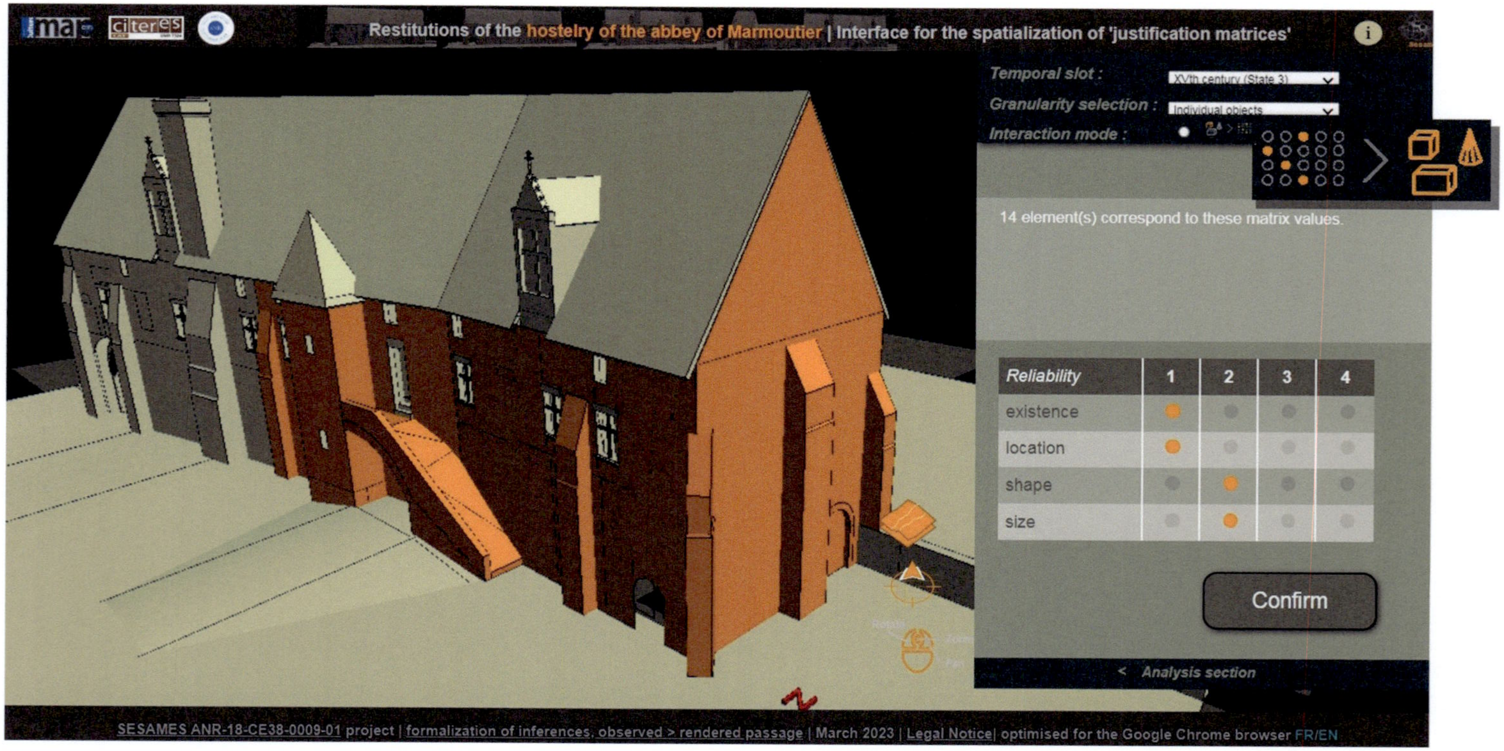

Figure 4.7. *Interaction mode 2*, illustrated on the third synchronic state (15th century). All components in the 3D virtual reconstructions with a justification matrix that corresponds to the user's selection (the right part of the interface) are highlighted in orange. Note the spatial consistency of elements sharing a common justification matrix, and the change of colour for the last part of the building (a part currently destroyed, raising more questions in terms of plausibility).

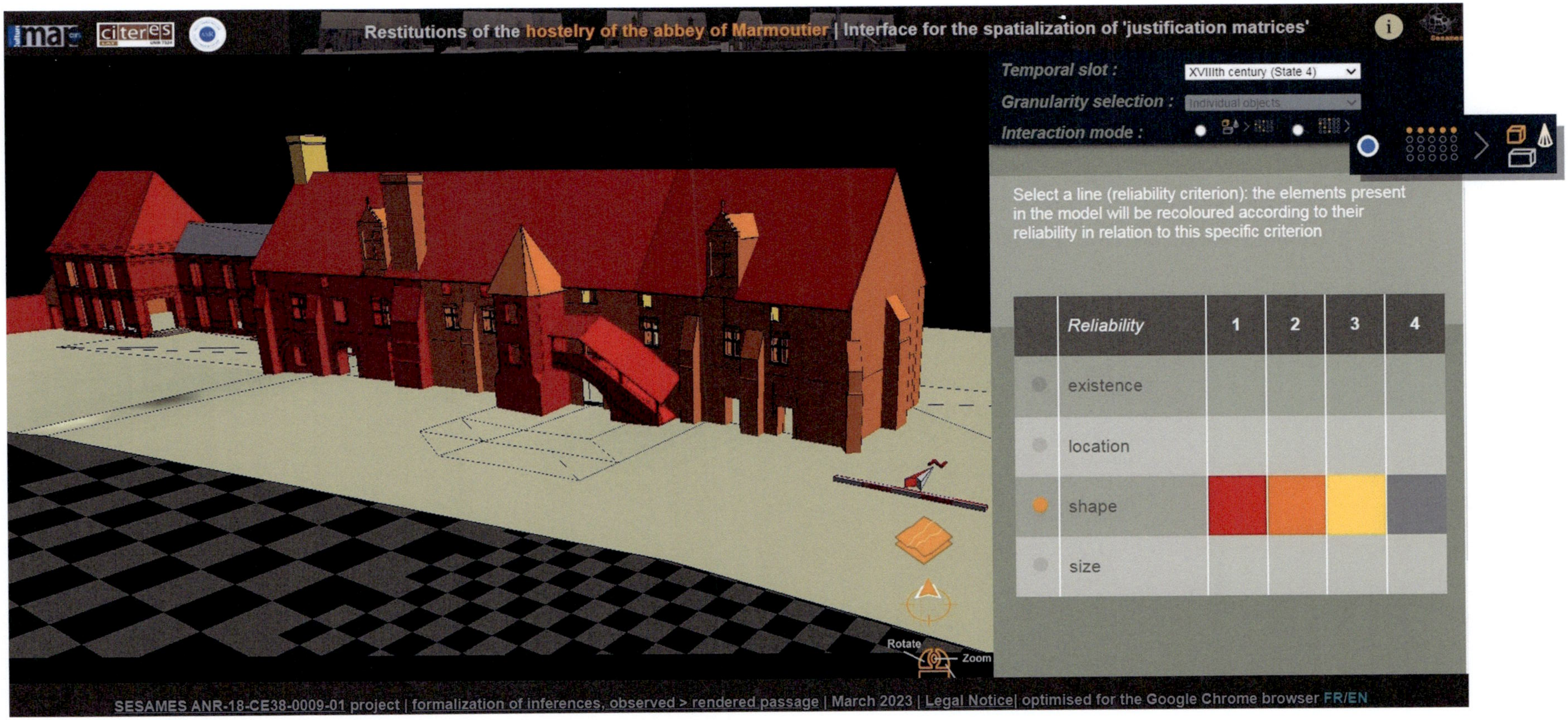

Figure 4.8. *Interaction mode 3*, illustrated on the fourth synchronic state (18th century). Each component in the 3D virtual reconstructions is attributed a colour that corresponds to its plausibility in terms of shape. Note the use of the colour "grey" (value 4) that indicates that no evaluation of plausibility of the element has yet been done – a way to assess visually the completion or not of the plausibility evaluation effort.

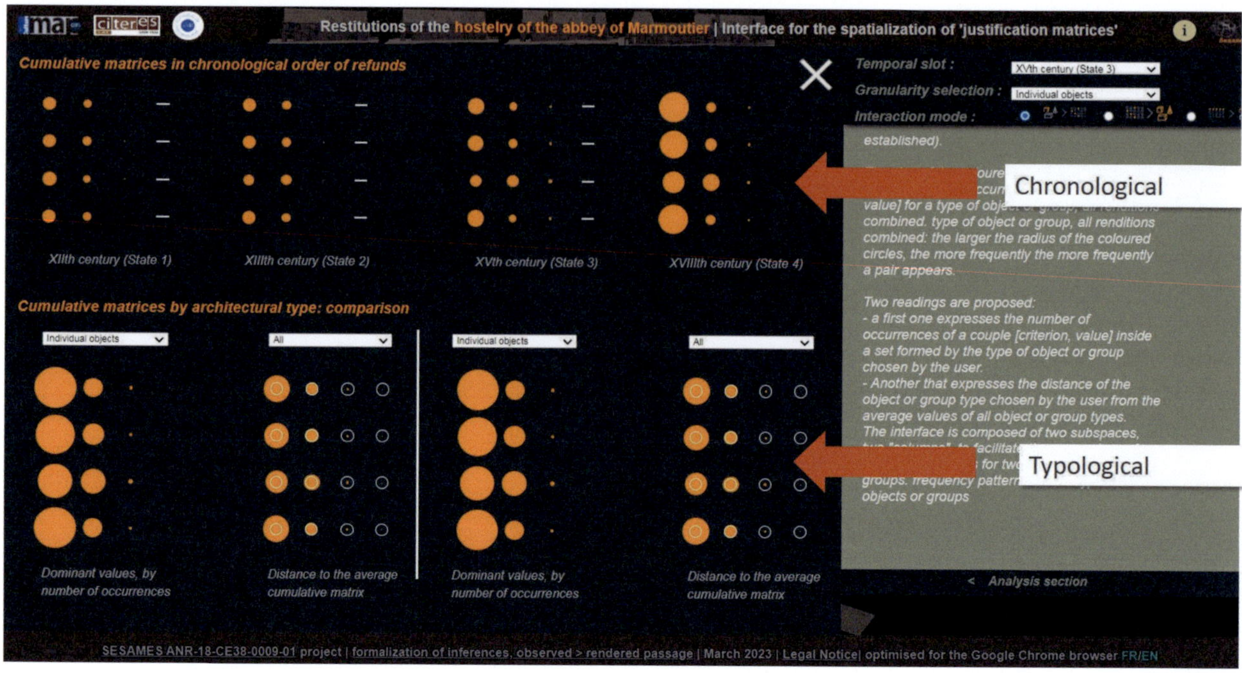

Figure 4.9. Visual display of the cumulative matrices, a means to analyse the collection of objects based on chronological or typological factors.

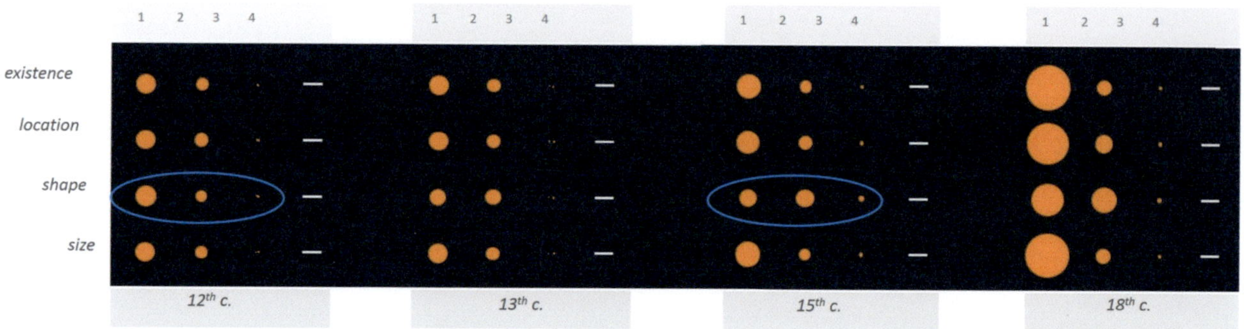

Figure 4.10. Cumulative matrices for the four synchronic states – the graphic shows, for instance (circled in blue), that for the third synchronic state the plausibility of shapes is lower than for the first synchronic state, a somewhat counter-intuitive finding. The circles for the last synchronic state appear far bigger than for the previous states – this is because the edifice was significantly enlarged, and as a result the overall number of architectural elements is bigger – and so are the number of [criterion, value] pairs. What is primarily displayed here are relative proportions, line per line, column per column.

- the first (left matrix) expresses the number of occurrences of a [criterion, value] pair inside a set formed by the type chosen by the user. It helps spotting the plausibility pattern for the type chosen by the user.
- the second (right matrix) expresses the distance of the architectural type chosen by the user to the mean average value for all types. It helps to unveil specificities in terms of informational patterns for the specific type that the user has chosen.

4.6.3 Implementation

The system architecture combines classic components in 3D web development – RDBMS/PHP/Massive javascript (three.js). We have considered the option of developing a so-called responsive interface but remain somewhat undecided on the relevance of this self-imposed development constraint. The issue is not technical, but a matter of readability: does it really make sense to navigate inside a complex 3D monument, with user interactions inside the 3D scene, on six inches screens (the average size of mobile phones)? Moving inside or rotating the 3D

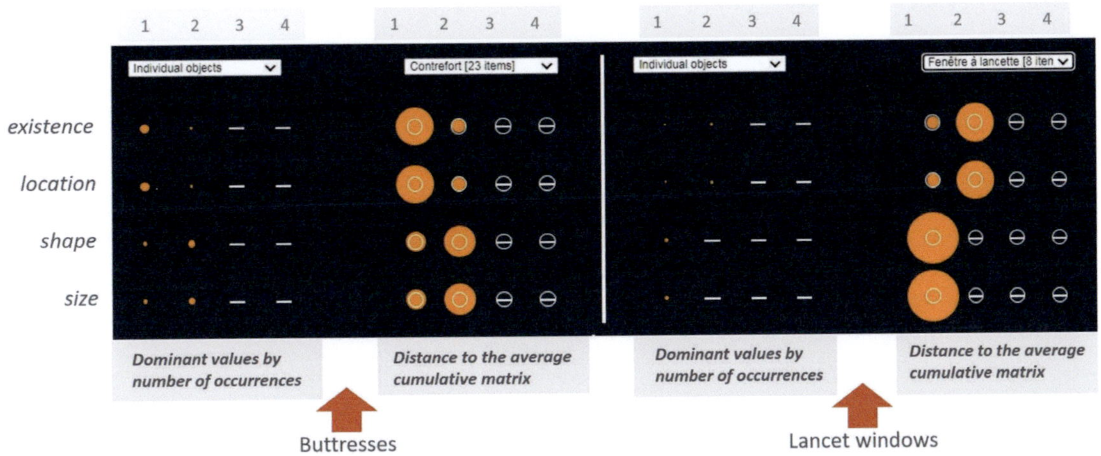

Figure 4.11. Cumulative matrices for buttresses (left) and for lancet windows (right). The graphics clearly shows divergent information patterns. The white circles correspond to the mean value of each [criterion, value] pair across the collection of architectural elements. White dashes correspond to [criterion, value] pairs that are never found for the architectural type under scrutiny.

model in those conditions is workable, but fine-grained interactions are not. This aspect of the research remains unexplored but would be a potential perspective – however falling outside the scope of this contribution.

4.7 Discussion, limitations and conclusion

The prototype we present in this contribution has been designed as a tool aimed at distributing in a 3D space, and analysing visually, the scientific justification behind so-called *3D virtual reconstructions*. In this section we first comment on the prototype's current limitations, some of which are significant, and justify considering the experiment primarily as a proof of concept. We then conclude with lessons learned, on the relevance of re-examining the issue today, and on what could be done to go further.

4.7.1 Limitations

Our contribution focuses on how to convey visually, in a 3D environment, *the result of an expertise* through which 3D architectural elements present in a virtual reconstruction are associated with a formal model expressing their plausibility (justification matrices). It does not address the issue of how to document and model the experts' cognitive processes, their choices, reasoning paths, and decisions concerning a shape and the corresponding matrix. There are ways to do so – starting from Gardin's logicism to today's MEMORIA IS (Dudek and Blaise 2019) – but commenting on these approaches is beyond the scope of this paper (though it remains a key issue). When sticking to this contribution's core components various significant limitations must be clearly stated:

- The plausibility analysis was carried out *a posteriori* (several years after the creation of the 3D models), and not by the 3D models' creators but by a colleague, who had limited information on why a specific modelling choice was made. What we present is a method, no conclusive results on this specific case should be expected. Significant insights about a specific case would require conducting the plausibility analysis task while the 3D model is created, or at least in direct interaction with the expert that made the key modelling choices.
- An in-depth evaluation of the applicability and efficiency of the matrix itself is needed – this could be done by reapplying the approach to other cases, for instance. Labels and values of the justification matrix as defined in this paper should be seen as a provisional methodological proposal, requiring further debate and experimentation.
- The model's discretization is architecture-based: 3D elements present in the reconstruction are consistent from the point of view of the architectural language (a wall, an opening, a buttress) but obviously the reality can be far more complex. Typically, sometimes within one consistent architectural element (a wall) there are sub-parts that would call for different plausibility evaluations. As an answer we have introduced a grouping mechanism (alternative granularities) but we acknowledge the solution is at this stage partial.

4.7.2 Lessons learned and conclusions

Shortly said, the experiment has resulted in a number of lessons learned on methodological aspects (real-case evaluation of the matrix formal model) and on

Figure 4.12. An illustration of the prototype as it stands today, with URL connection links (Open Access).

technological aspects (interactions in the 3D scene, visual encoding, 3D models reuse with a shift from proprietary 3D format to a web-enabled Javascript-based 3D interface). But due to the above-mentioned limitations we do not put forward any assertions concerning the informational patterns that would characterise this particular case study. What we report on in this contribution is a *potential*, backed up by a proof-of-concept experiment (Figure 4.12).

Obviously, the approach can only be workable and lead to significant observations and informational patterns on a specific case study if enough is known or remembered about the making of the 3D models (and here we mean the intellectual choices of the experts).

However, we hope such an experiment can act as food for re-thinking what type of knowledge can be expressed in a 3D virtual reconstruction. Said differently, we view this experiment as an opportunity to re-question the issue of sensemaking in 3D environments. The result we present is somewhere between Gardin's demanding approach to documenting 3D models (oriented on decision processes that are conducted while selecting this or that shape, this or that spatial arrangement), and traditional 3D models in which nothing is assessed as far as plausibility, human choices are concerned.

More generally, it seems to us that the technology, and the research agenda, may today open an opportunity to reconsider the information spaces connectable to 3D datasets, to enhance the interpretability of 3D scenes, as well as the repurposability of 3D components. The next step is probably to apply the method while producing the 3D models, and in the meantime collect feedback on potential benefits as perceived by users.

To conclude, we argue in this paper that besides the most current research topics in and around the architectural heritage (acquiring 3D data, trying to store and share it in FAIR-like ways), providing researchers with means to visually analyse and reason about (rather than document) data and information sets are also key issues (regardless of whether the focus is on 3D data or not). The experiment we have conducted is basically a proof-of-concept research, illustrating the fact that 3D datasets – when talking about concrete implementation of the FAIR principles – should be repurposable materials, i.e., content that can be reused to convey or discover new pieces of knowledge, or information patterns (in our case about uncertainty or plausibility). In that sense, our experiment is a renewed attempt to reason about heritage data sets by drawing on practices from the InfoVis field. Regardless of whether readers consider the experiment as significant or anecdotal, it definitely is thought of, on our side, as a call to design and discuss in the scientific community new ways of visualising architectural data, information, and pieces of knowledge.

Acknowledgments

The authors wish to thank all colleagues from the CITERES-LAT team who provided material and input for this study, as well as P. Bénistant (MAP team) for his technical support.

Funding

This research was funded by the ANR, the project-based funding agency for research in France, under the id ANR-18-CE38-0009-01.

Conflict of interest disclosure

The authors declare that they comply with the PCI rule of having no financial conflicts of interest in relation to the content of the article.

Data, scripts, code, and supplementary information availability:

The prototype is available online: https://page.hn/lop9b2.

Author Contributions

Conceptualisation, G.S, J.-Y.B. and I.D; data curation, L.B, G.S and J.-Y.B; formal analysis, J.-Y.B., I.D and G.S; Investigation, J.-Y.B., G.S; and I.D; Methodology, J.-Y.B., I.D and G.S; formal analysis, J.-Y.B., I.D and G.S; Software L.B. and J.-Y.B.; resources, G.S.; writing – original draft preparation, J.-Y.B. and G.S.; writing – review and editing, J.-Y.B., I.D and G.S; visualization, J.-Y.B. and I.D.; supervision, J.-Y.B.; project administration, J.-Y.B.; funding acquisition, J.-Y.B.

Peer review

This article has been reviewed and recommended by PCI Archaeology.

Carvalho, Daniel. 2023. "3D Models, Knowledge and Visualization: a prototype for 3D virtual models according to plausible criteria" *Peer Community in Archaeology* 100339. DOI:10.24072/pci.archaeo.100339.

References

Aigner, Wolfgang, Silvia Miksch, Heidrun Schumann, and Christian Tominski. 2011. *Visualization of Time-Oriented Data.* Human-Computer Interaction Series. London: Springer Science & Business Media. https://dl.acm.org/doi/10.5555/2016703.

Alkhoven, Patricia. 1993. "The Changing Image of the City: A Study of the Transformation of the Townscape Using Computer-Aided Architectural Design and Visualization Techniques: A Case Study: Heusden." PhD diss., Utrecht University.

Bertin, Jacques. 2010. *Semiology of Graphics: Diagrams, Networks, Maps (Orig. Edition in French 1967).* Translated by William J. Berg. Redlands, CA: Esri Press.

Blaise, Jean-Yves, and Iwona Dudek. 2002. "3D Models as Visual Interfaces for Internet: An Application to a Multimedia Documentation on Architectural Evolutions." In *Proceedings of the International Conference on Computer Vision and Graphics (ICCVG 2002), Zakopane, 25-29 Sept. 2002,* 250–6. https://shs.hal.science/halshs-00261887.

Blaise, Jean–Yves, and Iwona Dudek. 2005. "From Artefact Representation to Information Visualisation: Genesis of Informative Modelling." In *Smart Graphics, 5th International Symposium. Frauenwörth Cloister, Germany. 22-24 August 2005*, edited by Andreas Butz, Brian Fisher, Antonio Krüger, and Patrick Olivier, 230–6. Berlin / New York: Springer. DOI:10.1007/11536482_21.

Blaise, Jean-Yves, and Iwona Dudek. 2006. *Modélisation Informationnelle/ Informative Modelling.* MIA Journal. Vol. 1S (numéro spécial). Marseille: CNRS.

Blaise, Jean-Yves, Iwona Dudek, and Tudor Driscu. 2008. "Infosphere: One Artefact, Two Metaphors, Three Sort Criteria." In *Digital Heritage, Proceedings of VSMM 2008 - Virtual Systems and Multimedia,* edited by Marinos Ioannides, Andreas Georgopoulos, Loukas Kalisperis, and Alonzo Addison, 362–7. Budapest: Archeolingua.

Blaise, Jean–Yves, and Iwona Dudek. 2020. "Exploring Visually the Known and the Ill-Known about Krakow's Centre Urban Evolution: An Information Visualisation Perspective." In *Digital Cities: Between History and Archaeology*, edited by Maurizio Forte and Helena Murteira, Illustrated edition, 72–105. New York: Oxford University Press. DOI:10.1093/oso/9780190498900.001.0001.

Dallas, Costis. 2015. "Jean-Claude Gardin on Archaeological Data, Representation and Knowledge: Implications for Digital Archaeology." *Journal of Archaeological Method and Theory* 23 (1): 305–30. DOI:10.1007/s10816-015-9241-3.

Davies, Norman. 1997. *Europe: A History*. London: Pimlico.

Dudek, Iwona, and Jean-Yves Blaise. in press. "Enabling the Comparability of Research Workflows: A Case Study." in *Proceedings CAA2019 CAA Series Computer Applications and Quantitative Methods in Archaeology.* Accessed October 30, 2024. https://shs.hal.science/halshs-02927631.

Kienreich, Wolfgang. 2006. "Information and Knowledge Visualisation: An Oblique View." *MIA Journal,* Modélisation Informationnelle, Vol0 (1): 1–17.

Maeda, John. 2006. *The Laws of Simplicity*. Cambridge, MA: MIT Press.

Messemer, Heike. 2016. "The Beginnings of Digital Visualization of Historical Architecture in the Academic Field." In *Virtual Palaces, Part II. Lost Palaces and Their Afterlife. Virtual Reconstruction between Science and the Media*, edited by Stephan Hoppe and Stefan Breitling, 21–54. DOI:10.11588/arthistoricum.83.79.

Morandi, Simona, and Marco Tremari. 2017. "Interactive Past: From 3D Reconstruction to Augmented and Virtual Reality Applied to Archaeological Heritage. The Medieval Site of Bastia St. Michele (Cavaion Veronese, Verona, Italy)." In *Proceedings of the 2017 23rd International Conference on Virtual System & Multimedia (VSMM)*, edited by A. Addison and L. Goodman, 1–8. Dublin: IEEE. DOI:10.1109/VSMM.2017.8346278.

Pfeiffer, M., C. Carré, V. Delfosse, P. Hallot, and R. Billen. 2013. "Virtual Leodium: From An Historical 3d City Scale Model To An Archaeological Information System." *ISPRS Annals of the Photogrammetry, Remote Sensing and Spatial Information Sciences* II-5-W1:241–6. DOI:10.5194/isprsannals-II-5-W1-241-2013.

Reimer, Andreas W. 2010. "Understanding Chorematic Diagrams: Towards a Taxonomy." *The Cartographic Journal, The World of Mapping* 47 (4): 330–50. DOI:10.1179/000870410X12825500202896.

Rosenberg, Daniel, and Anthony Grafton. 2010. *Cartographies of Time: A History of the Timeline*. New York: Princeton Architectural Press.

Schuller, Gerlinde. 2009. *Designing Universal Knowledge*. Baden, CH: Lars Müller Publishers.

Skeels, Meredith, Bongshin Lee, Greg Smith, and George G. Robertson. 2010. "Revealing Uncertainty for Information Visualization." *Information Visualization* 9 (1): 70–81. DOI:10.1057/ivs.2009.1.

Sylaiou, Stella, and Petros Patias. 2004. "Virtual Reconstructions in Archaeology and Some Issues for Consideration." *Journal for Culture and Technology* 4:180–91.

Thomson, Judi, Elizabeth Hetzler, Alan MacEachren, Mark Gahegan, and Misha Pavel. 2005. "A Typology for Visualizing Uncertainty." In *SPIE Proceedings 5669, Visualization and Data Analysis 2005*. 5669:146–57. DOI:10.1117/12.587254.

Zuk, Torre, and Sheelagh Carpendale. 2007. "Visualization of Uncertainty and Reasoning." In *Smart Graphics, 8th International Symposium, SG 2007, Kyoto, Japan, June 25-27, 2007, Conference Proceedings*, edited by Andreas Butz, Brian Fisher, Antonio Krüger, Patrick Olivier, and Shigeru Owada, 164–77. Berlin; Heidelberg: Springer. DOI:10.1007/978-3-540-73214-3_15.

5 Archaeology specific BERT models for English, German, and Dutch

Alex Brandsen
Leiden University
a.brandsen@arch.leidenuniv.nl
ORCID 0000-0003-1623-1340

Abstract

This short paper describes a collection of BERT models for the archaeology domain. We took existing language specific BERT models in English, German, and Dutch, and further pre-trained them with archaeology specific training data. We then took each of these three archaeology specific models and fine-tuned them for Named Entity Recognition.

Keywords: BERT; Natural Language Processing; Named Entity Recognition; Large Language Models

5.1 Introduction

Archaeology deals with a deluge of data (Bevan 2015), and this of course includes text data. To efficiently analyse large amounts of texts, such as the hundreds of thousands of grey literature reports, Natural Language Processing (NLP) techniques are needed, such as Named Entity Recognition (NER), which tries to extract relevant concepts from text. In the case of our project, the entities we are looking for are artefacts, time periods, locations, materials, contexts, and species. Traditionally, NER was often performed using Conditional Random Fields (CRF) (Brandsen et al. 2019) or rule-based methods (Vlachidis et al. 2013).

With the rise of Deep Learning, BERT (Bidirectional Encoder Representations from Transformers) models can leverage large amounts of unlabelled text to create a language model, which can then be fine-tuned to perform specific NLP tasks – such as NER – with a smaller amount of labelled data (Devlin et al. 2019). This pre-training phase gives the model linguistic context before even seeing the labelled data, which has led to state-of-the-art results on many tasks. In previous research we showed that a BERT model for Dutch archaeology outperforms all other methods (Brandsen et al. 2022). In this paper, we present the same model types, but also for English and German.

In *Advances in Digital Archaeology. Proceedings of the 2023 conference Computer Applications and Quantitative Methods in Archaeology – 50 years of synergy*, edited by J.W.H.P. Verhagen, J. Waagen, A. Brandsen, A. Queffelec, R.M. Visser and D. Taelman, 71–76. Leiden: Sidestone Press.

Model name	Language	Task	HuggingFace URL
ArchaeoBERT	English	Fill-mask	https://huggingface.co/alexbrandsen/ArchaeoBERT
ArchaeoBERT-NER	English	NER	https://huggingface.co/alexbrandsen/ArchaeoBERT-NER
bert-base-german-cased-archaeo	German	Fill-mask	https://huggingface.co/alexbrandsen/bert-base-german-cased-archaeo
bert-base-german-cased-archaeo-ner	German	NER	https://huggingface.co/alexbrandsen/bert-base-german-cased-archaeo-NER
ArcheoBERTje	Dutch	Fill-mask	https://huggingface.co/alexbrandsen/ArcheoBERTje
ArcheoBERTje-NER	Dutch	NER	https://huggingface.co/alexbrandsen/ArcheoBERTje-NER

Table 5.1. Overview of the six BERT models, including links to HuggingFace.

Method	Language	Precision	Recall	F1
CRF	Dutch	0.773	0.564	0.643
General BERT	Dutch	0.762	0.688	0.723
Archaeo BERT	Dutch	**0.784**	**0.731**	**0.757**
CRF	German	0.677	0.325	0.414
General BERT	German	**0.698**	0.634	0.664
Archaeo BERT	German	0.681	**0.702**	**0.692**
CRF	English	0.774	0.592	0.655
General BERT	English	0.766	0.716	0.740
Archaeo BERT	English	**0.768**	**0.730**	**0.749**

Table 5.2. Overview of precision, recall and F1 on the NER task, comparing the archaeology specific BERT model versus the generic BERT model and CRF. Highest scores per language are highlighted in bold.

5.2 Methods

We started with the three existing fill-mask BERT models for English, German, and Dutch. We provide the model name, HuggingFace (Wolf et al. 2020) name, and citation for each:

- English: bert-base-cased (Devlin et al. 2019);
- German: bert-base-german-cased (Chan et al. 2021);
- Dutch: bert-base-dutch-cased (De Vries et al. 2019).

We then used the HuggingFace `run_mlm.py`[1] script to further pre-train these existing models with archaeology specific, unlabelled data. See the file `run_mlm_on_commandline.sh` in the code folder for the parameters used.

For English, we used roughly 44k documents (~264 million tokens) from the ADS library[2], for German we used about 21k documents (~107 million tokens) from the Heidelberg university library[3], and for Dutch we used around 60k Dutch excavation reports (~650 million tokens) from the DANS data archive[4]. Unfortunately, as a large proportion of the texts is copyrighted, under embargo, or otherwise access-protected, we cannot share this training data publicly.

This process creates an archaeology-specific fill-mask BERT model for each language, but these can't do NER yet. So, we fine-tuned them on labelled NER data, creating NER prediction models for each language. Table 5.1 shows an overview of all the models we trained. The labelled NER data was annotated by students, this data and the labelling process is further described in a previous paper (Brandsen et al. 2020).

1 https://github.com/huggingface/transformers/blob/main/examples/pytorch/language-modeling/run_mlm.py
2 https://archaeologydataservice.ac.uk/library/index.xhtml.
3 https://digi.ub.uni-heidelberg.de/en/sammlungen/archaeologie.html.
4 https://easy.dans.knaw.nl/ui/home.

5.3 Results

To see how well the models performed, we evaluated the recall, precision, and F1 score on a set of annotated NER data for each language. The results can be found in Table 5.2. We see that except for precision in German, the archaeology specific BERT models outperform the other methods. We also see that the increase in performance with the archaeology specific model is smaller for English than for the other two languages, something we will investigate in future research. For a more in-depth error analysis of the Dutch BERT model entity predictions, as well as more information about the CRF methods, please see Brandsen et al. (2022).

5.4 Usage

How to use these models depends on the task you are trying to perform. In the simplest case, the models can be used to do NER predictions on new text by importing the HuggingFace transformers package, loading the models from the HuggingFace repository, setting up a predictor, and running inference, in just a few lines of code. See the example below, using Transformers v4.37.0, where we imported the English Archaeology NER model and ran it on a sentence:

```
from transformers import pipeline

pipe = pipeline("token-classification", model="alexbrandsen/ArchaeoBERT-NER")

predictor = pipeline(
    'ner',
     model=model,
     tokenizer=tokenizer,
     device = 0,
     grouped_entities = False
)

sentence = "We have found a cup in a Medieval well."
entities = predictor(sentence)
```

Which will return the entities cup (artefact), Medieval (time period), and well (context):

```
[
    {'entity': 'B-ART', 'score': 0.9598702, 'index': 5, 'word': 'cup', 'start': 16, 'end': 19}
    {'entity': 'B-PER', 'score': 0.9939248, 'index': 8, 'word': 'Medieval', 'start': 25, 'end': 33}
    {'entity': 'B-CON', 'score': 0.58865726, 'index': 9, 'word': 'well', 'start': 34, 'end': 38}
]
```

Some possible uses for entities extracted from archaeological text are information retrieval (Brandsen 2022), enriching metadata, and as a preprocessing step for further knowledge extraction, such as knowledge graph creation or entity linking.

If you want to use the models for a task other than NER, you will need to fine-tune the fill-mask model(s) for your chosen task. This is a bit more involved than just running inference and is outside the scope of this paper. Full instructions on how to do this can be found in the HuggingFace documentation pages.[5]

Another possible use for the fill-mask models is to further pre-train them even further, with even more (or more specific) training data. In this case, the `run_mlm_on_commandline.sh` script in the code folder on Zenodo (Brandsen 2024) can be pointed to your own data, and this will update the model. Note that large amounts of text are needed for this, at least 50 million tokens are recommended.

5 https://huggingface.co/docs/transformers/training

5.5 Discussion

Of course, since the release of GPT-3 and its associated ChatGPT service (Brown et al. 2020), BERT has largely been overtaken in terms of performance by these Large Language Models (LLMs). However, for specific domains and low-resource languages, BERT can still outperform LLMs. We ran a quick trial using Meta's Llama model (Touvron et al. 2023) trying to do NER in English, and found it difficult to control the output, while the results were mediocre. For example, we used this prompt

> *"You are an expert archaeologist, who is annotating sentences with archaeological named entities, including artefacts, places, time periods, materials, locations, contexts and species. You are given an input as plain text and should output CONNL format. The input is: 2 pots were uncovered near London, dated to the Late Medieval period"*, which returned:

```
> 2 P
pots W
U
cove
r O
near O
London B-LOC
,
dated O
to O
the L
ate M
edieval P
e
r
i
o
d B-PER
```

It is clear that Llama sort of understands the task, but the output is not correct, nor correctly formatted in the CONLL format. More research is needed to see if this new generation of language models can help us for this specific task. At the same time, it is worth noting that the BERT models are at least intelligible and appropriate for the domain specific work one might want to do with them.

Also, something to keep in mind is that BERT is already a very computationally intensive model, using up much electricity and CO_2 (Bender et al. 2021), and these new LLMs are even bigger and more energy consuming, and this should be kept in mind when using these methods. Is the (sometimes small) increase in performance worth the extra time, expertise, and energy required for these models?

5.6 Conclusion

In this paper, we presented six BERT models for use in NLP in archaeology, in three languages. We also provide the methods on how to further pre-train models, and hope to either see models in other languages by other researchers, or we will train models ourselves, hopefully leading to an ecosystem of language models for archaeology.

Acknowledgements

We would like to thank the DANS archive, the ADS library, and Heidelberg University for sharing the data that these models were trained on. The models were trained using the compute resources from the Academic Leiden Interdisciplinary Cluster Environment (ALICE) provided by Leiden University.

Funding

The project in which this research has been carried out has been funded by NWO (The Dutch Research Council) under the "Future directions in Dutch archaeological research" programme.

Conflict of Interest Disclosure

The author declares that they comply with the PCI rule of having no financial conflicts of interest in relation to the content of the article. The author declares the following non-financial conflict of interest: the author is a recommender of PCI Archaeology.

Data, Scripts, Code, and Supplementary Information Availability

The code needed to further pre-train BERT models and to run inference with the models is included in the "models-and-code" zip file in the Zenodo archive (Brandsen 2024).

As for the data, as a large proportion of the texts is copyrighted, under embargo, or otherwise access-protected, we cannot share this training data publicly.

Peer review

This article has been reviewed and recommended by PCI Archaeology.

di Buono, M. 2024. "Multilingual Named Entity Recognition in archaeology: an approach based on deep learning". *Peer Community in Archaeology* 100394. DOI:10.24072/pci.archaeo.100394.

References

Bender, Emily M., Timnit Gebru, Angelina Mcmillan-Major, and Shmargaret Shmitchell. 2021. "On the Dangers of Stochastic Parrots: Can Language Models Be Too Big?" In *FAccT '21: Proceedings of the 2021 ACM Conference on Fairness, Accountability, and Transparency*, 610–23. Canada: ACM. DOI:10.1145/3442188.3445922.

Bevan, Andrew. 2015. "The Data Deluge." *Antiquity* 89 (348): 1473–84. DOI:10.15184/aqy.2015.102.

Brandsen, Alex. 2022. "Digging in Documents: Using Text Mining to Access the Hidden Knowledge in Dutch Archaeological Excavation Reports." PhD diss., Leiden University. https://hdl.handle.net/1887/3274287.

Brandsen, Alex. 2024. "Archaeology specific BERT models for English, German, and Dutch (Version v5)". *Zenodo*. DOI:10.5281/zenodo.10650835.

Brandsen, Alex, Karsten Lambers, Suzan Verberne, and Milco Wansleeben. 2019. "User Requirement Solicitation for an Information Retrieval System Applied to Dutch Grey Literature in the Archaeology Domain." *Journal of Computer Applications in Archaeology* 2 (1): 21–30. DOI:10.5334/jcaa.33.

Brandsen, Alex, Suzan Verberne, Karsten Lambers, and Milco Wansleeben. 2022. "Can BERT Dig It? - Named Entity Recognition for Information Retrieval in the Archaeology Domain." *Journal on Computing and Cultural Heritage* 15 (3): 1–18. DOI:10.1145/3497842.

Brandsen, Alex, Suzan Verberne, Milco Wansleeben, and Karsten Lambers. 2020. "Creating a Dataset for Named Entity Recognition in the Archaeology Domain." In *Proceedings of the 12th Language Resources and Evaluation Conference*, 4573–7.

Marseille: European Language Resources Association. https://www.aclweb.org/anthology/2020.lrec-1.562.

Brown, Tom B., Benjamin Mann, Nick Ryder, Melanie Subbiah, Jared Kaplan, Prafulla Dhariwal, Arvind Neelakantan, et al. 2020. "Language Models Are Few-Shot Learners." In *NIPS'20: Proceedings of the 34th International Conference on Neural Information Processing Systems*, 1877–1901. Vancouver: ACM. DOI:10.5555/3495724.3495883.

Chan, Branden, Stefan Schweter, and Timo Möller. 2021. "German's Next Language Model." In *Proceedings of the 28th International Conference on Computational Linguistics*, 6788-96. Barcelona: International Committee on Computational Linguistics. DOI:10.18653/v1/2020.coling-main.598.

Devlin, Jacob, Ming Wei Chang, Kenton Lee, and Kristina Toutanova. 2019. "BERT: Pre-Training of Deep Bidirectional Transformers for Language Understanding." In *Proceedings of the 2019 Conference of the North American Chapter of the Association for Computational Linguistics: Human Language Technologies*, 1:4171–86. Minneapolis, MN: Association for Computational Linguistics. DOI:10.18653/v1/N19-1423.

Touvron, Hugo, Thibaut Lavril, Gautier Izacard, Xavier Martinet, Marie-Anne Lachaux, Timothée Lacroix, Baptiste Rozière et al. 2023. "Llama: Open and efficient foundation language models." ArXiv. DOI:10.48550/arXiv.2302.13971.

Vlachidis, Andreas, Ceri Binding, Keith May, and Douglas Tudhope. 2013. "Automatic Metadata Generation in an Archaeological Digital Library: Semantic Annotation of Grey Literature." *Studies in Computational Intelligence*, 458: 187–202. DOI:10.1007/978-3-642-34399-5_10.

Vries, Wietse De, Andreas van Cranenburgh, Arianna Bisazza, Tommaso Caselli, Gertjan van Noord, and Malvina Nissim. 2019. "BERTje: A Dutch BERT Model." ArXiv. https://arxiv.org/abs/1912.09582.

Wolf, Thomas, Lysandre Debut, Victor Sanh, Julien Chaumond, Clement Delangue, Anthony Moi, Pierric Cistac, et al. 2020. "Transformers: State-of-the-Art Natural Language Processing." In *Proceedings of the 2020 Conference on Empirical Methods in Natural Language Processing: System Demonstrations*, 38–45. Stroudsburg, PA: Association for Computational Linguistics. DOI:10.18653/v1/2020.emnlp-demos.6.

6 Inferring shellfishing seasonality from the isotopic composition of biogenic carbonate

A Bayesian approach

Jordan Brown
Corresponding author
University of California
Berkeley
Correspondence:
jordanbrown@berkeley.edu

Gabriel Lewis
University of Massachusetts
Amherst

Abstract

The problem of accurately and reliably estimating the annual distribution of seasonally-varying human settlement and subsistence practices is a classic concern among archaeologists, which has only become more relevant with the increasing importance of holistic studies of social and ecological systems aimed at establishing deep historical baselines to ground current practical work in socioenvironmental management. In this paper, we present a novel approach to the analysis of shellfishing seasonality using stable isotope measurements on biogenic carbonate (e.g., mollusc shell). Our approach uses a Bayesian mixture model framework to construct an estimate of the annual distribution of shellfish harvesting activity (within some particular historical context) on the basis of isotope measurement sets from a sample of shell specimens (derived from some corresponding archaeological entity). This framework enables two major advances beyond current isotope sclerochronological methods for archaeological seasonality analysis: (1) flexible specimen-level seasonality assignments that may be as precise or diffuse as the data warrant and may respond to unforeseen seasonal signatures, unrelated to conventional seasons and perhaps only recoverable by mathematical analysis, and (2) full characterization of uncertainty accompanying the estimated density of shellfish harvesting activity at all points throughout the year, all of which may be displayed concisely in a single plot with an estimated density curve and uncertainty envelope. These features of our approach focus analysis and interpretation on the seasonally-varying human practice under study, as well as on exactly the state of our knowledge regarding the annual pattern of variation in that practice, including the portions of this pattern that remain poorly constrained. By treating these issues clearly, we address some common obstacles to the advancement of archaeological seasonality research, particularly as regards the appraisal of sampling adequacy requirements at various scales of analysis and the principled integration of diverse and possibly contradicting lines of evidence in broadly transdisciplinary research in the historical sciences. We hope that further elaboration of the methodological core presented here will aid the ongoing development of the creative and collaborative traditions

In *Advances in Digital Archaeology. Proceedings of the 2023 conference Computer Applications and Quantitative Methods in Archaeology – 50 years of synergy*, edited by J.W.H.P. Verhagen, J. Waagen, A. Brandsen, A. Queffelec, R.M. Visser and D. Taelman, 77–86. Leiden: Sidestone Press.

of scholarship that have emerged around studying local and regional histories of social and ecological relationships, with the aim of healing and strengthening these relationships in the present and future.

Keywords: archaeomalacology, Bayesian statistics, historical ecology, molluscs, paleoclimatology, sclerochronology, seasonality, shellfishing, shells, stable isotope analysis, zooarchaeology

6.1 Introduction

Seasonal rhythms of settlement and subsistence are a long-standing concern of archaeological scholarship, with implications for a wide variety of research themes ranging across social-environmental dynamics (Prendergast et al. 2018), long-distance communication and political integration (Graeber and Wengrow 2021), and the development of Indigenous intellectual traditions (Hadden et al. 2022). To detect seasonal rhythms in the archaeological record, archaeologists have employed numerous proxies, many based on recovering archaeological remains of seasonally-available plant or animal species, warranting inferences about both the seasonal utilization of the species in question and the seasonal occupation of the site (Monks 1981). Besides seasonally-restricted species, archaeologists have often studied seasonality using biogenic structures (e.g., mollusc shells, fish otoliths) that are grown by accretion over the course of an organism's lifetime, allowing the investigator to fix the organism's season of death by establishing relationships between time of year and organismal growth rates and/or structures (e.g., Mellars et al. 1980; Clark 1979) or geochemical signatures of seasonally-variable environmental parameters (e.g., Shackleton 1973; Killingley 1981).

This latter approach is of particular relevance for computational archaeology, as it relies on quantitative data (e.g., oxygen isotope composition [$\delta^{18}O$] of biogenic carbonate) for which statistical relationships have been established with environmental parameters (e.g., sea-surface temperature [SST]) whose patterns of seasonal variation may also be quantified (Kwiecien et al. 2022). However, despite the amenability of geochemical sclerochronological methods of seasonality determination to quantitative treatment, the standard for data analysis in these types of studies remains nonquantitative, erecting unnecessary barriers to the advancement of seasonality studies using these techniques. In what follows, we present a Bayesian framework for this style of quantitative seasonality analysis, focusing on the common case in which $\delta^{18}O$ of biogenic carbonate (e.g., of marine molluscs) is used as a proxy for seasonal variations in SST (Urey et al. 1951). We first formulate the problem in general terms for a single specimen and then develop an approach to estimating the distribution of harvest intensity over the year by modelling the isotope measurement sets from a sample of archaeological shell specimens as a mixture of regression distributions relating time of year to oxygen isotope composition, with the harvest intensity at different times of year modulating the mixing proportions (Ferguson 1983).

Our analytical approach advances the effectiveness and theoretical defensibility of isotope seasonality studies in two major ways:

1. It supports reliable detection of a wide variety of seasonality patterns by recording season-of-death estimates at fine resolution (days to weeks) and with full uncertainty characterization. We thereby avoid the risk of obscuring or distorting anthropologically important seasonal contrasts that is inevitable under the common analytical strategy of dividing the year a priori into artificially coarse and arbitrarily positioned seasonal bins, chosen primarily for having visually-identifiable signatures in the annual SST curve.
2. It focuses attention on exactly what the analysis tells us *about the seasonally-varying human practice of interest* (including how the precision of our knowledge may differ at different points of the year) by reporting results in the form of an estimate of the annual distribution of shellfishing intensity that also quantifies the degree of uncertainty involved in different portions of this estimate. We thereby avoid the confusion around how much confidence should be placed in the results of a given study that arises from the common practice of reporting essentially just a description of the sample that the study in question has analysed, rather than using that sample to make an inference about the theoretical population from which it was drawn.

The theoretical objections to shell seasonality studies that we answer here—regarding coarse, arbitrary seasonality assignments and unclear targets of inference and standards of evidence—were raised in essentially similar form by Claassen (1991) in her classic review of North American research traditions regarding shell-bearing sites. Claassen's discussion mentions only growth-line seasonality studies, but the issues apply to isotope studies just as well; see Deith (1985) for a comparison. Claassen attributes these problems to archaeologists' persistently simplistic treatment of both the structure of shell-bearing sites and the shell-depositing human practices involved in their development (see also Ambrose 1967; Meehan 1982; Waselkov 1987). In the decades since, much work has been done within archaeology to improve the effective excavation and interpretation of shell-bearing archaeological sites and deposits (e.g., Stein 1992;

Luby et al. 2006; Milner et al. 2007; Marquardt 2010; Roksandic et al. 2014; Villagran 2014; Letham et al. 2019), as well as the biological and ecological foundations and laboratory techniques of isotope sclerochronology (e.g., Kennett and Voorhies 1996; Jones et al. 2008; Schweikhardt et al. 2011; Hallmann et al. 2013; Burchell et al. 2018; West et al. 2018; Jazwa et al. 2020; Kwiecien et al. 2022). However, little progress has been made in the final stage of data analysis, with current strategies generally employing a variant of either Shackleton's (1973) temperature-and-trend classification scheme (e.g., springtime is characterized by low SST that is increasing), Killingley's (1981) SST wiggle-matching approach, or some combination of the two (see, e.g., Hadden et al. 2022; Cuthrell 2013; Burchell et al. 2018).

In paleoclimatology, researchers have made significant strides in the quantitative analysis of seasonally-resolved archives, including mollusc shells (e.g., Wilkinson and Ivany 2002; de Brauwere et al. 2009; Ivany 2012; Wang et al. 2015; de Winter et al. 2021; Kwiecien et al. 2022), but these methods are generally designed for the analysis of long-term, high-resolution data collected from a relatively small number of specimens (but see Zimmt et al. 2019, for a paleobiological counterpoint), with the aim of accurately characterizing variations in the seasonal climate regime over a long period. These techniques are therefore not particularly well suited to the needs of archaeological seasonality studies, which require a comparatively large number of specimens and are interested primarily in the final portion of the shell-producing organism's lifespan. This difference in focus warrants a different allocation of resources that increases the number of specimens per assemblage and decreases the number of samples per specimen, which is in fact reflected in the existing data base of isotope determinations from archaeological seasonality studies (see Palmer et al. 2022). Note that the same is not generally true of paleoclimatic seasonality studies conducted using archaeological materials.

The method we describe below is designed to fill this gap, allowing reproducible and rigorous quantitative analysis of the existing archaeological isotope seasonality database in a transparent fashion, while presenting a platform for further methodological development by incorporating more sophisticated anthropological, biological, depositional, and ecological process models increasingly under development. This approach also facilitates analysis of the larger samples necessary to address intra- and inter-site and diachronic variability and offers a principle for combining the diverse lines of evidence that bear on settlement and subsistence seasonality, while properly accounting for the uncertainties of each.

In what follows, we present first a simple, computationally inexpensive method for estimating the death date (i.e., day of year) of a single organism, in order to outline the basic problem of seasonality determination clearly in statistical terms. We then describe a powerful approach to estimating the annual distribution of shellfishing intensity on the basis of an assemblage composed of many specimens, which makes use of a mixture model framework to characterize the uncertainty in our estimate of the distribution of shellfish harvesting activity over the year.

6.2 Methods

The present section will discuss the key features of our approach to statistical modelling of isotope-based shellfishing seasonality determination. For additional mathematical detail, as well as implementation of this modelling framework with fully reproducible scripted examples in R and Stan (R Core Team 2023; Stan Development Team 2022; Stan Development Team 2023), please see the R Markdown document that accompanies this article (Lewis and Brown 2023).

6.2.1 Estimating the season of death of an individual shell

Suppose we have a good regression model for the distribution of SST (y) over days of the year (w) at a given location, with parameters θ: $p(y|w, \theta)$. We also assume that the oxygen isotope composition of seawater at this location remains constant throughout the year, so that we may disregard the effect of ambient seawater $\delta^{18}O$ fluctuations on the $\delta^{18}O$ of carbonate precipitated in this environment (Epstein et al. 1951, 1953; Kim & O'Neil 1997). Provided we are working with an organism with a reliable carbonate paleothermometer ($\delta^{18}O$ ~ SST) relationship so that parameter uncertainties can be disregarded, we are then essentially trying to predict the day of the year on which an observed SST time-series ended. For now, we do not model w, making $p(w)$ a uniform distribution. This choice is defensible only for the purpose of illustrating what we can learn from each shell individually. We assume that our regression is homoskedastic (equal variances in SST across different times of year) and make the large-sample approximation so that we can treat our parameters as concentrated entirely at their point estimates. We also stipulate that we know precisely the time-displacement between carbonate samples, equivalent to assuming a known constant shell growth rate throughout the year. None of these assumptions are strictly justified and can indeed be relaxed, but they do not trivialize the problem and add greatly to the ease of presentation for our purposes here.

We can then formulate a multivariate normal density function calibrated to the annual SST regression model and known spacing between carbonate samples, which will allow us to calculate the likelihood that a hypothetical organism dying on a given day would produce a particular SST time-series: $p(y = y^*|w^*)$. This likelihood can then be 'inverted' by summing over all possible death-dates to yield the probability that a real sampled organism producing an observed SST time-series in fact died on a particular day:

1. $p(w^*|y = y^*) = \frac{p(y=y^*|w^*)p(w^*)}{\int p(y=y^*|w)p(w)\,dw}$

6.2.2 Estimating the annual distribution of shellfishing activity

We would like to go a step further and do away with the theoretically indefensible practice of treating each shell as though its death was influenced by an entirely unique set of causes. Instead, we would like to learn precisely about the common causes involved in the death of all shells in an assemblage from a given place and time, i.e., the human practices of seasonally-varying shellfish harvesting activity. So, we model w explicitly, so that we are working with the full joint probability model: $p(y,w|\theta,\lambda)=p(y|w,\theta)p(w|\lambda)$, where λ represents the parameters of the prior distribution of harvest intensity over the year.

For each shell i, we have n_i observations ordered in time. Each observation $(y^j_i,\Delta w^j_i)$ comprises a temperature y^j_i which occurred at some time w^j_i that is unobserved; we observe only the corresponding time-displacement $\Delta w^j_i = w^j_i - w^{ni}_i$, where w^{ni}_i is the unobserved time-of-harvest. We will assume that temperatures are normally distributed around a sinusoidal mean-function $\mu(w_i,\theta)$ with some covariance $V(w_i,\theta)$, so: $p(y_i|w_i,\theta) = N(y_i|\mu(w_i,\theta),V(w_i,\theta))$

The joint probability distribution of the data then is:

2. $p(y_i,\Delta w_i|\theta,\lambda,\gamma) = \int p(y_i|\Delta w_i,w^{ni}_i,\theta,\lambda,\gamma)p(\Delta w_i|w^{ni}_i,\theta,\lambda,\gamma)p(w^{ni}_i|\theta,\lambda,\gamma)$

The displacements Δw_i and final time w^{ni}_i together contain exactly the same information as the times w_i themselves, so $p(y_i\,|\,\Delta w_i,w^{ni}_i,\theta,\lambda,\gamma)= p(y_i\,|\,w_i,\theta,\lambda,\gamma)$. We stipulate that $y_i\,|\,w_i$ is indeed modeled using only the regression parameters θ: $p(y_i\,|\,w_i,\theta)$. We then assume that the marginal distribution of harvest-times has its own parameters λ which do not include the other parameters and also, as above, that the displacements Δw_i are fully determined by w^{ni}_i and a known spacing-vector γ_i. Thus, $p(\Delta w_i\,|\,w^{ni}_i,\theta,\lambda,\gamma)$ effectively drops out of the integration and we can dispense with the parameter γ:

3. $p(y_i,\Delta w_i|\theta,\lambda) = \int p(y_i|\Delta w_i,w^{ni}_i,\theta)p(w^{ni}_i|\lambda)$

Suppose we know there are arbitrarily many possible harvest-times w°_j, where j=1,...,J, with corresponding probabilities λ_j. The data-generating distribution is then a finite mixture of regression distributions, mixing over possible harvest times w°_j with probabilities λ_j:

4. $p(y_i,\Delta w_i|\theta,\lambda) = \sum_j p(y_i|\Delta w_i,w^\circ_j,\theta)\,\lambda_j$

Each probability λ_j may be interpreted as the harvest intensity at time w°_j, so inferences about λ_j are of primary interest. All that is required further is to place prior probability distributions on θ and λ and translate the model into Stan to draw samples from the posterior distribution of λ.

Note that we may still draw inferences about individual shells. For each posterior draw of λ, we simply calculate:

5. $\Pr(w^*_i=w^\circ_k|y_i,\theta,\lambda) = \frac{p(y_i|w^\circ_k,\theta)\lambda_k}{\sum_{j=1}^{J} p(y_i|w^\circ_j,\theta)\lambda_j}$

We can see from the above expression that we may still draw fairly precise inferences about an individual shell even if the harvest distribution (described by λ) remains largely unknown.

6.3 Results

A full quantitative assessment of the performance of the above methods will await their testing on a range of both real-world and simulated datasets (cf. de Winter et al. 2021). For now, we will just describe the basic successful operation of these tools and some of the desirable attributes of the results produced. The results and figures discussed are available in full detail, along with reproducible generating scripts, in the R Markdown document that accompanies this article (Lewis and Brown 2023).

The procedure for drawing inferences about a single shell described above allows us to do a similar kind of analysis as has for decades been the standard in archaeological applications of isotope sclerochronology, in which a set of isotope measurements from a specimen is compared to the pattern of seasonal variation in a relevant environmental variable in order to infer the time of year at which the organism died and shell growth ceased (Fig. 6.1). However, our results improve upon the current state of the art in several important ways. First, the assumptions on which the analysis is based are made explicit and all steps are automated so that the entire analysis is reproducible and much more time-efficient than visual analysis of each set of measurements. The analysis is also statistically modeled so that results may be reported with proper characterization of uncertainty, which more faithfully and flexibly conveys what can be learned about the specimen's season of death, while simultaneously removing the need for any a priori delineation of coarse seasonal bins of potentially questionable anthropological relevance. Additionally, by modeling the set of isotope values likely to be recorded under a particular shell carbonate sampling strategy (e.g., samples drilled at 0 mm, 1 mm, 2 mm, and 2.5 mm from the shell terminus) as a multivariate normal distribution, we employ *all* of the data we have toward inferring the specimen's season of death, as opposed to the analytically inefficient practice of collapsing the data in some way

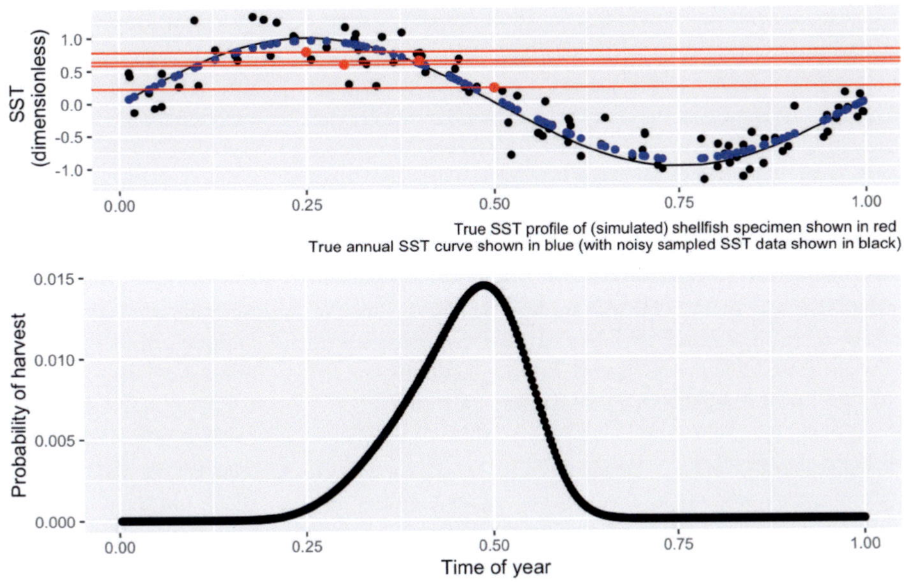

Figure 6.1. Estimating mollusc death date from multiple isotope measurements at intervals along shell growth axis.

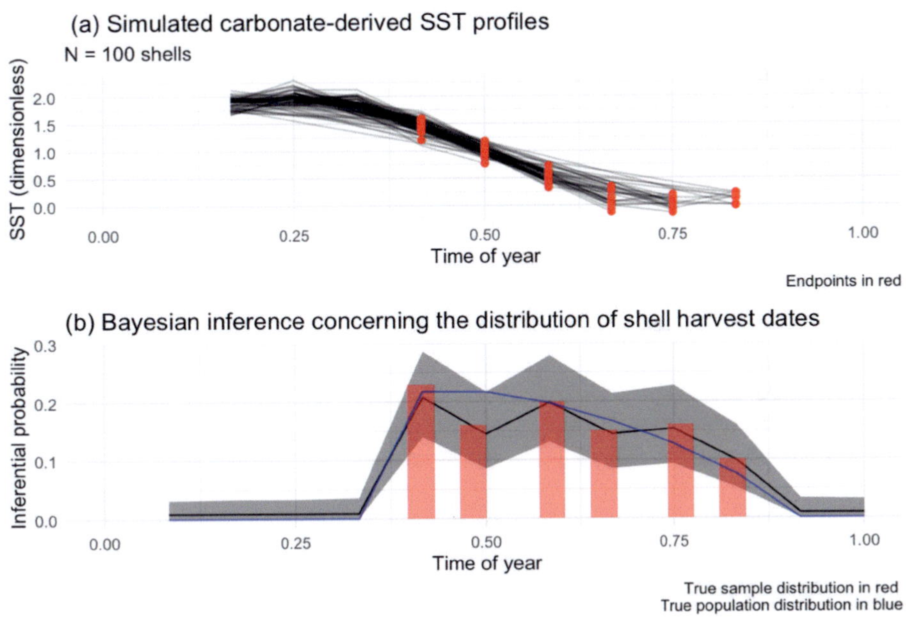

Figure 6.2. Estimating the annual distribution of shellfishing activity.

in order to make it tractable for nonstatistical visual or semi-quantitative analysis (see, e.g., Culleton et al. 2009; Mannino et al. 2011; Eerkens et al. 2013; Hadden et al. 2022).

The procedure we present for analyzing a sample of multiple shells in tandem explicitly to construct an estimate (with uncertainty) of a population distribution of interest apparently has no equivalent in the literature on isotope sclerochronology for season-of-death determination. All other studies that we are aware of derive their inferences about samples of multiple shells (and only implicitly the larger statistical populations they represent) just by tabulating and aggregating individual determinations of season of death on single specimens. This strategy is needlessly conservative: archaeologists study not one but many archaeological shells because we believe at least some of them to have been harvested according to some shared set of practices common to a human group at some place and time. Therefore, we should pool all specimens that we believe to have been harvested under related conditions and study them collectively, using all of this data to constrain the parameters of the population distribution from which we understand this sample to have been drawn. It is this style of analysis that our method enables and encourages, which offers both greater inferential power and a sounder theoretical underpinning than the alternative. Figure 6.2 shows the results of a run of the mixture model described above using simulated data (shown in the upper panel). The estimated annual distribution of harvest intensity (lower panel) matches both the sample and population distributions of shell death dates quite well. The uncertainty (shown in gray) represents how tightly constrained by the data our estimate of harvest intensity is during different portions of the year. Note that our uncertainty-bounded *estimate* of the population distribution of season of death is a better characterization of the true population distribution than is even the *true* sample distribution, not to mention the estimate thereof that we could construct in a real-world case.

6.4 Discussion

The key contribution of these results is to demonstrate the feasibility and value of deriving carbonate isotope composition-based estimates of subsistence (or settlement) seasonality that both characterize seasonal signatures with full flexibility and also transparently report the (nonuniform) uncertainty envelope around the estimated seasonality distribution. These features are essentially the usual merits of a fully modeled (esp. Bayesian) statistical approach, in which the processes understood to be responsible for generating the data are clearly described in quantitative terms, making plain the relationship between the sample of observations submitted to analysis and the unobserved (and here unobservable) statistical population from which this sample is understood to have been drawn. By defining the theoretical population explicitly, it becomes possible to assess the extent to which the sample is adequate to confidently characterize the population parameters of interest, a problem that has affected archaeological isotope seasonality research throughout its history (see Claassen 1991) and still presents difficulties today. Without a clear statistical framework, uncertainty as to what would constitute an adequate sample size (i.e., number of specimens) has often led conscientious researchers to follow the practice of paleoclimatologists and opt for fewer specimens with more isotope measurements per specimen, in order to increase confidence about season-of-death assignment per specimen (e.g., Hallmann et al. 2013; Burchell et al. 2018). Our method offers some balance to this tendency by quantifying analytical uncertainty at the level of both the specimen and the assemblage in order to find the most efficient strategy to reduce the overall uncertainty about the target of inference (e.g., the seasonality of shellfishing practices of a community at a particular place and time) in the case in question, facilitating better planned and even multi-step adaptive sampling programs, such as that implicitly described by Bailey et al. (1983). The transparent characterization of uncertainty in our approach also helps to ameliorate the common issue of isotope seasonality determinations appearing to contradict other sources of seasonality evidence, particularly historical and ethnographic (e.g., Jones et al. 2008; Hallman et al. 2013). With a clear sense of the precision of the isotope seasonality analysis, researchers have a straightforward path to reasoning about possible compromises between evidentiary bases with differing strengths or ranges of application.

An additional benefit of the population-oriented method we present is that it may also be applied to different groupings of the same set of specimens (including the extreme case of studying each specimen separately), in order to use isotope seasonality evidence to inform delineation of archaeologically-relevant units of study for other purposes. This 'reverse' application is one example of a variety of potential uses for this methodology within the diverse inferential ecosystem of archaeological research (see Wylie 2002; Currie 2018). Brown (2023) discussed these potential applications in more detail, describing how they relate to what are often viewed as sources of deleterious uncertainty by researchers seeking seasonality determinations. For example, though temporal variation in mollusc shell growth rates complicates the determination of season of death (Schöne 2008), this fact also implies that, if season of death can be established with some certainty (e.g., by fixing on some clear cultural pattern of shellfish harvesting), then we may be able to use this information to learn about growth rate variation in a species or population under certain conditions. This goes somewhat further than the admirable recognition by paleoclimatologists of the potential climatological value of isotope measurement datasets produced originally for archaeological seasonality-determination purposes (e.g., Palmer et al. 2022): not only may the data be mobilized to different ends, but rather the data can most fruitfully be viewed as the complex outcome of a range of diverse processes (climatological, biological, anthropological, etc.), which are nevertheless intimately connected and about which it is precisely these interconnections that are turning out to be most interesting and worthy of study, often with some sense of urgency (Prendergast et al. 2018; Kwiecien et al. 2022).

By extending the core model presented here with additional components treating the quantitative impacts (and uncertainty) of organismal physiology and ecology, subannual autocorrelation of climate time-series, interannual climatic variation, paleoclimatic and paleoenvironmental reconstructions, and knowledgeable modification and development of subsistence and settlement strategies by local human communities, we can create the opportunity to learn across these diverse systems, all of which are understood with varying levels and types of uncertainty. It is this sort of holistic, omnivorous (sensu Currie 2018) approach to research that characterizes archaeology at its best (Wylie 2002) and especially the specific tradition of Indigenous-led eco-archaeological scholarship from which the work presented here ultimately derives (Lightfoot et al. 2021). Some tentative steps toward demonstrating how a fully modeled quantitative treatment of the isotope seasonality problem can provide benefits for a wide variety of different research themes are taken by Apodaca et al. (2025), employing an earlier method developed by co-author Brown (2024) and applying this to the study of mollusc isotope data from three sites in Santa Cruz County, California, particularly with regard to physiological and anthropological processes (e.g., growth rate, choice of shellfish gathering location) that interact with the seasonality determination problem. Brown's earlier method differs from that presented here, in that it is based on measuring the correlation of an individual specimen's isotope measurement profile with portions of an empirical historical SST seasonality database and constructing only a 'point' estimate of the annual distribution of shellfishing activity without characterizing uncertainty around this estimated distribution. However, it still shares some of the essential features of the method described above, namely, allowing fully flexible high-resolution seasonality estimates (i.e., without preselected coarse bins) and reproducibly incorporating assumptions regarding biological, climatic, and environmental variables into the analysis, thereby allowing for sensitivity testing and exploration of the relationship between these assumptions and the seasonality conclusions reached.

The substantially more powerful Bayesian framework presented here can be extended much further in a similar direction, to holistically address larger questions of rhythmic interactions between biological and environmental dynamics and communal human traditions and innovations regarding the management of social and ecological systems (Hadden et al. 2022), as well as the more narrowly disciplinary concern of synthesizing a wide variety of seasonal and temporal indicators across the history of settlement at an archaeological site or within a region (Monks 1981). Such study of complex human eco-management systems articulates well with the distinct but allied goals of paleoclimatologists working to refine high-resolution studies of individual archives (de Winter et al. 2021), simultaneously offering a window onto the spatial and temporal structure of human engagements with dynamic environments (Prendergast et al. 2018). Many published datasets already exist that could support such large-scale research aims (Palmer et al. 2022), but for problems of comparability between different sample sizes and sampling routines that are difficult to resolve without a clear statistical formulation of the research problem (Claassen 1991). The explicitly statistical method presented here allows us to leverage these legacy datasets without costly physical reanalysis, while also providing a way to update analyses with the latest high-resolution results. We hope that such retrospective and summary-oriented application of this framework in the near future will provide guidance for the planning and development of integrative, transdisciplinary work on biogenic recorders of seasonal cycles, with proper respect for the anthropogenic archives—often actively stewarded by Indigenous peoples as part of millennia-long relationships with ancestral and sacred places—in which they are catalogued and held.

Acknowledgements

The authors gratefully acknowledge the Amah Mutsun Tribal Band for generously inviting our contributions as new collaborators in their work to reinvigorate Indigenous stewardship of the coastal ecosystems of Central California, as well as for their and their ancestors' incalculable efforts to create and conserve deep knowledge of these landscapes and seascapes for present and future. Every time we learn from archaeological data held in their traditional lands and waters, we learn from them and from their ancestors. We also thank Kent Lightfoot, Rob Cuthrell, Mike Grone, and Alec Apodaca for their interest in things statistical and for many stimulating conversations about the archaeological and scholarly context of the kinds of data whose interpretation we hope to have ameliorated somewhat here.

Funding

The authors declare that they received no specific funding for this study.

Conflict of interest disclosure

The authors declare that they comply with the PCI rule of having no financial conflicts of interest in relation to the content of the article.

Data, scripts, code, and supplementary information availability

Scripts are available online (in R Markdown format with explanatory text and annotations): DOI:10.5281/zenodo.7986873 (Lewis and Brown 2023).

Peer review

This article has been reviewed and recommended by PCI Archaeology.

Cortell-Nicolau, A. and Carrignon, S. 2024. "Mixture models and seasonal mobility." *Peer Community in Archaeology* 100419. DOI:10.24072/pci.archaeo.100419.

References

Ambrose, Wallace R. 1967. "Archaeology and shell middens." *Archaeology and Physical Anthropology in Oceania* 2 (3): 169-87.

Apodaca, Alec J., Jordan Brown, and Michael Grone. 2025. "Seasonality Of Mussel Harvesting At Three Holocene Sites On The Santa Cruz Coast: Insights From Isotopic Variation In Marine Mollusks." In *The Study of Indigenous Landscape and Seascape Stewardship on the Central California Coast: The Findings of a Collaborative Eco-Archaeological Investigation*, edited by Kent G. Lightfoot, Michael Grone, and Gabriel Sanchez. Berkeley: University of California Archaeological Research Facility.

Bailey, Geoffrey N., Margaret R. Deith, and Nicholas J. Shackleton. 1983. "Oxygen isotope analysis and seasonality determinations: limits and potential of a new technique." *American Antiquity* 48 (2): 390–8.

Brauwere, Anouk de, Fjo De Ridder, Rik Pintelon, Johan Schoukens, and Frank Dehairs. 2009. "A comparative study of methods to reconstruct a periodic time series from an environmental proxy record." *Earth-Science Reviews* 95 (3–4): 97–118. DOI:10.1016/j.earscirev.2009.04.002.

Brown, Jordan. 2023. "A data analysis framework for stable isotope sclerochronology and the interpretation of shell-bearing sites." Paper presented at the Annual Meeting of the Society for California Archaeology, Oakland, CA, March 2023.

Brown, Jordan. 2024. "Seasonality of Mussel Harvesting at Three Holocene Sites on the Santa Cruz Coast: Insights from Isotopic Variation in Marine Mollusks (Supplementary Material)." Zenodo. DOI: 10.5281/zenodo.14280026.

Burchell, Meghan, Marianne P. Stopp, Aubrey Cannon, Nadine Hallmann, and Bernd R. Schöne. 2018. "Determining seasonality of mussel collection from an early historic Inuit site, Labrador, Canada: Comparing thin-sections with high-resolution stable oxygen isotope analysis." *Journal of Archaeological Science: Reports* 21: 1215–24. DOI:10.1016/j.jasrep.2018.02.016.

Claassen, Cheryl. 1991. "Normative thinking and shell-bearing sites." *Archaeological Method and Theory* 3: 249–98.

Clark, George R. 1979. "Seasonal growth variations in the shells of recent and prehistoric specimens of Mercenaria mercenaria from St. Catherines Island, Georgia." *Anthropological Papers of the American Museum of Natural History* 51: 161–79.

Culleton, Brendan J., Douglas J. Kennett, and Terry L. Jones. 2009. "Oxygen isotope seasonality in a temperate estuarine shell midden: a case study from CA-ALA-17 on the San Francisco Bay, California." *Journal of Archaeological Science* 36 (7): 1354–63. DOI:10.1016/j.jas.2009.01.021.

Currie, Adrian. 2018. *Rock, bone, and ruin: An optimist's guide to the historical sciences*. MIT Press.

Cuthrell, Robert Q. 2013. "An Eco-Archaeological Study of Late Holocene Indigenous Foodways and Landscape Management Practices at Quiroste Valley Cultural Preserve, San Mateo County, California." PhD diss., UC Berkeley.

Deith, Margaret R. 1985. "Seasonality from shells: an evaluation of two techniques for seasonal dating of marine molluscs." In *Palaeoenvironmental investigations: research design, methods and data analysis*, edited by N.R.J. Fieller, D.D. Gilbertson and N.G.A. Ralph, 119–30. Oxford: B.A.R.

Eerkens, Jelmer W., Brian F. Byrd, Howard J. Spero, and Anna K. Fritschi. 2013. "Stable isotope reconstructions of shellfish harvesting seasonality in an estuarine environment: implications for Late Holocene San Francisco Bay settlement patterns." *Journal of Archaeological Science* 40 (4): 2014–24. DOI:10.1016/j.jas.2012.12.018.

Epstein, Samual, Ralph Buchsbaum, Heinz A. Lowenstam, and Harold C. Urey. 1951. "Carbonate-water isotopic temperature scale." *Geological Society of America Bulletin* 62 (4): 417–26.

Epstein, Samual, Ralph Buchsbaum, Heinz A. Lowenstam, and Harold C. Urey. 1953. "Revised carbonate-water isotopic temperature scale." *Geological Society of America Bulletin* 64 (11): 1315–26.

Ferguson, Thomas S. 1983. "Bayesian density estimation by mixtures of normal distributions." In *Recent advances in statistics*, edited by M. Haseeb Rizvi, Jagdish S. Rustagi and David Siegmund, 287-302. New York: Academic Press.

Graeber, David and David Wengrow. 2021. *The dawn of everything: A new history of humanity*. London: Penguin UK.

Hadden, Carla S., Gregory A. Waselkov, Elizabeth J. Reitz, and C. Fred T. Andrus. 2022. "Temporality of fishery taskscapes on the north-central Gulf of Mexico coast (USA) during the Middle/Late Woodland period (AD 325–1040)." *Journal of Anthropological Archaeology* 67: 101436. DOI:10.1016/j.jaa.2022.101436.

Hallmann, Nadine, Meghan Burchell, N. Brewster, Andrew Martindale, and Bernd R. Schöne. 2013. "Holocene climate and seasonality of shell collection at the Dundas Islands Group, northern British Columbia, Canada – A bivalve sclerochronological approach." *Palaeogeography, Palaeoclimatology, Palaeoecology* 373: 163–72. DOI:10.1016/j.palaeo.2011.12.019.

Ivany, Linda C. 2012. "Reconstructing paleoseasonality from accretionary skeletal carbonates – challenges and opportunities." *The Paleontological Society Papers* 18: 133–66. DOI:10.1017/S108933260000259X.

Jazwa, Christopher S., Christopher A. Wolfe, Elaine Y. Chu, and Kyra E. Stull. 2020. "The effects of vertical position in the intertidal zone on the δ18O and δ13C composition of Mytilus californianus shell carbonate." *Journal of Archaeological Science: Reports* 34: 102587. DOI:10.1016/j.jasrep.2020.102587

Jones, Terry L., Douglas J. Kennett, John P. Kennett, and Brian F. Codding. 2008. "Seasonal stability in Late Holocene shellfish harvesting on the central California coast." *Journal of Archaeological Science* 35 (8): 2286–94. DOI:10.1016/j.jas.2008.03.002

Kennett, Douglas J., and Barbara Voorhies. 1996. "Oxygen isotopic analysis of archaeological shells to detect seasonal use of wetlands on the southern Pacific coast of Mexico." *Journal of Archaeological Science* 23 (5): 689–704. DOI:10.1006/jasc.1996.0065.

Killingley, John S. 1981. "Seasonality of mollusk collecting determined from O-18 profiles of midden shells." *American Antiquity* 46 (1): 152–8. DOI:10.2307/279994.

Kim, Sang-Tae, and James R. O'Neil. 1997. "Equilibrium and nonequilibrium oxygen isotope effects in synthetic carbonates." *Geochimica et Cosmochimica Acta* 61: 3461–75. DOI:10.1016/S0016-7037(97)00169-5.

Kwiecien, Ola, Tobias Braun, Camilla Francesca Brunello, Patrick Faulkner, Niklas Hausmann, Gerd Helle, Julie A. Hoggarth, Monica Ionita, Christopher S. Jazwa, Saige Kelmelis, Norbert Marwan, Cinthya Nava-Fernandez, Carole Nehme, Thomas Opel, Jessica L. Oster, Aurel Perşoiu, Cameron Petrie, Keith Prufer, Saija M. Saarni, Annabel Wolf, and Sebastian F.M. Breitenbach. 2022. "What we talk about when we talk about seasonality – A transdisciplinary review." *Earth-Science Reviews* 225: 103843. DOI:10.1016/j.earscirev.2021.103843.

Letham, Bryn, Andrew Martindale, Kisha Supernant, Thomas J. Brown, Jerome S. Cybulski, and Kenneth M. Ames. 2019. "Assessing the scale and pace of large shell-bearing site occupation in the Prince Rupert harbour area, British Columbia." *The Journal of Island and Coastal Archaeology* 14 (2): 163–97. DOI:10.1080/15564894.2017.1387621.

Lewis, Gabriel and Jordan Brown. 2023. "Inferring shellfishing seasonality from the isotopic composition of biogenic carbonate: A Bayesian approach (Supplementary material)." Zenodo. DOI:10.5281/zenodo.7986873.

Lightfoot, Kent G., Robert Q. Cuthrell, Mark G. Hylkema, Valentin Lopez, Diane D. Gifford-Gonzalez, Roberta A. Jewett, Michael A. Grone, Gabriel M. Sanchez, Peter A. Nelson, Alec J. Apodaca, Ariadna Gonzalez, Kathryn Field, Jordan Brown, Alexii Sigona, and Paul V. A. Fine. 2021. "The Eco-Archaeological Investigation of Indigenous Stewardship Practices on the Santa Cruz Coast." *Journal of California and Great Basin Anthropology* 41 (2): 187–205.

Luby, Edward M., Clayton D. Drescher, and Kent G. Lightfoot. 2006. "Shell mounds and mounded landscapes in the San Francisco Bay area: an integrated approach." *Journal of Island and Coastal Archaeology* 1 (2): 191–214. DOI:10.1080/15564890600935365.

Mannino, Marcello A., K. D. Thomas, M. J. Leng, R. Di Salvo, and Michael P. Richards. 2011. "Stuck to the shore? Investigating prehistoric hunter-gatherer subsistence, mobility and territoriality in a Mediterranean coastal landscape through isotope analyses on marine mollusc shell carbonates and human bone collagen." *Quaternary International* 244 (1): 88–104. DOI:10.1016/j.quaint.2011.05.044.

Marquardt, William H. 2010. "Shell mounds in the southeast: middens, monuments, temple mounds, rings, or works?" *American Antiquity* 75 (3): 551–70.

Meehan, Betty. 1982. *Shell bed to shell midden.* Canberra: Australian Institute of Aboriginal Studies.

Mellars, Paul A., Michael R. Wilkinson, and N. R. J. Fieller. 1980. "Fish otoliths as indicators of seasonality in prehistoric shell middens: the evidence from Oronsay (Inner Hebrides)." In *Proceedings of the Prehistoric Society* 46: 19–44. Cambridge: Cambridge University Press.

Milner, Nicky, Oliver E. Craig, and Geoffrey N. Bailey(eds). 2007. *Shell Middens in Atlantic Europe*. Oxford: Oxbow Books.

Monks, Gregory G. 1981. "Seasonality studies." *Advances in Archaeological Method and Theory* 4: 177–240.

Palmer, Hannah M., Veronica Padilla Vriesman, Roxanne M. Banker, and Jessica R. Bean. 2022. "Compilation of a database of Holocene nearshore marine mollusk shell geochemistry from the California Current System." *Earth System Science Data* 14 (4): 1695–1705. DOI:10.5194/essd-14-1695-2022.

Prendergast, Amy L., Alexander J. Pryor, Hazel Reade, and Rhiannon E. Stevens. 2018. "Seasonal records of palaeoenvironmental change and resource use from archaeological assemblages." *Journal of Archaeological Science: Reports* 21: 1191–7. DOI:10.1016/j.jasrep.2018.08.006.

R Core Team. 2023. *R: A Language and Environment for Statistical Computing.* Vienna: R Foundation for Statistical Computing. https://www.R-project.org

Roksandic, Mirjana, Sheila Mendonça de Souza, Sabine Eggers, Meghan Burchell, and Daniela Klokler (eds). 2014. *The cultural dynamics of shell-matrix sites.* Albuquerque: University of New Mexico Press.

Schöne, Bernd R. 2008. "The curse of physiology – challenges and opportunities in the interpretation of geochemical data from mollusk shells." *Geo-Marine Letters* 28: 269–85. DOI:10.1007/s00367-008-0114-6

Schweikhardt, Peter, B. Lynn Ingram, Kent G. Lightfoot, and Edward M. Luby. 2011. "Geochemical methods for inferring seasonal occupation of an estuarine shellmound: a case study from San Francisco Bay." *Journal of Archaeological Science* 38 (9): 2301–12. DOI:10.1016/j.jas.2011.04.004.

Shackleton, Nicholas J. 1973. "Oxygen isotope analysis as a means of determining season of occupation of prehistoric midden sites." *Archaeometry* 15 (1): 133–41. DOI:10.1111/j.1475-4754.1973.tb00082.x.

Stan Development Team. 2022. *Stan Modeling Language Users Guide and Reference Manual, 2.33*. https://mc-stan.org.

Stan Development Team. 2023. *RStan: the R interface to Stan*. https://mc-stan.org

Stein, Julie. 1992. *Deciphering a shell midden*. New York: Academic Press.

Urey, Harold C., Heinz A. Lowenstam, Samuel Epstein, and Charles R. McKinney. 1951. "Measurement of paleotemperatures and temperatures of the Upper Cretaceous of England, Denmark, and the southeastern United States." *Geological Society of America Bulletin* 62 (4): 399–416. DOI:10.1130/0016-7606(1951)62[399:MOPATO]2.0.CO;2.

Villagran, Ximena S. 2014. "A redefinition of waste: Deconstructing shell and fish mound formation among coastal groups of southern Brazil." *Journal of Anthropological Archaeology* 36: 211–227. DOI:10.1016/j.jaa.2014.10.002.

Wang, Ting, Donna Surge, and Jonathan M. Lees. 2015. "ClamR: a statistical evaluation of isotopic and temperature records in sclerochronologic studies." *Palaeogeography, Palaeoclimatology, Palaeoecology* 437: 26–32. DOI:10.1016/j.palaeo.2015.07.008.

Waselkov, Gregory A. 1987. "Shellfish gathering and shell midden archaeology." *Advances in Archaeological Method and Theory* 10: 93–210. DOI:10.1016/B978-0-12-003110-8.50006-2.

West, Catherine F., Meghan Burchell, and C. Fred T. Andrus. 2018. "Molluscs and paleoenvironmental reconstruction in island and coastal settings: variability, seasonality, and sampling." In *Zooarchaeology in Practice*, 191–208. Cham: Springer. DOI:10.1007/978-3-319-64763-0_10

Wilkinson, Bruce H. and Linda C. Ivany, L. C. 2002. "Paleoclimatic inference from stable isotope profiles of accretionary biogenic hardparts – a quantitative approach to the evaluation of incomplete data." *Palaeogeography, Palaeoclimatology, Palaeoecology* 185 (1-2): 95–114. DOI:10.1016/S0031-0182(02)00279-1

Wylie, Alison. 2002. *Thinking from things: Essays in the Philosophy of Archaeology*. Berkeley: University of California Press.

Winter, Niels de, Tobias Agterhuis, and Martin Ziegler. 2021. "Optimizing sampling strategies in high-resolution paleoclimate records." *Climate of the Past* 17 (3): 1315–40. DOI:10.5194/cp-17-1315-2021.

Zimmt, Joshua B., Rowan Lockwood, C. Fred T. Andrus, and Gregory S. Herbert. 2019. "Sclerochronological basis for growth band counting: A reliable technique for life-span determination of Crassostrea virginica from the mid-Atlantic United States." *Palaeogeography, palaeoclimatology, palaeoecology* 516: 54–63. DOI:10.1016/j.palaeo.2018.11.029.

7 The Dynamic Collections

A 3D Web Platform of Archaeological Artefacts designed for Data Reuse and Deep Interaction

Marco Callieri
Visual Computing Lab, ISTI-CNR, Pisa, marco.callieri@isti.cnr.it

Åsa Berggren
Department of Archaeology and Ancient History, Lund University

Nicolò Dell'Unto
Department of Archaeology and Ancient History, Lund University

Paola Derudas
Department of Archaeology and Ancient History, Lund University

Domenica Dininno
Department of Archaeology and Ancient History, Lund University

Fredrik Ekengren
Department of Archaeology and Ancient History, Lund University

Giuseppe Naponiello
Department of Archaeology and Ancient History, Lund University

Abstract
The Dynamic Collections project is an ongoing initiative pursued by the Visual Computing Lab ISTI-CNR in Italy and the Lund University Digital Archaeology Laboratory (DARKLab), Sweden. The aim of this project is to explore the possibilities offered by a deep, structured interaction with a large set of digital replicas of archaeological artefacts. The project developed and deployed a web-based platform containing a large number of digital artefacts, and a set of dedicated tools to interact with them at a both artefact- and collection-level. This platform has been used in university courses and research activities with positive feedback from the community. In this contribution, we want to describe various aspects of the management of the project, its evolution, and discuss the roadmap of future developments and research directions.

Keywords: Archaeological collection; Online publishing; 3D models; 3D annotation; Collaborative platform

7.1 Introduction
Over the past decade, significant investments have been made worldwide to promote mass digitisations, and to build data platforms to support large-scale research and innovation in the cultural heritage sector. While undoubtedly useful, these platforms were not originally designed to facilitate deep interaction with digital materials or to encourage new research approaches. The COVID-19 pandemic highlighted the limitations of these platforms as digital collections became the only available sources for research, underlining the urgent need to explore strategies to define digital collections as primary research tools and to fully support scholars working in the digital space.

To date, no attempt has been made to systematically and rigorously investigate the potential and limitations of digital collections as a primary research support asset, or the impact of these platforms on how digital collections are constructed and how knowledge generation is facilitated through this construction. When we examine how information is organised in physical archives, we find that space and records are part of the same design. These environments are built to allow users to retrieve, read, compare and, most importantly, enjoy the records. How can we bring these elements into the virtual space, and what characteristics should a virtual environment have in order to trigger such a dynamic interaction?

In *Advances in Digital Archaeology. Proceedings of the 2023 conference Computer Applications and Quantitative Methods in Archaeology – 50 years of synergy*, edited by J.W.H.P. Verhagen, J. Waagen, A. Brandsen, A. Queffelec, R.M. Visser and D. Taelman, 87–96. Leiden: Sidestone Press.

The Dynamic Collections project was created in a collaboration between the Visual Computing Lab ISTI-CNR in Italy and the Lund University Digital Archaeology Laboratory DARKLab, Sweden, and officially launched the online platform in December 2020 (Ekengren et al. 2021). The initial aim of the project was to create a 3D archive to showcase the archaeological reference collection used in the courses in artefact analysis at the Department of Archaeology and Ancient History, Lund University. Once the digital artefacts were available, they were used by different teachers who, after testing the dynamic collections, began to suggest new artefacts to be included and new functionalities to be added. As a result of this socio-technological development, Dynamic Collections was implemented with new interactive tools and with further artefacts from the Historical Museum of Lund University, and later with artefacts from the Blekinge Museum and the Historical Museum in Stockholm. The number of digital artefacts continues to grow, and currently includes 430 high-resolution archaeological artefacts from the Stone Age to the Middle Ages in Scandinavia. The web system has been implemented to facilitate data re-use and to support multiple interpretations and narratives. Currently the Dynamic Collections are part of the Swedish National Infrastructure for Digital Archaeology and are the largest 3D data repository for archaeological artefacts in Sweden.

7.2 Related work

Tools and techniques for recording artefacts have increased significantly in recent years. Awareness of the potential loss of cultural heritage and limited access to tangible historical objects has driven this growth. As a result, an increasing number of curators are turning to 3D technologies for tasks such as documenting, preserving, analysing and sharing artefacts (Arnold and Kaminski 2014; Wachowiak and Karas 2009).

However, despite the various advances in 3D visualisation, determining the precise role and potential of 3D archives in generating new knowledge remains a challenge. This leads us to question whether these 3D archives will significantly impact higher education and research, and in what ways they can have an impact on current practice. One possible strategy for addressing these questions is to begin to develop strategies and tools aimed at transforming 3D archives into valuable assets capable of effectively facilitating dynamic and multimodal engagement with and between users (Drennan 2009; Hurcombe 2007; Di Giuseppantonio Di Franco et al. 2018).

Three-dimensional models offer the ability to perform tasks that cannot be replicated with physical objects. This data opens up opportunities for users to explore new ways of interacting with the represented material (Campanaro et al. 2015), helping to reveal details that often go unnoticed using more traditional methods. However, for these data to be useful in education and research, they need to meet certain quality standards and should be shared on platforms that allow for easy interaction and reuse (Scopigno et al. 2017).

For 3D artefacts to be truly effective, they need to comply with the FAIR principles (Findable, Accessible, Interoperable, Reusable; Wilkinson et al. 2016) and to be made available on digital platforms that support advanced learning and the formulation of new questions.

7.3 The Dynamic Collections

The core idea of the project was to build a digital equivalent to the reference collections typically used in academic institutions and museums. What we wanted was an archive of digital objects that could give the user the possibility to interact with 3D models in a meaningful, effective way, but also make it possible to create/interact with, and/or collaborate on customised dynamic sets of those objects.

Ideally, a digital collection must be something more than just a list of 3D models with some attached metadata. It should be able to include all those elements that might be used by scholars and teachers to effectively employ those objects in their everyday work in a cohesive and structured way; elements such as notes, reasoning elements, object-specific annotations, cross-links between entities, schemes, etc.

The online system (Lund U. and ISTI-CNR, 2023) presents, through a standard web interface, the objects of the archive (Figure 7.1). Objects are displayed as cards, with a thumbnail and some basic info. A more comprehensive view of all the attached meta- and para-data can be easily accessed by clicking on the card. A simple filtering/search functionality helps the user in navigating the archive. Each object in the archive can be viewed in detail using a 3D viewer in a dedicated page. The viewer page contains multiple rendering options, navigation helpers, and measuring tools. This page also offers a way to annotate the object, by adding text notes, saving views and rendering parameters (including the currently active measurements) as visual bookmarks with associated text, and placing customisable hotspots localised on the surface with associated text. These annotations of single objects can then be exported as a JSON file, to be shared and/or saved for future use.

The 3D viewer is based on the 3DHOP tool (Potenziani and Callieri 2015), an open-source framework for the creation of web-based visualisation of complex 3D models (https://3dhop.net/). 3DHOP can be easily configured and customised to implement specific interaction schemes and interfaces. The project exploited this possibility to design an interface that promotes a multi-faceted and versatile use of the 3D object, by providing simple but flexible navigation, coupled with multiple rendering options, and diverse methods to measure the geometry. The annotation interface

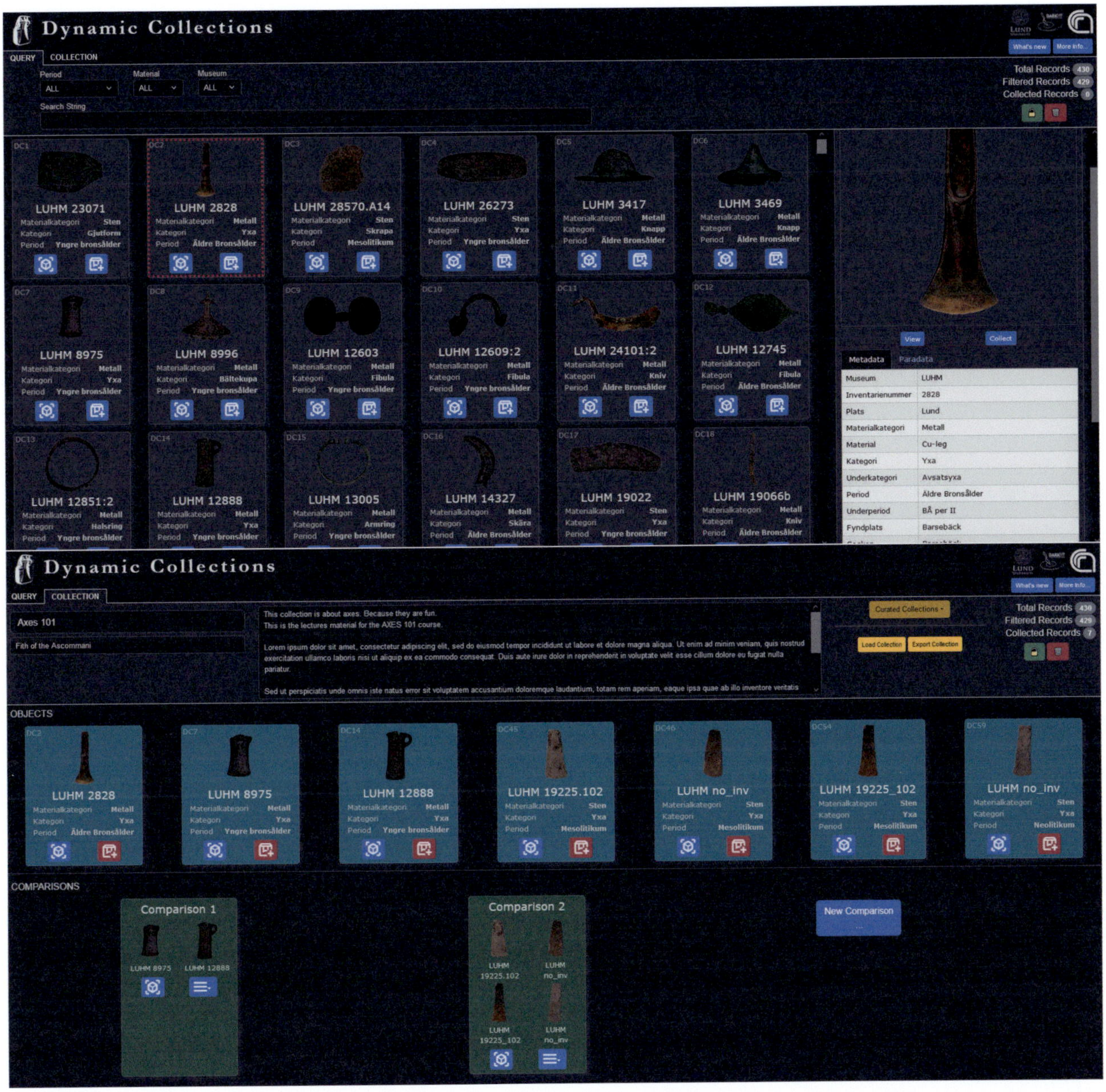

Figure 7.1. The online platform, showing all the objects in the archive, with details and metadata (top) and an annotated collection (bottom).

lets the user add a layer of information geo-referenced on the object geometry (Figure 7.2).

Thanks to the multiresolution scheme used in 3DHOP (NEXUS), the high-resolution digital data is stored in a compressed format on the server and streamed in an effective way to the client. The multi-resolution scheme also helps the real-time visualisation, as the rendering is optimised according to the point-of-view, framerate, memory, and network limits.

The most interesting functionalities, however, are related to the concept of custom-built collections. The user can select objects from the archive, dynamically building a personalised collection that suits their needs. Text notes and other metadata info can then be added to this custom collection. Furthermore, each of the objects in the collection can be annotated using the tools described above; the annotations become part of the collection, thus creating a fully annotated collection. This annotated collection can be exported as a JSON data structure for future use and sharing.

Upon this concept of annotated collections, it is possible to build complex interactions and workflows between colleagues and students, to pursue a collaborative working/teaching environment.

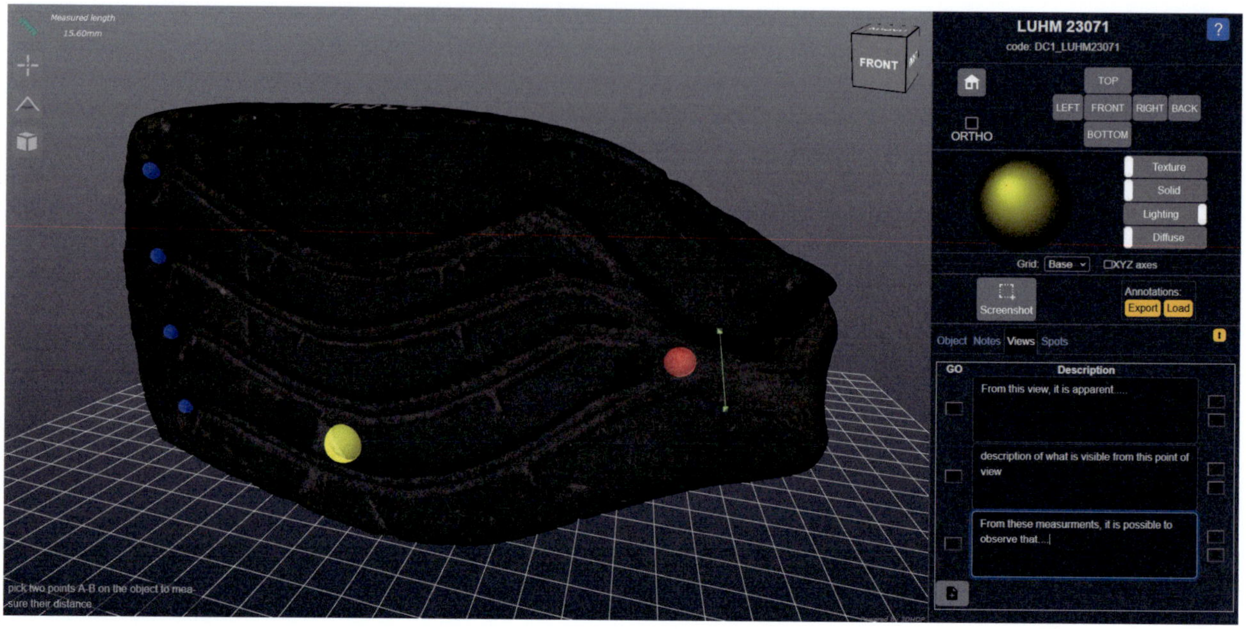

Figure 7.2. The single-object viewer, showing an annotated high-resolution 3D model.

An annotated collection may be used to represent the working notes, shared between the authors of an oncoming paper. They might contain the candidates for the identification and classification of a newly excavated specimen. Assembled by a teacher, they may be used as a course material, distributed to students, or used as slides during lessons. Compiled by the students, they may be used to take lecture notes directly on the 3D models. Students and teachers may also send the collections back and forth in dialogue, since annotations (analyses, interpretations, feedback etc.) can be added over existing ones. A collection may also be used for specific assignments or tasks to be sent back to the teacher.

An interesting detail of this setup is the clear separation between user data and system data. Everything that is user-created (the selection of objects and their annotations) is contained in the collection data structure, which references the entities in the archive through IDs; conversely, all the 3D data and the relative meta- and para-data are stored only in the online system. Moreover, the creation of the annotated collection is entirely client-side, nothing is ever stored on the remote server: user data is always under the control of its creator. This detail, initially due to a limitation of the platform, became a "selling" point of the tool, as its target audience values this kind of privacy and freedom of use.

7.4 Managing and sustaining the project

The core concepts of the projects have been developed in a purely scientific collaboration between Lund University and ISTI-CNR. A number of experiments were done to try working online, for teaching and study purposes, with digital replicas of artefacts. From these experiments, it became clear that, in order to obtain meaningful results, it was necessary to reach a critical mass of 3D objects to interact with and, at the same time, provide multiple ways to interact with these 3D entities.

The generous support from the Thora Ohlsson Foundation made it (and still makes it) possible to start building the digital archive in a systematic way and support the development and curation of the online tools. This initial funding enabled the purchase of 3D scanning and photographic equipment, as well as the recruitment of specialists in 3D capture and data post-processing. At that point, it was clear that the Dynamic Collections was a useful and promising platform, and it was necessary to change how the project was managed, going from an experiment towards a more structured, sustainable initiative, able to survive over a longer period of time.

Further funding was received from the Einar Hansen Foundation in 2020, which enabled the design and development of a new database to expand the Dynamic Collections into a new, more sustainable future. Beside the mere financial stability, in order to grow, it was necessary to establish connections with entities and existing initiatives and projects, since 2022, the Dynamic Collection project is supported by the Swedish National Infrastructure for Digital Archaeology – SweDigArch. The consortium focuses on linking a large number of Swedish archaeological databases (http://swedigarch.se) to facilitate the production of aggregated and harmonised datasets. Among its many aims, SweDigArch is charged with developing and implementing national strategies for the integration and dissemination of the broad range of digital data and information produced in archaeology.

Due to its ability to generate dynamic interpretations through various interactive tools, the Dynamic Collections platform is currently being used to support ongoing experiments within the activities of TETRARCHs (Telling Stories with Archaeological Data), a project funded by the European Union's Horizon 2020 research and innovation programme, which aims to explore different methods of collecting archaeological data to support different forms of storytelling (https://www.tetrarchs.org/index.php/about).

7.5 Growing together

It is also noteworthy how the development of the Dynamic Collection project influenced and was in turn influenced by other projects carried out by the involved partners.

An almost exact copy of the online tools of the Dynamic Collections have been used in another Scandinavian initiative: BItFROST, headed by the University of Oslo. Similarly to the main Dynamic Collections installation, the aim was to provide a more structured access to the archive of 3D objects produced by the University Museum of Cultural History. Testing the system on a different archive made all its components more robust, and the different needs emerging from the personnel working in this sister project helped define new possible interactions, analysis, and visualisation options.

The ARIADNE+ infrastructure is an EU-financed (Horizon 2020) project aimed at bringing together archaeological archives and providing services for the common access and use of this data. Among the different services maintained in this framework, the Visual Media Service provides a way to create customisable viewers for high-resolution media. The 3D viewer is based on 3DHOP and integrates some of the interaction components and widgets developed for the Dynamic Collections.

ISTI-CNR was involved in the development of online tools for the digital infrastructure supporting the restoration of Notre-Dame de Paris. Also in this case, some of the components developed for the Dynamic Collections were adapted to the visualisation of a specific class of objects: the stones of the collapsed rib vault. The specificity of this task helped in making the components more generic, robust, and reusable. Some of the specific measurement tools developed for this application were later integrated in the Dynamic Collections viewer.

- These connections between projects thus have a positive impact for all the involved parties.
- They help in widening the scope of the projects, as well as defining their needs and approaches, as the presence of different datasets and diverse users provide new problems, requirements, and perspectives.
- They make the development process more sustainable, thanks to the reuse of code and the opportunity to test the tools on multiple, diverse datasets.
- They create an ecosystem of tools, all linked by similar interaction paradigms and data management strategies. This, in turn, influences the community of users, helping the adoption of the involved technologies and approaches.

The presence of a completely open software layer helps this kind of interaction, as it is possible to readily integrate new solutions in the platforms.

7.6 Building up the archive

As the project aim was to replicate the concept of a reference collection, we started by digitising artefacts belonging to the local collection of the Historical Museum of Lund University. We started from small-to-medium size objects (5-50cm), as this is the most frequent range in object size, and we based the guidelines of the project archive on this initial selection. We are now expanding towards different classes of objects, especially unmovable ones, like runestones, to also explore and evaluate the benefit of providing this kind of access to objects that are normally not available for manipulation and shared access like the physical reference collections. This will probably require different viewer templates, to cope with the specificity of diverse object classes.

Another direction of development that we are pursuing is the support of multiple 3D models for each object. This development will make it possible to manage and interact with composite objects (this option is already supported in the platform, but it needs a better integration with the rest of the tools), objects with reconstruction parts (mixing measured data with hand-modelled 3D models), and objects with models of different time stages (e.g., before-after a restoration).

To achieve a higher level of shareability of the data in the archive, we are planning to associate to each of the digital entities a DOI. This permanent identifier will make it much easier to use the work done in the Dynamic Collections system in scientific papers and research projects, as it will be possible to "cite" the digital entities. The process will rely on the upcoming possibility of having Lund University directly assign DOIs.

Data reuse has been a focus of the project since the beginning. The data of the digitised objects has been stored for future (re)use, keeping both the master models in an interoperable format and the raw data. The amount of data stored so far (for the 430 objects) is still manageable at the level of the Lund University, but as the archive grow, the storage policy will have to rely on national infrastructures for data storage, of which the project is already part (SweDigArch). Hopefully, in the future, it would be possible to also rely on international infrastructures like the upcoming EU initiative for a Collaborative cloud for Cultural Heritage (ECCCH). Some of the models of the archive come from pre-existing digitisations, and from different institutions. This ingestion required a small step of metadata normalisation and minimal processing to conform the 3D objects with our conventions. We know that, going forward with the project, the problem of normalisation and data ingestion will become more relevant, and we are preparing for this task through dedicated tools that we are integrating in the new version of the platform.

As a further way to connect the project with university training, MA students have been involved in the acquisition of some of the objects for the archive, as part of their internship within the project. This activity proved to be an interesting and articulate task for the students, as it went beyond the standard "creating any 3D model". They were given the opportunity to create 3D models suitable for a specific project, following specific rules, conventions, and methodologies, simultaneously providing the project with feedback on the acquisition methods and workflow.

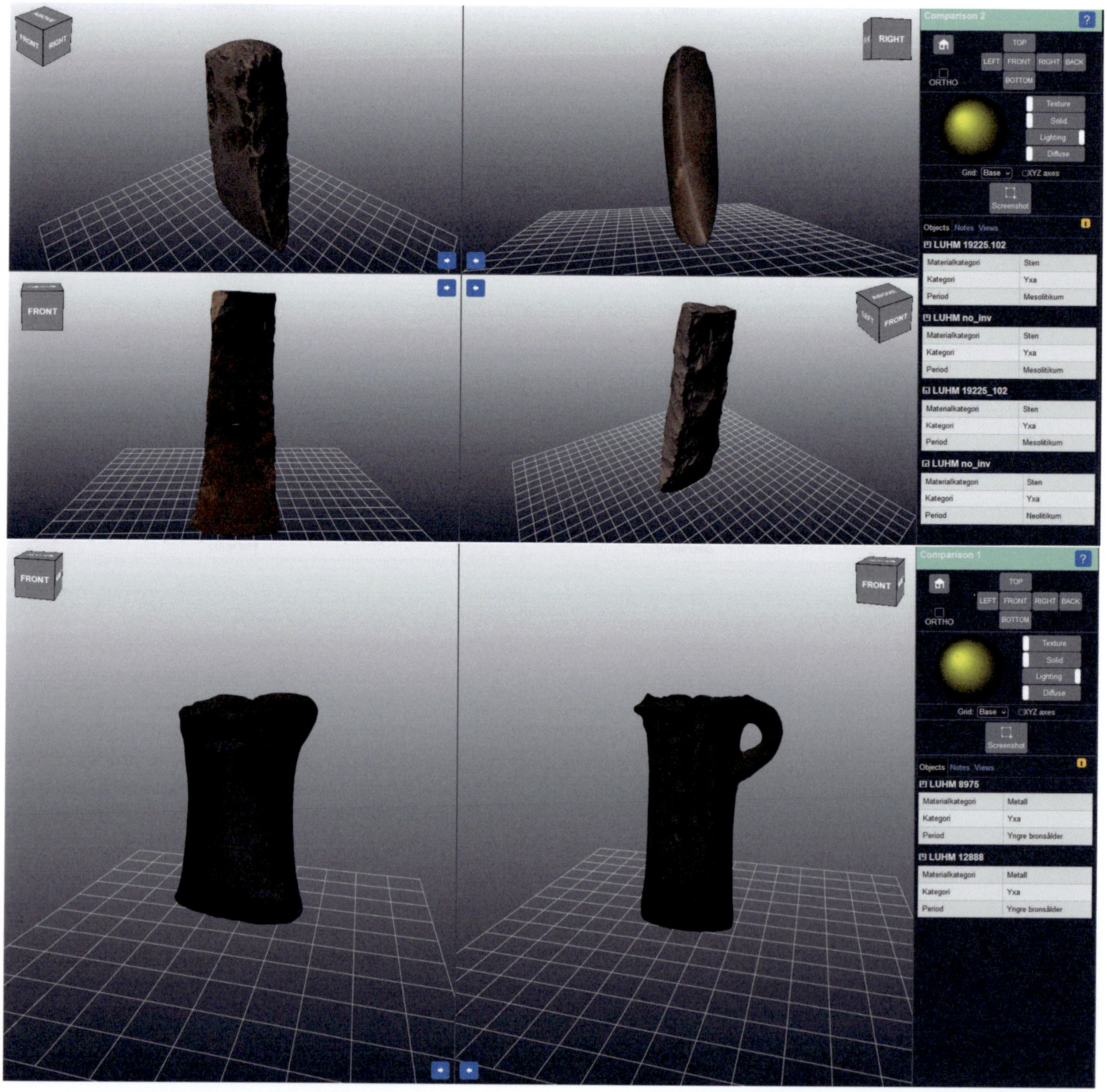

Figure 7.3. The new "comparison" entity in the collection can be used to create side-by-side multi-object visualisation and annotation.

7.7 Improving the deep interaction

The core concept of the Dynamic Collections is the deep interaction with the entities in the archive, and how the idea of a dynamically assembled collection may be used for multiple purposes: teaching, study, analysis, discussion, and the sharing of information.

7.7.1 Comparisons

The collection should not be just a set of objects with some attached annotations but should contain other user-created elements representing cross-object relationships and reasoning. A development direction is to design and implement more ways to manipulate and combine the objects in a collection, providing the user with more ways of working with the available entities. The first of these new tools being added to the online platform is the direct comparison of multiple objects inside a collection (Figure 7.3).

The chosen objects are shown in multiple viewer panels on the same page. The interaction and rendering options are similar to the ones in the single-object page viewer; each viewer panel can be controlled independently, but specific functionalities are available to sync the view and the scale across the panels, for a localised side-to-side comparison. Similarly to the single-object viewer, the user can annotate the comparison, adding notes, and saving specific combinations of views and rendering opinions across the viewers. These comparisons are then stored as new elements of the collection, following the principle of storing in the collection all the user-created data.

The new comparison functionalities are currently in their first test version and have been made available to all users in the last update.

7.7.2 Support to teaching

When the system was first designed, one of the main aims was the support of teaching. An annotated collection could be used as teaching material, akin to slides and handouts. The ability to create annotated collections can already be used as a form of assignment, but it could be possible to support other aspects of a course.

The system could be expanded to provide specific tools for the creation and evaluation of tests. The teacher would compile a collection, selecting the object to be included in the test. Then, on a restricted page, assemble a test starting from templates of questions and activities. This authored test would still be an annotated collection, containing new structures representing the individual questions and activities, but still fully interoperable with the rest of the platform.

On another specific page, the students would log and take the test, interacting with 3D models following the teacher-authored questions. The compiled test would also be stored as an annotated collection structure, using other dedicated data structures. To maximise their usefulness, these pages should be compliant with the existing online systems used by universities to manage courses and student activities. This could be achieved by using the university systems as identity providers, and serving the test pages inside the university service, thus managing the annotated collection through a secure connection.

Another interesting problem would be making these components (both the pages and the data structures) resilient to cheating and user manipulation, possibly without compromising the open and interoperable nature of the collection data structure.

Finally, this research direction would also be able to explore the topic of the use of 3D models in an academic test, in terms of interaction, visualisation, and the underlying geometry functions. This feature is currently being discussed and designed, but the real development has not started yet.

7.8 Towards a semantic management of metadata

The main focus of the project has been the interaction with 3D data. For this reason, in the first iteration of the system, we limited to a minimum the amount of meta- and para-data included in the archive. This additional data layer was just meant to help in organising/filtering the objects of the archive and providing the user some background information when inspecting a specific object. However, as the number of objects grows, and the scope of the project widens (in terms of involved partners and available interaction tools) this choice is falling short.

To make the metadata more informative and usable, to help the process of metadata normalisation and ingestion, and to support an easier inter-connection between our project and other existing repositories and archives, we are moving to a fully semantically mapped management (O'Neill and Stapleton 2022; Doerr et al. 2007) of the metadata of the entities in the archive (Figure 7.4). The use of semantic-based metadata is also becoming mandatory in many countries for digital archives of cultural data, and it is in line with the upcoming EU efforts related to the European Collaborative Cloud for Cultural Heritage (ECCCH).

To be compliant with the existing standards of semantic management of data, the new version of the online system will be based on OMEKA-S, a semantic web CMS (https://omeka.org/s/). This open-source platform supports modern linked data access paradigms, with an API and support to existing ontologies and vocabularies. OMEKA is an open tool, has a lively development community, and it is becoming more and more widespread across research bodies and public institutions.

This choice also responds to another current limitation of the system: not having a structured back-end server. By adding this component to the project, we will be able to provide more structured services, data persistence, and more complex interaction between users. Notwithstanding

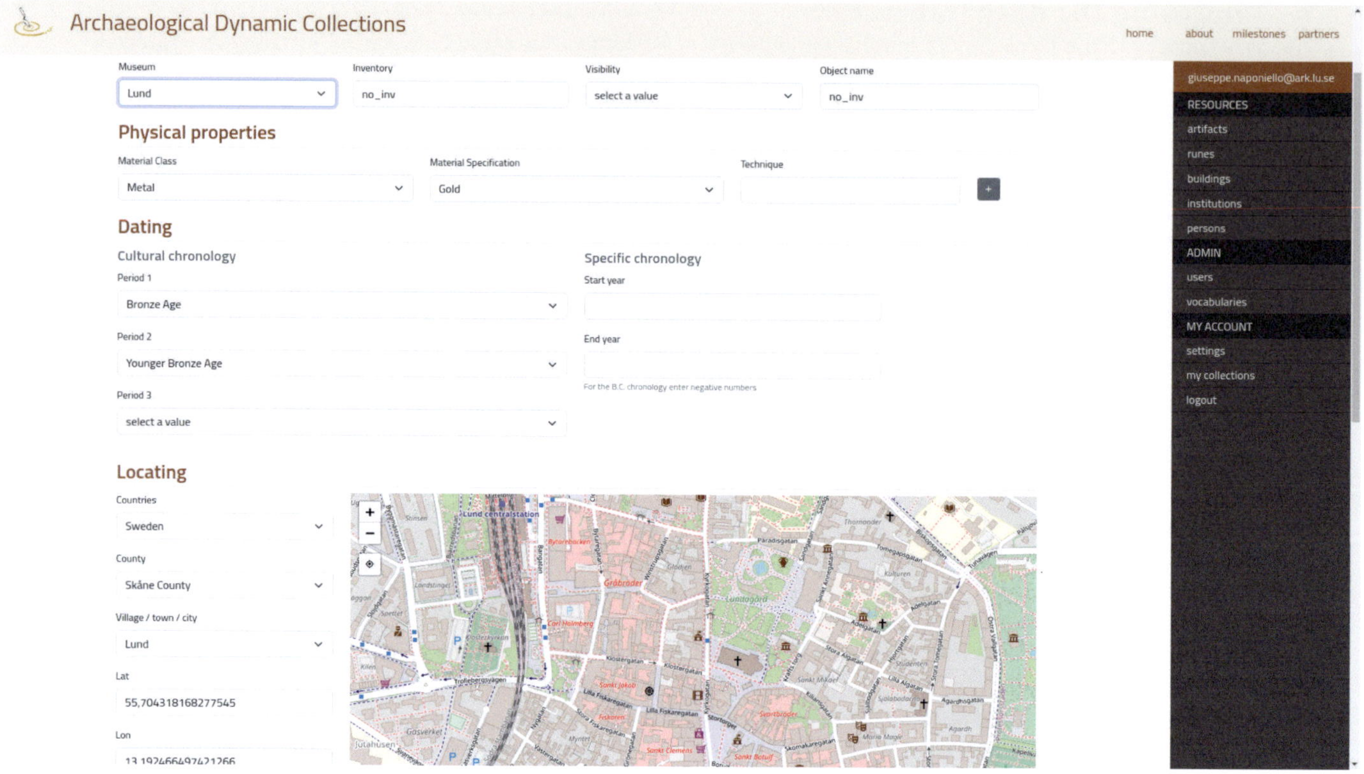

Figure 7.4. To support the new semantically mapped metadata, the authoring tool makes use of existing, established ontologies and vocabularies.

these advantages, we still strongly believe the usefulness and relevance for the community of being able to use the system without the need of a login and to keep all the data on client side, and for this reason we will strive to preserve this alternative workflow.

The use of consolidated ontologies and vocabularies will surely make this project more interoperable with existing online archives and research projects, but a promising direction would also be the definition of specific ontologies and semantic mapping for entities that are not currently available, such as the concepts related to the 3D aspects of the dataset. A comprehensive semantic mapping would make much easier the interoperable use of things like the 3D scene components, their arrangement and meaning, the interaction and navigation, and all the different ways to annotate the models that are already part of the platform (and the ones in development).

7.9 Conclusions

The Dynamic Collection is an ongoing project, but it has already proved the potentialities of a deep, structured interaction with a digital collection. This has been achieved not just by defining an abstract interaction paradigm, but by implementing and making it accessible as an online platform, to foster experimentation and practical usage. The most interesting contribution of the project is the concept of the annotated customised collection, and the different ways this data structure can be exploited to build complex and practical workflows in the framework of teaching and study activities in the archaeological field. The ongoing work of design and development is building upon these results, to provide new ways to interact and work with the digital replicas of the artefacts, but also to improve the platform to offer a more integrated experience.

Acknowledgements

We would like to express our sincere gratitude to Lund University Historical Museum and Blekinge Museum for their invaluable support in facilitating the scanning of artefacts and making them openly accessible. This research would not have been possible without their collaboration and dedication.

We are also deeply grateful to the Department of Archaeology and Ancient History at Lund University and the Joint Faculties of Humanities and Theology for generously providing the necessary infrastructure and hosting space. Their collective contribution to making the Dynamic Collections platform digitally accessible has greatly enriched our research.

Funding

The Dynamic Collections project has been generously funded by the Thora Ohlsson Foundation, the Einar Hansen Foundation, and the Swedish Research Council as part of the activities of the Swedish Digital Archaeology Infrastructure SweDigArch.

Conflict of interest disclosure

The authors declare that they comply with the PCI rule of having no financial conflicts of interest in relation to the content of the article.

Data, scripts, code, and supplementary information availability

Data are available online:
https://models.darklab.lu.se/dynmcoll/Dynamic_Collections (Lund U. and ISTI-CNR, 2023).
Supplementary information is available online:
https://www.darklab.lu.se/digital-collections/dynamic-collections (Lund U. and ISTI-CNR, 2023).

Peer review

This article has been reviewed and recommended by PCI Archaeology.
Hageneuer, Sebastian. 2023. "A comparative teaching and learning tool for 3D data: Dynamic Collections." *Peer Community in Archaeology* 100401. DOI: 10.24072/pci.archaeo.100401.

References

Arnold, David, and Jaime Kaminski. 2014. "3d Scanning and Presentation of Ethnographic Collections – Potentials and Challenges." *Journal of Museum Ethnography* 27: 78–97.

Chazan, Michael. 2018. *The Reality of Artifacts: An Archaeological Perspective*. London: Routledge. DOI: 10.4324/9781315439280.

Campanaro, Danilo Marco, Giacomo Landeschi, Nicoló Dell'Unto, and Anne-Marie Leander Touati. 2016. "3D GIS for Cultural Heritage Restoration: A 'White Box' Workflow." *Journal of Cultural Heritage* 18: 321–32. DOI: 10.1016/j.culher.2015.09.006.

Doerr, Martin, Christian-Emil Ore, and Stephen Stead. 2007. "The CIDOC Conceptual Reference Model – A New Standard for Knowledge Sharing." In *Tutorials, Posters, Panels and Industrial Contributions at the 26th International Conference on Conceptual Modeling - Volume 83*, edited by. JohnGrundy, Sven Hartmann, Alberto H. F. Laender, Leszek Maciaszek and John F. Roddick. Sydney: Australian Computer Society. DOI: 10.13140/2.1.1420.6400.

Di Giuseppantonio Di Franco, Paola, Fabrizio Galeazzi, and Valentina Vassallo. 2018. *Authenticity and Cultural Heritage in the Age of 3D Digital Reproductions*. Cambridge: McDonald Institute for Archaeological Research. DOI: 10.17863/CAM.27029.

Drennan, Robert D. 2009. *Statistics for Archaeologists: A Commonsense Approach*. Dordrecht: Springer. DOI: 10.1007/978-1-4419-0413-3.

Ekengren, Fredrik, Marco Callieri, Domenica Dininno, Åsa Berggren, Stella Macheridis, and Nicolò Dell'Unto. 2021. "Dynamic Collections: A 3D Web Infrastructure for Artifact Engagement." *Open Archaeology* 7 (1): 337–52. DOI: 10.1515/opar-2020-0139.

Hurcombe, Linda M. 2007. *Archaeological Artefacts as Material Culture*. London: Routledge. DOI: 10.1017/S0959774310000351.

Lund University, and ISTI-CNR. 2023. "The Dynamic Collections webpage and online platform." https://models.darklab.lu.se/dynmcoll/Dynamic_Collections.

O'Neill, Brenda, and Larry Stapleton. 2022. "Digital Cultural Heritage Standards: From Silo to Semantic Web." *AI & SOCIETY* 37 (3): 891–903. DOI: 10.1007/s00146-021-01371-1

Potenziani, Marco, Marco Callieri, Matteo Dellepiane, Massimiliano Corsini, Federico Ponchio, and Roberto Scopigno. 2015. "3DHOP: 3D Heritage Online Presenter." *Computers & Graphics* 52: 129–141. DOI: 10.1016/j.cag.2015.07.001.

Scopigno, Roberto, Marco Callieri, Matteo Dellepiane, Federico Ponchio, and Marco Potenziani. 2017. "Delivering and using 3D models on the web: are we ready?" *Virtual Archaeology Review* 8 (17): 1–9. DOI: 10.4995/var.2017.6405.

Wachowiak, Melvin J., and Basiliki Vicky Karas. 2009. "3D Scanning and Replication for Museum and Cultural Heritage Applications." *Journal of the*

American Institute of Conservation 48(2): 141–158. DOI: 10.1179/019713609804516992.

Wilkinson, Mark D., Michel Dumontier, IJsbrand Jan Aalbersberg, Gabrielle Appleton, Myles Axton, Arie Baak, Niklas Blomberg, et al. 2016. "The FAIR Guiding Principles for Scientific Data Management and Stewardship." *Scientific Data* 3 (1): 160018. DOI: 10.1038/sdata.2016.18.

8 Spaces of funeral meaning

Modelling socio-spatial relations in burial contexts

Aline Deicke
Academy of Sciences and Literature | Mainz / Philipps-University Marburg
aline.deicke@uni-marburg.de
ORCID 0000-0001-7347-7625

Abstract

Burials have long been one of the most important sources of archaeology, especially when studying past social practices and structure. Unlike archaeological finds from settlements, objects from graves can be assumed to have been placed there for a certain purpose. The same logic holds true for *where* these objects were placed: We must also understand the (ritual) acts of deposition and construction as intentional practice that moves the spatial configurations created by their placements into focus. Indeed, since the advent of the spatial turn, ideas of space as a social and cultural construct have also affected how archaeologists research and think about graves. However, the spatiality of burials as an expression of social structure has yet to be explored by means of digital methods. The paper wants to take a first step in filling this gap by conceptualizing a data model drawing on the sociology of space by Martina Löw that can then be used to facilitate computational analyses of socio-spatial relations. For this purpose, it introduces a first version of a model created using the CIDOC CRM, the compatible models CRMinf and CRMsoc, as well as additional custom classes to extend the model to adequately represent the social actions making up the construction of these relationships.

Keywords: Data modelling; CIDOC CRM; Sociology of Space; Mortuary Archaeology

8.1 Introduction

Burials have long been one of the most important sources of archaeology, especially when studying past social practices and structure. Unlike archaeological finds from settlements, objects from graves can be assumed to have been placed there for a certain purpose. Therefore, the way the deceased are presented is not to be understood as a "mirror image" (Haffner 1989) of their lives but instead as an intentional selection of artefacts and architectural features materializing different social identities (Saxe 1970) or a "social persona" (Binford 1971) to be communicated through their burial.

The same logic holds true for *where* these objects were placed: We must also understand the (ritual) acts of deposition and construction as intentional practices that move the spatial configurations created by their placements into focus. In the same way as the typochronological characteristics of grave goods allow inferences on status, gender, or even age, the arrangements of the burial space must be assumed to carry a variety of communicative meanings which, while not always reconstructable, can still – at least in parts – be observed.

This focus on space as a social variable is not new but in line with a number of ideas connected to the so-called spatial turn (for example, Lefebvre 1974; Simmel 2009;

In *Advances in Digital Archaeology. Proceedings of the 2023 conference Computer Applications and Quantitative Methods in Archaeology – 50 years of synergy*, edited by J.W.H.P. Verhagen, J. Waagen, A. Brandsen, A. Queffelec, R.M. Visser and D. Taelman, 97–106. Leiden: Sidestone Press.

Werlen 1993) that understands space as a social and cultural construct and considers "space's key role in the process by which people construct their understandings of the world" (Blake 2007, 230). As such, the spatial turn has also affected how archaeologists research and think about graves (among others, Arnold 2002; Bejko 2016; Hofmann and Attula 2017). As Helaine Silverman summarises in the introduction to a special issue of the *Archaeological Papers of the American Anthropological Association* on "the Space and Place of Death", studies now deal with "issues such as the siting of mortuary facilities; the interplay of agency and expressive style in the funerary context as these relate to the physical space and taking place of mortuary custom; and the recognition, cultural reconstruction, and explanation of death landscapes" (Silverman 2002, 1).

Mostly, these phenomena have been studied with approaches of traditional archaeology, focusing on a comparison of individual finds and sites. In fact, there seems to be a gap in applying these theories to analyses by means of digital methods which in this paper, includes formal, quantitative approaches, for example network analysis, but does explicitly not rule out qualitative applications. Still, especially if focused on the second aspect mentioned by Silverman, i.e. "the interplay of agency and expressive style", a relational perspective on and analysis of the subject matter promises large potential for research on a variety of topics: For example, the analysis of associations between grave goods, or between grave goods and the body could lead to insights into functions and socio-political significances of these artefacts; relational deposition patterns could be identified and connected to ritual activities or indicate zones materialising different aspects of identities; which, in general, could allow inferences on social practices and processes.

However, to exploit these potentials of formal analysis, basic questions of knowledge management have yet to be addressed. To begin, ontologies and exemplary data models that allow for the expression of non-geodetic conceptions of space are needed.

This paper wants to introduce a first version of a data model representing the construction of social space in a burial context. For this purpose, the paper draws on theories by Martina Löw on the sociology of space which will be explained further below. Then, it introduces a specific case study of elite burials of the Late Urnfield Period which motivated this research. After a review of existing standards and their suitability to model this type of spatial configuration, focusing on the CIDOC CRM and its compatible models, it suggests a possible model and an exemplary mapping which, in a next step, can be tested against a larger dataset and extended or adapted as needed. In doing so, the paper centres on one specific spatial configuration, namely the placement of objects in relation to each other in the grave. Finally, next steps and challenges are discussed.

8.2 Materials and methods

8.2.1 The Sociology of Space

To create a model representing socially constructed spaces, it is first necessary to understand and conceptualise exactly what should to be modelled. Many theories exist that could serve as a starting point, yet, in this study, the "Sociology of Space" as developed by Martina Löw has been chosen (Löw 2001; 2016; cited in this paper is the English translation). This was mainly because of her emphasis on social practice, and her understanding of space as inherently relational. She identifies two processes or social actions involved in the constitution of space: the "placing of social goods and people or [...] the positioning of markings that are primarily symbolic to identify ensembles of goods and people", which she calls *spacing*; and an *operation of synthesis* in which these arrangements are "amalgamated to spaces by way of processes of perception, imagination, and memory" (Löw 2016, 134–35).

For mortuary studies, it is important to note that Löw acknowledges the unconscious nature of the *spacing* process but also emphasises how "people are able to understand and explain how they create spaces" (Löw 2016, 137). This corresponds to the intentionality assumed for funeral assemblages as detailed above: While the concrete materialisation of social identities of the deceased follows unconscious knowledge of social structures and structure of the burial community, their selection is performed with intent and purpose.

Another benefit of this theory is that, coming from modern sociology, it asks questions about people and societies archaeologists might not be able to answer, but which are important to consider and reflect upon nevertheless to arrive at more thorough conceptions of the past. Some examples include the role of people as arranging spaces but also as being arranged or arranging themselves to become part of these spaces, or the external effectuality of objects and people, for example scent and sound, which can critically influence the outcome of the *synthesis* (Löw 2016, 165–66, 188).

8.2.2 Elite burials of the Late Urnfield Period

The other starting point for this paper was a case study analysing representations of elite identities in burials of the Late Urnfield period (Deicke 2021). The area of research covers a region north of the Alps that stretches from the East of France to the entrance of the Carpathian Basin. Here, the custom of elaborate burial re-emerges at the dawn of the Bronze Age after a period when depositional activity predominantly manifested in hoards. While the main focus of this study was on a network analysis of grave goods and features and their entanglements in extraordinary burials, a first foray into modelling and analysing spatial relationships was also undertaken. Basic relations, i.e., "next to", "above", "under" etc., were experimentally added to the existing graph database. This tentative exploration resulted in insights that enriched the original study: The explicit and formal documentation of spatial arrangements showed that knives, which were before seen as a homogeneous category, could be differentiated in function based on their material. Bronze knives were placed mainly in or on top of ceramic vessels and accompanied by animal bones (most likely a meat offering or remains of a funeral feast), while iron knives showed a distinctive association with the remains of the body, independent of its actual treatment as cremation or inhumation (Deicke 2021, 152–53). As far as can be observed, this pattern showed in some form at all sites in the dataset where iron knives appeared[1]. While these findings might seem trivial at first, the different treatment of the same type of object depending on its material ties into the increasingly widespread adoption of iron at the transition from Bronze to Iron Age. The deposition of the iron knife not in a utilitarian context but as part of the personal accoutrements of the deceased hints at the important role of this new technology in elite strategies of preservation, consolidation, and attainment of power. Additionally, this pattern could not consistently be observed in graves which contained only bronze knives[2]: While it held true at sites where iron knives had already been introduced[3], at the cemetery of Künzing, bronze knives–where they appeared–were placed with the ashes of the cremation[4].

These emerging patterns reveal a complexity that requires a large-scale analysis to study further. Based on this experimental approach, a research process can be derived that would ideally result in similar insights into function and meaning of other grave goods or architectural elements. First, contexts of spatially connected objects and features need to be identified, as in this case the associations of bronze knives with animal remains and iron knives with the body. Next, functional interpretations and semantic meanings need to be attributed to these spatial contexts, i.e., connotations of (ritual) feasting or personal items, possibly connected to an elevated socio-political status. Finally, these attributions would allow inferences on socio-political, -economical or -cultural practices and phenomena, exemplified here in the rise of iron metallurgy and the emergence of new forms of status representation.

However, as outlined above, to realise and further develop this methodology, more formal and standardised ways to encode the processes of *spacing* and *synthesis* in the burial context as data structures have to be considered.

8.2.3 Modelling space: a short review of existing standards

When modelling data from the domain of cultural heritage, the CIDOC CRM[5] and its compatible models[6] are the obvious starting points. The main model as well as, for example, CRMgeo (Hiebel et al. 2015) or CRMba (Ronzino et al. 2016) provide ample possibilities to understand and express location and relations between locations. Additionally, the focus of the CIDOC CRM on events as "central […] and essential for almost all modelling tasks" (Bekiari et al. 2022, 33) corresponds well with the emphasis on social actions and processes put forth by Löw's theories. Yet, before applying these classes and properties to a data model of the social construction of space, it has to be evaluated to which extent their semantics are in accordance with this purpose. As an ontology is commonly understood as "an explicit, formal specification of a shared conceptualization" (Studer, Benjamins, and Fensel 1998, 184), non-semantic use of these models contradicts their logic and limits the potentials arising from the use of a well-known standard ontology such as interoperability or the potential application of reasoning-approaches. Therefore, a short review of existing standards in regard to their ability to describe space and spatial relationships has to be conducted.

The CIDOC CRM itself focuses on "positioning in space of what has happened and the things involved, as well as reasoning about respective spatial relations". As such, it covers the documentation of geometric expressions of place, relations between places, and the history of object or actor locations, among others. Central to the CRM's understanding of space is the class *E53 Place* which can be specified by *E94 space*

1 Those sites consist of (from West to East): France: Saint-Romain-de-Jalionas (dép. Isère), "Les Tâches", Tumulus Géraud: iron knife to the right of the inhumation, bronze knife across animal bones (Brun 1987, 216–17). – Austria: Franzhausen, Gde. Nußdorf ob der Traisen (Bez. Sankt Pölten-Land), Franzhausen-Kokoron, grave 119: fragments of two iron knives inside urn, bronze knife across remains of a vessel with animal bones (Lochner and Hellerschmid 2016b, table 71); Stillfried an der March (Bez. Gänserndorf), grave 6: fragment of an iron knife, possibly inside urn (table 7 and 8 of the original publication show differing placements), bronze knife next to animal bones (Kaus 1984, table 7–8). – Slovakia: Senica (okr. Senica), Grab 1: iron knife by body (Romsauer 1999, 169, fig. 2,3). – Czech Republic: Brno-Obřany (okr. Brno-město), grave 169: iron knife on top of sword pointing at human remains (Adámek 1961, 95 fig. 99); Hostomice (okr. Teplice), Hostomice 2: three iron knives and a bronze knife, placement not documented (Kytlicová 2007, 263–64).

2 However, it has to be noted that for most of the graves in the dataset containing bronze knives, detailed documentation was not available.

3 Austria: Franzhausen-Kokoron, grave 31: bronze knife with animal bones placed on ceramic bowl (Lochner and Hellerschmid 2016b, table 15); Stillfried an der March (Bez. Gänserndorf), grave 38: bronze knife in assemblage with animal bones and ceramic sherds (Kaus 1984, table 7).

4 Grave 2 (Schopper 1995, 195 fig. 17, 4); grave 141 (Schopper 1995, 269 fig. 36, 6); grave 143 (Schopper 1995, 269 fig. 36, 2).

5 In this paper, version 7.1.2 as the last official version of the CRM is referenced (Bekiari et al. 2022).

6 https://www.cidoc-crm.org/collaborations (accessed 10 August, 2023).

primitive, e.g. coordinates. Temporal changes of location can be expressed through the *E9 Move* of a *E18 Physical Thing*. To express relations between places, a range of properties can be applied, namely *P189 approximates*, *P89 fall within (contains)*, *P122 borders with*, and *P121 overlaps with* (Bekiari et al. 2022, 37–38). In this understanding it is not objects that have spatial relations, but the places that these objects occupy. While this necessity to define individual places for all elements of a grave might appear slightly unwieldy at first, it is consistent with theories of the spatial turn that differentiate between place and space. As Löw phrases it, "[p]laces emerge through placements, but are not identical with the placement [...]" (Löw 2016, 167).

However, while these properties are able to encode the type of relation, they do not necessarily carry directional meaning, i.e., to which side the place of an object borders another one. This might be due in part to the fact that the choice of directional categories (right and left, or West and East, for example) is bound to depend on the goals and theoretical framework of a specific project. On the other hand, relations such as "under", "above", or "inside" can already be expressed by the precise application of these properties.

Some of the compatible models build on this condensed envisioning of space and spatial relations. Yet, most of them are clearly intended for the documentation of different cases and research questions than presented in this paper. For example, the CRMgeo states as its primary purpose "integrating all kinds of geoinformation that is available in GIS formats into CIDOC CRM representations" (Hiebel et al. 2015, 4) which constitutes precisely the perception of spatial information that this exercise intends to move away from. The CRMarchaeo focuses on "describing stratigraphic genesis and modifications and the natural phenomena or human intervention that led to their creation [...]." While its understanding of stratigraphy as the result of a production event potentially induced by human intentions carries definite potential for the analysis of the production of socially configured spaces, the original intent of describing "the nature and shape of existing stratifications and surfaces" in the context of the archaeological excavation process must be respected and prohibits its application to the semantics of space (Doerr et al. 2020, 5). The same holds true for the CRMba that contains additional properties dedicated to the description of spatial relations as well, but explicitly deals with the documentation of archaeological buildings (Ronzino et al. 2016).

While these models deal with the factual characterisation of space and spatial relations, other models can also be considered to add encodings of prehistoric social processes or reasoning decisions by modern researchers. The CRMinf or "argumentation model" aims to document "the management, integration, mediation, interchange and access to data about reasoning by a description of the semantic relationships between the premises, conclusions and activities of reasoning" (Stead et al. 2019, 3). As such, it seems especially suited to integrate the processes of assigning meaning and of interpretation that infer various spatial contexts from social *spacings* into the model.

Understanding a burial as the result of social practices and ritual actions further suggests the inclusion of these underlying processes into the model. While the case study presented in this paper has not yet reached the phase to deduce these types of social relations, potentially, their encoding could be provided by the CRMsoc. This model aims to "document social phenomena and constructs", and to "represent and relate social facts and life" (Alamercery et al. 2019, 2). As of the writing of this paper, the specification is published as version 0.1 and is still in its draft stage. Still, the model might serve as a fruitful addition to formally express the hypothesised social structures behind the finds and architecture of the burial.

Finally, the question must be asked if for such a specific research question that seems to lie beyond the intended applications of the CIDOC CRM and its compatible model, other ontologies or schemata could prove useful. To this end, some standards were evaluated, for example the Basic Formal Ontology (BFO), an upper ontology mainly used in the biomedical domain (Smith 2015). Yet, this evaluation shows that as the case study is clearly situated in the domain of cultural heritage, centring archaeological finds and features as the basis for its interpretative acts, the advantages of using a domain ontology such as the CIDOC CRM outweigh the disadvantages represented by the gaps identified in the process. Therefore, a first version of a data model was created by drawing on the CIDOC CRM which will be presented in the next chapter.

8.3 Results

8.3.1 A formal model of funeral spatial arrangements

While in many cases from business applications, data modelling focuses not only on a purposeful description of the domain but also on usage aspects such as "balancing the needs of the application, the performance characteristics of the database engine, and the data retrieval patterns"[7], in research-driven database design, the structure of the data will generally aim to express the structure of the domain from the perspective of a specific research question or purpose.[8] In this case, this means that while the model should support a certain degree of interoperability, for example by using a widely known

7 See also documentation of the popular database solution MongoDB (https://www.mongodb.com/docs/manual/core/data-modeling-introduction, accessed August 10, 2023).

8 See also Flanders' and Jannidis' distinction between curation- and research-driven modelling (Flanders and Jannidis 2019, 86).

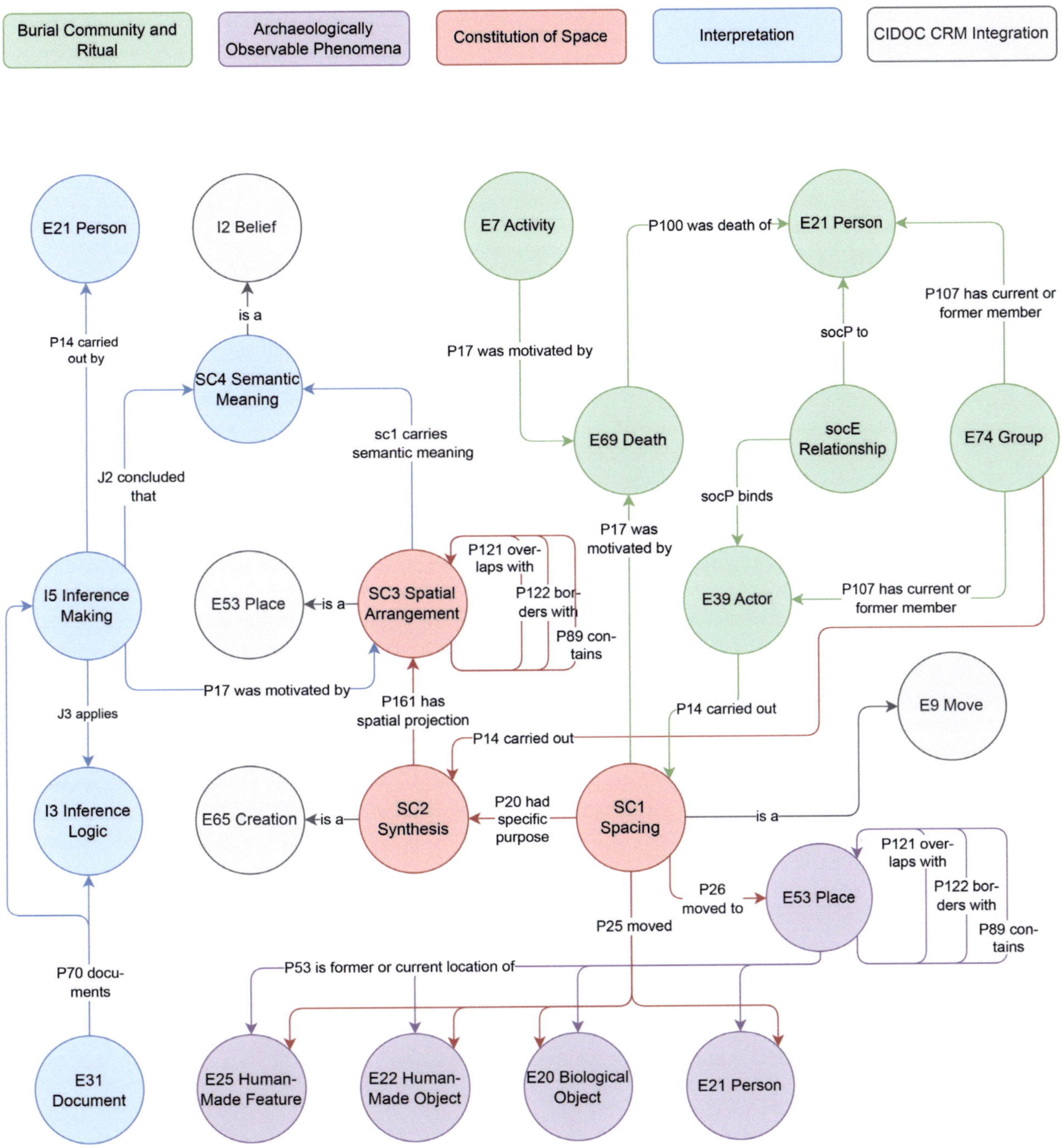

Figure 8.1. Conceptual model of the construction of social space through the acts of spacing and synthesis according to Martina Löw (2016). Created with diagrams.net (Jgraph Ltd. 2023).

standard ontology as a common frame of reference, the specific research purpose of modelling space as a social structure takes precedent.

Furthermore, in this case, the exercise of creating a data model can also be understood as ontological work in the original philosophical sense: identifying entities and conceptualising their relationships in the process of constructing social spaces and spatial arrangements (Arp, Smith, and Spear 2015, xxi). Accordingly, three components can be identified to map out the construction of social space according to Löw (2016, 132-5):

1. The "building blocks of space", i.e., living beings and social goods
2. Their relationships with each other
3. The acts of *spacing* and *synthesis*

Additionally, a fourth components needs to be added: as the interpretation of the spatial arrangements, of spacings, and even more so of synthesis and semantic meaning is highly subjective, this process, its actor(s) and their reasoning for arriving at these conclusions should also be added to the model:

4. Interpretative process

As a first result of the modelling exercise[9], it turned out that the CIDOC CRM proved to be largely sufficient to represent the processes of *spacing* and *synthesis* as conceptualised by Löw, supplemented by classes from the compatible models CRMinf and CRMsoc. Merely some classes and one property had to be added to satisfy the requirements of the specific use case, creating a first suggestion of a custom ontology.

In this process, the four components listed above were not translated one-to-one into modules of the model (Figure 8.1). Rather, the "building blocks" are represented by archaeologically observable phenomena (purple) as well as the assumed actors of the burial community and ritual (green); their relationships are manifested in properties of the CIDOC CRM, but also in the class *socE Relationship*; for the acts of *spacing* and *synthesis* additional classes were created which make up the process of the constitution of space (red); and the interpretative process was mapped out as a first experiment by adding classes of the CRMInf (blue). Following, some considerations that went into the model will be explained in more detail.

As mentioned above, the social processes and rituals surrounding the burial itself were not yet the focus of the research project, so this part of the model presents only a rough outline of the burial community, the relationship between its members, and their actions. The *E69 Death* of a person motivates an *E39 actors* to initiate the *SC1 Spacing*-activity that constitutes the first step of the construction of the burial space. It is important to note that in accordance with the CRM specification (Bekiari et al. 2022, 83), this node can signify one or more actors as it is unclear how many persons were effectively involved in the construction of an Urnfield burial. To account for the probability of further ritual actions surrounding the burial, another *E7 Acitivity* is added, though this part of the model should certainly only be seen as a stand-in for a more thorough exploration of ritualistic practice.

The person(s) construct(s) the grave by adding elements through *SC1 Spacing*, which constitutes an *E9 Move*-event, to *E53 places* that in their entirety constitute the burial space itself. These elements can be *E22 Human-Made Objects*, i.e., grave goods, *E20 Biological Objects*, i.e., animal bones, even *E21 Persons* itself as cremation or inhumation, but also *E25 Human-Made Features*. This accounts for the fact that architectural elements of the grave are understood as carriers of semantic meaning as well. Examples are the close links of sword depositions, tumuli, and inhumation rites that evolve in the late Urnfield and early Hallstatt Culture (Deicke 2021, 151; Kurz 1997, 108–9, 119; 123), or the association of elaborate grave architecture with the concept of energy expenditure, implying political control over human labour forces (Tainter 1975, 2; Wason 2004, 137–38). For Löw, living persons themselves are also a part of the spatial arrangement, yet, while this can be expressed by the model, it is not explicitely considered due to the challenges in accounting for contributions by living actors to the funeral placements with archaeological means.

One or more *SC1 Spacing*-events correspond to a *SC2 Synthesis* which is seen as heavily influenced by social routines, norms and structure of the burial community (Löw 2016, 144), and therefore, is carried out by the respective *E74 Group*. It is conceptualised as a subclass of *E65 Creation*. Yet, to some extent, *E81 Transformation* could fit better in this context as the *SC1 Spacing* also marks a transformation, moving living beings or social goods from the context of the living to the context of the dead (see also Deicke 2020, 44–50). Yet, according to the CRM specification, *E81 Transformation* only applies to *E18 Physical Thing*, not to abstract ideas such as spatial conceptions (Bekiari et al. 2022, 103). The two actions of *SC1 Spacing* and *SC2 Synthesis* lead to the creation of a *SC3 Spatial Arrangement* that carries *SC4 Semantic Meaning*. This meaning is concluded in an interpretative act expressed through classes from the CRMinf. Modelling *SC4 Semantic Meaning* as a *I2 Belief* and as the product of a *I5 Inference Making* positions it as an inversion of the *synthesis*–the interpretative act that gave meaning to a certain spatial configuration of objects has to be retraced by today's scholars to decipher this meaning. Both *I5 Inference Making* and *I3 Inference Logic* that was applied to arrive at this conclusion can be documented by *E31 Document*, if already published, and should otherwise be explained directly in the database. Lastly, it should be mentioned that just as the places inhabited by individual objects can overlap, border, or contain each other, so can the composite spaces of the *SC3 Spatial Arrangements*, to form new *spacings* and *syntheses*.

8.3.2 Example mapping: Grave 119 of Franzhausen-Kokoron

Technically, the next step of the knowledge engineering process would be the creation of a logical data model to reduce complexity and to facilitate implementation in a database, data entry, and querying. Yet, to better illustrate the intentions of the conceptual model, an exemplary partial mapping of a burial containing iron as well as bronze knives is presented below. Grave 119 of the

9 The model presented in this paper is an updated version of the one presented at the conference itself. Changes were made according to discussions in and around the session.

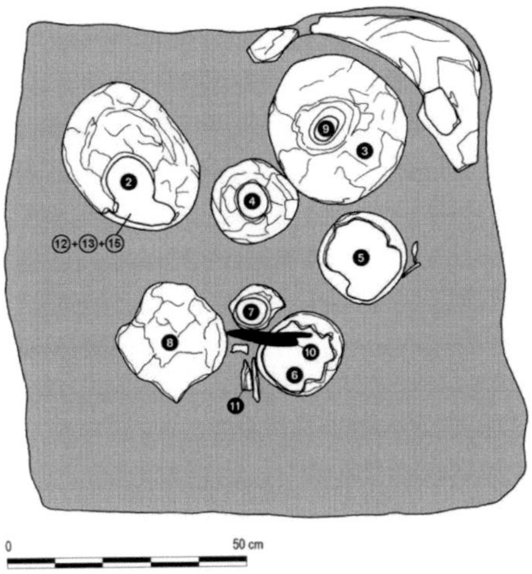

Figure 8.2. Grave 119 of Franzhausen-Kokoron. 2 – urn; 6, 7 – ceramic vessel; 10 – bronze knife; 11 – animal bones (sheep); 13, 15 – fragments of two iron knives (Lochner and Hellerschmid 2016b, table 71).

cemetery of Franzhausen (Nußdorf ob der Traisen, Lower Austria) contained fragments of two iron knives placed inside the urn alongside the ashes of a cremated body, and a bronze knife that was laid across the remains of a vessel and accompanied by animal bones (fig. 2; Lochner/Hellerschmid 2016, Grab 119).

Due to the complexity of the model, the mapping (Figure 8.3) incorporates only those entities of the inventory connected to the iron knives and their possible functions, namely the urn (*E22*), the iron knives (*E22*, combined into one node), and the cremation as the remains of the person of the deceased (*E21*). This last *E21*-node also represents the *E21 Person* whose death motivates the acts of *spacing and synthesis*, who is part of the burial community of Franzhausen-Kokoron (*E74*), and who can be assumed to have had a specific relation to the *E39 Actor* performing the placement.

At the centre of the mapping are the three *SC1 Spacing* events referring to the placement of the urn, iron knives, and cremation, and the spatial relations between them. They are connected to two events of *SC2 Synthesis* which, in turn, create three specific *SC3 Spatial Contexts* with different *SC4 Semantic Meanings*. One of those presents the initial decision of the original excavator, Johannes-Wolfgang Neugebauer, to define this assemblage of finds and features as a burial (Neugebauer 1993, 85-6). The second and third one document the interpretative acts of ascribing these arrangements meaning for the expression of social status and a connection to iron metallurgy by the author, documented in the study introduced above.

In summary, the mapping documents *spacing*-events in grave 119, and how different researchers group these *spacing*-events to draw conclusions on the assemblage as a whole (Neugebauer: grave) and in its parts (Deicke: social status). In making these processes explicit and their interpretation transparent, the mapping facilitates their analysis and ensures the reproducibility of the results.

8.4 Discussion and Outlook

In summary, a general model of the construction of burial spaces was created using the CIDOC CRM, the compatible models CRMinf and CRMsoc, as well as additional custom classes to extend the model to adequately represent the social actions behind this construction process. While the model contains substantial complexity, the decision of how much of this complexity is necessary to implement depends on the specific research project; certainly, parts such as the interpretative process or the representation of the burial community and rituals could be substituted by a careful qualitative contextualisation and description. As said in the beginning, part of this exercise was aimed at philosophical ontological work, to envision which entities and relationships are participating in the process of the construction of social spaces. In this regard, it must be noted that not all elements of Martina Löw's theories have been included in this version of the model, as, for example, the "external effectualities" mentioned above are not yet represented.

In a next step, the model will be transferred into a logical data model for a graph database containing the data from the case study. Two approaches are considered for quantitative analysis: (a) the development of algorithms based on the extended CRM that allow for the querying of this knowledge base and could point researchers to other patterns such as the one described above; and (b) the export of the selected relationships and analysis of these using methods and measures of network analysis.

As mentioned above, the ensuing research pipeline will be tested and, if necessary, the model will be adapted accordingly. For this process, some challenges remain to be considered. For example, the question remains if the existing properties of the CIDOC CRM that describe spatial relations are expressive enough to adequately illustrate the arrangements between grave goods, architecture, and organic remains, or if it will prove necessary to develop a more detailed controlled vocabulary. Also, it might be fruitful to integrate additional categories into the model that potentially influence *spacing* and *synthesis*, such as gender or age of the deceased, or the materiality of objects, that are now subsumed into the respective *E22 Human-Made Object*-nodes.

Still, with this first modelling effort, an important step has been taken to lay a foundation for the study of socially constructed space by means of digital methods. It opens a wide range of potentials for future studies to detect patterns of mortuary spatial arrangements, to contribute to a more detailed understanding of past funeral norms, function and meaning of grave goods and architecture, and consequently, to draw inferences on the social structure of the burial community in which these spaces were produced.

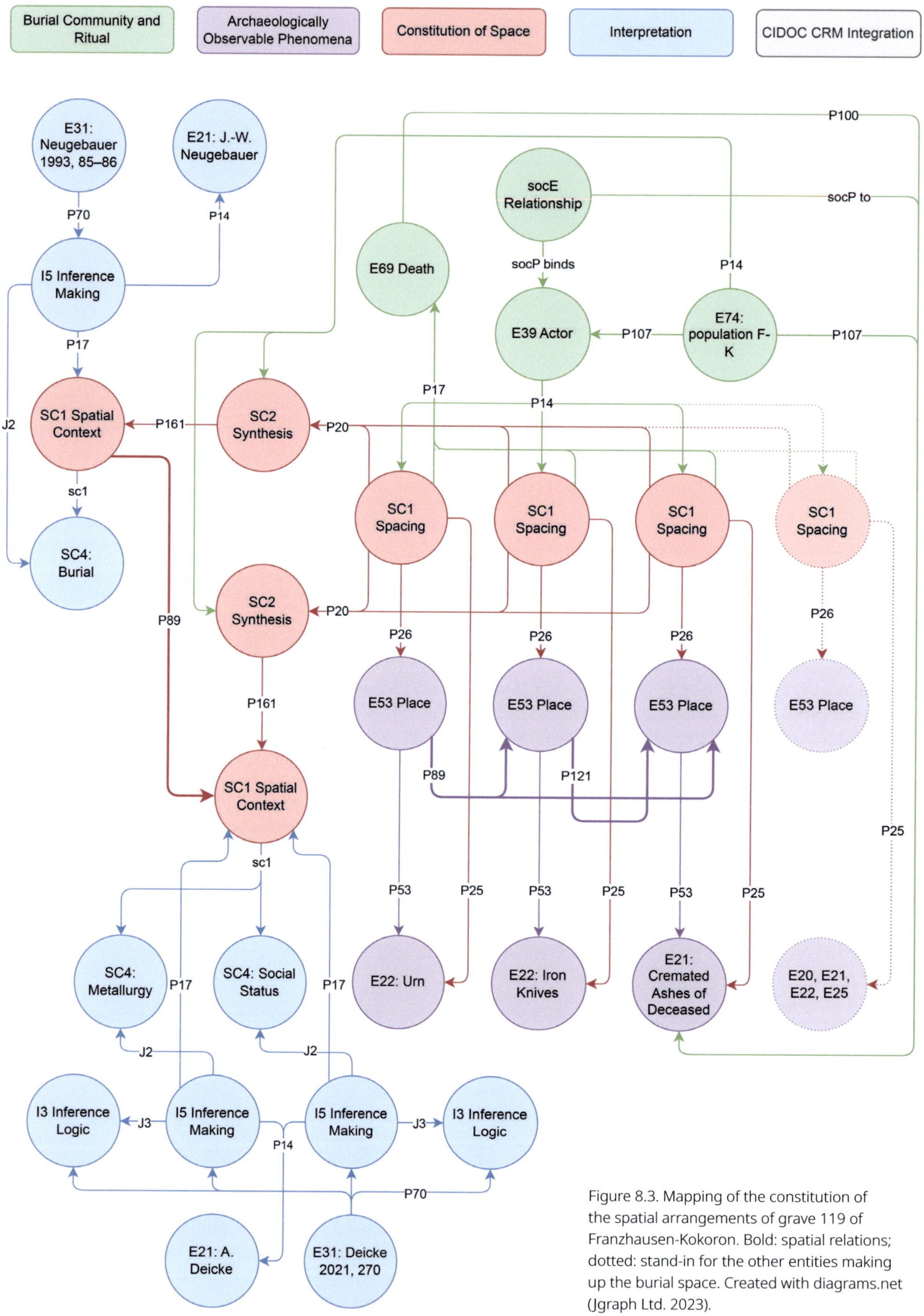

Figure 8.3. Mapping of the constitution of the spatial arrangements of grave 119 of Franzhausen-Kokoron. Bold: spatial relations; dotted: stand-in for the other entities making up the burial space. Created with diagrams.net (Jgraph Ltd. 2023).

Acknowledgements
The author thanks Asuman Lätzer-Lasar (Philipps-University Marburg) and Sarah Pittroff (Academy of Sciences and Literature | Mainz) for their insights and for lively discussions on the subject of the paper.

Conflict of interest disclosure
The author declares that she complies with the PCI rule of having no financial conflicts of interest in relation to the content of the article.

Peer review
This article has been reviewed and recommended by PCI Archaeology.

Lätzer-Lasar, A. 2024. "A new approach to a data ontology for the qualitative assessment of funerary spaces." *Peer Community in Archaeology* 100414. DOI: 10.24072/pci.archaeo.100414.

References
Adámek, František. 1961. *Pravěké Hradisko u Obřan*. Brno: Monografické Práce Moravského Muzea v Brně 1.

Alamercery, Vincent, Francesco Beretta, George Bruseker, Martin Doerr, Robert Sanderson, and Athanasios Velios. 2019. *Definition of the CRMsoc. An Extension of CIDOC CRM to Support Social Documentation. Version 1.0*. ICOM/CIDOC Documentation Standards Group/CRM Special Interest Group. https://cidoc-crm.org/sites/default/files/CRMsoc_20190326.pdf.

Arnold, Bettina. 2002. "A Landscape of Ancestors: The Space and Place of Death in Iron Age West-Central Europe." *Archaeological Papers of the American Anthropological Association* 11 (1): 129–43. DOI: 10.1525/ap3a.2002.11.1.129.

Arp, Robert, Barry Smith, and Andrew D. Spear. 2015. *Building Ontologies with Basic Formal Ontology*. Cambridge, MA: The MIT Press.

Bejko, Lorenc. 2016. "Social Landscape and Tumuli Burials in Late Bronze and Early Iron Age Southeastern Albania." In *Tumulus as Sema Space, Politics, Culture and Religion in the First Millennium BC*, edited by Olivier Henry and Ute Kelp, 75–88. Berlin: De Gruyter. DOI: 10.1515/9783110267501-008.

Bekiari, Chryssoula, George Bruseker, Erin Canning, Martin Doerr, Philippe Michon, Christian-Emil Ore, Stephen Stead, and Athanasios Velios. 2022. *Volume A: Definition of the CIDOC Conceptual Reference Model. Version 7.1.2*. ICOM/CIDOC Documentation Standards Group/CRM Special Interest Group. https://cidoc-crm.org/sites/default/files/cidoc_crm_v.7.1.1_0.pdf.

Binford, Lewis R. 1971. "Mortuary Practices: Their Study and Their Potential." *Mem. Soc. Am. Anthr.* 25: 6–29.

Blake, Emma. 2007. "Space, Spatiality, and Archaeology." In *A Companion to Social Archaeology*, edited by Lynn Meskell and Robert W. Preucel, 230–54. Malden: Blackwell Publishing. DOI: 10.1002/9780470693605.ch10.

Brun, Patrice. 1987. *Princes et Princesses de La Celtique: Le Premier Âge Du Fer En Europe 850-450 Av. J.-C.* Paris: Errance.

Deicke, Aline. 2020. "Entangled Identities. Processes of Status Construction in Late Urnfield Burials." In *Archaeological Networks and Social Interaction*, edited by Lieve Donnellan, 38–63. Abingdon: Routledge.

Deicke, Aline. 2021. *Zwischen Individuum Und Communitas. Identitätskonstruktion Späturnenfelderzeitlicher Eliten Im Spiegel Funeraler Statusnetzwerke*. Bonn: Habelt.

Doerr, Martin, Achille Felicetti, Sorin Hermon, Gerald Hiebel, Athina Kritsotaki, Anja Masur, Keith May, et al. 2020. *Definition of the CRMarchaeo. An Extension of CIDOC CRM to Support the Archaeological Excavation Process. Version 1.5.0.* Florence: PIN, University of Florence.

Flanders, Julia, and Fotis Jannidis. 2019. "A Gentle Introduction to Data Modeling." In *The Shape of Data in Digital Humanities. Modeling Texts and Text-Based Resources*, edited by Julia Flanders and Fotis Jannidis, 26–95. London: Routledge. DOI: 10.4324/9781315552941.

Haffner, Alfred. 1989. *Gräber, Spiegel des Lebens. Zum Totenbrauchtum der Kelten und Römer am Beispiel des Treverer-Gräberfeldes Wederath-Belginum.* Mainz: Zabern.

Hiebel, Gerald, Martin Doerr, Øyvind Eide, and Maria Theodoridou. 2015. *CRMgeo: A Spatiotemporal Model An Extension of CIDOC-CRM to Link the CIDOC CRM to GeoSPARQL through a Spatiotemporal Refinemen. Version 1.2*. ICOM/CIDOC Documentation Standards Group/CRM Special Interest Group. https://site2024.cidoc-crm.org/sites/default/files/CRMgeo1_2.pdf.

Hofmann, Kerstin P., and Regina Attula. 2017. "Funerary Spatial Concepts and Spatial Practices in South-Eastern Sicily during the Eighth to Fifth Centuries BCE." In *Theoretical Approaches to the Archaeology of Ancient Greece: Manipulating Material Culture*, edited by Lisa C. Nevett, 249–72. Ann Arbor: University of Michigan Press.

JGraph Ltd. 2023. "Diagrams.Net." https://github.com/jgraph/drawio.

Kaus, Margarete. 1984. *Das Gräberfeld Der Jüngeren Urnenfelderzeit von Stillfried an Der March. Ergebnisse Der Ausgrabung 1975-1977. Forschungen in Stillfried 6.* Wien: Stiglmayr.

Kurz, Siegfried. 1997. *Bestattungsbrauch in Der Westlichen Hallstattkultur: Südwestdeutschland, Ostfrankreich, Nordwestschweiz.* Münster: Waxmann.

Kytlicová, Olga. 2007. *Jungbronzezeitliche Hortfunde in Böhmen.* Stuttgart: Steiner.

Lefebvre, Henri. 1974. *La Production de l'espace.* Paris: Éditions Anthropos.

Lochner, Michaela, and Irmtraud Hellerschmid. 2016a. *Dokumentation Franzhausen-Kokoron: Ein Gräberfeld Der Jüngeren Urnenfelderkultur Aus Zentraleuropa. Erweiterte Interaktive Datenbank Mit Illustrationen Und Fundbeschreibungen. Version 03/Epub.* Vienna: Verlag der Österreichischen Akademie der Wissenschaften. DOI: 10.1553/KatalogUFK.

Lochner, Michaela, and Irmtraud Hellerschmid. 2016b. *Fundmaterial und Befunde des urnenfelderzeitlichen Gräberfeldes von Franzhausen-Kokoron – Tafelformat (Onlinepublikation).* Vienna: Österreichische Akademie der Wissenschaften. https://www.austriaca.at/?arp=0x00344254.

Löw, Martina. 2001. *Raumsoziologie.* Frankfurt am Main: Suhrkamp.

Löw, Martina. 2016. *The Sociology of Space: Materiality, Social Structures, and Action.* New York: Palgrave Macmillan US. DOI: 10.1057/978-1-349-69568-3.

Neugebauer, Johannes-Wolfgang. 1993. *Archäologie in Niederösterreich: St. Pölten Und Das Traisental.* St. Pölten: Verlag Niederösterreichisches Pressehaus.

Romsauer, Peter. 1999. "Zur Frage Der Westgrenze Der Mezőcsát-Gruppe." In *Archaeology of the Bronze and Iron Age: Experimental Archaeology, Environmental Archaeology, Archaeological Parks*, edited by Erzsébet Jerem and Ildikó Poroszlai, 167–76. Budapest: Archaeolingua.

Ronzino, Paola, Achille Felicetti, Martin Doerr, and Franco Niccolucci. 2016. *Definition of the CRMba. An Extension of CIDOC CRM to Support Buildings Archaeology Documentation. Version 1.4.* ICOM/CIDOC Documentation Standards Group/CRM Special Interest Group. https://cidoc-crm.org/crmba/ModelVersion/version-1.4.

Saxe, Arthur A. 1970. *Social Dimensions of Mortuary Practices.* Ann Arbor: University Microfilms, Inc.

Schopper, Franz. 1995. *Das urnenfelder- und hallstattzeitliche Gräberfeld von Künzing, Lkr. Deggendorf (Niederbayern).* Regensburg: Universitätsverlag Regensburg.

Silverman, Helaine. 2002. "Introduction: The Space and Place of Death." *Archaeological Papers of the American Anthropological Association* 11 (1): 1–11. DOI: 10.1525/ap3a.2002.11.1.1.

Simmel, Georg. 2009. *Sociology: Inquiries into the Construction of Social Forms.* Edited by Anthony J. Blasi, Anton K. Jacobs, and Mathew Kanjirathinkal. Leiden: Brill.

Smith, Barry. 2015. *Basic Formal Ontology 2.0. Specification and User's Guide.* https://raw.githubusercontent.com/BFO-ontology/BFO/master/docs/bfo2-reference/BFO2-Reference.pdf.

Stead, Stephen, Martin Doerr, Christian-Emil Ore, and Athina Kritsotaki. 2019. *CRMinf: The Argumentation Model. An Extension of CIDOC-CRM to Support Argumentation. Version 0.10.1 (draft).* ICOM/CIDOC Documentation Standards Group/CRM Special Interest Group. https://cidoc-crm.org/sites/default/files/CRMinf%20ver%2010.1.pdf.

Studer, Rudi, V. Richard Benjamins, and Dieter Fensel. 1998. "Knowledge Engineering: Principles and Methods." *Data & Knowledge Engineering* 25 (1): 161–97. DOI: 10.1016/S0169-023X(97)00056-6.

Tainter, Joseph A. 1975. "Social Inference and Mortuary Practices: An Experiment in Numerical Classification." *World Archaeology* 7 (1): 1–15.

Wason, Paul K. 2004. *The Archaeology of Rank, 2nd Ed.* Cambridge: Cambridge University Press. DOI: 10.1017/CBO9780511521195.

Werlen, Benno. 1993. *Society Action and Space: An Alternative Human Geography.* New York: Routledge.

9 HORAI

An integrated management model for historical information

Pablo del Fresno-Bernal
Sistemes de Gestió del Patrimoni SCCL
Barcelona
ORCID ID 0000-0001-8775-9113

Sonia Medina-Gordo
Universitat de Barcelona
somego12@gmail.com
ORCID ID 0000-0002-3921-3025

Esther Travé-Allepuz
Universitat de Barcelona
ORCID ID 0000-0002-6769-4487

Abstract

The archiving process goes beyond mere data storage, requiring a theoretical, methodological, and conceptual commitment to the sources of information. We present HORAI as a semantic-based integration model designed to facilitate the development of information systems that promote seamless communication across diverse disciplines within the field of Historical Sciences. This model adopts a data-centric approach, and uses principles and methods derived from Archival Science and Information Studies. Along with the model, we present a few experiences currently developed in different parts of Spain. Within this framework, this research has produced useful insight pertaining to the dynamics of data production and collaborative information management.

Keywords: Management Systems; Past construction; Slow Science; Historical knowledge; CRM

9.1 Introduction

The archiving process becomes an essential activity in a significant portion of historical studies. Firstly, as part of a comprehensive data management plan, it involves determining what is deemed to be archived; that is, what information is considered relevant and useful for conducting a study on a specific element of the past (Opgenhaffen 2022, 1). Secondly, it is during this stage that the researcher or research group bears the responsibility of selecting the objects from which knowledge will be generated. Consequently, careful consideration is given to the modes and formats of information recording, employing the necessary standards, tools and techniques accordingly. Hence, we deduce that this practice of information management extends beyond mere data storage, requiring a theoretical, methodological and conceptual commitment to these sources, as they are the foundation of our narratives. This inference is particularly noticeable in contemporary digital contexts, where certain ***data imaginaries*** shape our approach to historical sources to a greater or lesser extent (Huggett 2022a, 270-278).

In data-driven approaches, potentially problematic dynamics seem to be emerging, for example, the development of large-scale analysis strategies without considering whether the extracted and cleaned data align to comparable conceptions. Chippindale (2000) already addressed this aspect by distinguishing between *data* (raw data) and *capta* (theory-laden data), suggesting the need for a prior theoretical approach to the latter in order to (re)utilise them (Wylie 2017). In these scenarios, one of the

In *Advances in Digital Archaeology. Proceedings of the 2023 conference Computer Applications and Quantitative Methods in Archaeology – 50 years of synergy*, edited by J.W.H.P. Verhagen, J. Waagen, A. Brandsen, A. Queffelec, R.M. Visser and D. Taelman, 107–118. Leiden: Sidestone Press.

main challenges lies in striking a balance between the interpreted value and the epistemic trust elements (Mickel and Byrd 2021; Sandoval 2021) when constructing our narrative about the past, given the substantially artefactual and multifaceted nature of historical data (Owens 2011; Schöch 2013). While not exclusive, these observations are indeed noteworthy within disciplines where methodological tradition has been subject to reflection, such as Archaeology, since its parallel development with the use of new technologies has not always been accompanied by theoretical reflection on the implications that these digital means have on the articulation of knowledge (Huggett 2015; 2021).

Furthermore, when the study of a historical element requires the convergence of multiple disciplines, the aforementioned commitment becomes even more challenging to systematise, especially when the goal is to offer a comprehensive interpretation. In such situations, the knowledge alignment can be hindered by the difficulty to coordinate the approaches and methods used for data gathering by each specialist. This may explain why some research teams manage to aggregate (*complement*) data obtained from diverse sources of information (Costa Badia and Sancho i Planas 2022), but struggle to effectively match (*integrate*) them, despite it being the intended objective. While such results are valuable, they fail to address the necessary understanding among scholars from different fields from a wider perspective. Dealing with this aspect, Moreland (2006) provides a historiographic overview of its repercussions, focusing on the relationship between documentalists and archaeologists in recent decades. From this perspective, A. Woolf (2009, 6-7) argues that the challenge lies in the interpretative frameworks employed by each group and calls for a shift away from perceiving disciplines as autonomous and insurmountable domains of knowledge.

Given the outlined panorama, we believe that the problem does not reside in the data recording process itself, but rather in how we reason about the foundations of its production, particularly to avoid what some scholars have begun to refer to as "data deluge" (Bevan 2015). As an alternative starting point, Niccolucci (2020) has recently suggested a shift in perspective. The author proposes a data-centric viewpoint aimed at enhancing our engagement with different information archiving proposals, whether they come from one or multiple disciplines. Echoing these insights, we argue that one possible way for overcoming this issue could be through data modelling. We consider that without a shared conceptual model and a coherent management structure enabling interoperable information recording (including written, archaeological, or heritage-related data, among others), the accessibility and transferability of the generated knowledge could remain challenging for both specialists and other stakeholders. A constructed knowledge, therefore, should transcend the confines of archaeological studies and encourage collaborative synergies with other domains of expertise, despite the challenges and difficulties–and occasionally contradictions–intrinsic to standardisation (Hugget 2023, 28).

In view of this context, we introduce HORAI[1] as a semantic-based integration model aimed at facilitating the creation of information systems that foster smooth communication among the various disciplines encompassed within the so-called Historical Sciences. To achieve this, HORAI adopts a data-centric approach, prioritising the very data, and at the same time addressing the processes inherent to a project by drawing upon principles and methods derived from Archival Science and Information Studies. This methodological proposal emerges from previous experiences gained in diverse research contexts, each characterised by its own premises, objectives, and informational foundations. Over time, the refinement of the model has allowed us to set HORAI as a semantic tool that underpins the development of other applications, management processes, or technologies within the realms of Historical or Heritage Research. In this regard, two crucial aspects needed to be addressed: (1) the need to mitigate the risks of insular information management and (2) the need to facilitate a robust records management structure that ensures the consistent traceability of the research process along with the preservation of the generated information.

9.2 Delving into a key concept: *integration*

The aforementioned problem of insular management is related to the lack of interoperability that turns our knowledge bases into isolated systems. Technically, this management framework corresponds to the challenge of sharing data repositories with third parties. Conceptually, problems arise when a data model cannot employ concepts nor extend its applicability to other contexts. By referring to the concept of *integration*, we intend to highlight the importance of providing an operational inter-system reciprocity both for our repositories and for our models of abstract data representation. In our case, the minimum information units of the HORAI model, namely Unit of Topography (UT), Unit of Stratigraphy (US), and Actor (Ac), play a key role (Mauri Martí 2006; Travé-Allepuz et al. 2020). In previous publications, we delved into these concepts through various case studies (Del Fresno-Bernal et al. 2020; Travé-Allepuz et al. 2021a; Travé-Allepuz and Medina-Gordo 2021; Medina-Gordo and Travé-Allepuz 2021). Here we seek to highlight their significance in the archival processes.

1 https://horai.es/

9.2.1 Information exchange between heterogeneous research contexts

In the field of Humanities and Social Sciences, there is a growing number of projects committed to enhancing data exchange. This is evidenced by the proliferation of initiatives that facilitate the coordination of different systems, such as projects like Arachne[2], Arches[3], and PARTHENOS[4]. This proliferation is particularly prominent in these contexts due to the complexity and heterogeneity of the information handled, especially in cases that involve multidisciplinary frameworks. However, little theoretical attention has been paid to the thin line between compatibility and interoperability. In the former, systems can coexist and share data but have limitations in direct (inter)communication. In the latter, interoperability enables smooth data exchange and ensures data integrity, as long as common conceptual standards are adopted. It is important to consider that each scholar or research group usually adheres to their own management schemes, and data recording often aligns to the specific focus of each project. Matching this diversity of situations and preventing informational isolation is possible through both compatible and interoperable schemes, but it is only through the latter that effective data integration can be achieved.

Considering these premises, designing a digital environment that coordinates the storage and mutual understanding of systems is not misguided. Nonetheless, it is not the ideal option for the integrated management processes we pursue. Data integration also requires a conscious, explicit, and unambiguous association between the value of data and the meaning we attribute to it (Uschold and Gruninger 1996; Gruber 1995). This is why proposals based on ontologies or conceptual models seem to be better received in the development of systems capable of synchronising knowledge, as the conceptual definition of system elements forms the basis for associating the semantics of our data with those of other environments (Guarino 1997). This makes them highly competent approaches for information management, with models such as CIDOC CRM[5] serving as widely recognised and adaptable references among heritage and historical documentation managers. However, adopting this research line is not exempt of challenges, as the tension between the *generic* and the *specific* is sometimes not considered fully.

In our commitment to data, we must be able to establish a scale of knowledge representation and determine to what extent it satisfies the defined requirements of another system. Indeed, this idea has to do with the abstraction problems that occur when adapting data models, which can blur the integration process. A few years ago, González-Pérez and Martín-Rodilla (2024) reflected on these issues when they presented their Conceptual Reference Model CHARM[6], along with a mechanism they called *gradual refinement of models*, which minimises the problems we have discussed. If we revisit the question of epistemological equivalence across disciplines, the potential of this methodology allows for versatility in working with data that have rarely been explored in depth. It enables us to access information gathered in different systems, yet aligned to the same conceptual model, without the need to reconstruct each one's organisational or recording architecture. This coincides with the objectives of HORAI, providing a platform that bridges our databases, rather than imposing or adopting specific norms and standards for records management.

9.2.2 A proposal for an integrated Historical Science

We still have to develop how the concepts we presented at the beginning assist us in achieving this objective of integrating data obtained from sources of different origin, nature and support within a system that makes them fully shareable and that allows for joint exploitation. Taking a closer look at archaeological (field)work, Lucas (2001) reflected on the hermeneutics that enable the construction of archives in this discipline. Acknowledging the argumentative limitations that justify the recording of a portion of this work, the author proposed reconsidering the archaeological archiving process not as a copy of the intervened heritage entity, but as a substitution for it. What is interesting about this idea is that, in this process of conceptualisation and information management, the outcome constitutes not just a representation but a *displacement* of the object itself to the archive, ultimately allowing archaeological data to be reinterpreted by others (Lucas 2001, 44). As mentioned above, although dynamics vary among teams, this archiving procedure typically revolves around a widely recognised minimum unit of information in archaeology: the US. However, the challenge lies in conceptually representing the material data separately from the interpreted one (Martín-Rodilla et al. 2016), and this is where the use of the UT paves the way for data integration.

As suggested by A. Mauri Martí (1995), the management of the past turns around two key notions: time and space. From this perspective, historical logic involves, among other things, recognising certain actions within space that can be chronologically related (Mathieu 2021). In our model, a US is an instance of a UT insofar as it informs us about an action that occurred at a specific time and

2 https://arachne.dainst.org/.

3 https://www.archesproject.org/.

4 http://www.parthenos-project.eu/.

5 https://www.cidoc-crm.org/.

6 http://www.charminfo.org/.

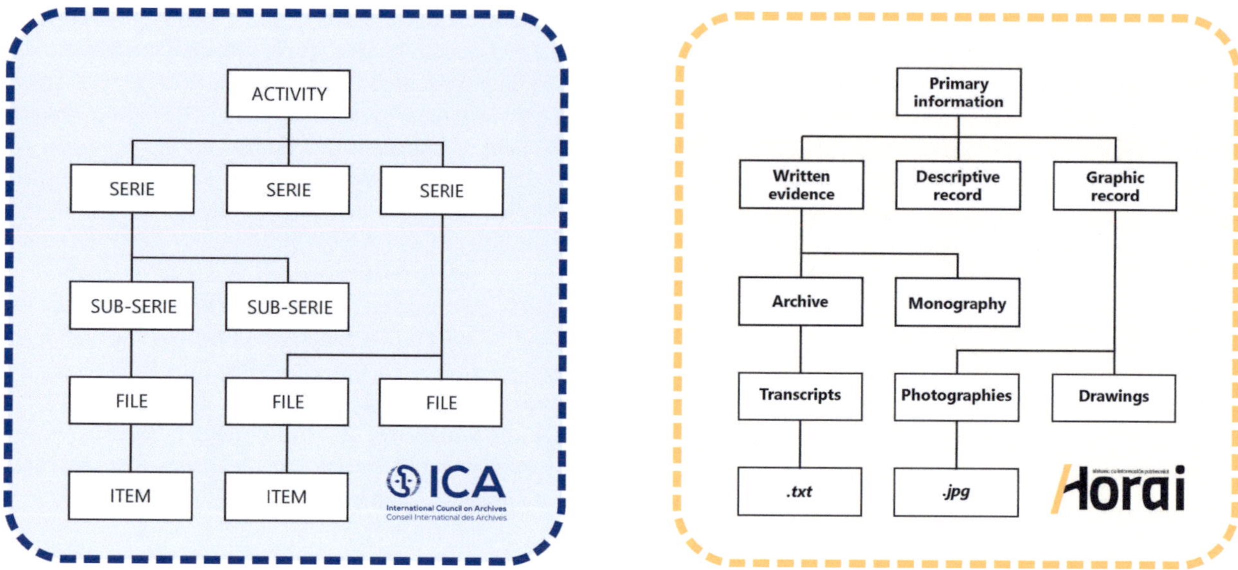

Figure 9.1. Comparison chart between the standards of archival description proposed by the International Council of Archives and an example of a classification chart used in HORAI for the *primary information* activity and sub-processes during the datafication context.

space, leaving a material trace (Harris 1989; Travé-Allepuz et al. 2020, 14). This physical evidence, as we mentioned, is characteristic of archaeological work, but it is not the only clue that the discipline searches for to reconstruct the historical narrative. There are other types of vestiges that may lack materiality and can be detected through the combined interpretation of different USs (e.g., Carandini 1997, 139–42), and that we could capture in the form of UTs. Under these terms, the concept of UT expands upon that of US because the identification of the action is possible regardless of its materiality, making it versatile enough for its application in any Historical Science.

As we will see later, each project can adjust (*refine*) their respective data models using these units according to their aims and incorporate them into management processes regardless of the nature of the information sources we employ. The interoperability of systems is possible through the use of common concepts, and in domains like History, where epistemic value has traditionally been given greater importance (Topolski 1992, 36–47), the use of UT represents a significant methodological step forward because it is possible to reproduce its work with common sources for the discipline, such as written sources. On the other hand, the UT/US/Ac model makes it possible to work with notions such as *spatiality* (Shoorcheh 2019), and thus to record the interaction between space and society at a given moment. For archives constructed as a result of archaeological work routines, we cannot identify the agency in the analysed past; we could recognise who documented an action, but then we would dig into aspects more related to meta-information (Martín-Rodilla and González-Pérez 2019; Huvila 2022). However, identifying the social dimension, the Ac, is operable in sources such as texts or photographs, and its conceptual representation through HORAI enables effective integration of the recorded data.

9.3 Archival Science applied to heritage-related records management

Along with data integration, HORAI addresses other processes related to record management, thus building on principles and methods of Archival Science. These premises should be connected to the advantages of maintaining traceability throughout the different stages of project progress, allowing for easy access and reproduction of the information generated and stored at any given time. In collaborative contexts, we believe it is important to have control over the sequence of processes carried out before, during, and after data management to trace their development from start to finish. We advocate for its significance because, on the one hand, it facilitates the exchange of files from our archives with different project participants and, on the other hand, it allows us to identify potential inconsistencies in the information and easily address them in all the elements that constitute an archival bond to that information (Stančić and Bralić 2021, 2-3). In order to define the context and content of what is archived, we propose a structured framework inspired on certain descriptive units (Figure 9.1), which are defined according to the General International Standard Archival Description.

Within this framework, we can further divide the process into four management phases that roughly correspond to the following:

1. The context of project management. This refers to all the aspects that need to be considered in terms of time, resources, and the number of people involved in the project's execution, among others. As these are the initial steps, this phase also coincides with the beginning of the data capture process, as it involves the design of the study, the obtention of funding and excavation licenses, the access to relevant documents, the establishment of a bibliographic state-of-the-art. These activities contribute to the datafication of our archival collection (Figure 9.1).
2. Data gathering and management, as a primary form of information management. In this phase, activities such as (systematic) data extraction from sources, development of storage protocols, and insertion of metadata are addressed. It is important to note that we are still in a stage of information extraction, but now overlapping with the phase of digitalisation. During this process, we observe the *de-contextualisation* of data (Leonelli 2014, 4), their displacement from their original context, while simultaneously reflecting on how we document them (in a digital format).
3. Data processing, as a form of secondary information management. For illustrative purposes, we can mention the processes of exploitation and interpretation of primary data, or those of derived documents, such as statistical exploration, laboratory analyses, and computational simulations. Moreover, it is in this phase that the identification of HORAI's units of information converges, and the focus shifts from extracting information to constructing knowledge. Therefore, this stage is distinct from both of the above-mentioned as it involves the *re-contextualisation* of data (Leonelli 2014, 4–5), considering the context in which they were originated and offering (our) new perspectives on them.
4. Data participation, or the final sharing stage where both the data and the information produced are disseminated. Within the framework of HORAI, we aim to explore how sharing information not only enables its reuse (Leonelli 2014, 5–6) but also foster its evolution, allowing it to take new forms and adapt to different contexts (Huggett 2022b, 104). The involvement with the construction of knowledge is possible through various means (academic, educational, administrative...), formats (open access, under license...), and forms (computer files, interactive computational platforms, web applications...).

As can be seen, the lifecycle of data in the primary management of information extends beyond the project because this work of reflection and commitment allows us to set the bases for its potential use in the form of new questions or theoretical contexts. The ability to interoperate this information with other systems ensures such situations, since the direct interaction between them creates scenarios for the evolution of data that, process after process, accumulate experiences and keep them as dynamic elements of management. Furthermore, as we mentioned before, the general guidelines proposed by HORAI are not incompatible with the needs of each research context, which is why the use of specific vocabularies and varied tools is expected (for instance, Del Fresno-Bernal and Mauri Martí 2020; Travé-Allepuz et al. 2021b, 7–9). In any case, we are interested in highlighting two concluding ideas from the procedure: on the one hand, this approach to record management ensures organised collaboration among the participants by aligning them all to the proposed description scheme for a project. On the other hand, it promotes information preservation by stimulating the review of data obsolescence, which is characteristic of digital media.

9.4 Some current experiences

The issues raised so far are the cornerstone of the systems we introduce below. In this section we will introduce and comment on ANATOLE, GREYWARE and an additional database for historical research, as examples of current experiences of the HORAI model implementation. These three tools have been refined over the past years within a research team consisting of companies, universities, museums, and local cultural entities, creating an environment for sharing diverse experiences and knowledge, while fostering constructive dialogue. Each of these systems was created in response to specific challenges and entails different levels of complexity and objectives. Nevertheless, the information management processes and archival dynamics are shared and aligned to the previously outlined framework, and provide more detailed and practical insight into our reflections on the subject. For their presentation, we have focused on the elements that help us understand them within the context in which they are developed, as it is not the purpose of this study to delve into the technical aspects.

9.4.1 The archaeological information management system ANATOLE

ANATOLE emerges from a previous experience, SigArq, whose specificities (Del Fresno-Bernal 2016), proposed improvements (Fructuoso Fernández 2018), and application to various case studies have offered opportunities for enhancing *HORAI*. This web application was part of an Archaeological Information System aimed at organising, processing, and standardising the results obtained from fieldwork and archaeological research (Del Fresno-Bernal et al. 2021). Among other features, SigArq offered a protocol to the users for entering archaeological information, allowing them to store and access primary data. However, it was restrictive in that, in order to incorporate it into other projects, these projects had to adhere to pre-established standardisation guidelines, which could require reorganising data recording protocols in cases where studies did not start from scratch. This characteristic hindered its applicability in archaeological sites studied by groups not linked with the SigArq development team. Therefore, being aware of this limitation, we sought to overcome any technological dependency through HORAI.

ANATOLE focuses on the management of heritage-related records. The process of uploading, classifying, and retrieving records involves the development of a project, and the management system is built upon the concept of US in its descriptive, graphic, cartographic, and temporal dimensions, whereas the UT corresponds in this case to the stratigraphic synthesis. Moreover, ANATOLE enables the spatial exploration of gathered information either through raw or synthesised data. So far, ANATOLE is used by various heritage scholars and curators, thus managing archaeological sites of different chronology, typology, and geographical location in Spain.

9.4.2 The GREYWARE Information System

The research project GREYWARE [PID2019-103896RJ-I00] explores the processes of change and continuity related to a specific type of material: the reduced-fired pottery or *GREYWARE*, diachronically. This study proposal builds upon previous experiences acquired in Medieval and Post-Medieval pottery studies (Padilla Lapuente 1984; Travé-Allepuz 2009; Travé-Allepuz and Vicens Tarré 2018). On these bases, our interest lies in delving deeper into how social changes influence the production and consumption patterns of these materials, particularly during transitional periods (Travé-Allepuz 2021). This approach has led to the development of a homonymous information system focused on the study of this specific object (Travé-Allepuz et al. 2021b), requiring robust management mechanisms due to the volume and heterogeneity of the information available. This empirical reality encompasses data about the ceramic object itself, as well as information about the agents involved in its production (Vicens Tarré and Travé-Allepuz 2018, 120–24) and other related secondary data (Travé-Allepuz et al. 2014; Travé-Allepuz 2022). While we have proposals that allow us to systematise some of this data (for instance, Adroher Auroux et al. 2016), the challenge lies in processing them within the framework of the conceptual adequacy mentioned in previous sections.

Through HORAI, it is possible to manage data that aligns to the required abstraction model for each defined entity and establish direct communication with other digital repositories whose information had already been generated prior to the project and needed to be integrated. These entities reveal typologies, ceramic fabrics or productions that, based on the UT concept, can be compared according to the level of precision in our analysis, whereas the Ac concept incorporates the social component.

9.4.3 A historical information management system

The third system is an outcome of an ongoing PhD research that pursues a dual objective. On the one hand, it aims at achieving reconciliation and traceability of interpretative frameworks in disciplines such as History, Archaeology, and Remote Sensing (Medina-Gordo and Travé-Allepuz 2021). On the other hand, it seeks to reflect on the marginalised nature of mountain landscapes during the Early Middle Ages, whose history often seems to start *in media res*, following a sudden, passive integration of the people inhabiting them into the structures of external societies characterised by a certain dominance. The study area considered is the southern region of the Sierra de la Demanda, located between the current provinces of Burgos and Soria. For this region, we have studies that have generated complementary interpretations of written and archaeological evidence (Pastor Díaz de Garayo 1996; Escalona Monge 1996), but they have hardly modified the explanatory bases of previous works exclusively based on documents (Álvarez Borge 1991). Besides, the marginality of this area has been considered only in relation to secular forms of domination (Escalona Monge 1996) and the distribution of known archaeological sites in relation to a few environmental features (Pastor Díaz de Garayo 1996, 62–6; Álvaro Rueda 2012, 51–98).

Therefore, we are not starting from scratch, but the work done so far prompts a reflection on the mechanisms used to build this construction of the past, both from the point of view of interpretative and information management. To explore the articulation of these landscapes, we identify the notion of power, not as an element of dominance, but as a manifestation of human agency. Precisely, the conceptualisation of data by means of HORAI allows us to model the dialogue between the traces of this agency – either material or symbolic – in the form of UT, and the agents who participate in making those traces, in the form of Ac (Medina-Gordo et al. 2022).

9.5 Discussion: data sharing or engaging data?

Each of the aforementioned tools are based on the principles of conceptual reconciliation and efficiency in historical information management that we advocate for. On the one hand, regardless of the technological support employed, all of them allow for a direct exchange of the information and generated knowledge while maintaining their own objectives and study frameworks. These procedures enable an environment of data interoperability

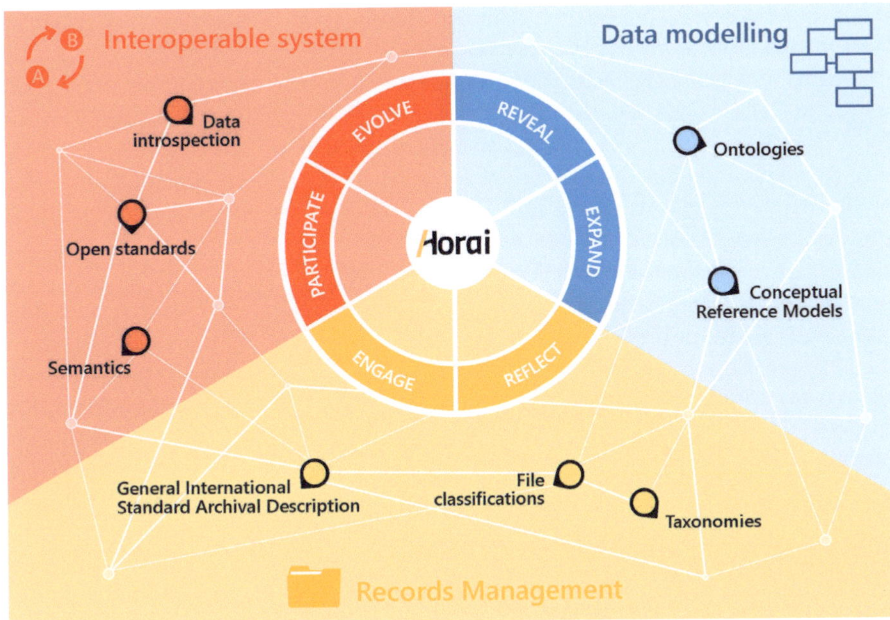

Figure 9.2. Pie chart of HORAI's chances and principles in research, inspired by the proposal of Hugget (2022b).

as the systems are built upon a conceptual model of data integration, shifting the complementary character of these data towards knowledge matching practices based on semantics. On the other hand, they also enable us to define our work's traceability, at least from the perspective of Records Management and administrative organisation of archives. This not only ensures transparency in workflows but also their monitoring. At this point, we question to what extent this investment of time in understanding data is allowing us to *decelerate* methodological processes characterised by streamlining and simplification of information (Marila 2019) and gain awareness of the past from the very underpinnings upon which we build it (Thibodeau 2019; 2021).

To address this issue, Marila (2019) examines the works that have been thriving within what is known as *fast science*. The author expresses concern regarding the direction this approach is taking, as the necessity to establish a valid way of conducting science, based on an empirical logic, and the systematisation of these principles, are leading to an increasing separation between scientific practice and the effective generation of knowledge. Similarly, Orman (2015) shares related concerns when exploring what he terms the "information paradox". Orman delves into issues such as production costs, the sense of obsolescence, and competition across various levels, resulting in a high volume of data with a limited quality of information. Likewise, data modelling can yield a reductionist representation of historical complexity if we fail to consider the narrative within the data. An excessive simplification risks erasing nuances, contexts, and fundamental connections contained in the data. Therefore, a more reflective approach to information management should integrate strategies that preserve contextual complexity, thereby enabling a more precise and thoughtful understanding of the past.

All these insights are not isolated concerns but have also been assessed from different perspectives by other authors (e.g., Gero 2007; Rączkowski 2020; Lucas and Witmore 2022; Marila 2022). From the perspective of working with information, we believe that the recent reflections by Huggett (2022b, 103–106) provide a complementary theoretical dimension to the proposal we advocate for. As we have mentioned before, our way of making information available is not solely aimed at its publication, but we hope that our work provides users with the necessary tools to critically evaluate the knowledge generated once it will be reused. In these kinds of data use, we acknowledge that the usual knowledge management process of paradigms like Big Data, when properly implemented (Liu et al. 2021), facilitates such reuse. However, we must also note that in this increased process of reusability we may end up neglecting aspects such as the original significance of data. Therefore, we believe that the forthcoming research agenda for those exploring traces of the past should promote alternative approaches to mere data sharing, fostering greater reflection and engagement with the data.

Taking as a reference point the comparison of positions regarding data lifecycle outlined by Huggett (2022b, 104), and considering the working perspectives we propose, we would like to conclude by assessing three key pillars of the HORAI model, which we have somewhat delineated throughout the previous sections (Figure 9.2). Firstly, data modelling ensures that we go beyond tasks such as data identification and capture, as the creation of a model brings forth (*reveals*) and adds dimension (*expands*) to the data. In this line, the works that promote the definition of ontologies (Van Helden et al. 2018) or Conceptual Reference Models (González-Pérez and Parcero-Oubiña 2012) are significant. Secondly, Records Management offers alternative tools for data validation and preservation, as we can discern how they have been constructed (*reflect*) and enhance our involvement (*engage*) with them. Although not exclusive, the tasks of creating taxonomies or file classification systems are two examples within this field, as exemplified in Figure 9.1. Lastly, interoperability extends beyond data sharing environments, as it allows us to be part of their (re)creation (*participate*) and to dynamise (*evolve*) its use, for which a closer examination of information (Tobalina-Pulido and González-Pérez 2020) or its semantics (Vlachidis et al. 2013) is relevant, along with the promotion of open standards for data management (Richards 2009; Huggett 2012; Kansa 2012).

9.6 Concluding remarks

HORAI allows us to reason, document, and communicate complex phenomena such as historical research and heritage management. In our effort in contributing to the construction of the past, we have presented a proposal that is based on conceptual modelling as the basis to address such complexity, while also providing mechanisms for Records Management of the elements involved in a project's development. As we have observed, both characteristics facilitate the construction of interoperable ecosystems as long as the management systems align with the model's minimum units of information. Within this framework, the research plan has brought to light issues that are related to the dynamics of data production and use. Based on the results obtained, we conclude that the challenges that lie ahead in this context of information management are diverse, with technological constraints being the most prominent. As HORAI does not depend on any specific technology, the way we interconnect each of the digital tools planned for a study development – its virtual environment – is an area that is still being refined, and we expect to obtain results in the coming years.

Acknowledgements

The authors wish to acknowledge Ms Noemí Travé for language edition and review. Alfred Mauri provided useful insights and inspiration during the development of this contribution. All colleagues involved in the past and still today in the development of the HORAI system deserve our most sincere gratitude. Naming every one of them singularly will add a never-ending list. We express our deep acknowledgement to them all.

Funding

This piece of research is an outcome of the HORAI Research Project coordinated by the company Sistemes de Gestió del Patrimoni SCCL. One of the information systems has been matured as part of the GREYWARE research project (PID2019-103896RJ-I00), funded by the Spanish Ministerio de Ciencia e Innovación (MCIN/AEI/10.13039/ 501100011033). Another has been developed thanks to a PhD grant supported by the Secretariat for Universities and Research of the Ministry of Business and Knowledge of the Government of Catalonia and the European Social Fund (2022 FI_B1 00021). The whole study is part of the current research tasks carried out by the Medieval and Postmedieval Archaeology Research Group GRAMP.UB (2021SGR-00236-GRC), at the University of Barcelona, and supported by an Archaeological Research Project (CLT/2022/ARQ001SOLC/110) developed in Martorell and co-funded by the local Town Council.

Conflict of interest disclosure

The authors declare no potential conflicts of interest with respect to the research, authorship, and/or publication of this paper.

Peer review

This article has been reviewed and recommended by PCI Archaeology.

Huvila, Isto 2024. "A novel management model for historical information." *Peer Community in Archaeology* 100387. DOI:10.24072/pci.archaeo.100387.

References

Adroher Auroux, Andrés María, César Carreras Monfort, Rui De Almeida, Adolfo Fernández Fernández, Jaime Molina Vidal, and Catarina Vegas. 2016. "Registro para la cuantificación de cerámica arqueológica: estado de la cuestión y una nueva propuesta. Protocolo de Sevilla (PRCS/14)." *Zephyrus* 78: 87–110. DOI:10.14201/zephyrus20167887110.

Álvarez Borge, Ignacio. 1991. "Estructura social y organización territorial en Castilla La Vieja. Los territorios entre el Arlanzón y el Duero en el siglo X." PhD diss., Universidad de León.

Álvaro Rueda, Karen. 2012. "El poblamiento altomedieval y sus manifestaciones funerarias en la cuenca del Alto Arlanza (s. IX y XI)." PhD diss., Universitat de Barcelona. http://hdl.handle.net/10803/80651.

Bevan, Andrew. 2015. "The Data Deluge." *Antiquity* 89 (348): 1473–84. DOI:10.15184/aqy.2015.102.

Carandini, Andrea. 1997. *Historias en la tierra*. Barcelona: Editorial Crítica.

Chippindale, Christopher. 2000. "Capta and Data: On the True Nature of Archaeological Information." *American Antiquity* 65 (4): 605–12. DOI:10.2307/2694418.

Costa Badia, Xavier, and Marta Sancho i Planas. 2022. "La cartografía Digital Como Herramienta dinámica E Integrativa Para El Estudio Del Poblamiento Medieval. La Propuesta metodológica Del Proyecto "Muntanya Viva"." *Cuadernos de Arqueología de la Universidad De Navarra* 30 (2): 185–210. DOI:10.15581/012.30.2.009.

Del Fresno-Bernal, Pablo. 2016. "Sistema de Información Arqueológica: propuesta de normalización, desarrollo conceptual e informático." PhD diss., Universidad del País Vasco / Euskal Herriko Unibertsitatea.

Del Fresno-Bernal, Pablo, and Alfred Mauri Martí. 2020. "Una propuesta de sistematización para la gestión de la documentación e información arqueológica (SIA)." In *I Simposio Anual de Patrimonio Natural y Cultural: ICOMOS España*, edited by José Luis Lerma, Víctor Manuel López-Menchero Bendicho, and Alfonso Maldonado, 585–93. Valencia: Editorial Universitat Politècnica de València. DOI:10.4995/icomos2019.2020.11711.

Del Fresno-Bernal, Pablo, Alfred Mauri Martí, and Esther Travé-Allepuz. 2020. "Documentació d'intervencions de restauració en jaciments arqueològics i patrimoni edificat: cap a la construcció d'un sistema d'informació." In *Documentar en la conservació-restauració. Mètodes i noves tecnologies: XVI Reunió Tècnica de conservació-Restauració. 12-13 novembre 2020*, edited by Kusi Colonna-Preti, and Natàlia Sánchez, 75–90. Barcelona: CRAC.

Del Fresno-Bernal, Pablo, Esther Travé-Allepuz, and Alfred Mauri Martí. 2021. "Sistemas de Información Arqueológica: procesos de gestión integrada del patrimonio arqueológico para la investigación interdisciplinar." In *Las Humanidades Digitales como expresión y estudio del patrimonio digital*, edited by María Ángela Celís Sánchez, 227–35. Cuenca: Ediciones de la Universidad de Castilla-La Mancha.

Escalona Monge, Julio. 1996. "Transformaciones sociales y organización del espacio en el Alfoz de Lara en la Alta Edad Media." PhD diss., Universidad Complutense de Madrid. https://hdl.handle.net/20.500.14352/61722.

Fructuoso Fernández, Xènia. 2018. "Proposta de classificació terminològica per a l'elaboració d'un vocabulari arqueològic normalitzat." BA diss., Universitat Autònoma de Barcelona.

Gero, Joan M. 2007. "Honoring Ambiguity/Problematizing Certitude." *Journal of Archaeological Method and Theory* 14: 311–27. DOI:10.1007/s10816-007-9037-1.

González-Pérez, César and Patricia Martín-Rodilla. 2014. "Integration of Archaeological Datasets through the Gradual Refinement of Models." In *CAA2014: 21st Century Archaeology. Concepts, methods and tools. 42nd Annual Conference on Computer Applications and Quantitative Methods in Archaeology*, edited by F. Giligny, F. Djindjian, L. Costa, P. Moscati, and S. Robert, 193–204. Oxford: Archeopress.

González-Pérez, César and César Parcero-Oubiña. 2012. "A Conceptual Model for Cultural Heritage Definition and Motivation." In *CAA2011: Revive the Past. 39th Annual Conference on Computer Applications and Quantitative Methods in Archaeology*, edited by Mingquan Zhou, Iza Romanowska, Zhongke Wu, Pengfei Xu and Philip Verhagen, 234–44. Amsterdam: Pallas Publications.

Gruber, Thomas R. 1995. "Toward principles for the design of ontologies used for knowledge sharing." *International Journal of Human-Computer Studies* 4 (5–6): 907–28. DOI:10.1006/ijhc.1995.1081.

Guarino, Nicola. 1997. "Semantic matching: Formal ontological distinctions for information organization, extraction, and integration." In *Information Extraction. A Multidisciplinary Approach to an Emerging Information Technology*, edited by Maria Teresa Pazienza, 139–70. Berlin: Springer. DOI:10.1007/3-540-63438-X_8.

Harris, Edward C. 1989. *Principles of archaeological stratigraphy*. London: Academic Press Limited.

Huggett, Jeremy. 2012. "Lost in information? Ways of knowing and modes of representation in e-archaeology." *World Archaeology* 44 (4): 538–52. DOI:10.1080/00438243.2012.736274.

Huggett, Jeremy. 2015. "A Manifesto for an Introspective Digital Archaeology." *Open Archaeology* 1 (1): 86–95. DOI:10.1515/opar-2015-0002.

Huggett, Jeremy. 2021. "Algorithmic Agency and Autonomy in Archaeological Practice."

Open Archaeology 7 (1): 417–34. DOI: 10.1515/opar-2020-0136.
Huggett, Jeremy. 2022a "Data Legacies, Epistemic Anxieties, and Digital Imaginaries in Archaeology." *Digital* 2 (2): 267–95. DOI: 10.3390/digital2020016.
Huggett, Jeremy. 2022b. "Is less more? Slow Data and Datafication in Archaeology." In *Critical Archaeology in the Digital Age*, edited by Kevin Garstki, 97–110. Los Angeles: UCLA Cotsen Institute of Archaeology Press.
Huggett, Jeremy. 2023. "Deconstructing Digital Infrastructures Supporting Archaeological Knowledge." *Current Swedish Archaeology* 31: 11–38. DOI: 10.37718/CSA.2023.08.
Huvila, Isto. 2022. "Improving the usefulness of research data with better paradata." *Open Information Science* 6 (1): 28–48. DOI: 10.1515/opis-2022-0129.
Kansa, Eric. 2012. "Openness and archaeology's information ecosystem." *World Archaeology* 44 (4): 498–520. DOI: 10.1080/00438243.2012.737575.
Leonelli, Sabina. 2014. "What difference does quantity make? On the epistemology of Big Data in biology." *Big Data & Society* 1 (1). DOI: 10.1177/2053951714534395.
Liu, Pengfei, Sabine Loudcher, Jérôme Darmont, and Camille Noûs. 2021. "ArchaeoDAL: A Data Lake for Archaeological Data Management and Analytics." In *25th International Database Engineering & Applications Symposium (IDEAS 2021)*, edited by Bipin C. Desai, Jeffrey Ullman, Richard McClatchey, and Motomichi Toyoma, 252–62. New York: Association for Computing Machinery. DOI: 10.1145/3472163.3472266.
Lucas, Gavin. 2001. "Destruction and the Rhetoric of Excavation." *Norwegian Archaeological Review* 34 (1): 35–46. DOI: 10.1080/00293650119347.
Lucas, Gavin, and Christopher Witmore. 2022. "Paradigm Lost: What Is a Commitment to Theory in Contemporary Archaeology?" *Norwegian Archaeological Review* 55 (1): 64–77. DOI: 10.1080/00293652.2021.1986127.
Marila, Marko M. 2019. "Slow science for fast archaeology." *Current Swedish Archaeology* 27 (1): 93–114. DOI: 10.37718/CSA.2019.05.
Marila, Marko M. 2022. "A Theoretically Committed Archaeology is a Civilised Archaeology." *Norwegian Archaeological Review* 55 (1): 78–80. DOI: 10.1080/00293652.2021.2010123.
Martín-Rodilla, Patricia, and César González-Pérez. 2019. "Metainformation scenarios in Digital Humanities: Characterization and conceptual modelling strategies." *Information Systems* 84: 29–48. DOI: 10.1016/j.is.2019.04.009.
Martín-Rodilla, Patricia, César González-Pérez, and Patricia Mañana-Borrazas. 2016. "A Conceptual and Visual Proposal to Decouple Material and Interpretive Information About Stratigraphic Data." In *CAA2015: Keep the revolution going. Proceedings of the 43rd Annual Conference on Computer Applications and Quantitative Methods In Archaeology*, edited by S. Campana, R. Scopigno, G. Carpentiero, and M. Cirillo, 201–11. Oxford: Archeopress.
Mathieu, Jon. 2021. "Is Historical Temporality "Heterogeneous" and "Contingent"? William H. Sewell's Cultural Turn." *Histories* 1 (1): 12–21. DOI: 10.3390/histories1010005.
Mauri Martí, Alfred. 1995. "La aplicació del Mètode Harris a l'estudi del territori." In *Actes del 3r curs d'arqueologia d'Andorra, del 30 de setembre al 4 d'octubre de 1991. La vida medieval als dos vessants del Pirineu*, edited by Patrimoni Cultural d'Andorra, 8–24. Andorra: Patrimoni Cultural d'Andorra, Servei de Recerca Històrica.
Mauri Martí, Alfred. 2006. "La configuració del paisatge medieval: el comtat de Barcelona fins al segle XI." PhD diss., Universitat de Barcelona. http://hdl.handle.net/10803/2065.
Medina-Gordo, Sonia, Karen Álvaro Rueda, and Esther Travé-Allepuz. 2022. "Integración de datos y procesos de registro de la información: un estudio de caso en el Alto Arlanza." *Cuadernos de Arqueología de la Universidad de Navarra* 30 (2): 161–84. DOI: 10.15581/012.30.2.008.
Medina-Gordo, Sonia, and Esther Travé-Allepuz. 2021. "Developing integrated research in Historical Science: Transdisciplinary strategies for information management and exploitation." In *16th Iberian Conference on Information Systems and Technologies (CISTI), Chaves, Portugal*, 1–6. IEEE. DOI: 10.23919/CISTI52073.2021.9476336.
Mickel, Allison, and Nylah Byrd. 2021. "Cultivating trust, producing knowledge: The management of archaeological labour and the making of a discipline." *History of the Human Sciences* 35 (2): 1–26. DOI: 10.1177/09526951211015855.
Moreland, John. 2006. "Archaeology and Texts: Subservience or Enlightenment." *Annual Review of Anthropology* 35: 135–51. DOI: 10.1146/annurev.anthro.35.081705.123132.
Niccolucci, Franco. 2020. "From Digital Archaeology to Data-Centric Archaeological Research." *magazén* 1 (1): 35–54. DOI: 10.30687/mag//2020/01/002.
Opgenhaffen, Loes. 2022. "Archives in action. The impact of digital technology on archaeological recording strategies and ensuing open research archives." *Digital Applications in Archaeology and Cultural Heritage* 27: e00231. DOI: 10.1016/j.daach.2022.e00231.
Orman, Levant. V. 2015 "Information Paradox: Drowning in Information, Starving for Knowledge." *IEEE Technology and Society Magazine* 4: 63–73. DOI: 10.1109/MTS.2015.2494359.

Owens, Trevor. 2011 "Defining Data for Humanists: Text, Artifact, Information or Evidence?" *Journal of Digital Humanities* 1 (1).

Padilla Lapuente, José Ignacio. 1984. "Contribución al estudio de las cerámicas grises catalanas de época medieval: El taller, los hornos y la producción de Casampons." *Acta historica et archaeologica mediaevalia* 2: 99–143.

Pastor Díaz de Garayo, Ernesto. 1996. *Castilla en el tránsito de la Antigüedad al Feudalismo. Poblamiento, poder político y estructura social: del Arlanza al Duero (siglos VII-XI)*. Valladolid: Junta de Castilla y León.

Rączkowski, Włodzimierz. 2020. "Power and/or Penury of Visualizations: Some Thoughts on Remote Sensing Data and Products in Archaeology." *Remote Sensing* 12 (18): 2996. DOI:10.3390/rs12182996.

Richards, Julian. D. 2009 "From anarchy to good practice: the evolution of standards in archaeological computing." *Archeologia e Calcolatori* 20: 27–35.

Sandoval, Gustavo. 2021 "Single-Context Recording, Field Interpretation and Reflexivity: An Analysis of Primary Data In Context Sheets." *Journal of Field Archaeology* 46 (7): 496–512. DOI:10.1080/00934690.2021.1926700.

Schöch, Christof. 2013. "Big? Smart? Clean? Messy? Data in the Humanities." *Journal of Digital Humanities* 2 (3).

Shoorcheh, Mahmood. 2019. "On the spatiality of geographic knowledge." *Asian Geographer* 36 (1): 63–80. DOI:10.1080/10225706.2018.1463854.

Stančić, Hrvoje, and Vladimir Bralić. 2021. "Digital Archives Relying on Blockchain: Overcoming the Limitations of Data Immutability." *Computers* 10 (8): 91. DOI:10.3390/computers10080091.

Thibodeau, Kenneth. 2019. "The Construction of the Past: Towards a Theory for Knowing the Past." *Information* 10 (11): 332. DOI:10.3390/info10110332.

Thibodeau, Kenneth. 2021. "Discerning Meaning and Producing Information: Semiosis in Knowing the Past." *Information* 12 (9): 363. DOI:10.3390/info12090363.

Tobalina-Pulido, Leticia, and César González-Pérez. 2020. "Valoración de la calidad de los datos arqueológicos a través de la gestión de su vaguedad. Aplicación al estudio del poblamiento tardorromano." *Complutum* 31 (2): 343–60. DOI:10.5209/cmpl.72488.

Topolski, Jerzy. 1992. *Metodología de la Historia*. Madrid: Cátedra.

Travé-Allepuz, Esther. 2009. "Producció i distribució d'una terrisseria medieval: Cabrera d'Anoia." PhD diss., Universitat de Barcelona. http://hdl.handle.net/10803/2072.

Travé-Allepuz, Esther. 2021. "Building traditional craftsmanship. Some thoughts about endurance and change." *Academia Letters* 4309. DOI:10.20935/AL4309.

Travé-Allepuz, Esther. 2022. "Statistical Analysis of Morphometric Data for Pottery Formal Classification: Variables, Procedures, and Digital Experiences of Medieval and Postmedieval GREYWARE Clustering in Catalonia (Twelfth-Nineteenth Centuries AD)." *Open Archaeology* 8 (1): 1269–85. DOI:10.1515/opar-2022-0269.

Travé-Allepuz, Esther, Pablo del Fresno Bernal, and Alfred Mauri Martí. 2020. "Ontology-Mediated Historical Data Modeling: Theoretical and Practical Tools for an Integrated Construction of the Past." *Information* 10 (4): 182. DOI:10.3390/info11040182.

Travé-Allepuz, Esther, Pablo del Fresno Bernal, Alfred Mauri Martí, and Sonia Medina-Gordo. 2021a. "The Semantics of History. Interdisciplinary Categories and Methods for Digital Historical Research." *International Journal of Interactive Multimedia and Artificial Intelligence* 6 (5): 47–56. DOI:10.9781/ijimai.2021.02.002.

Travé-Allepuz, Esther, Sonia Medina-Gordo, Pablo del Fresno Bernal, Joan Vicens Tarré, and Alfred Mauri Martí. 2021b. "Towards an Ontology-Driven Information System for Archaeological Pottery Studies: The GREYWARE Experience." *Applied Sciences* 11 (17): 7989. DOI:10.3390/app11177989.

Travé-Allepuz, Esther, and Sonia Medina-Gordo. 2021. "Explotación de documentación contable para el estudio de las sociedades mercantiles en la Baja Edad Media: Ontología del sistema FENIX y gestión integrada de Big Data." In *Las Humanidades Digitales como expresión y estudio del patrimonio digital*, edited by María Ángela Celís Sánchez, 259–72. Cuenca: Ediciones de la Universidad de Castilla-La Mancha. https://hdl.handle.net/10578/30437.

Travé-Allepuz, Esther, Patrick S. Quinn, M. Dolores López Pérez, and José Ignacio Padilla Lapuente. 2014. "One hundred sherds of grey: compositional and technological characterization of Medieval GREYWARE pottery production at Cabrera d'Anoia, Catalonia, Spain." *Journal of Archaeological and Anthropological Science* 6: 397–410. DOI:10.1007/s12520-014-0179-2.

Travé-Allepuz, Esther, and Joan Vicens Tarré. 2018. "Terrissa negra i canvi social: pervivències i transformacions en l'ús de ceràmica de cocció reductora a Osona i les comarques gironines a partir de la recerca arqueològica i documental." *Ausa* 28: 829–50.

Uschold, Mike, and Michael Gruninger. 1996 "Ontologies: Principles, methods and applications." *The Knowledge Engineering Review* 11 (2): 93–136. DOI:10.1017/S0269888900007797.

Van Helden, Daniël, Yi Hong, and Penelope Allison. 2018 "Building an Ontology of Tablewares using 'Legacy Data'." *Internet Archaeology* 50. DOI:10.11141/ia.50.13.

Vicens Tarré, Joan, and Esther Travé-Allepuz. 2018. "La terrissa popular de Josep Escortell i

Cerqueda: la tipologia de Quart." *Estudis del Baix Empordà* 37: 97–129.

Vlachidis, Andreas, Ceri Binding, Keith May, and Douglas Tudhope. 2013. "Automatic Metadata Generation in an Archaeological Digital Library: Semantic Annotation of Grey Literature." In *Computational Linguistics. Applications*, edited by A. Przepiórkowski, M. Piasecki, K. Jassem, and P. Fuglewicz, 187–202. Berlin: Springer. DOI: 10.1007/978-3-642-34399-5_10.

Wylie, Alison. 2017. "How Archaeological Evidence Bites Back: Strategies for Putting Old Data to Work in New Ways." *Science, Technology, & Human Values* 42 (2): 203–25. DOI: 10.1177/0162243916671200.

Woolf, Alex. 2009. "A dialogue of the deaf and the dumb: Archaeology, history and philology." In *Approaching Interdisciplinarity: Archaeology, History and the Study of Early Medieval Britain, c. 400–1100*, edited by Zoe L. Delvin, and Caroline N. J. Holas-Clark, 3–9. Oxford: Archaeopress.

10 Supporting the analysis of a large coin hoard with AI-based methods

Chrisowalandis Deligio
Goethe-Universität Frankfurt am Main
chrisowalandis.deligio@gmail.com
ORCID 0000-0002-5708-4271

Karsten Tolle
Goethe-Universität Frankfurt am Main
K.Tolle@em.uni-frankfurt.de
ORCID 0000-0002-9953-7638

David Wigg-Wolf
Römisch-Germanische Kommission
Frankfurt am Main
david.wigg-wolf@dainst.de
ORCID 0000-0002-8604-544X

Abstract

In the project "Classifications and Representations for Networks: From types and characteristics to linked open data for Celtic coinages" (ClaReNet) we had access to image data for one of the largest Celtic coin hoards ever found: Le Câtillon II with nearly 70,000 coins. Our aim was not to develop new processes, but rather to demonstrate how existing tools can be used to support the numismatic task of processing and analysing large complexes of coins, thus validating the enormous potential of IT-based methods. The main steps involved are the pre-sorting of coins by size (denomination), the attribution of individual coins to classes or types, and finally the identification of which coins were struck by individual dies.

The process from digitisation of a hoard as images to an actual die study is lengthy and work-intensive. In testing methods to support each of the steps, we focused particularly on methods that do not need any prior knowledge of the material, in order to explore whether these methods can be applied to a dataset for which there is no more information than the images themselves. The different steps were evaluated against information provided by the numismatist working on the hoard (class and die attributions of the coins), who was also involved in different stages of the process.

The result is a workflow that can be used in future work on large coin finds, thus supporting numismatists and significantly speeding up the work of identification and analysis.

This paper also presents tools, visualisation methods and extensions that proved useful, both for the individual processes, as well as for communicating with the numismatists and integrating their expertise. Earlier phases of our work were presented at CAA 2022 in Oxford.

Keywords: Machine Learning; Celtic coins; Unsupervised Learning; Classification; Object Detection

10.1 Introduction

In our project Classifications and Representations for Networks (ClaReNet), we are exploring and evaluating the application of computer-based methods for the classification of three different Celtic coin series. One of the series consists of the billon staters attributed to the Coriosolitae, a tribe from Brittany, that were included in the hoard of Le Câtillon II found in Jersey in 2012. We are grateful to our collaboration partner Philip de Jersey and Jersey Heritage for allowing us to work on this huge dataset of 120,000 images (some 60,000 for

In *Advances in Digital Archaeology. Proceedings of the 2023 conference Computer Applications and Quantitative Methods in Archaeology – 50 years of synergy*, edited by J.W.H.P. Verhagen, J. Waagen, A. Brandsen, A. Queffelec, R.M. Visser and D. Taelman, 119–130. Leiden: Sidestone Press.

each side of the coins). Before our work began, Jersey Heritage (including 25 volunteers) had invested a huge amount of labour and time in dismantling the hoard, taking the photos and making a first identification of each coin. They provided us with this data during the course of the project.

In order to analyse such an enormous dataset and to generate the data, numismatists conduct a series of tasks with different goals. The process is often a top-down approach, starting with the separation into immediately recognisable groups – in this case different sizes of coins (denominations) – followed by attribution to individual classes or types of coins, and finally even identifying coins produced by the same die. At the same time, damaged, or poorly preserved or corroded coins may be separated, as they are harder to identify and may require more intensive work. As the granularity increases, so do the skill and domain knowledge required. It is this process of analysing a dataset in the several stages into which a numismatist divides the work that forms the focus of this paper. By specifically using different IT-based methods for each stage, the aim is to use well-tried methods to support the process in terms of time benefits, while at the same time ensuring data quality.

The stages are:

1. Pre-sorting – removing those coins that are fragmented or in bad condition and would therefore interfere with or bias later steps.
2. Sorting by size (denomination) – in our specific case separating the staters from the smaller quarter stater and *petits billons* also contained in the hoard.
3. Identifying the coins by class or type – in this case attributing the staters to the six classes of the standard numismatic classification of the coin series.
4. Identifying the coins struck by individual dies within the six classes – such die studies are a basic numismatic tool for reconstructing production processes and economic networks.

For evaluation of our results, we had additional information provided by the Jersey team: a) a list containing the class assignments of the staters as determined by the numismatists, (the ground truth) and b) the results of a die study of the smallest of the six classes of the staters (class VI), containing about 1300 coins. We also included the numismatic expert in all stages of our process, in particular in order to improve the data quality of the ground truth and to receive feedback on the value of the tools and processes that we developed. Finally, we developed a method of visualising the results of the tool for supporting a die study that we developed so that the numismatic expert could test it for the other five classes of staters. It should be noted that the expert estimated the time needed by a single person to fulfil this task in the traditional way, without our tool, would be 150 years.

The paper first introduces the dataset and how it was provided, followed by the pipeline that we developed to mirror the different stages into which numismatists divide such work. First, an object detection method was used to prepare the data and crop the images of the coins, a process which includes size approximation. This was followed by the use of an unsupervised method to filter out corroded or damaged coins and to pre-sort the rest, ideally into classes. Using the result and the information provided, we then moved to a supervised approach on coins that were not filtered or sorted out. The last part focuses on the die study, including methods that were developed to support it, as well as an interactive visualisation tool powered by the Orange Data Mining software.

10.2 A look at the bigger picture

Coins as a more-or less standardised mass product have already been analysed and classified with IT tools for many years. For modern coins, with their machine-based production, many systems can reach over 99% accuracy in identification (Shatrughan and Bawa 2012). Ancient coins are very different, since dies for their production were hand-made and the coins themselves hand-struck, so that both can vary greatly. On top of this, the quality of preservation of individual coins can differ a lot depending on their intensity of circulation (wear) and how corroded they are. In most cases, the coins used for computer vision approaches have come from collections with many well-preserved individual specimens. A good example of this is the Roman Republic Coin Dataset (RRCD) that can be downloaded via Github[1] consisting of some 17,546 images of coins of 100 different classes (coin types). While such a dataset is ideal for comparing computer vision approaches, as done by Anwar et al. (2021), it does not reflect the reality faced by numismatists who deal with coin finds, as exemplified by the coins and photos used here.

For die studies, Heinecke et al. (2021) attempted an automatic approach based on well preserved gold and silver coins, in contrast to our material. So far, attempts at providing an online service or the relevant code have not been successful, although the code for the CADS system (Taylor 2020) is available in GitHub. Essentially, we employed a very similar approach to CADS, but for visualisation of and interaction with the results we decided to simply adopt Orange Data Mining widgets instead of implementing a new system, thus greatly reducing any maintenance problems. We also tailored the system to assist the numismatist in carrying out an actual die study.

1 https://github.com/saeed-anwar/CoinNet?tab=readme-ov-file.

Figure 10.1. Variations in the photos and conditions of the coins (Photos: Jersey Heritage).

Generally, it is important to keep the domain expert in the loop, as this will help increase the usability and practicability of the pipeline and tools developed, as well as create trust in and acceptance of such approaches by future users.

10.3 Data

The dataset made available to us consisted of about 60,000 photos for each face of the coins and included not just the staters that we planned to study, but also smaller coins such as quarter staters and *petits billons*. The photos themselves mostly included not only the coins, but also a scale bar, and sometimes further information such as the inventory number assigned to the coin (ID), or occasionally the class to which the numismatist assigned the coin. Both the coins and the photos were of very mixed quality: there were broken, worn and corroded coins, as well as blurred, overexposed and underexposed photos (Figure 10.1). The variance in the photos was due to them being taken by a number of volunteers without any standardisation. For our projects we focused on the staters, as they are the most common coins in the hoard (about 50,000) and numismatic research on them is more advanced than for the quarters and the *petits billons*. The staters are generally divided by numismatists into six classes (I to VI), a classification which was originally based on the obverse, or "heads" face of the coin (Colbert de Beaulieu 1957). Therefore, we concentrated our work on the obverse. Central information that we had in order to evaluate our work was:

- Staters have an average diameter of about 22 mm, quarter staters and *petits billons* about 13 mm.
- The numismatist provided us with information about the denomination (size) of the coins (stater, quarter stater, ...) and the class they were assigned to (ground truth).
- For one class of the staters (VI for which we had some 1300 images) the numismatist had already carried out an unpublished die study.

10.4 Overview of the pipeline

In order to identify the staters among the 60,000 coins for which we had images we followed a divide and conquer methodology. The aim is to sequentially divide the dataset into smaller batches in order to analyse each one more efficiently. Our pipeline thus included the following steps:

Pre-sorting and size estimation based on Object Detection – Since the focus of our work was the image of the coin itself, the coins need to be detected and cropped from the photos. At the same time the size of the coin can be calculated by detecting the scale bar on the photo, thus allowing a first sorting process to identify the staters based on their being larger than the quarters and *petits billons*.

Further pre-sorting based on unsupervised learning – The intention was to use only the images as input, so that initially we employed methods that do not require any further domain knowledge. This step of the pipeline was repeated in order to identify groups of high similarity that corresponded to the expert's classification, while removing corroded and worn coins to eliminate any bias they might cause.

Classifying the coins by class based on supervised learning – The results of step two were checked against the classification of the expert, and the groups that corresponded to the expert's classification used to train a model to assign the coins from the other batches to the numismatic classes. The domain expert was also involved in the process.

Implementing a die study – By checking the results against the die study already carried out by the expert for one of the classes, we compared different approaches (unsupervised, supervised and feature detection) for their effectiveness in the task. Finally, we implemented a system based on Orange Data Mining in order to support the expert in their ongoing work on the remaining five classes to accelerate the process.

For the steps one to three we used a divide and conquer approach, meaning that we divided the dataset step by step in order to facilitate better analysis at the next step. The

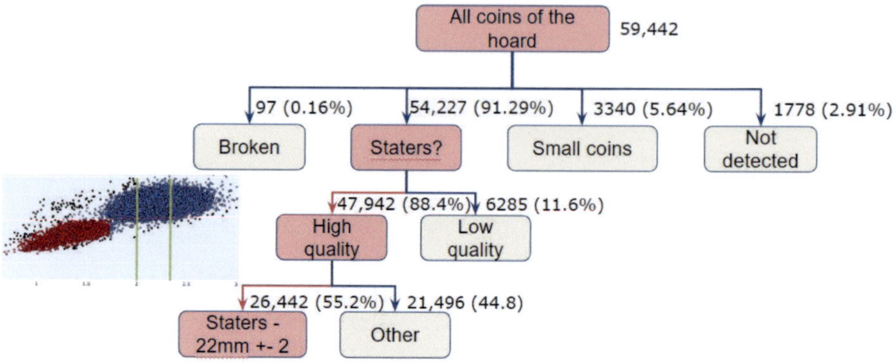

Figure 10.2. Using the divide and conquer methodology, the dataset could be divided step by step into more easily analysable parts (Graphic: C. Deligio).

first division into large/small and broken coins (second row) is the result of object detection and the calculation of the approximate size of the coins. The second division into high and low quality is produced by the unsupervised method, the last one is the result of the application of size identification (step one) together with step two (high/ low quality).

10.5 Object Detection

This step can be seen as a pre-processing step, based on standard approaches in the IT field, with no major training effort needed. Its primary purpose was to crop the coins from the photos so that we could focus on them. At the same time, we were able to use this step to determine the size of the coins using the information in the image itself, thus exploring the potential utility of the method to identify the staters autonomously. As already mentioned, the quality of the photos varied greatly, but their format was generally consistent. For most of the photos, four areas could be defined: the inventory number (ID), the coin, the scale and the class (rare), of which the last two were sometimes missing, in particular the class. For us, the coin and the scale were relevant, while the ID can be retrieved via the file name and the class was available in the spreadsheet provided by the expert (Figure 10.3).

The implementation was carried out with a typical supervised object detection process in which two classes, coin and scale, were defined, and a training and a test dataset were created. As "scale" we defined and labelled the black section of the scale bar representing one centimetre, and not the scale bar itself. It provides the information needed to calculate the size of the coin. The position of the two objects on the images was consistent and the scale was a less complex target due to its representation as a simple black box. Given this consistency, we decided to select only a relatively small dataset in order to first evaluate the procedure: 100 images were chosen as training data, and 25 as test data. They were chosen on a more or less random basis, although it was also important to include small and large, as well as broken coins. Annotation of the data was done using the open-source tool labelImg.[2] The evaluation of the test dataset after training gave a mean average precision of 95% for the calculation of the size. The evaluation for the whole dataset could not be given as a percentage, but by calculating the size of the coins it was possible to identify outliers and thus improve the procedure in a targeted way. In addition to the outliers detected by size, we also manually re-measured 10 coins to check the quality of the result, which was indeed accurate. Finally, we cropped the images of the coins and verified whether they were still completely displayed. Although 100 coins was only a small sample, it did prove that this number of images was sufficient for the task. An overall evaluation would require the annotation of all data, which would be extremely time-consuming and is not essential for the further process. For the implementation, we used Tensorflow's Object Detection API[3] and its Model Zoo[4] in order to select a model architecture. We did not attempt to evaluate the different architectures against each other but decided to use the CenterNet Hourglass104 512x512 architecture by Duan et al. (2019) because it had a good balance between time and accuracy. In Model Zoo, benchmarks are given that have been calculated on the COCO dataset[5], such as the mean average precision, and these can be used as a guide when choosing an architecture.

Once the model had been trained and tested, it was applied to the entire dataset. Each image was cropped and the size was calculated. An optimal result is shown in Figure 10.4. The size calculation is intended to sort the dataset, rather than to calculate minimum and maximum diameter exactly.

Therefore, we decided to take only two measurements: the width and height of the bounding box of the coin that was detected. The size of the coin in centimetres is given

2 labelImg v1.8.1 (2018); https://github.com/HumanSignal/labelImg.
3 https://github.com/tensorflow/models/tree/master/research/object_detection.
4 https://github.com/tensorflow/models/blob/master/research/object_detection/g3doc/tf2_detection_zoo.md.
5 https://cocodataset.org/#home.

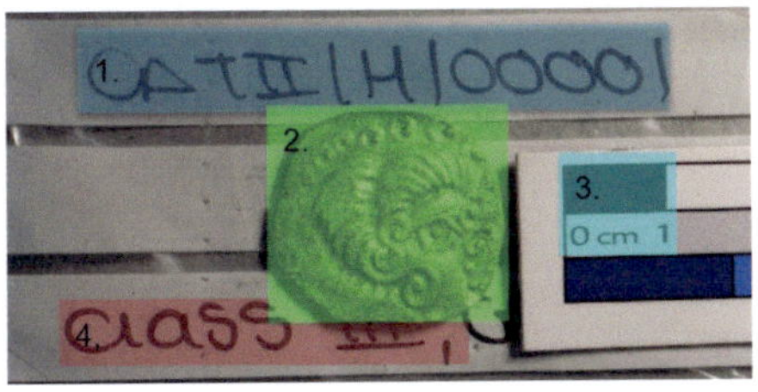

Figure 10.3. The positions of the four defined areas are consistent overall. (Photo: Jersey Heritage).

Figure 10.4. Optimal Prediction of the model. Calculated values: height: 2.321cm, width: 2.194cm. (Photo: Jersey Heritage. Graphic: C. Deligio).

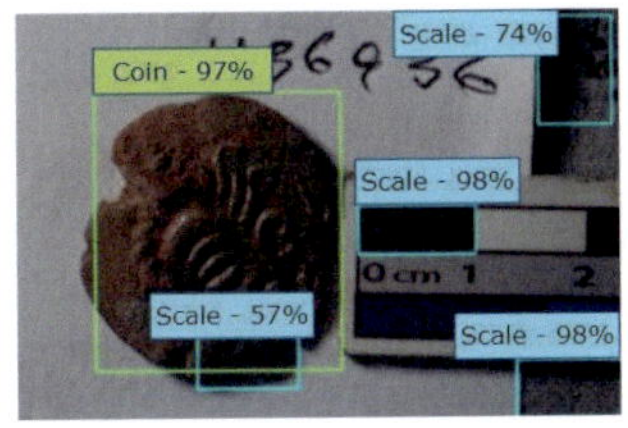

Figure 10.5. Shadowy areas can lead to an incorrect prediction by the model, resulting in a false calculation of size. (Photo: Jersey Heritage. Graphic: C. Deligio).

by dividing these two values for the coin by the width of the bounding box for the scale. The cases where the size calculated for the coin differed greatly from the majority, and was therefore to be classified as an outlier, were considered separately. Figure 10.5 shows such a case. There are several reasons for an incorrect calculation. Sometimes darker or shadowy areas in the image are erroneously classified as the scale, a problem when the target is a black box. In the example in Figure 10.5 there is also an area for which the same percentage as the scale itself was attributed, causing selection problems during the calculation. Where problems were apparent, the images were annotated, thus broadening the training base, as were other suitable images (e.g. images with shadows).

The calculation was made for each photo, i.e. for both sides of the coin, resulting in four measurements for each coin. Comparing the values for both sides can also act as a quality check, and cases where the values were very different were examined more closely. The calculated values in centimetres are visualised in a scatter plot in Figure 10.6. The colour coding is as follows: coins with a height and width deviation of more than 40% are defined as damaged and marked in black. Small coins (probably quarter staters and *petit billons*) are marked in red and large coins (probably staters) are marked in blue. Where we can separate the different groups exactly needs to be examined more closely, but the visualisation shows that there is a gap at about 1.75cm, so we chose this as the boundary. The blue area is the focus of our work because it should contain the staters. But as we want to analyse it in more detail first, we will call this group the "Staters?".

If we look at the peaks of the two point clouds, most of the results are at around 1.3 cm and 2.2 cm. These two values correspond to the information provided by the expert and thus provide first confirmation of the validity of our process. The dataset can therefore be divided into four groups: "Staters?" (54.227 – 91.29%), "Small Coins" (3.340 – 5.64%), "Damaged" (97 – 0.16%) and "Not Detected" (1.778 – 2.91%) (Figure 10.2). The latter contains photos where no scale was available or it was not detected, and therefore no calculation could be carried out.

10.6 Unsupervised learning for pre-sorting

Taking our divide and conquer approach one step further, we selected the "Staters?" group as the dataset for unsupervised learning. The main aim was to see if we can pre-sort the coins into the numismatic classes successfully and compare the results with the classification by the numismatist. Deep Learning and convolutional neural networks (CNNs) were our first choice for image classification, and a promising approach proved to be the DeepCluster method developed by Caron et al. (2018) as illustrated in Figure 10.7. This combines a convolutional neural network with a clustering algorithm for unsupervised training of a CNN. The idea behind this approach is to use the clusters generated as pseudo-labels to train the CNN, and the extracted features in turn serve as input to the clustering algorithm. This process is then repeated for the desired number of epochs.

We used the VGG16 architecture, and as the clustering algorithm k-Means. The required inputs for the system were the images of the coins and the number of desired clusters (k). The choice of k was initially a challenge, for Caron et al. (2018) recommend a much larger k (e.g. the best results are obtained with a k 10 times larger than the actual number of classes). On the other hand, the number of expected classes was known (6), but since we wanted to analyse the dataset without using any prior information, we started with a k equal to 100. To measure another factor of the effectiveness of the method, for our first exercise we entered both the obverse and reverse photos of the coins to see if they would be separated. For the evaluation of the resulting clusters, we avoided the use of any additional information and performed it manually. Based on this manual evaluation, the following observations were made (Figure 10.8):

- Obverse and reverse were generally not mixed within the clusters → showing that the method already works at a high level.

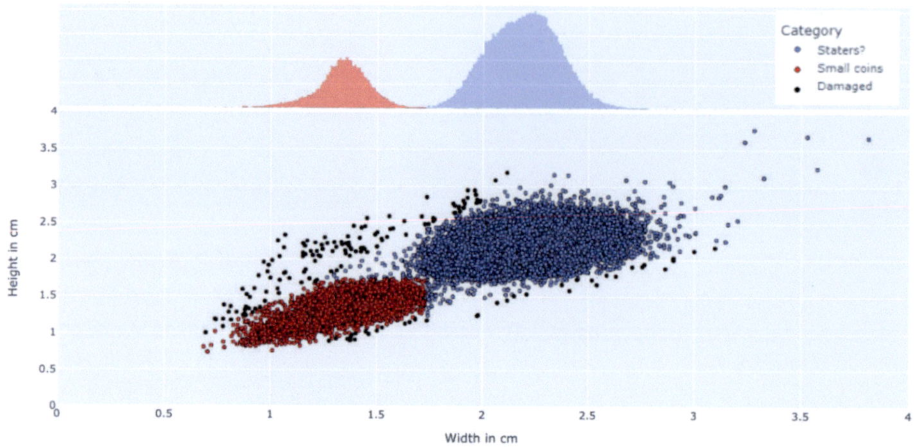

Figure 10.6. Scatter plot of the approximated diameter. (Graphic: C. Deligio).

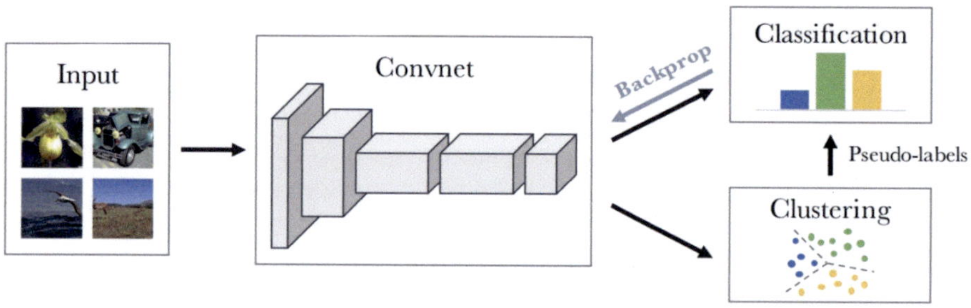

Figure 10.7. DeepCluster implements a method of unsupervised training of a CNN, (Caron et al. 2018).

- Coins in poor condition were grouped together → showing the potential to clean up the dataset for further processing.
- Clusters with different levels of wear were identified.
- There were mixed clusters with no common features → CNNs are complex, often being described as black boxes, and it is not always clear how the clusters were generated.

Many clusters showed strong similarity (based on our manual evaluation), while clusters which had identified corroded and poorly preserved coins were sorted out. This allowed us to divide the dataset into "High Quality" – clusters with a high similarity and well-preserved coins – and "Low Quality" – corroded and worn coins – as well as clusters with a significant mix. In order to have a further degree of certainty we focused on the coins at the centre of the size point cloud, i.e. 2.2 cm ± 0.2 cm (Figure 10.5). This was done to be absolutely sure that only actual staters were present in the dataset (Figure 10.8). Additionally, for the next step we only used the obverse images.

The goal for this new, reduced dataset (c. 26,000 images) was to divide them into the six existing classes for staters defined by numismatists. Running the unsupervised approach with just six classes would generate clusters that are too big and not very useful, so we decided to run it with k=25 (25 clusters), which we then evaluated against the spreadsheet provided by the numismatist of his class attributions (ground truth). The first evaluation was to determine whether our selection did contain only staters, something that was confirmed. By comparing our results with the expert's spreadsheet, we could also check exactly which classes were represented in each cluster: the result was that 18 out of 25 clusters (15,063 images) contained at least 79% of coins of only one single class (the actual values ranged from 79% in cluster 7 to 99,7% in cluster 20). Of those 18 clusters, only 8% of the coins (1208 images) did not correspond to the class given in the numismatist's spreadsheet. One negative result was that we did not manage to find any clusters with only class VI coins, partly since it is by far the smallest class in the dataset with only some 1300 examples present in the hoard. The images of class VI coins were mostly mixed into clusters of class V, or sometimes IV, which is probably a result of the relative similarity with these classes. In total, the attribution by the CNN of 13,855 coins (23% of the total dataset of c. 60,000 coins) were confirmed by the comparison with the spreadsheet. This dataset, verified by two systems, 1) by deep learning and 2) the expert's classification, now formed the basis for the supervised approach (represented by the green segment in the pie chart in Figure 10.9).

10.7 From unsupervised to supervised

This validated dataset was now used as the basis for building a supervised, trained CNN model. As the dataset was highly unbalanced (ranging from 615 to 5317 images per class) and we could not automatically extract class VI

Figure 10.8. Example of clusters generated. (Photos: Jersey Heritage).

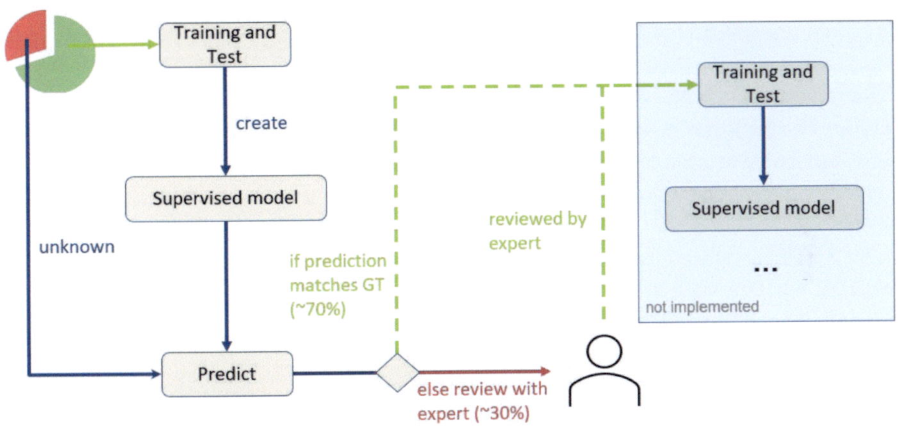

Figure 10.9. The 13,855 images from the previous step were selected as the first training base (green). The 1208 wrongly selected images were used as the first test set (red). The percentages are the results of the predictions for the test set. (Graphic: C. Deligio).

with our method, we adapted the dataset slightly. In order to be able to identify class VI, we added the coins validated by the expert as class VI. Furthermore, we rebalanced the dataset by downsampling to the smallest class. For the CNN architecture we again used VGG16. After training, we used this model to predict the coins that had been clustered wrongly (represented by the red segment of the pie chart in Figure 10.9). For the outcome we involved the numismatic expert because the predictions could have two results: where the prediction matched the ground truth of the spreadsheet, it was basically confirmed. Cases where the prediction differed were not automatically classified as false, but instead saved separately to be reviewed.

Whether the prediction of the CNN or the class given in the ground truth provided by the numismatist was correct had to be decided by someone with domain knowledge, and therefore we involved the numismatist. To do this we created a list with the images of the coins with the ID, together with two values: the CNN's prediction and the class assignment in the ground truth. But which was which was masked so that the numismatic expert could not see it. He could then choose which value was correct, or even specify a new one. Comments by the expert were also encouraged, especially in the case of difficult decisions, as they could help us as non-experts to understand the difficulties. In our first test set (illustrated in Figure 10.9), the CNN model diverged from the ground truth for 30% of the coins (328 out of 1208 images). The

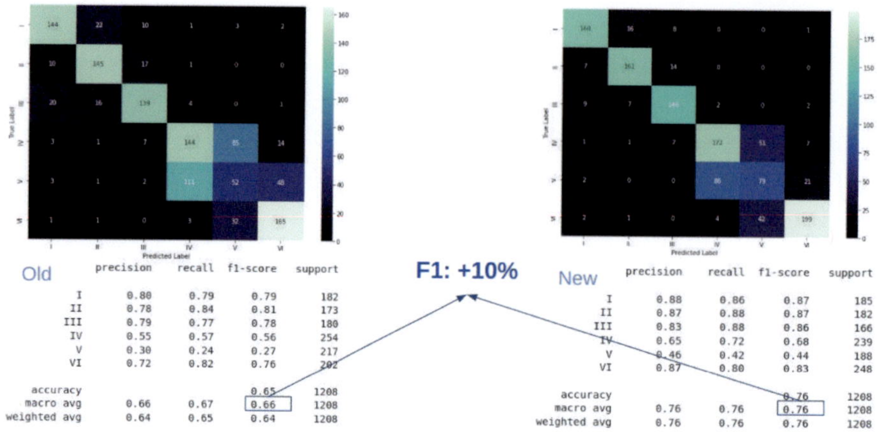

Figure 10.10. Same predictions, different results. Comparison between two classifications (old vs revised). (Graphic: C. Deligio).

review by the expert for these cases could be divided into four cases:

1. The class assigned in the ground truth was actually wrong and was improved by the model → data quality improvement (115 cases – 35%).
2. The class assignment was not clear → problematic cases (26 cases – 8%).
3. The model was wrong (175 cases – 53%), mostly between class IV and V (126 cases).
4. Both were wrong (12 cases – c. 4%).

The model mainly had problems distinguishing between classes IV and V, but the expert had the same problem. We also distributed the list to our project team (i.e. to non-experts) and they also had problems with exactly these two classes. Figure 10.10 presents the CNN's evaluation of the 1208 images with the old classification (the one originally supplied by the expert), together with the result when the expert's revised classification is considered. With the revised classification, the F1 metric increased by 10%. This demonstrates above all that the performance of such a model cannot be calculated exclusively on the basis of metrics, but that the underlying data quality must be taken into consideration.

A next step would be to improve the supervised model by repeating the process (the blue box in Figure 10.9) with the remaining coins, starting by predicting the classes of the coins in the remaining seven of the original 25 stater clusters. This process could then be repeated step by step for the remaining coins that had been excluded in the pre-sorting process.

An important question we also asked ourselves was how to deal with the coins that we defined as "low quality": to what extent could our model be useful for these coins. Using a random sample of 20 images per class from this set, we conducted a small case study. It was of particular interest to see if the model that had been trained on very good images could be applied. Our case study achieved an accuracy of 47%. Figure 10.11 shows the confusion matrix. The figure also shows three examples visualised with GradCam (Selvaraju et al. 2019). It can be seen that the regions that are of most relevance to the class assignment (such as the hair or eye) are focussed on, but that there is also a bias due to the condition of the coins as these are their best-preserved areas. The two images on the left are correctly classified by the model.

This was only a preliminary test, but it demonstrated not only the important role played by the ground truth, but also that the ground truth can and should be questioned. It is also clear that in order to improve the model, more such material should be integrated to counteract the bias of the condition of the coins.

10.8 Supporting a die study

In order to investigate how we might support a die study, we dug further into a single class in order to try to identify coins struck with individual dies. As noted above, for one of the six classes (VI with about 1300 images) an unpublished die study was available to us in order to evaluate our methods. Die recognition brings new challenges for, although there is less data to deal with, the coins are very similar (being of the same class) and there are many dies. Previously we had about 60,000 images with the goal of distinguishing six classes, but now we had only 1300 images of coins struck with some 30 or more dies (based on the unpublished die study). For the implementation, we tested three methods against each other:

1. Reapplying DeepCluster (k=45, as an approximation of the defined die classes).
2. Using our trained supervised model to extract features and then cluster them.
3. Employing algorithms that compare the key points in the image, which has been successfully used on other coinages.

The first two methods are similar in principle but differ in the trained CNN that is used. In (1) the CNN is trained from

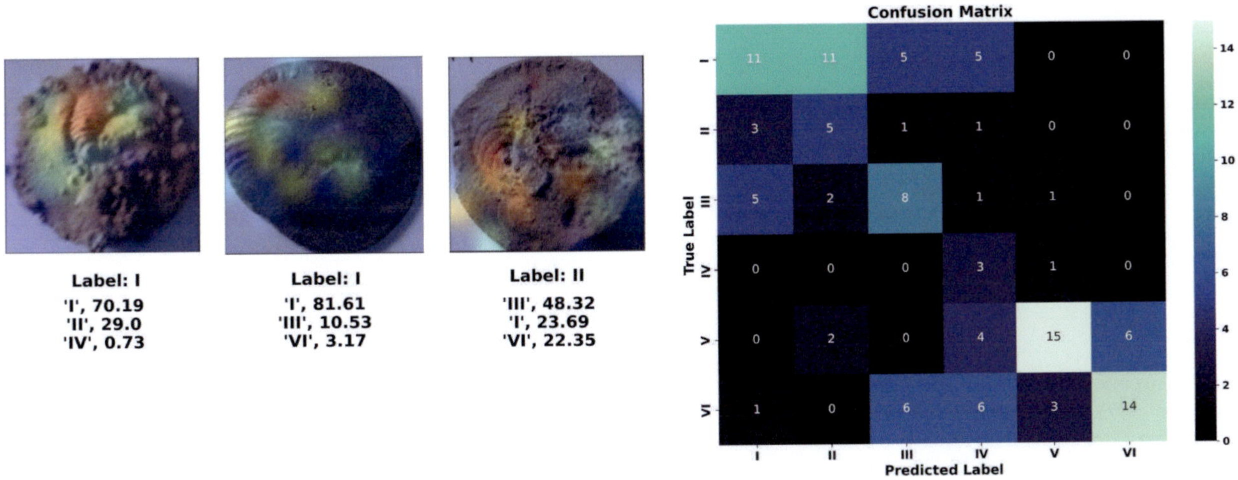

Figure 10.11. Left: the visualisation of the prediction with the top 3 values; right: the matrix of the 120 predictions. An F1 value of 44% and an accuracy of 47% were achieved. (Photos: Jersey Heritage. Graphic: C. Deligio).

scratch using the DeepCluster algorithm, in (2) we used our model that was trained on the six classes in order to extract features. (3) is a very different method to the CNNs and is discussed briefly here. The algorithms used are from the field of image matching, the best known of which are probably SIFT (Scale-invariant feature transform) by Lowe (2004), and SURF (Speeded Up Robust Features) by Bay et al. (2006). Both algorithms are patented, but a popular open-source alternative is ORB (Oriented FAST and rotated BRIEF) by Rublee et al. (2011). Feature matching algorithms have been successfully applied to ancient coins in various publications (Kampel and Zaharieva 2008; Taylor 2020; Heinecke et al. 2021) and for our procedure we used ORB. Some pre-processing steps were employed that had a positive effect on the results in terms of reducing bias (such as scratches arising from the coins' use and wear). The images were converted to greyscale in order to avoid a colour bias and were blurred and contrast adjusted (Heinecke et al. 2021). Finally, a circle crop was applied to remove the edges of the coins and to focus only on the motif. Examples of the input are shown in Figure 10.12.

The process is as follows: the first step consists of key point detection and matching the key points between two images. This comparison is carried out in pairs between all images, a process that mirrors how numismatists conduct analogue die studies, comparing each coin individually with all other coins. The matches found are captured as a vector for each image (resulting in an n x n matrix). The exact method of calculating the key points in ORB is explained in Rublee et al. 2011.

The second step is the same for all three methods. The features from (1) and (2), which are also stored as a vector, and the result from (3) are used as input to a clustering algorithm, in our case hierarchical clustering. We used the Orange Data Mining tool for calculating distances (based on the Spearman distance metric), clustering and visualisation. Figure 10.13 shows the visualisation of the clustering as a dendrogram, using a hierarchical clustering with a complete linkage (already implemented in Orange). The result of the clustering is compared with the existing die study carried out by the expert. In order to evaluate the three methods equally, there are various possibilities; we decided to evaluate them all with the same distance value.[6] We started with the image matching method (3), for which the distance value 0.3 proved to be optimal, and this was also chosen for the other two methods for direct comparison. Table 1 is a summary of the results that were obtained with this value. It shows the best value achieved within a cluster in terms of the number of coins from an individual die that were identified, the mean value of all clusters, and the total number of clusters formed.

The DeepCluster method performs better with a larger amount of data and in this case struggled with the relatively high number of classes for the small number of images. The second method, our supervised trained model, performed somewhat better, with the added advantage that the model already existed, and no additional training time was required. The third method based on ORB worked best. Looking more closely at the results of the third method of the 256 clusters, 208 had at least 70% coins from the same die. Furthermore, 194 of them had only coins of just one die. These 194 clusters contained 489 coins, that is 40% of the dataset.

6 To calculate the distance, we used the Spearman metric.

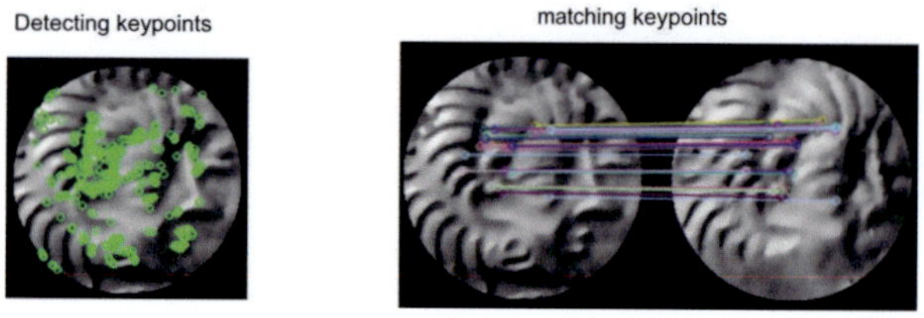

Figure 10.12. Left, an image with detected keypoints. Right, an example of two coin struck with the same die according to the ground truth and their matches. (Photos: Jersey Heritage. Graphic: C. Deligio).

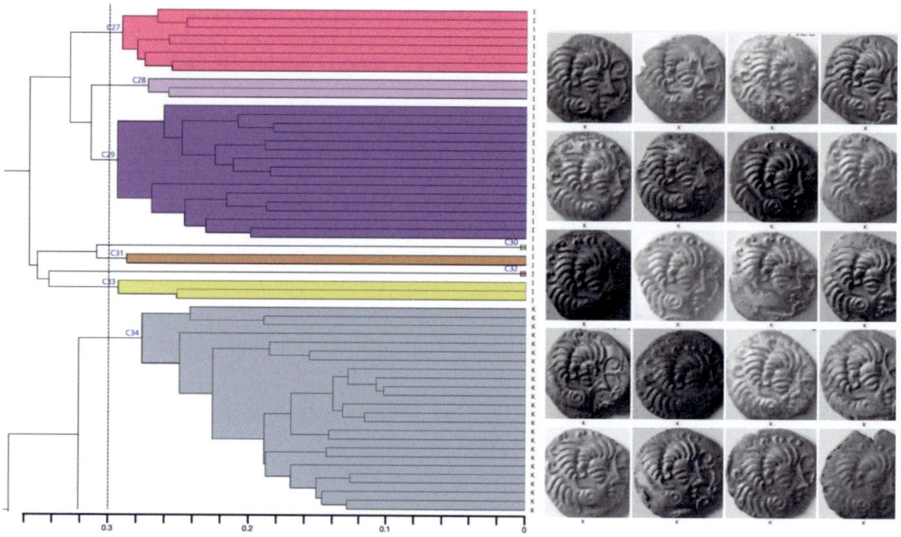

Figure 10.13. Left, part of the dendrogram created with the hierarchical clustering widget in Orange using the Spearman distance, based on the results of ORB. Right, overview of a cluster that contained only coins struck by one die. (Photos: Jersey Heritage. Graphic: C. Deligio).

10.8 Recapitulation and outlook

We started this research by treating the dataset as if it were a case study of a new find, with no information about the coins available at the outset. With the first step of object detection, it was possible to automatically crop the images and, using the scale bar, to calculate the size of the coins and to carry out pre-sorting. This helps to identify the staters, which were the coins with which we wished to work. The IT methods used are standard and, in our case, required little effort/training.

The next step of unsupervised learning still does not need any input from numismatists as domain experts, but the resulting clusters must be evaluated manually. A first process with 100 clusters allowed us to exclude about 12% of the coins, which were identified as unsuitable, badly preserved pieces. The dataset was further narrowed down by taking only staters with a calculated diameter of 22 mm ± 2 mm (the standard size as defined by the numismatist), and the unsupervised method was repeated to produce 25 clusters. Since we had received a spreadsheet from the numismatic expert providing his classification of the coins, it was possible to verify that a) this dataset did indeed contain only staters, and b) that 18 of the 25 clusters mainly contained coins of the same class. The best result was 0.997% (cluster 20: only two of 772 coins are not of the same class). In a situation where the domain expert has not yet classified the coins, it is clear that the pre-sorting into clusters would significantly speed up his task (as is also the case for the method to support a die study that we developed). However, generating a ground truth is mandatory for training a supervised classification model.

Re-evaluating the data with a supervised method led to a significant improvement in data quality. It also showed that experts and AI had similar problems, in particular in distinguishing classes IV and V, which may indicate that the border between the classes is not sharp. Our experience showed that in such cases it is necessary to involve the domain expert in the evaluation process. Specific modifications can be made to influence the areas or features on which the AI concentrates in order to create a model that is closer to the criteria employed by the numismatic expert, for example concentrating on specific areas (e.g. the nose). But since this was not within the scope of our project, we only briefly looked into this direction.

A CNN is a system that learns to distinguish different classes, which includes learning different levels of abstraction from the individual coins. When it comes to studying coins, however, such abstractions are generally not productive because in most cases the amount of data is too small and the differences between the coins can be minimal. It therefore proved useful to look at other

Method	DeepCluster (k=15)	Supervised model (CNN)	Keypoint detection & matching (with ORB)
Nr. of clusters at distance threshold (0.3)	45	172	256
Highest correspondance	60%	75%	100%
Mean	24%	37%	84%

Table 10.1. Supporting a die study. To compare the methods, we used the same threshold (0.3). We calculated two values to evaluate the performance: Highest correspondence with the ground truth in a cluster, and the mean for all clusters.

algorithms (in terms of complexity and computing power required), in our case image matching (ORB). This approach is particularly suitable for small datasets, especially when there are many classes and a high similarity of data, as is shown by the positive results for our die study. Selecting the right approach and algorithm is still a challenge, even for IT experts. This is partly because each approach also requires various subtasks (e.g. different methods of preprocessing or augmentation) and has different possibilities for fine tuning (e.g. the number of clusters, hyperparameter settings, choosing the best loss function for the task).

The results of our work clearly demonstrate that semi-automatic processes can be extremely helpful in sorting and classifying large complexes of coins and can even support a work-intensive and time-consuming die study. We believe that the system we built around Orange Data Mining will speed up the die study for the other five classes of staters in the Le Câtillon hoard. Furthermore, our experience has shown that a human centric approach that involves close cooperation with domain (numismatic) experts can be a good way to increase trust and acceptance of IT methods and achieve a high success rate.

Funding

The Classifications and Representations for Networks (ClaReNet) project on which this report is based was funded by the German Federal Ministry of Education and Research under grant number 01 UG2126A. Responsibility for the content of this publication lies with the authors.

Conflict of interest disclosure

The authors declare the following non-financial conflict of interest: David Wigg-Wolf is a recommender for PCI Archaeology.

Data, scripts, code, and supplementary information availability

Implementations used in this paper: https://github.com/Frankfurt-BigDataLab/2023_CAA_ClaReNet.

Official implementation of DeepCluster by Caron et al. (2018): https://github.com/facebookresearch/deepcluster.

Annotation tool used: https://github.com/heartexlabs/labelImg.

Implementing an object detection model: https://github.com/sglvladi/TensorFlowObjectDetectionTutorial.

For implementing a supervised model: https://www.tensorflow.org/tutorials/images/transfer_learning.

Useful augmentations library: https://albumentations.ai.

Tool for visualising results (and more): https://orangedatamining.com.

Peer review

This article has been reviewed and recommended by PCI Archaeology.

Brandsen, Alex. 2024. “A demonstration of the use and finetuning of existing machine learning tools for analysing large complexes of coins.” *Peer Community in Archaeology* 100397. DOI: 10.24072/pci.archaeo.100397.

References

Anwar, Hafeez, Saeed Anwar, Sebastian Zambanini, and Fatih Porikli. 2021. “Deep Ancient Roman Republican Coin Classification via Feature Fusion and Attention.” *Pattern Recognition* 114: 107871. DOI: 10.1016/j.patcog.2021.107871.

Bay, Herbert, Tinne Tuytelaars, and Luc Van Gool. 2006. “SURF: Speeded Up Robust Features.” In *Computer Vision – ECCV 2006. Lecture Notes in Computer Science Vol. 3951*, edited by Aleš Leonardis, Horst Bischof, and Axel Pinz. Berlin: Springer. https://link.springer.com/chapter/10.1007/11744023_32.

Caron, Mathilde, Piotr Bojanowski, Armand Joulin, and Matthijs Douze. 2018. “Deep Clustering for Unsupervised Learning of Visual Features.” arXiv. DOI: 10.48550/arXiv.1807.0552.

Colbert de Beaulieu, Jean-Baptiste. 1957. “Le trésor de Jersey-11 et la numismatique celtique des deux Bretagnes.” *Revue Belge de Numismatique* 103: 47–88.

Duan, Kaiwen, Song Bai, Lingxi Xie, Honggang Qi, Qingming Huang, and Qi Tian. 2019. "CenterNet: Keypoint Triplets for Object Detection." arXiv. DOI:10.48550/arXiv.1611.10012.

Heinecke, Andreas, Emanuel Mayer, Abhinav Natarajan, and Yoonju Jung. 2021. "Unsupervised Statistical Learning for Die Analysis in Ancient Numismatics." arXiv. DOI:10.48550/arXiv.2112.00290.

Huang, Jonathan, Vivek Rathod, Chen Sun, Menglong Zhu, Anoop Korattikara, Alireza Fathi, Ian Fischer, Zbigniew Wojna, Yang Song, Sergio Guadarrama, and Kevin Murphy. 2017. "Speed/Accuracy Trade-Offs for Modern Convolutional Object Detectors." arXiv. DOI:10.48550/arXiv.1611.10012.

Kampel, Martin, and Maia Zaharieva. 2008. "Recognizing Ancient Coins Based on Local Features." In *Advances in Visual Computing. ISVC 2008. Lecture Notes in Computer Science Vol. 5358*, edited by George Bebis, Richard Boyle, and Bahram Parvin, 11–22. Berlin: Springer. DOI:10.1007/978-3-540-89639-5_2.

Karami, Ebrahim, Siva Prasad, and Mohamed Shehata. 2017. "Image Matching Using SIFT, SURF, BRIEF and ORB: Performance Comparison for Distorted Images." arXiv. DOI:10.48550/arXiv.1710.02726.

Lowe, David G. 2017. "Image Features from Scale-Invariant Keypoints." *International Journal of Computer Vision* 60: 91–110. DOI:10.1023/B:VISI.0000029664.99615.94.

Rublee, Ethan, Vincent Rabaud, Kurt Konolige, and Gary Bradski. 2011. "ORB: An Efficient Alternative to SIFT or SURF." In *2011 International Conference on Computer Vision, Barcelona, Spain*, 2564–71. IEEE. DOI:10.1109/ICCV.2011.6126544.

Selvaraju, Ramprasaath R., Michael Cogswell, Abhishek Das, Ramakrishna Vedantam, Devi Parikh, and Dhruv Batra. 2019. "Grad-CAM: Visual Explanations from Deep Networks via Gradient-Based Localization." *International Journal of Computer Vision* 128: 336–359. DOI:10.1007/s11263-019-01228-7.

Shatrughan, Modi, and Seema Bawa. 2012. "Image Processing Based Systems and Techniques for the Recognition of Ancient and Modern Coins." arXiv. DOI:10.48550/arXiv.1312.6599.

Taylor, Zachary McCord. 2020. "The Computer-Aided Die Study (CADS): A Tool for Conducting Numismatic Die Studies with Computer Vision and Hierarchical Clustering." Honors diss., Computer Science, Trinity University.

11 Study and enhancement of the heritage value of a fortified settlement along the Limes Arabicus

Umm ar-Rasas (Amman, Jordan) between remote sensing analysis, photogrammetry and laser scanner surveys

Francesca Di Palma
University of Bari 'Aldo Moro' / Institute of Heritage Science of the Italian National Research Council (CNR-ISPC), Lecce
francescadipalma1@cnr.it
ORCID 0009-0004-9695-0197

Roberto Gabrielli
Institute of Heritage Science of the Italian National Research Council (CNR-ISPC), Rome
ORCID 0000-0002-9603-252X

Pasquale Merola
Institute of Heritage Science of the Italian National Research Council (CNR-ISPC), Lecce
ORCID 0000-0001-8631-8957

Ilaria Miccoli
Institute of Heritage Science of the Italian National Research Council (CNR-ISPC), Lecce

Giuseppe Scardozzi
Institute of Heritage Science of the Italian National Research Council (CNR-ISPC), Lecce,
ORCID 0000-0002-8931-4887

Abstract

The Limes Arabicus provides an excellent opportunity to experiment with historical remote sensing data in identifying and mapping fortified centres along the eastern frontier of the Roman and Byzantine Empires. Remote sensing, combined with modern surveying techniques and tools such as photogrammetry and laser scanners, enables the identification, documentation, and study of ancient settlements. It also facilitates the development of site valorisation programmes, including the design of real and virtual routes for better use of archaeological areas. This is a preliminary contribution to the site of Umm ar-Rasas (Amman, Jordan), a fortified town located to the east of the Via Traiana Nova. The paper discusses investigations conducted between 2021 and 2022. During this period, a series of analyses and elaborations were carried out on historical and recent satellite data, including Corona KH-4B, Hexagon KH-9, Pléiades-1A, and Pléiades Neo 4, as well as field research. The purpose was to document aerially recognized emergencies and to survey and locate them from the ground. Moreover, a photogrammetric and laser scanner survey of the castrum has been conducted in recent years.

Keywords: Limes Arabicus: Remote Sensing analysis; High-resolution satellite images; Laser scanner survey; Photogrammetry; Historical landscape

11.1 Introduction

Umm ar-Rasas, the current governorate of Amman, is situated approximately 30 km southeast of Madaba (Figure 11.1a). It is an archaeological site renowned for its Byzantine mosaics, which characterise its churches. These mosaics were excavated between the second half of the 1980s and the early 2000s.

In *Advances in Digital Archaeology. Proceedings of the 2023 conference Computer Applications and Quantitative Methods in Archaeology – 50 years of synergy*, edited by J.W.H.P. Verhagen, J. Waagen, A. Brandsen, A. Queffelec, R.M. Visser and D. Taelman, 131–146. Leiden: Sidestone Press.

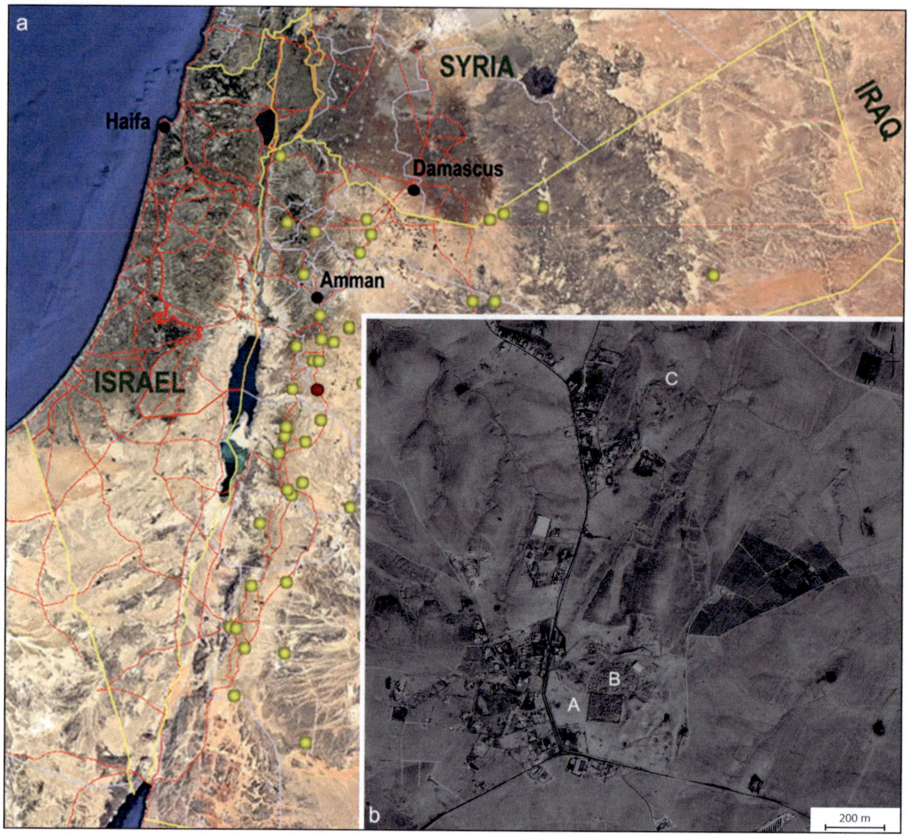

Figure 11.1. a) Site location (Google Earth, © Maxar Technologies, map by Francesca Di Palma); b) Framing of the archaeological area: castrum (A); Byzantine-Umayyad village (B); Stylite tower complex (C) (Pléiades 1-A from 30/10/2020, edited by Francesca Di Palma).

The site is characterised by the presence of three settlement units: the castrum (A), which dates to the end of the third and beginning of the fourth centuries AD; the Byzantine-Umayyad village, which is located to the north (B); and the Stylite tower complex, which is situated approximately 2 km to the north (C; Figure 11.1b).

11.1.1 State of art

Umm ar-Rasas in Arabic means "mother of lead". The toponym probably refers to the size and colour of the stones that distinguish the castrum. It was the destination of explorations since 1800 (Burchardt 1822; Irby and Mangles 1823; Buckingham 1825; Robinson 1837; Seetzen 1854, Palmer 1871, 498–500; Tristram 1874; Layard 1887; Vailhé 1896; Germer-Durand 1897; Clermont-Ganneau 1898; Lagrange 1898; Wilson 1899; Brünnow and Domaszewski 1905, 63–72; Musil 1907; Glueck 1934; Savignac 1936; Saller and Bagatti 1949, 244–5). In 1986, two inscriptions discovered in mosaic floors of the Lion Church and St. Stephen's Church permitted to link the site to the biblical and historical *KASTRON MEFA*. *Mefaat* was the city of the Ruben tribe (Gs. 13, 18; 21, 37; 1Cr. 6, 64; Ger. 48, 21), the *φρούριον* mentioned in the *Onomasticon* of Eusebius (*Onomasticon* 128, 21) and the Roman camp of *Equites Promoti Indigenae* mentioned in the *Notitia Dignitatum* (*NotitiaDignitatum*, p. 81, n. 19).

In 1939, the site was explored from the air by Sir Marc Aurel Stein. Between 1986 and 2006, the Studium Biblicum Franciscanum of Jerusalem excavated the churches of the Byzantine village immediately north of the castrum (Abela and Acconci 1997; Abela and Pappalardo 1998; 2002; 2004; Piccirillo 1986; 1987; 1998a; 1988b; 1989; 1991b; 1992b; 1995; 1996; 1997; 1999; 2001; 2002; 2003; 2006; Piccirillo and Alliata 1994; Piccirillo and Attiyat 1986; Piccirillo, Abela, and Pappalardo 2005; 2007). Finally, the Swiss Max van Berchem Foundation (1988–2000) studied a tiny part of the castrum. The gates, particularly the east gate, as well as the south-east portion of the walls, comprising the twin churches, were explored (Bujard 1992; Bujard 2008; Bujard and Joguin 1995; Bujard and Haldimann 1988). In 2004, Umm ar-Rasas was designated a UNESCO World Heritage Site (Abu Dayyeh 2002).

11.1.2 The Kastrum Project

In 2013, Roberto Gabrielli began a project aimed at documenting, enhancing, and musealising the archaeological area of Umm ar-Rasas (Figure 11.2). Seven successful missions incorporating the churches of the Saint Stephen complex and the Stylite Tower were carried out between 2013 and 2019 (Cozzolino et al. 2019; Gabrielli et al. 2016, 236–40; Malinverni et al. 2019). Various topographic surveys were undertaken throughout those

Figure 11.2. Kastrum Project, Umm ar-Rasas, 2013. Laser scanner and photogrammetric tests (Roberto Gabrielli ©).

years, as well as 3D surveys of structures and mosaic floors utilising GPS, photogrammetry, and laser scanners. Several tests have been carried out over the years to establish a method that would allow for the comprehensive documentation of the mosaic flooring in high resolution utilising photogrammetry techniques with a significant number of pictures and approximately thirty scans for the church (Gabrielli et al. 2017).

Since 2021, the already multidisciplinary study team has expanded even more, and research on the castrum and its surroundings has resumed, utilising remote sensing analyses and surveys (architectural, archaeological, photogrammetric, and laser scanners).

11.1.3 Research aims

This paper presents the results of the most recent field campaigns. The primary objective was the aerotopographic study of the site and the laser scanning survey of the castrum. The aim of the study and surveys was twofold: firstly, to address a series of questions concerning the structure of the castrum and the extent of the Byzantine settlement that had not been answered by previous research; secondly, to create an updated archaeological map of the area. The goal of this map is not only to locate all the relevant archaeological evidence, but also to enhance the area as a useful tool for the design of itineraries for tourists visiting.

11.2 Methods, tools and results

This section presents the methods and tools used during the last two years of remote sensing and fieldwork at Umm ar-Rasas. The research has focused on the study of Umm ar-Rasas (castrum and settlement) and its surroundings, using mostly unpublished historical and recent remote sensing data. Research has also focused on ground, architectural, photogrammetric and laser scanning surveys. In particular, photogrammetric and laser scanning surveys were carried out on the walls of the castrum All features verified on the ground were identified through the application of remote sensing analysis.

11.2.1 Remote sensing analysis

The study commenced with a remote sensing analysis, the principal research tools employed being historical aerial photographs taken by Sir Marc Aurel Stein in 1939 during a flight over Umm ar-Rasas and satellite panoramic camera photographs taken by Corona KH-4B. However, the most significant contribution has been the recently declassified Hexagon KH-9, which has been instrumental in contextualising the site. Finally, the use of recent high- and very high-resolution satellite images (0.50–0.30 m ground resolution) has enabled the recording of the current state of preservation of the traces and the discovery of new ones (Di Palma 2025).

Sir Marc Aurel Stein was a Hungarian-born, naturalised English explorer of late 19th and early 20th centuries. In the late 1930s, he conducted significant aerial and ground surveys of the Roman Eastern Frontier between Iraq and Jordan, following the work of Father Antoine Poidebard in Syria (Poidebard 1934). Stein left the Sinjar in the spring of 1938 and completed the mission in May of 1939. On his journey, he used the Kirkut-Haifa oil pipeline and then explored the archaeological sites of the Eastern Roman Limes to the Aqaba Gulf (Stein 1938;1940). In May 1939, Stein flew to Umm ar-Rasas and made four aerial photographs, one vertical and three oblique, at heights of 1200 and 600 feet, respectively (Figure 11.3). These photographs enable us to recreate the topography and landscape of the archaeological site. They capture a desert landscape marked by the pure presence of ruins. A desert landscape is crossed by roads and wadis but without modern overlays, such as urbanisation or new agricultural land use.

Figure 11.3. Umm ar-Rasas May 6, 1939. The aerial photographs taken by Stein. I) a vertical view of the castrum from 1200 feet above ground; II-III) oblique views of the castrum and village from the northeast and south, respectively, at a height of 600 feet; IV) an oblique view of the Stylite complex from the north, also at a height of 600 feet (British Academy of London Archive).

Historical satellite photographs, in particular a Hexagon KH-9 from 1974, suggest a landscape very similar to that photographed by Stein. Hexagons are well-known panoramic satellite images taken by American spy satellites between 1971 and 1984. Their accuracy on the ground ranges from 0.60 to 1.20 metres. In addition to the three settlement units (A – the Tetrarchic Castrum, with its water reservoir, in the south; B – the Byzantine-Umayyad settlement, immediately to the north of castrum; C – the Stylite complex tower, about two kilometres to the north), the 1974 Hexagon allowed us to better contextualise the archaeological evidence. From the north to the south, these comprised quarries and material extraction sites (marked in yellow on the plan); irrigation and hydraulic systems (dams and canals – D), which describe the surrounding zone; and a large dam to the NE (about 1.5 km from the castrum – E) (Figure 11.4). More specifically, we can make out a series of roadways

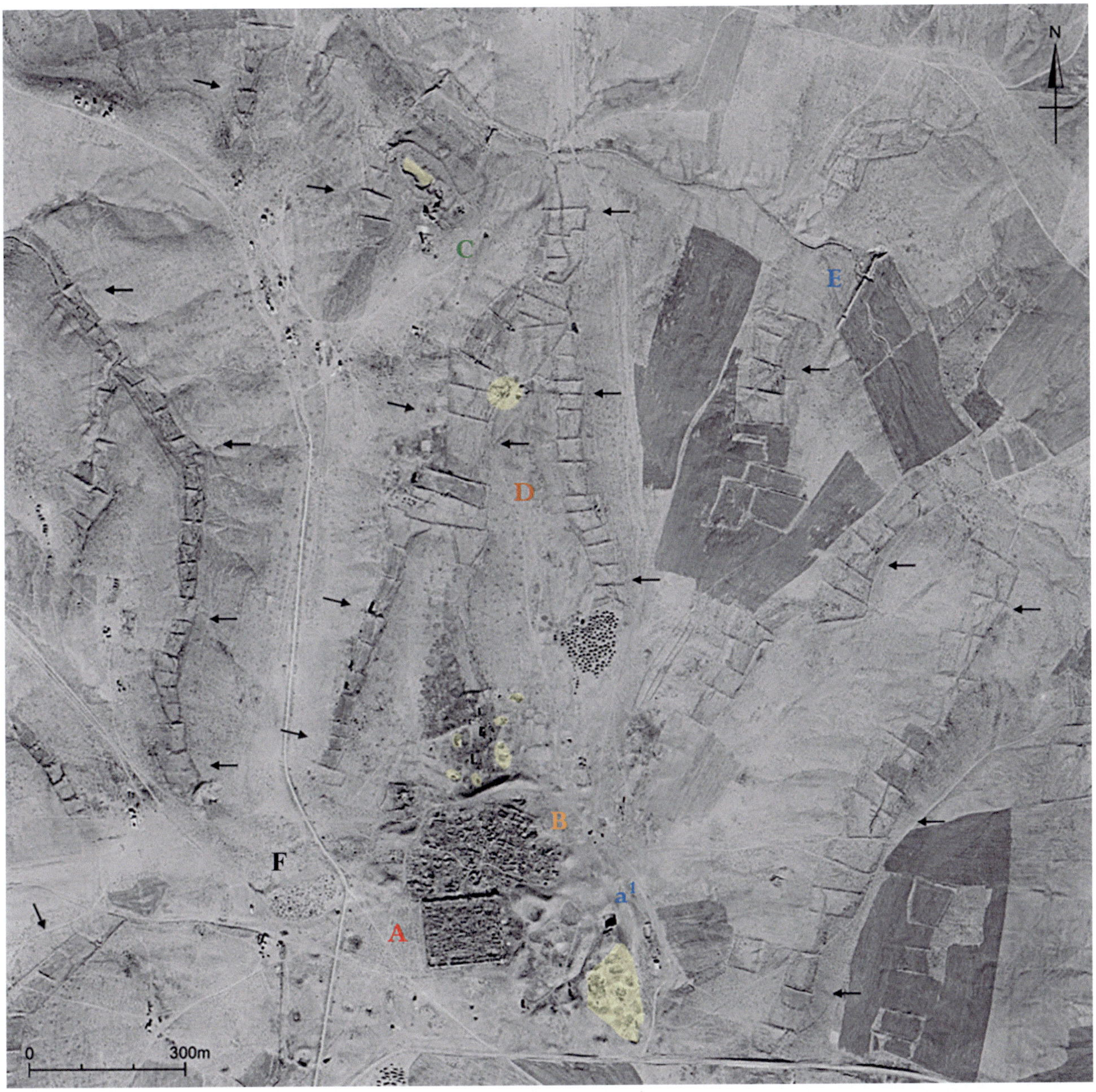

Figure 11.4. Umm ar-Rasas. Hexagon KH-9 images 1974/12/01, ground resolution: 1.20-0.60 m. Featured: A Roman castrum; a[1] hydraulic reserve; B Byzantine and Umayyade settlement; C Stylite tower complex; D System of irrigated plots (channels and dams); E the dam ; F the Byzantine cemetery. Quarries and material extraction points are highlighted in yellow, whilst arrows indicate hydraulic channelling systems (Hexagon acquired from USGS and edited by Francesca Di Palma).

that lead to, cross, or border the Byzantine hamlet, the cemetery (F), as well as a network of canals and water storage facilities southeast and east of the castrum. The northernmost component, the Stylite tower complex, clearly displays canal-dam systems (Figure 11.4.). We can assess the conservation state of the traces of the fossilised agricultural ecosystem seen on the Hexagon by comparing them to a recent and high-resolution satellite image, Pléiades 1-A from 2020 (Figure 11.5).

Additionally, archaeological features from published maps were georeferenced and vectorised using the 2020 Pléiades-1A. Furthermore, it was essential to validate, georeference, and vectorise (in QGIS) any data observed through on-site remote sensing analysis.

In order to make archaeological and palaeoenvironmental traces and remains more legible, the Pléiades-1A satellite image was lastly processed utilising data fusion and different enhancing techniques.

Figure 11.5. Umm ar-Rasas. The Pléiades 1A satellite's image acquired on October 30, 2020, ground resolution 0.50m. Featured: A Roman castrum; a[1] hydraulic reserve; B Byzantine and Umayyade settlement; C Stylite tower complex; D System of irrigated plots (channels and dams); E the dam. The hydraulic channelling systems remain visible, albeit less prominent than depicted in the Hexagon image (acquired from Planetek Italia srl and edited by Francesca Di Palma).

The image processing of optical satellite data, carried out using specific software (see below) in order to facilitate the identification and examination of archaeological marks and anomalies, represents one of the possibilities offered by the remote sensing application for archaeology.

A satellite image is a matrix of pixels, and the value of each is related to the solar energy reflected by the corresponding portion of the earth's surface. This energy is divided into various bands of the electromagnetic spectrum: a small portion of this radiation, divided into the blue, green, and red bands, gives an image similar to that of an aerial photo; another portion, wider and particularly important, especially for archaeological studies, is occupied by the Red Edge (720 nm) and Near Infrared (840 nm) channels, which allow the investigation of elements and phenomena of the earth's surface otherwise not visible to the human eye. These two bands are very important for archaeological applications because they are particularly sensitive to stress factors in vegetation growth, which, as is known, is one of the main mediating elements of the archaeological features (crop marks). The presence of positive buried ancient structures (wall structures, floors,

Figure 11.6. Umm ar-Rasas area in the panchromatic band of Pléiades 1A image.

ruins) affects the vegetation growth, while the negative archaeological structures or even palaeo-elements of the ancient landscape (ditches, canals, excavated trenches, but also depressions and palaeo-riverbeds) favour full vegetation growth thanks to ideal conditions in the humus soil layer that is very drained of humidity.

Over the years, numerous methodologies and techniques have been developed to improve these images, i.e., processing classes that operate on the particular radiometric, spectral, and geometric properties of satellite data (Lasaponara and Masini 2012). These elaborations are necessary to increase the readability of the images and to better discriminate small differences in tone and colour, which, as is well known, are useful indicators in the identification of marks related to buried or semi-surfaced ancient structures.

Therefore, the availability of two very high-resolution satellite images that capture the Umm ar-Rasas area – the first image acquired on October 30, 2020, by the Pléiades-1A satellite and the other acquired on January 25, 2022 by the Pléiades Neo-4 satellite – has allowed us to test the potential of remote sensing applications through specific data processing chains for the investigation of the ancient topography of the site and its territory. Compared with its predecessors Pléiades constellation, which provides four multispectral bands, Blue, Green, Red and Near Infrared (Pléiades satellites provide images with a resolution of 0.5 m in panchromatic mode and a resolution of 2 m in multispectral mode, https://earth.esa.int/eogateway/catalog/pleiades-esa-archive), Pléiades Neo images have a better spatial resolution and have two additional bands, the Deep Blue and the Red Edge, thus adding important information on the earth's surface characteristics (Pléiades Neo satellites provide images with a resolution of 0.3 m in panchromatic mode and a resolution of 1.2 m in multispectral mode, https://earth.esa.int/eogateway/missions/pleiades-neo).

Pléiades Neo data products are characterised by two images: the RGB image, with Red, Green and Blue bands, and NED image, with and Near-infrared, Red Edge and Deep Blue bands. As anticipated, Red Edge is very important for

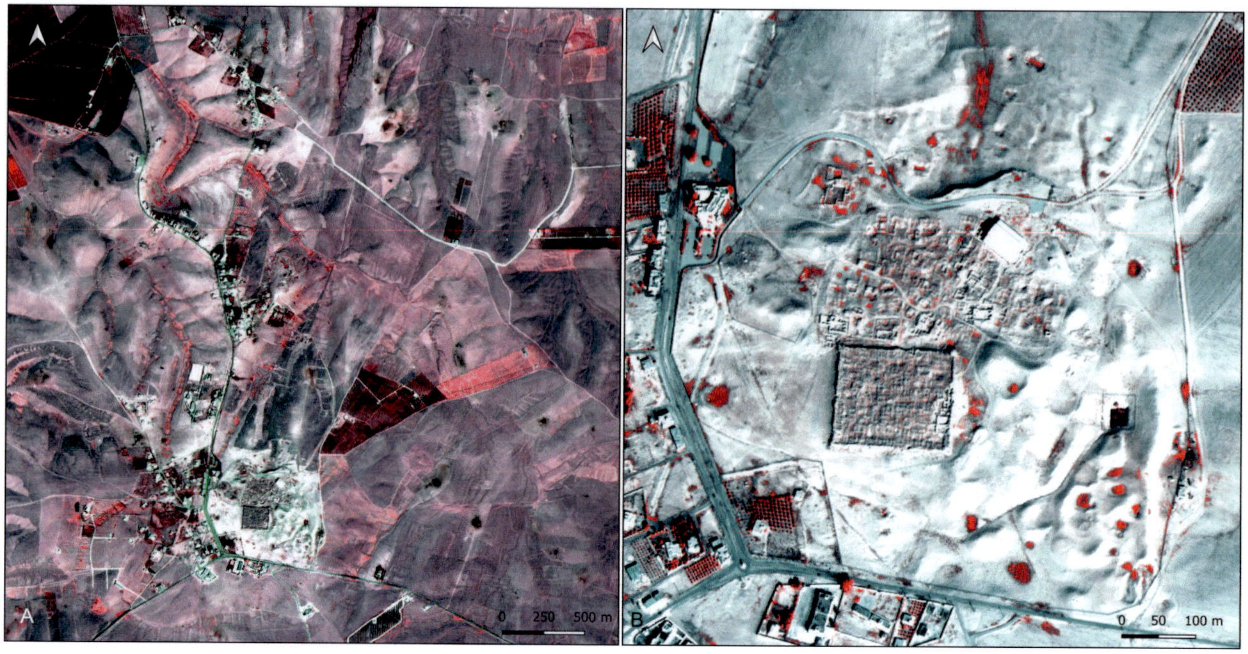

Figure 11.7. (A) Umm ar-Rasas. RGB Colour Composite in false colour of the Pléiades 1A image showing the general view of the Umm ar-Rasas area, and (B) of the Pléiades Neo-04 image showing a detailed area of the Late Antique castrum and the Umayyad village (processing and editing by Ilaria Miccoli).

archaeological applications because it is used for analysis of vegetation status through detailed photosynthesis characterization. Thanks to the availability of the images in Standard Ortho mode (the product is a georeferenced image in Earth geometry and is corrected from acquisition and terrain off-nadir effects), the pre-processing operations, which involve the geometric and radiometric correction of the image, have been skipped.

For the two images of Umm ar-Rasas, the most performing processing chains were then applied for the identification of the archaeological traces and are already widely used in consolidated remote sensing studies applied to archaeology: the RGB Colour Composite, the Datafusion and the Principal Component Analysis. The software used was ENVI 4.7. A necessary and preparatory first step to the subsequent image processing phases was a qualitative examination based on the visual inspection of each band.

This phase was necessary to verify the visibility of the different types of traces and their immediate surroundings and to evaluate which bands guarantee more effective discrimination of their spectral or radiometric separability. The evaluation showed that, to the detriment of the spectral information, the panchromatic band proved to be very useful in the identification of the micro-reliefs produced by buried or semi-buried ancient structures because its very high spatial resolution allows the detailed visualisation of the micro-reliefs (Figure 11.6). On the other hand, the spectral bands, in particular the near infrared, the red edge, and the red, allow us to investigate characteristics of the soil surface, such as the surroundings of buried elements that appear more vegetated or humid. Once the properties of each band have been examined in depth, the effective processing chain has begun.

Among the most basic processing techniques, there is undoubtedly the RGB Colour Composite, which allows viewing the image with a different order of band overlapping, useful for perceiving some information better than others. So, the image is displayed with an appearance similar to what the human eye perceives in the "true colour combinations", while in other combinations, called "false colour combinations", the near infrared or red edge band, invisible to the human eye, appears in place of the red and green bands.

In the case of the Umm ar-Rasas site, the simple composition of bands with false colours facilitated, making it more visible, the preliminary visual analysis of the more humid and vegetated surfaces, normally difficult to identify in these geographical contexts characterised by very arid conditions but potentially indicative of disappearing elements of the ancient landscape. This result is particularly clear in the false-colour composition of the Pléiades 1A image, acquired in October, a period when the soil is not excessively dry. The infrared band (visible in red) and the red band (visible in green) show a consistent network of small wadis exploited through reclamation and regimentation works to obtain cultivable areas (Figure 11.7A). While other interesting features are more

Figure 11.8. Pansharpened product of the data fusion technique by panchromatic and multispectral data of Pléiades Neo-04 image (processing and editing by Ilaria Miccoli).

evident in the false colour composition of the Pléiades Neo image, the small vegetated and rounded depressions that are highlighted within the remains of the buried village could correspond to disused cisterns (Figure 11.7B).

Other image processing techniques, useful for obtaining the maximum information in qualitative and quantitative terms, were therefore employed. The data fusion technique of the panchromatic and multispectral data of the Pléiades Neo-04 of 2022, exploiting the high spatial resolution of the panchromatic image (0.30 m) and the high spectral resolution of the multispectral image (6 bands), was performed to obtain an optimal result. This operation, carried out using the "Gram-Schmidt" method of the ENVI routine, produced a "pan-sharpened image", a new image where the spectral resolution of the colour bands has been adapted to the resolution of the panchromatic data (Lasaponara et al. 2007, 213–17).

The result obtained was a good qualitative image for the discrimination of spatial details and a good quantitative image for the discrimination of a series of crop marks and dump marks highlighted, as mentioned before, by the responses in the infrared band, the red edge, and red (Figure 11.8).

The choice to apply Principal Component Analysis technique (PCA) using the pansharpened bands and to minimise the redundancy in information in some areas seemed quite effective (Lasaponara et al. 2010, 486–90). Among the six new bands obtained, the best ones were the first (PC1) and second (PC2) bands of the RGB image and of the NED image (Figure 11.9).

At this point, some operations were tested to combine the products obtained from the individual enhancement techniques into a new false colour composition; this operation does not improve the analysis of the anomalies much, but overall, it offers a more immediate perception of some feature traces.

Finally, since the outputs of the various processing products were exported in geotiff format, their loading into a GIS platform was sufficient to implement the information layers of the project. After a further visual examination and interpretation of the images based on other contextual information, the traces and anomalies identified were vectorised (Di Palma's remote sensing analysis was updated and presented in Cozzolino et al. 2025).

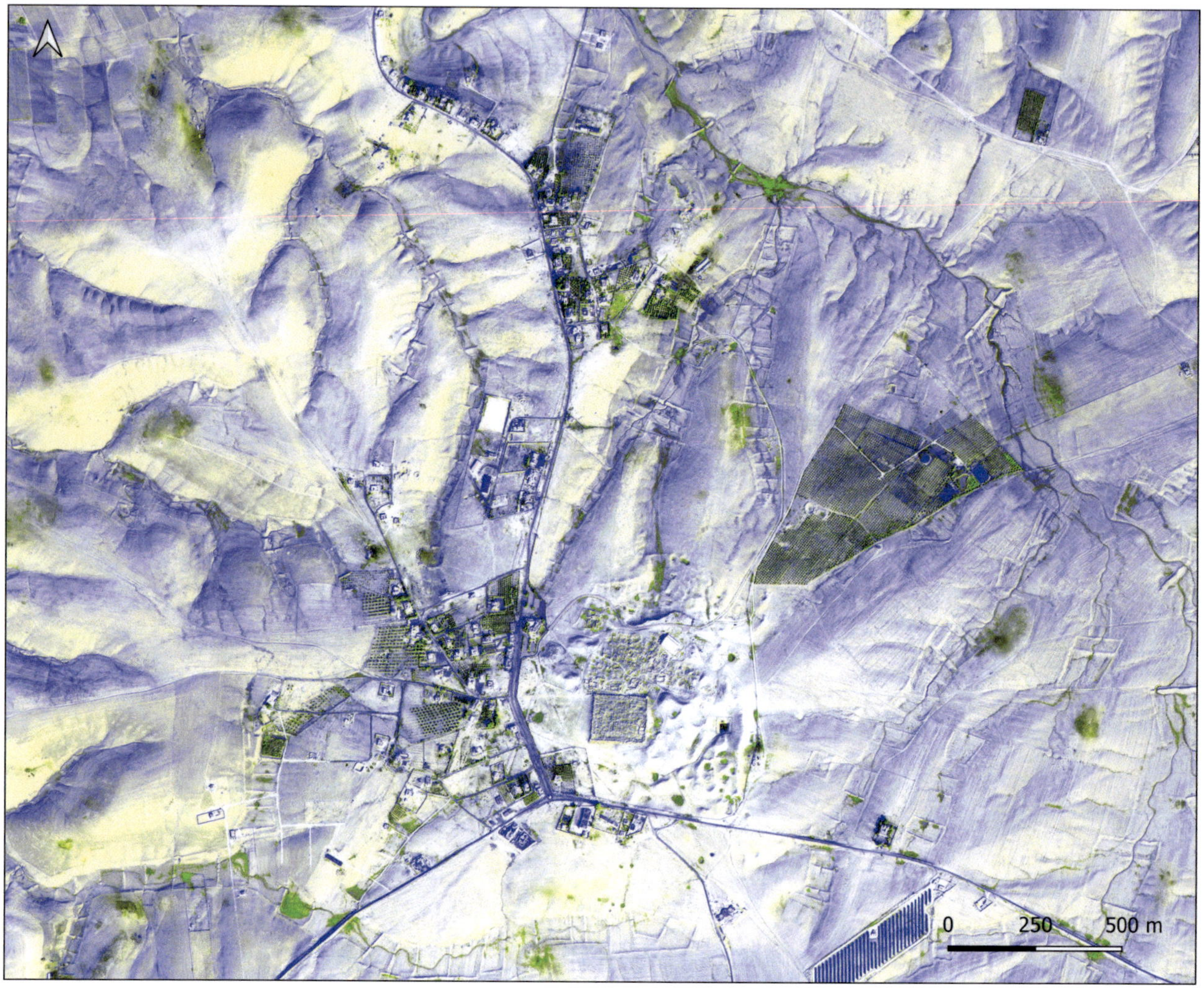

Figure 11.9. RGB colour composite in false colour of the Pléiades Neo-04 multispectral image processed by PCA technique. R: PC1 band of RGB data; G: PC1 band of the NED data; B: PC2 band the NED data (processing and editing by Ilaria Miccoli).

11.2.2 From the air to the ground

The remote sensing analysis was then followed by the verification of all the proof discovered from above. All quarries, irrigation systems, and water canalization have been mapped in detail. Forty reservoirs, dozens of quarries, and dozens of canal systems have been mapped in total. In addition, hypogean settings probably going back to the Bronze Age, such as those found in Amman's Citadel, have been identified. One thing to note about the water reservoirs: we recognised their primary role as a quarry in at least five or six of them.

Finally, a fantastic result was obtained with the discovery of a dam to the north-east of Umm ar-Rasas. It was made possible by Hexagon analysis and a later check survey on the ground. The dam has not been photographed by Stein and has never been studied before. The Jordanian Department of Antiquities itself didn't know about the existence of this dam. Through ground observations, we were able to determine that the dam's construction period for building materials, dimensions, and block fabrication can most likely be considered contemporaneous with the castrum or of the same period as the castrum.

11.2.3 Laser scanner and photogrammetric surveys

They were then carried out during the Kastrum Project 2021 and 2022 missions: preliminary architectural and stratigraphic analysis; study and documentation (photographic and graphic) of architectural components; photogrammetric surveys and processing of the walls (tests); laser scanner surveys and processing; archaeological-architectural surveys inside the walls.

For the research and documentation of the castrum walls, a specific form has been developed.

Despite significant obstacles, photogrammetric acquisition of the castrum's exterior walls began in 2021.

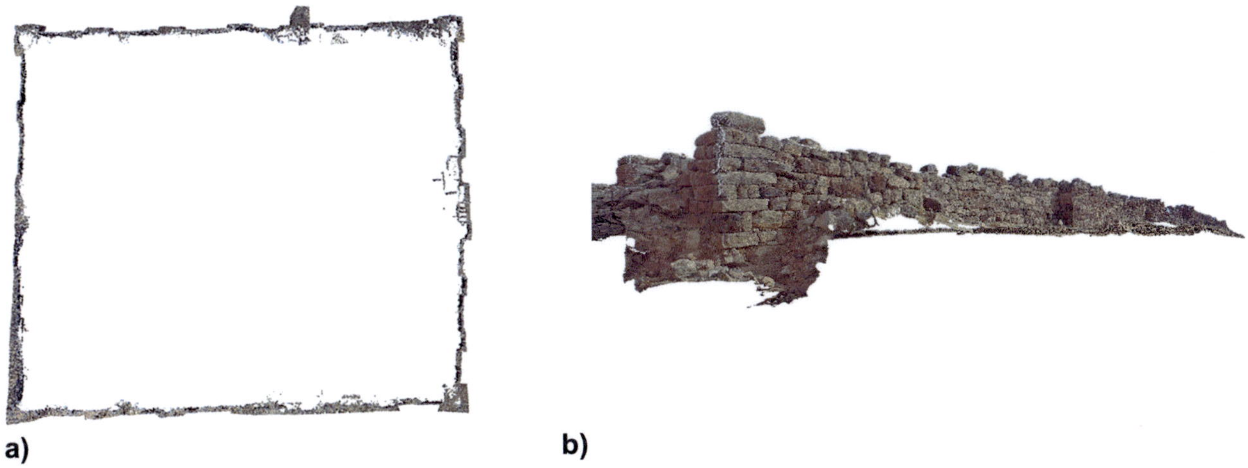

Figure 11.10. Kastrum Project 2022. (a) Print screen processing of all wall reliefs completed; (b) Detail of the west wall, print screen processing in progress (processing by Francesca Di Palma).

Figure 11.11. Kastrum Project 2022–2023. Print screen processing of all wall reliefs completed: the external walls were identified in their natural colours (relief 2022); the interior of the castrum was characterised by a distinctive colour mapping (inclination) (relief 2023 – by Francesca Di Palma).

Difficulties brought on by the following factors: a large castrum (159 × 138 m approx.); numerous collapses; and (of course) the Mission's short duration. Even so, a first photogrammetric test of the walls' full external circuit has been completed (Figure 11.10).

As a result, a first laser scanner acquisition campaign was run during the 2022 expedition (completed in 2023, Figure 11.11), allowing accurate documentation of the masonry and the castrum's state of conservation. Two pieces of equipment, the FARO Focus 3D S120 (which can scan objects up to 120 m away and measure at speeds of up to 976,000 points per second, with an optimal distance of 50 to 60 m) and the FARO Focus X 330 HDR (can scan objects up to 330 m away and measure at speeds of up

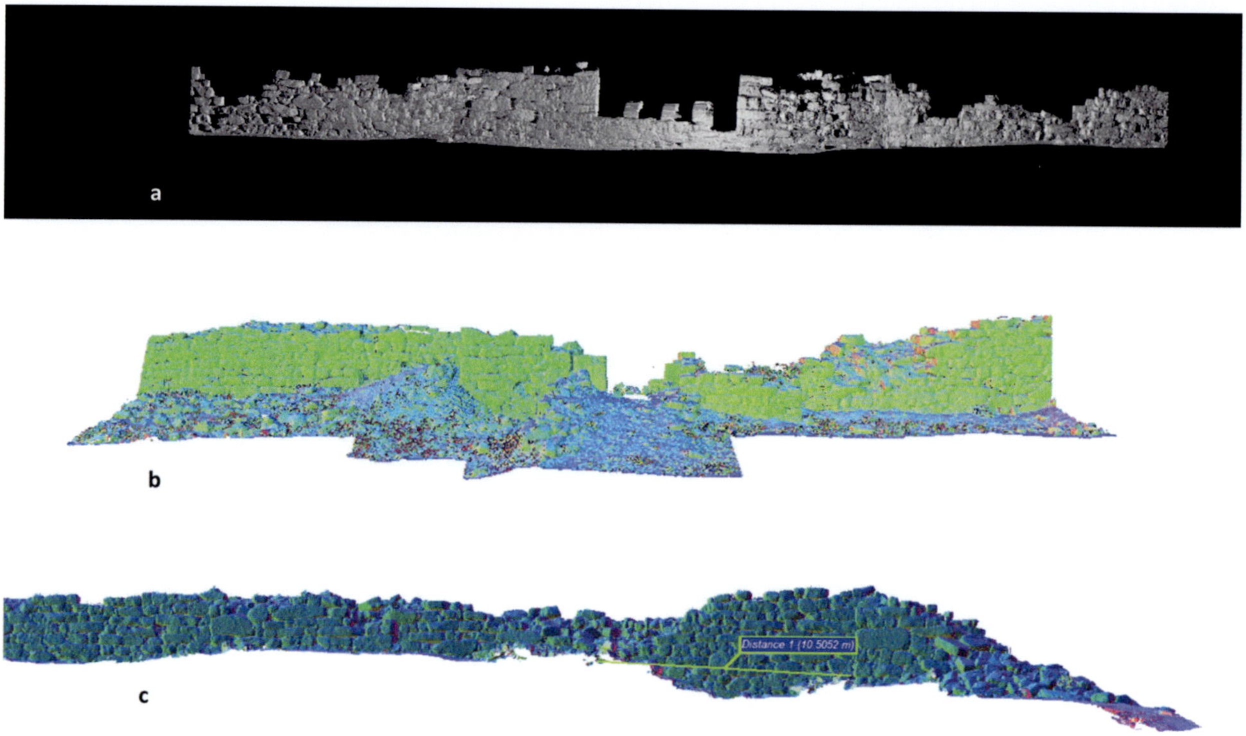

Figure 11.12. a) Results of the data processing phase: Ortho-image of East Gate; b) North Gate. Data processing phase. Colour mapping: inclination; c) A section of West wall. Colour mapping: inclination (processing by Francesca Di Palma and Roberto Gabrielli).

to 976,000 points per second, with an optimal distance between 208 and 290 m), were used to conduct the laser scanner surveys. Two instruments were employed to expedite the measurements due to the limited amount of time available. One point every three millimetres at a distance of ten metres was the resolution that the two laser scanners had been calibrated to.

The two laser scanners were positioned less than 50 m from the castrum walls and 10 m apart from one another (they were spaced this way to provide sufficient scan overlap). This shows that the two instruments performed at their highest level.

The scans were processed using Reconstructor 4.4, a software created by a Brescia University spin-off (https://gexcel.it/it/software/reconstructor). Before being registered automatically, the scans were manually pre-registered. This procedure has never had more than 2 mm of average inaccuracy.

However, this is a comprehensive survey that enables us to create a 3D model that can be remotely measured and analysed (Figures 11–12).

11.3 Discussion and forthcoming perspectives

In summary, the material, construction, stratigraphic, and structural degradation characteristics of the masonry were identified. We also finished the photogrammetric and laser scanner surveys of the exterior walls to accurately record the structures, create a 3D model that can be remotely measured and analysed, plan future research and preservation efforts, and improve accessibility.

The systematic analysis of (unpublished) remote sensing data (Table 11.1), both historical and recent, in terms of a territorial scale allowed the identification of new archaeological sites (hypogeum environments/graves of the Bronze Age emptied and used as dwelling/shelter in the Umayyad period until recent times, dams and the dam, etc.) and the reconstruction of the historical landscape (specifically water channels, dams, quarries, reservoirs and systems of irrigated plots) associated with the Byzantine-Umayyad settlement. In a more detailed perspective (i.e., around the castrum), the analysis of remote sensing data (in particular historical data), combined with a preliminary survey on the ground, allowed the identification of ancient wall remains (Figure 11.13). These walls could be associated with the castrum or with a previous and smaller fortification (of Severian age?). In this regard, a fragmentary Latin inscription indicating a Roman presence in 306 and 307, as well as many pottery shards from the 2nd-3rd centuries AD, have been found (Scarpati 1991; Lewin 2001; Bujard 2008, 22, 35). After all, there are several references in the bibliography to Severan fortresses that were later incorporated into much larger Tetrarchic fortifications (Arce 2010; 2015).

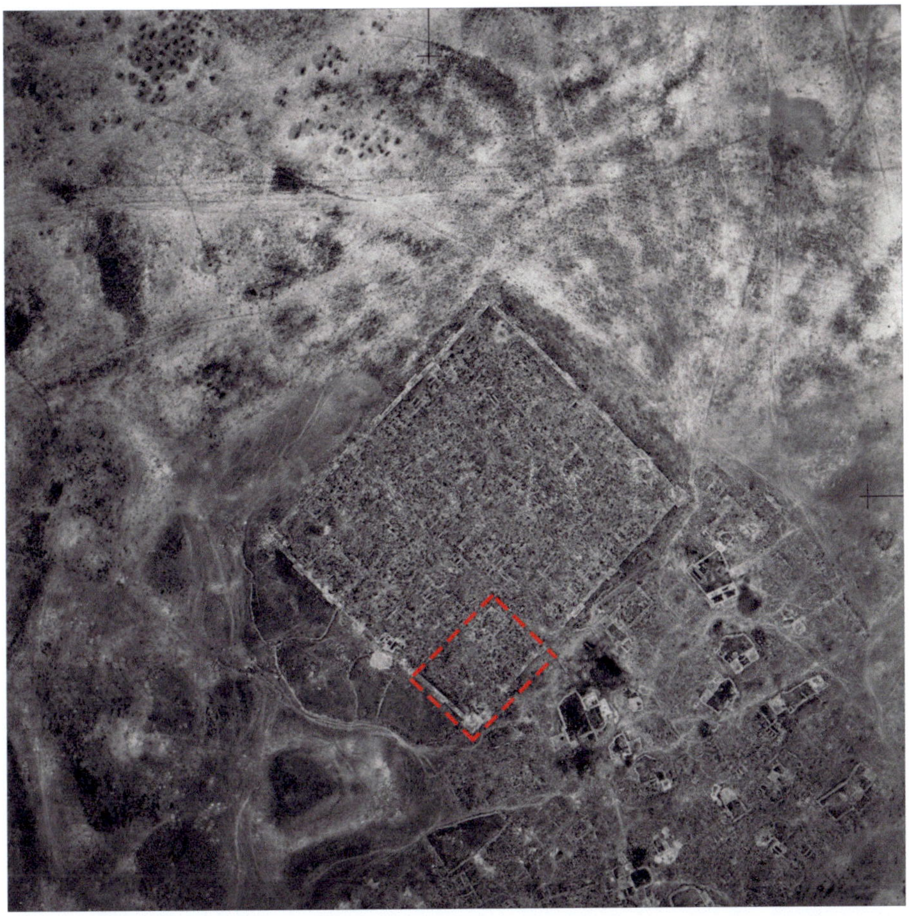

Figure 11.13. Umm ar-Rasas. Highlighting the site where remains of ancient walls have been found, either from the earlier and smaller fortress of Umm ar-Rasas (Severan period) or from the same period as the castrum wall (Tetrarchic period).

BA*	Aerial Photograph	Dates	Hours	Flying height	Figure 11.s
ASA/3/618	oblique	1939/5/6	10:10	600 ft	2, III
ASA/3/619	oblique	1939/5/6	10:12	600 ft	2, II
ASA/3/620	oblique	1939/5/6	10:17	600 ft	2, IV
ASA/3/594	vertical	1939/5/6	12:00	600 ft	2, I, 13
Satellite Images	**ID**	**Dates**	**Spatial Resolution**	**Sensors**	**Figure 11.s**
Hexagon KH-9	1209-200214F019	1974/12/1	1.20–0.60 m	Panchromatic	4
Pléiades-1A	202010300836510	2020/10/30	0.50 m	Multispectral	5-7A
Pléiades Neo	202201250826144	2022/01/25	0.30 m	Multispectral	7B-9

Table 11.1. A summary table of the aerial photographs and satellite images utilised, along with their respective characteristics. *British Academy of London

In summary, Umm ar-Rasas has recently been used as an experimental lab for interdisciplinary searches. Research aimed at understanding and optimising a location with substantial potential. A considerable amount of work remains to be done.

Regarding the prospects for the future, aerial photogrammetric and laser scanner surveys will be used to finish the surveys. Figure 11.11 illustrates the initial processing of the relief from above conducted in 2023 using a laser scanner. This processing will require further improvement and implementation, which will be achieved through additional aerophotogrammetric tests and the use of laser scanners in order to improve the map of the military camp during the Tetrarchic period. We plan to use electrical resistivity tomography to investigate the area inside the castrum walls in order to find and confirm structures that were present at the time the castrum was built as well as to find and confirm the presence of earlier structures (previous fortification).

We intend to define the extent of the Byzantine and Umayyad settlement in the north, confirm the existence of walls surrounding the Byzantine settlement (This goal was achieved during the November 2023 mission, see Cozzolino et al. 2025), and investigate the hydraulic systems of the settlement using geophysical surveys, processing, and archaeological interpretation of new remote sensing data.

Author Contributions

Conceptualization, F.D.P., I.M., G.S., P.M. and R.G.; methodology, F.D.P. and I.M.; validation, G.S., P.M. and R.G.; formal analysis, F.D.P. and I.M.; investigation, F.D.P.; resources, F.D.P., G.S., I.M., R.G. and P.M.; data curation,F.D.P. and I.M.; writing—original draft preparation, F.D.P. and I.M.; writing—review and editing, F.D.P., I.M., G.S., P.M. and R.G.; visualization, F.D.P., I.M., G.S., P.M. and R.G.; project administration, R.G.; funding acquisition, R.G.; F.D.P. All authors have read and agreed to the published version of the manuscript.

Acknowledgements

We greatly appreciate the support and collaboration of the Jordanian Department of Antiquities. We wish to express our gratitude to inspectors Aktam Oweidi and Hussein Dahbour, as well as the director, Fadi Al-Balawi.

We would like to express our gratitude to the British Academy in London for providing the photographic documentation of the archive, in particular to the archivist Sharon Messanger for her invaluable assistance.

We would also like to express our gratitude to Pasquale Galatà, Technical Officer of CNR ISPC, for his invaluable assistance in the field and in the processing of the laser-scanner reliefs.

Funding

The research in Umm ar-Rasas was supported by the Institute of Heritage Science of the Italian National Research Council (CNR-ISPC) as well as the Italian Ministry of Foreign Affairs.

The present study forms part of a larger research project conducted by Francesca Di Palma, entitled *Border roads and construction. An aerotopographic study of the East Limes between Iraq and Jordan: from aerial photos of Sir Aurel Stein to historical and recent satellite images* for a PhD in Archaeological, historical, architectural Mediterranean landscape heritage (PASAP_med – XXXVI cycle) of the University of Bari 'Aldo Moro'.

Conflict of interest disclosure

The authors declare that they comply with the PCI rule of having no financial conflicts of interest in relation to the content of the article.

Peer review

This article has been reviewed and recommended by PCI Archaeology.

Brucato, A. 2024. "Integrating remote sensing and photogrammetric approaches to studying a fortified settlement along the Limes Arabicus: Umm ar-Rasas (Amman, Jordan)." *Peer Community in Archaeology* 100404. DOI:10.24072/pci.archaeo.100404.

References

Abela, John, and Alessandra Acconci. 1997. "Umm al-Rasas Kastron Mefa'a. Excavation Campaign 1997. Church of St. Paul: northern and southern flanks." *Liber Annus* 47: 484–8.

Abela, John, and Carmelo Pappalardo. 1998. "Umm al-Rasas, Church of St. Paul: Southeastern flank." *Liber Annus* 48: 542–6.

Abela, John, and Carmelo Pappalardo. 2002. "Umm al-Rasas – Kastron Mefaa Archaeological Campaign 2002." *Liber Annus* 52: 475–8.

Abela, John, and Carmelo Pappalardo. 2004. "Umm al-Rasas 2004, Excavation Report." *Liber Annus* 54: 419–24.

Abu Dayyeh, Abdel Sami. 2002. *Nomination of the old city of Um er-Rasas (Kastrum Mefa'a) for the World Heritage List*. Jordan: Department of Antiquities. https://whc.unesco.org/document/168869

Arce, Ignacio. 2010. "Qasr Hallabat, Qasr Bshir and Deir El Kahf. Building techniques, architectural typology and change of use of three quadriburgia from the limes arabicus. Interpretation and significance." In *Arqueología de la construcción, II:*

Los procesos constructivos en el mundo romano: Italia y 8 provincias orientales (Congreso, Certosa di Pontignano, Siena, 13–15 de noviembre de 2008), edited by Stefano Camporeale, Hélène Dessales, and Antonio Pizzo, 455–81. Madrid: Consejo Superior de Investigaciones Científicas.

Arce, Ignacio. 2015. "Severan Castra, Tetrarchic Quadriburgia, Justinian Coenobia, and Ghassanid Diyarat: patterns of transformation of Limes Arabicus forts during Late Antiquity." In *Roman Military Architecture on the Frontiers Armies and Their Architecture in Late Antiquity*, edited by Rob Collings, Matthew Symonds, and Meike Weber, 98–122. Oxford: Oxbow Books.

Brünnow, Rudolf Ernest, and Alfred Domaszewski. 1905. *Die Provincia Arabia, II.* Strasbourg: Trübner.

Buckingham, James Silk. 1825. *Travels among the Arab tribes inhabiting the countries east of Syria and Palestine.* London: Longman.

Bujard, Jacques. 1992. "Les Églises Géminées D'Umm Er-Rasas, Fouilles de la mission archéologique Suisse (fondation Max van Berchem)." *Annual of the Department of Antiquities of Jordan* 36: 291–301.

Bujard, Jacques. 2008. "Kastron Mefaa, un bourg à l'époque byzantine: Travaux de la Mission archéologique de la Fondation Max van Berchem à Umm al-Rasas, Jordanie (1988–1997)." PhD diss., University of Fribourg.

Bujard, Jacques, and Marc-André Haldimann. 1988. "Fouilles de la mission archéologique Suisse ("fondation Max van Berchem) a Umm er-Rasas et Umm al-Walid en 1988." *Annual of the Department of Antiquities of Jordan* 32: 291–301.

Bujard, Jacques, and Michelle Joguin. 1995. "La fortification de Kastron Mayfa'a / Umm ar-Rasas." *Studies in the History and Archaeology of Jordan* 5: 241–9.

Burchardt, John Lewis. 1822. *Travels in Syria and the Holy Land.* London: John Murray.

Clermont-Ganneau, Charles. 1898. "L'inscription de Oumm er-Rasas." *Recueil d'Archéologie Orientale* 2: 185–8.

Cozzolino, Marilena, Roberto Gabrielli, Pasquale Galatà, Vincenzo Gentile, Giorgia Greco, and Eleonora Scopinaro. 2019. "Combined use of 3D metric surveys and non-invasive geophysical surveys at the stylite tower (Umm ar-Rasas, Jordan)." *Annals of geophysics* 62 (3): 1–9. https:// doi.org/10.4401/ag-8060.

Cozzolino, Marilena, Di Palma, Francesca, Gabrielli, Roberto, Mauriello, Paolo, Scardozzi, Giuseppe. 2025. "A Top-Down, Multi-Method and Multi-Scale Approach to Studying the Byzantine–Umayyad Settlement of Ummar-Rasas (Amman, Jordan)." *Heritage* 2025, 8, 177. https://doi.org/10.3390/heritage8050177.

Di Palma, Francesca. 2025. Dal Laboratorio Sperimentale del Limes Orientale al Laboratorio Interdisciplinare di Umm ar-Rasas (Amman, Giordania). In *Infrastrutture e Strutture di Confine. Lo Studio Aerotopografico del Limes Orientale Tra Iraq e Giordania: Dalle Foto Aeree di Sir Aurel Stein alle Immagini Satellitari Storiche e Recenti*. Ph.D. Dissertation, University of Bari 'Aldo Moro', Bari, Italy, 5 February 2025.

Gabrielli, Roberto, Antonio Salvatori, Alessandra Lazzari, and Damiano Portarena. 2016. "Il sito di Umm ar-Rasas – Kastron Mefaa – Giordania." *Scavare documentare conservare, viaggio nella ricerca archeologica del CNR*. Roma: CNR Edizioni.

Gabrielli, Roberto, Damiano Portarena, and Mauro Franceschinis. 2017. "Tecniche di documentazione dei tappeti musivi del sito archeologico di Umm al-Rasas Kastron Mefaa (Giordania)." *Archeologia e calcolatori* 28 (1): 201–18. DOI:10.19282/AC.28.1.2017.12.

Germer-Durand, Joseph. 1897. "Frontières de l'Empire Romain en Arabie." *Echos de Notre-Dame de France* 50: 37.

Glueck, Nelson. 1934. "Exploration in Eastern Palestine." *The Annual of the American School of Oriental Research* 14: 39.

Irby, Charles Leonard, and James Mangles. 1823. *Travels in Egypt and Nubia, Syria, and Asia Minor; during the years 1817 and 1818.* London: White.

Lagrange, Marie Joseph. 1898. "Oumm er-Rasas." *Revue Biblique* 7: 168.

Lasaponara, Rosa, and Nicola Masini. 2012. *Satellite Remote Sensing: A New Tool for Archaeology*. New York: Springer.

Lasaponara, Rosa, Nicola Masini, and Giuseppe Scardozzi. 2007. "Immagini satellitari ad alta risoluzione e ricerca archeologica: applicazioni e casi di studio con riprese pancromatiche e multispettrali di QuickBird." *Archeologia e Calcolatori* 18 (2): 187–227.

Lasaponara, Rosa, Nicola Masini, and Giuseppe Scardozzi. 2010. "Elaborazioni di immagini satellitari ad alta risoluzione e ricognizione archeologica per la conoscenza degli insediamenti rurali del territorio di Hierapolis di Frigia (Turchia)." In *Il dialogo dei Saperi – Metodologie integrate per i Beni Culturali* edited by Francesco D'Andria, Daniele Malfitana, Nicolas Masini, and Giuseppe Scardozzi, 479–494. Naples: Edizioni scientifiche italiane.

Layard, Henry. 1887. *Early Adventures in Persia, Susiana and Babylonia*. London: John Murray.

Lewin, Ariel Samuel. 2001. "Kastron Mefaa, the equites promoti indigenae and the creation of a late Roman frontier." *Liber Annus* 51: 293–304.

Malinverni, Eva Savina, Roberto Pierdicca, Francesco Di Stefano, Roberto Gabrielli, and Alessandra Albiero.

2019. "Virtual Museum enriched by GIS data to share science and culture. Church of Saint Stephen in Umm ar-Rasas (Jordan)." *Virtual Archaeology Review* 10 (21): 31–9. DOI: 10.4995/var.2019.11919.
Musil, Alois. 1907. *Arabia Petraea I, Moab*. Vienna: Alfred Holder.
Palmer, Edward Henry. 1871. *The Desert of the Exodus, II*. Cambridge: Deighton Bell and Co.
Piccirillo, Michele. 1986. "Prima campagna di scavo a Um er-Rasas." *Liber Annus* 36: 351–4.
Piccirillo, Michele. 1987. "Um er-Rasas-Kastron Mefaa. Seconda Campagna, 1987." *Liber Annus* 37: 401–3.
Piccirillo, Michele. 1988a. "The Mosaics at Umm er-Rasas in Jordan." *The Biblical Archaeologist* 51 (4): 208–13, 227–31.
Piccirillo, Michele. 1988b. "Um er-Rasas – Kastron Mefaa. Terza campagna, 1988." *Liber Annus* 38: 458–9.
Piccirillo, Michele. 1989. "Excavation at Mount Nebo – Umm Er-Rasas 1989." In *DoA: Registration and Documentation Section*. Unpublished report.
Piccirillo, Michele. 1991a. "Il complesso di Santo Stefano a Umm al-Rasas – Kastron Mefaa in Giordania." *Liber Annus* 41: 327–64.
Piccirillo, Michele. 1991b. "Sesta campagna a Umm er-Rasas – Kastron Mefaa." *Liber Annus* 41: 522–6.
Piccirillo, Michele. 1992a. "La chiesa dei Leoni a Umm al-Rasas -Kastron Mefaa." *Liber Annus* 42: 199–226.
Piccirillo, Michele. 1992b. "Settima Campagna di scavi a Umm al-Rasas 1992." *Liber Annus* 42: 366–9.
Piccirillo, Michele. 1995. "Archaeological Campaign at Umm al-Rasas." *Liber Annus* 45: 513–5.
Piccirillo, Michele. 1996. "A New Church amongst the ruins of Umm al-Rasas – Kastron Mefa'a in Jordan." *Liber Annus* 46: 409–13.
Piccirillo, Michele. 1997. "La chiesa di San Paolo a Umm al-Rasas – Kastron Mefaa." *Liber Annus* 47: 375–94.
Piccirillo, Michele. 1999. "Excavation Report on the Tombs of The Lion's and St. Paul Churches at Um Er-rasas." In *DoA: Registration and Documentation Section*. Unpublished report.
Piccirillo, Michele. 2001. "Um Er-rasas archaeological campaign." In *DoA: Registration and Documentation Section*. Unpublished report.
Piccirillo, Michele. 2002. "Um Er-Rasas archaeological campaign." In *DoA: Registration and Documentation Section*. Unpublished report.
Piccirillo, Michele. 2003. "La Chiesa della Tabula Ansata a Umm al-Rasas." *Liber Annus* 53: 285–302.
Piccirillo, Michele. 2006. "La Chiesa del Reliquiario a Umm al-Rasas." *Liber Annus* 56: 375–88.
Piccirillo, Michele, and Eugenio Alliata. 1994. *Umm al-Rasas Mayfa'ah. Vol. I. Gli scavi del Complesso di Santo Stefano*. Jerusalem: Edizioni Custodia di Terra Santa.
Piccirillo, Michele, and Taysir Attiyat. 1986. "The complex of Saint Stephen at Umm er-Rasas –Kastron Mefaa." *Annual of the Department of Antiquities of Jordan* 30: 341–51.
Piccirillo, Michele, John Abela, and Carmelo Pappalardo. 2005. "Umm al-Rasas 2005, Excavation Report." *Liber Annus* 55: 494–8.
Piccirillo, Michele, John Abela, and Carmelo Pappalardo. 2007. "Umm al-Rasas – campagna 2007. Rapporto di scavo." *Liber Annus* 57: 660–8.
Poidebard, Antoine. 1934. *La trace de Rome dans le désert de Syrie : le limes de Trajan à la conquête arabe; recherches aériennes 1925 – 1932*. Paris: Geuthner.
Robinson G. 1837. *Travels in Palestine and Syria. Vol. 1–2*. London: Henry Colburn.
Saller, Sylvester John, and Bellarmino Bagatti. 1949. *The town of Nebo*. Jerusalem: Franciscan Press.
Savignac, Raphael. 1936. "Sur les pistes de Transjordanie méridionale." *Revue Biblique*: 235–262.
Scarpati, Dario. 1991. "Un'iscrizione latina da Umm al Rasas." *Liber Annus* 41: 363–4.
Seetzen, Ulrich Jasper. 1854. *Reisen durch Syrien, Palästina, Phönicien, die Transjordan-Länder, Arabia Petrarca und Unter-Aegypten (1–2)*. Berlin: Verlag Georg Reimer.
Stein, Marc Aurel. 1938. "Note on Remains of the Roman Limes in North-Western 'Iraq." *The Geographical Journal* 92 (1): 62–6. DOI: 10.2307/1787358.
Stein, Marc Aurel. 1940. "Surveys on the Roman Frontier in 'Iraq and Trans-Jordan." *The Geographical Journal* 95 (6): 428–38. DOI: 10.2307/1788428.
Tristram, Henry Baker. 1874. *The Land of Moab, London*.
Vailhé, Siméon. 1896. "Dans les montagnes bleues." *Echos de Notre-Dame de France* 37: 230.
Wilson, Charles William. 1899. "Address Delivered at the Annual Meeting of the Fund." *Palestine Exploration Fund Quarterly Statement* 31 (4): 304–16.

12 Research workflows, paradata, and information visualisation

Feedback on an exploratory integration of issues and practices – MEMORIA IS

Iwona Dudek
UMR 3495 CNRS/MC MAP
Marseille
iwona.dudek@map.cnrs.fr

Jean-Yves Blaise
UMR 3495 CNRS/MC MAP
Marseille

Abstract

The paper presents an exploratory web information system developed as a reaction to practical and epistemological questions, in the context of a scientific unit studying the architectural heritage (from both historical sciences perspective, and engineering sciences standpoint). The article presents the methodological and analytical potential of this system for the description, analysis and information sharing of research workflows.

The MEMORIA prototype is first and foremost an effort to build a tool that should help us to ensure the traceability, transmissibility and verifiability of scientific results and fulfil the challenges of open science (providing free access to the content produced). The specificity of the system is to empower a formal characterisation of processes that led to a particular research result by listing the most important elements necessary for a proper understanding of the result. An important point is the ambition to deploy visual interfaces providing access to resources and enabling direct analysis of the information collected. Ultimately, the project aims at depicting cognitive and methodological approaches behind scientific results using the possibilities offered by Information Visualisation.

The paper presents and defines the key concepts behind our approach and describes how they develop in practice. The theoretical aspects are illustrated with practical examples. The paper concludes with an analysis of the benefits and potential of the systematic approach to scientific process documentation that we introduce, highlighting its advantages and discussing its limitations.

Keywords: Web-based Information System; Paradata; Scientific results; Research workflows; Information Visualisation; Historical Sciences

12.1 Introduction

Documentarists, archaeologists, cultural historians, computer scientists and ICT practitioners – more and more frequently stress the lack of reliable tools for documenting multiple aspects of research processes (i.e., its intellectual/cognitive, methodological, technological, tacit elements). The research initiative that we propose to discuss bases on the

In *Advances in Digital Archaeology. Proceedings of the 2023 conference Computer Applications and Quantitative Methods in Archaeology – 50 years of synergy*, edited by J.W.H.P. Verhagen, J. Waagen, A. Brandsen, A. Queffelec, R.M. Visser and D. Taelman, 147–162. Leiden: Sidestone Press.

idea that beyond metadata describing outputs themselves, the scientific community is awaiting "paradata" that would include means to ensure traceability, verifiability and comparability of research workflows. This means sharing procedural knowledge and it is known not to be a straightforward task.

Doing things does not require the same skills as careful documenting, especially when the purpose of documentation is to picture comprehensively, the *how* and *why* of the overall "production" process. In the *Journal of Documentation* Swedish researchers analyse how archaeologists document their work practices within archaeological reports. They stress that sharing procedural knowledge is difficult "because of the lack of experience in thinking of their doings in terms of documentation" (Huvila et al. 2021, 1109).

Describing and documenting, like perhaps all competences, require organisation, structure and practice. Not surprisingly, then, practitioners themselves find it difficult to describe what they do, as this refers to their personal knowledge (acquired by learning) and recollections – two interrelated but distinct aspects of memory.

First of all, *knowledge has to be acquired.* If someone has not learnt how to document, he or she will probably struggle to do it well. Documenting needs to be taught.

Secondly, different processes involves *different types of knowledge* (Carper 1978) identified four fundamental *patterns of knowing* in nursing: empirical, personal, aesthetic, and ethical knowing. Others, following Michael Polanyi, classify knowledge into *explicit knowledge* (knowing-that) and *tacit knowledge* (knowing-how) (Halonen and Laukkanen 2008; Gamble 2020). Depending on the problem we focus on, knowledge can be furthermore categorised as *declarative* or *procedural* (ten Berge and van Hezewijk 1999; Burgin 2016), *contextual* (Bakken and Dobbs 2016; Brezillon and Pomerol 1999), *somatic* (Bakken and Dobbs 2016; Green 2002; Horst 2008), *a posteriori* or *a priori* (Tahko 2011), and so on. This diversity reflects the complex nature of a knowledge to be transmitted. It encompasses at the same time facts, models, taxonomies, know-how, intuition, ethical components of a given practice, perception, mind-body action and reaction, the ability to identify one's own individual biases affecting the quality of work, etc.

In addition, human memory is unreliable, imprecise and subject to distortions. Our ability to remember detailed information about what we are doing and why we are doing it is limited – in quantity, quality and time (Neisser and Harsch1992). Some experts highlight the inevitability of forgetting:

> "[forgetting] *is not a failure of memory, but a function of it* [...] *The brain is always trying to forget the information it's already learnt*" (Gravitz 2019, 13).

It is therefore difficult for one to reconstruct a sequence of actions (activity types, decisions, their cause-and-effect relationship, their temporal sequence, instruments employed, people involved, etc.) within a longer process.

Finally, numerous frontline practitioners tend to understand their practice as the "doing". In her thesis, Rosemary Doyle (2009) explores the relationships between practice ("doing") and documenting activity in social work. She points out that social work practitioners consider "describing and documenting" practices as "secondary, bureaucratic concerns, with no material effect on the core processes and outcomes" of their work practice (Doyle 2009, 11). The statement that such a state of affairs is also observable in other areas of human activity – including heritage sciences – is not likely to stir up much controversy.

This paper presents the methodological and analytical potential of the MEMORIA web-based information system for the description, analysis and information sharing of research workflows. The system has been conceived and developed as a reaction to the practical and epistemological questions, in the context of a scientific unit studying the architectural heritage. The main purpose of the system is to identify various results obtained through scientific studies and to describe formally the processes that led to a specific result. Elements taken into account include the structure of a research process, methods and approach used in the investigation, tools and instruments, actors and their roles within the process, scientific context (e.g., organisational framework, objectives), sources, inputs *(e.g., outputs produced previously and described by a specific process)*, dates, etc.

Before detailing how the concept of paradata develops in practice in the aforementioned information system, it is important to clarify a set of basic concepts related to it.

12.1.1 Metadata, paradata, provenance, process, workflow, pipeline – terminological confusion

The concepts of *metadata, paradata, provenance, process, workflow and pipeline* are increasingly used across disciplines. However, these terms lack sharp and commonly accepted definitions.

12.1.1.1 Metadata and paradata

A recent study on the use of the "paradata" concept in a corpus of scholarly texts from archaeology and cultural-heritage studies (Sköld et al. 2022) points out a considerable disagreement about *what paradata is* and *what its purpose might be.* Some consider *paradata* as a subset or a type of metadata (Brusaporci 2017; Huvila 2022) – calling them *provenance metadata* (Australian Research Data Commons 2020), or *reference metadata* (Karr 2020). Others perceive them clearly as information distinct from *metadata* (Kreuter and Casas-Cordero 2010), or assess concepts of *metadata, paradata* and *provenance* as partially overlapping (Karr 2020; Moreau and Groth 2022). However, a common consensus can be found: paradata refers to information about productive process.

In the context of our work, in line with the definition given by Australian Research Data Commons (2020), we view "metadata" as *data/information about an object or resource* that describes its characteristics such as content, quality, format, location and data administrative information.

In turn, "paradata" should be understood as *data/ information about a process by which an outcome was achieved* including: methods (why and how the object or resource was "produced"), intellectual processes (decisions, reasoning paths, ...) circumstances under which results have been achieved (scientific context of the process, organisational framework,...), and the resources engaged (what tools, sources, inputs and approaches were involved in the successive stages of object or resource production, who was involved and when, ...).

12.1.1.2 Process, workflow and pipeline

A similar cloud of semantic ambiguity surrounds the concepts of *"process"*, *"workflow"* and *"pipeline"*. Depending on the sphere of application – business, art or a specific scientific field – these terms may carry different conceptual meaning that can range from abstract concepts (e.g., "workflow" which refers to enterprise activities (Barga and Gannon 2007) to very specific, tangible elements (e.g., workflow and pipeline referring to scripts or codes; Leipzig 2017; Mazzu 2022).

Often used as synonyms, these terms can be associated with tools (e.g., management of document flows), diagrams (e.g., timeline or concept flow diagrams), modelling methods, sequences of real-life actions, etc. However, what seems to be the common denominator, is that they all refer to *a sequence of tasks leading from a trigger to an outcome.*

In the context of our work, we will use these terms in the following sense:

- a "process" will be understood as *a series of actions or steps taken in order to achieve a particular end.* In other words, it is the actual, real work as it is done ("doing").
- a "workflow" will be considered as a *view or representation of actual work* – just as a map is a representation of a territory.
- a "pipeline" will refer to *a linear predefined sequence of steps or instructions.*

It is important to underline that a "workflow", as opposed to a "process" or a "pipeline", is most often a selection (deliberate or not) of actions through which a piece of work passed from initiation to completion.

The formal descriptions of workflows may vary from a purely verbal, linear, textual form (SSHOC 2022a; Mauri et al. 2020), to diagrammatic multipath representations (Aigner et al. 2011; Carlsson 2012; Mauri et al. 2020; McLachlan and Webley 2021). Visual representation of processes by diagrams is a well-established practice. They are widespread in business (Barga and Gannon 2007) and scientific research (Goble et al. 2020), but they are also used in law (McLachlan and Webley 2021), construction management (Carlsson 2012), health risk communication (Ancker et al. 2006), chronic disease care (Mclachlan et al. 2020) or education (Mauri et al. 2020).

Workflows are commonly used to keep a *record of what has been done*, or to visualise a series of steps on the way towards the project objectives, as well as current problems and potential disruptions. Their visual character helps to understand patterns and relationships between activities, improves the accuracy of quantitative reasoning and, therefore, may improve problem solving and decision-making.

Thanks to their inherent property of displaying and ordering the relations between data over time and facilitating contextual and targeted reading of the data/ information they present, workflow diagrammatic representations can convey protocols progression more easily than words alone. Tufte claims that: *"well-designed graphics are far more effective than words in showing observations"* (Tufte 2006, 87).

Yet, one should not assume that all graphics are clearer and more understandable than a text. In this context, the role of the information "recipient" must not be overlooked. Research surveys indicate that individuals' interpretation of the information graphics depends on their expertise (familiarity with the topic and prior knowledge) and instruction (graphic interpretation skills; Ancker et al. 2006; Glazer 2011; Phillips 1997).

12.1.2 Statement of need

In 2014, because of the lack of systematic documentation and archiving of research results within our team, as well as of the fluctuation of the people involved in research works, we noticed certain partial but significant information losses. We lost information about what was done, by whom, what the original objectives were and what limitations were encountered, which files contain what, how to open them, and so on. Data and information collected in the course of numerous projects and results of their analyses at various stages of progress were – and unfortunately still are – organised and described in an idiosyncratic manner. The central research problem of the MEMORIA project,[1]

1 The MEMORIA project is a long-term project initiated in 2014 by members of the MAP-Gamsau team (UMR 3495 CNRS/MC MAP); http://memoria.gamsau.archi.fr/projet/objectives.php?lang=en.

Figure 12.1. The presence or absence of metadata for each element of the system is visually expressed by a "film frame" metaphor which summarises the completion of the documentation effort.

launched to address the above difficulties, is to elaborate methods and technical means to depict scientific results, with indicators (metadata and paradata) that would allow for a better understanding of our research results as well as of the processes through which these results were obtained, and to make this information searchable and available for others.

In the following sections we present the methodological approach we have developed and adopted to structure, preserve and analyse *metadata* and *paradata*. First, we define the key concepts behind our approach, and present objectives that guided us. Theoretical aspects are illustrated with practical examples in the *Results* section. Finally, we present the benefits and the potential of the approach, highlighting its advantages and discussing its limits.

12.2 Methods

Our approach to the preservation and analysis of metadata and paradata is based on the following principles:

- the system should describe the *results of research activities* – this is where we have to decide what we consider to be a "result", what types of results should be taken into account and what is the relevant information (metadata) we should record,
- for each result we should be empowered with means to depict the *process* that led to it – a process should structure the key elements necessary for a proper understanding and verification of the result by presenting the succession of actions and decisions in the form of a workflow diagram enabling *focus-plus-context* interpretation,
- the information collected should be accessible and queryable. It should serve as a basis for *comparative analyses* building on InfoViz practices.

12.2.1 Results of research activities (output, composition and publication)

Research activities may lead to highly heterogeneous results ranging from scientific outputs *per se* to dissemination products. Our choice was to distinguish three types of results that we call respectively *outputs*, *compositions* and *publications*. They are characterised by a series of descriptors (metadata) describing both the container (e.g, title, creator(s), format), and the content (e.g, one or more objects of study, temporal coverage).

The conceptual differences between output, publication and composition are reflected in the categories of metadata describing them (Figure 12.1).

Metadata provide only cursory information about what has been achieved, and where it is possibly available. Metadata alone do not allow to describe – and therefore to understand – what exactly the results are (e.g., data quality), how they should/can be interpreted, to which extent they can be exploited. In short, they do not allow an evaluation of the usefulness of the results nor their proper interpretation. This information is to be found in the "process workflow" (a formal description of a research protocol that led to an outcome's creation) and in the paradata that have been integrated into it (Figures 12.6 and 12.8).

12.2.2 Representing processes as workflows

In heritage sciences at large where observation, interpretation, subjective choices, specific and general

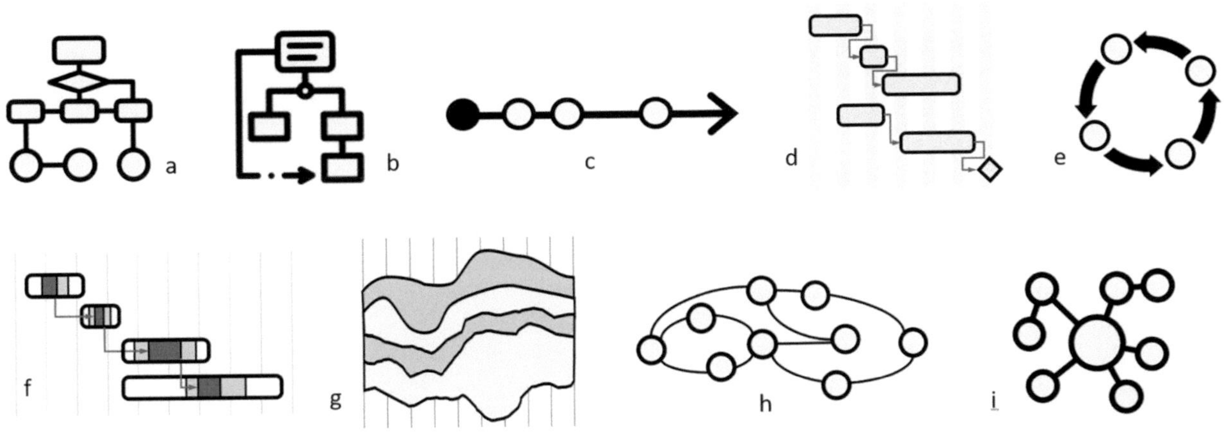

Figure 12.2. Diagrams which are most frequently used to represent processes: a) flowcharts, b) UML activity diagrams, c) timelines, d) Gantt charts, e) lifecycle diagrams f) PlanningLines, g) streamgraphs, h) twist of pearls graph and i) mind maps. (cf. Aigner et al. 2011; McLachlan and Webley 2021).

knowledge, analogies, inference based on source selection intermingle throughout the scientific process, it is impossible to automatically trace the sequence of steps and decisions taken. Whether we choose to use an ethnic language or a diagrammatic representation to express the sequence of steps taken, the final result will show our *mental map* of the process.

Processes can be described by words. However, "a language [...] requires a linear progression of thoughts that may mask the interconnectedness of knowledge" (Bank and Heidberger 2020, 2).

The examples of text-based workflows inherit the above-mentioned limitations, for example research workflows proposed by SSH Open Marketplace[2] (SSHOC 2022b), designed to represent sequences of operations (pipelines) performed on research data during its lifecycle.

A research workflow is often a complex and non-linear array of sequences of steps. In that context diagrams allow the representation of relationships between objects, from a simple order to complex correlated relations (networks). They may be used to enhance *visual* (non-verbal) *reasoning skills* and exploit *iconic memory*. The desire to promote visual reasoning to support users' cognitive abilities was the starting point for the design of MEMORIA workflow diagrams.

2 The goal of SSH Open Marketplace scientific workflow is to enable sharing and re-use of workflows that are essentially a short, step-by-step guides. A workflow is composed of a sequence of paragraphs representing successive steps. Each step can be associated with the TaDIRAH metadata and linked to various digital items (papers, web pages, reports) called *useful resources*. From the legibility point of view these workflows resemble a hypertext (with similar difficulties in grasping the whole problem at once; Vocabs n.d.).

12.2.3 Workflows from the InfoViz perspective

A process (a series of actions or steps) develops over time, therefore its visual representation (workflow), must be tailored to time-oriented data. In visual formalisms, time may be modelled in four different aspects: scale, scope, arrangement and viewpoint (Aigner et al. 2011).

The set of the most commonly used process-oriented diagrams includes flowcharts, UML activity diagrams, lifecycle diagrams, timelines, Gantt charts, concept maps and mind maps (Figure 12.2). Some of them may be adapted to support different scales, scopes, arrangement or viewpoints, but each visual formalism has its own intrinsic limits.

For example, a *flowchart* – the most commonly used process-oriented diagram – originally designed (in 1949) to plan computer algorithms, is tailored to represent decision making processes. It offers a terminology and "syntax" dedicated to this purpose (e.g., input, process, decision, output, initialisation). Flowcharts and the family of similar process-oriented diagrammatic formalisms, including UML activity diagrams or DRACON diagrams, allow the representation of iterations, parallel and concurrent processing, but do not allow the distinction between *repetitive* or *iterative* activities (see Figure 12.3). Since they were designed to plan computer algorithms, they do not take into account actions that take place simultaneously or occur without any regular sequential order – typical of humans. Moreover, their graphical language may be off-putting. This may seem like an exaggeration, but graphics quality, is of major importance in helping to understand difficult schemes: "people may not accept or attend to graphics they dislike" (Ancker et al. 2006, 609).

Further analysis of the inherent limitations of the above visual formalisms is beyond the scope of this paper.

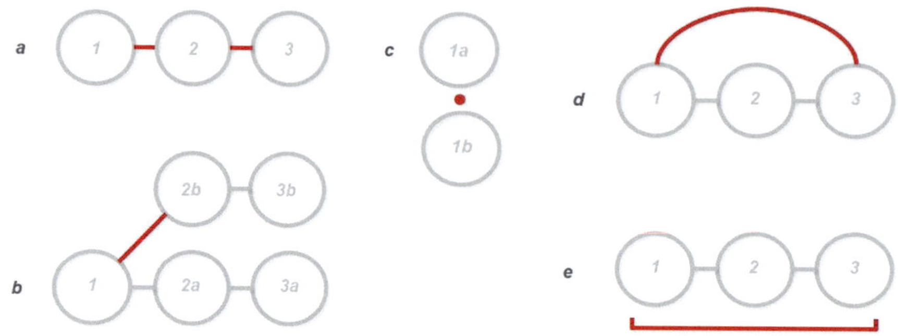

Figure 12.3. Links between workflow nodes organise and structure time-oriented relations between activities, using following typology (the red colour indicates the symbol used to encode the relationship) : a) chain – a sequence of a successive activities over time (displaying their order), b) parallel sequences of activities – activities that run concurrently in time, c) knot of activities – a set of activities that take place simultaneously or occur without any sequential order that could be determined, d) iterative sequences or activities (i.e., cyclic repetition of activities or their sequences on the same item, e) repetitive sequences or activities (i.e., repetition of the same operations on multiple items. In particular cases, when the information about the order of activities is missing, the order of execution of the activities within a process can remain unspecified.

12.2.4 MEMORIA workflow diagrams

In order to avoid getting locked into pre-existing constraints, we decided to design *workflow diagrams* by thinking outside of the box. We have, however, built on our prior knowledge to draw on various existing visualisation formalisms. The main goal was to provide a diagrammatic representation that could serve as food for thought, enabling a *focus-plus-context*[3] interaction, preserving graphical simplicity and respecting the *data-ink ratio*[4] principle. The resulting diagram is a type of *cognitive map*, in other words: a visual representation of a person's (or a group's) mental model for a given process (Gibbons 2019). Of all the formalisms known to us, concept maps are by far the ones closest to MEMORIA workflow diagrams. In order to highlight the specificity of MEMORIA workflow diagrams, we will describe them in comparison to this formalism.

Concept maps are visual formalisms for organising and representing knowledge in a form of a graph, where nodes represent concepts (names) and labelled and directed links – that organise and structure information – represent the relationships between them (linking words). Concepts are (in principle) represented in a downward-branching hierarchical structure – the most general concepts are arranged at the top of the map and the more specific ones,

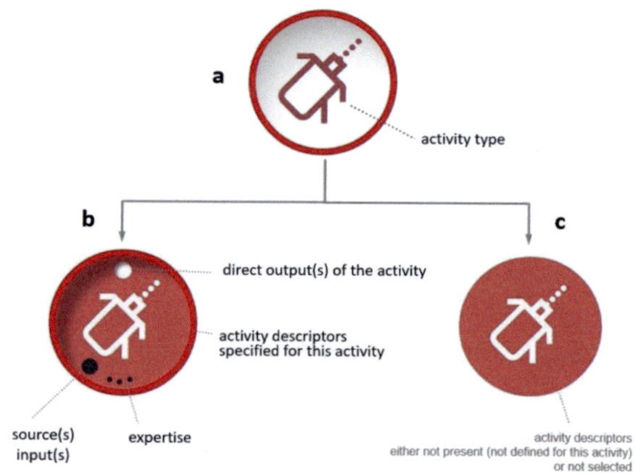

Figure 12.4. An example of a MEMORIA workflow node (laser distance measurement activity) – red colour refers to the activity's group (data collection and acquisition). a) declared, but not yet described activity, b-c) described activities: the background colour refers to a given group of activity, the presence of visual elements indicates advancement in activity's characterisation (paradata).

are organised hierarchically below. Each node can have more than one parent, therefore nodes in a concept map are often cross-connected. The aim of concept maps is usually to explore relationships among several concepts (Novak and Cañas 2008).

The MEMORIA workflow diagram is basically a concept-map-based graph (DAG – directed acyclic graph)[5], where nodes represent activities and the connections between them represent temporal relations. The key particularities of this graph may be summed up as follows:

3 The main idea of *focus plus context* visualisations is to provide viewers with the opportunity to see the object of interest presented in all its details (focus) while having the big picture – all the surrounding information (i.e., context) – available (infoVis:Wiki 2005).

4 A concept introduced by Edward Tufte. Data-ink is the *"non-erasable core of a graphic, the non-redundant ink arranged in response to variation in the numbers represented"*. If the data ink is removed from the image, the graphic loses its content. *Non-data-ink* does not transport the information (e.g., background colour, edges; Tufte 2006, 93).

5 Directed acyclic graph – a graph that does not have a closed loop.

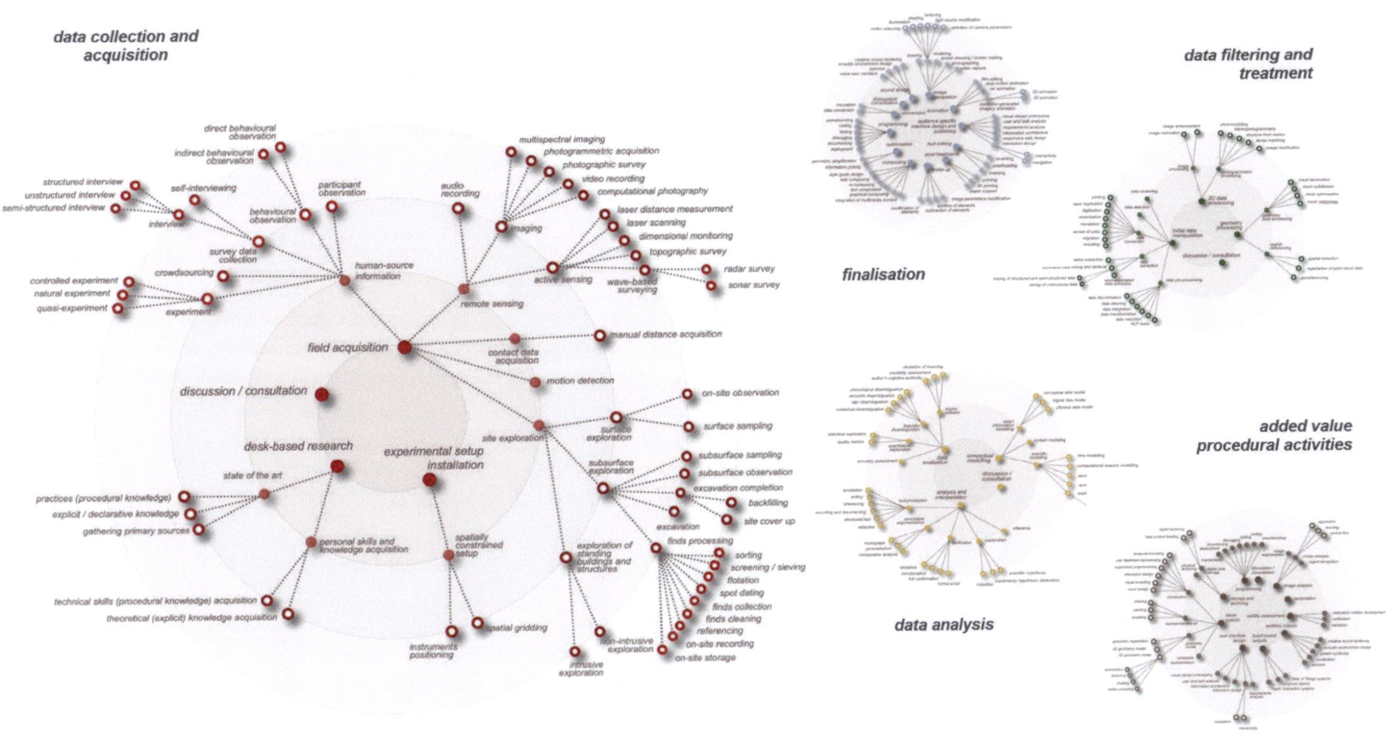

Figure 12.5. Wheels of activities organise a set of activities specific to our laboratory in a systematic way that allows them to be easily retrieved and selected. Each activity is represented by a multidimensional icon indicating the category of the activity (colour), its type (glyph) and its hierarchical position. The result of this effort has been recently published (https://shs.hal.science/halshs-03744846).

- MEMORIA workflows diagrams are *time-oriented graphs* – conventionally, time expands in a rightward direction,
- links between nodes are not labelled, instead, their shape represents the type of time-oriented relationship (Figure 12.3),
- a workflow diagram is endowed with a set of symbols to annotate the process (e.g., milestone notes – a brief record of observations about a particular stage in a process, infrastructure used as a support during the process, link to the preceding process(es),
- a formal identification of the moments in the workflow where results appear, differentiation of the type of these results (output, composition or publication),
- general data describing the process itself (e.g., name, project(s) within which the process is/was conducted, remarks) accessible behind icons.

Another noteworthy difference between MEMORIA workflow diagram and a conventional concept map lies in the visual encoding of the nodes.

12.2.4.1 Nodes (activities)

In a typical concept map a node is a labelled concept. By contrast, MEMORIA nodes encode the following information without the use of ethnic languages: activity type (glyph), its affiliation to one a particular group of activities (colour) and the presence of paradata provided for each individual activity (Figure 12.4).

Activities (nodes) are picked up by users via interactive *"wheels of activities"* – diagrams showing activities (with definitions and examples) distributed into five consistent groups (Figure 12.5). We have not based our model on any pre-existing example but on our data and our experience. All activities have been structured into five groups gathering goal-oriented activities dedicated to: A) data collection and acquisition, B) data filtering and treatement – transformation of the raw data into a form suitable for analysis, output production or finalisation needs, C) data analysis – encompassing methods of gaining of theoretical, explicit knowledge, D) added value procedural activities – the research phase centred on the use of procedural knowledge such as scientific procedures and technological protocols, E) finalisation – the research process that is specifically undertaken in dissemination contexts, such as publication, communication, etc.

Activities were collectively identified and structured during a long-term elicitation[6] cycle (Dudek and

6 The phase of elicitation was a long and complex process during which we sought to identify the structure of the professional practice of experts in the field. The process consisted of various phases in which forms of direct interaction with experts (e.g. focus groups), individual interviews or individual desk-based research were interwoven.

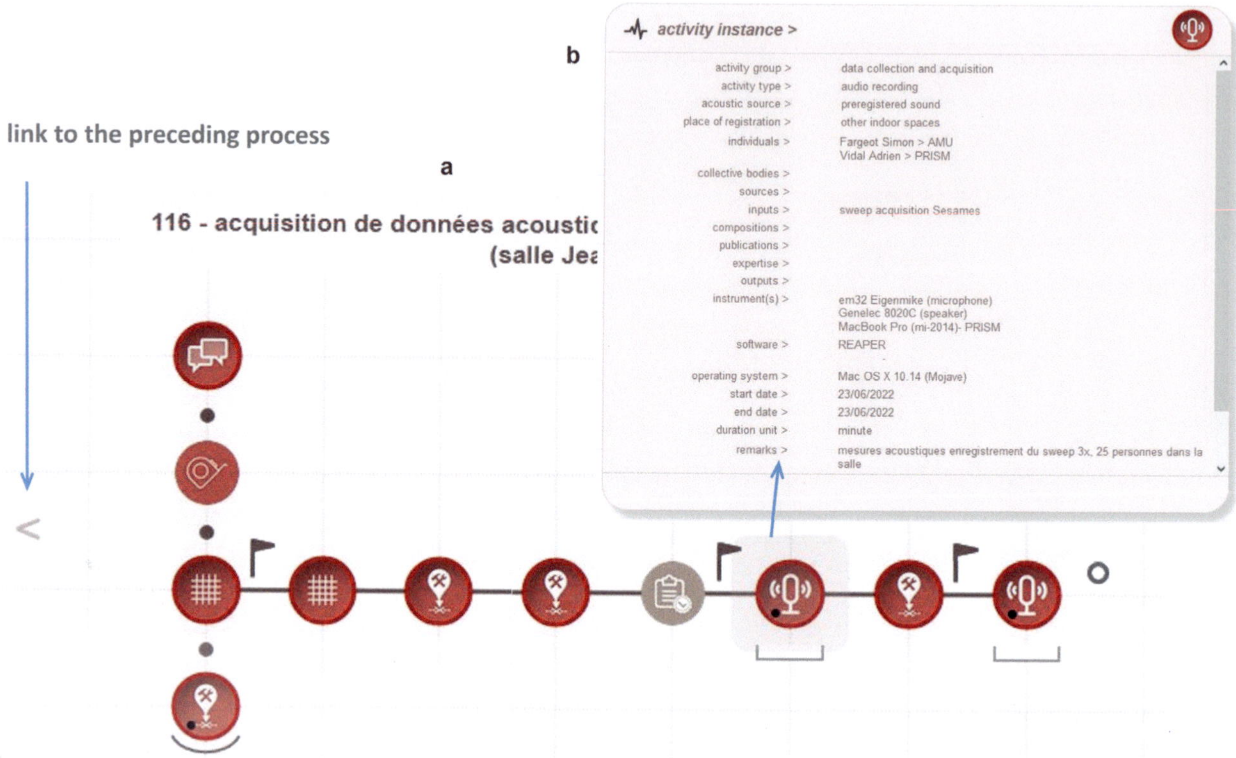

Figure 12.6. The structure of the process acts as the structural backbone of the paradata declared and organised within each activity. a) Example of MEMORIA workflow diagram illustrating an acoustic data acquisition process. Instruments were positioned basing on a protocol applied a few weeks earlier. Upon casual inspection, this workflow showcases the linear structure of the process, composed predominantly of nodes corresponding to data acquisition. b) outputs' paradata declared within the highlighted activity (audio recording).

Blaise 2020). This elicitation step is a crucial and recurring stage in the MEMORIA IS (Information System) construction. It was recently undertaken in cooperation with a group of archaeologists and the system was extended to explore its potential in archaeology – more precisely in a phase of archaeological fieldworks. The division of activities into the above-mentioned five groups is sometimes perceived – especially in data science circles – as an approach based on data lifecycle. We comment on this aspect in Appendix 1 (DOI: 10.5281/zenodo.8311129).

12.2.4.2 From the mental model of a process to its Memoria workflow diagram

Structuring one's own mental model of a process into a temporally organised diagram is a way for a researcher to interpret and question his/her own research protocol, but also to foster exchanges with other scientists on the basis of a shared description. However, as mentioned before, an individual's interpretation of the information graphics and their capability to model and structure their own knowledge depends on their graphic interpretation skills. Hopefully these skills can be learned, trained and refined.

At this stage of development, the system is functional and allows to describe and structure a process associated with the "production" of one or more outcomes. Navigation through the *wheels* allows the selection of activities – all selected activities are stored within an "activity tray", from where they can be dragged and dropped inside a composition grid and structured into a process by specifying relationships between activities (e.g., order of execution, iterative or repetitive segments, etc.). From then on, activities dropped inside the composition grid can be documented with paradata (activity by activity). A workflow diagram is a sort of a backbone for the "body of the process". Paradata depicting each activity are anchored on it, they are freely accessible, searchable, editable (Figure 12.6). Organised by the means of a workflow, they are stored in an RDBMS (relational database management system). They can be queried, compared and visualised.

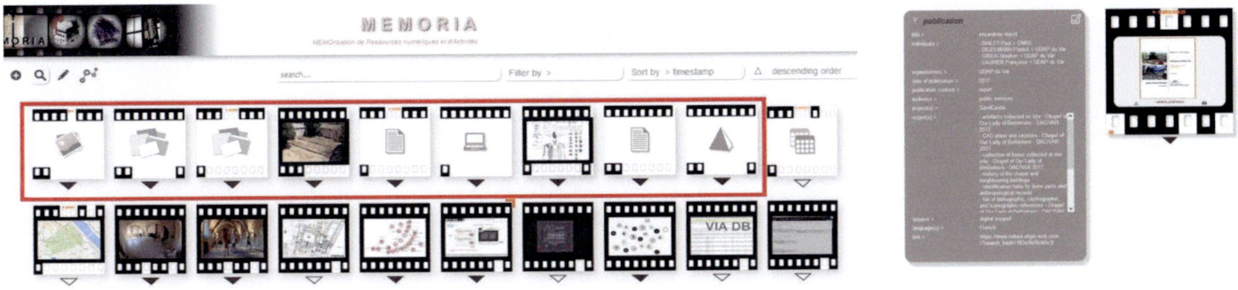

Figure 12.7. Nine outputs identified (and partially described) for the illustrative example of archaeological fieldwork. On the right, metadata on the report, using the form of a film metaphor, illustrates the level of completion of the publication's description (https://sandbox.memoria.map.cnrs.fr/is/enter.php?show=publication&id=20).

12.3 Results

The majority of the Memoria IS exploratory interface was developed and tested as part of the SESAMES ANR project.[7] During this period over 240 results – stemming from six independent projects – were identified and described (most of them are outputs). The mainstream of our work deals with study of architectural heritage, although not from a perspective of archaeology, so examples of workflows already present within the system may be thematically distant from archaeological practice – and therefore may be hard to comprehend. We have therefore chosen to overcome this complication by constructing a hypothetic project representing archaeological fieldwork based on a real-life example. We will use this example to concisely illustrate the particularity, usability and potential benefits of our exploratory system.

12.3.1 How to create a workflow diagram? From the identification of a result to workflow description

The hypothetical example we will present below is based on the analysis of an actual archaeological fieldwork report.[8]

12.3.1.1 Identification of results

Based on the report's content, we have identified a set of ten outcomes (Figure 12.7). Nine of them, categorised as outputs and one as a publication, were described within the MEMORIA-sandbox platform – the IS familiarisation tool. The next step was to interpret the report in order to structure the excavation process into a MEMORIA workflow diagram.

7 ANR (Agence Nationale de la Recherche) project ANR-18-CE38-0009-01; http://anr-sesames.map.cnrs.fr/index.html.

8 Digelman (2017); the interpretation was done by I. Dudek (an architect with no practical experience in archaeological excavations), therefore the reader is asked to bear in mind the hypothetical and instructional nature of this demonstration, which is intended only to illustrate the functionality of the system.

12.3.1.2 Workflow diagram as an answer to a question

Let us return again to the comparison of workflow with concept maps. Their inventor, J.D. Novak, points out that the sensible approach to construct concept maps is to work with reference to a *focus question*: "a particular question we seek to answer" (Novak and Cañas 2008).

A similar approach should be taken when trying to shape a workflow within the MEMORIA IS. Within our system, the focus question is: *how did I proceed to obtain this result? What were my subsequent steps?* In this hypothetical example the question became: *How did this group of archaeologists proceed to obtain these ten results? What were their subsequent steps?*

The answer to this question was particularly perplexing. The core of the report focuses on the presentation of the results of the operation and the research context (archaeological, geographical and geological …). It contains exhaustive administrative data, but the section on methods and means is relatively short and contains not enough details to properly reconstruct the sequence and succession of the actions taken. The workflow diagram presented below is one of the numerous options we considered (Figure 12.8). This diagram certainly does not reflect the actual progress of the work, for which more detailed information would be needed (i.e., field notes, layer forms …). However, it is a version from which it is possible to start the reflection and discussion.

12.3.1.3 The real reasons for describing the process

An important decision is to make it clear for ourselves *why* and *for whom* we are documenting. What elements of the process we may consider as relevant (i.e., activities, milestone notes) and which paradata we will be willing to provide depends on the reason for documenting. The effort put into the description differ from case to case. If someone is documenting for themselves to prevent forgetting, then he/she will select the fragments that are

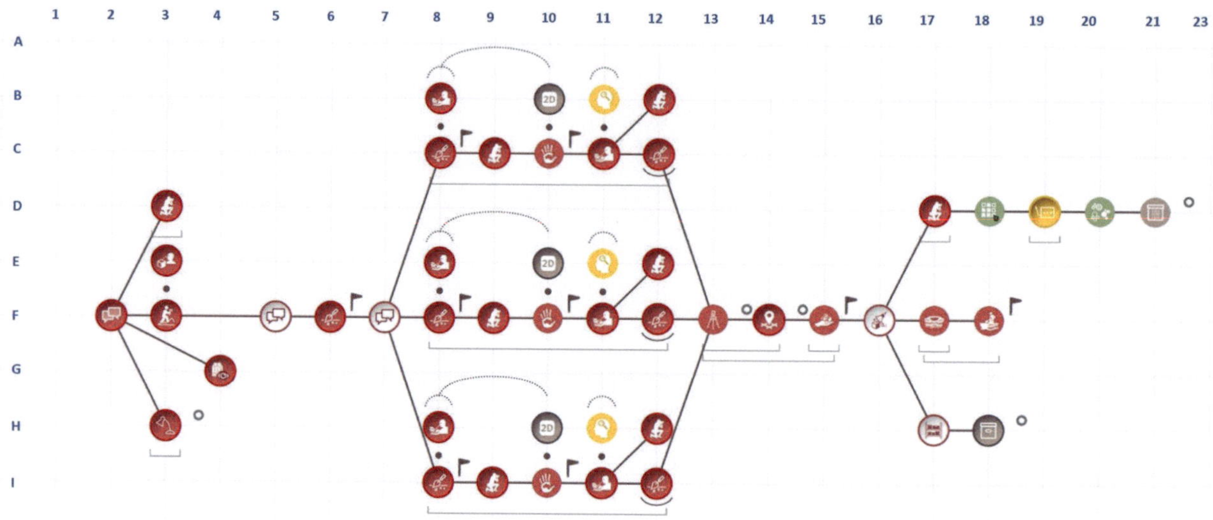

Figure 12.8. MEMORIA workflow diagram – archaeological survey based on an archaeological report (https://sandbox.memoria.map.cnrs.fr/is/enter.php?show=process&_op=set&id=118). The small grey rings indicate the moments at which the output data (identified in the system) appears. The story the diagram tells is detailed in Appendix 2 (DOI:10.5281/zenodo.8311129).

important to him/her. The knowledge about a process will be structured differently for colleagues from the same discipline (who are familiar with the methods, objectives and approaches used) and for specialists from other disciplines (who know neither the objectives nor the specifics of the approach).

In the current state of implementation, the MEMORIA IS allows documentation of real-case (past and ongoing) processes. We identified two other potential uses for workflow diagrams – *"theoretical process"* and *"project process"*. The concept of *theoretical process* has a potential of passing on know-how and expertise of an individual or a research team – it could serve as a basis for tacit knowledge consolidation and transfer. One case study has already been tested.

Planned operations (project process) could also be recorded using a MEMORIA workflow diagram. A major opportunity in this case would be to enable documentation of the project during its execution using its project workflow diagram. A later comparison of the planning and execution diagrams could be used, for example, to highlight unanticipated elements. Both components – theoretical and project process – are pending implementation and testing.

12.3.1.4 Putting the concepts of metadata and paradata into practice in MEMORIA IS

As outlined earlier, we consider *metadata* as data/information about characteristics of an object or resource. Their role in the system is to facilitate the findability and filtering of results, and to enable their comparative analysis. *Paradata* refer to the process of the production of results. Their function in the system is to allow the recording, sharing, explanation of the protocols used to produce the results, and to enable their comparative analysis.

The ultimate aim of these analyses would be enlarging epistemological awareness of the methods and approaches we use (identification of biases and errors for example), the influence of tools we use on the outputs we obtain, etc. In order to approach this goal, it is necessary to enter the sufficient amount of data into the system. However, the crucial and, possibly, inherent obstacle is that as people actively involved in scientific research, we often do not take time to document sufficiently our work. An in-depth analysis of this issue is beyond the scope of this document, but we will nevertheless shortly comment on it in the *Discussion* section.

12.3.1.5 What we have learnt from examining our case-study archaeological report?

Our attempt to describe this archaeological report in the form of a MEMORIA workflow diagram helped to highlight the nature and objectives of this document. It is a publication presenting several outputs to a given public (regional archaeological service) in the context of exploratory archaeological survey. It sums up results achieved in a systematic and organised way. An accurate and truthful description of the process based solely on the information contained in this type of document is impossible. The crux of the matter is that an archaeological report answers the questions posed *prior* to the operation – i.e., evaluation of the condition of the preserved archaeological layers and of the existence of previous occupation levels, supplementing the chronological phases already partially established.

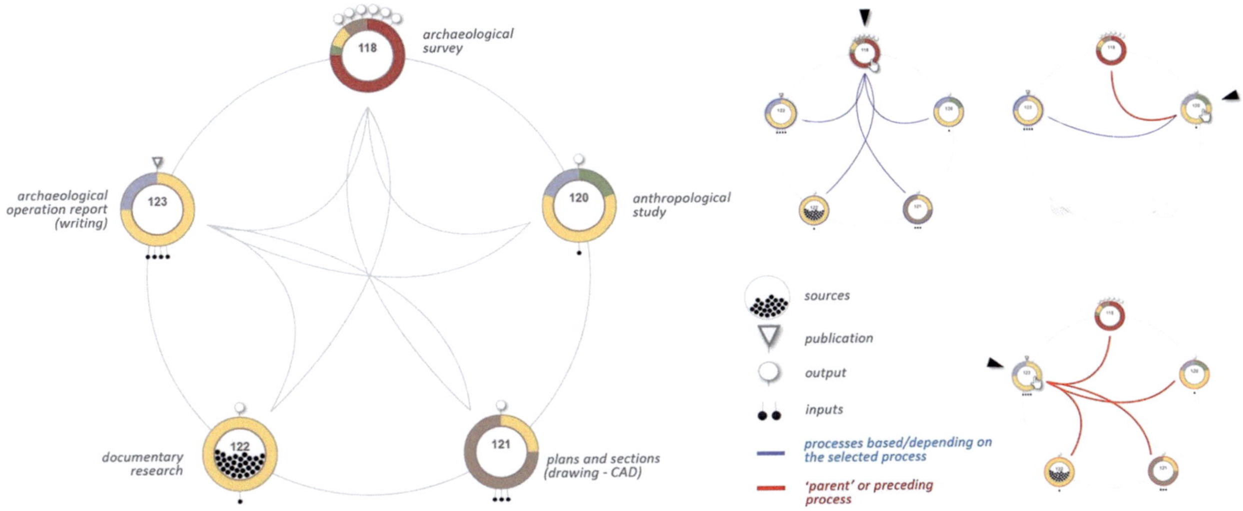

Figure 12.9. Process as activities' proportion rings, one of the system's data visualisation tool designed to provide an answer to the question: What are the relative proportions of each group of activities inside a process, and how many inputs, outputs/results and sources are concerned? On the left, the case-study of archaeological fieldworks – six outputs identified in this process, a prevailing number of data acquisition activities (red colour) with a predominance of photographic survey, excavation and subsurface observation activities, missing paradata concerning tools, dates, and instruments. On the right, the conceptual modelling process of the controlled vocabulary employed in the MEMORIA IS – the apparent predominance of data analysis (yellow colour) and huge quantity of sources used within the process (black feeling of the interior of the activities ring).

It therefore presents a selection of outcomes and summarises roughly the course of action.

The *metadata* describing the results of this operation is relatively complete (Figure 12.7). What is missing relates to file formats, instruments and software used to produce the outputs. The paradata that can be extracted from the report are more limited. Technological and methodological elements, such as the organisational and temporal pattern of the process, the role of each person in particular activities, the techniques used to uncover remains, the different phases of excavation strategy, the instruments and tools used, the obstacles encountered, the decisions taken, or the ethical and legal elements (legal restrictions, copyright) are not presented in a sufficiently precise manner in the report.

12.3.1.6 The role of Information Visualisation within the system

> *"To see is to forget the name of the thing one sees"* (Valéry and Degas 2017, 159).

The basic principle which has guided us from the very beginning of the project is based on the reinforcement and facilitation of non-verbal thinking in all phases of the system's use – in the phases associated with data feeding (filling in and recording the data), in the knowledge elicitation (process structuring), in the searching and filtering of the data and, above all, in the data analysis phase.

At the current stage of development, the MEMORIA IS helps the user to access structured metadata related to outputs and processes in read mode (the what, where, when and how of an output, etc.) and for all types of results to retrieve structured metadata in PDF format. The system provides data visualisation tools that can be used to exploit the content collected (metadata or paradata) to obtain a visual answer to a given question such as:

- what are the main categories of activities that make up an individual's operational profile?
- what are the relative proportions of each group of activities inside a process, and how many inputs, outputs/results and sources are concerned (Figure 12.9)?
- what are the relations between the various processes conducted within a project (Figure 12.10)?

Multiple interactions are possible with the activities' proportion rings, for example display of percentage of activities from various groups, links to and information about the process's results (outputs, compositions, publications) and about elements the process is based on (sources, inputs, expertise).

The system interface is intended to provide the user with a visually stimulating environment, free of unnecessary embellishments (i.e., not carrying extra information), but showing variation in the data and drawing attention to the meaning and substance of the data.

Figure 12.10. Process variability chord diagram – a data visualisation tool displaying relations between processes conducted within a given project. On the left, the case-study of archaeological survey composed of five processes (four of them are non-data-driven study, drafted only as an example). Processes are represented as activities' proportion rings and ordered chronologically (clockwise) according to the start date of the first activity declared within a process. On the right, examples of user interactions – an onmouseover event* highlights the processes declared as being related to the process that is being pointed to. In this case study, archaeological fieldworks produce outputs used as inputs in all subsequent processes. The anthropological study bases on archaeological fieldworks and serves the archaeological operation report.

* The onmouseover event occurs when the mouse pointer enters an element (https://www.w3schools.com/jsref/event_onmouseover.asp).

A recent study on documentation in archaeological field reports points out that:

> *"reports have had a relatively poor renommée as being uninspiring to read* [...] *and according to critics, too often superficial, uninformative and of low scholarly value"* (Huvila et al. 2021, 1111).

The scientific reports are probably not very thrilling either. We believe that a certain dose of visual stimulation can substantially deepen knowledge and understanding of processes and considerably reduce the discomfort barrier, making the work of the reporter and of the reader easier. This type of advantage, however, has its price – a detailed description of sequences of activities takes time. It requires determination and honesty, if the whole effort is to lead to understanding rather than to misinformation or camouflage of our failures.

12.4 Discussion

The MEMORIA exploratory prototype is, first and foremost, an effort to build a tool that should help us meet the requirements of scientific integrity (e.g., ensuring the traceability, transmissibility and verifiability of scientific results) and the challenges of open science (providing free access to the content produced), allowing methodological comparisons within the framework of intra-, inter- and multidisciplinary work. A central point of the approach is the will to develop visual interfaces providing access to resources and empowering a direct analysis of the information gathered.

The MEMORIA visual interface gives access to *metadata*, *paradata* (structured within workflow diagrams) and dynamic visualisation tools. It allows the human analyst to interact with complex, abundant data about research results and the history of their production. But any tool – like a knife or an information system – can be used properly or inappropriately, for good and bad purposes. And so the MEMORIA IS has its potential – without recognising it, we would not have committed ourselves for eight years to its slow, successive construction – and, unsurprisingly, it also has limitations. It is difficult to list them all in an organised way, because whether one sees them as advantages or not can be relative. Positive aspects of the system and its benefits include:

- *documentary potential* – an archive of traces of our professional activity, allowing us to store and share thematically structured collections of metadata and paradata, which can be translated to other formats (e.g., XML, JSON, text),
- potential role of the *theoretical/tacit knowledge-sharing environment* – possibility of sharing experiences and

practical (tacit) knowledge with others (cf. "theoretical process"),

- *innovative/creative visual analytical framework* – using collected data/information to analyse relations, trends and exceptions using dynamic visualisation tools,
- *support for the planning of scientific protocols* based on records of previous experiments (cf. "project process"),
- possibly a groundbreaking approach to *meaningful documenting*[9] – using the system can allow us to look at our own work from a different perspective. It helps to be aware of *a whole* research process, of what has been done or abandoned, and of how it was achieved. It puts a spotlight on the need to take notes focusing on choices during the execution ("doing") phase.

However, each of the abovementioned points presents some methodological and practical limitations. Some of these are linked to our early choices. Its novel character puts a potential user on a steep initial learning curve, one that requires an intellectual involvement based on one's deontology. Structuring the MEMORIA workflow diagrams requires being ready to model one's own knowledge and this exercise may be time-consuming. Additionally, potential users should be open to learn meaningfully, and this requires an emotional and intellectual involvement to gain new insights through an autonomous discovery.

It should not be expected that this approach will suit everyone. A variety of reasons can be mentioned, such as:

- individuals may vary in their ability to describe the protocols in which they participated (e.g., due to the dilemmas of what is important to be included or difficulty in coherently conveying complex information),
- users may lack experience in conceptual modelling or graphic interpretation skills,
- users may lack willingness to explore ways of passing their experience to others,
- they may simply lack reliability or accuracy.[10]

The first and second set of difficulties is not insurmountable – these skills can be learned, trained and refined. Other limitations are more fundamental. The very fact of using an information system is, in a sense, a limitation and a difficulty in itself, related to the issue of the *longevity and sustainability of web-based information systems*. The constant development and evolution of technology requires continuous mobilisation to ensure functionality of such systems (e.g., maintenance, development, user support and funding).

The documentary potential of the MEMORIA system is inherently restricted by its *purely digital nature entailing a certain fragility* of the stored data. For decades we have been cautioned about the necessity of digitalisation. Now we face an ever-increasing volume of digital documents occupying the disks of servers around the world. The risks involved include ensuring the long-term accessibility and readability of this data. Digital data are not less fragile than analogue ones, they are just different[11]. The numerical/analogue data archiving procedures considered in the 1990s[12] could be a good solution, for example, for archiving export files in PDF format.

The MEMORIA system may play the role of a *knowledge-sharing and knowledge-generating environment*. This requires reliable data within the system, and the correctness of the data entered depends entirely on its users. So far, the willingness to pursue a systematic description of our work – even of parts of it – is not prevalent within our community. The main – and relatable – argument is lack of time. Still, it should be clear that without a documentary effort and without making the documented data and associated scientific protocols openly available, our achievements may fail to survive and serve others, or enter the bloodstream of science, nourish and revitalise it.

Our actions depend predominantly on an acute awareness of their purpose. For what purpose and to whom should the data we collect be useful? Why and for what purpose should we document?

Furthermore, all the data, information and publications being produced today will not be stored indefinitely. Not only because of the increased costs incurred to store and keep them continuously available, but for purely pragmatic reasons: not all files deserve to be stored (Australian Research Data Commons 2020). Determining how to sort the wheat from the chaff is a very difficult question, beyond our competence and the scope of this paper – we have not reached that point yet. For now, we are looking for ways to encourage "harvesting". P. Fox recommends to:

> *"develop incentives to induce data providers to develop metadata and data products that will be usable by both narrow initial users of data and the wider community of interdisciplinary users reusing data for other purposes"* (Fox 2011, 22).

Among the incentives, he indicates wider data use and data citations. Among the deterrents, he proposes contingent funding and contingent publication of papers.

9 In reference to the notions of *rote learning* and *meaningful learning* (Novak and Cañas 2008).

10 The use of collected *meta-* and *paradata* to ***design new scientific processes and protocols***, despite its potentially encouraging nature, can also have its dark side – e.g., the "copy and paste" syndrome. We know from experience that the misuse of this procedure, which speeds up the work to some extent, leads to an ill-considered, automatic use of one's own or third-party contributions.

11 One solar storm in the near or distant future may erase them.

12 Digital to microfilm, for example.

12.4.1 Necessity of "sticks and carrots"

It is only fair to admit that documenting is not particularly exciting. Most people we consulted on this issue seemed visibly crestfallen when they heard about the need for record-keeping. Within the MEMORIA IS, we have tried to incorporate several incentives such as a neat working environment to support the intellectual effort of description, involving visual thinking, design of visualisation tools that provide answer to user's questions, or offering converted metadata in a stable, human-readable format (PDF). Further improvements are possible. Introduction of the possibility of grouping the completion of certain metadata/paradata common to various activities to allow swifter form filling. The paradata structured within workflow diagrams could be accessible as a text and read aloud using a text to speech voice reader for visually impaired persons.

Nevertheless, there are also some "carrots" over which we have no influence, like those recommended by P. Fox, or their variations, for example establishing regulations enabling for the publication of open data enriched with how-to (i.e., paradata) to become an act of publication of equal or increased value as compared to the publication of an academic research paper.

The "sticks" are also necessary, but these are not at all within our reach (e.g., authorisation of research structures on condition that they have internal regulations requiring members to work systematically with open data + paradata, support research and applications aimed at improving cross- and inter-disciplinary discovery and reuse of data and results (Fox 2011).

Without a subtle and well-thought-out combination of reward and correction, to challenge the inherent human inertia.

By designing and developing MEMORIA IS, we have tried to address the problem of a shortage of metadata and paradata in documentation practices at the local level (our lab). Our aim is not to convince anyone to abandon existing documentation practices, but rather to encourage an interdisciplinary reflection on the use, in one way or another, of theoretical principles or practical solutions proposed by the system.

Acknowledgements

Collaborators who provided an effective contribution to this work: Pascal Bénistant (UMR 3495 MAP, Marseille): resources and software; and Gaël Simon (UMR 7324 CITERES, Tours): support in data curation and investigation.

Funding

This work was supported by the Département de la Recherche, de l'Enseignement Supérieur et de la Technologie, Ministère de la Culture / Department of Research, Higher Education and Technology, French Ministry of Culture (2016-2020) and the Agence Nationale de la Recherche [ANR-18-CE38-0009-01, project SESAMES, 2019-2023].

Data, scripts, code, and supplementary information availability

Link to the MEMORIA IS website: http://memoria-dev.gamsau.archi.fr/is/enter.php.

Link to the MEMORIA "sandbox" – a "hands on" platform that allows potential users of the MEMORIA IS to try out the system and to explore the notions of output, composition, publication, processes and activities, or expertise: https://sandbox.memoria.map.cnrs.fr/is/enter.php.

Link to the MEMORIA project website: http://memoria-dev.gamsau.archi.fr/projet/objectives.php?lang=en.

The classification of the 285 activities present in the MEMORIA information system in May 2022 (PDF): https://shs.hal.science/halshs-03744846.

Author Contributions

I.D.: Conceptualisation, Data curation, Formal analysis, Investigation, Methodology, Software –designing and testing, Project administration, Supervision, Validation, Visualisation, Writing – original draft, Writing – review & editing,

J.-Y.B.: Conceptualisation, Data curation, Methodology – expertise and feedback, Writing – original draft, Writing – review & editing, Funding acquisition.

Peer review

This article has been reviewed and recommended by PCI Archaeology.

Huvila, Isto. 2023. "Using information visualisation to improve traceability, transmissibility and verifiability in research workflows" *Peer Community in Archaeology* 100330. DOI:10.24072/pci.archaeo.100330.

References

Aigner, Wolfgang, Silvia Miksch, Heidrun Schumann, and Christian Tominski. 2011. *Visualization of Time-Oriented Data, 2nd Ed.* London: Springer. https://dl.acm.org/doi/10.5555/2016703.

Ancker, Jessica S., Yalini Senathirajah, Rita Kukafka, and Justin B. Starren. 2006. "Design Features of Graphs in Health Risk Communication: A Systematic Review." *Journal of the American Medical Informatics Association* 13 (6): 608–18. DOI: 10.1197/jamia.M2115.

Australian Research Data Commons. 2020. "Data Provenance Metadata: Building Trust in Research | ARDC." https://ardc.edu.au/article/data-provenance-metadata-builds-trust-credibility-and-reproducibility.

Bakken, Richard, and James Dobbs. 2016. "The Relevance of Four Types of Knowledge for Leader Preparation in Radically Different Settings: Reflections on Data from a Case Study in Qatar and Teaching at a United States Military Academy." *Creighton Journal of Interdisciplinary Leadership* 2 (2): 17–23. DOI: 10.17062/CJIL.v2i2.47.

Bank, Carl-Georg, and Heidi Daxberger. 2020. "Concept Maps for Structuring Instruction and as a Potential Assessment Tool in a Large Introductory Science Course." *Journal of College Science Teaching* 49 (6): 65–75. DOI: 10.1080/0047231X.2020.12290666.

Barga, Roger, and Dennis Gannon. 2007. "Scientific versus Business Workflows." In *Workflows for E-Science: Scientific Workflows for Grids*, edited by Ian J. Taylor, Ewa Deelman, Dennis B. Gannon, and Matthew Shields, 9–16. London: Springer. DOI: 10.1007/978-1-84628-757-2_2.

Berge, Timon ten, and René van Hezewijk. 1999. "Procedural and Declarative Knowledge: An Evolutionary Perspective." *Theory & Psychology* 9 (5): 605–24. DOI: 10.1177/0959354399095002.

Brezillon, Patrick, and Jean-Charles Pomerol. 1999. "Contextual Knowledge and Proceduralized Context." In *Proceedings of the AAAI-99 Workshop on Modeling Context in AI Applications, Orlando, Florida, USA, July. AAAI Technical Report*, 16–20. Orlando: AAAI Press.

Brusaporci, Stefano. 2017. "The Importance of Being Honest: Issues of Transparency in Digital Visualization of Architectural Heritage." In *3D Printing: Breakthroughs in Research and Practice*, 333–60. Hershey, PA: IGI Global. DOI: 10.4018/978-1-5225-1677-4.ch018.

Burgin, Mark. 2016. *Theory Of Knowledge: Structures And Processes*. Singapore: World Scientific Publishing. DOI: 10.1142/8893.

Carlsson, Linnea. 2012. "Visual Planning in Construction: A Study of Its Use in Construction Projects." MA diss., KTH Stockholm. https://urn.kb.se/resolve?urn=urn:nbn:se:kth:diva-96390.

Carper, Barbara A. 1978. "Fundamental Patterns of Knowing in Nursing." *Advances in Nursing Science* 1 (1): 13–24. DOI: 10.1097/00012272-197810000-00004.

Digelman, Patric. 2017. *Diagnostic archéologique. Commune de Bras, Var. Chapelle Notre Dame de Betléem. Rapport d'opération archéologique, Bras, 12-21 Juin 2017.* Département du Var, Direction des Affaires Culturelles, Service du Patrimoine et de l'Archéologie. https://www.culture.eligis-web.com/?search_hash=16729f97a2570f.

Doyle, Rosemary. 2009. "Doing, Describing and Documenting : Inscription and Practice in Social Work." PhD diss., University of St Andrews. https://research-repository.st-andrews.ac.uk/handle/10023/766.

Dudek, Iwona, and Jean-Yves Blaise. 2020. "Enabling the Comparability of Research Workflows: A Case Study." *CAA Series Computer Applications and Quantitative Methods in Archaeology*. https://shs.hal.science/halshs-02927631.

Fox, Peter. 2011. "Data Management Considerations for the Data Life Cycle." Presented at the NRC STS Panel 2011, Washington DC, November 17. https://www.google.com/search?client=firefox-b-d&q=Data+Management+Considerations+for+the+Data+Life+Cycle+fox+NRC+STS+Panel.+2011.

Gamble, Jordan R. 2020. "Tacit vs Explicit Knowledge as Antecedents for Organizational Change." *Journal of Organizational Change Management* 33 (6): 1123–41. DOI: 10.1108/JOCM-04-2020-0121.

Gibbons, Sarah. 2019. "Cognitive Maps, Mind Maps, and Concept Maps: Definitions." Nielsen Norman Group. https://www.nngroup.com/articles/cognitive-mind-concept.

Glazer, Nirit. 2011. "Challenges with Graph Interpretation: A Review of the Literature." *Studies in Science Education* 47 (2): 183–210. DOI: 10.1080/03057267.2011.605307.

Goble, Carole, Sarah Cohen-Boulakia, Stian Soiland-Reyes, Daniel Garijo, Yolanda Gil, Michael R. Crusoe, Kristian Peters, and Daniel Schober. 2020. "FAIR Computational Workflows." *Data Intelligence* 2 (1–2): 108–21. DOI: 10.1162/dint_a_00033.

Gravitz, Lauren. 2019. "The Forgotten Part of Memory." *Nature* 571 (7766): S12–S12. DOI: 10.1038/d41586-019-02211-5.

Green, Jill. 2002. "Somatic Knowledge: The Body as Content and Methodology in Dance Education." *Journal of Dance Education* 2 (4): 114–18. https:/ doi.org/10.1080/15290824.2002.10387219.

Halonen, Raija, and Elisa Laukkanen. 2008. "Managing Tacit and Explicit Knowledge in Organisational Teams." In *2008 Third International Conference on*

Digital Information Management, London, UK, 292–97. IEEE. DOI: 10.1109/ICDIM.2008.4746707.

Neisser, Ulric, and Nicole Harsch. 1992. "Phantom Flashbulbs: False Recollections of Hearing the News about Challenger." In *Affect and Accuracy in Recall: Studies of 'Flashbulb' Memories*, edited by Eugene Winograd and Ulric Neisser, 9–31. Cambridge: Cambridge University Press. DOI: 10.1017/CBO9780511664069.003.

Horst, Tara. 2008. "The Body in Adult Education: Introducing a Somatic Learning Model." In *Adult Education Research Conference*. St. Louis, MO. https://newprairiepress.org/aerc/2008/papers/28.

Huvila, Isto. 2022. "Improving the Usefulness of Research Data with Better Paradata." *Open Information Science* 6 (1): 28–48. DOI: 10.1515/opis-2022-0129.

Huvila, Isto, Olle Sköld, and Lisa Börjesson. 2021. "Documenting Information Making in Archaeological Field Reports." *Journal of Documentation* 77 (5): 1107–27. DOI: 10.1108/JD-11-2020-0188.

InfoVis:Wiki. 2005. "Focus-plus-Context – InfoVis:Wiki." InfoVis:Wiki. https://infovis-wiki.net/wiki/Focus-plus-Context.

Karr, Alan F. 2020. "Metadata and Paradata: Information Collection and Potential Initiatives." US National Institute of Statistical Sciences. https://www.niss.org/research/metadata-and-paradata-information-collection-and-potential-initiatives.

Kreuter, Frauke, and Carolina Casas-Cordero. 2010. *Paradata*. Berlin: Rat für Sozial- und Wirtschaftsdaten. https://www.econstor.eu/handle/10419/43631.

Leipzig, Jeremy. 2017. "A Review of Bioinformatic Pipeline Frameworks." *Briefings in Bioinformatics* 18 (3): 530–36. DOI: 10.1093/bib/bbw020.

Mauri, Michele, Maria de los Angeles Briones, Beatrice Gobbo, and Gabriele Colombo. 2020. "Research Protocol Diagrams as Didactic Tools to Act Critically in Dataset Design Processes." In *INTED2020 Proceedings*, 9034–43. Valencia: IATED. DOI: 10.21125/inted.2020.2470.

Mazzu, Greg. 2022. "Bioinformatics Pipeline & Tips For Faster Iterations." WEKA. https://www.weka.io/blog/hpc/bioinformatics-pipeline/.

Mclachlan, Scott, Evangelia Kyrimi, Bridget J. Daley, Kudakwashe Dube, Max Marsden, Sarah Finer, Graham A. Hitman, and Norman E. Fenton. 2020. "Incorporating Clinical Decisions into Standardised Caremaps." In *2020 IEEE International Conference on Healthcare Informatics (ICHI), Oldenburg, Germany*, 1–2. IEEE. DOI: 10.1109/ICHI48887.2020.9374381.

McLachlan, Scott, and Lisa C. Webley. 2021. "Visualisation of Law and Legal Process: An Opportunity Missed." *Information Visualization* 20 (2–3): 192–204. DOI: 10.1177/14738716211012608.

Moreau, Luc, and Paul Groth. 2022. *Provenance: An Introduction to PROV*. Switzerland: Springer Nature.

Novak, Joseph D., and Alberto J. Cañas. 2008. *The Theory Underlying Concept Maps and How to Construct and Use Them*. Florida: Florida Institute for Human and Machine Cognition. https://cmap.ihmc.us/publications/ResearchPapers/TheoryUnderlyingConceptMapshq.pdf.

Phillips, Richard J. 1997. "Can Juniors Read Graphs? A Review and Analysis of Some Computer-Based Activities." *Journal of Information Technology for Teacher Education* 6 (1): 49–58. DOI: 10.1080/14759399700200005.

Sköld, Olle, Lisa Börjesson, and Isto Huvila. 2022. "Interrogating Paradata." In *Proceedings of the 11th International Conference on Conceptions of Library and Information Science, Oslo Metropolitan University, May 29 - June 1, 2022*. Borås: University of Borås. DOI: 10.47989/colis2206.

SSHOC. 2022a. "How to Create a Workflow in the SSH Open Marketplace?" Social Sciences & Humanities Open Marketplace. https://marketplace.sshopencloud.eu/workflow/hmGpmv.

SSHOC. 2022b. "World Digital Library – Content Workflow." Social Sciences & Humanities Open Marketplace. https://marketplace.sshopencloud.eu/training-material/vbob91.

Tahko, Tuomas E. 2011. "A Priori and A Posteriori: A Bootstrapping Relationship." *Metaphysica* 12 (2): 151–64. DOI: 10.1007/s12133-011-0083-5.

Tufte, Edward R. 2006. *The Visual Display of Quantitative Information*. Cheshire, CT: Graphics Press.

Valéry, Paul, and Edgar Degas. 2017. *Degas Danse Dessin. Fac-Simile de l'éd. de Paris : A. Vollard, 1936*. Paris: Gallimard.

Vocabs. n.d. "ACDH-CH/DARIAH Vocabularies: TaDiRAH: Taxonomy of Digital Research Activities in the Humanities." Vocabs. Accessed October 22, 2022. https://vocabs.dariah.eu/tadirah/en.

13 Creating an Additional Class Layer with Machine Learning to counter Overfitting in an Unbalanced Ancient Coin Dataset

Sebastian Gampe
Big Data Lab
Goethe-Universität
Frankfurt am Main
gampe@em.uni-frankfurt.de
ORCID 0009-0002-8700-3505

Karsten Tolle
Big Data Lab
Goethe-Universität
Frankfurt am Main
k.tolle@em.uni-frankfurt.de
ORCID 0000-0002-9953-7638

Abstract

We have implemented an approach based on *Convolutional Neural Networks* (CNN) for mint recognition for our *Corpus Nummorum* (CN) coin dataset as an alternative to coin type recognition, since we had too few instances for most of the types (classes). However, this shift increased an existing problem with our dataset: the extremely unbalanced number of instances per class. While some of our classes consist of only 20 instances, others consist of several hundred. After training our VGG16 model we unsurprisingly observed an overfitting of these "big" classes within the confusion matrix. To reduce this problem, we tried to split the dominating classes with the most images into several smaller ones and called them additional class layers. We use three different *Machine Learning* (ML) approaches to perform this breakdown. One is an unsupervised clustering method without additional manual work. The other two are supervised approaches which explicitly take into account the motifs of the coins themselves: a) an Object Detection model that predicts trained entities, and b) a *Natural Language Processing* (NLP) method to find entities in the textual descriptions of the coins. Based on the combination of obverse and reverse results from these two approaches new additional class layers were defined for each of them independently. After retraining our mint recognition model with these new classes, we evaluated the results based on the confusion matrix. In our case, the best results could be observed by forming an additional class layer based on the NLP method. Unfortunately, in our situation the overfitting problem could only be reduced and not eliminated.

Keywords: Machine Learning; Image Recognition; Convolutional Neural Networks; Unbalanced Dataset; Ancient Coins

13.1 Introduction

In our current project D4N4 – Data quality for Numismatics based on Natural language processing and Neural Networks (D4N4 n.d.) we want to implement a Machine Learning (ML)-based coin type recognition model that covers as many coin types as possible from

In *Advances in Digital Archaeology. Proceedings of the 2023 conference Computer Applications and Quantitative Methods in Archaeology – 50 years of synergy*, edited by J.W.H.P. Verhagen, J. Waagen, A. Brandsen, A. Queffelec, R.M. Visser and D. Taelman, 163–176. Leiden: Sidestone Press.

CNN Architecture	Class Type	Additional Class Layer	Number of Perinthos / Pergamon classes	Top-1 Accuracy	Top-5 Accuracy
VGG16	Types	None	1	82%	98%
VGG16	Mints	None	1	79%	94%
VGG16	Mints	DeepCluster	15 / 15	73%	91%
VGG16	Mints	DeepCluster	10 / 10	74%	92%
VGG16	Mints	Object Detection	8 / 10	78%	93%
VGG16	Mints	Object Detection	4 / 4	77%	93%
VGG16	Mints	NLP	16 / 16	76%	92%
VGG16	Mints	NLP	8 / 9	78%	93%

Table 13.1. Metrics for the models with and without the additional class layers.

Figure 13.1. The merged images of CN coin 2377 (CN type 763; mint: Maroneia) and CN coin 18232 (CN type 11944; mint: Pergamon) with black bars for the quadratic input format of the CNNs (Photos: Münzkabinett Berlin).

the "Corpus Nummorum" (CN) (Corpus Nummorum n.d.) dataset. The goal is to use it to improve and verify the data quality of existing data, and use it to help the process of entering new coins. The CN dataset features about 19,600 different coin types and more than 49,000 coins from four different ancient landscapes (Thrace, Moesia Inferior, Troad and Mysia). This dataset contains coins from several different museums, institutions and collectors. The largest part of our images comes from the Berlin-Brandenburgische Akademie der Wissenschaften, the Münzkabinett Berlin and the Bibliothèque nationale de France, Département des Monnaies, médailles et antiques. We published the images from these three institutions (due to existing copyrights) as a dataset for ML research on Zenodo (Corpus Nummorum 2023). A coin in the database is generally represented by images of the obverse and reverse of the original, or by a plaster cast. In rare cases, both representations are assigned to a coin record. For our ML dataset, we merged the obverse and reverse images of a coin into a single image showing both (as can be seen in Figure 13.1).

The biggest challenge for our type recognition is the ratio of an average of approximately two coin images per type. In previous experiments we learned that 20 coin images per class threshold is a reasonable starting point to achieve good results in the training for our data. This means that for most of the types our dataset currently has too few coins (Gampe 2021) (Gampe and Tolle in print 2019). Currently only 179 of the 19,600 type classes can meet the condition. The VGG16 model, which was pretrained on the ImageNet dataset (ImageNet 2021), achieves a Top-1 Accuracy of 82% (Table 13.1) based on those types that meet the threshold (>20 images), with the drawback that 99% of the type classes in the CN dataset are not part of the training[1]. We are constantly increasing the number of our images and we have been able to double the number of trainable types since the start of the project.

In order to get better coverage and still generate something useful, we trained a different model to recognise another important aspect of our coins: the mint in which the coin was produced. Predicting a coin's mint could also reduce the workload for our numismatists since the presorting of a larger number of coins by mint can save a lot of time. We kept our VGG16 setup and only needed to change the training and test set. Currently there are 122 mints in our data set. With the 20-coin image threshold, 98 of them are eligible for training. This way we could use about 40,000 (~80%) of our images for this approach. The remaining 24 mints have less than 200 images combined. The accuracy values here are comparable to the type recognition (Top-1 Accuracy: 79%, tab. 1) in spite of the fact that the individual mint classes are much more disparate than the type classes. Most mint classes consist of several different coin types which differ more or less from each other, Pergamon for example has 653 different coin types (630 are currently published on the website)[2].

However, we still encounter the problem of having an unbalanced dataset when training the mint recognition. The advantage of the significantly higher number of usable

1 The Top-1 Accuracy shows the percentage of correct results of the predictions with the highest probability. The Top-5 Accuracy is the percentage of correct predictions within the five most likely predictions.

2 Overview of the 630 published types in the CN dataset: https://www.corpus-nummorum.eu/search/types?type=quicksearch&mints%5B%5D=74 [accessed 15 December 2023].

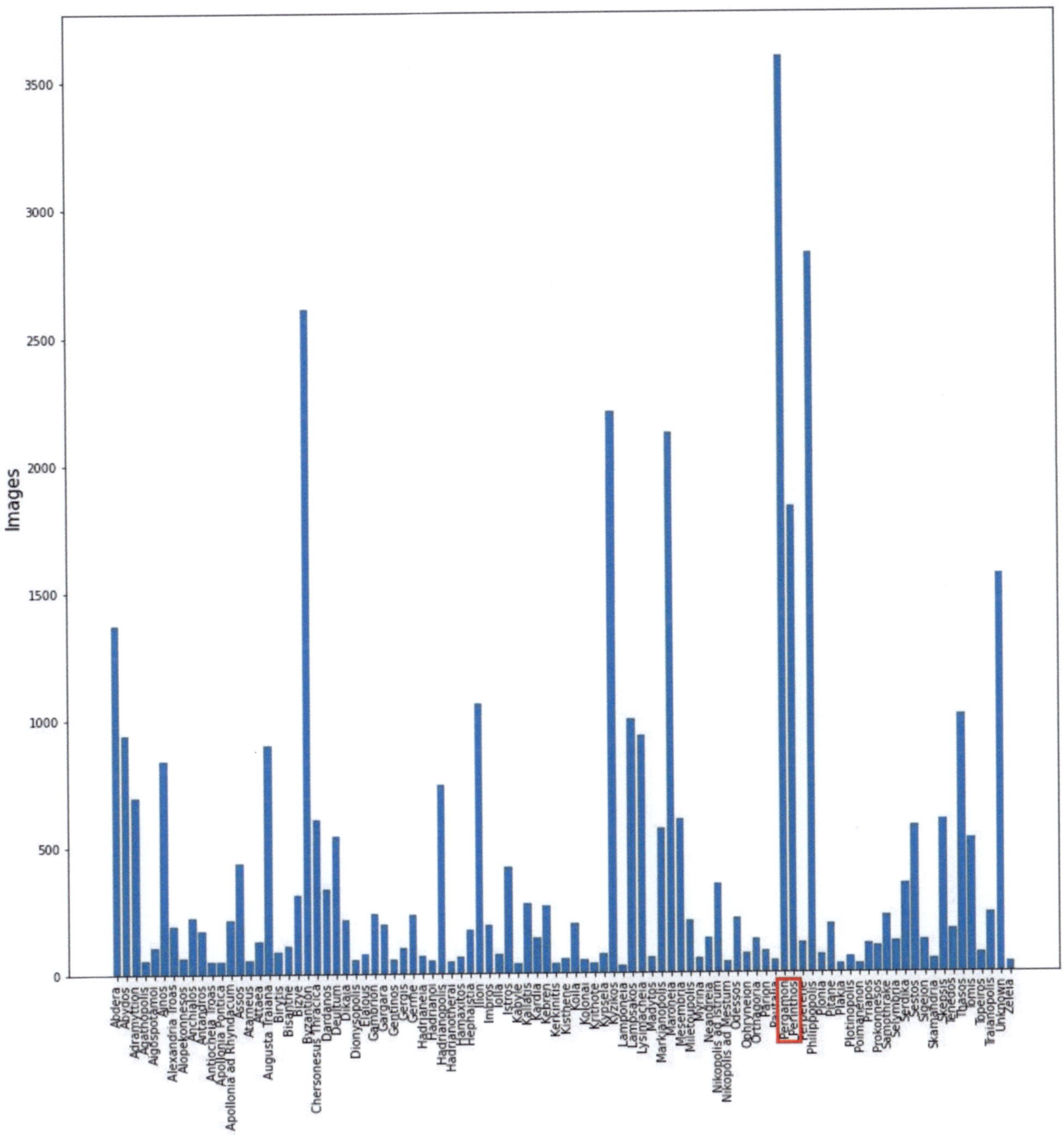

Figure 13.2. Number of images for each mint in the Corpus Nummorum dataset. (Graphic: S. Gampe, Big Data Lab).

images comes with the problem of a clearly higher number of instances in a single class. Due to the different production patterns of the mints and the disparity in the number of coins of each ancient city in our area of interest, we also have significantly different coin image numbers for each city. Some of them have only the threshold value of 20 images while others have several hundred (Figure 13.2).

Such big differences in the number of images per class can lead to a phenomenon known as overfitting. A CNN model learns to recognise some classes better than others due to the larger number of images, with the result that the weights in the trained network can be more tuned to these classes during training. Subsequently, it is possible that images of other smaller classes are predicted preferentially as belonging to one of these overfitted classes. Overfitting can also appear by running too many epochs during the training. In our case and in this paper this source for overfitting is neglected and we concentrate on the

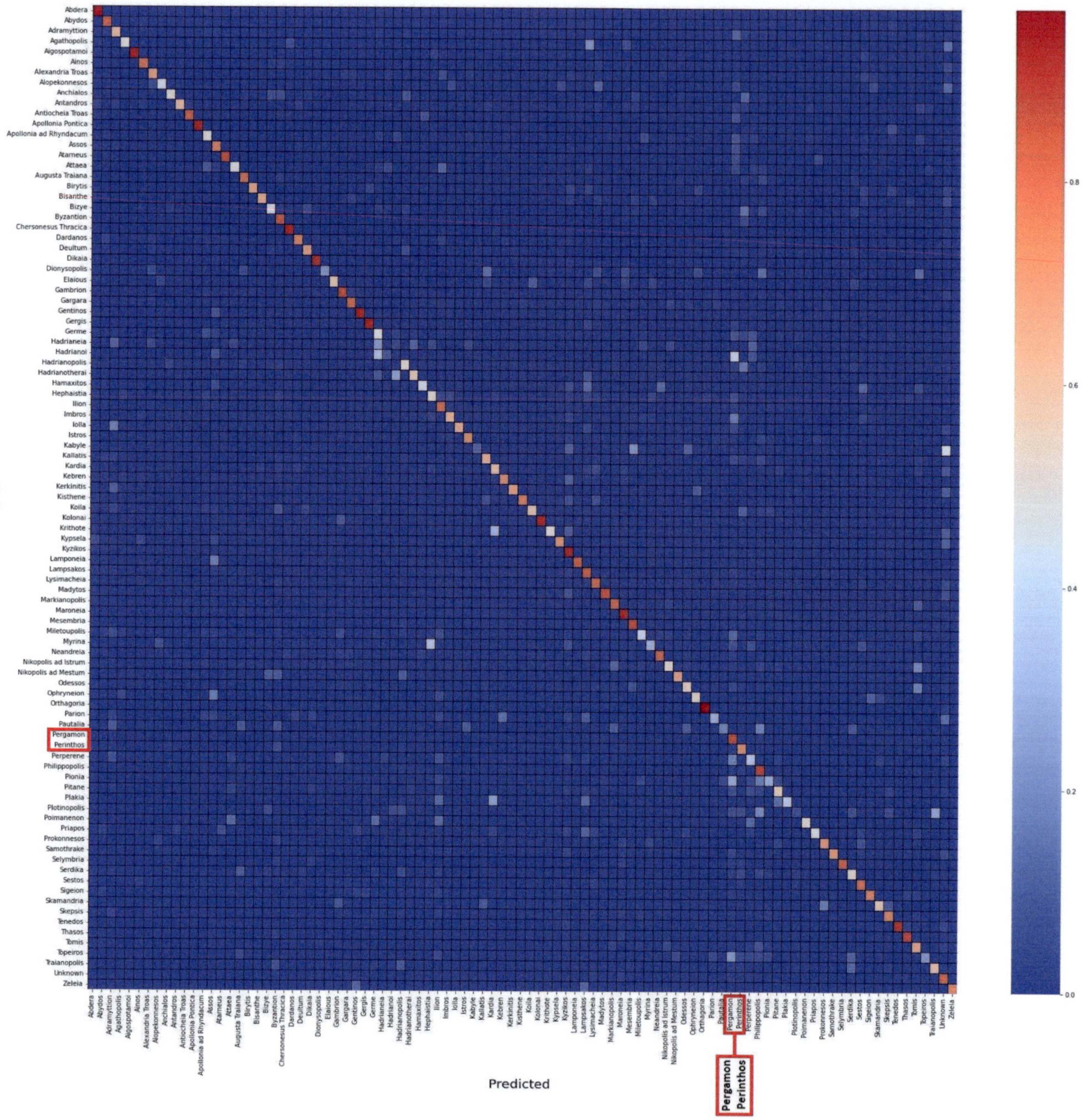

Figure 13.3. Confusion matrix for the mint model without the additional class layer. (Graphic: S. Gampe, Big Data Lab).

inhomogeneity of the data set as a basis for overfitting. A good way to determine if overfitting is present in a model is to create the so-called Confusion Matrix (CM) (Figure 13.3). The CM is a common way to make overfitting visible for individual classes in a multiclass problem. In the CM the predictions of the model and the true classes (ground truth) are confronted. In the case of a model that is 100% correct for all predictions, the diagonal of this matrix should be deep red. Recurring errors for one class create visible points off the diagonal. Traces of vertical lines for one or more classes are a good indicator for the overfitting problem. The CM of our most recent model shows these traces (Figure 13.3). They are clearly visible for the cities that have the most associated images like Pergamon and Perinthos (Figure 13.2). Every city with more than 1500 assigned images shows clear signs of overfitting on the CM. This overfitting is probably also responsible for the poorer performance of the model. The Pergamon line is the most prominent. Although Perinthos also has a large number of images, the overfitting problem is less pronounced here

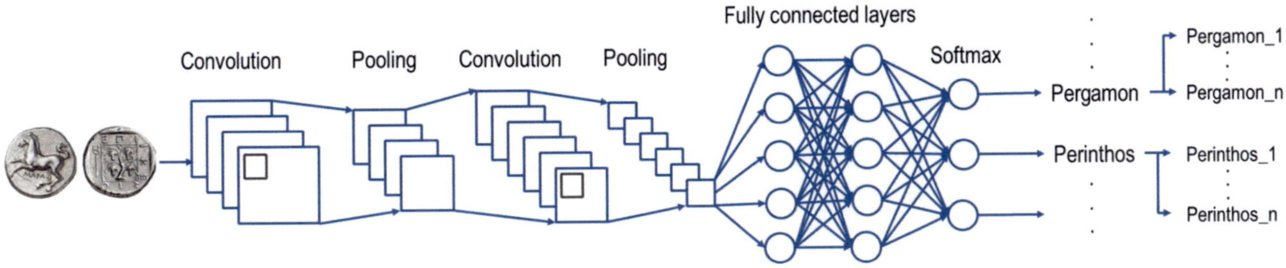

Figure 13.4. Overview of a Convolutional Neural Network, its different layers and the additional class layer. (Photo: Corpus Nummorum. Graphic: S. Gampe, Big Data Lab).

than with Pergamon. These differences, and the fact that both mints produced very different looking coin types and thus present a challenge when dividing into new smaller classes, make them a good case study in our view.

One idea for solving the overfitting problem is limiting the number of training images per class. The problem for the image limitation is the number of types which belong to a mint. For example, for the mint Pergamon there are over 3600 coin images, which are split over 653 different coin types. This means that if we want to represent each type with at least one coin image in the training set the Pergamon class would still be significantly larger than many other classes. A limited dataset can also lead to lower model performance because mint classes whose coins occur very often in archaeological finds will not have proper training for their range of types. The accuracy for the types which are very common in that mint will not be as good as it could be with an unlimited training set. Another method we tried in the overfitting context is the "compute_class_weight" algorithm from the scikit-learn package (scikit-learn n.d.). It computes class weights for every class for an unbalanced dataset like ours in order to avoid overfitting. The computed weight of a class with many images is significantly lower than that of a class with few images. Unfortunately, the performance of the trained model with such class weights was unacceptable. We got a Top-1 Accuracy of less than 1%. We also experimented with the "sparse categorical focal loss" function for our case (focal-loss n.d.). The function makes easy-to-classify images contribute less than hard-to-classify images during the training. However, training with this loss function had no positive effect at all.

This paper deals with the problems we encountered when applying an image recognition (IR) approach to an ancient coin dataset. The focus is on our main challenge of a very unbalanced dataset consisting of classes with very few images and others with several hundred images. This means we focus here not on the improvement of Machine Learning (ML) algorithms as such, but on the setup, in particular the handling of the datasets and the definition of the result classes for the training.

The goal was to improve our mint recognition model by breaking down large classes with many input images into several smaller ones. For this purpose, we used three different methods: 1. DeepCluster – an unsupervised clustering method, 2. Object Detection based on a Region Based – Convolutional Neural Network (R-CNN) and 3. our Natural Language Processing (NLP) pipeline (Gampe and Tolle in print). The DeepCluster model is available on GitHub (GitHub – facebookresearch / deepcluster n.d.). The Object Detection approach trained for this paper is based on TensorFlow and Keras (Keras n.d.; TensorFlow n.d.). The already existing NLP Pipeline was developed with the spaCy application programming interface (spaCy n.d.). Our Image Recognition models, which are based on a pretrained VGG16 model, are implemented with TensorFlow and Keras (Gampe and Tolle in print 2019) (TensorFlow n.d.; Keras n.d.). All of the above methods run on Jupyter Notebook and are written in the Python programming language.

In another Project (ClaReNet) the DeepCluster Method was used to cluster a coin hoard with celtic coins. The already existing typology and the allocation of coins to them was checked with the method. The R-CNN based Object Detection was utilised to crop the area of a portrait on imperial Roman coins to prevent a CNN from making decisions based on the legend (Gampe 2021). Our NLP approach has been in development for some time (Klinger et al. 2018; Gampe and Tolle in print) and is now also used for other reasons within the CN-project. We therefore wanted to check whether it could also be used to solve our overfitting problems.

Our idea for addressing this problem is to break down big classes like Pergamon and Perinthos into smaller ones. We call this the *additional class layer*. The term "layer" is well known from neural networks like the CNN, which has different layers (Figure 13.4). The last layer in such networks is called the softmax and is responsible for transforming the incoming numerical values from the preceding layers into the class's probabilities (Amidi and Amidi n.d.). We also call this layer the class layer. Our idea is to add an additional layer for large classes on top of the existing ones (Figure 13.4).

In this process, classes like Pergamon are divided based on the similarity of their different types and new smaller classes are added. Then we add the old class layer with the new ones to get a new train and test set. To realize this approach, we use three different Machine Learning based methods:

1. Unsupervised "DeepCluster"
2. Region Based – CNN based Object Detection
3. Natural Language Processing

By creating these new classes and reducing the old large ones we tried to reduce the amount of overfitting and potentially increase the accuracy of our models. To test these approaches, we applied them to two different mints: Pergamon with c. 3600 images and Perinthos with c. 1800 images. Pergamon was chosen because it is the mint with the most associated images. In contrast Perinthos has just half as many images, however, this city has types that differ greatly from those from Pergamon since the city belongs to another region (Pergamon – Mysia, Perinthos – Thrace). These differences are important to ensure the applicability of the three approaches to different mints.

13.2 Related Work

The first automated classification approaches on coins were based on modern coins which, due to their uniformity in production and design, represent a more manageable challenge compared to ancient coins (Fukumi 1992; Davidsson 1996). In the 2000s, the first computer vision approaches dealing with ancient coins were published. Most of these approaches usually use balanced datasets. In 2007, Zaharieva et al. used a small dataset of three coin types with 10 to 16 coins per type for the classification and the identification of individual ancient coins (Zaharieva et al. 2007). A year later the ILAC (Image-based Classification of Ancient Coins) project was presented for the first time. One of their most important goals was to create a new database with coin types to support the coin classification algorithms (Kampel et al. 2008). Five years later an automated image-based classification system was developed for Roman Republican coins based on several methods like SIFT. The used dataset consisted of 180 coin reverse images split equally over 60 classes (Kavelar et al. 2013). Two years later, Kim and Pavlovic used several other techniques to train a Roman emperor recognition (15 different emperors) with approximately 2800 coin images (Kim and Pavlovic 2015). Shortly after that the CNN age started with a mobile app approach for modern coins (Capece et al. 2016). Schlag and Arandjelovic adapted that type of deep neural network for their Roman emperor recognition (Schlag and Arandjelovic 2018). For their training of 83 classes, they used a dataset consisting of approx. 30,000 coin images. Due to the class imbalance in this dataset, they trained two models, one with the original imbalanced dataset and another with an "synthetically" balanced set and tested these models on two other datasets. The balanced model performed only a few percentage points worse in terms of the emperor recognition. A combination of unstructured text analysis and a CNN image recognition approach was trained to recognise five smaller iconographic elements ("horse", "cornucopia", "patera", "eagle" and "shield") of ancient coins images with five separate models (Cooper and Arandjelovic 2019; Cooper and Arandjelovic 2020). They used a bigger set of coin images extracted from 100,000 coin auction lots. By training separate models for each image element and using the stratified sampling method they were able to work around the problem of unbalanced classes. Another small and balanced dataset (4 classes with 100 images each) was used by Ma and Arandjelovic for their "histogram of hue-based" and "histogram of colour-word-based representation" approach (Ma and Arandjelovic 2020). The RRCD – Roman Republican Coin Dataset was first introduced by Anwar et al. (2020) for their CoinNet project which uses Feature Fusion and Attention to recognise the backside motifs on their coin images. Their aim was to use a dataset that is more representative of the challenges of coin classification in numismatics due to the larger number of coins and classes. It consists of approx. 18,000 images divided into 100 classes and is somewhat unbalanced (RRCD-main). Most of the classes have 100 to 200 images but 15 classes clearly exceed the 200 image boundary (class 70 has 620 images). However, they have not limited the number of images per class. Unfortunately, the effects of this imbalance on the performance of individual classes have not been mentioned. In 2021, the CNN based AnCoins approach was presented by Kiourt and Evangelidis (2021). They created a new dataset with the coins of 12 Thracian cities, but they only use one side of the coin with the motif characteristic of the city (e.g., horse for Maroneia). Their dataset was also quite balanced with 35 to 50 coins per class. Another CNN based coin classification was carried out by Manzoor et al. on the RRCD dataset from Anwar et al. and the smaller Roman coin dataset from Kavelar et al. (Manzoor et al. 2022, Anwar et al. 2020, Kavelar et al. 2013). They have also not changed the imbalance of classes in the RRCD dataset. Due to the latest trends in Machine Learning, a Vision Transformer model was used by Guo et al. to recognise emissions from Roman emperors (Guo et al. 2023). They explicitly mention that they want to solve the problem of the large number of classes with fewer or even no images for training. Therefore, they focus their model on learning a representation that can generally distinguish classes from each other and thus does not require images for each class to be trained. The Transformer model was trained on 524 obverse images of 24 different issues (as they call it in their paper – it can be seen in this case as a synonym for type), of which only one had significantly more images than the others. The test set contained 7605 issues of 196 depicted persons. The results achieved with this small data set seem very promising for numismatic classification problems beyond the often delicate type identification.

General approaches for dealing with unbalanced data are not easy to find. The problem is usually dealt with in the different subject areas themselves. In 2021 a review of different classification methods related to unbalanced data was published by Wang et al. (2021). For Deep Learning models like CNNs they recommend using class weights (see above).

As this overview of ancient coin related approaches has shown, the various projects and the scientists involved in them have demonstrated that different approaches for classifying ancient coins can deliver very good results. The goal of most of the work is to prove that the algorithms and Machine Learning-based methods used can be applied to numismatic material. However, we want to provide a usable tool to support the classification work of numismatists in the context of Corpus Nummorum. We therefore have to deal with the problems like highly unbalanced class sizes, mixture of real coin images and images from plaster casts and the situation that many types are limited to very few instances.

13.3 Unsupervised "DeepCluster"

Our first method, *DeepCluster* from Facebook Research (Caron et al. 2018), combines unsupervised and supervised elements. An integrated CNN extracts features from the input images. Afterwards, these features are clustered with a k-means algorithm and the resulting clusters are used as pseudo labels. These newly labeled images serve as input for further CNN training. The number of clusters depends on the input parameter "k", which can be freely selected before the start (Caron et al. 2018). One big benefit of this approach is the fact that DeepCluster needs no time-consuming adaptations to our problem. Values for a few parameters have to be chosen, such as the number of clusters "k" and the amount of training epochs. We chose 200 epochs for each attempt. The number of clusters was set to 15 and 10 because we didn't want to create a large number of small classes. DeepCluster's Algorithm uses all of our images from Pergamon and from Perinthos to form the 15 clusters for each mint separately. This means that both original classes have been completely split up and therefore no longer exist as classes in the training. However, it is possible that DeepCluster forms very heterogeneous clusters with a lot of different looking types.

For our first attempt of dividing the Pergamon and Perinthos classes into smaller ones we had 15 clusters each (Pergamon_01 to Pergamon_15 and Perinthos_01 to Perinthos_15). Although both classes have different numbers of images, we have chosen an equal number of new classes to investigate the effects on these different sized classes. After the training most clusters had a size of 50 to 100 images for Perinthos and 100 to 200 for Pergamon. Both mints also had one cluster with many more images than the others: DeepCluster tends to build what we call "garbage clusters", which contain all images that could not be assigned to the other clusters (Pergamon_10 and 12, Perinthos_02 and 11). They are somewhat comparable to the original classes with the leftover images from our two other approaches (see below). The 30 clusters built with DeepCluster are now incorporated as new classes in our train and test set replacing the original Pergamon and Perinthos classes. After the training we could observe that the Top-1 and Top-5 Accuracy values were below those from the unmodified model (Table 13.1). We also created the confusion matrix for the new model on the test set (Figure 13.5).

What is immediately noticeable is that there is a clear vertical line in the area of the new classes. This means that these classes are often confused with each other. A look at the composition of the clusters indicates that this is due to the inhomogeneity of the assigned images within each cluster. While many clusters share images of the same or very similar types, the two biggest "garbage clusters" from both mints (Pergamon_12 and Perinthos_11) are clearly visible on the CM. These share a particularly large number of coin types with the other new classes. For Pergamon, the overfitting problem has diminished, but some of the brighter points from the unmodified class columns are now spread across the vertical lines of the new classes. For Perinthos we could also observe a slight decrease of the overfitting. However, new overfitting problems can also arise, as it is apparent in the Byzantion column at the level of the new Perinthos classes. We repeated this test with a smaller number of clusters. This time we executed DeepCluster with 10 clusters as preset. However, the result barely changed. The confusion between the new classes is still there and the overfitting for both mints is nearly the same as with 15 clusters. We also found a reduction of the Top-1 Accuracy of about 5% in both tests. These results have led us to conclude that the DeepCluster method is not suitable for our problem.

13.4 Region Based – CNN based Object Detection

Our second approach is an Object Detection model from Keras (n.d.). It is based on a Region Based Convolutional Neural Network (R-CNN) which produces a set of region proposals that are likely to contain objects and uses a CNN to extract features from each region proposal to classify objects within these regions. (Girshick et al. 2014). The way new classes were created here followed a different concept. We trained the R-CNN model on frequently occurring subjects on the coins like "head" or "sitting person". Most of these subjects are among the most common objects and animals in the CN database (Wirth 2021). The new classes

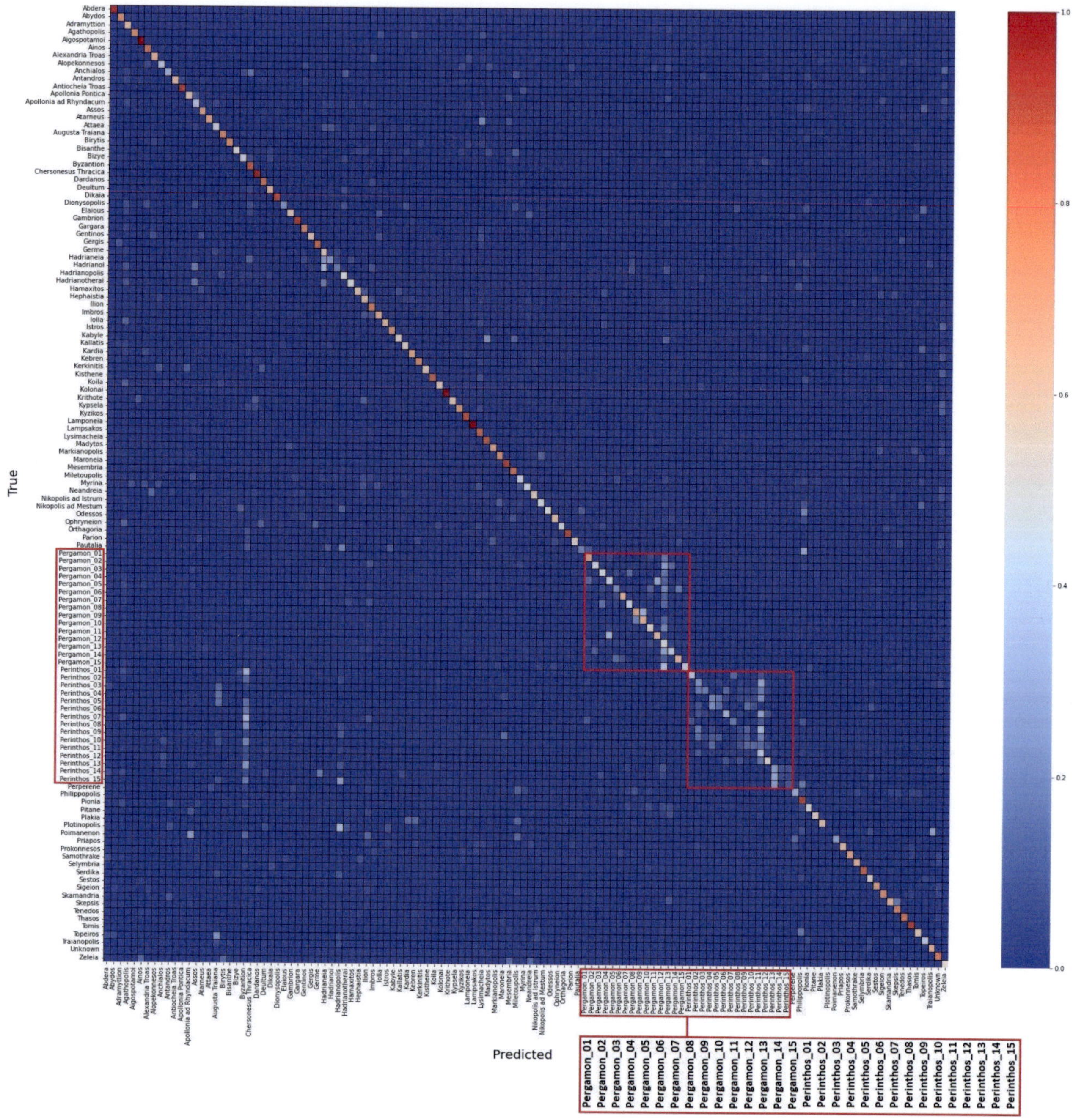

Figure 13.5. Confusion matrix for the DeepCluster approach. (Graphic: S. Gampe, Big Data Lab).

were built based on the combinations of these subjects in the dataset.[3] The training of the R-CNN model was carried out by Huy Long, who wrote his master's thesis on this topic (Long 2022). He annotated 20 to 30 images for every subject with a polygonal annotation and with bounding boxes. With a polygonal annotated training set the model can predict the contour of an object, but annotation is more time consuming compared to the annotation of bounding boxes. After training the Object Detection model, it was used to predict subjects on each coin image of Pergamon and Perinthos. Based on these results, new classes had been built manually based on the resulting combinations

3 The following subjects were used for the combinations: 1. Pergamon: "sitting_person", "head", "serpent_box", "owl", "serpents", "eagle", "podium", "bull", "bow". 2. Perinthos: "sitting_person", "head", "podium", "bull", "quadriga", "double_horse", "club", "laurel_wreath", "price_crown", "ship", "table", "pot", "standing_person".

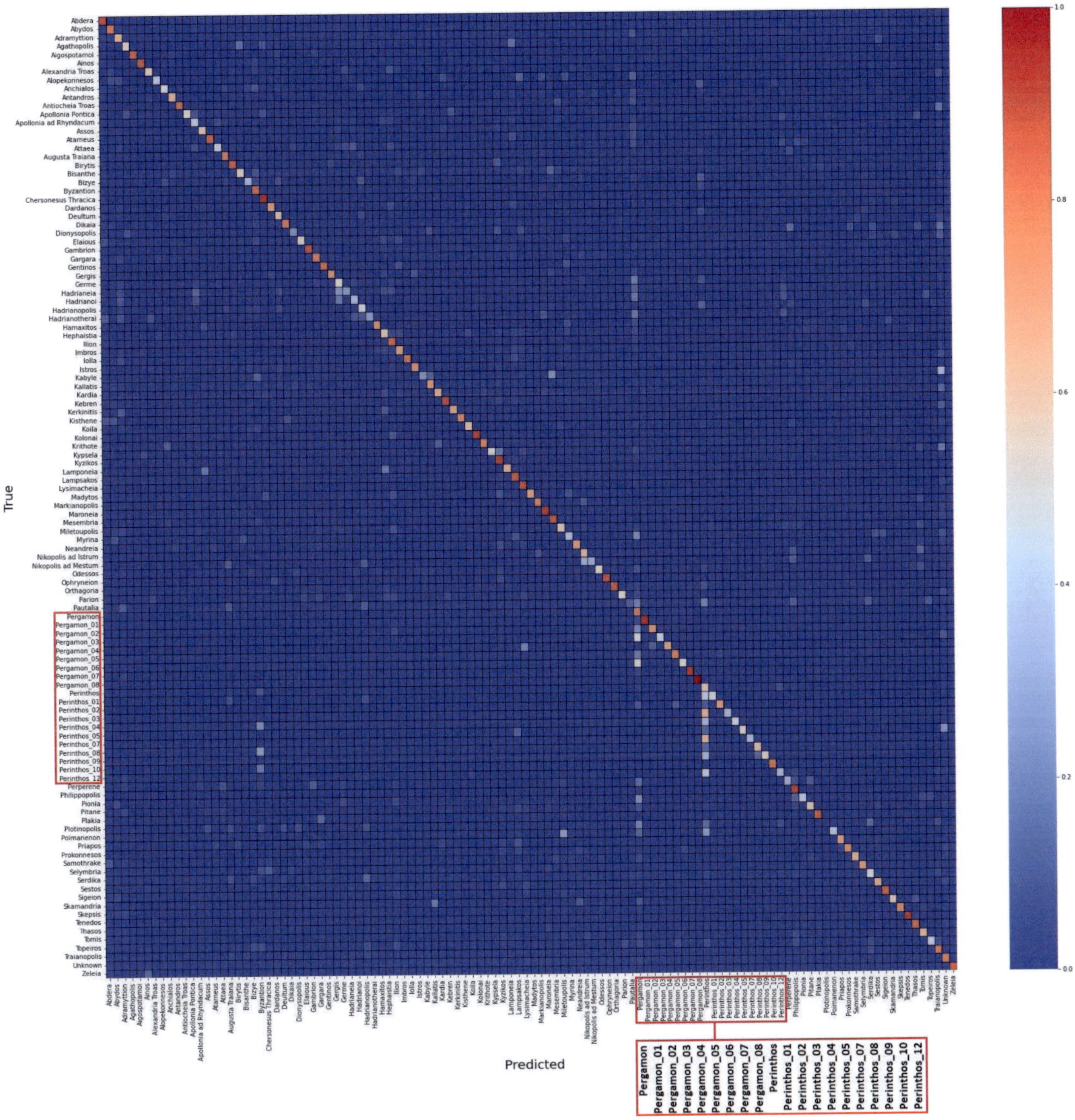

Figure 13.6. Confusion matrix for the Object Detection approach. (Graphic: S. Gampe, Big Data Lab).

of obverse and reverse subjects (e.g., "Head–Owl"). For Pergamon this generated eight classes and for Perinthos ten classes. These classes have different sizes with around 20 to 200 images assigned to them. This way we reduced the number of images in the original Pergamon and Perinthos classes to 2520 and 1170. After training our VGG16 model on the updated train and test set we observed that the Top-1 and Top-5 Accuracy has hardly changed (Table 13.1). But the resulting CM shows a problem similar to the DeepCluster approach (Figure 13.6). Images of the new classes are often attributed to the reduced Pergamon and Perinthos class. Furthermore, the overfitting for both original classes was not reduced as the CM shows. We repeated this test with a reduced number of new classes, where the images of some of the smaller classes had been manually merged back to the Pergamon and Perinthos classes. After retraining, beside a small decrease in the accuracy values, the overfitting problem also remained.

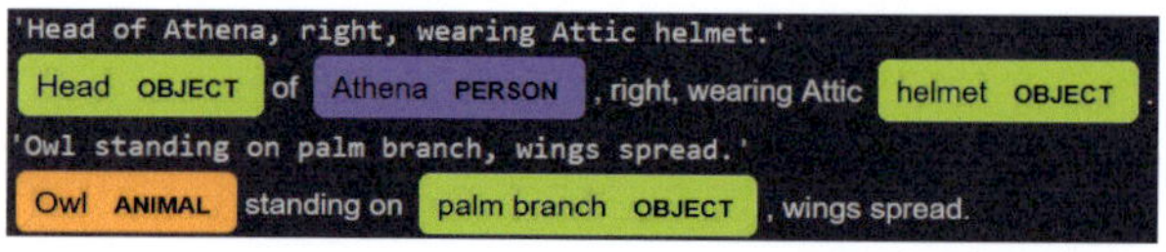

Figure 13.7. Coin image descriptions and entities found by the NLP model. These descriptions are used for different coins and/or coin types (Figure 13.1), e.g., coins https://www.corpus-nummorum.eu/coins/53267?lg=en and https://www.corpus-nummorum.eu/coins/53408?lg=en [accessed December 15, 2023] for the Athena description shown here. (Graphic: S. Gampe, Big Data Lab).

Clearly this approach is unfortunately not suitable for solving, or at least reducing our problem. An explanation for this could be the performance of the R-CNN Object Detection model. When examining the new classes, it became apparent that quite a few objects had not been detected by the Object Detection model. The new classes were not really well distinguishable from the Pergamon and Perinthos ones. The annotation used seems not to cover the whole range of several subjects.

13.5 Natural Language Processing

Our final method for dealing with mint overfitting is the application of our Natural Language Processing (NLP) pipeline. We already have trained an NLP model for the textual descriptions of our coins in the CN database (Gampe and Tolle in print; Klinger et al. 2018). This model can find numerous entities like "Athena" or "Spear". The list of trained entities includes four different categories: persons, objects, animals and plants. We wrote a query for grouping all coins with the same entities on the obverse and reverse and sorted them by the frequency of these individual combinations. To create the new classes, we had to filter these combinations manually because a coin's description can have several entities assigned to it and overlaps are possible. The example (Figure 13.7) shows all entities in a coin's obverse and reverse description. For example, this coin can be assigned to the combination "Athena–Owl" and "Head–Palm Branch". Filtering is a time-consuming but mandatory step due to the large number of combinations. We also wanted to avoid new classes sharing coin images.

After the filter step the new classes could be built from the remaining combinations. We assembled 16 new classes for Pergamon and Perinthos with different combinations of entities.[4] These classes contained mostly different types that share a similar appearance. The number of images for each class varied from 40 to 400 for Pergamon, and 40 to 300 for Perinthos. Using the NLP model, we were able to reduce the number of images in the original Pergamon and Perinthos classes to 1201 and 629. This is a significantly larger reduction than that with Object Detection. Compared to the original model, the values of the metrics after the training are only slightly lower (Table 13.1).

However, as the confusion matrix shows, the new classes are again often confused with the original Pergamon and Perinthos classes (Figure 13.8). The overfitting of Pergamon was slightly reduced with this attempt, but the vertical line in the original Pergamon class fields (outside the new classes) is still visible. The reduction of the overfitting for Perinthos, on the other hand, is clearly visible. Due to the confusion of the old with the new classes, both overfitting reductions had no influence on the metrics. We repeated this experiment again with a lower number of new classes (eight for Pergamon and nine for Perinthos). However, this had no positive effect on the overfitting problem for Pergamon. In fact, it became worse than before. The overfitting of Perinthos remained at the same level as in the first NLP attempt.

For this approach we can say that the NLP method required the most manual work of all three approaches. Our efficient NLP pipeline helped us best to separate the types that share a similar appearance for the new classes from the original classes. It also gave the best results for the overfitting problem based on the observation of the CM. However, the confusion between the new classes shows that the types of one mint very likely share some common features. This is something that could be further explored.

13.6 Summary and Conclusion

Due to our limited dataset and the high number of types, a training on types with sometimes only two or three instances per type results in an unacceptable performance (34% Top-1 Accuracy). By switching to mints (accumulating all types of a mint to one training class), a very unbalanced dataset was generated with some mints (classes) dominating the training. While the performance of our trained models seems sufficient, we saw traces of overfitting for the dominating mints in the confusion matrix. The problem of unbalanced data sets is very common in the domain of numismatics and archaeology in general. The overall preservation quality of the coins we used was relatively good, especially compared to excavation finds where additional problems and uncertainties occur. However, our work could lay the basic foundation to expand the models also to less well preserved material. It is therefore important to solve problems before dealing with less optimal material.

We conducted three different Machine Learning based experiments to solve this overfitting problem with the

4 The following entities were used for the combinations: 1. Pergamon: "Athena", "laurel_wreath", "owl", "Augustus", "crepidoma", "bust", "Asclepius", "emperor", "Telesphorus", "cista", "serpent", "figure", "head", "bow", "heads", "temple", "trophy", "paludamentum", "Zeus". 2. Perinthos: "bust", "ears_of_corn", "Herakles", "lyre", "palm_branch", "patera", "torch", "cuirass", "apples", "head", "altar", "athlete", "club", "Dionysos", "horses", patera, "Isis", "apis", "radiate_crown", "board".

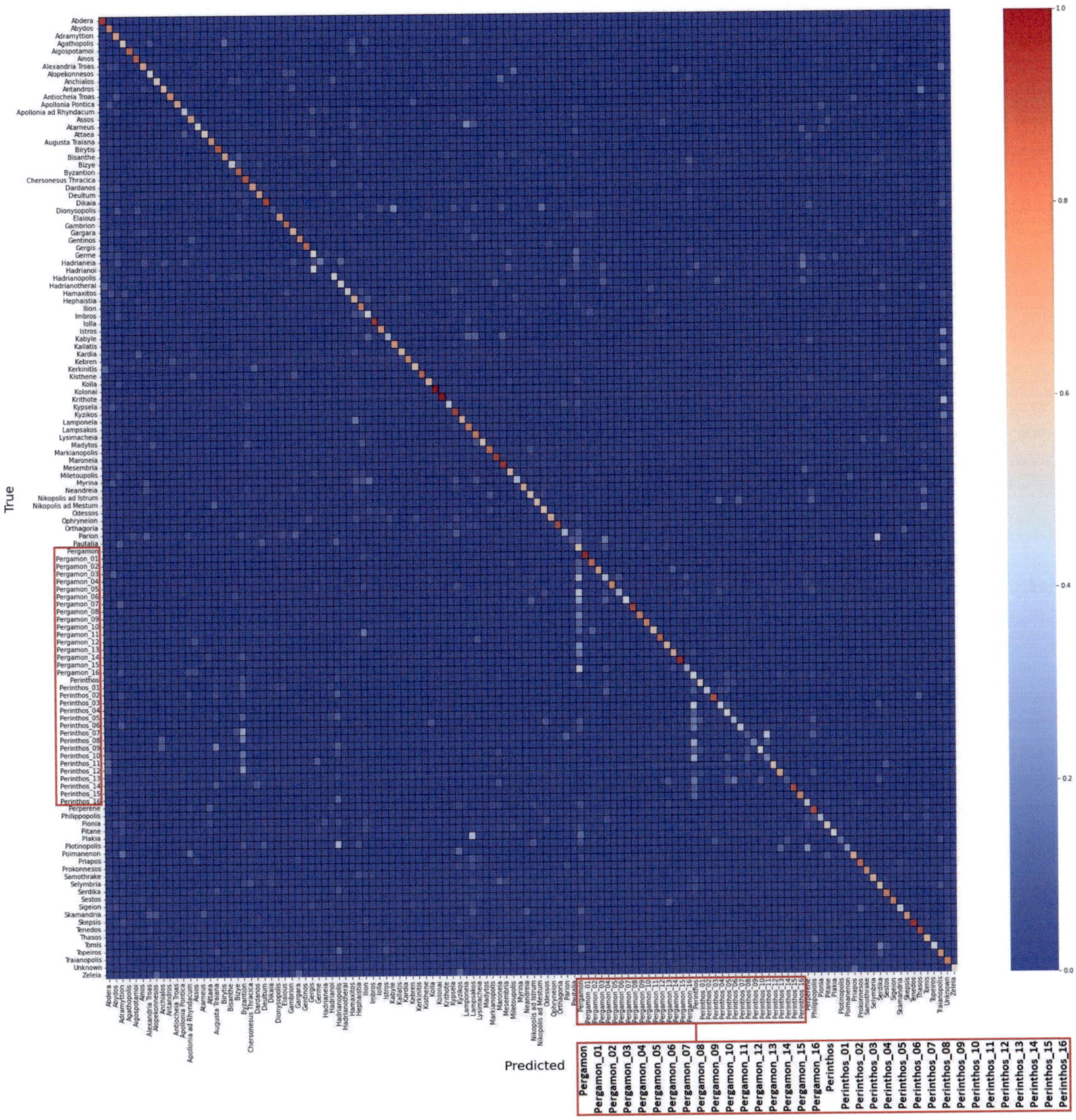

Figure 13.8. Confusion matrix for the NLP approach. (Graphic: S. Gampe, Big Data Lab).

unbalanced Corpus Nummorum dataset. To do this, we split two mint classes with a large number of images and created an additional class layer for them, and generated another training and test set with it. In our first attempt we created several new classes based on DeepCluster (unsupervised). The generated clusters contained too many different looking coin types (based on a human judgment) which negatively affected the learning process of our VGG16 model. In the second attempt the class layer was created with an Object Detection approach. This generated only a few smaller extra classes and the remaining coins without objects detected still formed a dominating class. It must be stressed that the Object Detection approach was only trained for some very common objects and the overall performance was still limited. Both approaches did not produce appropriate solutions for our problem. In the third approach classes were generated with Natural Language Processing. They were the most distinguishable from the original classes and this approach reduced overfitting the most. However, due the amount of manual work and the confusion of new and old classes, we are currently not following this path either. The accuracy of all newly trained models was below the original mint model. Even the observed visual reduction of the overfitting for the original Pergamon and Perinthos classes in the NLP experiment had no positive impact on model performance. This means that so far, we could not solve our overfitting issue with mint prediction in a sufficient way.

These approaches might be useful methods in other cases. However, it shows that a generic approach to an overfitting due to dominant classes has not been found. We are therefore investigating additional ways to tackle this problem. This includes the creation of new coin images using ML-based methods for the individual classes. It can be seen as an augmentation approach for the smaller classes in order to reduce the domination of some huge classes. Furthermore, we started to compare other model approaches than just CNN (VGG16), like vision transformers or multimodal approaches.

Our next steps in the D4N4 project are:
The domain experts are trying to improve the CN dataset by including more images, especially for smaller classes. We are also working on a Generative Adversarial Network (GAN) approach to create virtual new coin images (that never existed) for those classes with very few coins. Finally, we published our CN dataset for other scientists and students to test their own ML methods, for example those that were recently part of a data challenge course at the Goethe-University (Corpus Nummorum 2023).

Funding

The D4N[4] project is funded by the Deutsche Forschungsgemeinschaft (DFG) in the program "e-research-Technologien".

Conflict of interest disclosure

The authors declare that they comply with the PCI rule of having no financial conflicts of interest in relation to the content of the article.

Data, scripts, code, and supplementary information availability

Google Colab notebook for testing our type and mint model is available online: https://github.com/Frankfurt-BigDataLab/IR-on-coin-datasets.

NLP pipeline code, models and a Google Colab Notebook for testing are available online: https://github.com/Frankfurt-BigDataLab/NLP-on-multilingual-coin-datasets.

The code for running our type, mint and NLP models is also included in this Zenodo archive: https://zenodo.org/doi/10.5281/zenodo.8298077.

The Corpus Nummorum image dataset is available online: DOI: 10.5281/zenodo.10033993.

Peer review

This article has been reviewed and recommended by PCI Archaeology.

Brandsen, Alex. 2024. "A significant contribution to the problem of unbalanced data in machine learning research in archaeology." *Peer Community in Archaeology* 100395. DOI: 10.24072/pci.archaeo.100395.

References

Amidi, Afshine, and Shervine Amidi. n.d. "Convolutional Neural Networks cheatsheet." Accessed August 8, 2023. https://stanford.edu/~shervine/teaching/cs-230/cheatsheet-convolutional-neural-networks.

Anwar, Hafeez, Saeed Anwar, Sebastian Zambanini, and Fatih Porikli. 2020. "Deep Ancient Roman Republican Coin Classification via Feature Fusion and Attention." *Pattern Recognition* 114. DOI: 10.48550/arXiv.1908.09428.

Capece, Nicola, Ugo Erra, and Antonio Vito Ciliberto. 2016. "Implementation of a Coin Recognition System for Mobile Devices with Deep Learning." In *2016 12th International Conference on Signal-Image Technology & Internet-Based Systems (SITIS)*, edited by Kokou Yetongnon, Albert Dipanda, Richard Chbeir, Giuseppe De Pietro, and Luigi Gallo 186–92. Naples: IEEE. DOI: 10.1109/SITIS.2016.37.

Caron, Mathilde, Piotr Bojanowski, Armand Joulin, and Matthijs Douze. 2018. "Deep Clustering for Unsupervised Learning of Visual Features." arXiv. DOI: 10.48550/ARXIV.1807.05520.

Cooper, Jessica, and Ognjen Arandjelovic. 2019. "Understanding Ancient Coin Images." arXiv. DOI: 10.48550/arXiv.1903.02665.

Cooper, Jessica, and Ognjen Arandjelović. 2020. "Learning to Describe: A New Approach to Computer Vision Based Ancient Coin Analysis." *Sci* 2 (2): 27. DOI: 10.3390/sci2020027.

Corpus Nummorum. n.d. "Corpus Nummorum." Accessed August 8, 2023. https://www.corpus-nummorum.eu.

Corpus Nummorum. 2023. "Corpus Nummorum – Coin Image Dataset." Zenodo. https://zenodo.org/doi/10.5281/zenodo.10033992.

D4N[4]. n.d. "Data quality for Numismatics based on Natural language processing and Neural Networks." Accessed August 8, 2023. http://www.bigdata.uni-frankfurt.de/d4n4.

Davidsson, Paul. 2022. "Coin Classification Using a Novel Technique for Learning Characteristic Decision Trees by Controlling the Degree of Generalization."In *Industrial and Engineering Applications of Artificial Intelligence and Expert Systems, 1st Ed.*, edited by Takushi Tanaka, Setsuo Ohsuga, and Moonis Ali, 403–11. London: CRC Press. DOI: 10.1201/9780429332111-70.

focal-loss. n.d. "focal_loss.sparse_categorical_focal_loss." Accessed August 8, 2023. https://focal-loss.readthedocs.io/en/latest/generated/focal_loss.sparse_categorical_focal_loss.html.

Fukumi, Minoru, Sigeru Omatu, Fumiaki Takeda, and Toshihisa

Kosaka. 1991. "Rotation-Invariant Neural Pattern Recognition System with Application to Coin Recognition." In [Proceedings] *1991 IEEE International Joint Conference on Neural Networks. Vol. 2*, 1027–32. Singapore: IEEE. DOI: 10.1109/IJCNN.1991.170532.

Gampe, Sebastian. 2021. "Neuronale Netze zur Bestimmung römischer Kaiser auf Bildern antiker Münzen." MA diss., Goethe-Universität Frankfurt am Main. http://www.bigdata.uni-frankfurt.de/wp-content/uploads/2022/05/Masterarbeit_Sebastian_Gampe_online.pdf.

Gampe, Sebastian, and Karsten Tolle. in print. "Combination of Machine Learning Methods of Image and Natural Language Recognition of Ancient Coin Data." In *Computer Applications & Quantitative Methods in Archeology (CAA), Proceedings of the conference in Krakow 2019.*

Girshick, Ross, Jeff Donahue, Trevor Darrell, and Jitendra Malik. 2013. "Rich Feature Hierarchies for Accurate Object Detection and Semantic Segmentation." arXiv. DOI: 10.48550/ARXIV.1311.2524.

GitHub – facebookresearch / deepcluster. n.d. "Deep Clustering for Unsupervised Learning of Visual Features." Accessed August 8, 2023. https://github.com/facebookresearch/deepcluster.

Guo, Zhongliang, Ognjen Arandjelović, David Reid, Yaxiong Lei, and Jochen Büttner. 2023. "A Siamese Transformer Network for Zero-Shot Ancient Coin Classification." *Journal of Imaging* 9 (6): 107. DOI: 10.3390/jimaging9060107.

ImageNet. 2021. "ImageNet." https://www.image-net.org/update-mar-11-2021.php.

Kavelar, Albert, Sebastian Zambanini, Martin Kampel, Klaus Vondrovec, and Kathrin Siegl. 2013. "The ILAC-PROJECT: Supporting Ancient Coin Classification by Means of Image Analysis." *The International Archives of the Photogrammetry, Remote Sensing and Spatial Information Sciences* XL-5/W2 (July): 373–8. DOI: 10.5194/isprsarchives-XL-5-W2-373-2013.

Keras. n.d. "Keras: Deep Learning for humans." Accessed August 8, 2023. https://keras.io.

Kim, Jongpil, and Vladimir Pavlovic. 2015. "Improving Ancient Roman Coin Recognition with Alignment and Spatial Encoding." In *Computer Vision – ECCV 2014 Workshops*, edited by Lourdes Agapito, Michael M. Bronstein, and Carsten Rother, 149–64. Cham: Springer. DOI: 10.1007/978-3-319-16178-5_10.

Kiourt, Chairi, and Vasilis Evangelidis. 2021. "AnCoins: Image-Based Automated Identification of Ancient Coins Through Transfer Learning Approaches." In *Pattern Recognition. ICPR International Workshops and Challenges*, edited by Alberto Del Bimbo, Rita Cucchiara, Stan Sclaroff, Giovanni Maria Farinella, Tao Mei, Marco Bertini, Hugo Jair Escalante, and Roberto Vezzani, 54–67. Cham: Springer. DOI: 10.1007/978-3-030-68787-8_4.

Klinger, Patricia, Sebastian Gampe, Karsten Tolle, and Ulrike Peter. 2018. "Semantic Search Based on Natural Language Processing – A Numismatic Example." *Journal of Ancient History and Archaeology* 5 (3). DOI: 10.14795/j.v5i3.334.

Long, Hui. 2023. "Klassifizierung von Motiven auf antiken Münzen mit Mask R-CNN." MA diss., Goethe-Universität Frankfurt am Main. http://www.bigdata.uni-frankfurt.de/wp-content/uploads/2023/02/Masterthesis-Huy-Luong.pdf.

Ma, Yuanyuan, and Ognjen Arandjelović. 2020. "Classification of Ancient Roman Coins by Denomination Using Colour, a Forgotten Feature in Automatic Ancient Coin Analysis." *Sci* 2 (2): 37. DOI: 10.3390/sci2020037.

Manzoor, Sehrish, Nouman Ali, Muhammad Raees, Khan Awais Khan, Muhammad Usama, and Afzal Ahmed. 2022. "Ancient Coin Classification Based on Recent Trends of Deep Learning." https://ceur-ws.org/Vol-3266/paper2.pdf.

Kampel, Martin, Klaus Vondrovec, Maia Zaharieva, and Sebastian Zambanini. 2008. "Image-based Classification of Ancient Coins." In *Proceedings of the 14th International Conference on Virtual Systems and Multimedia. Project Papers*, edited by Marinos Ioannides, Alonzo Addison, Andreas Georgopoulos, and Loukas Kalisperis, 341–8. Budapest: Archaeolingua.

Schlag, Imanol, and Ognjen Arandjelovic. 2017. "Ancient Roman Coin Recognition in the Wild Using Deep Learning Based Recognition of Artistically Depicted

Face Profiles." In *2017 IEEE International Conference on Computer Vision Workshops (ICCVW)*, 2898–2906. Venice: IEEE. DOI:10.1109/ICCVW.2017.342.

scikit-learn. n.d. "sklearn.utils.class_weight.compute_class_weight." Accessed August 8, 2023. https://scikit-learn.org/stable/modules/generated/sklearn.utils.class_weight.compute_class_weight.html.

Selvaraju, Ramprasaath R., Michael Cogswell, Abhishek Das, Ramakrishna Vedantam, Devi Parikh, and Dhruv Batra. 2020. "Grad-CAM: Visual Explanations from Deep Networks via Gradient-Based Localization." *International Journal of Computer Vision* 128 (2): 336–59. DOI:10.1007/s11263-019-01228-7.

spaCy. n.d. "spaCy: Industrial-strength Natural Language Processing in Python." Accessed August 8, 2023. https://spacy.io.

TensorFlow. n.d. "Tensorflow Object Detection API." Accessed August 8, 2023. https://github.com/tensorflow/models/tree/master/research/object_detection#tensorflow-object-detection-api.

Wang, Le, Meng Han, Xiaojuan Li, Ni Zhang, and Haodong Cheng. 2021. "Review of Classification Methods on Unbalanced Data Sets." *IEEE Access* 9: 64606–28. DOI:10.1109/ACCESS.2021.3074243.

Wirth, Alicia. 2021. *Einfluss von Bildannotationstechniken auf die Genauigkeit von Machine Learning-Modellen zur Objekterkennung.* Frankfurt am Main: Goethe-Universität. http://www.bigdata.uni-frankfurt.de/wp-content/uploads/2021/12/2021_FP_Alicia_online.pdf.

Zaharieva, Maia, Reinhold Huber-Moerk, Michael Noelle, and Martin Kampel. 2007. "On Ancient Coin Classification." In *VAST: International Symposium on Virtual Reality*, edited by David Arnold, Franco Niccolucci and Alan Chalmers, 55–62. Aire-la-Ville: The Eurographics Association. DOI:10.2312/VAST/VAST07/055-062.

14 Similarity Network Fusion

Understanding Patterns and their Spatial Significance in Archaeological Datasets

Timo Geitlinger
University of Zurich
timo.geitlinger@uzh.ch

Abstract

Since its earliest application in the 1970s, network analysis has become increasingly popular in both theoretical and GIS-based archaeology. Yet, applications of material networks remained relatively restricted. This paper describes a specific kind of material network, so called similarity networks, and presents a new network analysis method: Similarity Network Fusion (SNF).

Most archaeological applications of material networks approach similarity by simply quantifying the number of co-occurrences of certain traits between two nodes, without considering the relative importance of these traits for the whole network. Statistical similarity measures have so far only been applied to a handful of case studies. The similarity network analysis outlined in this paper relies on SNF, a method common in genomic studies. SNF is based on the iterative integration of similarity networks derived from multiple datatypes for the same set of samples, allowing the application of a wide range of similarity indices. It has proven to be particularly robust to heterogenous and noisy datasets containing a small number of samples, but a large number of measurements, scale differences, and collection biases.

In a case study, I applied SNF to Early Bronze Age, Middle Bronze Age, and Late Iron Age burial sites in Dorset, drawing on data published by the Grave Goods Project. To enhance the understanding of the resulting networks and topological clusters, the network was spatially represented and the clusters were correlated with five further attributes; physiographic areas, the sex of the buried individuals, the ratio of objects per grave, whether isotopic analyses suggest that the buried people were local inhabitants or moved into the area of their burial, or whether there is an association between clusters and a finer chronological subdivision of sites. The network analysis and the topological clustering of the sites revealed at least two possible spatial clusters and two statistically significant correlations between clusters and further attributes of the burial sites. These results clearly suggest the great potential of SNF for analysing archaeological datasets, unveiling patterns within the archaeological record, and understanding the significance of these patterns for the structuration of the past landscape.

Keywords: Networks; Burial practices; GIS; Prehistory; Dorset

In *Advances in Digital Archaeology. Proceedings of the 2023 conference Computer Applications and Quantitative Methods in Archaeology – 50 years of synergy*, edited by J.W.H.P. Verhagen, J. Waagen, A. Brandsen, A. Queffelec, R.M. Visser and D. Taelman, 177–196. Leiden: Sidestone Press.

	Node 1	*Node 2*	*Node 3*	*Node 4*	*Node 5*	*Node 6*
Node 1			2	0.75		
Node 2					3	
Node 3	2			1		
Node 4	0.75		1		0.75	
Node 5		3		0.75		0.5
Node 6					0.5	

Adjacency Matrix

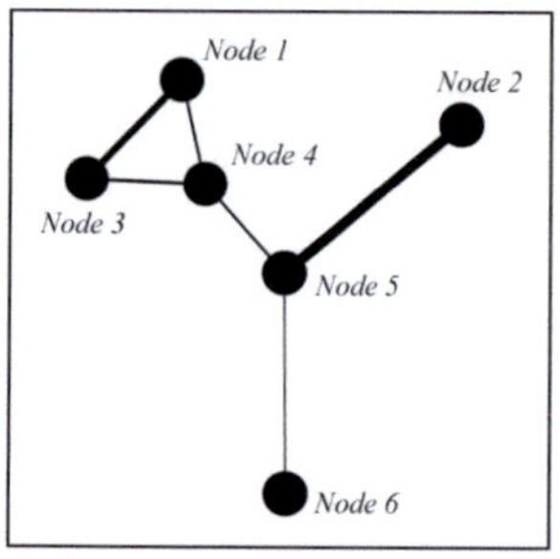

Node-Link-Diagram

Edge ID	Source Node	Target Node	Edge strength
1	1	3	2
2	1	4	0.75
3	3	4	1
4	5	2	3
5	5	4	0.75
6	5	6	0.5

Edge List

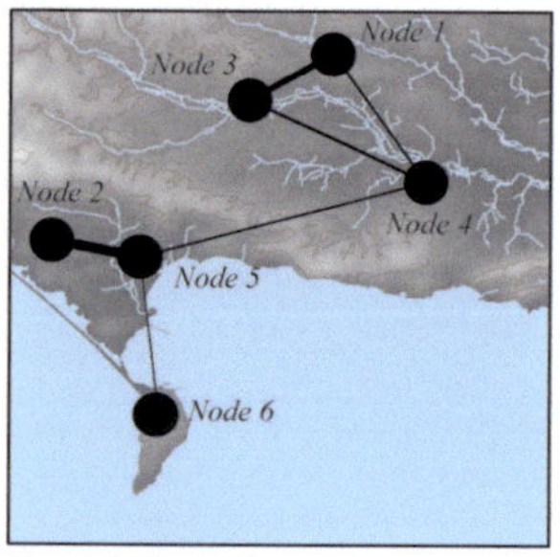

Spatial Network

Figure 14.1. Different types of network representations of the same Network. After Brughmans and Peeples (2020, Figure 15.1). Background © Environment Agency.

14.1 Introduction

Network analysis[1] has proven to be a powerful analytical tool to study and visualise the significance of relationships between past and present social, cultural, and material entities (Collar et al. 2015). For archaeological applications, it has been argued that one of the major advantages of network analysis is its great flexibility and versatility in use. Depending on the research question, virtually every entity can be studied meaningfully through a network approach, regardless of its size or materiality. Similarly, edges can represent a multitude of different relationships such as social connections, economic interactions, flows of ideas and goods, geographical proximity, or material similarity (Brughmans et al. 2016). Furthermore, due to the spatial reference of archaeological data, networks in archaeology can be analysed and visualised both in relational space, for example through adjacencies matrices or node-link-diagrams (Figure 14.1), or in absolute space within a geographical information system (Knappett 2013; Brughmans and Peeples 2020). Archaeological networks, therefore, have the potential of bridging simultaneously a diverse range of social and geographical scales of analysis and overcoming the problematic split between geometric and relational perspectives (Knappett 2011; Knappett 2013; Knappett 2016). Network analysis, moreover, provides archaeology with a multitude of well-established exploratory network techniques and statistical network measures, representing powerful tools to detect patterns and clusters in networks as well as to describe local and global measures, revealing structural properties of single nodes or of the network as a whole (Brughmans and Peeples 2020).

Since its earliest application in the 1970s and particularly in the last decade, network analysis became increasingly popular in both theoretical and GIS-based archaeology (Prignano et al. 2017; Brughmans and Peeples 2020; Donnellan 2020). However, applications of material networks remained astonishingly restricted. Material networks are a specific kind of archaeological network whose edges are defined by aspatial contextual information such as geochemically sourced materials, shared presence of certain objects, or similarities in material assemblages (Brughmans and Peeples 2020, 277). By relating these networks to the geographical space, material networks appear particularly suitable to study the structuration of past landscapes and understanding the spatial significance of past social and cultural processes.

In this paper I will further explore the potential of material network analysis. The focus of the paper is on a specific kind of material network, so called similarity networks. I will investigate similarity networks through a case study, conducted with data from the numerous Prehistoric burials in Dorset (UK), and a new network analysis technique developed for genomic studies: Similarity Network Fusion (SNF).

14.2 Similarity Networks

In general, similarity networks are a set of material network analysis methods, which use measures of similarity to

1 A network is a representation of the structure of relationships or connections (often called edges) between certain kinds of elements (often called nodes) of interest (Brughmans and Peeples 2020, 273). For further reading: Brughmans et al. (2023).

define edges among archaeological sites (Brughmans and Peeples 2020, 277). Originally, similarity networks are simple bipartite networks, consisting solely of two classes of nodes; the archaeological context (i.e., a site), and attributes associated with this context (i.e., artefact types). However, unlike normal binary affiliation networks, the strength of the edges between nodes is weighed by the frequency of their shared attributes (Prignano et al. 2017). Within similarity network analysis, the strength of similarity between archaeological assemblages is often interpreted as proxy of exchange, interaction, population movement, transmission of knowledge, or cultural relatedness (Peeples et al. 2016; Prignano et al. 2017).

Most archaeological applications of material culture networks rather seem to approach similarity by simply quantifying the number of co-occurrences of certain traits between two nodes, without considering the relative importance of these traits for the whole network (i.a., Sindbaek 2007; Mizoguchi 2009; Blake 2013; Östborn and Gerding 2015; Feugnet et al. 2017). In order to approach the relative importance of a network connection, statistical similarity measures need to be applied. There are many different similarity measures which all have slightly different contextual meaning and have different suitabilities for certain archaeological questions (cf. Habiba et al. 2018). Yet so far only a handful of archaeological case studies have used such similarity coefficients. Probably the first application of a similarity coefficient in archaeology was undertaken by Morgan and Whitelaw (1991), using dissimilarity indices to relate different Geometric pottery assemblages in the Greek Argive region. More than 20 years later, Golitko et al. (2012) used the Brainerd-Robinson coefficient to analyse similarities among the composition of obsidian sources of Mayan stone tool assemblages, while Mills et al. (2013) applied the same approach to pre-Hispanic ceramic and obsidian assemblages from the south-western United States. De Groot (2019) resorted to Jaccard and Kulczynski-2 measures in order to assess similarity between Neolithic pottery assemblages in Eastern Anatolia, the Aegean, and the Balkans. Bourgeois and Kroon (2017), lastly, used the cosine similarity index for the estimation of the similarity between Northern European Corded Ware graves. For the cosine similarity index each observation consisting of different variable attributes is converted to a vector in virtual space; the similarity between two observations is expressed as differences between the angles of their vectors (Bourgeois and Kroon 2017).

The similarity network analysis outlined in the case study below relies on so called Similarity Network Fusion (SNF), a method commonly applied in genomic studies (Wang et al. 2014). SNF is based on the integration of similarity networks derived from multiple datatypes (i.e., different object types) for the same set of samples (i.e., sites). In a first step, SNF calculates a similarity network between each pair of samples for each of the datatypes, allowing the application of a wide range of similarity indices. Secondly, all of these networks are fused into a single similarity network, by using a nonlinear, iterative approach; based on message-passaging theory, every network is updated and made more similar to the other networks after each iteration, before finally converging to a single network. In the iterative process, strong similarities tend to be emphasised, while weak similarities are down-weight through a K-nearest neighbours procedure, reducing the noise in the final network and only retaining weak relationships, being consistent across the whole dataset. SNF has proven to be particularly robust to heterogenous and noisy datasets, containing only a small number of samples, but a large number of measurements, scale differences, and collection biases. Arguably, these data conditions are not only common for genomic datasets but are also typical for archaeological data. Furthermore, apart from integrating data, SNF provides a set of additional network techniques (i.e., spectral clustering), which are especially suitable for detecting subtypes and clusters in topological networks.

14.3 Case Study

14.3.1 Material and Methods

To further expand on the functionality, performance, and potential of similarity networks and SNF for archaeological purposes, I conducted a similarity analysis of Late Prehistoric burial sites in Dorset. Subsequently, I understand burials as materialisation of past social, ritual, and cultural actions, both representing and constituting social and cultural meaning (cf. Ekengren 2013). By representing material networks between roughly contemporary burial sites, the objective of the analysis is to get insights into the social, cultural, and ritual structuration of the landscape. Central to a landscape perspective is a more holistic view of human actions, taking into consideration the relationship between sites as well as humanly and non-humanly created features. As such, landscape is understood as cause and outcome of human actions, crossing the distinction between nature and culture (cf. Gosden et al. 2021, 18).

The data used for conducting the SNF analysis were derived from the published database of the *Grave Goods project* (Cooper et al. 2022). Within six regional study areas, the Grave Goods project analysed diachronically and at a series of scales material culture and mortuary contexts during the Neolithic to the Iron Age period. The six regions were chosen, taking into account strong histories of investigation, the accessibility of records, and grave goods traditions (Cooper et al. 2020, 2). The database is based on information from the Historic Environment Record and was further enhanced by published and unpublished data (Cooper et al. 2020). Though the burial data were subject to extensive analyses, which were only recently published

Dataset 1	
Categories:	*Examples:*
Grave Hierarchy	Primary, secondary
Grave Type	Cist, mound, etc.
Human Remains	Inhumation, cremation
Monument Type	Burial, barrow, etc.
Placement of the Object	Torso, head, etc.
Grave Good Type	Ceramics, Dagger, etc.
Materials	Bronze, gold, etc.
Number of Buried Individuals	1, 2, 3...

Table 14.1. Dataset 1, showing all categories of the burial data included in the holistic SNF analysis and examples for the kind of information recorded by the grave goods project for each datatype.

Dataset 2	
Categories:	*Examples:*
Grave Good Type	Ceramics, dagger, etc.
Placement of the Object	Torso, head, etc.

Table 14.2. Dataset 2, showing all categories of the burial data included in the object-related SNF analysis and examples for the kind of information recorded by the grave goods project for each datatype.

(Cooper et al. 2022), neither addressed the project explicitly a network approach to the collected data, nor appears the abundant contextual burial information, yielded by the project, to be exploited to its full potential.

I choose Dorset as area of investigation for the SNF analysis, as it is the region with the most extensive site record analysed by the Grave Goods project. To roughly fulfil the presupposition of contemporaneity, I only used similarity measures for sites dating to the same subperiod. Additionally, I solely took sites dating to the Early Bronze Age (EBA, 2200-1500 BCE, 115 burials), Middle Bronze Age (MBA, 1500-1150 BCE, 46 burials), and Late Iron Age (LIA, 100 BCE-40 CE, 23 burials) into consideration, as from remaining subperiods the burials did not appear numerous enough for meaningful network analyses. Since the Grave Goods project stored the spatial data on the level of the site, I defined inter-site relations as scale of analysis.

In order to explore similarity-relationships, I prepared two sets of different datatypes for the sites of each subperiod. The first set attempted to give a more holistic impression of burial rituals covering a great variety of aspects of the burial data. Namely, the datatypes encompassed grave hierarchy, grave type, human remains, the associated monument types, numbers of buried individuals, the unspecific grave good type, the placement of the objects in relation to the body, and the materials of the grave goods (Table 14.1).

Since archaeology traditionally assigns to the type of object high cultural and chronological significance (Ekengren 2013), the second set of datatypes focused on the grave goods themselves. This set solely included the specific grave good type and the placement of the objects in relation to the buried body (Table 14.2).

Since SNF analyses need contingency tables as input, each datatype first needed to be reformatted accordingly. This pre-processing was conducted in Excel and SPSS and resulted in tables, containing information about the absence or presence of all attributes of a datatype for each site. In conducted SNF analysis in Python, using the SNFpy package (cf. Markello 2018; RMARKELLO 2022). A recent study (Prignano et al. 2017) reached the conclusion that Network measures such as Weighted Degree Centrality and Betweenness Centrality indexes of the Brainerd-Robinson coefficient, which is the most common coefficient in archaeological applications of similarity network analysis, highly depend on the number of samples. For incomplete datasets, the Brainerd-Robinson coefficient therefore does not seem to be the best performing similarity index to study the strongest network connections. Instead, I applied the well-established cosine coefficient for the creation of the similarity networks for the different datatypes (cf. Bourgeois and Kroon 2017), which is particularly effective for datasets with many different attributes and to consider non-uniform significance (Habiba et al. 2018). The python SNF algorithm displays the fused network as adjacency matrix, showing the similarity between each pair of sites. After all networks had been fused with each other, I determined the optimal number of clusters in the network using the get_n_clusters function and grouped the sites accordingly. The get_n_cluster function is based on a spectral clustering approach (RMARKELLO 2022). In spectral clustering, the eigenvalues or spectrum of the similarity matrix are used to reduce dimensions and translate the similarities in a Laplacian graph. K-means clustering is then applied to the eigenvectors of the Laplacian graph to establish the optimal number of clusters.

Together with the fused similarity matrix, I subsequently exported the resulting clusters of sites. The fused similarity network was reformatted as edge list and imported into ArcGIS pro. Since the results of the SNF analysis roughly vary between values of 0 and 0.6, in ArcGIS Pro I used the Standardize Field tool (Esri 2022a) to exclude outliers of very high similarity values, occurring due to the great similarity which samples have with themselves, and to rescale the remaining values between 0 and 1. Between all sites of each period, I created a non-planar Origin-Destination Cost Matrix (Esri 2022b), defining each site as a node connected by edges to every other site. The edges of the network were then joined with the results of the SNF analysis. To get an assessable impression of possible relationships in the area of research, I restricted the representation of the edges to the 25 highest similarities and weighed them according to their network importance. The cluster classification of the sites was joined with the nodes of the networks, enabling a representation of the topological clusters in geographical space.

14.4 Discussion

Dorset is a county in southern England, bordering the English Channel to the south. Apart from a long stretching coastline, Dorset is characterised by a varied hinterland with chalk downs, limestone ridges, and low-lying clay valleys. In the earliest part of the EBA, burials were mainly constructed as single inhumation graves with a large number of deposits under mounds of a diverse range of sizes and forms (Cullingford 1980). Not uncommonly, these mounds were designed as multiphase monuments. In the later EBA, cremations under single-phase mounds predominated (Bradley 2019, 173; Garwood 2007). In the MBA, cremation burials likewise prevailed. Some were still placed under barrows, while occasionally, they also occurred in cemeteries. MBA burials were usually associated with ceramic vessels and less commonly with metalwork and other objects (Cooper et al. 2022). In the LIA, inhumation graves were usually organised in cemeteries. They were associated with a variety of objects such as objects of personal adornment, tools, or ceramics.

Except for the clusters reconstructed from EBA burials (Figures 14.3 and 14.6), most clusters derived from the first and second dataset appear quite different from each other (Figures 14.4 and 14.7, and Figures 14.5 and 14.8). In general, the topological clusters reveal hardly any clear patterns in geographical space. Some notable exceptions are conspicuous clusters of LIA burials in southern Dorset, visible on both the extensive and the object focused network analysis (black cluster Figure 14.5, white cluster Figure 14.8) as well as clusters of MBA sites derived from the network analysis with the first set of datatypes (Figure 14.4); taking the spatial distribution of the white and the black clusters into account, it almost appears as if these groups separate into a northern and a southern pattern. However, the third, most comprehensive red cluster seems to distort this clear picture. Furthermore, in both datasets and across almost all periods some clusters seem to be more closely connected than others. Most obvious this can be seen in the network of MBA sites derived from dataset 1 (Figure 14.4). Here, the strongest network connections are almost exclusively between points of the white cluster.

To enhance the understanding of the meaning and relevance of the topological clusters and strongest network edges, I evaluated the spatial correlations of the clusters with five further attributes. Namely, these five attributes were the association of the burials with specific physiographic areas, the sex of the buried individuals of a site, the ratio of objects per grave, whether isotopic analyses suggest that the buried people were local inhabitants or moved into the area of their burial, or whether there is an association between clusters and a finer chronological subdivision of sites.

14.3.1 Landscape

The association of burial clusters with a certain landscape was approached by using the National Character Area Profiles (Natural England 2022). National Character Areas are a classification of England by regions, which have a recognisable character and are bounded by natural lines in the landscape. Though the character of landscapes arguably has significantly changed since the Late Prehistory and strongly relies on our modern way of perceiving these areas, since National Character Areas are based on the natural structuration and appearance of the landscape, they seem a more accurate approximation of possible past landscape divisions than modern political borders.

In total, the area of Dorset consists of nine National Character Areas (Figure 14.2). Yet, depicting the different networks against the background of the National Character Areas does not suggest a correlation between the topological clusters and these nine regions. In fact, apart from the geographically very restricted clusters visible in the LIA object network (white cluster Figure 14.8), there seems to be not a single cluster which exclusively is located in only one National Character Area.

14.3.2 Sex Affiliation

The association of a site with a specific sex was reconstructed on the basis of data of anthropological sex determinations of human remains available within the Grave Goods project database. Since some sites encompassed several human remains with different sexes, for the purpose of this analysis the sites were reclassified in the attributes Male, Female, Subadult, and Mixed according to their predominant association with a certain sex.

Similar as with the landscape classification, there does not seem to be an obvious correlation between the burial clusters and the different sex categories; while within the EBA and LIA networks there is no cluster consisting solely or predominantly of one sex class (Figures 14.5 and 14.8), the white cluster in the MBA network derived from a diverse set of datatypes only comprises female burials (Figure 14.4). However, since most sex affiliations of the cluster's sites are unknown and the potential relationship between the cluster and burials does not seem to be mutually exclusive, it appears rather doubtful that there is a correlation between the cluster and the sex classes at all.

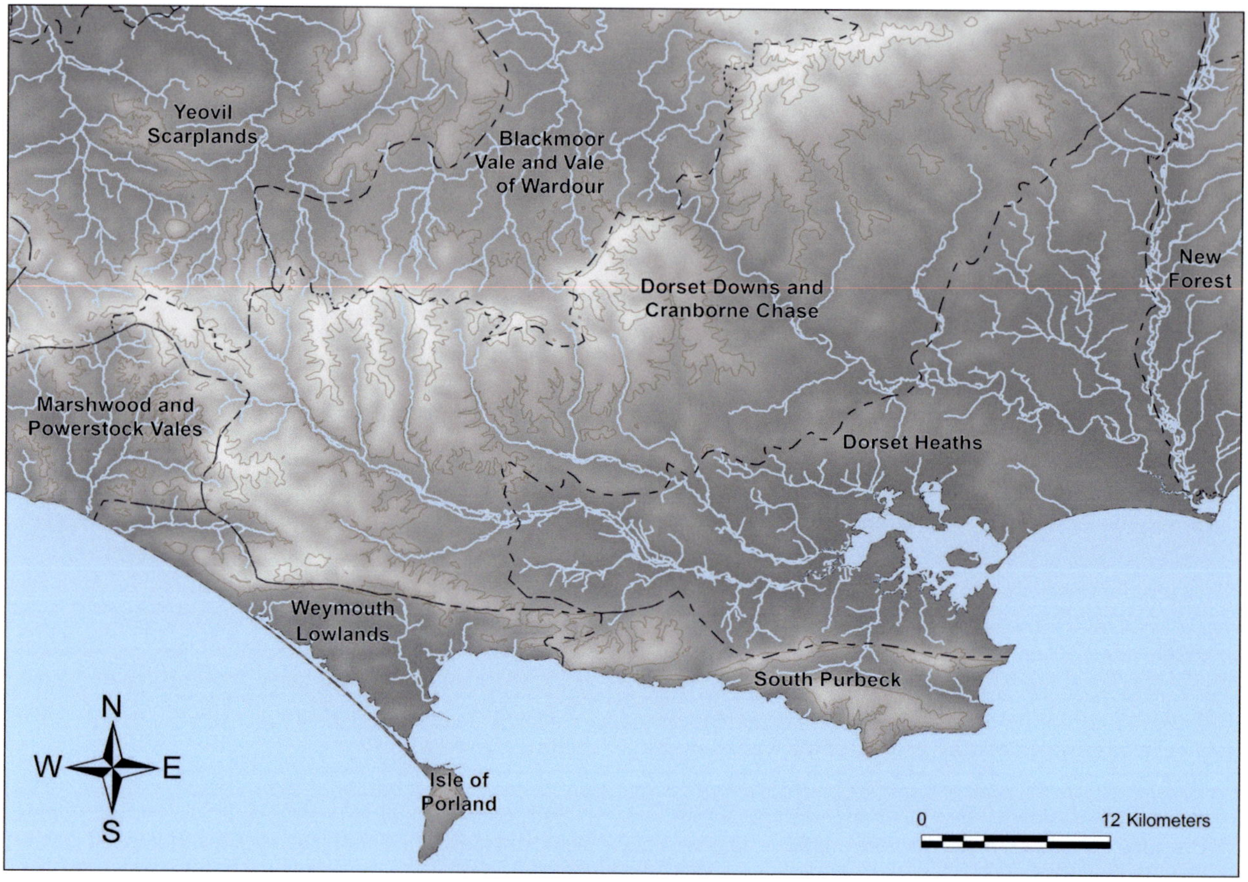

Yeovil Scarplands
Blackmoor Vale and Vale of Wardour
Dorset Downs and Cranborne Chase
New Forest
Marshwood and Powerstock Vales
Dorset Heaths
Weymouth Lowlands
South Purbeck
Isle of Porland
N
W
E
S
0
12 Kilometers

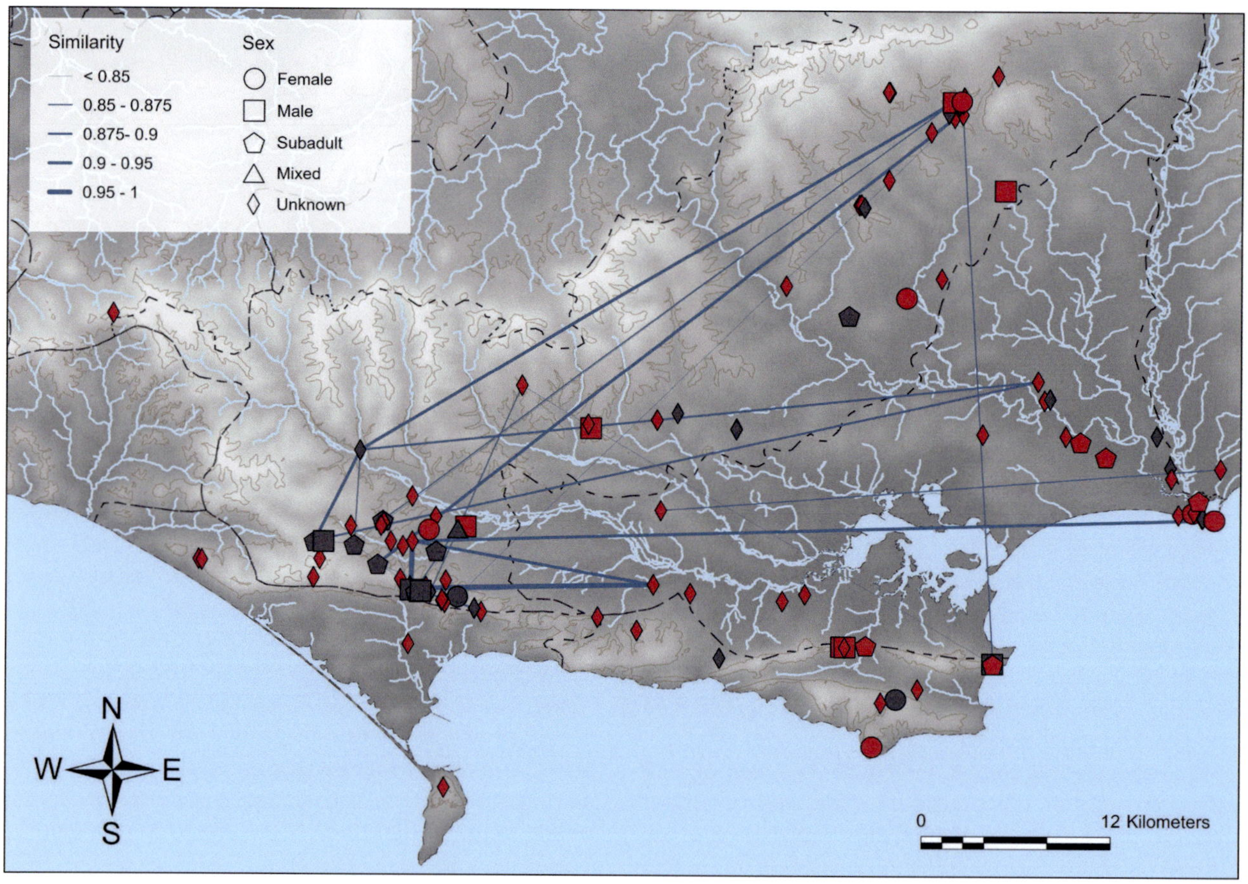

Similarity
< 0.85
0.85 - 0.875
0.875- 0.9
0.9 - 0.95
0.95 - 1
Sex
Female
Male
Subadult
Mixed
Unknown
N
W
E
S
0
12 Kilometers

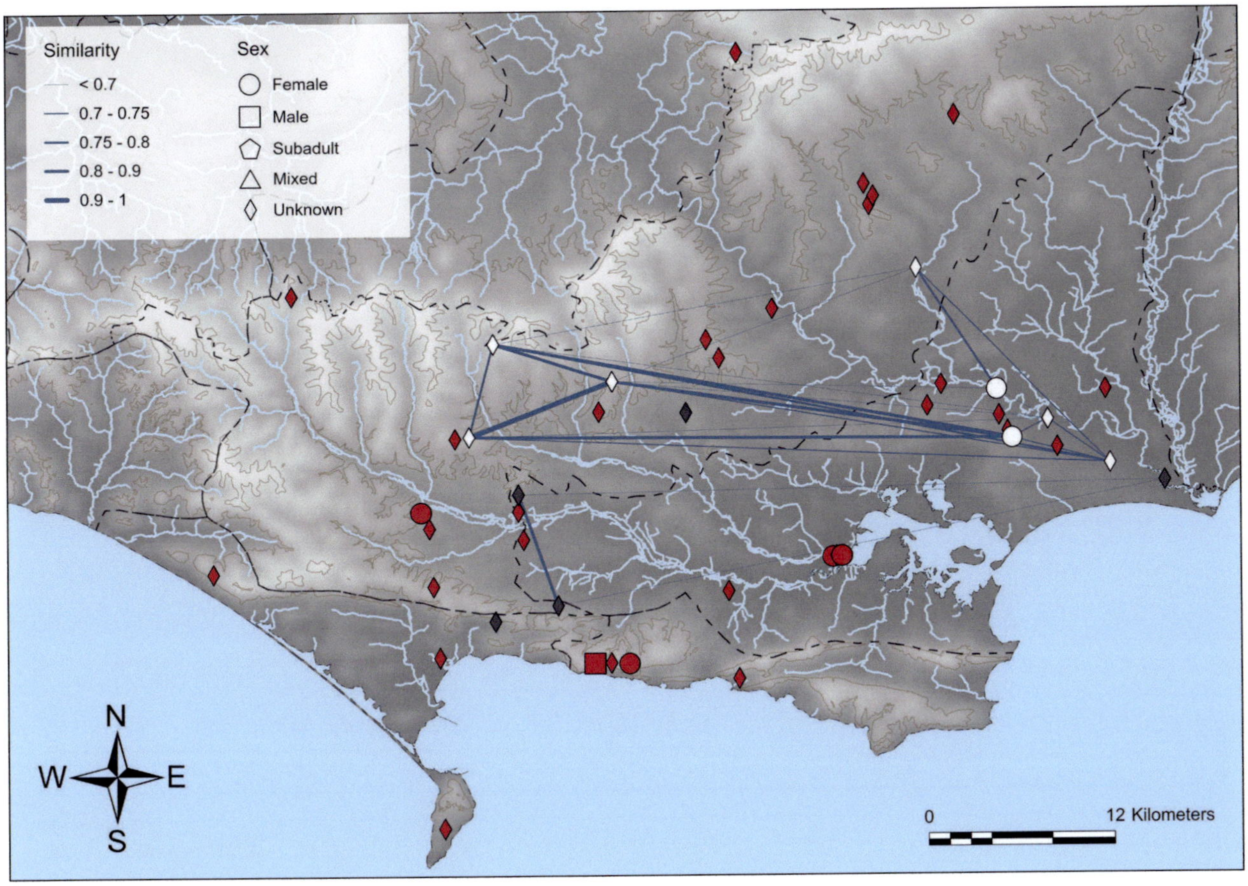

Figure 14.4. Similarity network derived from the first datatypes of Middle Bronze Age sites in Dorset, depicting the 25 strongest network connections, topological clusters (black, red, white), and sex classification of sites. Background © Environment Agency. Natural character areas © Natural England.

(Opposite page, top) Figure 14.2. National Character Areas of Dorset. Background © Environment Agency. Natural character areas © Natural England.

(Opposite page, bottom) Figure 14.3. Similarity network derived from the first datatypes of Early Bronze Age sites in Dorset, depicting the 25 strongest network connections, topological clusters (black, red), and sex classification of sites. Background © Environment Agency. Natural character areas © Natural England.

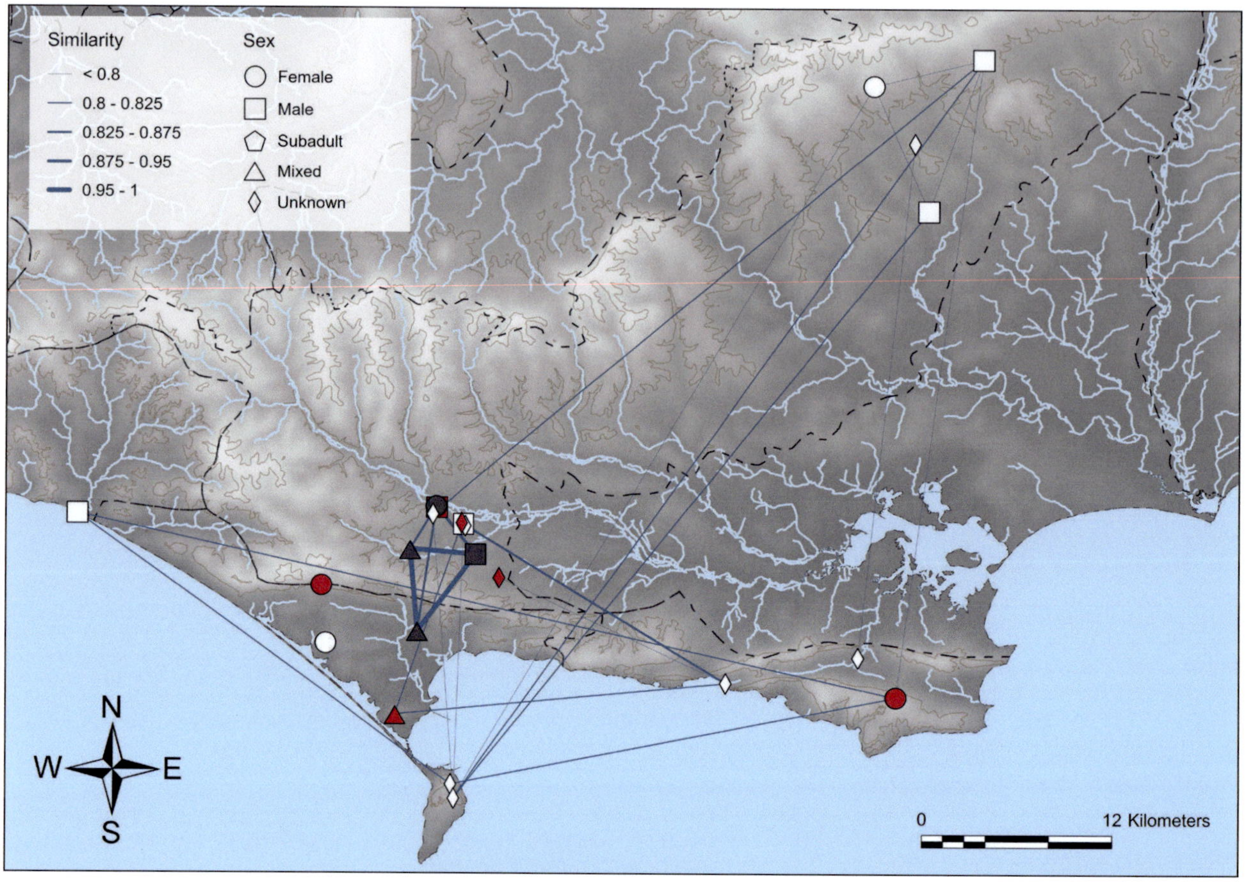
Similarity
< 0.8
0.8 - 0.825
0.825 - 0.875
0.875 - 0.95
0.95 - 1
Sex
Female
Male
Subadult
Mixed
Unknown
N
W
E
S
0
12 Kilometers

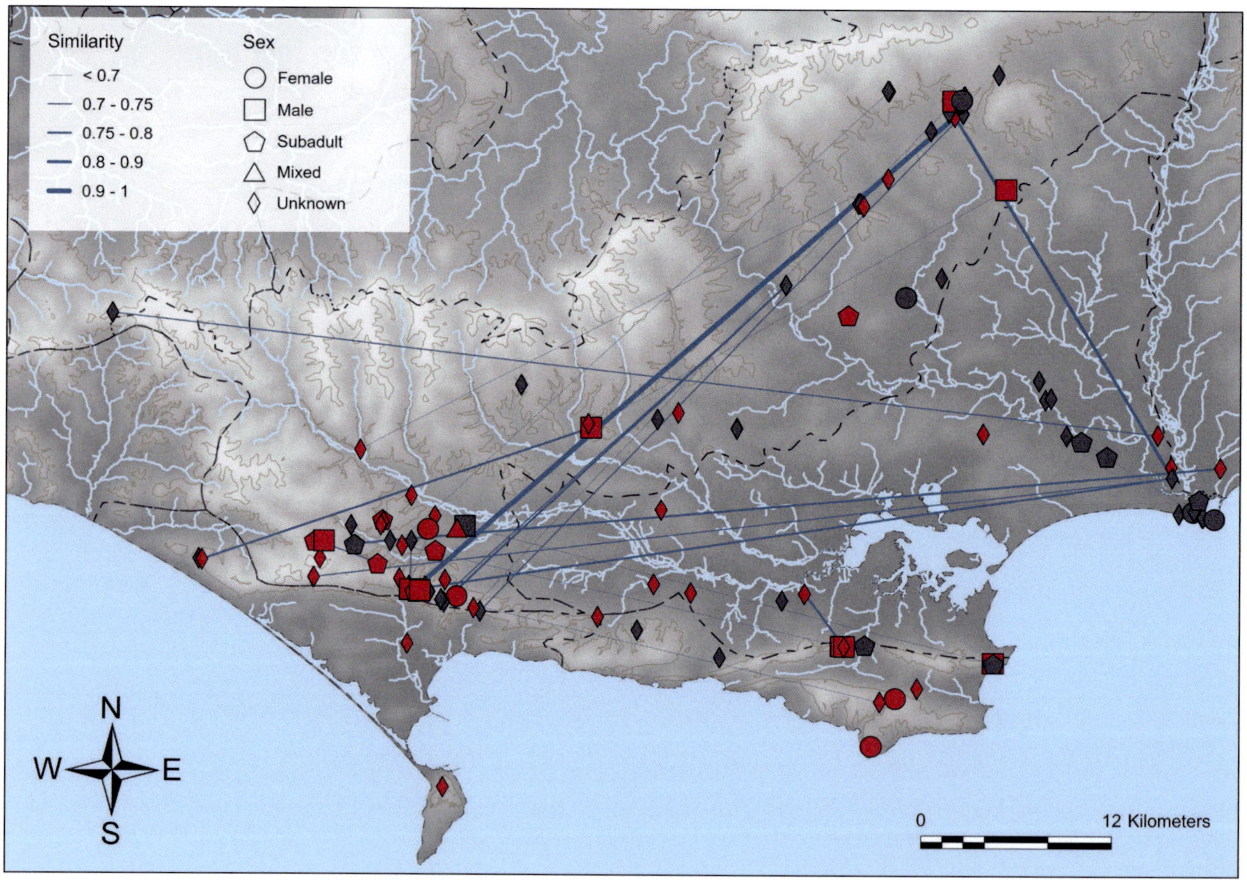
Similarity
< 0.7
0.7 - 0.75
0.75 - 0.8
0.8 - 0.9
0.9 - 1
Sex
Female
Male
Subadult
Mixed
Unknown
N
W
E
S
0
12 Kilometers

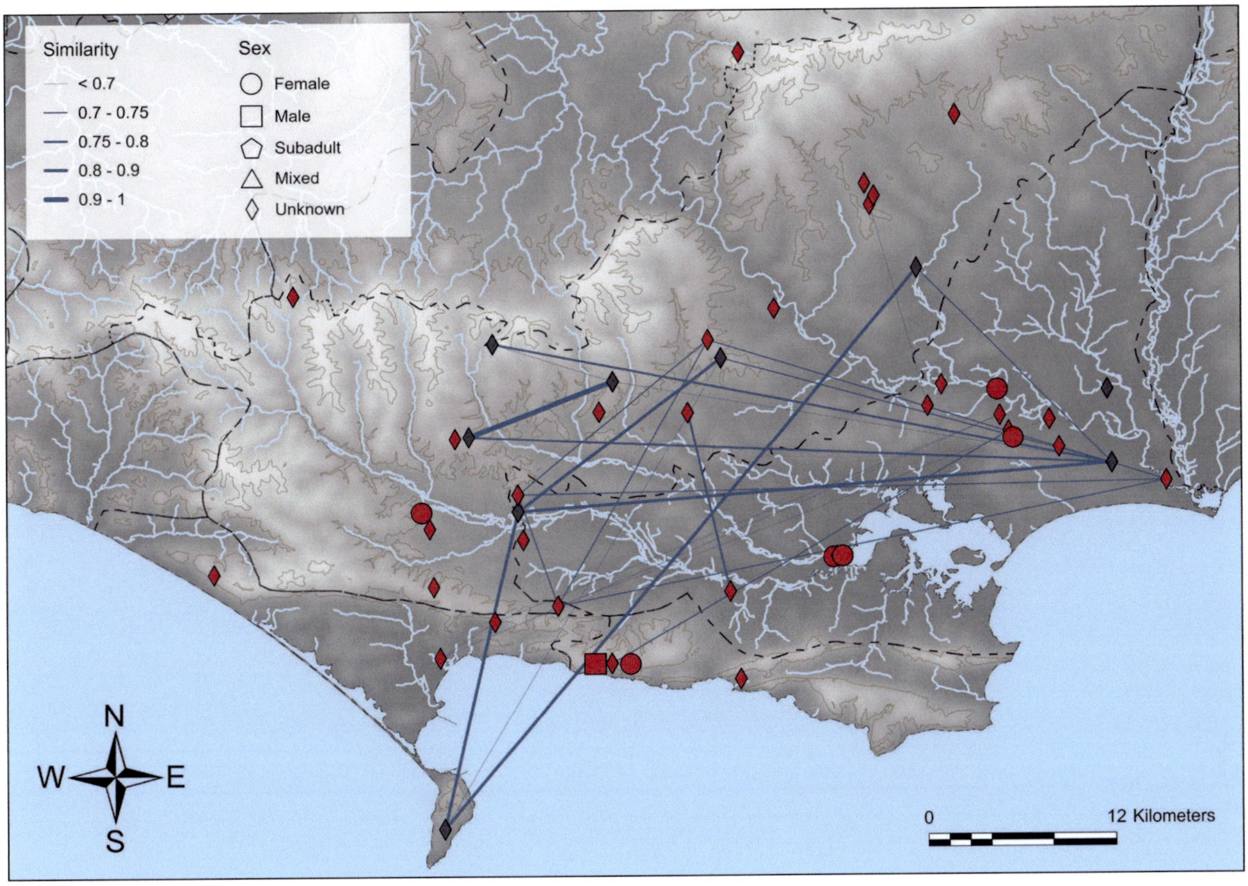

Figure 14.7. Similarity network derived from the second datatypes of Middle Bronze Age sites in Dorset, depicting the 25 strongest network connections, topological clusters (black, red), and sex classification of sites. Background © Environment Agency. Natural character areas © Natural England.

(Opposite page, top) Figure 14.5. Similarity network derived from the first datatypes of Late Iron Age sites in Dorset, depicting the 25 strongest network connections, topological clusters (black, red, white), and sex classification of sites. Background © Environment Agency. Natural character areas © Natural England.

(Opposite page, bottom) Figure 14.6. Similarity network derived from the second datatypes of Early Bronze Age sites in Dorset, depicting 25 strongest network connections, topological clusters (black, red), and sex classification of sites. Background © Environment Agency. Natural character areas © Natural England.

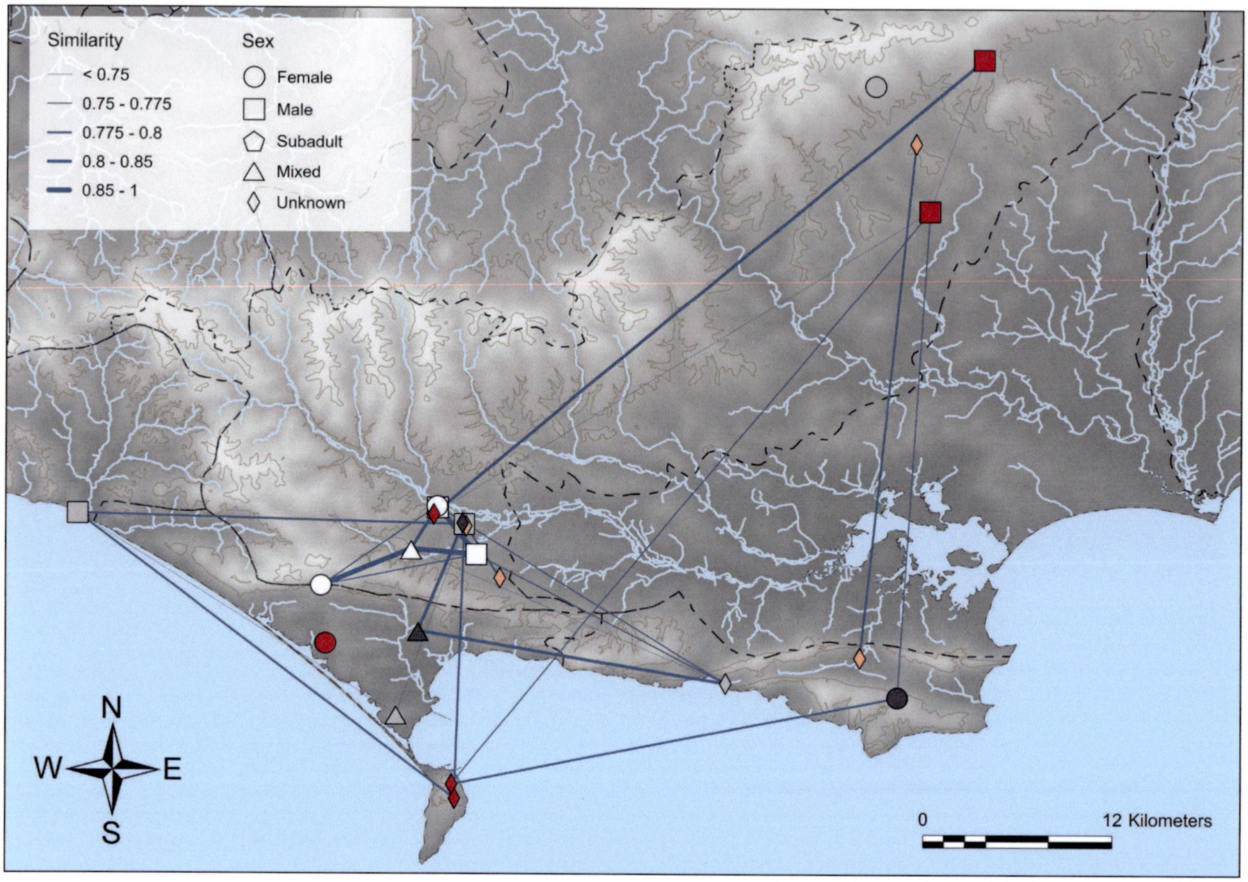
Similarity
< 0.75
0.75 - 0.775
0.775 - 0.8
0.8 - 0.85
0.85 - 1
Sex
Female
Male
Subadult
Mixed
Unknown
N
W
E
S
0
12 Kilometers

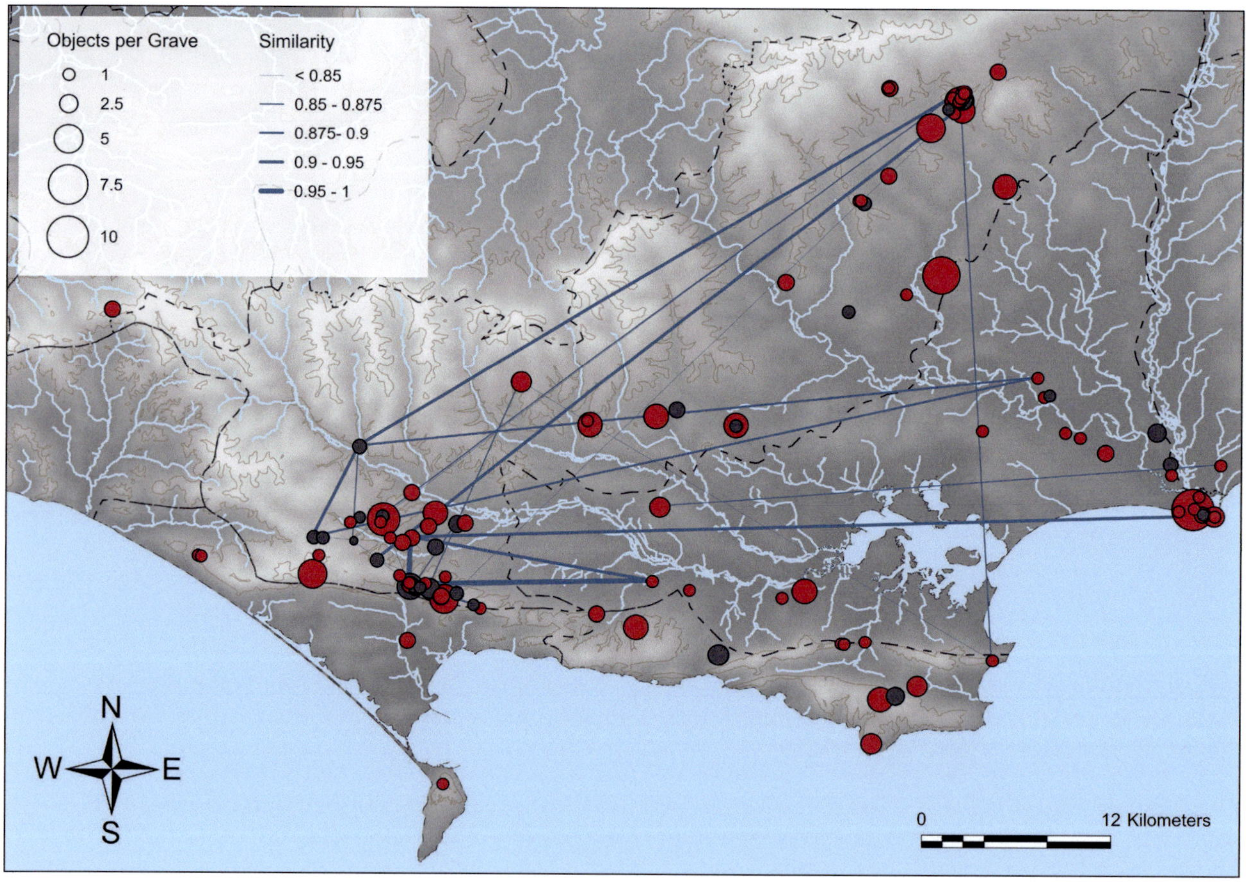
Objects per Grave
1
2.5
5
7.5
10
Similarity
< 0.85
0.85 - 0.875
0.875- 0.9
0.9 - 0.95
0.95 - 1
N
W
E
S
0
12 Kilometers

14.3.3 Burial Goods per Grave

As potential proxy of social differences, from the Grave Goods project data the average amount of burial goods per grave were determined for each site (Figures 14.9–14.14). Traditionally, differences in numbers of objects have been interpreted as proxy of differences in the richness of the graves and, thus, in social status or prestige of the deceased or the bereaved. Even though this line of argument tends to oversimplify the diverse, context-dependent ways graves symbolically communicated meaning (Ekengren 2013), the potential correlation appears intriguing.

The average amount of grave goods per site was established through the number of graves and objects found at a site. Indeed, there is a strong correlation between most of the different clusters and the number of graves and objects, which even can be statistically affirmed through an analysis of variance (ANOVA; Table 14.3). Within dataset 1 there is, for example, throughout all periods one cluster consisting solely of sites with single burials (red cluster Figure 14.9, red cluster Figure 14.10, and white cluster Figure 14.11) that can be separated from the other clusters also including sites with multiple burials. Though the number of burials and burial goods apparently influences other aspects of the burial ritual, from a data perspective this seems hardly surprising, as most of the categories used to create the networks (Tables 14.1 and 14.2) are more or less directly related to the number of graves or goods. Contrary to expectations, these potential correlations do not hold true for all datasets. For instance, the number of objects does not necessarily have a provable influence on the formation of the EBA object-based clusters (dataset 2), as suggested by a probability above a level of significance of 5%. Looking at the original data, EBA burials are characterised by a great variety of different object materials and types, whose selection for a burial seems to be unrelated to the total amount of the interred objects.

On the contrary, for most datasets there is no significant correlation between the average amount of grave goods per grave and the determined clusters (Figures 14.9–14.14). One notable exception is the MBA network derived from dataset 1. The network divides the sites into one cluster with more (Figure 14.13, black cluster) and one with fewer (Figure 14.13, red cluster) grave goods per grave. As a statistical analysis of variance (ANOVA) revealed, the difference ($F(1, 43) = 6.448, p = 0.015$) in the amount of burial goods per grave of the black ($M = 3.59, SD = 5.82$) and the red cluster ($M = 1.19, SD = 0.38$) is statistically significant. Looking at the strength of the network connections, the strongest edges furthermore seem to be located between sites of the black cluster. Yet, during the MBA in Dorset, ceramic vessels used as cremation urns were almost exclusively found as burial goods. Since hardly any other objects are recorded in the MBA graves, it seems rather unlikely that these differences in the average amount of objects should be related to clear social differences. Instead, they rather seem to represent small variations and deviations in an otherwise very uniform grave goods tradition.

14.3.4 Mover or Local

A differentiation between individuals who were born and died at different locations, thus moved or were moved during or after their lifetime, and individuals who were born and died at the same location, was made on the basis of the isotopic data gathered by the Beaker People Project (Parker Pearson et al. 2019). Though the main focus of the Beaker people project was laid on the Beaker period, during the project abundant of nitrogen, carbon, sulphur, strontium, and oxygen isotope data was sampled and

		Number of Graves		Number of Grave Goods	
		F-score	Probability	F-score	Probability
Dataset 1	EBA	157.370	< 0.001	48.642	< 0.001
	MBA	28.582	< 0.001	10.837	< 0.001
	LIA	8.612	0.002	12.655	< 0.001
Dataset 2	EBA	5.471	0.021	3.607	0.060
	MBA	11.888	< 0.001	17.616	< 0.001
	LIA	1.944	0.147	3.315	0.034

Table 14.3. F-scores and probabilities of the analysis of variance of the clusters with the number of graves and grave goods.

(Opposite page, top) Figure 14.8. Similarity network derived from the second datatypes of Late Iron Age sites in Dorset, depicting the 25 strongest network connections, topological clusters (black, red, white, grey, orange), and sex classification of sites. Background © Environment Agency. Natural character areas © Natural England.

(Opposite page, bottom) Figure 14.9. Similarity network derived from the first datatypes of Early Bronze Age sites in Dorset, depicting the 25 strongest network connections, topological clusters (black, red), and average grave goods per grave per site. Background © Environment Agency. Natural character areas © Natural England.

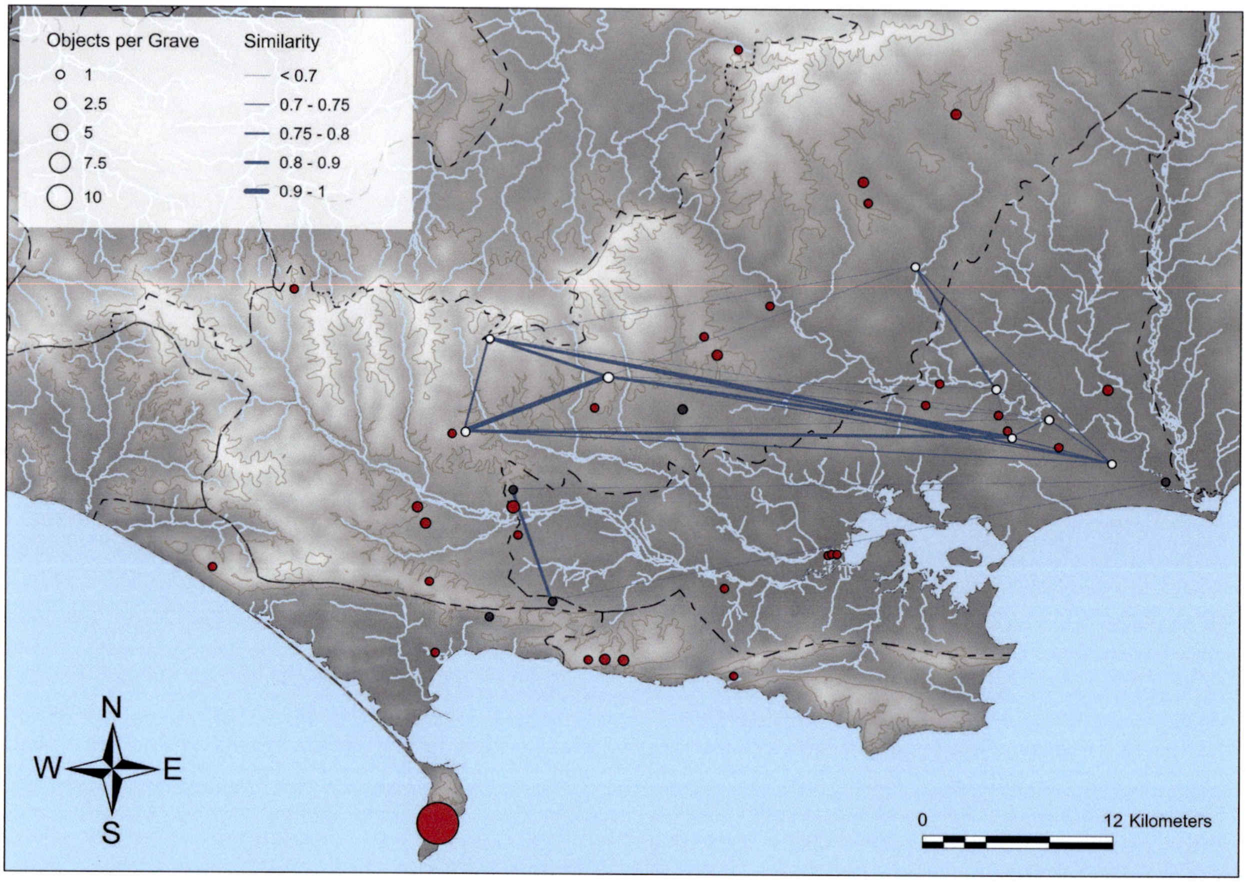

Objects per Grave
1
2.5
5
7.5
10
Similarity
< 0.7
0.7 - 0.75
0.75 - 0.8
0.8 - 0.9
0.9 - 1
N
W
E
S
0
12 Kilometers

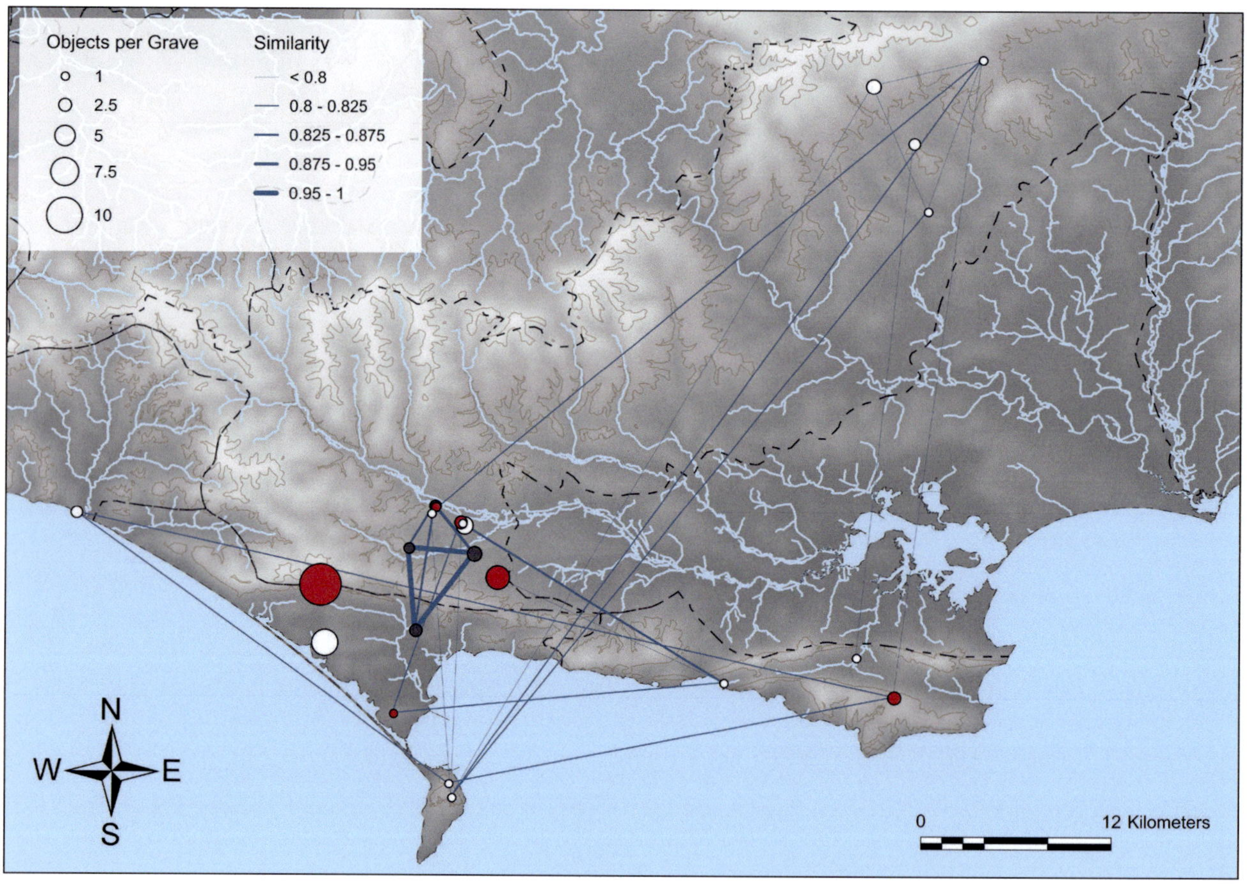

Objects per Grave
1
2.5
5
7.5
10
Similarity
< 0.8
0.8 - 0.825
0.825 - 0.875
0.875 - 0.95
0.95 - 1
N
W
E
S
0
12 Kilometers

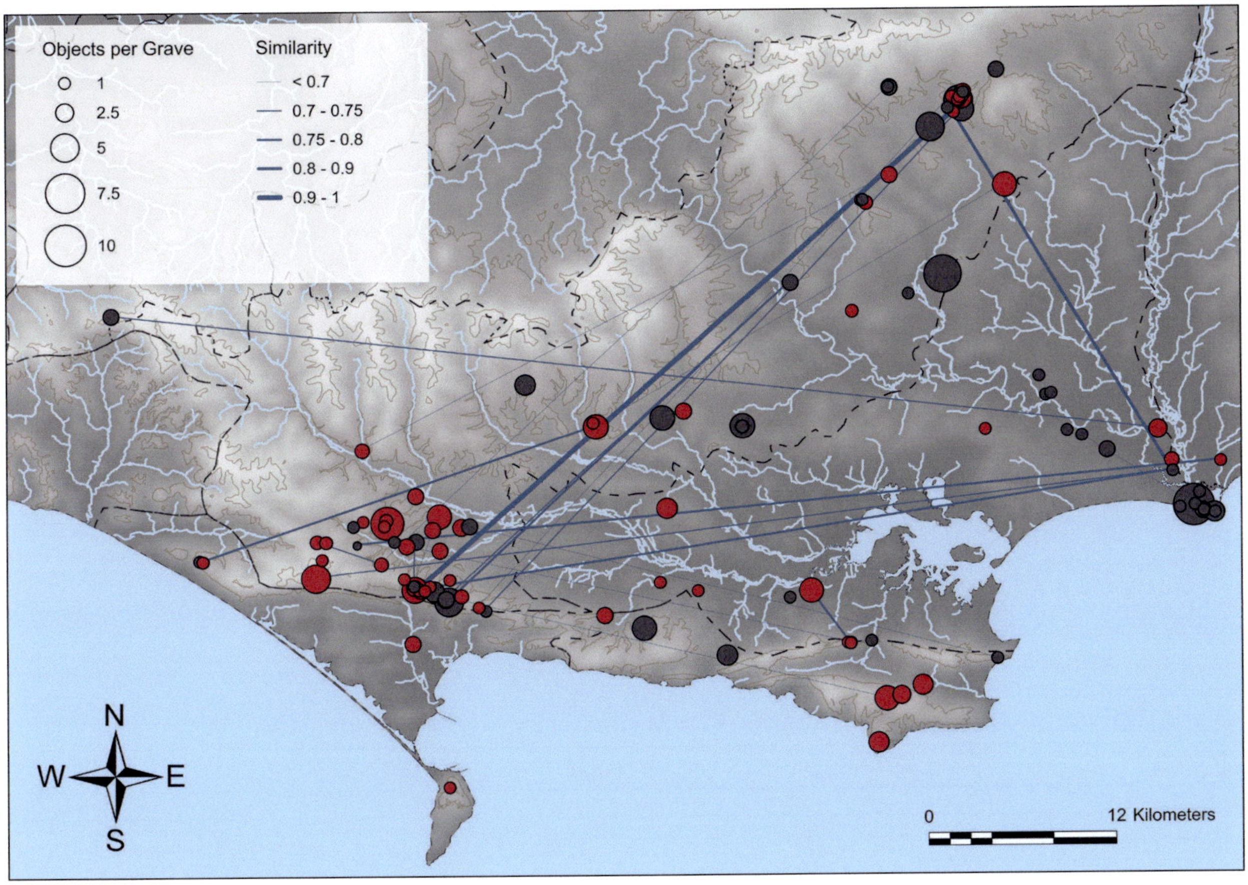

Figure 14.12. Similarity network derived from the second datatypes of Early Bronze Age sites in Dorset, depicting the 25 strongest network connections, topological clusters (black, red), and average grave goods per grave per site. Background © Environment Agency. Natural character areas © Natural England.

(Opposite page, top) Figure 14.10. Similarity network derived from the first datatypes of Middle Bronze Age sites in Dorset, depicting the 25 strongest network connections, topological clusters (black, red, white), and average grave goods per grave per site. Background © Environment Agency. Natural character areas © Natural England.

(Opposite page, bottom) Figure 14.11. Similarity network derived from the first datatypes of Late Iron sites in Dorset, depicting the 25 strongest network connections, topological clusters (black, red, white), and average grave goods per grave per site. Background © Environment Agency. Natural character areas © Natural England.

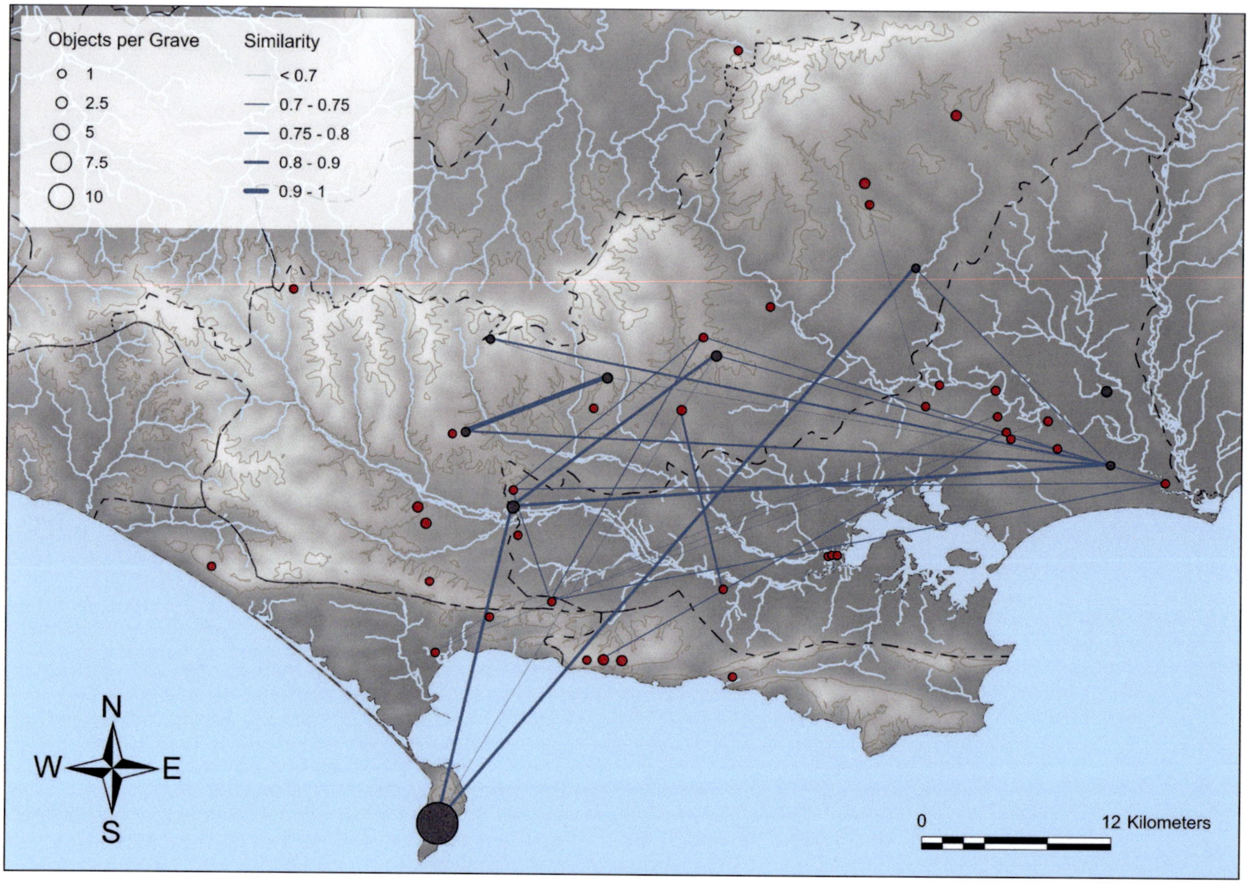
Objects per Grave
1
2.5
5
7.5
10
Similarity
< 0.7
0.7 - 0.75
0.75 - 0.8
0.8 - 0.9
0.9 - 1
N
W
E
S
0
12 Kilometers

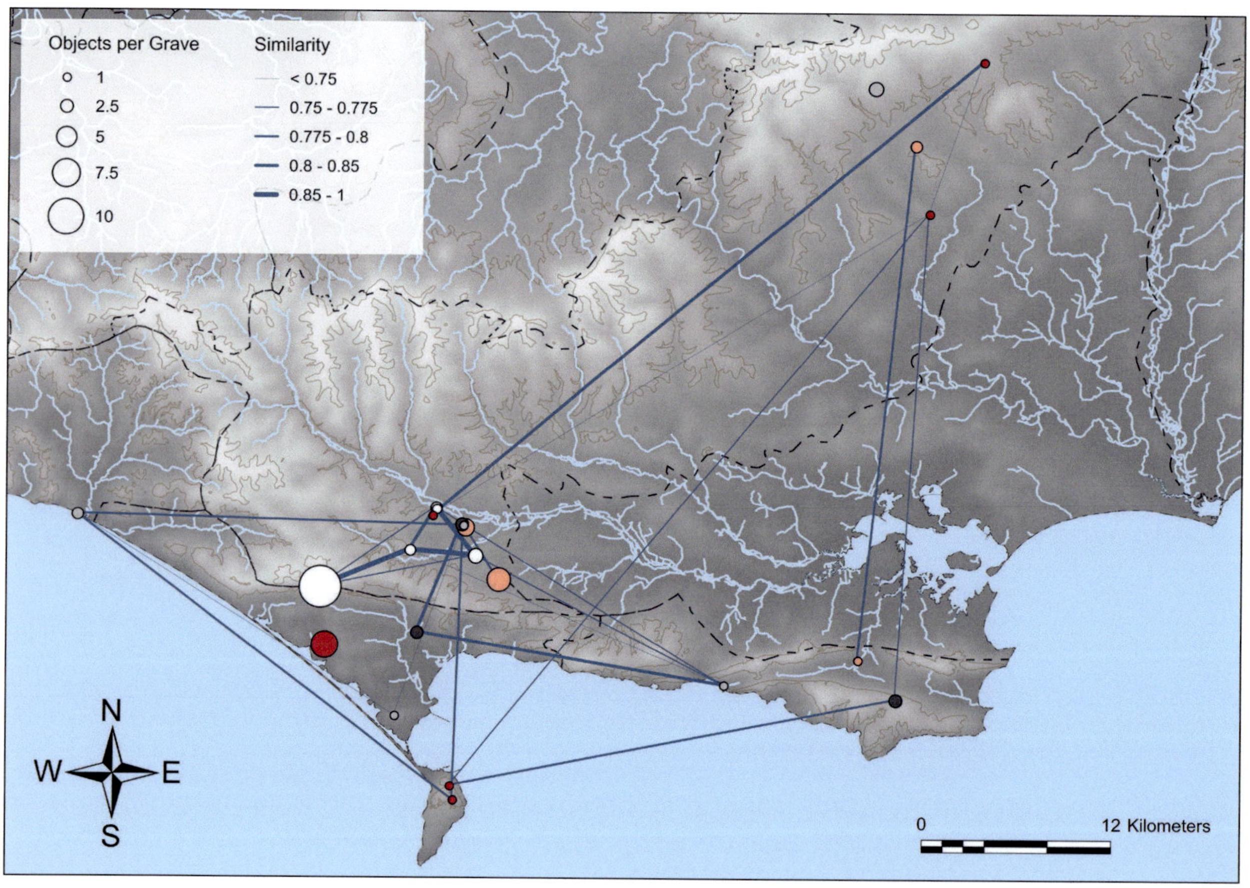
Objects per Grave
1
2.5
5
7.5
10
Similarity
< 0.75
0.75 - 0.775
0.775 - 0.8
0.8 - 0.85
0.85 - 1
N
W
E
S
0
12 Kilometers

gathered across many time periods and regions. Yet, for EBA, MBA, and LIA Dorset, only individuals from six sites were sampled and could be attributed to the category *local* or *mover*. This sample size is not considered sufficient to make a reasonable statement on potential correlations with network clusters. Nevertheless, even though EBA burials, which make up four of the six samples and consisting of three locals and one mover are evenly distributed across both clusters rather not suggesting any correlation, the ever-increasing availability of isotope data might be a promising trajectory to further explore similar patterns in the future.

14.3.5 Chronology

For a set of objects, the Grave Goods project database provides more precise information of the durations of their use. On the supposition that these durations roughly represent the date of their occurrence in burials, these objects were used to refine the period classification of the graves. The refinement of the chronology was solely undertaken for the EBA period, as only for this period the available quantity of information was considered abundant enough. I classified the objects according to whether their duration of occurrence indicated with a greater likelihood that they were used in the early (2200-1900 BCE) or late (1900-1500 BCE) EBA period. By this means, I could differentiate 42 burials in total, consisting of ten early and 32 late EBA graves.

However, the interpretation of a possible correlation of the refined chronological classification with the EBA network clusters does not appear straightforward at all (Figures 14.15 and 14.16); superficially, the cluster derived from the network with several aspects of the burial ritual seems to suggest a balanced distribution of early and late EBA burials in the black cluster, while the red cluster appears clearly dominated by the late EBA burials (Table 14.4). However, considering that there are three times more burials, which are classified as late EBA, the red cluster appears less significant, while a bias of the black cluster towards early EBA burials seems possible. A similar pattern becomes also apparent for the clusters of the object-based network; the black cluster seems even more clearly biased towards late EBA burials, while a dominance of the early EBA burials in the red cluster can only be theorised, by taking the unbalanced nature of the dataset into consideration (Table 14.4).

An ANOVA defining affiliation with early EBA as 0 and late EBA as 1 revealed that both, the correlation between the first cluster and the classification into early ($M = 0.5$, $SD = 0.52$) and late ($M = 0.009$, $SD = 0.3$) EBA ($F(1, 40) = 9.638$, $p = 0.003$) as well as the correlation between the object cluster and the classification into early ($M = 0.4$, $SD = 0.52$) and late ($M = 0.81$, $SD = 0.4$) EBA ($F(1, 40) = 7.128$, $p = 0.011$) are statistically significant. This correlation is very intriguing, but – especially for the object-derived network – not surprising at all; for relative chronologies or seriation methods, changes in object types are often interpreted as manifestation of time lapse (cf. Ekengren 2013). If this correlation gets confirmed and refined further, for example through the inclusion of radiocarbon dates, this will open new possibilities, as both spatial and temporal development can be effectively analysed and represented in absolute space.

14.5 Conclusion

Material networks are powerful heuristic and analytical tools to understand and visualise relationships between archaeological phenomena. Especially the applied SNF technique proved an effective method for the incorporation of various similarity networks derived from different datatypes into one single network. Moreover, due to its robusticity against small and noisy datasets, this technique also appears to have great potential for other applications and fields in archaeology coping with similar datasets, such as archaeobotany or archaeozoology, and seems to

	Early	Late
Total	10	32
Red	5	28
Black	5	4

Table 14.4. Association between Dataset 1 of the EBA burials and the sub-period classification.

	Early	Late
Total	10	32
Red	6	6
Black	4	26

Table 14.5. Association between Dataset 2 of the EBA burials and the sub-period classification.

(Opposite page, top) Figure 14.13. Similarity network derived from the second datatypes of Middle Bronze Age sites in Dorset, depicting the 25 strongest network connections, topological clusters (black, red), and average grave goods per grave per site. Background © Environment Agency. Natural character areas © Natural England.

(Opposite page, bottom) Figure 14.14. Similarity network derived from the second datatypes of Late Iron Age sites in Dorset, depicting the 25 strongest network connections, topological clusters (black, red, white, grey, orange), and average grave goods per grave per site.

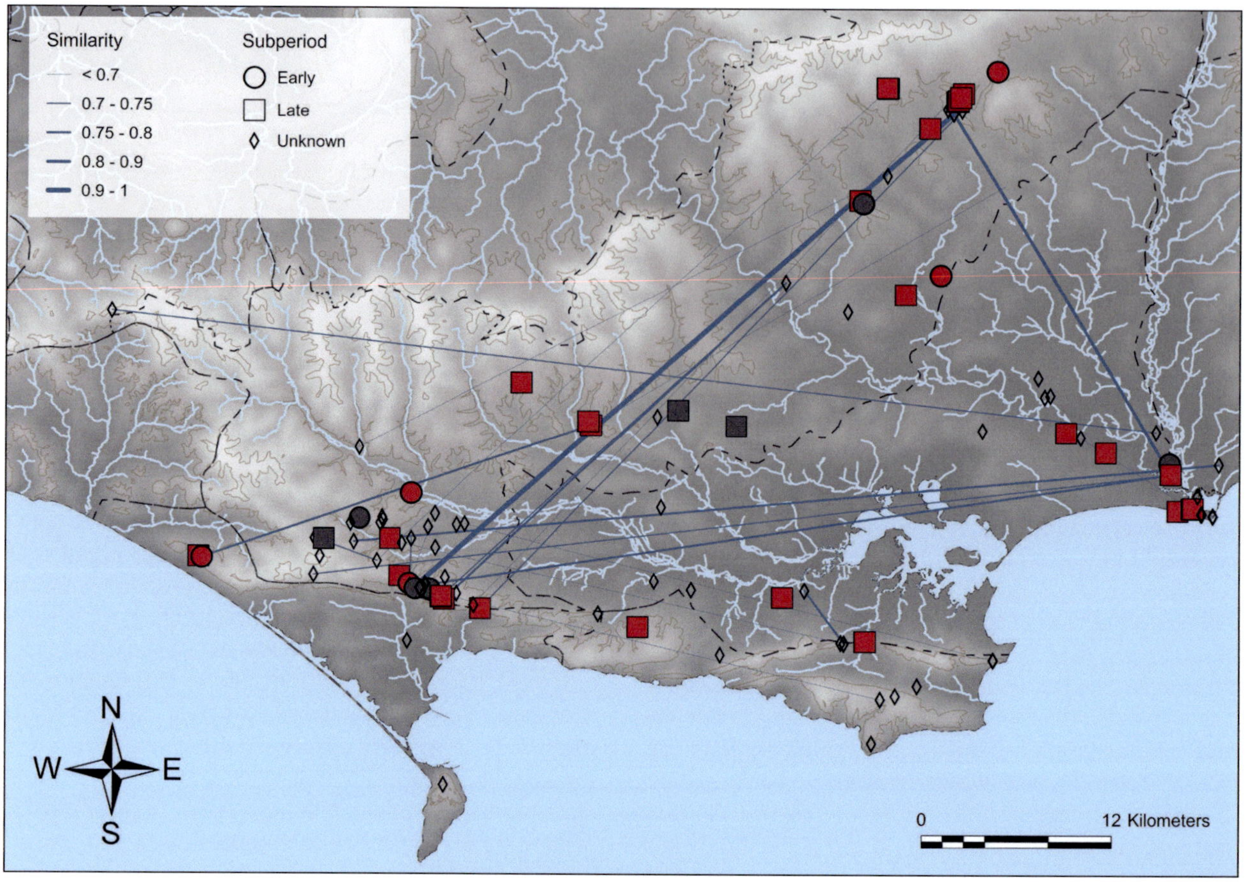
Similarity
< 0.7
0.7 - 0.75
0.75 - 0.8
0.8 - 0.9
0.9 - 1
Subperiod
Early
Late
Unknown
N
W
E
S
0
12 Kilometers

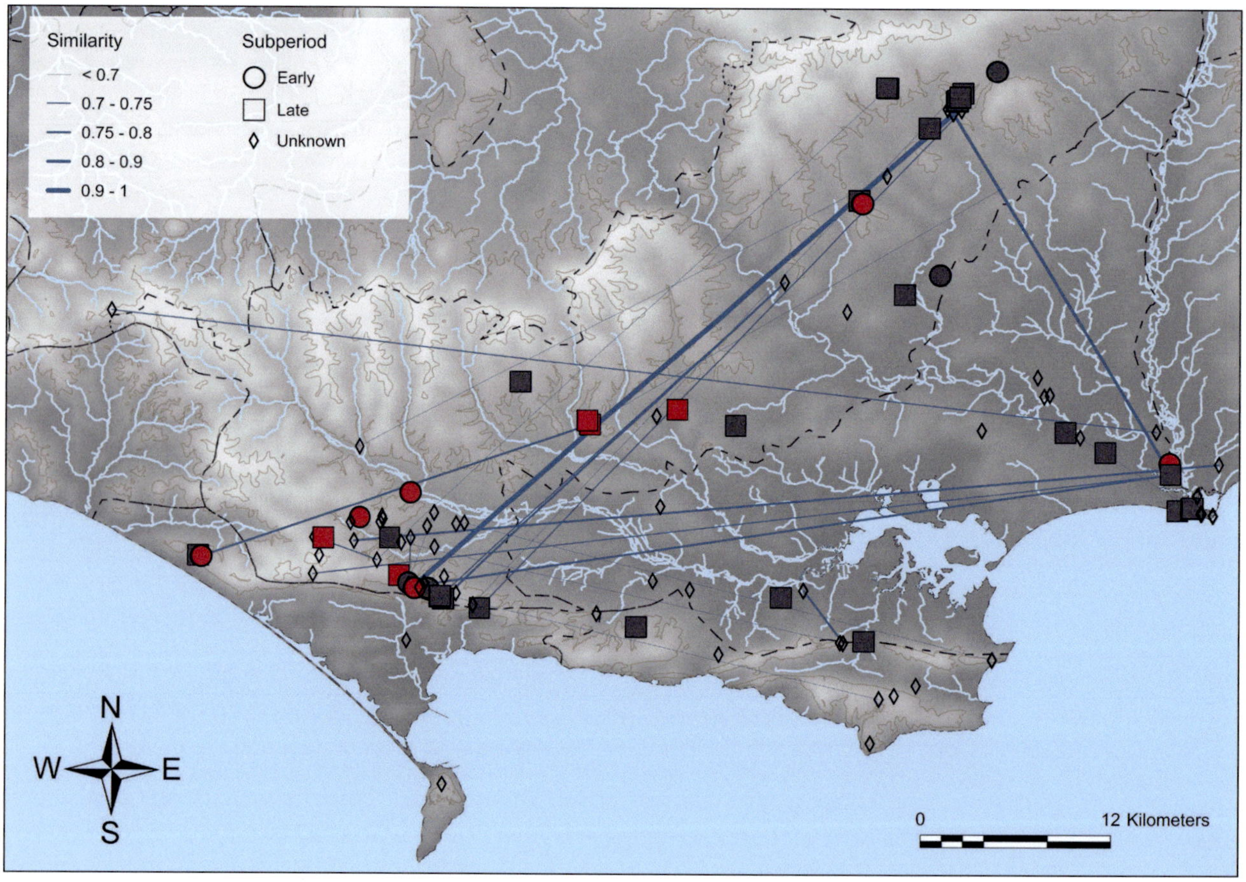
Similarity
< 0.7
0.7 - 0.75
0.75 - 0.8
0.8 - 0.9
0.9 - 1
Subperiod
Early
Late
Unknown
N
W
E
S
0
12 Kilometers

complement other multivariate statistical approaches such as correspondence or cluster analysis.

Many of the typical methodological and interpretive constraints and challenges of network analysis in archaeology also manifest themselves in the discussed case study on late prehistoric burials in Dorset; the area of research could only be inadequately bounded and mainly followed modern borders and the broader data availability. Though for the investigated periods there is a relatively high density of sites across the area of research, the incompleteness and biases of the dataset and their influence on the results of the analysis is unknown. Finally, as past interactions can only be approximated through material culture, the exact meaning of the specific similarity network is difficult to assess and can only indirectly be approached through correlations of different data attributes.

Nevertheless, the network analysis and the topological clustering of the sites revealed at least two possible spatial clusters within the EBA and LIA networks and two statistically significant correlations between clusters and further attributes of the burial sites. The aim of the case study was to shed light on the past landscape and its structuration. Indeed, it seems likely that the distinctions manifesting in the two spatially significant clusters are expressions of diverging cultural behaviour. On the assumption that these differences were conceivable and recognisable in the past, they were contributing to the constitution of the past landscape. The other two statistically significant correlations might have no spatial significance, but as has been argued above they potentially form part of a past social or cultural reality which yet has to be further investigated.

The exploration of the meaning of the topological clusters does not seem to be exhausted by the discussed five attributes; the inclusion of further landscape derived characteristics such as potential trajectories of movement or visibility measures (cf. Woodward 2000) seems to be particularly promising to understand the spatial location of the topological clusters. Finally, the case study also points to the potential of approaching and re-evaluating freely accessible archaeological data gathered by past research projects with new questions and methods.

Acknowledgments

Many thanks to Dr. John Pouncett, under whose supervision this project was realised and who enriched my paper with valuable advice and criticism. Special thanks also to the Swiss Study Foundation for supporting me and my education financially as well as my parents for patiently proofreading many of my pieces of writing.

Funding

This project was financially supported by the Annual Scholarship of the Swiss Study Foundation.

Data, Scripts, Code, and Supplementary Information Availability

All data and codes to reproduce the results of the SNF and statistical analyses are found on an online repository (Geitlinger 2024): DOI:10.5281/zenodo.10890531. To enhance the reusability, instructions on implementing the code and further information about the data are deposited as README file and as Markdown section included in the python code.

Peer review

This article has been reviewed and recommended by PCI Archaeology.

Santos, Joel. 2024. "A different approach to similarity networks in Archaeology – Similarity Network Fusion." *Peer Community in Archaeology* 100347. DOI:10.24072/pci.archaeo.100347.

(Opposite page, top) Figure 14.15. Similarity network derived from the first datatypes of Early Bronze Age sites in Dorset, depicting the 25 strongest network connections, topological clusters (black, red), and sub-period classification. Background © Environment Agency. Natural character areas © Natural England.

(Opposite page, bottom) Figure 14.16. Similarity network derived from the second datatypes of Early Bronze Age sites in Dorset, depicting the 25 strongest network connections, topological clusters (black, red), and sub-period classification. Background © Environment Agency. Natural character areas © Natural England.

References

Blake, Emma. 2013. "Social Networks, Path Dependence, and the Rise of Ethnic Groups in Pre-Roman Italy." In *Network Analysis in Archaeology: New Approaches to Regional Interaction*, edited by Carl Knappett, 203–11. Oxford: Oxford University Press. DOI: 10.1093/acprof:oso/9780199697090.003.0009.

Bourgeois, Quentin, and Erik Kroon. 2017. "The Impact of Male Burials on the Construction of Corded Ware Identity: Reconstructing Networks of Information in the 3rd Millennium BC." *PLOS ONE* 12 (10): e0185971. DOI: 10.1371/journal.pone.0185971.

Bradley, Richard. 2019. *The Prehistory of Britain and Ireland, 2nd Ed.* Cambridge: Cambridge University Press. DOI: 10.1017/9781108419925.

Brughmans, Tom, Anna Collar, and Fiona Coward. 2016. "Network Perspectives on the Past: Tackling the Challenges." In *The Connected Past: Challenges to Network Studies in Archaeology and History*, edited by Tom Brughmans, Anna Collar and Fiona Coward, 3–20. Oxford: Oxford University Press.

Brughmans, Tom, and Matthew A. Peeples. 2020. "Spatial Networks." In *Archaeological spatial analysis: a methodological guide*, edited by Mark Gillings, Piraye Hacıgüzeller, and Gary Lock, 273–95. London: Routledge. DOI: 10.4324/9781351243858.

Brughmans, Tom, Barbara J. Mills, Jessica Munson, and Matthew A. Peeples (eds). 2023. *The Oxford Handbook of Archaeological Network Research*. Oxford: Oxford University Press. DOI: 10.1093/oxfordhb/9780198854265.001.0001.

Collar, Anna, Fiona Coward, Tom Brughmans, and Barbara J. Mills. 2015. "Networks in Archaeology: Phenomena, Abstraction, Representation." *Journal of Archaeological Method and Theory* 22 (1): 1–32. DOI: 10.1007/s10816-014-9235-6.

Cooper, Anwen, Duncan Garrow, Catriona Gibson, Melanie Giles, and Neil Wilkin. 2020. "Grave goods: objects and death in later prehistoric Britain." https://archaeologydataservice.ac.uk/archives/view/grave_ahrc_2020/index.cfm, DOI: 10.5284/1052206.

Cooper, Anwen, Duncan Garrow, Catriona Gibson, Melanie Giles, and Neil Wilkin. 2022. *Grave goods: objects and death in later prehistoric Britain*. Oxford: Oxbow Books. DOI: 10.5284/1052206.

Cullingford, Cecil N. 1999. *A History of Dorset, 3rd Ed.* Chichester: Phillimore & Co. Ltd.

Donnellan, Lieve. 2020. "Archaeological networks and social interaction." In *Archaeological networks and social interaction*, edited by Lieve Donnellan, 1–19. London: Routledge.

Ekengren, Fredrik. 2013. "Contextualizing Grave Goods: Theoretical Perspectives and Methodological Implications." In *The Oxford Handbook of the Archaeology of Death and Burial*, edited by Liv Nilsson Stutz and Sarah Tarlow, 172–92. Oxford: Oxford University Press. DOI: 10.1093/oxfordhb/9780199569069.013.0010.

ESRI. 2022a. "Standardize Field (Data Management)." https://pro.arcgis.com/en/pro-app/2.8/tool-reference/data-management/standardizefield.htm.

ESRI. 2022b. "Generate Origin Destination Cost Matrix (Ready To Use)." https://pro.arcgis.com/en/pro-app/2.8/tool-reference/ready-to-use/itemdesc-generateoriginde stinationcostmatrix.htm#:~:text=An%20OD%20cost%20matrix%20is,that%20origin%20to%20each%20destination.

Feugnet, Aurélia, Fabrice Rossi, and Clara Filet. 2017. "Co-Presence Analysis and Economic Patterns: Mediterranean Imports in the Celtic World." *Frontiers in Digital Humanities* 4. https://www.frontiersin.org/articles/10.3389/fdigh.2017.00001.

Garwood, Paul. 2007. "Before the Hills in Order Stood: Chronology, Time and History in the Interpretation of Early Bronze Age Round Barrows." In *Beyond the Grave. New Perspectives on Barrows*, edited by Jonathan Last, 30–52. Oxford: Oxford University Press.

Geitlinger, Timo. 2024. "Similarity Network Fusion: Understanding Patterns and their Spatial Significance in Archaeological Datasets." Zenodo. DOI: 10.5281/zenodo.10890531.

Golitko, Mark, James Meierhoff, Gary M. Feinman, and Patrick Ryan Williams. 2012. "Complexities of Collapse: The Evidence of Maya Obsidian as Revealed by Social Network Graphical Analysis." *Antiquity* 86 (332): 507–23. DOI: 10.1017/S0003598X00062906.

Gosden, Chris, Chris Green, Anwen Cooper, Miranda Creswell, Victoria Donnelly, Tyler Franconi, Roger Glyde, Zena Kamash, Sarah Mallet, Laura Morley, Daniel Stansbie, and Letty ten Harkel 2021. *English Landscapes and Identities: Investigating Landscape Change from 1500 BC to AD 1086*. Oxford: Oxford University Press. DOI: 10.1093/oso/9780198870623.001.0001.

Groot, B. G. de. 2019. "A Diachronic Study of Networks of Ceramic Assemblage Similarity in Neolithic Western Anatolia, the Aegean and the Balkans (c.6600–5500 Bc)." *Archaeometry* 61 (3): 600–613. DOI: 10.1111/arcm.12450.

Habiba, Jan C. Athenstädt, Barbara J. Mills, and Ulrik Brandes. 2018. "Social Networks and Similarity of Site Assemblages." *Journal of Archaeological Science* 92: 63–72. DOI: 10.1016/j.jas.2017.11.002.

Knappett, Carl. 2011. *An Archaeology of Interaction: Network Perspectives on Material Culture and Society*.

Oxford: Oxford University Press. DOI: 10.1093/acprof:osobl/9780199215454.001.0001.

Knappett, Carl. 2016. "Networks in Archaeology: Between Scientific Method and Humanistic Metaphor." In *The Connected Past: Challenges to Network Studies in Archaeology and History*, edited by Tom Brughmans, Anna Collar, and Fiona Coward, 21–34. Oxford: Oxford University Press.

Knappett, Carl. 2013. "Introduction: Why Networks?" In *Network Analysis in Archaeology: New Approaches to Regional Interaction*, edited by Carl Knappett, 2–15. Oxford: Oxford University Press. DOI: 10.1093/acprof:oso/9780199697090.003.0001.

Markello, Ross. 2018. "snfpy: Similarity Network Fusion in Python." https://snfpy.readthedocs.io/en/latest.

Mills, Barbara J., Jeffery J. Clark, Matthew A. Peeples, W. R. Haas, John M. Roberts, J. Brett Hill, Deborah L. Huntley, Lewis Borck, Ronald L. Breiger, Aaron Clauset, and M. Steven Shackle. 2013. "Transformation of Social Networks in the Late Pre-Hispanic US Southwest." *Proceedings of the National Academy of Sciences* 110 (15): 5785–90. DOI: 10.1073/pnas.1219966110.

Mizoguchi, Koji. 2009. "Nodes and Edges: A Network Approach to Hierarchisation and State Formation in Japan." *Journal of Anthropological Archaeology* 28 (1): 14–26. DOI: 10.1016/j.jaa.2008.12.001.

Morgan, Catherine, and Todd Whitelaw. 1991. "Pots and Politics: Ceramic Evidence for the Rise of the Argive State." *American Journal of Archaeology* 95, 79–108. DOI: 10.2307/505158.

Natural England. 2022. "Natural England – National Character Area Profiles." https://nationalcharacterareas.co.uk.

Östborn, Per, and Henrik Gerding. 2015. "The Diffusion of Fired Bricks in Hellenistic Europe: A Similarity Network Analysis." *Journal of Archaeological Method and Theory* 22 (1): 306–44. DOI: 10.1007/s10816-014-9229-4.

Parker Pearson, Mike, Alison Sheridan, Mandy Jay, Andrew Chamberlain, Mike Richards, and Jane Evans (eds). 2019. *The Beaker people: isotopes, mobility and diet in prehistoric Britain*. Oxford: Oxbow Books.

Peeples, Matthew A., Barbara J. Mills, W. Randall Haas Jr, Jeffery J. Clark, and John M. Roberts Jr. 2016. "Analytical Challenges for the Application of Social Network Analysis in Archaeology." In *The Connected Past: Challenges to Network Studies in Archaeology and History*, edited by Tom Brughmans, Anna Collar, and Fiona Coward, 59–84. Oxford: Oxford University Press.

Prignano, Luce, Ignacio Morer, and Albert Diaz-Guilera. 2017. "Wiring the Past: A Network Science Perspective on the Challenge of Archeological Similarity Networks." *Frontiers in Digital Humanities* 4. DOI: 10.3389/fdigh.2017.00013.

RMARKELLO. 2022. "SNFPY." https://github.com/rmarkello/snfpy.

Sindbæk, Søren M. 2007. "Networks and Nodal Points: The Emergence of Towns in Early Viking Age Scandinavia." *Antiquity* 81 (311): 119–32. DOI: 10.1017/S0003598X00094886.

Wang, Bo, Aziz M Mezlini, Feyyaz Demir, Marc Fiume, Zhuowen Tu, Michael Brudno, Benjamin Haibe-Kains, and Anna Goldenberg. 2014. "Similarity Network Fusion for Aggregating Data Types on a Genomic Scale." *Nature Methods* 11 (3): 333–7. DOI: 10.1038/nmeth.2810.

Woodward, Ann. 2000. *British Barrows: A Matter of Life and Death*. Stroud: Tempus.

15 The transformation of an archaeological community and its resulting representations in the context of the co-development of open Archaeological Information Systems

Eric Lacombe
Nîmes University
eric.lacombe@unimes.fr

Dominik Lukas
University of Chicago
dlukas@uchicago.edu

Sébastien Durost
Bibracte EPCC
sebastien.durost@bibracte.fr
Glux-en-Glenne

Abstract

The adoption of Archaeological Information Systems (AIS) evolves according to multiple factors, both human and technical, as well as endogenous and exogenous. In consequence the ever-increasing scope of digital tools, which allow for the organisation of information in order to understand the transformations of an archaeological site, transforms the organisations that generate or manage these data. The transformations induced by digital methods are carriers of an antagonism between continuity and discontinuity, which leads to constant reorganisation. At the same time online collaboration and design (centred on and with the user) allow for open access to data, to code and to make the design process accessible to the greatest number. In this spirit, archaeology seeks interoperability and reusability (e.g., FAIR principles, LOUD data), which in return, leads to the emergence of new organisations of information, as for example, the definition of criteria for interoperability, data models dedicated to data exchange (e.g., CIDOC CRM), dissemination platforms, the scripting of treatments in order to make these reproducible, or the sharing of terminologies. Hereby interoperability takes on a dual sense: An "internal interoperability", encompassing the current process of retrieving data as it is stored in the primary recording system of the excavation and their transformation for their traditional publication or storage in digital repositories, and an "external interoperability", encompassing the effort of linking these "final" data with already existing data in order to facilitate exploitation by any kind of future research. In this contribution we present an approach to study the emergence of the relationship between the organisation of information and the transformation of the organisation. The study is conducted in view of the SIAMOIS project ("Mutualized

In *Advances in Digital Archaeology. Proceedings of the 2023 conference Computer Applications and Quantitative Methods in Archaeology – 50 years of synergy*, edited by J.W.H.P. Verhagen, J. Waagen, A. Brandsen, A. Queffelec, R.M. Visser and D. Taelman, 197–210. Leiden: Sidestone Press.

and Open Archaeological Information System based on Semantic Intelligence") which has the objective to master these relationships in a collaborative context.

In order to analyse these transformations, we propose a conceptualised analysis model, formalised in the T!O (Transformation, Information, Organisation) framework. This framework takes seriously the principle of "Tertium non datur" in classical logic by using a relational approach. In this way the differences expressed within the conventional binary logic are not understood as conflicting opposites, but as a source for a dynamic equilibrium where the actualisation of one state is simultaneous with the potentialisation of the other. Thereby a formalised representation of the organisation of an archaeological community is produced and the processes constituting the generation of knowledge are brought into view and can become the object of particular attention.

As a use case, the paper analyses the production of archaeological knowledge by modelling excavation processes and the establishment of discourse based on typologies which are employed in publications, in order to show how the T!O framework allows for reflecting on institutional processes at the same time as it indicates the necessary parameters to organise and record archaeological data. Modelling these processes brings "silences" in the archaeological data to the fore, which are either generally left unconsidered as implicit knowledge, or at least problematised when the attempt is made to transform the same knowledge by way of ontologies. Our approach shows that only magnifying the individual processes of knowledge production in a research project ultimately allows for those "shared conceptualisations" that are sought when aligning AIS and ontologies under the objective of publishing archaeological data.

Keywords: Archaeological Information System; Interoperability; Knowledge Production; Organisational Modelling; Ontology; Thesaurus

15.1 Introduction

Archaeology collects, identifies, describes and quantifies in order to understand and explain ancient material realities and connections among them – in other words, Archaeology writes a rational history of human societies based on the traces they leave behind. Archaeological research programs are held to report all of these stages when publishing the results of this process. The completeness of the transmitted information to the scientific community is essential as it supports the argumentation within the scientific discourse by accounting for the hypotheses formulated based on the observed remains and further knowledge used, to generate a conclusive interpretation. Actualisations of the discourse are part of a continuous process, which requires recurrent publication.

Present approaches to publishing archaeological knowledge leave considerable parts of this process untraceable. In the present paper we identify three primary processes with an increased need for transparency. On the one hand we need to deal with an "internal interoperability", encompassing the current process of retrieving data as it is stored in the primary recording system of the excavation and their transformation with a view to their traditional publication or storage in digital repositories. On the other hand, "external interoperabilities", encompass the effort of linking these "final" data with already existing data in order to facilitate exploitation by any kind of future research, including interests in other regions, pertaining to other periods, conducted by archaeologists using other methodologies or even interdisciplinary research. While these processes are already managed in databases at present, albeit not necessarily distinguished there, a third aspect is consistently missing from archaeological recording systems: the contextual information containing the who-does-what, why and how of research.

As we will show, the two interoperabilities are thoroughly entwined, as decisions made during the conceptualisation of a recording system require ontological decisions right from the onset and on the same level as the well-known reflections to further external interoperability of data by using ontologies. The similarity between the initial and the ultimate stage of ontological reflection can be seen as one of the main reasons why these two processes are not distinguished in recording systems. Ultimately it is this third aspect, the in-depth investigation of the specific archaeological processes within individual projects, which will allow for resolving issues of interoperability.

15.2 Retrotheorisation and Shared Conceptualisation

In order to understand the intricate relationship of internal and external interoperability, a brief look into the history of archaeological information systems is revealing. Even before the invention of the personal computer, excavation data had been integrated in mainframe computers by way of databases which were mostly developed either by computer scientists with an affinity to archaeology, or – and that was surprisingly often the case – archaeologists themselves invested their time in programming. In consequence, the first knowledge systems were brought to use in the 1970s and while these systems were initially dedicated to singular excavation projects, later systems like Plutarch ("Program Library Useful To ARCHaeologists" – see Wilcock 1974) or Syslat (Roure et al. 2021) were conceived for implementation on multiple sites.

The logical architecture of these systems engaged the technology available at the time and were mostly implemented as hierarchical and then increasingly as relational databases. Following the advancement of Artificial Intelligence (AI) during the 1970s, archaeologists also began developing expert systems, which required the modelling of conceptual schema reflecting the field of research in question. While these applications did not yet use ontology as a label, expert systems slowly gave way to the idea of computational ontologies and if in theory not properly formalised, the archaeological knowledge systems in use did very much follow Thomas Gruber's oft-cited definition of ontologies as "formal, explicit specification of a shared conceptualization" (Gruber 1995). Although probably reflecting the most common understanding of ontologies, this definition is not the only notion of ontology. As another example, Grenon et al. (2004) define an ontology as grasping "the entities which exist within a given portion of the world at a given level of generality". They point to the metaphysical problem of ontologies – the question of the relationship between data and the world from which the data is extracted. While Gruber focuses on "collective conceptualization" and the idea that the user group accepts data as adequate (and that each user discusses the relationship between data and reality for themselves), Grenon et al. use a definition of ontology in the classical philosophical sense. As Khazraee and Lin (2011) point out, the term "ontology" finds nearly anarchic use today and if before the onset of computer ontologies, the term ontology was primarily understood based on its metaphysical connotation, now and especially with the work of Philippe Descola (2013) and Eduardo Viveiros de Castro (2015) ontologies are limited to relativism. This development is parallel with the loss of objectivity in the aftermath of the linguistic turn (Rorty 1991), and subsequent investigations into the modalities of research practices (e.g., Knorr-Cetina 1981; 1999; Latour 1999; Latour and Woolgar 2013; Daston and Galison 2010). Where archaeological theory in the same vein until the 1980s attempted to unify research by implementing models of explanation (for a detailed summary see Salmon 1982 and Salmon 1992) research today seems more driven by the continuous recalibration of theoretical conceptions to determine the validity of a statement.

Independent of the metaphysical status of either approach to ontology, for the present discussion the definition of ontologies as "shared conceptualizations" shall suffice. With this definition ontologies (and other conceptualised knowledge systems) can at least be understood as reflections or even materialisations of epistemic cultures (Knorr-Cetina 1999) and as such the interactions of researchers within these cultures can be shown as being in tension with either advancing their research or being constrained by the inherent structures of the systems. On a temporal trajectory, knowledge systems evolve and their positionality changes over time as they are continuously realigned. Just as Neurath's ship (Quine 1960) shows, knowledge is in a constant state of transformation (e.g., CIDOC-CRM is at version 7 now): Neurath describes a vessel which cannot be docked in a harbour and therefore repairs as well as remodelling must be executed while at sea. Similar to the "ship of Theseus," Neurath's ship is a metaphor for the constant endeavour of producing knowledge whilst never being able to start from scratch. In consequence knowledge is always fluid and can only be grasped as perspectival reflections. Without recourse to metaphysics, ontologies are then merely determined by their social context – a group committing to the defining criteria and the interdependencies of the classes and properties constituting them. In order to determine which ontology is most suitable for a given situation or social context, it is necessary to clarify the decision-making processes for each entity structuring the data. Either a group comes to an informed decision to employ a pre-existing ontology, or by establishing their own structure and defining the groups' ideas of how knowledge should be formed in their domain. Unfortunately, these considerations are more often than not taken by a very restricted group of a research team (the project director, a database/software developer, sometimes even including field directors and directors of specialist laboratories) and leave the majority of participants to the project outside of that development process. Only in rare cases (e.g., excavations conducted following a reflexive approach[1]) data highlighting the details of the excavation process are recorded. These missing types of data include names of archaeologists beyond those listed as authors of research reports, their specialties, the tools used, the methods implemented, the configuration parameters of the digital recorders – or even more generally the conditions which make the excavation possible, such as its financing, or further circumstantial data. Failing to record these data, makes it difficult to retrace this information when inquiring into the original datasets or attempting to use automatic inferencing on a repository, where an AIS potentially ends up for long-term storage. While some projects take the participants to a project more seriously, collaboration at the moment of initial development of the informational structure is certainly a rare feat.

Considering our initial distinction of internal and external interoperability, the historical sketch of AIS development allows for understanding the similarities between the development of a new recording system and the procedures leading to an appropriate mapping of an existing data structure. In fact, the CIDOC-CRM (Bekiari et al.

1 A most recent example discussing the relationship of reflexivity and excavation data can be found in Taylor et al. (2018). In a similar vein, projects appreciating "paradata" recognize the intricate details of the excavation process as they take serious what Huggett (2020) called the "silences of knowledge in digital archaeology".

2021) has not only been used as a reference model for final publications of closed databases, but also as a catalogue of guidelines to define the inherent logic for new research projects – e.g., AIR (Derudas et al. 2023), Himat (Hiebel et al. 2014), Arches (Carlisle et al. 2014) or ResearchSpace (Oldman and Tanase 2018). Quite unsurprisingly, the above-mentioned deliberations during the development of an AIS and the mapping of data onto an existing ontology concern the definition of appropriate containers for archaeological information as they are conceived by the group constituting a research project. The main difference then is merely the temporal perspective, stressing futurity when arguing that an ontology in question is acceptable as underlying structure of an AIS or underscoring historicity when research data are published, and the structures of an ontology and a domain conceptualisation are being negotiated. Either an AIS is developed in regard to its theoretical implications, or the potential interoperability of a system with a certain ontology (after having used a recording system for a while), is done by retrotheorisation. This again is most often achieved without the developers of the initial conceptualisation and especially without the people involved during the actual excavations. The process of transforming data towards interoperability is therefore isolated (truncated) from the process of conceptualisation and generation of data at all stages of transformation. Theseus' ship would surely present a dire picture if it was treated like that.

15.3 Modelling the organisation of knowledge: stratigraphic unit vs. excavation unit

In order to clarify how differences in defining certain classes of data have effects on the interpretation of the resulting datasets as a whole, it is beneficial to focus on one of archaeology's central concepts: the stratigraphic unit. Here archaeological research broadly follows E. Harris' (1979) approach to capture bodies of sediments – the "stratigraphic units" – as they are encountered during the process of excavation, and how perceivable differences between those bodies can be documented. According to Harris a stratigraphic unit is determined by the identification of its interface and the identification of its chronologically significant limits. Stratigraphic units are characterised by their role in the processes of erosion, sedimentation, weathering and soil formation, as well as by their importance for historical and cultural interpretation. They are used for the contextual study of material remains and as an anchor to relate archaeological material with an absolute measure of time. Harris emphasizes the importance of interfaces for inferring chronological relationships between stratigraphic units, defined as the smallest perceptible units of soil anterior and posterior to neighbouring units. This approach implicitly considers stratigraphic units to be archaeologically isotropic, which implies a uniform cultural and chronological interpretation at every point in their volume, despite their heterogeneous physical composition. Harris implicitly excludes the possibility of archaeologically significant "continuous" variations that would not be materialised by a contact surface.

Whatever the categories of interpretation used and the level of detail of that interpretation, interpreting the stratigraphic units in historical and cultural terms is an essential condition for developing a synthetic discourse on the evolution of the site, going beyond simple chronology. We agree with Bruno Desachy (2008) that the question of the cultural and historical significance of the stratigraphic unit must also be asked of the stratigraphic relationship between two units. In fact, a relationship is not simply a type of physical contact (superposition, overlap, etc.) reflecting the process of formation of the terrain, nor is it limited to an element of strict relative chronology (before/after), but also bears witness to a transition from one historical state of the site to another and to the inadequacy of stratigraphic chronology alone to give an account of what can be called the "cultural lifespan" of stratigraphic units (Carver 1990; Paice 1991).

Although stratigraphy provides a chronological order, the temporal durations represented by the stratigraphic units and their relationships are generally not preserved by stratification, resulting in a loss of temporal information. To estimate this lost chronology, it is necessary to use timing indicators, such as historical data, physicochemical analyses or studying the archaeological material. These indicators must be formalised in the same way as the stratigraphic record if they are to be applied correctly to date stratigraphic units, otherwise erroneous conclusions will be drawn. Despite its importance, the way in which relative stratigraphic chronology is incorporated into absolute chronology remains unclear.

Confronted with this ambiguity, in the following sections we will examine an exemplary approach of modelling the archaeological process in general and stratigraphic information in particular. We will focus on the Archaeological Information Systems (AIS) in use at the site of Bibracte in France. Located on Mount Beuvray (821 m) in the heart of Burgundy (20 km to the west of Autun), Bibracte is considered as the ancient capital of the *Aedui* people of the first century BC. According to historical sources (e.g., *De Bello Gallico*) Vercingetorix received the command of the Gallic coalition there in the summer of 52 BC, and Julius Caesar might even have completed writing his *De Bello Gallico* here. It is a major archaeological site discovered by Jacques-Gabriel Bulliot in the nineteenth century and it allowed Joseph Déchelette to characterise the oppida as paradigmatic fortified places, typical of the European late Iron Age (Lukas 2014). With the founding of the Centre Archéologique Européen du Mont Beuvray in 1984, Bibracte has become synonymous with the international research program and the Musée de la Civilisation Celtique inaugurated there in 1996.

Bibracte's approach to research data and scientific publications has focused on a documentation management system (bdB) launched in 1996-1997.[2] Initially, the dissemination of results was based on traditional research reports and exhaustive publications for completed excavation sectors, which often led to delays in data sharing. To meet the growing demand for immediate access to data, a review of the dissemination process was undertaken from 2012 onwards (Desachy et al. 2012). The aim of this development was to streamline the dissemination process, which led to the creation of "Bibracte Numérique", a multi-year programme (2018-2021) to promote an integrated approach and collaboration with other archaeological entities.[3] Since 2017, efforts have been made to systematise dissemination methods, facilitating the ongoing production of archaeological information.

Since the time of bdB's original implementation, digital advances have considerably transformed the field of archaeology, impacting not only the technical aspects, but also the very nature of the data used in research. With the emergence of new archaeological methods, such as the growing use of geo-referenced data, documentation management systems must constantly evolve to effectively integrate these new elements. bdB features a unique tree-like architecture, designed to capture a multitude of material realities, from excavation sites to samples taken, in line with the archaeological data collection process.

As is the case for many AIS, the above-mentioned ambiguities to relate stratigraphic information and absolute chronology, are also apparent in bdB. While stratigraphic relationships which are observed during excavation can be formalised as diagrams, the stages of quantification and the reasoning involved in characterising the "cultural life" of stratigraphic units remain practically undocumented here. Yet in contrast to the traditional "stratigraphic unit" as conceptualised by Harris, in bdB archaeological contexts are classified as "excavation unit" or "*unité de fouille*" – an attempt to increase the level of processual detail stored with the mere stratigraphical information. This concept, which forms the basis for recording in bdB, allows units to be defined, either as stratigraphic units by recording stratigraphic relationships, or as grouping units based on criteria other than the interfaces identified in the field. This is very useful, for example, for grouping together the same type of material as part of a typological study, or for recording old documentation, such as the data produced by 19th century excavations. While amplifying possible approaches to determine stratigraphically relevant data, also in the case of the "excavation unit" the individual rationales that justify these groupings are only insufficiently explicated and remain circumstantial to the normalised data. In order to incorporate this information with the traditional data regime, the actual processes of encountering, identifying, documenting and interpreting archaeological contexts need to be analysed and formalised. In that respect progress is being made at Bibracte with the SIAMOIS 2024-2026 project, which aims to develop an open-source Archaeological Information System (AIS) using web technologies and digital humanities practices. Hereby the analysis of the archaeological process is conducted based on a modelling approach developed by the first author in his doctoral thesis in information and communication sciences (Lacombe 2021). While the original model was intended for the analysis of the digital transformation of networked organisations, and more specifically the potential of dynamic information schematisation, here the model enables a more detailed view on the different factors involved in the production of archaeological data.

15.4 T!O

Following Lacombe (2021), the T!O model is directly derived from the logic of energy ("the logic of the included third") developed by Stephane Lupasco (1951). Lupasco (1900-1988) was a French philosopher of Romanian origin. Inspired by the advances of quantum physics, he defined a logical system, of which classical logic can be considered a particular case. This type of logic is based on the dialectic inherent to energy. Following Lupasco, this logic is not merely reduced to the science of reasoning, but they understand it as a logic of all that exists – allowing for the model to be considered as the logic of the living.[4]

Following Lupasco the classical logic of the excluded third is a binary logic which allows for something to either be the case or not to be the case. Classical logic then is a logic of opposition with an inherent antagonism inside everything that is being asserted. According to the logic of the included third, the antagonism of classical logic is not an appropriate reflection of reality. An antagonism

2 While bdB enabled research data to be recorded digitally only within the facilities of the local research center, the actual fieldwork-recording has mostly remained paper-based. Attempts to establish a computer-based recording system for digital on-site recording were initially undertaken by research teams from partner universities (as early as 1999; see Fleischer and Schrickel 2004) and most recently on the occasion of the research program Digital Bibracte (Thivet 2019).

3 One of the challenges of this program was to support the process of disseminating Bibracte results via the digital services of the Very Large Research Infrastructure (TGIR) Huma-Num (CNRS Joint Service Unit).

4 Lupasco's influence on twentieth-century thought is still little studied. Yet, Joseph Brenner has recently made his work available in English in the book "Logic in reality" (Brenner 2003).

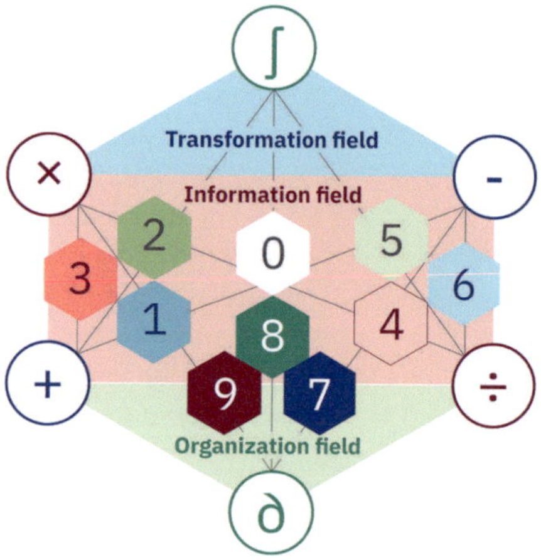

Figure 15.1. T!O-model – description logic to represent the transformation of organisation.

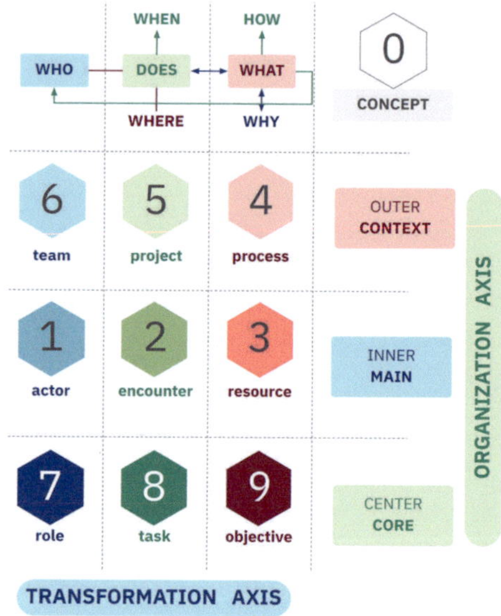

Figure 15.2. Information seeds: table to determine the descriptors of organisation.

should not be conceived as an either/or-decision, but as a generative force. Something that is stated is then not only opposed to what is not being stated, but that which is being stated is only one possible statement out of the vast array of potential assertions. In that sense, what is being stated – the fact – is actualised in that it is being specified and as having been stated it is also immune to modifications. In consequence, what had been a binary opposition is now described by its position between actualisation and potentialisation. Actualisation and potentialisation form an antagonistic pair that opens a spectrum of how we might speak about that fact. Whatever we can say about the fact is in continuous movement and what in the end will be said is contingent on the context of whoever speaks about it. Whoever, whenever, wherever.

By taking the continuous movement of the stated antagonism into account, the spectrum which is opened up, encompasses also all that which has not been said – that which in consequence is called the "included third." Allowing for the included third to become a constitutive part to what is being said, allows for the emergence of knowledge. Interestingly this will be the case, independent of an assertion or a failed acknowledgement of the included third during the description process. In case we leave it out, it will constitute what we call "implicit" knowledge, and if we care for it, we allow for its investigation in order to better understand how our knowledge has been constituted. Traditional conceptions of knowledge do not consider the implications of the "included third", following an Aristotelian, binary conception. As discussed above, examples to store archaeological information by inclusion of the included third are rare but do exist: these systems either apply a reflexive method or attempt the storage of so called "paradata". Potentially whatever can come out of bottom-up approaches like DIY fieldwork documentation systems might also advance the recognition of these furtive data.

Applying the logic of the "included third" the static antagonism can now be modelled as a dynamism (Figure 15.1), to become generative as a field of transformation. The model is not constituted by fixed parameters, but assertions are constrained by a set of poles – the attractors (Lacombe 2023). The use of attractors reflects a resolutely relational approach (Deleuze 1968; Bitbol 2010). In regard to the discussed antagonism, the two attractors are represented by mathematical operators – the multiplier (x) and the reducer (-). The multiplier creates diversity, variations, dimensions and discontinuity. On the opposing end, the reducer erases the differences, it is a source for continuity. The conjunction of these opposites consists in an integration, represented by a third attractor, the integrator (∫). The relational triangle described here can be called the transformation field.

As shown in Figure 15.1, the transformation field is in specular opposition to the organisation field. Organisation is understood as the result of integration, in symmetry to transformation. This field is dynamic as well, translated by the three attractors of the adder (+), the separator (÷) and the derivator (δ). In symmetry to the integrator of the Transformation field, the derivator spans open the organisation field, with the organising centre oscillating between inner and outer spaces. It is important to note that the model is conceptualised as pan-scalar and can therefore be applied on different levels of organisation: an organ, an organism, or a social organisation. The analogy with living organisms can help to specify the function of the attractors of the Organisation field further: the adder illustrates the organisation as being fed by way of the adder, while extracting resources from the environment by way of the separator.

In between the two described fields, the information field is opened (Figure 15.2). It is constituted by a set of elementary units of meaning – the "information seeds". The term "seed" hereby refers to the elementary nature of what the information seed entails. Sticking with the biological analogy, a seed already contains all the potential growth of the plant it derives from, and it is about to grow into.

The seeds fall into two categories, descriptors and interpreters. The descriptors are concrete markers that make it possible to describe a situation by crossing two axes, one operational, translated by "who-does-what" evoking the canonical structure of the sentence (subject, verb, complement), the other organisational on 3 levels, "main-context-core" (i.e., "inner-outer-centre" or "body-context-heart"), ultimately determining 9 species of descriptors.

On each organisational level descriptors are organised following the same structure and position on the operational axis, resulting in a matrix multiplication allowing to determine the specific configuration of each information seed. Concerning the "context", descriptor 4 – which could be transcribed as the "context of the what" – allows for the generation or processing of a set of resources and can be understood as a container for "services". For instance, if we were to model the concept of "book" and everything that was involved in its production, descriptor 4 would reflect the services provided by the publishing house that publishes several works, the printing house that produces them, the distribution platform that distributes them, the bookstore that sells them or the media library that lends them out, right up to the recycling centre that recovers unsold copies. Returning to archaeology, descriptor 4 could be a certain method to be applied during fieldwork.

Following the described logic, the other 8 descriptors can be understood accordingly: Descriptor 5 (or the "context of the does") groups together a series of events or situations that respond to a common purpose; it designates the project, the program or the mission or – again specifically for archaeology – the excavation project or fieldwork campaign. Descriptor 6 ("context of who") represents any group of actors, whatever its size, an individual being potentially linked to different groups – the group of researchers bound up within a research project

The "heart level" is part of an internal register: descriptor 7 ("heart of who") expresses the capacity, the potential of the actor or the group, attached to their role or mission and translating a competence. An excavator in an archaeological project would find their specific role determined here. Descriptor 8 ("heart of does") designates the action, an elementary temporal unit, knowing that only the actions that are significant for the discourse are memorised. Again, translated to the field of archaeology, the actual application of a chosen method is expressed with an action – the taking of a sample or the extraction of a quantity of soil from a designated archaeological unit. Descriptor 9 ("heart of what") at last represents the idea, the objective, the intention, translating a reason for being, or in archaeological terms a research goal.

In addition to these 9 species of descriptors, there is the interpreter, 0 the "concept", an abstraction designating a category, a theme or a keyword. The 10 seeds are identified by the same reduced set of attributes, in particular contextualisation attributes, such as domain, author, space or time, which are therefore not represented by seeds. The order of description is left free, the attributes remain optional. By analogy with the seed in botany, an information seed is a concentrate. It develops by putting it into relationships, thus forming a multidimensional structure, a graph called a schema, comparable to a rhizome. If seeds are formally defined as reifications of relationships between the 3 transformation attractors, and the 3 organisational attractors, they are themselves linked by 6 types of relationship, describing either transformational or organisational processes. The three transformational relations are correlation, formation (i.e., causality) and conjunction, whereby the correlation is the default relation which is at the basis of any more complex relationality that can be established. A change of objective is thus expressed by two seeds "9" linked by causality, the end date of the first corresponding to the start date of the second. The three organisational relations are appropriation – in the sense of acquiring extracted resources to respond to a need for an energetic imbalance ("unity makes strength"), domination – in the sense of mastering life or achievement ("divide and conquer"), and opposition. As mentioned above, by default information seeds are linked by mere correlation – the fact that there is a relationship, and that relationship has a scientific value. With increasing depth of investigation of the excavation process, a certain directionality between the seeds becomes apparent. This directionality could either mean a direction of transformation, or at the same time a type of causality between the seeds in question. The third relationship of the "tuner of the organisation" is less tangible, but it is the relationship responsible for the emergence of knowledge because it signifies the informational effect of the interaction of seeds.

The model as it has been described so far, has been introduced at the *Centre Archéologique Européen du Mont Beuvray*, a research centre with the scope to conduct research at the late Iron Age oppidum Bibracte. By allowing its members to model their organisation, they were able to discuss and develop the constitutional processes in use at Bibracte in order to identify processes that work well and others that are in need of improvement.

15.5 T!O and bdB

Within SIAMOIS modelling the process of an archaeological excavation with T!O assists the identification of necessary aspects of recording and identifying shared as well as disparate conceptualisations at the partner institutions. In the following section T!O is applied to model the processes of excavation and typological analysis in order to show how modelling these processes can help understanding the requirements as well as conceptual divergences in archaeological discourses on the fundamental level of data recording.

15.5.1 Modelling the excavation process

The process of an archaeological excavation as modelled with T!O is illustrated in 6 steps (Figures 15.3A–15.3F).

In a first step (Figure 15.3A) the information seeds for actor (1) and encounter (2) are situated on the axis for the internal space. In order to model an actor who relates themselves to encounter something like an archaeological context, the actor is transformed from their being related to the unique attractor, towards being related to the organisational attractor. In other words, the individual actor engages towards an activity which is integrated with the organisation. The relations activated here are that of correlation – the relation that is active by default – and the transformation.

In a second step (Figure 15.3B) the encounter happens on the spatial axis, but an activity involving the archaeological context requires a transformation from the unique attractor to the multiple attractors. Again, in other words, the actor extends themselves onto the location of the archaeological context. Besides correlation and transformation, we recognise the relation of appropriation as the encounter enables the actor to move onto the resource. Throughout this transformation and taking into consideration the dynamics of continuous movement between actualisation and potentialisation underlying all processes, the actor continuously examines their relationality with the context and themselves – in fact an expression of reflexivity during that process. The encounter in which the actor is involved translates (original meaning of "*translatio*") them towards actualisation.

A third step (Figure 15.3C) models the actor's activity predetermined by them being part of a research project from which they derive their specific role (information seed 7). Therefore, the actor is organised in a determined space, and they are transformed by adopting a causal directionality, which gives them their role on site. The primary relationships in this situation are transformation and conjunction so that acting following that role, the actor becomes their role. Framed by that role they can make decisions and decide on how that directionality becomes manifest.

In the next step (Figure 15.3D) the actor's relation with the context following a certain role moreover implies following general directives defined by the project. These constraints are modelled as an actor fulfilling their role to become instrumental for the progress of the excavation. The primary relation being transformation, the organised is transformed from an integrated being towards expansion specifying the actual interaction with the archaeological context. In other words, the potential excavator is being actualised by way of their objective.

At the same time (Figure 15.3E), the general directives are prone to being modified in regard to specific circumstances. The dynamism is expressed by issuing specific tasks or staying with the model, transforming from being related to a multiple attractor towards being integrated. The general role finds its necessary configuration for the task at hand and the overall excavation strategy becomes manifest.

Finally (Figure 15.3F) the excavator, equipped with a role, directives and an outline for their task is enabled to move into the archaeological context and begins digging. Thereby the organisational aspects of the directive are transformed towards a spatial contraction and the resource identified during the initial encounter is now actualised by the actor's intention. The relationship with the resource is thereby that of transformation but also predation, as the context is being processed and extracted. As we can see, the resulting model allows for reflecting on the complex interaction of the excavator with their context, considering the different levels of organisational rules embedded in general strategies, directives and definition of tasks.

Already modelling this basic and partial aspect of the archaeological process with T!O shows a set of aspects that are for now ignored within bdB. First, the transformation from seeds 2 to 3 (encounter towards resource) shows that the actor never escapes their environmental context, which makes it necessary to examine these parameters continuously and document the effects of the process. Secondly, the movement from seeds 1 to 7 is practically expressed by the actors making decisions, again an important element to be documented in order to understand the data resulting from that process.

On a general level, the model shows as well that the actor's presence with their context is only complete by taking into account the temporal aspects of the same activity. In consequence an information system treating excavation data necessitates the recording of the temporal structure of these activities.

Regarding the ambiguities of the concept of "stratigraphic unit", the model underscores the increased attention to alternative ways of grouping archaeological data, similar to those enabled by the use of the "excavation unit". Allowing for a differential documentation depending on whether a unit is a traditional stratigraphic unit, a unit of grouped material in view of the facilitation of typological studies or even the attribution of historical excavation units established in the 19th century, the "excavation unit" is a

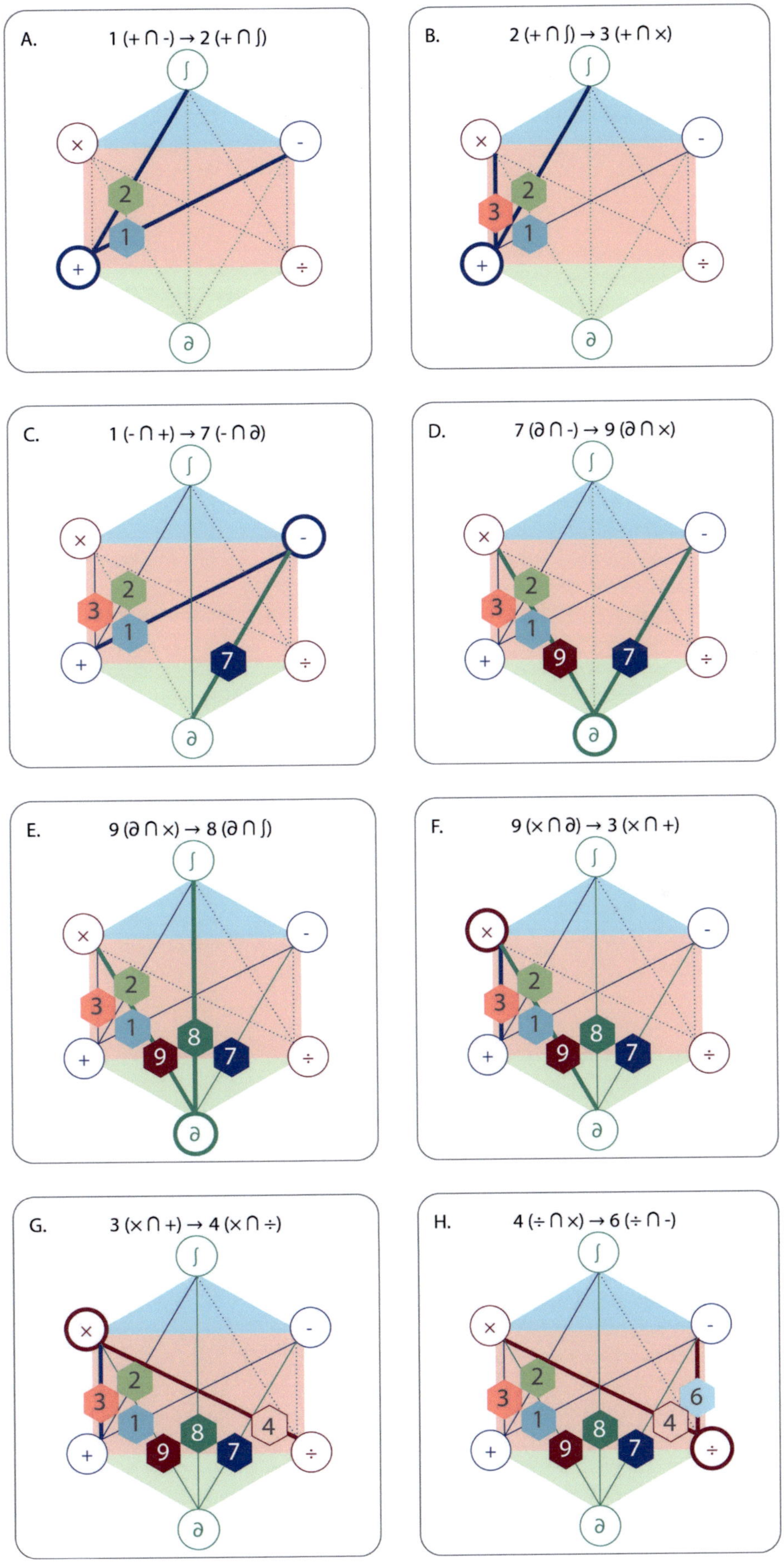

Figure 15.3. The process of archaeological excavation and reasoning as modeled with T!O

more appropriate reflection of actual excavation processes. Breaking this process down with T!O now moreover allows for the identification of moments within the process, where information should be gathered in order to enable a more detailed recording of the reasoning process involved in the definition of such a unit. Each movement on the network of information seeds holds potential data in that respect. The proposed model therefore allows for reflecting on institutional processes at the same time as it indicates the necessary parameters to organise and record.

15.5.2 Modelling archaeological reasoning

Modelling the process of soil extraction obviously reflects only a small part of the archaeological process. As discussed above, large parts of the archaeological discourse are recorded in vernacular language, which are fluid but disconnected from the data. In order to expand the present example accordingly, modelling the process of confronting excavated objects with research documents will shed light on the requirements to digitally encode both discourse and data to enable their connection (interoperability), ultimately allowing them to delegate to machines some of their memory and processing capabilities (sorting and calculation).

In archaeology it is quite common for a vocabulary to be specifically created or reorganised based on a particular case study and for the same term to refer to different, evolving realities depending on the context (cultural, chronological, etc.) and viewpoints, without specialists always being aware of it. Therefore, the process of extracting an object is further modelled by its confrontation with a typology (Figure 15.3G).

In Figure 15.3H, the typology itself is modelled as an authoritative set of rules issued by the related research community, but the retrieved objects have initially formed the basis for the creation of the very typology and throughout the prolonged interaction on site, the authoritative document is transformed as well. As a term used as a keyword in a catalogue or a database may not necessarily refer to the same material or conceptual realities according to its users. In consequence, this issue of polysemy affects documentation management, and even casts doubt on the comparison of archaeological corpora since the meaning of vocabularies used to index data often varies from one dataset (database or publications) to another.

The polysemy apparent in the example is typically clarified in scientific publications by referencing the bibliographical information that includes the producer's surname and the year of term creation – what we refer to as the "vintage". This reliance on the vintage has emerged as an obvious and functional solution in the presentation of competing and contextualised controlled vocabularies by appending a bibliographic citation call to the term label: name(s) + year. Stemming from this choice, the understanding of a term is embedded within the same vintaged bibliographic context.

Acknowledging the situation of polysemy of terms and its resolution merely outside of the recording system by way of traditional publications, the Bibracte project conducted an experiment as part of the publication "La vaisselle céramique de Bibracte" (Barrier and Luginbühl 2021). In parallel to it being published as a traditional book, the specialised vocabulary used to characterise and describe pottery fragments was furthermore published by using the thesaurus manager Opentheso (https://opentheso.huma-num.fr/opentheso). Opentheso is compliant with the ISO 25964 standard (https://www.iso.org/en/standard/53657.html) that guides the development of controlled vocabularies (Durost et al. 2022). One of the rules of the standard establishes the impossibility of presenting two strictly identical terms in the same thesaurus while associating them with different semantic spaces (position in the hierarchy of terms, relationships, definition).

The definition (in the sense of the ISO 1087-2019 standard: "representation of a concept by an expression that describes it and differentiates it from related concepts") serves to individualise the concept by qualifying its properties. It specifies the researcher's paradigm for comprehending their subject of study, which, through the alignment of terms from different thesauri, can be confronted with the multiplicity of viewpoints presented therein and thus become part of a knowledge network. Furthermore, for a given type of artifact, the methods of study and analysis can change depending on the research question, the researcher's perspective, and taphonomic conditions (i.e., all the physicochemical processes that occur after the object is abandoned). In case objects of an unknown type are retrieved, the typology requires modification. In our example the discovery of a lid (and the recipient covered by it) are from now on to be considered as a potential object not merely from a settlement context but also as a funerary object. While the process is obviously known and a common event in archaeology, the actualisation process of modifying the typology is rarely recorded with information systems in use. Even less the means of modification of authoritative rules by way of which retrieved objects were used to modify the typology.

Consequently, and as a further issue for internal interoperability, the archaeologist creates their own vocabulary and/or draws part or all of their terminology from a reference already used elsewhere, adapting it to meet their needs. To accurately understand the vocabularies created or invoked by authors, it is necessary to have access to the corpus(es) upon which they are based. Connecting them for comparisons is a fundamental need, which in the digital age is expressed as the requirement for a technological networking of knowledge. A thesaurus manager is entirely capable of initiating this through its internal relationships (associations between concepts within the same thesaurus) and external relationships (alignments between concepts from different thesauri), as long as the organisation and networking of these vocabularies are extended by access to the data recorded and/or defined based on material or immaterial realities. Indeed, only by returning to the data can one appreciate the meaning of the vocabulary and the relevance of alignments with a comparative vocabulary, and therefore, its associated dataset.

In conclusion it is necessary to formalise the vocabularies used for data description by a researcher, that is, to expose the uniqueness of their perspective and the richness of their vocabulary, to be capable of understanding other paradigms, and to be able to compare their terminology within the semantic space of their colleagues.

15.6 Conclusion

The narration of a site's history involves arranging the collected data, which includes information derived from the data and their relationships, as well as the nature of the reasoning to achieve this, while maintaining a constant concern to be tested against archaeological facts. Currently, this work is carried out through the institutionalised dissemination of written publications, such as scientific reports, articles, or monographs, in vernacular language. Whether recording processes are established in collaboration or by way of retrotheorisation, it is necessary to describe these processes systematically. T!O allows for the investigation of archaeological processes in order to identify the necessary questions to be answered when attempting to define a projected knowledge structure. The questions (and answers) are both distinctive of the specific group of researchers while at the same time underscoring commonalities with other groups or the discipline in general. In the long run this approach allows for the assessment of potential mappings with already existing ontologies, thereby bridging not only internal but also external interoperabilities.

Updates in archaeological discourse are part of a permanent iterative process (Moberg 1969), oscillating (feedback) between the stages of archaeography (requesting / observing [archaeometry, archaeoscopy] / describing [ordering, classifying, sorting, generalising]) and those of producing discourse about the past (archaeology: Ἀρχαῖος, "ancient", and Λόγος, "discourse") proper (analysing, associating, interpreting, understanding, etc.). However, such a heuristic framework is hindered by a highly incomplete restitution of information. This methodological weakness has early on caught the attention of the French archaeological community (Gardin 1971; Tchernia et al. 1984).

Current digital technologies have undoubtedly reached the necessary maturity to address this techno-methodological question, but as it stands, this would constrain the archaeological community to condition its heuristic practice to the use of tools conceptualised outside its intellectual realm, which is not desirable for epistemological (their logic would elude it) and practical reasons (it wouldn't master them). Nevertheless, these digital solutions could reduce the excessive reliance on cumulative deductive abilities derived from each individual's experience and the common culture of the discipline, which places too much emphasis on the implicit and individual memorisation capacity. How can the transition be made, in collaboration with archaeologists (co-construction), from restitutions in vernacular language, fluid but disconnected from the data, to digital encodings faithful to both discourse and data, allowing them to be connected (interoperability), and ultimately enabling them to delegate to machines a portion of their memorisation and processing capabilities (classification and calculation)?

It would be appropriate to envisage a new system that would encourage and network both the diversity of the data and the accepted plurality of points of view. If ontologies are ideal candidates to map the common aspects of a recordings system, either in regard to the internal or external interoperability, what is then the best approach to develop the overall system by tolerating conceptual differences as well as retaining the potential for later integration with external databases? As we have seen, most AIS are far from being conceptualised in a collaborative fashion and retrotheorisation of existing systems is mostly left to a small group attempting to reproduce theoretical deliberations that were supposedly occurring during the development of an AIS. To address this limitation, a new system fostering diversity of data and viewpoints is necessary. This would enable a more comprehensive and collaborative synthesis of archaeological paradigms.

In emphasis to the above-mentioned difficulties to trace individual treatments of the archaeological context, this modelling approach takes seriously the fact that already AIS can be considered as shared conceptualisations in the sense of a group of researchers buying into their institutions' chosen organisation of knowledge.

T!O proposes a paradigm shift that goes beyond binary logic and invites us to consider ontologies from a dynamic point of view: invariants are limited to operations, not states. This approach has two major advantages: on the one hand, it is compatible with the living world, and on the other, it harmonises the understanding of phenomena currently dealt with in different disciplines, after translating specific terms into the T!O language. From a practical point of view, as the model is recent, it does not yet have specific tools to facilitate its deployment. However, this disadvantage is offset by the fact that it can be gradually implemented in existing information systems. In this way, SIAMOIS ultimately hopes to meet the primary requirement of ontologies as discussed by Gruber, thereby developing a genuine "shared conceptualisation" of archaeological research.

Acknowledgements

We thank Vincent Guichard, director of the Bibracte European archaeological center for hosting the SIAMOIS project. We are grateful to Miled Rousset for developing OpenTheso, which is a crucial part of the SIAMOIS software development. Many thanks to Jean-Pierre Girard (Archéorient, Lyon) and the partners of the SIAMOIS project.

Funding

The SIAMOIS project is supported by the state of France as part of the "Digitization of Heritage and Architecture" initiative within "France 2030", operated by the public sector financial institution "Caisse des Dépôts".

Conflict of interest disclosure

The authors declare that they comply with the PCI rule of having no financial conflicts of interest in relation to the content of the article.

Peer review

This article has been reviewed and recommended by PCI Archaeology.

Taylor, James Stuart. "Exploring The Role of Archaeological Information Systems in Improving Data Management and Interoperability." *Peer Community in Archaeology* 100409. DOI:10.24072/pci.archaeo.100409.

References

Barrier, Sylvie, Thierry Luginbühl, and Philippe Barral. 2021. *La vaisselle céramique de Bibracte: de l'identification à l'analyse*. Glux-en-Glenne: Bibracte.

Bekiari, Chryssoula, George Bruseker, Martin Doerr, Christian-Emil Ore, Stephen Stead, and Thanasis Velios. 2021. *Definition of the cidoc conceptual reference model v7.1.1. The CIDOC Conceptual Reference Model Special Interest Group*. DOI:10.26225/FDZH-X261.

Berggren, Åsa, Nicolo Dell'Unto, Maurizio Forte, Scott Haddow, Ian Hodder, Justine Issavi, Nicola Lercari, Camilla Mazzucato, Allison Mickel, and James S. Taylor. 2015. "Revisiting reflexive archaeology at Çatalhöyük: integrating digital and 3D technologies at the trowel's edge." *Antiquity* 89 (344): 433–48. DOI:10.15184/aqy.2014.43.

Bitbol, Michel. 2010. *De l'intérieur du monde: pour une philosophie et une science des relations*. Paris: Flammarion.

Brenner, Joseph E. 2008. *Logic in reality*. Dordrecht: Springer.

Carlisle, Philip K., Ioannis Avramides, Alison Dalgity, and David Myers. 2014. "The Arches Heritage Inventory and Management System: a standards-based approach to the management of cultural heritage information." In *CIDOC (International Committee for Documentation of the International Council of Museums) conference: Access and Understanding – Networking in the Digital Era, Dresden, Germany, September 6-11, 2014*.

Carver, Martin Oswald Hugh. 1990. "Digging for data; archaeological approaches to data definition, acquisition and analysis." In *Lo scavo archeologico: dalla Diagnosi all'Edizione, IIIe Ciclo di Lezioni sulla Ricerca applicata in Archeologia, Certosa di Pontignano (Siena), 6-18 novembre 1989*, edited by Riccardo Francovich and Daniele Manacorda, 45–120. Florence: Al Insegna del Giglio.

Chadwick, Adrian. 2003. "Post-processualism, professionalization and archaeological methodologies. Towards reflective and radical practice." *Archaeological Dialogues* 10 (1): 97–117. DOI:10.1017/S1380203803001107.

Daston, Lorraine, and Peter L. Galison. 2021. *Objectivity*. Princeton: Princeton University Press.

Deleuze, Gilles. 1968. *Différence et Répétition*. Paris: Epiméthée.

Derudas, Paola, Federico Nurra, and Andreas Svensson. 2023. "New AIR for the Archaeological Process? The use of 3D web Semantic for Publishing Archaeological Reports." *ACM Journal on Computing and Cultural Heritage* 16 (3): 1–23. DOI:10.1145/3594722.

Desachy, Bruno. 2008. "De la formalisation du traitement des données stratigraphiques en archéologie de terrain." PhD diss., Université de Paris 1.

Desachy, Bruno, Sébastien Durost, Myriam Giudicelli, and Vincent Guichard. 2012. "Rapports scientifiques de fouilles programmées et publications de Bibracte. Réflexions, acquis et perspectives." *Les nouvelles de l'archéologie* 130: 58–64.

Descola, Phillipe. 2013. *Beyond Nature and Culture*. Translated by Janet Lloyd. Chicago: University of Chicago Press.

Durost, Sébastien, Guillaume Reich, and Jean-Pierre Girard. 2022. "Terminologies, modèles de données archéologiques et thésaurus documentaires: réflexions à partir d'une typologie de céramiques." *Humanités Numériques* 6. DOI:10.4000/revuehn.3119.

Fleischer, F., and Marco Schrickel. 2004. "Alte Mauern–moderne Technik. Computerelektronik bei Ausgrabungen in Frankreich." *Universität Leipzig Uni Journal* 4: 20.

Gardin, Jean-Claude. 1971. *UNISIST, Study report on the feasibility of a World Science Information System*. Paris: UNESCO.

Grenon, P., B. Smith, B., and L. Goldberg. 2004. "Biodynamic ontology: applying BFO in the biomedical domain." In *Ontologies in Medicine*, edited by P.M. Pisannelli, 20–38. Amsterdam: IOS Press.

Gruber, Thomas R. 1993. "A translation approach to portable ontology specifications." *Knowledge Acquisition* 5 (2): 199-220.

Harris, Edward C. 1979. "The laws of archaeological stratigraphy." *World Archaeology* 11 (1): 111–7. DOI:10.1080/00438243.1979.9979753.

Hiebel, Gerald, Martin Doerr, Klaus Hanke, and Anja Masur. 2014. "How to put archaeological geometric data into context? Representing mining history research with CIDOC CRM and extensions." *International Journal of Heritage in the Digital Era* 3 (3): 557–77. DOI:10.1260/2047-4970.3.3.557.

Hodder, Ian. 2000. "Where is Çatalhöyük? Developing a Reflexive Method in Archaeology." In *Towards Reflexive Method in Archaeology: The Example at Çatalhöyük*, edited by Ian Hodder, 3–14. Cambridge: McDonald Institute for Archaeological Research.

Hodder, Ian. 2003. "Archaeological reflexivity and the "local" voice." *Anthropological Quarterly* 76 (1): 55–69.

Huggett, Jeremy. 2020. "Capturing the silences in digital archaeological knowledge." *Information* 11 (5): 278. DOI:10.3390/info11050278.

Khazraee, Emad, and Xia Lin. 2011. "Demystifying ontology." In *Classification & Ontology: Formal Approaches and Access to Knowledge, Proceedings of the International Udc Seminar 19-20 September 2011 the Hague, the Netherlands*, 41–53. Würzburg: Ergon Verlag.

Knorr-Cetina, Karin D. 1981. *The manufacture of knowledge: An essay on the constructivist and contextual nature of science*. Oxford: Pergamon Press.

Knorr-Cetina, Karin. 1999. *Epistemic cultures: How the sciences make knowledge*. Cambridge, MA: Harvard University Press.

Lacombe, Eric. 2021. "Transformation numérique des organisations en réseau : les potentiels d'une schématisation dynamique de l'information." PhD diss., Université Michel de Montaigne Bordeaux III. https://theses.fr/2021BOR30016.

Lacombe, Eric. 2023. "Vers un langage pour exprimer la complexité." *LHUMAINE* 2. https://hal.science/hal-04402428.

Latour, Bruno. 1999. *Pandora's hope: Essays on the reality of science studies*. Cambridge, MA: Harvard University Press.

Latour, Bruno, and Steve Woolgar. 2013. *Laboratory life: The construction of scientific facts.* Princeton: Princeton University Press.

Lukas, Dominik. 2014. "A historical-semantic approach to the concept of 'oppidum': The example of Bibracte." In *Paths to Complexity: Centralisation and Urbanisation in Iron Age Europe*, edited by Manuel Fernández-Götz, Holger Wendling, and Katja Winger, 84–100. Oxford: Oxbow Books.

Lukas, Dominik, Claudia Engel, and Camilla Mazzucato. 2018. "Towards a living archive: Making multi layered research data and knowledge generation transparent." *Journal of Field Archaeology* 43: S19–S30. https://doi-org/10.1080/00934690.2018.1516110.

Lupasco, Stéphane. 1951. *Le principe d'antagonisme et la logique de l'énergie. Prolégomènes à une science de la contradiction.* Paris: Hermann & Co.

Moberg, Carl-Axel and Holger Arbman. 1969. *Introduktion till arkeologi: jämförande och nordisk fornkunskap.* Stockholm: Tryckindustri.

Nicholson, Christopher, Sarah Kansa, Neha Gupta, and Rachel Fernandez. 2023. "Will It ever be FAIR? Making archaeological data findable, accessible, interoperable, and reusable." *Advances in Archaeological Practice* 11 (1): 63–75. DOI:10.1017/aap.2022.40.

Oldman, Dominic, and Diana Tanase. 2018. "Reshaping the knowledge graph by connecting researchers, data and practices in ResearchSpace." In *The Semantic Web–ISWC 2018: 17th International Semantic Web Conference, Monterey, CA, USA, October 8–12, 2018, Proceedings, Part II 17*, edited by Denny Vrandečić, Kalina Bontcheva, Mari Carmen Suárez-Figueroa, Valentina Presutti, Irene Celino, Marta Sabou, Lucie-Aimée Kaffee, and Elena Simperl, 325–40. Cham: Springer. DOI:10.1007/978-3-030-00668-6_20.

Paice, Patricia. 1991. "Extensions to the Harris matrix system to illustrate stratigraphic discussion of an archaeological site." *Journal of Field Archaeology* 18 (1): 17–28. DOI:10.2307/530148.

Quine, Willard Van Orman. 1960. *Word and Object.* Cambridge, MA: MIT Press.

Rorty, Richard. 1991. "Solidarity or objectivity?" In *Objectivity, Relativism, and Truth: Philosophical Papers, Volume 1*, edited by Richard Rorty, 21–32. Cambridge: Cambridge University Press.

Roure, Réjane, Hakima Manseri, Sébastien Munos, and Michel Py. 2021. "Towards an Archaeological Information System: the evolution of Syslat, an archaeological data management software." In *Big Data and Archaeology: Proceedings of the XVIII UISPP World Congress (4-9 June 2018, Paris, France) Volume 15, Session III-1*, edited by François Djindjian, and Paola Moscati, 62–70. Oxford: Archaeopress.

Salmon, Merrilee H. 1982. *Philosophy and archaeology*. New York: Academic Press.

Salmon, Wesley C. 1992. "Explanation in archaeology: An update." In *Metaarchaeology: Reflections by Archaeologists and Philosophers*, edited by Lester Embree, 243–53. Dordrecht: Springer Netherlands.

Taylor, James Stuart, Justine Issavi, Åsa Berggren, Dominik Lukas, Camilla Mazzucato, Burcu Tung, and Nicoló Dell'Unto. 2018. "'The Rise of the Machine': the impact of digital tablet recording in the field at Çatalhöyük." *Internet Archaeology* 47: 1. DOI: 10.11141/ia.47.1.

Tchernia, André, Jean-Claude Gardin, Jean-Paul Morel, Pierre Gros, Yvon Thébert, Pier Giovanni Guzzo, Olivier Picard, Didier Ozanam, Bernard Vincent, and Charles Pietri. 1986. "La publication en archéologie." *Mélanges de l'école française de Rome* 98 (1): 359–86.

Thivet, Matthieu, Quentin Verriez, and Damien Vurpillot. 2019. "Aspectus: développement d'une plateforme collaborative en ligne d'analyse des données 3D pour l'archéologie et le patrimoine." *In Situ. Revue des patrimoines* 39. DOI: 10.4000/insitu.21934.

Viveiros de Castro, Eduardo. 2015. *Cannibal metaphysics.* Minneapolis: University of Minnesota Press.

Wilcock, J. D. 1974. "The PLUTARCH System." In *Proceedings of the Annual Conference organised by the Computer Centre University of Birmingham, January 1974*, edited by J. D. Wilcock, and S. Laflin, 64–8. Birmingham: Computer Centre, University of Birmingham.

16 Linking Scars

Topology-based Scar Detection and Graph Modeling of Paleolithic Artifacts in 3D

Florian Linsel
Institute of Computer Science
Martin-Luther University
of Halle-Wittenberg
florian.linsel@informatik.uni-halle.de

an Philipp Bullenkamp
Institute of Computer Science
Martin-Luther University
of Halle-Wittenberg

Hubert Mara
Institute of Computer Science
Martin-Luther University
of Halle-Wittenberg

Abstract

Motivated by the concept of combining the archaeological practice of creating lithic artifact drawings with the potential of 3D mesh data, our goal in this project is not only to analyse the shape at the artifact level, but also to enable a more detailed analysis of stone tools at the scar and ridge level. For this purpose, we combine the archaeological interpretation, typically represented in 2D, with its corresponding 3D data. To achieve this goal, we propose a workflow that utilizes 3D datasets as the best means for shape analysis of lithic artifacts, which relies on one of the first open access repositories of 3D scanned lithic tools. In our four-step workflow, we start with a preprocessing in GigaMesh, followed by a scar segmentation using Morse theory-based algorithms, continue with a postprocessing and finally create a graph model-based representation of the lithic artifacts in 3D. This prototypical graph model can already be used to display and evaluate manual or parameterized operational sequences in 3D. The source code and the manually annotated ground truth data are available as open-access publications under a Creative Commons license.

Keywords: Scar detection; 3D meshes; Palaeolithic; Operational Sequences; Computational Archaeology; Lithic Technology

16.1 Introduction

Lithic artifacts display varying shapes and forms due to the differences in raw material quality and knapping techniques utilized during their production. Of particular interest is the knapping process. Palaeolithic artifacts remain unpolished, which allows the study of each production step inside the knapping process. These production steps leave convex and concave scars behind that are separated by ridges (Figure 16.1). In contemporary archaeology, drawings and images of artifacts, often supported by additional details, are the standard approaches to documenting them.

One of the pieces of information that can be added to a drawing, is the temporal relation between scars and ridges. In this complex analytical approach, scar-ridge patterns are utilized to establish the sequence of working steps or scars, leading to the analysis of an *operational sequence* (abbr. OS, fr. *chaîne opératoire*; Pastoors et al. 2015; Richter 1997; 2004). Because identifying scars and ridges can be time-consuming, it is easier to automate comparisons of the overall artifact shape.

In *Advances in Digital Archaeology. Proceedings of the 2023 conference Computer Applications and Quantitative Methods in Archaeology – 50 years of synergy*, edited by J.W.H.P. Verhagen, J. Waagen, A. Brandsen, A. Queffelec, R.M. Visser and D. Taelman, 211–224. Leiden: Sidestone Press.

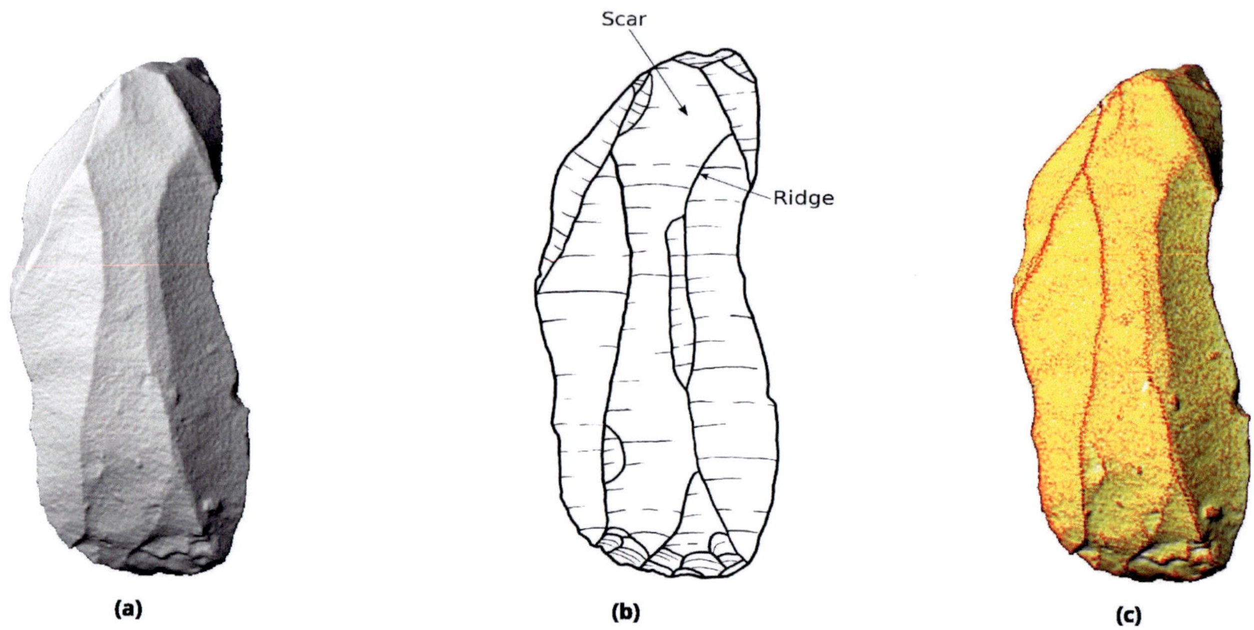

Figure 16.1. Images of artifact GdF 31: (a) orthographic projection of the scanned object; (b) drawing of the artifact; (c) MSII-curvature mapped as function value.

Since the introduction of Geometric Morphometrics methods in 2D, the analysis of outlines has become more common. Currently, standardized drawings can even be analysed at the level of individual scars (Gellis et al. 2022). However, the analysis of 3D models in archaeology is still in its early stages. Some approaches involve the use of manually placed landmarks to extract features from the surface of artifacts, such as the overall shape (Herzlinger and Grosman 2018) or the angle of the cutting edges (Weiss 2020).

Similar to drawings, users of lithic artifact annotations mark specific surface features on the 3D model. In the case of a drawing, the illustrator recognizes and draws the ridges, while in the case of annotation, the annotator does the same but annotates the scars. In both cases, scars and ridges are directly or indirectly determined. To our knowledge, only a few annotators are currently available, such as those for cuneiform tablets (Homburg et al. 2022) and for lithic artifacts (Pop 2019).

Besides the manual annotation of scars and ridges, they can also be (semi-)automatically segmented. 3D segmentation is a well-known practice to separate 3D models to smaller coherent areas. Segmentation is up to today an under-investigated practice in Palaeolithic archaeology. Only a handful of approaches are using 3D models to detect scars or ridges. While some approaches use 3D models to extract a 2D rendering in a drawing-like fashion (Barone et al. 2018), other approaches implemented algorithms to automatically segment them on the meshes. Pulla et al. (2001) proposed one of the first methods utilizing a watershed model and varied curvature measurements. The most well-known work in this field is Richardson et al. (2014). In this study, the authors utilized a principal curvature-based geodesic clustering to oversegment lithic artifacts. They merged weak borders and optimized the graph-cut to obtain the scar segmentation. Subsequently, they constructed an adjacency graph model.

The motivation of our research is to visualize labelled 3D models as 3D representations of OS's. Thus, it is necessary to analyse scar-ridge patterns for two objectives: firstly, to segment scars and secondly, to analyse OS's of lithic artifacts, as strongly suggested during our presentation's discussion. Therefore, we introduce a Morse theory-based segmentation approach and an adjacency graph model of neighbouring scars to simplify the 3D model. By considering the relative properties of the scar nodes, we have developed a definition of link direction based on parameters. In this study, we show our workflow leading from the annotation, over the segmentation towards a proof of concept for determining the link directions of scar-ridge graph models.

16.2 Archaeological Practice

16.2.1 Technical Drawings

For most artifacts, from ceramics, over bronze knives to lithic tools, one of the primary documentation techniques is a technical drawing. The process of depiction is, according to specialist, an essential part of the archaeological education. Each category of artifact has its own tradition of how it should be represented and drawn.

In the following, the most common way how Palaeolithic stone artifacts are depicted and drawn (Shea 2013) will be described. Due to the sequential information imprinted on the dorsal side of the artifact, the dorsal side gets depicted preferably while other views are additional. In a general analysis, all flakes and especially blades are orientated with the pointed side upwards (distal part at the top) and the point of impact, the striking platform, at the bottom of the main view. The artifacts are orientated according to their biggest extent in the y-axis. This digitisation standard applies only to two-dimensional depiction of artifacts, but relying on it, modern approaches using 3D models are following its lead.

16.2.2 Operational Sequences

To determine the OS's, multiple attributes are defined (Pastoors et al. 2015), which specify the ridge patterns of adjacent scars. One of these conditions of distinguishing the temporal relation between scars is that "a younger scar contours follows the older scar contour and cuts across it". This process leads to an overprinting and reducing of the more central, older scar. In general, a more central scar, which rings true especially for bigger artifacts like hand axes, is older than scars on the edge. Even if bifaces are not the subject of this research, similar considerations should also be applicable for blade and bladelets. Hence, the positional integration of the scar inside of a scar ridge pattern should be considered.

For a better understanding of artifacts, especially for the procedural relationship between the scars, a graph representation is helpful for understanding the scar-ridge connections (Richardson et al. 2014). Graph models in the form of Harris matrices are used to represent the relation between working stages of lithic artifacts (e.g., Pastoors 2000, Pastoors et al. 2015, and Richter 2004). In this research, they created Harris matrices from working stages, not from scars. In this line of thought, scars are assigned to working stages, which are considered to be procedural steps of the knapping. The representation of each scar in a Harris matrix is rather uncommon. However, by providing attributes to determine the relation between adjacent scars (Pastoors et al. 2015), a graph model of lithic artifacts is worth exploring. The basic concept was already applied to experimental data in the context of a refitting (Yang et al. 2017), but it was as far as we know, not applied to real archaeological data. The creation of graph models will serve as an important step towards real archaeological data and can give insights into the production patterns.

16.3 Material and Methods

16.3.1 Dataset

In this study, an open dataset of lithic artifacts from the *Grotta di Fumane* (GdF) site (Falcucci and Peresani 2022b) was used. GdF is a north-eastern Italian site, which is well-known for one of the earliest cave paintings in Europe as well as layers clearly associated with the Uluzzian. The Uluzzian, a transitional industry, is one of the earliest techno-complexes associated with the AMHs arrival in Europe (Marín-Arroyo et al. 2023). All artifacts from the dataset are attributed to the on this site following Proto-Aurignacian and are either made from blade or bladelet blanks. Many of the blades and bladelets, especially the intermediate slender blades stay unretouched (Falcucci et al. 2017).

From the 732 published artifacts, we selected 57 artifacts from the A1-A2 unit, which is dated between 42,000 and 39,250 cal BP. To gain a broader perspective, we included also 5 artifacts from the D3 unit (D3b, D3d and D3d base), which is dated between 40,000 and 37,750 cal BP (Higham et al. 2009; Marín-Arroyo et al. 2023). A total of 62 artifacts were selected according to their varying scar-ridge complexity.

To compensate for the absence of the original artifact, the annotation workflow was created to determine whether ridges and scars are applicable even when the artifact is not available. In order to get a better representation of the scar-ridge patterns than using conventional rendering techniques, the dataset was pre-processed using the 3D *Multi-Scale Integral Invariant* (MSII) filter and selecting the maximum curvature (Mara and Krömker 2013; Figure 16.2). It is recommended to use a dual monitor or widescreen monitor to use MeshLab (Cignoni et al. 2008) and GigaMesh side by side. While examining the ridges in GigaMesh, MeshLab's Z-painting tool is used to colour code the different segments of the mesh surfaces. This creates a dataset that approximates the *ground truth* (GT). It is worth noting that the annotations may vary when multiple experts are involved given the absence of a deterministic solution.

Each manually applied colour, i.e., graphical annotation represents a labelled connected component. This labelled dataset will serve first, as GT dataset to evaluate the segmentation results and second, to determine the precision of the adjacency graph models. Beside annotated meshes, for the evaluation of the directed graph models, manual OS's were needed. Due to the differing quality of the 3D models, which varies between 40,000 and 400,000 vertices, the relation between scars cannot be determined in some cases, e.g., GdF 710. For the GdF 207, we were able to reconstruct with a high confidence an OS. One additional OS was published in Falcucci et al. (2017), from which a directed graph model

Figure 16.2. Artifact (GdF 31) turned in position to be annotated: (a) original 3D mesh; (b) MSII values (GigaMesh) mapped 3D mesh; (c) with MeshLab colour painted 3D mesh.

was generated. The artifact is a multi-platform core (ID: GdF RF.c_49). It was not part of the initial GdF dataset (Falcucci and Peresani 2022b) and was added in the later version 2.1.1 (Falcucci and Peresani 2022a).

16.3.2 Methods

This section presents a four-step workflow for the analysis of lithic artifacts. In the first step, the 3D meshes are preprocessed in the GigaMesh software, then their scars are segmented using Morse theory. The third step is a postprocessing step, and the fourth step is to create an adjacency graph model-based on the annotation.

1. Preprocessing in GigaMesh (Mara et al. 2010)
    a. Orienting, Cleaning and Filling
    b. *3D Multi-Scale Integral Invariant* (MSII) Filtering
2. Scar Segmentation using Morse Theory
    a. Morse-Smale Complex
    b. Weak and Strong Ridges
    c. Oversegmentation (Morse Cells)
    d. Merging Morse Cells based on Ridges
3. Extracting Spatial Properties of Annotated 3D Meshes
4. Scar-Ridge-Patterns as Graph Models
    a. Scar-Ridge Graph as Source for Digital Drawings
    b. Directing the Graph Model by Parameter

This step-by-step process will be presented in the following subsections.

16.3.2.1 Preprocessing in GigaMesh

The workflow starts by automatically cleaning and filling the surface of the meshes using the command line tool in GigaMesh. Every 3D mesh by its nature has natural or artificial openings, holes, and gaps on its surface on one side and topological errors due to, e.g., imperfect scan alignment on the other side. Due to the simplicity of lithic artifacts, e.g., no natural and artificial holes, the default setting of the tool can be used.

The next step is to orient the artifact using a 3-step procedure. First, calculate the principal orientation based on vertex coordinates and check the mesh for mirroring. Second, a k-means clustering algorithm was utilized to distinguish between the dorsal (front) and ventral (back) sides. Third, the distal (top) and proximal (bottom) orientations are determined by the relationship between the centre of mass of the artifact and the location of the centroid of its bounding box (Maier et al. 2023).

Finally, the maximum of the MSII curvature is then calculated as an approximation of the maximum curvature (Mara and Krömker 2013).

16.3.2.2 Scar Segmentation using Morse Theory

The segmentation method used to detect scars originates from Morse theory, which is a technique from differential topology, that has a discrete counterpart introduced by Forman (2001). To use this discrete Morse theory, a mesh with vertices that have a scalar function assigned to them is required. The scalar function used for scar and ridge detection are the maximum MSII curvature values, since they already visually highlight the ridges.

16.3.2.3 Morse-Smale Complex

Following the algorithms described in Robins et al. (2011), discrete Morse theory allows to calculate a combinatorial gradient on the mesh, that leads to the detection of minima, saddle points and maxima (also called critical points) on the surface taking into account the underlying scalar function of the vertices. This allows to extract so-called Morse-Smale complexes (MS complexes) by calculating the adjacencies of these extremal points. The adjacency can be retrieved as lines, so-called separatrices, by following the steepest gradient from maxima to saddle points as well as the steepest gradient from saddle points to minima.

The resulting skeleton-like structure on the mesh can be seen in Figure 16.3a, which schematically depicts a hill and dale surface, with the height function as a scalar function for Morse theory. The maxima (blue), saddle points (green) and minima (red) are shown as well as the separatrices (arrows) connecting them. Note that, by definition, there are no separatrices connecting maxima to minima. Such

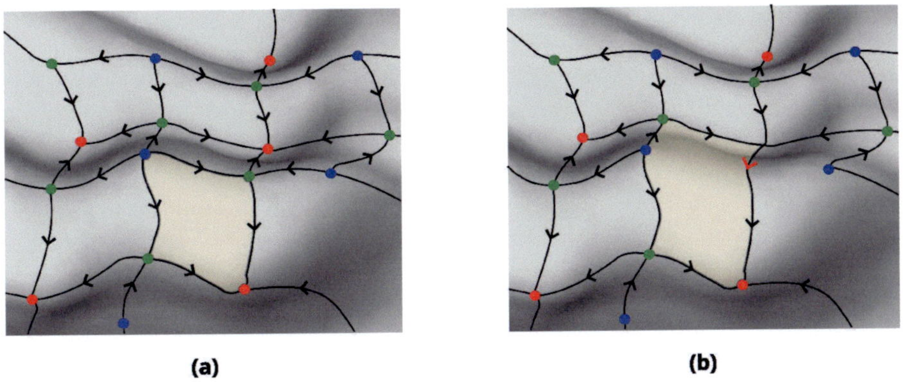

Figure 16.3. (a) MS complex; (b) simplified MS complex.

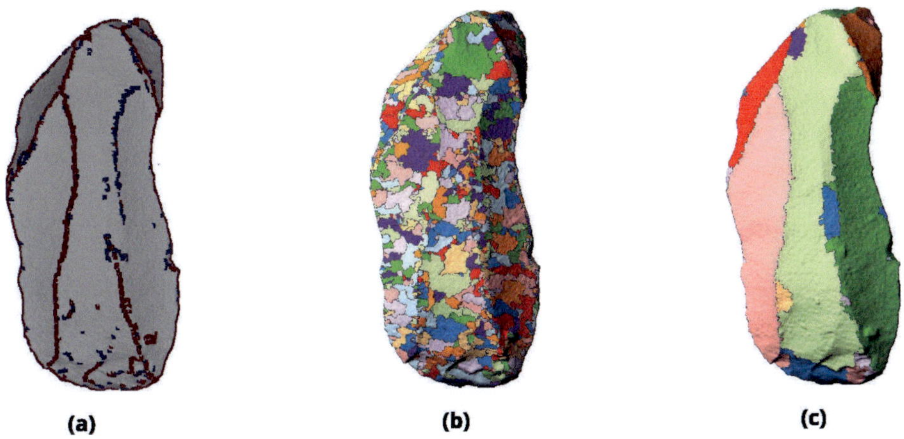

Figure 16.4. (a) Ridges: strong ridges (dark red), weak ridges (dark blue); (b) Over-segmentation; (c) Merging (result)

a MS complex on the mesh automatically indicates a segmentation and divides the surface into regions that are enclosed by separatrices, known as Morse cells. One is highlighted in Figure 16.3a as an illustration.

16.3.2.4 Weak and Strong Ridges

Separatrices represent extremal lines, so they can be used to filter for weak and strong ridges. The mean curvature value of the vertices of a separatrix is used as the importance measure and a double threshold is used to get weak and strong ridges, adding the weak ridges only if they are adjacent to a strong ridge. Figure 16.4a shows the resulting ridges on an example artifact. The advantage over a thresholding on the whole vertices lies in the nature of separatrices, as they are thin connected lines already and taking the mean curvature value along them allows to bridge short interruptions in the ridges.

16.3.2.5 Oversegmentation (Morse Cells)

The next step is getting an oversegmentation of the mesh that aligns with the already detected ridges. Morse theory already provides a natural segmentation, but real datasets contain noise and make this segmentation very fine grained. The skeleton can be simplified by removing small local minima or maxima when their function value distance to the next saddle is below a threshold. A possible step of such a simplification is shown in Figure 16.3b, which leads to enlarged Morse cells. For the segmentation method, Morse cells of a slightly simplified skeleton are taken. This removes noise and ensures that the oversegmentation has cells which are not too small and also keeps the detected ridges in between the Morse cells. Figure 16.4b shows such an oversegmentation.

16.3.2.6 Merging Morse Cells based on Ridges

Using the oversegmentation and the detected ridges, a weighted adjacency graph can be created using the Morse cells from the oversegmentation. The weights are defined as the percentage of detected ridge points along the boundary between two cells. As a final step, neighbouring cells that have no or not enough ridge points detected along their boundary can be iteratively merged. This leads to a final segmentation result (Figure 16.4c) that ensures that there is a predefined percentage of ridge points between all cells.

16.3.2.7 Extracting Spatial Properties of Annotated 3D Meshes

To demonstrate the process with a final, adjusted segmentation, the ground truth data is used; if done

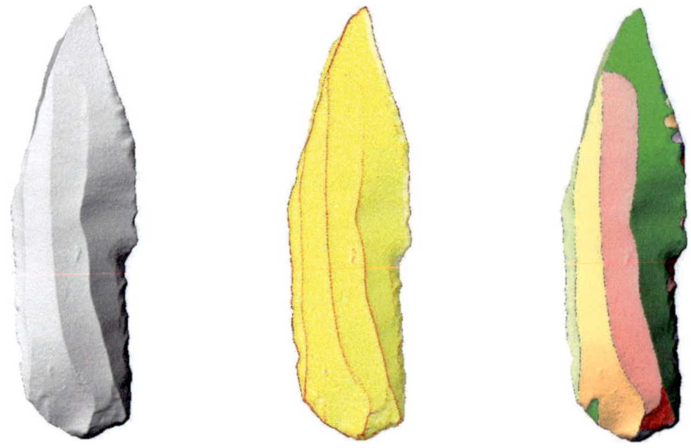

Figure 16.5. Rendered images of artifact GdF 207: (a) Solid view; (b) MSII light view (1.0 mm); (c) GT label view.

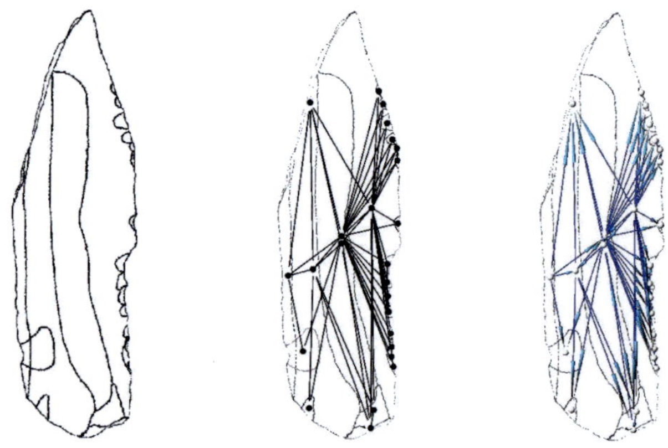

Figure 16.6. GdF 207 models: (a) 3D ridge model; (b) adjacency graph model and ridge model; (c) directed adjacency graph model (direction = manual).

correctly, the ground truth data should be the goal of the segmentation algorithm anyway. Once annotations have been obtained, all colours must be translated into respective labels. Here, due to the high number of scars and the limited number of easily accessible colours in MeshLab, colours can be used repeatedly. Consequently, colour values are collected, and the data is relabelled to isolate only connected components. Each connected component corresponds to one scar. These connected components are then used to divide the 2D manifold into distinct submeshes.

Each connected component has a contour, which can be represented as a polyline. A contour is a circular line consisting of vertices, where each vertex has neighbours from a different connected component. Additionally, each vertex of a contour has 2 neighbours that belong to the same connected component.

These connected components serve as basis for determining the ridges of an artifact. In fact, the contour set is determined by selecting every contour vertex and every face that contains only contour vertices. In a subsequent step, this set of contours can be divided into segments, each of which represents a ridge. Thus, a ridge can be defined as an area where two or more scars share adjacent contours.

16.3.3 Scar-Ridge-Patterns as Graph Models

In this section, the overall approach for representing the connections of scar-ridge patterns using a graph model gets introduced and analysed to determine the direction of their links. Additionally, the visualization of directed and undirected graph models in 3D will be introduced.

16.3.3.1 Scar-Ridge Graph as Source for Digital Drawings

The scar-ridge pattern serves as a source for digital drawings. From the scar-ridge patterns, an adjacency graph model can be abstracted. In this model, each scar is represented as a node. The existence of an undirected link between two nodes is determined by their neighbourhood. Therefore, each ridge can be represented as a link due to the adjacency of the scars. To answer the question of where a scar ends and the ridge begins, it is necessary to differentiate between a scar contour and a ridge segment. This will help to untangle the strong connection between scars and ridges.

While creating the graph model, various properties can be included to specify node or link parameters, such as spatial and non-spatial parameters of scars or ridges. Spatial parameters can include the area of the scar or the mean of a selected parameter, such as the mean MSII curvature values within a scar. In addition to imported scar or ridge parameters, graph parameters describing the relationships between nodes and links can be calculated and used.

In contemporary archaeological practice, the ideal representation of an artifact is a technical drawing that captures the ridges and ripple lines. Having a high-resolution 3D model allows to render alternative images as well as new means of representing a lithic tool assisting in determining the OS. So, two renderings were created, one similar to conceptual drawing and one as a graph model depicting the relations (or connections) between surface segments, i.e., scars and ridges.

In the following graph visualization, scars are represented by spheres. The location of the node is determined by the centre of mass of each scar. If the node must be on the surface of the manifold, the closest point to the centre of mass can be selected.

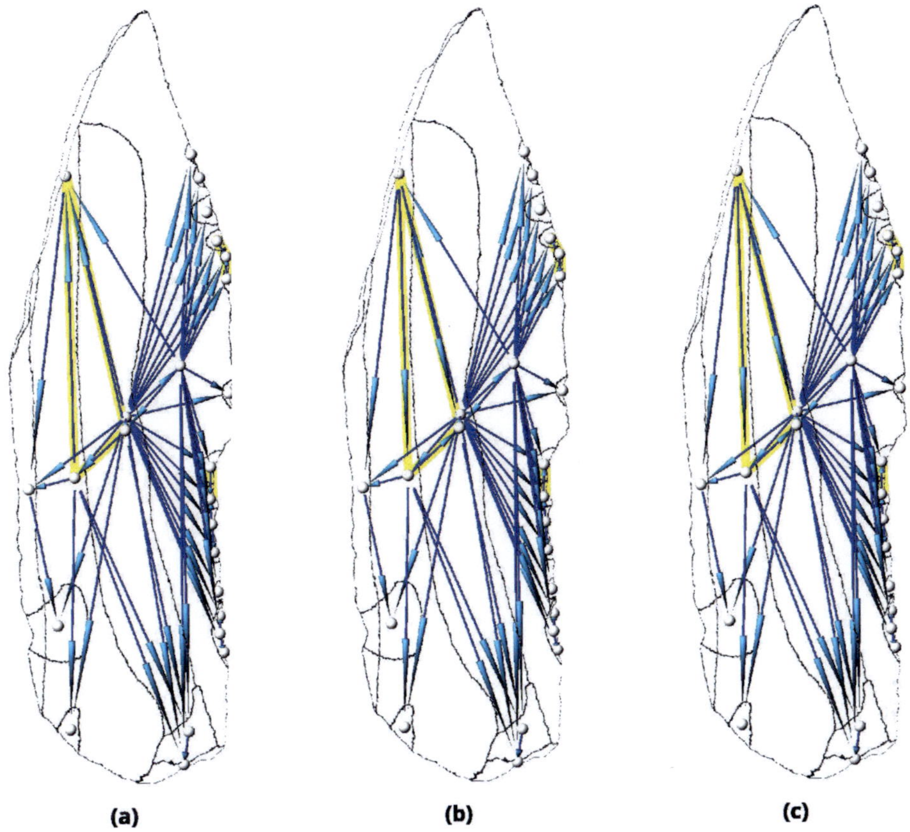

Figure 16.7. Directed 3D graph model of GdF 207 depicting differences in link orientations (yellow): (a) directed by scar area ("greater"); (b) directed by degree ("greater"); (c) directed by betweenness ("greater").

In addition to the scar properties, the segmentation of scar contours into ridges is another relevant parameter. The scar contour is an ordered list of vertices that form a circular closed polyline. When performed ideally, ridges can be viewed as the contour segment where two contours share neighbouring vertices. Thus, each ridge can be considered as two segments comprised of two contours and due to the right orientation of the faces, these are oppositely oriented. All vertices belonging to the ridge can also be considered as link properties.

In this study, we focus on visualizing all contours and therefore filter the mesh for faces consisting of contour vertices only (Figure 16.6a). In the final visualization of the ridge graph model, everything from the nodes over the ridges to the connections in the form of cylinders (Figure 16.6b) or arrows (Figure 16.6c) had to be combined and finally exported.

16.3.3.2 Directing the Graph Model by Parameter

Every undirected graph model possesses properties directly derived from the connectivity of each node and link, such as degree or betweenness centrality. The degree of a node in a graph is the number of nodes that are connected to it by links. Betweenness centrality measures node accessibility. A node with a high betweenness provides insight into the importance of the node in accessing other parts of the graph. A node's betweenness centrality is higher if it needs to be crossed more often to reach other nodes. Conversely, a node on the periphery has a low betweenness centrality.

The procedure for the three parameters is similar. First, an undirected graph model is created. Then the parameter of either the mesh or the graph is extracted and computed. Finally, the difference between two adjacent nodes is estimated. Specifically, the relative difference in area, degree, and betweenness centrality of two adjacent scars are examined to obtain the direction of a link. Due to the exploratory nature of the research, the difference between the nodes was defined as the links direction either from the node with the lower value to one with the higher value ("greater"), or vice versa ("lower"; Figure 16.7). In this context, indegree describes the number of directed links to a node, outdegree the opposite.

16.4 Results and Evaluation

The results presented in this study are divided into two parts: first, the segmentation, where quantitative data is available. Second, creating and visualizing graph models, where a proof of concept is provided.

16.4.1 Segmentation Results

The described segmentation method was implemented in Python and published in Bullenkamp et al. (2023).

The method requires four parameters: persistence for the level of simplification in the oversegmentation, weak and strong ridge thresholds for filtering ridges and a merging parameter for the weighted adjacency graph simplification. Determining these parameters can be laborious. However, the segmentation algorithm is accompanied by a graphical user interface. This allows the user to adjust parameters and obtain visual feedback rather than executing code and importing results into another software for each parameter combination. Furthermore, this article utilizes a pipeline approach to run the segmentation for various parameters and evaluate each combination with the ground truth data (Linsel et al. 2023). Taking the best result for each artifact enables a quantitative evaluation of the segmentation method. For the 62 artifacts with ground truths, the average percentage of correctly labelled vertices is 91.26%, ranging from 81.2% to 97.2%.

In Figure 16.8 some representative results are shown, including the best (e) and worst (d) results of the dataset. Artifacts b, d, and h all have cortex areas, that are supposed to be one label. However, given their rough surface, they have high curvature values that lead to false ridge detection and an oversegmentation of these areas. In Figure 16.8g there is an artifact that gives a good overall result, but two small scars on the right side are not detected. These scars are too small and the ridge between them and the large scar is too weak. Especially artifacts with clear ridges like Figure 16.8a, c, e and f show good results.

16.4.2 Proof of Concept of Graph Modelling

Due to the early stage of this approach, this study will only present prototypical approach of how to use and visualize graph models of lithic artifacts. Digital graph models of lithic artifacts extend the analytical potential of OS's from a manual towards data-driven approaches.

In the case of GdF 207, the relationship between the scars is not difficult to follow with a normal OS diagram for an expert, as shown in Figure 16.9a. But as the complexity of the scar pattern increases, the ability to understand the OS becomes a cognitive challenge. GdF 207 is a blade and has therefore been knapped from the surface of a core, and as a result shows only partly the negatives and hence the complexity of the OS before.

To change perspective and focus on a core, GdF RF.c_49 is analysed (Figure 16.9b, Figure 16.10). In addition, this artifact already had an OS in the form of a drawing (Falcucci et al. 2017). The possible applications of the scar and ridge properties of adjacency graphs are numerous, from simple statistical parameters that can be assigned to either the scars or the ridges, such as the mean, median, and standard deviation of a parameter, e.g., the surface area, to parameters derived directly or indirectly from the relationship between scars and ridges.

To obtain the direction of a connection and to evaluate this interpretation, this research uses the relative difference in area, degree, and betweenness of two adjacent scars. To calculate the area of the scars, submeshes of the labels were created and their surface area was calculated.

16.4.2.1 Parameter Directed Graphs and Evaluation

The accuracy of GdF 207 and GdF RF.c_49 differ and represent the range of accuracy of the graph computation. While the accuracy of GdF 207 ranges from 78 to 84 %, the accuracy of GdF RF.c_49 ranges from 49 to 53% (Table 16.1). The difference can be partly explained by their object categories: while GdF 207 is a retouched blade from which several small flakes have been removed along the edges, leading to a strong connection between dorsal and ventral scars along the edges without regard to their position in the OS, GdF RF.c_49 is a core from which flakes of more similar size have been removed. Due to the completely different ways in which Palaeolithic people handled these artifacts, one as a source for tools and the other as a tool itself, the scar patterns naturally differ.

In both cases, the relative area, degree and betweenness of the scars lead to similar results, with only a range of 6 % (GdF 207) and 4 % (GdF RF.c_49). This could possibly be explained by an underlying relationship between the size of a scar and its relevance in the graph. Figure 16.11 shows that GdF 207 contains prominent outliers that have an impact on all parameters considered.

Even without considering the poor results of GdF RF.c_49, the graph models for GdF 207 have difficulties detecting the correct relationship between dorsal scars, which are either similar in size or earlier scars have been overwritten by later ones. Furthermore, dorsal-ventral links are also prone to error, as the most prominent ventral scar is the largest scar on the artifact, considering that it is almost complete. This scar is the youngest scar on the artifact, not considering later retouches. But it is one of the earliest, according to all the data derived from the graph models.

As using graph models have been successfully used to describe complex situations allowing for queries and

Accuracy of the Graph Models

Parameter	*GdF 207*	*GdF.c_49*
Area	**84 %**	52 %
Degree	78 %	49 %
Betweenness	79 %	**53 %**

Table 16.1. Evaluation link directions of graph models according to area, degree and betweenness.

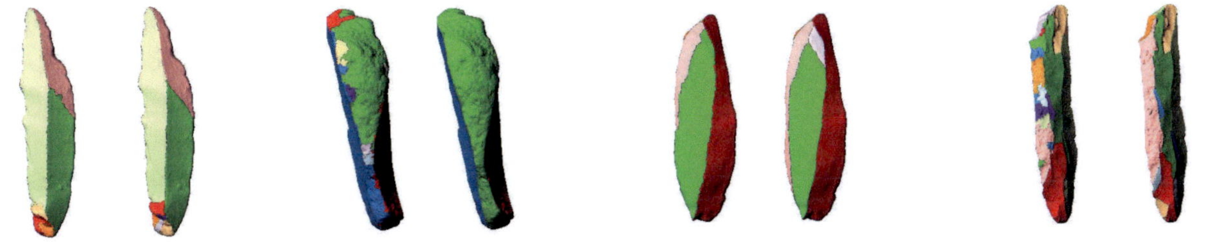

(a) GdF *713* (95.6%) **(b)** GdF *75* (84.6%) **(c)** GdF *2490* (93.6%) **(d)** GdF *6626* (81.2%)

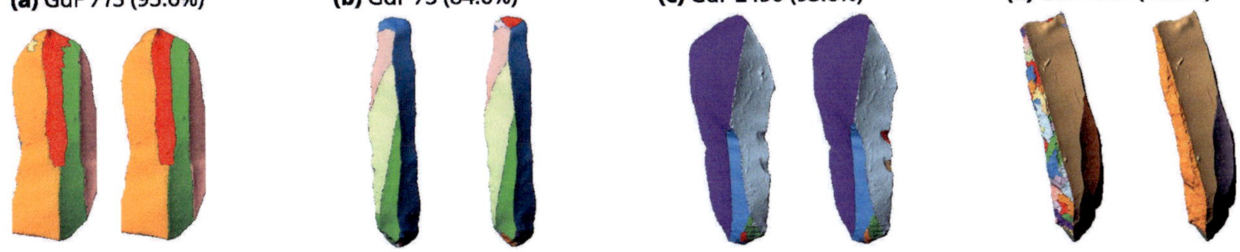

(e) GdF *10356* (97.2%) **(f)** GdF *752* (94.9%) **(g)** GdF *4501* (97.1%) **(h)** GdF *700* (83.4%)

Figure 16.8. Difference between results (left) and ground truths (right).

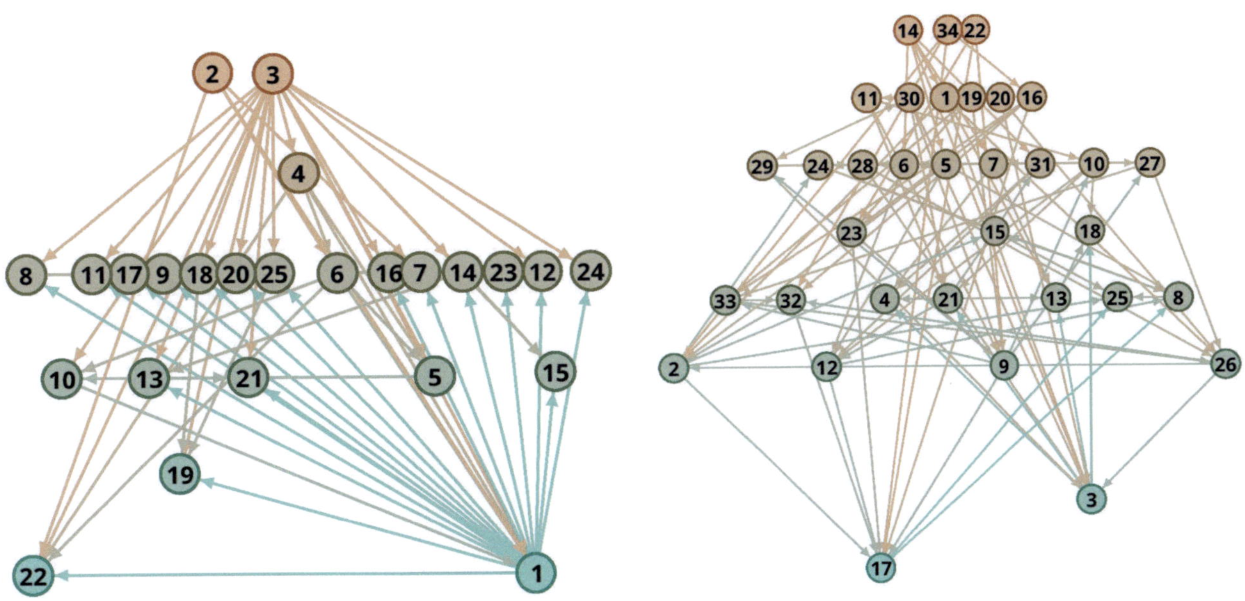

(a) **(b)**

Figure 16.9. Hierarchical graph diagram based on indegree created with Gephi (Bastian et al. 2009) (node colour = indegree (brown: low, turquoise: high), link colour = indegree of source node, y-position: indegree); (a) GdF 207; (b) GdF RF.c_49.

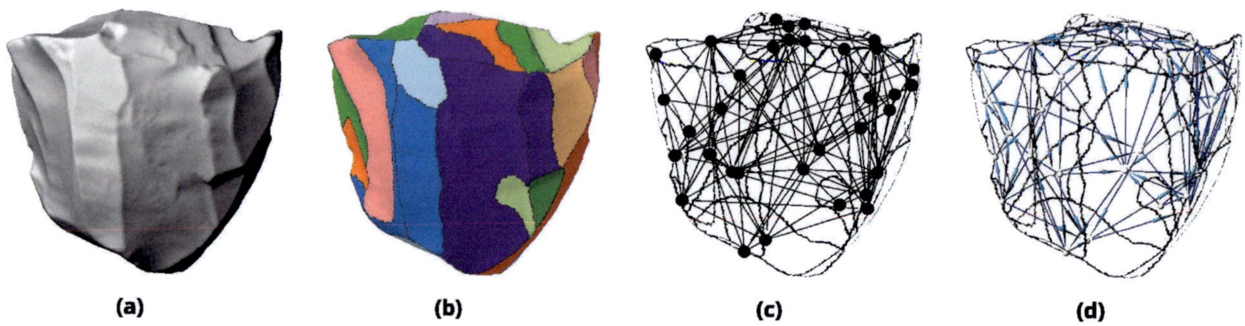

Figure 16.10. (a) 3D mesh of *GdF RF.c_49*; (b) ground truth label; (c) adjacency graph model; (d) graph model (direction = Falcucci et al. 2017).

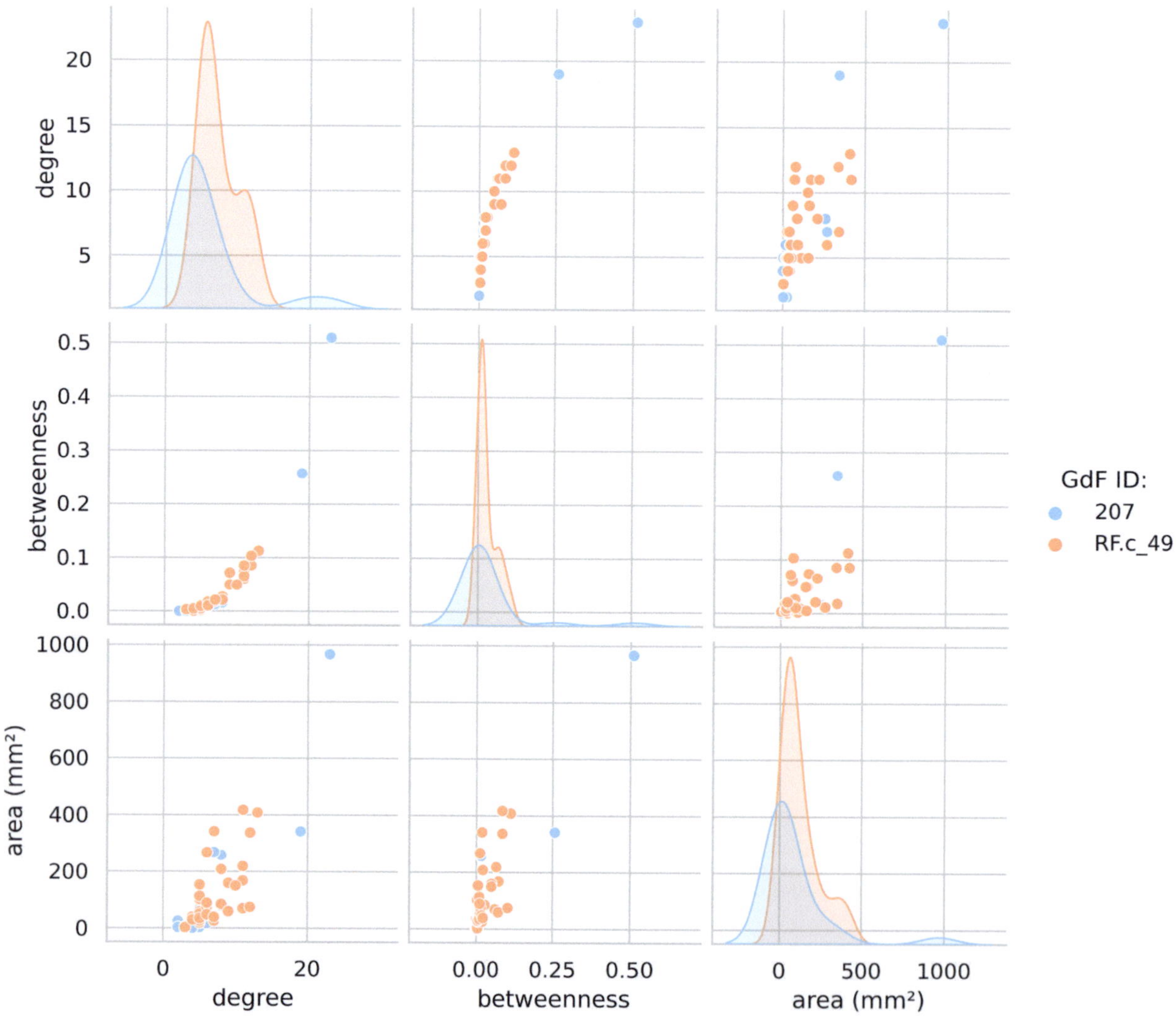

Figure 16.11. Comparison of area (mm^2), degree and betweenness of the scars of GdF RF.c_49 and GdF 207.

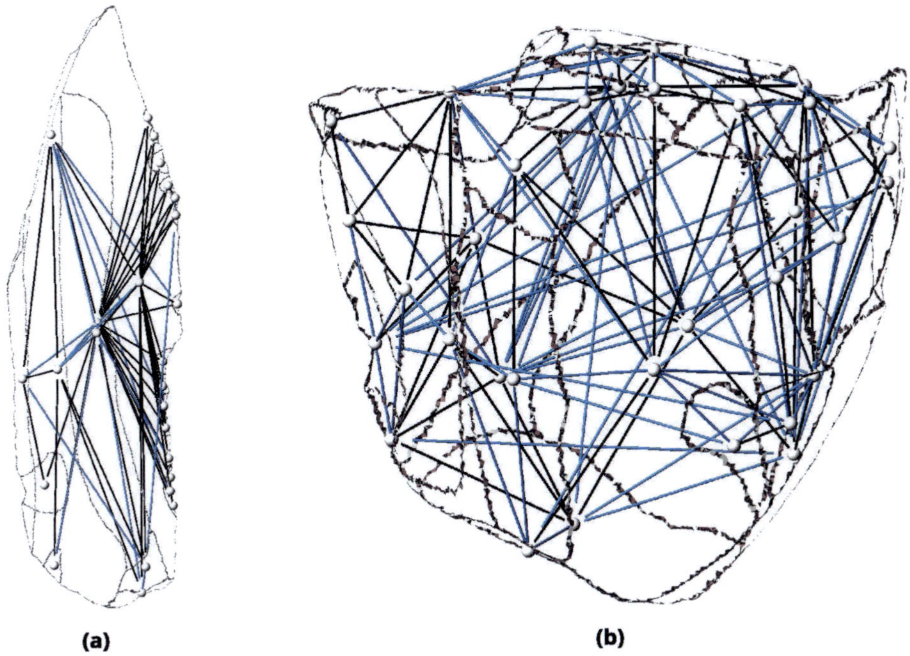

Figure 16.12. Evaluation of best performing directions (black = true; blue = false); (a) *GdF 207*: Area ("greater"); (b) *GdF RF.c_49*: Betweenness ("lower").

visualizations, it will help to understand the underlying patterns. A similar effect can be expected for the question of determining OS's. Having a small number of easily understandable parameters is by design to make the approach accessible for a wider range of users. Automatic determination of parameters will be a next step. Furthermore, the graph representation can also be useful for teaching OS's conceptually.

16.5 Outlook and further Applications

One of the central challenges in archaeology is the lack of open, digitized data that can be used to evaluate automated approaches, which applies in particular to 3D models, segmentations and OS's. This limits the development of new methods and ultimately restricts the scope of future research. To address this, we have published along this article our annotated dataset (Linsel et al. 2023), which we used to evaluate our segmentation algorithm (Bullenkamp et al. 2023). The OS's are still subject to ongoing research and will be published later. However, we are expanding our dataset to include more manually annotated artifacts by scanning lithic artifacts, e.g., leaf points from different sites, creating graph models, and adding OS's as well.

One of the key limitations of exclusively examining artifacts in the absence of their position within an OS is the dependency on surface properties and expert knowledge. To ensure the accuracy of an 3D OS dataset, we will aim to incorporate 3D data from experimental knapping series where the connection between positive and negative scars within an OS is documented in future work. Merging a complete OS Graph with 3D data will lead to the development of a more precise GT dataset, enabling us to adapt methods to real datasets.

16.5.1 Relative Chronology of Scars (OS)

We are currently working on new methods to determine OS's automatically. As discussed in this article, the results of the graph model-based OS are promising but due the univariate method, and the small dataset used to determine the direction, the results and the gained insights are limited. Hence, one of the next needed steps is to combine multiple parameters of more artifacts in the graph model to obtain a better insight of the internal mechanics of the knapping process and as a result of the OS's. In this regard, we are currently working on implementing two methods, which are derived from the archaeological practice described by Pastoors et al. (2015).

This research serves as a first step towards abstracting human lithic tools in a simplified and computer readable way. We do consider our graph models of individual tools as intermediate result being a data source for graph-based machine learning, which has shown great potential in recognizing cuneiform signs (Kriege et al. 2018), and ultimately as a stepping stone towards a more detailed understanding of lithic technologies.

Acknowledgements

We thank Jürgen Richter for his help in creating the operational sequences. We also thank Ernst Max Stötzner for his contributions to GigaMesh and Rebecca Gnau for her help in creating the validation data for the graph models. We thank Sebastian Hageneuer for his role as PCI recommender and to the two reviewers for sharing their valuable suggestions.

Funding

This research was directly funded by the Martin-Luther University Halle-Wittenberg and conducted at the Institute of Computer Science.

Conflict of interest disclosure

The authors declare that they comply with the PCI rule of having no financial conflicts of interest in relation to the content of the article.

Data, Script, Code and Supplementary Information Availability

In addition to this publication, we provide a code publication of the segmentation (Bullenkamp et al. 2023) and a data publication (Linsel et al. 2023). Due to the early stage of the graph models, which were heavily inspired by the discussion at the CAA conference, we cannot provide its code and data at this stage of our research.

Peer review

This article has been reviewed and recommended by PCI Archaeology.

Hageneuer, Sebastian. 2024. "A valuable contribution to automated analysis of palaeolithic artefacts." *Peer Community in Archaeology* 100413. DOI: 10.24072/pci.archaeo.100413.

References

Barone, Sandro, Alessandro Paoli, Paolo Neri, Armando Razionale, Maria De Santis, and Federico Mailland. 2018. "Automatic illustration of lithics from 3d scanned models." *IOP Conference Series: Materials Science and Engineering* 364: 012017. DOI: 10.1088/1757-899X/364/1/012017.

Bastian, Mathieu , Sebastien Heymann, and Mathieu Jacomy. 2009. "Gephi: an open source software for exploring and manipulating networks." In *Proceedings of the Third international AAAI conference on weblogs and social media, 17-20 May 2009, San Jose, California, USA*. AAAI Publications.

Bullenkamp, Jan Philipp, Theresa Häberle, and Hubert Mara. 2023. *MorseMesh*. Version v0.1. DOI: 10.5281/zenodo.8297368.

Cignoni, Paolo, Marco Callieri, Massimiliano Corsini, Matteo Dellepiane, Fabio Ganovelli, and Guido Ranzuglia. 2008. "MeshLab: an Open-Source Mesh Processing Tool." In *Eurographics Italian Chapter Conference*, 129–36. The Eurographics Association. DOI: 10.2312/LocalChapterEvents/ItalChap/ItalianChapConf2008/129-136.

Falcucci, Armando, Nicholas J. Conard, and Marco Peresani. 2017. "A critical assessment of the Protoaurignacian lithic technology at Fumane Cave and its implications for the definition of the earliest Aurignacian." *PLOS ONE* 12: 1–43. DOI: 10.1371/journal.pone.0189241.

Falcucci, Armando, and Marco Peresani. 2022a. *The Open Aurignacian Project. Volume 1: Fumane Cave in northeastern Italy*. Version 2.1.1. Zenodo. DOI: 10.5281/zenodo.7664308.

Falcucci, Armando, and Marco Peresani. 2022b. *The Open Aurignacian Project. Volume 1: Fumane Cave in northeastern Italy*. Version 1.0.0. Zenodo. DOI: 10.5281/zenodo.6362150.

Forman, Robin. 2001. "A User's Guide To Discrete Morse Theory." *Séminaire Lotharingien de Combinatoire* 48: B48c.

Gellis, Jason J., Camila R. Smith, and Robert A. Foley. 2022. "PyLithics: A Python package for stone tool analysis." *Journal of Open Source Software* 7: 3738. DOI: 10.21105/joss.03738.

Herzlinger, Gadi and Leore Grosman. 2018. "AGMT3-D: A software for 3-D landmarks-based geometric morphometric shape analysis of archaeological artifacts." *PLOS ONE* 13: 1–17. DOI: 10.1371/journal.pone.0207890.

Higham, Thomas, Fiona Brock, Marco Peresani, Alberto Broglio, Rachel Wood, and Katerina Douka. 2009. "Problems with radiocarbon dating the Middle to Upper Palaeolithic transition in Italy." *Quaternary Science Reviews* 28: 1257–67. DOI: 10.1016/j.quascirev.2008.12.018.

Homburg, Timo, Robert Zwick, Hubert Mara, and Kai-Christian Bruhn. May 2022. "Annotated 3D-Models of Cuneiform Tablets." *Journal of Open Archaeology Data* 10. DOI: 10.5334/joad.92.

Kriege, Nils. M., Matthias Fey, Denis Fisseler, Petra Mutzel, and Frank Weichert. 2018. "Recognizing Cuneiform Signs Using Graph Based Methods." arXiv. DOI: 10.48550/arXiv.1802.05908.

Linsel, Florian, Jan Philipp Bullenkamp, and Hubert Mara. 2023. *3D Data Derivatives of Grotta di Fumane: GigaMesh-processed, Annotations and Segmentations*. Version 1.0.0. Zenodo. DOI: 10.5281/zenodo.8288967.

Maier, Andreas, Robin John, Florian Linsel, Georg Roth, Walpurga Antl-Weiser, Lisa Bauer, Norbert Buchinger,

Levin Cavak, Helen Hoffmann, Janos Puschmann, Marcel Schemmel, Viola C. Schmid, Ulrich Simon, and Roswitha Thomas. 2023. “Analyzing Trends in Material Culture Evolution – a Case Study of Gravettian Points from Lower Austria and Moravia.” *Journal of Paleolithic Archaeology* 6: 15. DOI: 10.1007/s41982-023-00145-z.

Mara, Hubert, and Susanne Krömker. 2013. “Vectorization of 3D-Characters by Integral Invariant Filtering of High-Resolution Triangular Meshes.” In *2013 12th International Conference on Document Analysis and Recognition, Washington, DC, USA,* 62–66. IEEE. https://doi.org/10.1109/ICDAR.2013.21.

Mara, Hubert, Suzanne Krömker, Stefan Jakob, and Bernd Breuckmann. 2010. “GigaMesh and Gilgamesh 3D Multiscale Integral Invariant Cuneiform Character Extraction.” In *Proceedings of the 11th VAST International Symposium on Virtual Reality, Archaeology and Intelligent Cultural Heritage*, edited by Allessandro. Artusi, Morwena Joly-Parvex, Genevieve Lucet, Denis Pitzalis, and Alejandro Ribes, 131-138. The Eurographics Association. DOI: 10.2312/VAST/VAST10/131-138.

Marín-Arroyo, Ana B., Gabriele Terlato, Marco Vidal-Cordasco, and Marco Peresani. 2023. “Subsistence of early anatomically modern humans in Europe as evidenced in the Protoaurignacian occupations of Fumane Cave, Italy.” *Scientific Reports* 13: 3788. DOI: 10.1038/s41598-023-30059-3.

Pastoors, Andreas. 2000. “Standardization and Individuality in the Production Process of Bifacial Tools – Leaf-shaped Scrapers from the Middle Paleolithic Open Air Site Saré Kaya I (Crimea). A contribution to understanding the method of Working Stage Analysis.” In *Neanderthals and Modern Humans – Discussing the Transition. Central and Eastern Europe from 50.000 – 30.000 B.P.*, edited by J. Orschiedt, and G.-C. Weniger, 243–55. Mettmann: Neanderthal Museum.

Pastoors, Andreas, Yvonne Tafelmaier, and Gerd-Cristian Weniger. 2015. “Quantification of late Pleistocene core configurations: Application of the Working Stage Analysis as estimation method for technological behavioural efficiency.” *Quartär* 62: 62–84. DOI: 10.7485/QU62_3.

Pop, C. M. 2019. *cornelmpop/Lithics3D: v0.4.2*. Version v0.4.2. Zenodo. DOI: 10.5281/zenodo.2648097.

Pulla, S., A. Razdan, and G. Farin. 2001. “Improved curvature estimation for watershed segmentation of 3-dimensional meshes.” *IEEE Transactions on Visualization and Computer Graphics* 5: 308–21.

Richardson, Eitan, Leore Grosman, Uzy Smilansky, and Michael Werman. 2014. “Extracting Scar and Ridge Features from 3D-scanned Lithic Artifacts.” In *Archaeology in the Digital Era: Papers from the 40th Annual Conference of Computer Applications and Quantitative Methods in Archaeology (CAA), Southampton, 26-29 March 2012*, edited by G. Earl, T. Sly, D. Wheatley, I. Romanowska, K. Papadopoulos, P. Murrieta-Flores, and A. Chrysanthi, 83–92. Amsterdam: Amsterdam University Press.

Richter, Jürgen. 1997. *Sesselfelsgrotte III. Der G-Schichten-Komplex der Sesselfelsgrotte. Zum Verständnis des Micoquien.* Stuttgart: Franz Steiner Verlag.

Richter, Jürgen. 2004. “Copies of flakes: operational sequences of foliate pieces from Buran-Kaya III level B1.” *The Middle Paleolithic and Early Upper Paleolithic of Eastern Crimea* 3: 233–47.

Robins, Vanessa, Peter Wood, and Adrian Sheppard. 2011. “Theory and Algorithms for Constructing Discrete Morse Complexes from Grayscale Digital Images.” *IEEE transactions on pattern analysis and machine intelligence* 33: 1646–58. DOI: 10.1109/TPAMI.2011.95.

Shea, John J. 2013. “Lithics Basics.” In: *Stone Tools in the Paleolithic and Neolithic Near East: A Guide*, edited by John J. Shea, 17–46. Cambridge: Cambridge University Press. DOI: 10.1017/CBO9781139026314.003.

Weiss, Marcel. 2020. “The Lichtenberg Keilmesser – it's all about the angle.” *PLOS ONE* 15: 1–31. DOI: 10.1371/journal.pone.0239718.

Yang, Xi, Katsutsugu Matsuyama, and Kouichi Konno. 2017. “Interactive visualization of assembly instruction for stone tools restoration.” In *2017 IEEE Pacific Visualization Symposium (PacificVis), Seoul, Korea (South),* 270–4. IEEE. DOI: 10.1109/PACIFICVIS.2017.8031604.

17 A Focus on the Future of our Tiny Piece of the Past

Digital Archiving of a Long-term Multi-participant Regional Project

Scott Madry
Research Laboratories of Archaeology
The University of North Carolina
at Chapel Hill
madrys@email.unc.edu

Gregory Jansen
Advanced Information Collaboratory
The University of Maryland

Seth Murray
College of Humanities
and Social Sciences
North Carolina State University

Elizabeth Jones
Research Laboratories of Archaeology
The University of North Carolina
at Chapel Hill

Lia Willcoxon
College of Humanities
and Social Sciences
North Carolina State University

Ebtihal Alhashem
School of Information
and Library Sciences
The University of North Carolina
at Chapel Hill

Abstract

This paper will consider the practical realities that have been encountered while seeking to create a usable Digital Archiving system of a long-term and multi-participant research project. The lead author has been involved in archaeological and landscape research in the Burgundy region of France for the past 45 years. This long-lived project has continued across several generations, institutions, continents, and disciplines, and began in the mid-1970s before many of our commonly used digital data types and capabilities even existed. Over the decades, many individual researchers, students, and local community members have participated in our broadly defined research activities, conducting field and laboratory research, and they have, cumulatively, woven a tapestry of knowledge regarding some 2000 years of the interaction between peoples and their landscapes in our study area. Our project has endeavoured to understand how different societies, with their differing political and technological capabilities and limitations, have both impacted and have been formed by the landscape that they have inhabited over this time. We have conducted an explicitly interdisciplinary approach using many interwoven disciplinary techniques and perspectives to try to develop a comprehensive and integrated understanding of these questions, as well as developing and refining the various toolsets involved in our work. Many project participants have moved on to other interests and some have passed away. Homes and personal archives have sadly burned, and offices and labs have been flooded. All the while, an analogue method of work has transitioned to a new digital paradigm that is completely unrecognizable from how we began our journey. As this project slowly winds down, the issues of both analogue and digital data preservation and the means of providing continued access to other researchers who may be interested in accessing our vast repositories and datasets has become one of great interest to our group. How can we address the proper archiving and metadata of thousands of individual analogue and digital records and datasets located in multiple institutions and attics? How can we even accurately know what we all have? How can these be properly archived and preserved? And most importantly, how can other researchers gain access to these for future use after we are no longer here to share them?

Keywords: Digital archiving; Archaeology; Burgundy, France; Historical Ecology; Dataverse; Dryad

In *Advances in Digital Archaeology. Proceedings of the 2023 conference Computer Applications and Quantitative Methods in Archaeology – 50 years of synergy*, edited by J.W.H.P. Verhagen, J. Waagen, A. Brandsen, A. Queffelec, R.M. Visser and D. Taelman, 225–232. Leiden: Sidestone Press.

17.1 Introduction

Researchers have been conducting a long-term program of investigations in the southern portion of Burgundy, France since the mid-1970s (Crumley and Marquardt 1987; Madry et al. 2023). This unusually large and diverse project has amassed a very large and disparate amount of data in many formats over the decades. The data gathered over a span of 45 years by a plethora of researchers from diverse institutions encompasses a wide array of sources. This includes data from archaeological and aerial surveys, information derived from historical documents, geophysical and geological datasets, aerial imagery and remote sensing data, historical maps, Geographic Information System (GIS) data, Global Positioning System (GPS) location data, historical documents, and ethnographic interviews, among other data types.

Initially, these data were only "archived" by the individual researcher who collected the data, often kept in personal or university facilities, file drawers, and map cases. In the early days of the project, little thought was given to the concept of permanent archiving of these data, as the publications were considered the final products, and as the research world transitioned from an analogue to digital paradigm, many of the original records and data were simply ignored.

Digital archiving has become an established field of study, primarily within schools of library and information science. It integrates traditional library and archival methods and theory, computer science, databases, internet technologies, and the various disciplinary traditions of those seeking to properly archive their data. Digital archiving began more as an end-of-career records repository when researchers became concerned about preserving the integrity of their research holdings and ensuring continuity of access. But it has evolved to be a tool provided to new professionals to be used throughout one's career, providing an easily accessed repository while work is underway, and creating a lasting digital repository when a project or career is completed. This has also been a subject of important discussion within the archaeology community and the Computer Applications in Archaeology community (Huvila 2008; Wright and Richards 2018; Richards et al. 2021).

As our project has begun to wind down, and more of our team are nearing or in retirement, we have begun the process of considering what life after this project will be like, and what should happen to the large amounts of data that have been amassed. Commonly, for such projects, files were simply placed in cardboard boxes and, hopefully, these would be retained in a university storage somewhere. But oftentimes, these unique records were simply pitched out, either by the researchers themselves when they "downsized" or moved, or by family members who survived them, not knowing the importance of these records.

17.2 Methods

Our project began to consider what the options might be, and began a tentative and, frankly, uninformed process of trying to learn about what digital archiving was and what our options might be. Initially, we did some web searches and discovered the Dspace system (https://dspace.mit.edu), maintained by the Massachusetts Institute of Technology (MIT). We made a tentative attempt to download the system and begin an archive of our data, but we were not successful, partly due to the unfamiliarity with the nature of digital archives, partly due to our lack of experience in the field, and partly due to the large number of records and files that we held. Our first attempt was a failure, and we had to regroup and reconsider what our options might be.

Later, in our evolving discovery process, we evaluated several other currently available digital archiving environments and options, and we had the good fortune to meet and work with experts in the field, which enabled us to better understand the processes, strengths, and limitations of these various capabilities, and to comprehend how we and our specific data collections might fit into the modern digital archiving environment.

As our earlier attempt at archiving our large and disparate data collections ourselves using DSpace was not successful, due to the large amount of data and, as archaeologists, our unfamiliarity with the digital archiving world, we sought other options. The pressing importance of creating a permanent repository for our data within a reasonable amount of time with the resources and skills available to us has led to a different approach, and recently we conducted a comparative analysis of different digital archiving environments to assess their suitability for the preservation and dissemination of our archaeological data.

Having enlisted the assistance of experts in the field, we selected two digital archiving environments for consideration, based on their popularity, functionality, and accessibility: Dataverse, and Dryad. We evaluated their technical features, such as metadata standards, file formats, storage capacity, interoperability, and access control. These two environments were selected because two key members of our project maintain faculty status at two universities that maintain digital archive infrastructures for their faculty using these two environments, and we would, therefore, have access to professional archival support at our respective institutions.

Since two of our home institutions use Dataverse (UNC-CH) and Dryad (NCSU) for their digital repositories, these became obvious choices for us. Having an institutional repository, maintained by our universities and with skilled archivists available to support our activities was a clear improvement over our failed initial self-guided efforts. UNC-CH uses the Dataverse system for their digital data repository, originally developed by Harvard University and in use by nearly 100 institutions around the world (https://dataverse.org). This is managed by the UNC Odum Institute Data Archive (https://odum.unc.edu/archive), which has over 50 years of data management experience. Their mission is to provide trusted long-term preservation and stewardship of research data assets to broaden scientific inquiry, promote research producibility, and foster data fluency now and into the future. The Dataverse environment has a very flexible metadata system which is data driven and powered by "metadata blocks" that are defined in the User's guide. It also has multiple metadata customization options as well. Dataverse

> *"is committed to using standard-compliant metadata to ensure that a Dataverse installation's metadata can be mapped easily to standard metadata schemas and be exported into JSON format (XML for tabular file metadata) for preservation and interoperability."*[1]

Dryad (https://datadryad.org/stash) is used by NC State University, which provides free digital data archiving for its faculty and students using this system. The data repository (https://www.lib.ncsu.edu/do/data-management/dryad) has integration features with Zenodo, a useful tool in archaeological publication and research. Zenodo is an open repository developed and operated by CERN in Europe and permits the deposit of a wide range of documents, data, reports, and more in a structured and recoverable format. Dryad is a non-profit organization that provides a curated repository for data underlying scientific publications (Dryad n.d.). It supports a wide range of file formats, metadata standards, and identifiers. It also offers long-term preservation, data citation, and integration with journals and other repositories. Dataverse is generally comparable to Dryad in capability and features, but they are two separate systems.

To ensure the quality and reproducibility of our research, we follow the FAIR principles for data management promoted by both Dataverse and Dryad (FORCE11 n.d.). FAIR stands for Findable, Accessible, Interoperable and Reusable. This means that our data will be assigned persistent identifiers, stored in a public repository with clear metadata and licenses, compatible with multiple formats and tools, and available for reuse by other researchers with minimal barriers. In order to efficiently apply these principles, we began by creating and using an informational Excel spreadsheet that remained consistent with data organization standards for spreadsheets (Broman and Woo 2018).

Having made the choice of these two institutional repositories and their respective archiving environments, we began an initial data search and data preparation process to prepare our data for entry into the two archives. Upon completing the data preparation process, we will upload our datasets to our respective institutional repositories. During the upload process, we will assign appropriate metadata standards, file formats, and persistent identifiers to each dataset, following the recommendations of the respective platforms.

By using Dataverse and Dryad as digital archiving environments for our archaeological data, we seek to promote transparent, reproducible, and collaborative research practices, ultimately contributing to the advancement of the field. Our hope is that our data will prove useful to future researchers.

17.3 Process

Having decided on the use of these two institutional archiving systems, we have begun the initial analysis of our needs and goals, along with – given our inexperience – an initial investigation into what digital archiving is and is not, and what it, in its current state of evolution, can and cannot provide to our particular situation. It has been a steep learning curve for those of us without experience in this field, but we have been fortunate to have the assistance of subject matter experts who have eased our way. We have connected with some very experienced digital archivists at several institutions who have been extremely helpful and generous with their time and expertise to assist us.

17.3.1 Locating Data

As a practical first step, we have begun to amass the first order listing of all extant project data, in both analogue and digital formats, from both current and former project participants. Over 40 people have worked on the project at some point, and several are now retired and, sadly, several are no longer with us. We have reached out to current and former participants in our project and have asked them if they hold any data from the time of their involvement in the project, and if they would be willing to share their data with us to include in the digital repository. Several have responded positively and have provided us with trays of 35 mm slides, personal papers and recordings, and digital documents. Two previous project participants very regrettably suffered major house fires at various times, and there was a flooding event in the 1990s at Dr. Madry's lab at Rutgers university, resulting in the loss of important project data, some of which had no backup or duplicate copies. This reinforces the importance of creating and uploading such data while the project is ongoing, rather than simply storing data in the closet.

17.3.2 Cataloguing our Data

Our second step was to create the first order cataloguing of all extant project data, in both analogue and digital formats. This catalogue was created and designed to include information on general data type, amounts, condition,

1 https://guides.dataverse.org/en/latest/user/appendix.html

location, sensitivity, ownership, etc. An initial Google Sheets spreadsheet on a shared Google Drive was created to catalogue what and how much of each type of record has been located for use in this extended project.

17.3.3 Data

Our project, with its many individual components, has generated significant amounts of disparate data. Fortunately, over the years, much of our existing analogue data has already been scanned or is in the process of being scanned by project participants. These include large numbers of 35 mm slides (remember those?), paper field documents, field maps, paper aerial photographs, paper and digital historical documents and manuscripts, audio recordings, paper and scanned digital maps, and other field and lab documents and archival records. Most of these still do not have any item-level metadata, provenance, or keywords at this point, and this will be a vital component of our subsequent work. We are in the process of defining the final metadata standards for each of the two systems. While these are similar, we need to define a comprehensive metadata approach and are still in the process of defining this. At the same time, we are being guided by our experts in the creation of a comprehensive controlled vocabulary for the keywords. This is no small task, as it must include many disciplinary terms and geographical placenames, many of which have changed over time. For example, many of our historical maps have had four or even five spellings for the same town or location over the centuries. This work is ongoing.

17.4 Work Program and Project Strategy

Having chosen our two institutional digital archiving software systems and repositories and having learned what institutional support will be available to our project members, we next had to map out a realistic work program to populate our archives at our two respective institutions. We then began the actual process of creating, annotating, populating, and managing our digital project archives. We are using, as stated above, two different systems, because two major project participants are affiliated with different institutions using different digital archiving systems. While this is an unwelcomed complexity, we are working to ensure that we will end up with an archive that will be easily searched and accessed externally. We will not, as far as is practical, duplicate data, with each researcher archiving their own data at their own institution. In order to facilitate this, we are in the process of creating a web-based project archival website which will provide seamless external access to data regardless of which university archive the data are located in. Current state-of-the-art online finding aid structures will be developed in order to allow access to all project data located at either repository.

An overall digital archiving strategy was developed that outlines how the materials are to be digitized, stored, and made accessible. This strategy included factors such as the format and size of the materials, the required storage capacity, the sensitivity of the data, and the accessibility needs of future users. The proposed framework for the Burgundy digital archiving process began by evaluating these current digital archiving environments (Dataverse and Dryad) in this context. This involved assessing factors such as modes of use, scalability, and potential for integration or interoperability with other tools and platforms such as those made available by our institutions.

17.4.1 Initial Data Catalogue

An initial digital asset inventory of all existing data, in both analogue and digital formats, from all current and former project participants was generated in an online Google Sheets spreadsheet, as shown below in Figure 17.1.

This list includes information on the data type, rationale for archive, location, origin, producers, and contributors, medium, data format, current mode of access (analogue or digital), privacy and activity, data size, geotagging, keywords, and physical or digital repository location. A Google Sheets spreadsheet in a shared Google Drive folder, titled "Digital Asset Inventory", was created to catalogue the data, and track the progress of the project, so that all interested project participants had access and could provide input into the process, add additional data, and assist in the work. When cataloguing the resources found in our inventory, special care was taken to ensure that human subjects and sensitive archaeological site data were appropriately protected.

This "first order" spreadsheet was created, listing all the types of data, owner, security levels, keywords, etc., as shown above in Figure 17.1. After an initial review and much internal discussion and advice from our digital archiving experts, a total of 16 separate "buckets" of archival data types were decided upon, and individual, customized spreadsheets were then created for each of these, which contained details specific to each data type. These 16 data buckets are:

1. Ethnographic interviews and recordings
2. Documents in MS Word, Excel, and PowerPoint format, as well as those created with Google Docs Editors and OpenOffice
3. Digital GIS data in either raster or vector format
4. Digital remote sensing imagery from multiple satellite systems dating back to 1964
5. Scanned aerial photographs
6. Historical documents of many types
7. Data related to GNSS coordinates and times and geotagged photos
8. Academic papers and reports
9. Genealogy data
10. Websites and data in HTML format
11. Videos and movies, including computer visualizations

Product	Rationale	Origin	Producer(s)	Contributor	Medium	Format	Access	Repository	Owner
Maps	Maps of Burgundy	Multiple, IGN, BNF, AN, LOC	Multiple, IGN, BNF, AN, LOC		Paper	Analog		UNC Dataverse	S. Madry
Maps digital	Scanned maps	Multiple, IGN, BN	Multiple, IGN, BNF, AN, LOC		Digital	Digital		UNC Dataverse	S. Madry
Vertical aerials analog	1945 aerials	US DOD	US DOD			Analog		UNC Dataverse	S. Madry
Vertical aerials digital	1945 aerials	US DOD				Digital		UNC Dataverse	S. Madry
IGN aerials digital	IGN mapping ph	IGN				Digital		UNC Dataverse	S. Madry
Oblique aerials	aerail photos	Multiple				Analog		UNC Dataverse	S. Madry
Oblique aerials digital	aerail photos					Digital		UNC Dataverse	S. Madry
Remote Sensing data	Satellite imagery of various dates	Landsat, ESA, JAXA	US, ESA, Japan			Digital		UNC Dataverse	S. Madry
GPS files	GPS ground points		US GPS			Digital		UNC Dataverse	S. Madry
GIS files	GIS data		Multiple			Digital		UNC Dataverse	S. Madry
35mm slides	ground and aerial photos					Analog		NCSU/UNC	
35mm Scanned						Digital		NCSU/UNC	
Print photos	ground and aerial photos					Analog		NCSU/UNC	
Scanned photos						Digital		NCSU/UNC	
Videos and movies						Digital		UNC Dataverse	
GIS animations/flythroughs						Digital		UNC Dataverse	S. Madry
PowerPoint presentations						Digital		NCSU/UNC	
Poster papers						Digital		NCSU/UNC	

Figure 17.1. Spreadsheet of Digital Archive Catalogue

French Map Catalogue

Index Number	Date	Title	Produced By	Area	Features	Map Type	Map Media & Condition	Scale	Center X	Center Y	Width (cm) map area & sheet area	Height (cm) map area & sheet area
1	1759	Cassini No. 84	Jean Dominique and Jacques Cassini	Bourgogne; From Saulieu (north) to Couches (south); from Chateau Chinon	Autun, eastern Morvan, Mont Beuvray, Arroux River, Canal du Centre, Yonne River, Ouche	Shaded relief, hydrology (mills), woods, roads, towns, etc.	B&W reproduction on heavy paper; edges torn, tape on edges	1 cm = 1000 metres; 1 inch = 1000 toise	80,000 T à la M.	100,000 T à la P.	89.7 cm	55.6 cm

Storage Location	Map Source	Notes	Digital Photo for database/ file name	Digital Scan yes/no	Scanned Digital File Name	File Type	Image Resolution	Digital Storage	freatures extractyerd?Y?N	which features	Digital copies reside	Paper ma reside
Battle Hall, 3rd drawer map file	IGN	Just north of our research area commune and preliminary research area. Scale is not reproduced to exact size.	Map File 1	yes	cassininorth	JPEG	300 dpi	France Scans CDROM (copies Madry, Tickner, Jones)				

Figure 17.2. Spreadsheet for analogue cartographical data.

12. Paper maps
13. Map inventory of the Virunga Volcano project, Rwanda
14. Scanned 9x9 inch 1945 aerial mapping photographs
15. Data backups
16. References, articles, and related documents

Each of these bucket spreadsheets contain unique categories of information relevant to that specific data. A portion of the current working spreadsheet for our collection of over 200 paper maps is shown in Figure 17.2 below. This contains 26 categories of information for each map.

17.4.2 Data Preparation

The process of scanning and digitizing analogue data, including 35 mm slides, field and aerial photographs, historical documents and manuscripts, paper maps, audio and video recordings, and other field and lab documents and archival records has been ongoing piecemeal for several years, conducted at both NCSU and UNC-CH. NCSU has, over several years, provided student workers who have assisted us in this process, and this significantly accelerated our work. This involved selecting the appropriate hardware and software tools to ensure that the resulting digital copies are of sufficient quality and met appropriate preservation standards. Fortunately, NCSU has a 35 mm slide scanner, which was used to scan hundreds of these slides. UNC-CH had for several years a high-resolution flatbed colour scanner which was used to scan many maps and large drawings and our collection of 9x9 inch World War II aerial photos of the region.

Many paper maps, aerial photos, etc. had already been scanned over the years, but at low quality, and many of these were rescanned to meet modern archival standards. Additional searches were made for data, and we contacted many previous project participants, asking if they had data they would provide us. Several provided photos, 35 mm slides, and other files to us, which have been added to the workflow.

17.4.3 Data Formats

Given that our project has been going on for 45 years, we have had to deal with the fact that older project data existed in many different data formats, including many that are no longer commonly supported. These include 35 mm slides, CDs, VHS cassettes, Zip backup drives, Super 8 mm movie reels, audio cassettes, and more, as shown below in Figure 17.3. Many sets of data have gone through several generations of formats over the decades, from analogue to CD to Zip disks to external hard drives to the cloud. This is a problem common to many long-term research programs such as ours. A vital aspect of this work is the annotation of data with appropriate metadata and keywords such as the person who took the photo, the date, location, subject, etc. Sometimes, only one person knows these details, and some are dealing with data collected over 40 years ago, so this will be a lengthy process, but is vital to our project. Our intention is that individuals will be able to search the archives for specific locations, dates, subjects (mill ponds, forests, old roads, etc.) and individuals across all data types, and this will require detailed keywords and metadata, much of which does not yet exist. We recognize that this will be a prolonged (and unfunded) activity.

17.5 Project Status

In the summer of 2023, the data will undergo a final quality assurance process and creation of missing keywords and metadata. We will then begin to undertake the process of entering each of the 16 buckets of data into the Dataverse system at UNC-CH and the Dryad system at NCSU, depending on who created and archived the data. As we are going to use both two institutional data repositories, a dedicated project archival access website is also under development, so that people can find project data regardless of its institutional archival location. This will be constructed using standard online finding aid structures. Metadata and keywords remain to be added to much of the data, in order to allow searches by location, date, type of data, etc. Final decisions will be made on data access and permissions before the archival "system" goes live in the fall of 2023. Additionally, the existing document archives of Prof. Carole Crumley, already archived at UNC-CH, will be linked where possible. One outstanding concern is that the Odum Institute's archive only accepts digital data, and we do not know what will happen to all the paper maps, slides, and other data that we hold. We are seeking a proper repository for these, perhaps in partnership with the historical collections at one of our institutions' libraries.

17.6 Results

This is an ongoing project, and we do not yet have final results. But our situation is likely mirrored throughout the archaeological community. In our case, we followed a strategy based on digital archiving principles to guide our project steps, but we found it essential to adapt these standards to the specific challenges and needs of our extensive archive. We learned that digital archiving is not a linear process, but rather a cyclical and iterative process that requires constant evaluation and re-adjustment. Some of the challenges we faced included finding and using appropriate digital archiving tools, gaining access to some analogue or digital data, and ensuring the appropriate security and privacy of our data. We crafted our steps in a non-rigid process that began with locating data, researching digital archive tools, preparing a first-order list, ascertaining privacy, and creating a collective catalogue of our project. We anticipate that our next steps will include further securing and digitizing our data, uploading our data to the two servers, monitoring project progress, and disseminating our results to other researchers and community members. We are hopeful that these steps will contribute to the preservation and accessibility of our project in the long term, understanding that this project will take time to further establish and maintain.

Large landscape projects, including archaeological, historical ecology, and related activities, often consist of multiple researchers from many different disciplines, institutions, and academic perspectives. Each participant brings with them large amounts of disparate raw, intermediate, and finished data in both analogue and digital formats. Such projects can be very long-lived, continuing for several decades, with both people, technologies, data formats, media, and archival perspectives coming and going over time.

Such projects can generate massive amounts of data, both digital and analogue, which should be properly conserved and archived, and these should also be made available as a matter of course to the largest possible number of researchers, both within the project as well as beyond, after initial publication of results. Such archiving should be a part of all phases of work, including the initial planning and analysis work. Proper care must be taken for human subjects and sensitive archaeological site data, even after the specific project is ended, as well as anything that is copyrighted.

We have decided to include all information that we have retained in this project, in so far as is practical,

Figure 17.3. Data from our project in its many, outdated formats such as 35 mm slides, floppy drives, audio cassettes, Super 8 mm movie film, VHS videos, CD-ROMs, and Zip disks, none of which are supported today.

partly as we do not believe that we can know what information will be considered important in the future. All archaeological site location or human remains information will be included but will be appropriately restricted. It is important to note that no existing project data of any format are being deliberately excluded from this project, with the single expectation of some GIS data originally obtained from the French IGN mapping agency and some scanned cartographic maps provided by certain French archives which retain copyright. These data will not be included in our archive for copyright reasons, but pointers to these data will be included in our archive, so that future researchers can access them from the original sources for their own use if desired. All other data we retain will be included. Information on who originally collected the data, who processed it, and who conducted the analysis will be included wherever possible, with both metadata and paradata information included in so far as is possible. For example, some of our earlier paper data have limited such information. Regarding the data that was lost due to fires and floods, we are not able to recreate an accurate determination of what percentage of our total collection these represented, but it is relatively small and primarily focused on earlier periods of our work. Fortunately, some data were held by more than one person, so we believe that the total amount which was lost is relatively small and does not impact the overall value of the collection.

17.7 Discussion

Digital archiving and related tools now exist that can be incorporated into new projects directly as they begin, so that they become another tool for the use of the researchers, but this requires specific knowledge and expertise which is, under some circumstances, outside of our fields, which is not always available to archaeological projects. Our project has struggled to keep track of the data held by various participants over the years, and significant data has also been lost. Data retained by former participants is rarely scanned or catalogued, nor does it contain metadata or is it accessible using keywords or geotags.

Our strong advice to all is to please take digital archiving into consideration AT THE BEGINNING of your projects, and to incorporate digital archiving technologies and specialists in your work. Indeed, long-term data management strategies and plans are often now required components for many successful grant proposals at various public and private funding agencies. Key concepts such as digital data fixity, redundant backups, paradata, metadata, and appropriate keywords should become a part of all of our standard professional workflow, no matter what our particular discipline may be.

Once our data are uploaded and the archives "go live", the project will continue to be monitored and adjusted as necessary, with the goal of ensuring that the data remains available for a broad scope of researchers over time. Finally, information on the process and results of the digital archiving project will be collected and distributed to other researchers to benefit their own research and digital archive development.

We hope that our experiences in seeking, well after the fact, to incorporate this important new capability into our work will be useful not only for our project and researchers in our ongoing work, but also for those who may come after us working in this region. We also hope that our experiences will be helpful to the larger community, to assist others to incorporate these important tools into their future work as a matter of course.

Acknowledgements

We wish to acknowledge the participation of multiple people who have worked with us over the years. This includes Professor Carole Crumley, the numerous colleagues who collaborated with us on the project over the 45 years of its existence, and all the collaborators in this work, past and present. We also acknowledge the North Carolina State University undergraduate students Hannah Taylor, Duncan Anderson, Angel Ngo, Madeleine Guyant, Daniela Agostini, Charlotte Bulkeley, and Kaitlyn Bohn, who assisted us in scanning and documenting much of the data that will be archived. We also recognize and thank the many people of our French study area who so graciously supported and assisted us over the decades, and who shared their homes, fields, and archives with us. We also express our gratitude to the digital archiving experts who have so graciously assisted us, and the digital archiving staffs at UNC-CH and NCSU. We also acknowledge our two peer reviewers who improved this paper through their constructive criticism.

Funding

This digital archiving work is primarily unfunded and is being conducted on our own. NC State University has provided funding for several undergraduate and graduate students in support of this project to scan various analogue data.

Conflict of interest disclosure

The authors declare that they comply with the PCI rule of having no financial or other conflicts of interest in relation to the content of the article.

Data, Scripts, Code, and Supplementary Information Availability

Data will be made available online at the University of North Carolina at Chapel Hill's Odum Institute Data Repository: https://odum.unc.edu/archive and at North Carolina State University's Dryad Data Repository at https://www.lib.ncsu.edu/do/data-management/dryad.

Peer review

This article has been reviewed and recommended by PCI Archaeology.

Huvila, I. 2023. "A meticulous description of archiving research data from a long-running landscape research project." *Peer Community in Archaeology* 100334. DOI: 10.24072/pci.archaeo.100334.

References

Broman, Karl W., and Kara H. Woo. 2018. "Data Organization in Spreadsheets." *American Statistician, 72*(1): 2–10. DOI: 10.1080/00031305.2017.1375989.

Crumley, Carole.. 1987. *Regional Dynamics: Burgundian Landscapes in Historical Perspective.* San Diego: Academic Press.

Dryad. n.d. "Good data practices." Accessed April 15, 2023. https://datadryad.org/stash/best_practices.

FORCE11. n.d. "The FAIR Data Principles." Accessed April 15, 2023. https://force11.org/info/the-fair-data-principles.

Huvila, Isto. 2008. "Participatory archive: towards decentralized curation, radical user orientation, and broader contextualisation of records management." *Archival Science* 8: 15–36. DOI: 10.1007/s10502-008-9071-0.

Madry, Scott, Anna Westin, and Elizabeth Jones (eds). 2024. *Practicing Historical Ecology. Methods for the Collection, Analysis, and Integration of Interdisciplinary Regional Data.* Uppsala: SLU Swedish Biodiversity Centre, Swedish University of Agricultural Sciences.

Richards, Julian D., Ulf Jakobsson, David Novák, Benjamin Štular, and Holly Wright. 2021. "Digital Archiving in Archaeology: The State of the Art." *Internet Archaeology* 58. DOI: 10.11141/ia.58.23.

Wright, Holly and Julian. D. Richards. 2018 "Reflections on collaborative archaeology and large-scale online research infrastructures." *Journal of Field Archaeology* 43: S60-S67. DOI: 10.1080/00934690.2018.1511960.

18 Transforming the Archaeological Record Into a Digital Playground

A Methodological Analysis of *The Living Hill* Project

Samanta Mariotti
Department of Humanistic Research and Innovation
University of Bari 'Aldo Moro'
samanta.mariotti@uniba.it
ORCID 0000-0001-8958-9293

Abstract
Video games are now recognised as a valuable tool for disseminating and enhancing cultural heritage. In Italy, the recent institutionalisation of Public Archaeology programs and incentives for digital innovation has resulted in a proliferation of video games for archaeological heritage. However, critical evaluation of these projects is still needed.
This paper describes The Living Hill project dedicated to the Archaeological Park and Fortress of Poggio Imperiale in Poggibonsi, Italy and the methodological framework adopted: a) a preliminary deep analysis of the objectives, the context, and the expected audience; b) a multi-professional collaboration (between archaeologists, developers, graphic designers) to make the best choices based on the primary analysis; c) a (first) final UX evaluation.

Keywords: Archaeogaming; The Living Hill; Digital Public Archaeology; Methodology; UX Evaluation

18.1 Introduction

In recent decades, digital applications like AR, VR, and video games have revolutionised archaeological practice, serving as invaluable tools for studying sites, records, and promoting heritage through new methods able to fascinate new audiences (Bekele et al. 2018; Champion 2015; Champion 2021; Sanders 2014). More recently, the academic community, including archaeology professionals, has shown great interest in the relationship between digital games, research, education, and outreach (Ariese et al. 2021; Hageneuer 2020; Huggett 2019; Mol et al. 2017; Morgan 2019; Reinhard 2018) since, as pointed out by Champion (2015), these digital products offer a learning potential through tools focused on non-textual visualisation, in addition to their ability to convey stories and meanings by applying mechanisms able to engage the large public into an active state of lasting commitment and learning where players are motivated to create their own knowledge rather than to receive information passively (Mortara et al. 2014, 318).

The integration of video games with archaeology in Italy has been challenging due to academics viewing commercial products as providing unreliable information, the misconception that video games are childish entertainment, and the lack of

In *Advances in Digital Archaeology. Proceedings of the 2023 conference Computer Applications and Quantitative Methods in Archaeology – 50 years of synergy*, edited by J.W.H.P. Verhagen, J. Waagen, A. Brandsen, A. Queffelec, R.M. Visser and D. Taelman, 233–248. Leiden: Sidestone Press.

Typology	Title Example	Content
trivia, puzzles and mini-games	*Time Tales – Gli Etruschi* (2019)	educational game for children dedicated to the Etruscan civilization
gamified solutions of interactive exhibitions/visits	*ArkaeVision Archeo* (2018)	a mixed gamified experience (VR and MR) dedicated to the ancient city of Paestum
gamified solutions of interactive exhibitions/visits	*Inventum* (2018)	mobile AR application created to promote the National Archaeological Park of Venosa, Potenza
mobile applications for museums, touristic sites, exhibitions exploiting some reward/engagement mechanism	*Father & Son* (2017)	a narrative 2D game created for the National Archaeological Museum of Naples
mobile applications for museums, touristic sites, exhibitions exploiting some reward/engagement mechanism	*Mi Rasna* (2018)	a simulation game dedicated to the Etruscan civilization
mobile applications for museums, touristic sites, exhibitions exploiting some reward/engagement mechanism	*Past for Future* (2018)	a narrative 2D game created for the promotion of the ancient city of Taranto
mobile applications for museums, touristic sites, exhibitions exploiting some reward/engagement mechanism	*Beyond Our Lives* (2019)	an adventure game to promote the main ancient Etruscan cities in Tuscany
mobile applications for museums, touristic sites, exhibitions exploiting some reward/engagement mechanism	*Dive in the Past* (2021)	an adventure game developed as part of an European project to promote the underwater archaeological heritage
mobile applications for museums, touristic sites, exhibitions exploiting some reward/engagement mechanism	*Domitian* (2021)	a narrative puzzle game dedicated to the exhibition "Emperor Domitian: God on Earth"
mobile applications for museums, touristic sites, exhibitions exploiting some reward/engagement mechanism	*Hold the Hut* (2021)	a puzzle game dedicated to the discovery of a VIth century BC hut on the site of Serra a San Chirico Nuovo, Potenza
mobile applications for museums, touristic sites, exhibitions exploiting some reward/engagement mechanism	*Mediterranean* (2021)	a simulation game developed as part of an European project dedicated to the Phoenician civilization
mobile applications for museums, touristic sites, exhibitions exploiting some reward/engagement mechanism	*Taras' Gifts* (2022)	a narrative game created during the Covid pandemic for the exhibition "Taras and the Gifts of the Sea" at the Archaeological Museum of Taranto
virtual simulations of past events trough gesture based interaction	*Difendiamo le Mura!* (2014)	a virtual simulation game based on the siege of the city of Paestum by Alexander Molossus and available inside the local archaeological museum
adventures set in faithful reconstructions and/or digital counterparts of real sites	*A Night in the Forum* (2019)	an environmental narrative game for Sony PlayStation VR set in the Forum of Augustus, Rome
mixed experience (gaming, VR and AR) to explore and play in reconstructed archaeological sites	*Augustus* (2022)	app-game and PC game dedicated to four archaeological parks in Sicily

Table 18.1. Some relevant archaeogaming examples in Italy in the last decade.

understanding of the interactive industry by archaeologists (Giordano 2020; Modena 2019). Meanwhile, commercial interactive media producers have been meeting the public's desire for historical representations, but they often lack the expertise to meet archaeologists' high content standards (Mariotti 2020a).

However, the recent institutionalization of Public Archaeology programs in Italy (Bonacchi 2013) had the potential to face the interactive entertainment industry's encroachment into archaeology (Richardson 2013) and change these sentiments towards interactive entertainment (De Felice 2015; Volpe 2020; Volpe and De Felice 2014). As a result, the domain of cultural and archaeological heritage in Italy has recently seen an upsurge of interest in video games. This is largely due to the attention from museums and academics (Bertoldi and Mariotti 2022; Bonacini 2023; Bonacini and Giaccone 2022; Pescarin 2020) as well as the incentives provided for digital innovation by local administrations and the government (First Playable Found 2021).

The National Research Council of Italy has played a pivotal role over the years in the development of video games that promote archaeological sites (Pescarin 2020, 11–3; Pietroni 2020). As 3D and interactive technologies become more affordable and easier to use, Italian private companies and archaeological departments are increasingly involved in this field – even internationally as in the case of *Valete Vos Viatores* video game project (Andreu Pintado et al. 2022). This led to a significant increase in the creation of such games and their accessibility to the public. Moreover, it is now possible to cater to the growing demand by including a larger number of lesser-known archaeological sites, museums, and themes.

Various samples of recent archaeogaming projects in Italy, with clear promotional and educational purposes, are presented in Table 18.1, including examples retrieved from scientific literature and the Italian Videogame Program narrative archive (IVIPRO n.d.). A comprehensive review of archaeological video games developed in Italy between 2013 and 2023 is discussed in Mariotti (2025).

This paper presents a video game project, *The Living Hill*, developed within the Department of Historical Sciences and Cultural Heritage of the University of

Research	Tech. Development	References
Archeokids	Entertainment Game Apps Ltd.	Mariotti and Marotta (2020)
National Research Council of Italy	Digitalcomoedia, Beyond Tech.	Pagano et al. (2020)
Effenove s.r.l.s.	Effenove s.r.l.s., Pixel s.r.l., Jetbit Digital Agency	https://www.inventumgame.com
National Archaeological Museum of Naples, Tuo Museo	Tuo Museo	Solima (2018)
Etruscan Museum of Villa Giulia (+ national and local museums, various Superintendencies), Entertainment Game Apps Ltd.	Entertainment Game Apps Ltd.	Amoroso (2020); Bonacini and Giaccone (2022)
National Archaeological Museum of Taranto, Tuo Museo	Tuo Museo	https://museotaranto.beniculturali.it/en/past-for-future
Tuo Museo	Tuo Museo	https://www.beyondourlives.com
Campi Flegrei Archaeological Park, Central Institute for Restoration, University of Zara, Greek Ephorate, Ministry of Greek Culture	3D Research s.r.l.	Cozza et al. (2021)
University of Newcastle, Rijksmuseum van Oudheden	Entertainment Game Apps Ltd.	https://www.egameapps.com/gameapps/domitian
Soprintendenza Archeologia Belle Arti e Paesaggio della Basilicata	Effenove s.r.l.s.	Mutino et al. (2022)
La Rotta dei Fenici, Entertainment Game Apps Ltd.	Entertainment Game Apps Ltd.	https://www.egameapps.com/gameapps/mediterranean
University of Bari	Swipe Story	De Felice (2022)
National Research Council of Italy, Fondazione Paestum, University of Salerno	E.V.O.CA. s.r.l., National Research Council of Italy	Pietroni (2020)
National Research Council of Italy, Museo dei Fori Imperiali	VRTRON, National Research Council of Italy	Ferdani et al. (2020) Pescarin et al. (2020)
University of Palermo, National Research Council of Italy	ETT, Red Raion, AD Meridiem	Fazio et al. (2022) https://www.augustusgame.it

Siena. The game is dedicated to the excavation site located on the Poggio Imperiale hill of Poggibonsi (Siena, Italy; Francovich and Valenti 2007) which has been an emblematic case study for digital application to an archaeological project since its initial phases in the 1990s (Fronza et al. 2001) and the case study chosen to experiment with new dissemination methodologies such as VR and gaming applied to archaeological heritage between 2020 and 2022 (Bertoldi 2021; Bertoldi and Mariotti 2022; Mariotti 2020b). *The Living Hill* was developed starting from the scientific results of the Poggibonsi excavation and through a strict collaboration between academia and industry (Entertainment Game Apps, Ltd., the company that managed the programming and the graphics of the game is specialised in historical video games) in the framework of the C.A.P.I. project (Collina Accessibile di Poggio Imperiale – Accessibility of the Hill of Poggio Imperiale) whose aim was the digital enhancement of the archaeological heritage on the site. What is extraordinary in this case study is the nature of the archaeological context (spanning from Late Antiquity to the First Renaissance period) and the evident intentions in terms of public outreach that characterized the excavation project since the earliest approaches: from the creation of the archaeological park in 2007 to the building of the open-air museum in 2014 which pursues an in-progress full-scale reconstruction of the 17 structures found during the excavation of the Carolingian Age village (Figure 18.1).

After almost 30 years of archaeological research and interpretation on the site, the C.A.P.I. project faced a major challenge: how to use complex archaeological data, often related to small or poorly preserved structures, in a video game that would engage a broad range of learners in accessible ways? In a 2017 paper discussing whether archaeologists and games could mix, Erik Champion concluded:

> *"My solution is to suggest that rather than concentrate on the technology, archaeologists should focus on the expected audience. What do we want to show with*

Figure 18.1. The open-air museum on the hill of Poggibonsi. The remains of the XIIth century Church of Saint Agnes columns are still visible behind the huts.

digital technology, for what purpose, for which audience, and how will we know when we have succeeded?" (Champion 2017).

In this statement, the author highlights three key issues regarding the use of video games in archaeology that will be used as research questions and guidelines in this paper to illustrate *The Living Hill* project and its preliminary outcomes. First, different professionals with specific competencies are essential for a good result. Archaeologists should focus on historical and archaeological content, narrative, and storytelling, while other professionals should determine the technological aspects (Copplestone 2017). Nevertheless, this also means that since we, as archaeologists, are entering an entirely new way of communicating, we must at least understand the "new rules" of the video game form. Secondly, over the last decade, public engagement and communication of archaeological data have become significant concerns in Italian archaeology (Ripanti 2022). As a result, multiple strategies have been developed, utilizing various mediums, with technology playing a central role (Economou 2015; Moscati 2019). However, as archaeologists, we should focus on exploring the benefits of a gaming approach in expanding communication and outreach through education programs. To do this, a preliminary assessment of the public, themes, and objectives is essential. Lastly, it appears increasingly crucial to set out an experimental approach to evaluate the projects once finished and assess users' experience and the dissemination/education outcomes of the created video game (Bonacchi and Moshenska 2015, 9).

18.2 Connecting Audiences, Objectives and Methods

Following Champion's questions, one of the first issues we had to face when the C.A.P.I. project started in April 2020 concerned the identification and involvement of the public and the co-creation approach we had planned for the project development. We had scheduled an in-depth analysis of potential users (local community, middle and high school students, archaeology students, academics, and tourists) to collect suggestions and recommendations and to evaluate style choices that had to be made (Bollwerk 2015; Simon 2010, 187). Unfortunately, the Covid-19 pandemic and the subsequent lockdown forced us to change our plans. However, luckily, the open-air museum, in six years of activity, had provided us with a lot of valuable data concerning its heterogeneous public. Official data on tourist trends in Poggibonsi show continuous growth over the years since the creation of the open-air museum: from 42,453 visitors in 2014 to 73,849 in 2018. After a little downturn in 2019 (64,785 visitors) and the expected drastic drop in 2020 (19,522), renewed growth is already attested (32,236 visitors in 2021 and 51,462 in 2022; Camera di Commercio Arezzo-Siena 2023). The archaeological park, which includes the whole surface of the hill, is always open to the public, and every Sunday, archaeologists/reenactors who manage the area are there in their early-medieval costumes, ready to interact with visitors. Moreover, special events are organised throughout the year and, most of all, the open-air museum has become one of the most popular destinations for school trips. Thousands of students come every spring from all over Tuscany and beyond (1150 students in 2016, 1800 in 2017, 4500 in 2018, 4000 in 2019 according to museum records). In 2023, after three years of ceasing, an incredible number of schools booked their visit, and from February to June, about 6,000 students arrived in Poggibonsi. Another aspect that can be noted in the last two years is that, despite its dramatic effects, the Covid-19 pandemic had a positive impact on many schools' digital assets by forcing them to upgrade their technological equipment (Giovannella et al. 2022). Although interactive whiteboards (IWBs) were already quite common (Piano Nazionale Scuola Digitale 2015), various schools received funding to purchase tablets and computers to facilitate remote learning. However, the digital gap is still a persistent issue in Italy, particularly in peripheral areas (Di Pietro 2021).

Based on these data and through interviews and focus groups with the archaeologists who manage the open-air museum, interact with visitors and collect their impressions (Valenti and Salzotti 2017), a list of appreciated features was created. These were combined with project objectives established with the same archaeologists and the project director, Professor Marco Valenti. According to this first analysis, the majority of visitors (regardless of age, cultural level, digital skills or background) appreciate being able to explore a rebuilt environment and interact with objects and characters in an immersive experience (Valenti 2016).

So, the shared plan was to create a video game to allow people to have a visit experience as close as possible to reality to exploit the potential of the so-called "experiential learning" (Kolb 1984; Moon 2004) in a digital playground (Bogost 2007). Furthermore, we aimed to create a video game that could function as an educational tool for schools and as an alternative to physical visits during inclement weather or other obstacles. Moreover, we wanted the game to have an educational purpose for the general public to learn while exploring the historical setting in an enjoyable way (Boyan and Sherry 2011; Mortara et al. 2014). Additionally, we aimed to increase accessibility for individuals who are either geographically distant or have physical limitations, as digital tools can help overcome architectural barriers that are not always removable in archaeological settings. Last but not least, we aimed to expand visitors' knowledge of the site through the video game, showcasing two often overshadowed periods (late Medieval and early Renaissance) in addition to the well-known early medieval period already famous for being represented by the open-air museum village. That is the reason why we choose to create three different levels in the game, each one dedicated to a specific period, as if they were mini open worlds (Hiriart 2017, 171). The first one represents the early medieval village, and the selected topics are associated with the inhabitants' main occupations; the second level is dedicated to the late medieval city of Poggio Bonizio that flourishes during this period due to the passage of the Via Francigena; the third level is dedicated to the last phase of the site and it tells about the building of the renaissance fortress commissioned by Lorenzo il Magnifico of the Medici family.

To create a fully immersive experience, the History-Game Relations framework (Cassone and Thibault 2016) was utilized. The HGR framework is an analytic tool for scholars and designers alike, capable of taking into account all the layers and processes necessary to transform History in the setting of a game. In particular, the framework follows a semiotic approach and focuses on the intersection of the three processes needed for creating a historical discourse (setting, modelling and representing; Lozano 1987) and on the three translations that the past undergoes to become a game: perspectival, digital and ludic.

The Living Hill game revolves around a first-person story. The player's main quest is to return three objects collected by a little girl who used to visit their grandfather in Poggibonsi during the 1910s to their rightful owners, each of whom lives in one of the three periods. When starting the game, upon discovering a small box in the attic, the girl's ghost appears and transports the player back in time to each of the three epochs. Each period in the game has specific characters and missions that encourage players to explore the environment, collect items, and gain information to progress. Interactions with characters offer 2-3 options, each with different outcomes and reactions while several info points allow optional learning on specific objects and activities, similar to Discovery Tours in *Assassin's Creed* games (Poiron 2021; Politopoulos et al. 2019). However, despite the opportunity offered of exploring the three historical environments, *The Living Hill* differ from a walking simulator or a virtual tour since players' agency is fundamental to discover information within the system, advance in the game and complete the quests (Mortara et al. 2014, 318). As a video game, it engages players and teaches them things through procedural rhetoric, which players "read" through direct engagement and criticism (Bogost 2007, 233–261; Copplestone 2017, 86).

When discussing the visual aspects of the game, we must address the accuracy and perception of

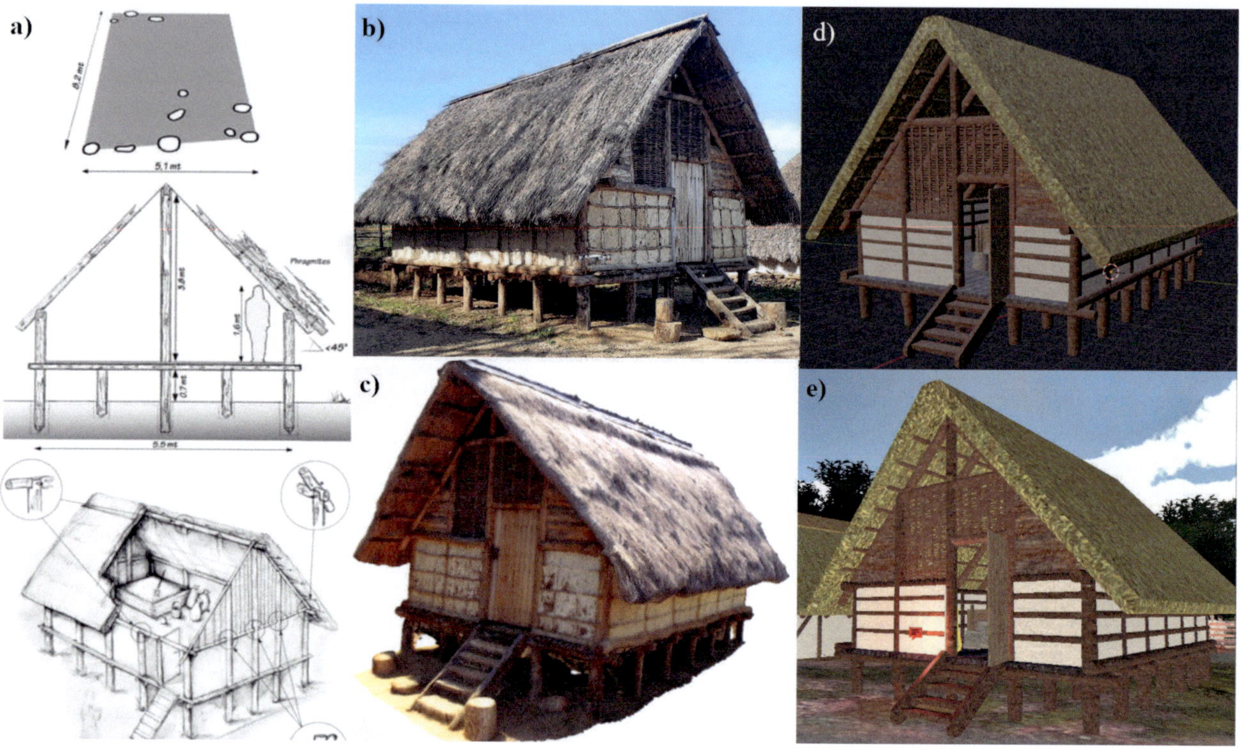

Figure 18.2. The reconstruction of the granary: a) the postholes identified during the excavation and the hypothetical reconstruction; b) the reconstructed structure at the open-air museum; c) the photogrammetric model; d) the hut in Blender; e) the hut in the game.

the reconstructions based on the archaeological record (Copplestone 2016). This is similar to the issue archaeologists faced when building the open-air museum and reconstructing huts. As archaeologists, our discipline deals with interpreting traces (or their absence), often related to poorly preserved structures or complex sequences of events rather than seeking "truth". When setting up the approach for the video game, we strictly followed archaeological methods for data interpretation, historical sources analysis, and case studies comparison to fill in gaps with plausible features (Figure 18.2). This goal required researchers, developers, and graphic designers to balance entertainment and scientific accuracy (Ibrahim and Ali 2018).

The 3D game environment reconstruction (Mortara and Catalano 2018) began with a photogrammetric survey of the hill using a DJI Phantom 4 drone. The digital images were then processed in Agisoft Metashape software (1.8.4 version) to obtain a 3D model of the terrain including the archaeological evidence and open-air museum structures. However, to allow players to explore inside digital replicas of huts, the entire game environment was rebuilt using 3D graphics software. A first attempt to test Unity 3D tools was unsatisfactory, so we switched to Blender (version 2.91). The 3D models were later imported into Unity (version 2020.3.19f1) for programming.

18.3 Preliminary Results: the Game Prototype

When *The Living Hill* project began, the strategy arranged with the archaeologists working on the site was to create a mobile video game. However, during development, a PC version was also considered to enhance the player's experience with the high-quality reconstructions. Nevertheless, in this regard, several accuracy issues needed addressing.

The reconstruction of the first-level environment was made easier by the physical reference of the open-air museum structures and the work of archaeologists in re-enactment activities, including costumes, character names, definitions, and storytelling (Valenti 2019). Even the characters' design was based on real archaeologists' appearance, making them easily identifiable for visitors. This high level of detail set a standard motivating us to maintain similar accuracy in designing the other two levels, despite lacking a comparable material asset for reconstruction.

The only remains of the XIIIth century settlement we planned to use as the second-level setting are a few layers of block stones at the centre of the hill (Francovich and Valenti 2007), now often hidden by grass. Fortunately, we had professional drawings made for the volume dedicated to the site and based on the archaeological record to rely on for our reconstructions (Inklink 2007). Since the settlement in this period was very large, we

Figure 18.3. Late Medieval remains on the hill and archaeological interpretation (the Via Francigena in red); 3D reconstruction in Blender based on a reconstructive drawing (the selected area and the Via Francigena in red); 3D environment texturized; game frame.

selected a specific area of the site represented by the main road (Via Francigena) connecting the two main churches. Today, this area (Figure 18.3) is still recognizable, as the remains of the churches are visible, and the present road closely follows the ancient path. For this level, the names of the characters were in some cases invented or omitted; in other cases, we adopted the names used by the same archaeologists during a one-time re-enactment event dedicated to this period, and in the case of the name of one of the notable men in Poggio Bonizio, we relied on the real name carved in a lead seal found during the excavation (Francovich and Valenti 2007, 184).

Lastly, we set the scene in front of the citadel for the third level dedicated to the construction of the Renaissance fortress at the beginning of the XVIth century. In this case, the reconstructed fortress walls limit the space unrealistically, as the area would have been more extensive during that time, even if it was empty due to the previous settlement being destroyed. We used one of the information points to clarify this creative choice to players. The primary reference for this level was another drawing from the main publication volume (Inklink 2007) and a book edited by the architect, Luciana Masi (1992), who studied the fortress construction site. While conducting her research, she also consulted the historical archives of the Medici family, which contain detailed records of the construction site's activities. These documents were useful for our project as they contain information regarding the names, roles, pay, and other interesting details of the individuals who worked at the construction site. This game level representing the ambitious architectural project included humble workers (such as a stonemason and a furnace men), suppliers of raw materials, the construction site manager for the Medici family, and the architect Antonio da Sangallo, brother of Giuliano, who had previously worked on the fortress design with Lorenzo il Magnifico.

At present, the game can only be accessed through the PC platform. The mobile version of the game still has some technical issues and bugs related to the mechanics. Moreover, we are also working on finding a solution to make it available in the app stores, as the file size of the game is quite large for a standard mobile application (around 1.5 GB). To address the issue, we attempted to optimize the file by reducing polygons and texture quality. However, this negatively impacted the game's visual resolution. The programmer suggested a potential solution involving partitioning the game into smaller packages that can be downloaded as needed, but this will require a significant restructuring of the game.

Currently, our plan is to continue with the testing with different audiences and then release the PC version on the open-air museum website as a free download. The team is also exploring the possibility of releasing the assets and game code as open source after the game's official launch. This will allow the community to create their own stories within the landscape and architecture of the project, which could be advantageous for increasing public outreach and community engagement. Moreover, in the future, we also aim to have the game accessible on dedicated computer stations located inside the fortress's citadel.

18.4 UX Evaluation: Pilot Testing and First Results

So, once a video game is created, how can we try to answer the last question prompted by Champion: "How will we know if we have succeeded?"

While several video games dedicated to archaeological and cultural content have been developed in Italy recently, the literature still stresses a lack of significant, extensive user tests. Games' effectiveness in learning outcomes is still understudied mainly due to the complexity of assessing intangible measures (Bellotti et al. 2013). Further research is necessary to investigate in greater detail the actual effectiveness of the various types of video games, to define a methodology based on metrics and evaluation tools (Bellotti et al. 2010), even more so those with cultural/archaeological content (Konstantakis and Caridakis 2020). Games applied to cultural heritage have proven to potentially be an independent instrument, capable of bringing information, lasting engagement, knowledge, and curiosity to a very diversified public. So, how do we assess these further aspects?

In order to answer this very complex question, a multi-level analysis was planned as a consistent extension of the project. Since *The Living Hill* aims to reach a broad audience, the study will use surveys, interviews, and focus groups to gather feedback from various group of players: middle and high school students, archaeology students and professionals, and the general public. The archaeologists managing the site have given positive feedback on the PC version during development, while evaluation of the general public's experience has only just begun.

In the general public case, the most complex one to be surveyed considering the diverse range of individuals involved, a prototype questionnaire was created and tested during a public event hosted by the Foundation of Musei Senesi (the network that brings together 45 museums in the territory of Siena, including the open-air museum of Poggibonsi) and the University of Siena at the Botanic Garden of the city. On this occasion, participants were given the chance to play the video game and provide feedback through answering questions about their experience (Dawson et al. 2020, 256–62).

Although the context was not suitable for an accurate survey, as players only experienced partial gameplay due to participating in almost 30 different activities proposed in various stands, leaving insufficient time to finish the game (it takes about one hour to complete it), and being disrupted by others walking and chatting around, it was still the first opportunity to test the game and the users' experience analysis method. Some promising assessments have already been made on similar occasions (Birchall et al. 2012; Pagano et al. 2015; Pagano et al. 2020), and the methodology adopted (test, observation, questionnaire and a cross-referenced data analysis) could be easily applied to *The Living Hill* case study.

The survey featured a comprehensive mix of closed-ended questions, a Likert-scale rating section, and targeted open-ended questions. It consisted of three main parts. The first included demographic questions about gender, age, affiliation, video game experience (also related to cultural heritage game projects), and knowledge of the archaeological site. The second section focused on players' experiences with *The Living Hill*, asking them to rate the game based on entertainment, education, immersion, and authenticity (Copplestone 2016). Participants were also asked to identify difficulties, most and least effective features, how they felt during the game, and aspects they would improve. Lastly, the survey explored players' willingness to play again and their learning perception.

During the four-hour event, 24 players from Siena and its surrounding areas filled out the questionnaire, with 12 male and 12 female participants aged between 12 and 56. The majority of respondents (almost 80%) were middle or high school students, while three were undergraduates and one held a Doctor of Philosophy degree. More than a third of the respondents (37.5%) had visited the archaeological park of Poggibonsi at least once. Fifteen respondents (all under 40) stated they liked video games. Of these, 73.3% (n = 11) play at least one hour a week (some of the most cited titles are *Minecraft*, *Call of Duty*, *Roblox*, *The Last of Us*, and *Fifa Mobile*), mostly (80%) using a computer (nearly half of them also uses a console) while 20% prefers mobile devices. None of the respondents had ever played a video game created for an archaeological site, ancient civilization or historical period with educational purposes before.

In the second section of the survey, it was noted that none of the players were able to reach the second level of the game. As a result, the players' experience was limited to the early-medieval village level as expected. During the testing phase of the game, the average duration of a single game session ranged between 10 and 20 minutes. However, there were three players, all over 40 years old, who gave up almost immediately (they were not included in the survey). On the other hand, there were also four players who returned to play the game later, when the public pressure was less intense. This was mainly due to the fact that only two computers were available for testing the game.

The overall satisfaction level, entertainment, education, authenticity, immersion grades, and site enhancement were rated on a 5-grade scale, from value = 1 to value = 5 (Table 18.2). From the question regarding the authenticity

	Total	Group 1	Group 2	Group 3	Group 4	Group 5	Group 6	Group 7	Group 8
Overall Satisfaction	3.62	3.75	3.50	3.71	3	3.2	4.3	3.75	3.5
Entertainment	3.50	3.50	3.50	3.57	3	3.2	4	3.75	3.25
Education	4	3.75	4.25	4.14	3	4.2	3.67	4	4
Authenticity	3.71	2.67	4.50	3.5	5	3.2	5	4.25	4
Immersion	3.43	2.33	4.25	3.17	5	3	4.5	3	3.75
Site Enhancement	4.43	4	4.75	4.33	5	4.2	5	4.33	4.5

Table 18.2. Mean Values from the Statistics of Likert-scale rating questions (section two). Comparative analysis of how various groups of players evaluated general attractiveness, entertainment grade, educational grade, authenticity grade, immersion grade, and site enhancement. Note: Group 1 = male players; Group 2 = female players; Group 3 = under-forty age group; Group 4 = over-forty age group; Group 5 = players with high-level gaming experience; Group 6 =players with low-level gaming experience; Group 7 = players who had visited the archaeological park; Group 8 = players who had not visited the archaeological park.

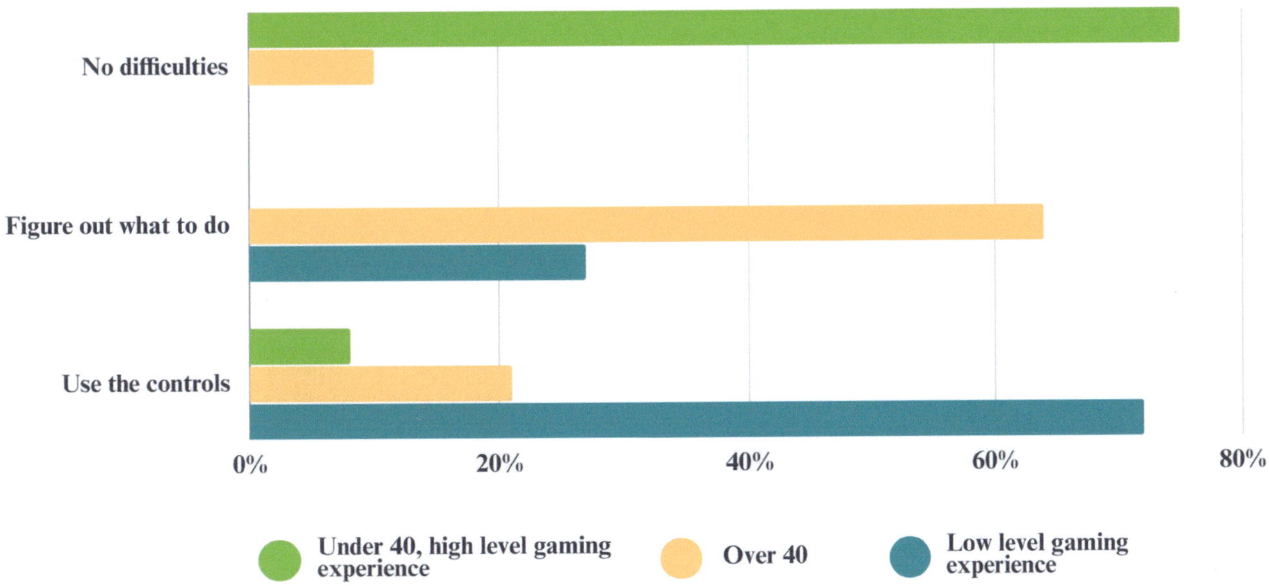

Figure 18.4. Difficulties encountered during the game session (percentages; n=21).

grade, the number of respondents was 21. The analysis was inspired by the UX approach applied by Dawson et al. (2020).

As underlined in Figure 18.4, when asked about the difficulties encountered during the game session, most players under 40 with a high gaming experience reported no problems. On the contrary, players over 40 with a lower level of gaming experience declared they had difficulty figuring out what to do and how to use the controls (WASD keys in combination with mouselook). However, during game sessions, players' abilities improved in just a few minutes of testing, as reported by respondents.

The game received praise for its dialogues, engaging character interactions, narrative which allows players to go back in time, and historical reconstruction. The responses provided were consistent with the results of the initial analysis conducted on the public of the open-air museum. However, younger users criticized the static graphic design of characters and suggested adding more detail (as emerged in Poullis et al. 2019). As a matter of fact, making them walk or perform activities linked to their occupation was already part of our plans to improve realism.

During the game session, players were also asked to report their attitude and feelings by selecting from a list of definitions and providing their perception. The results were in line with their game experience: "interested" (n=11), "free" (n=7), "challenged" (n=7) were selected by those who reported an overall positive experience while "frustrated" (n=2, in combination with "interested" and "challenged") was selected by those players who had difficulties.

In the last part of the survey, as illustrated in Figure 18.5, players were asked to evaluate the project from a promotional and educative point of view. During the game, 66.7% of players (n=16) reported learning something new, including details about life in an IXth century

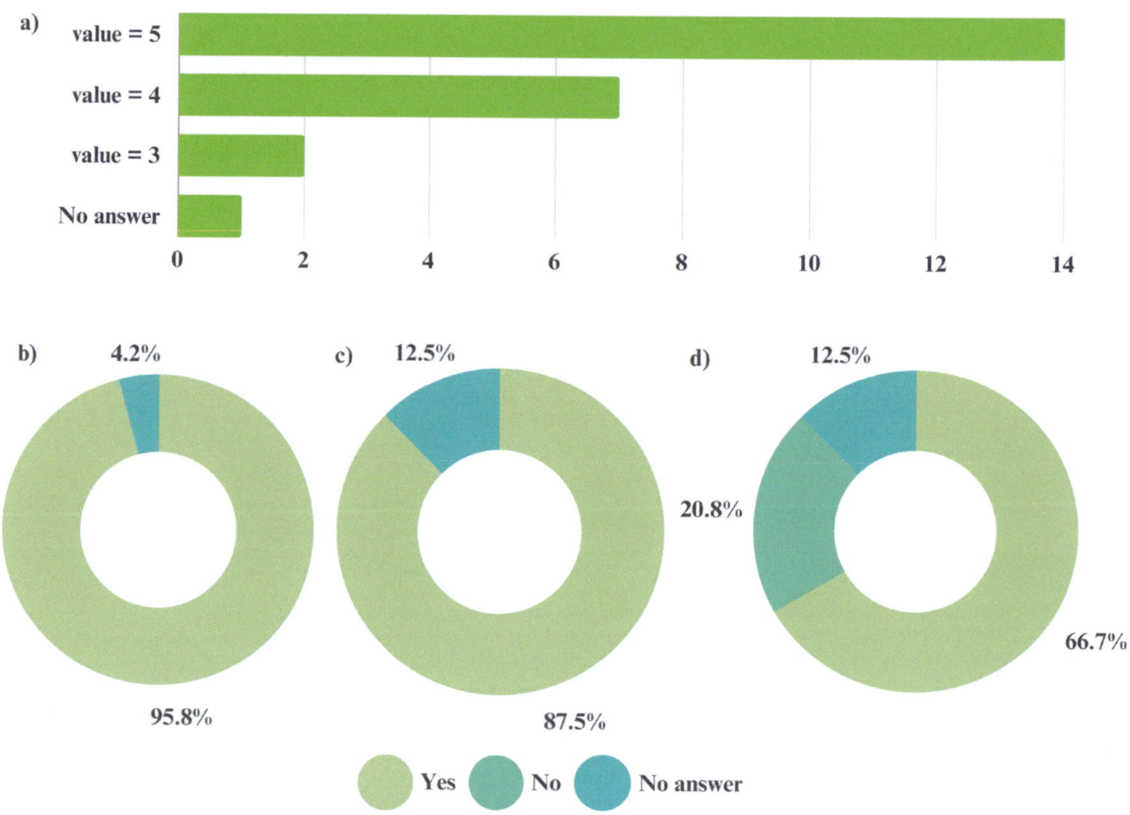

Figure 18.5. Responses (n=24) to the questions; a) "How effective do you think a game like *The Living Hill* can be to promote and make people appreciate an archaeological site?"; b) "Would you like to play similar video games dedicated to other archaeological sites, museums, ancient civilisations, or historical periods?"; c) "Would you like to play *The Living Hill* again?"; d) "Do you think you learned something you did not know by playing this game?".

village, various occupations of the inhabitants, and how to use a video game. Additionally, three players expressed increased engagement and interest in the historical period and wished to play again.

To summarise, general observations of users revealed a great sense of curiosity towards the game application as observed by Pagano et al. (2015) and Merchán et al. (2023). The first evaluation identified that players with low game experience found it difficult to manage controls and showed some bias towards video games. Younger players noted a lack of realism, especially in character animation, due to their familiarity with AAA titles (Poullis et al. 2019, 12).

As expected, the virtual exploration requires interaction skills that enable users to learn cultural aspects and gaming abilities through the learn-by-doing doctrine. Although the first moments may be challenging, even non-gamers can benefit. The most appreciated features (engaging storytelling, accurate reconstruction and characters' interaction) are helpful in situating the learning (Catalano et al. 2014), stimulating the "irrational" part of individuals and generating motivation (Shih et al. 2015, 206-207). This is the first aspect that pushes people to adopt technological solutions and facilitates the learning process (Goleman 1995). Eventually, the overall consideration of the project objectives (education and site enhancement) and the curiosity generated by an "unusual" medium to promote knowledge and participation look promising.

According to the analysis, *The Living Hill* project provides an immersive and (pro)active digital cultural heritage experience through storytelling, emotional features, and accurately reconstructed environments, resulting in success as confirmed by other works (Konstantakis and Caridakis 2020; Rice 2014). However, additional investigation is needed, especially to better evaluate the components analysed in Table 18.2. The results may have been affected by the testing context and limited time, particularly in regard to the sense of immersion, which had the lowest values.

18.5 Conclusion

In the previous sections, the workflow adopted for creating of *The Living Hill* was illustrated with particular attention to context and expected audience. The choices were explained in relation to the project's objectives, the analysis conducted on the average visitors of the open-air museum, and the contingent issues we had to face during the development phase. The accuracy issues with the game's narrative and visual environment were easily resolved since the archaeologists working on the site were compelling in explaining why accuracy should have been an integral aspect of this kind of game, and the developers agreed. It was obvious to everyone how the objectives of the C.A.P.I. project were intrinsically tied to the potential of video games to act as authoritative sources of information for a cultural heritage project.

This does not mean that video games should be automatically applied to any cultural site/museum/content without a critical analysis of the purposes, a precise choice of themes, a particular focus on a) the expected audience, b) an appropriate understanding of the video game system and c) an excellent knowledge of the historical/cultural context. A thorough analysis of these factors may lead to alternative choices for game type, narrative, and visuals or even lead to entirely different kinds of tools for communicating our research, even if creating a video game for cultural heritage is currently popular (some recent examples are presented in Table 18.1 and discussed in Bonacini and Giaccone 2022; Mariotti 2021). The cited titles are among those listed in the map of games fully or partially based in Italy and involving to the Italian cultural heritage and landscape created by the Italian Videogame Program (IVIPRO n.d.).

Nowadays, video games serve multiple purposes, including meeting archaeological aims and acting as a valuable medium for archaeological heritage dissemination and enhancement (Mariotti 2021). However, video games dedicated to cultural heritage cannot become a panacea or, worse, a cool and innovative excuse for not seriously dealing with significant actions to promote knowledge and public involvement. That is why a serious examination should be conducted to assess how video games affect users' learning and knowledge of a specific context before and after creating the game.

In conclusion, a meaningful project cannot be separated from a) a previous careful analysis of the objectives, the context, and the expected audience; b) a contextual effort to collaborate between the various domain experts (archaeologists, developers, graphics designers) to make the best choices based on the primary analysis; c) a final evaluation of the project (Bonacchi and Moshenska 2015) to identify its strengths and weaknesses, and eventually solve the latter.

Meeting visitors' needs and expectations within cultural spaces and providing people with significant experiences regarding the past is crucial to stimulating knowledge and learning, engaging visitors, and making them care about cultural heritage. Since the proliferation of video games dedicated to the past, the development of a creation and evaluation methodology to suggest a series of best practices to be applied to different case studies and measure users' experience will be helpful and meaningful for many researchers and practitioners not only in the heritage field but also for those working in digital applications companies.

Acknowledgements

The author acknowledges Professor Marco Valenti, Doctor Federico Salzotti and all the archaeologists/reenactors working at the archaeological park and open-air museum in Poggibonsi for their thoughtful insights, and Maurizio Amoroso and Francesco Rossini for their professional support in developing *The Living Hill.*

Funding

The research program of C.A.P.I. was funded by the Tuscany Region, the University of Siena, the Foundation of the bank Monte dei Paschi di Siena, Archeòtipo Ltd. (the private company that manages the archaeological area on the hill of Poggibonsi and the open-air museum), and Entertainment Game Apps, Ltd. (a private company specialised in the development of historical serious games).

The UX research was carried out as part of the PhD research project of the author, funded by a scholarship of the University of Bari 'Aldo Moro'.

Conflict of interest disclosure

The author declares no financial conflicts of interest related to the content of this article.

Data, Scripts, Code, and Supplementary Information Availability

The raw data file related to the questionnaire is available at DOI: 10.5281/zenodo.8305896.

Peer review

This article has been reviewed and recommended by PCI Archaeology.

Hageneuer, Sebastian. 2023. "Gamification of an archaeological park: *The Living Hill* Project as work-in-progress." *Peer Community in Archaeology* 100399. DOI: 10.24072/pci.archaeo.100399.9

References

Amoroso, Maurizio. 2020. "Videogame archeologici e storici: luci, ombre e lezioni imparate con Mi Rasna." In *Videogames, Ricerca, Patrimonio Culturale*, edited by Sofia Pescarin, 55–9. Milano: Franco Angeli.

Andreu Pintado, Javier, Pablo Serrano Basterra, and Iker Ibero Iriarte. 2022. "Old wine in new wineskins: a video game with epigraphic content." In *Valete vos viatores. Travelling through Latin inscriptions across the Roman Empire*, edited by Javier Andreu, Armando Redentor, and Elena Alguacil, 63–94. Coimbra: Imprensa da Universidade de Coimbra.

Ariese, Csilla E., Krijn H. J. Boom, Bram van den Hout, Angus A. A. Mol, and Aris Politopoulos (eds). 2021. *Return to the Interactive Past. The Interplay of Video Games and Histories*. Leiden: Sidestone Press.

Bekele, Mafkereseb Kassahun, Roberto Pierdicca, Emanuele Frontoni, Eva Sabina Malinverni, and James Gain. 2018. "A survey of augmented, virtual, and mixed reality for cultural heritage." *Journal on Computing and Cultural Heritage* 11 (2): 1–36. DOI:10.1145/3145534.

Bellotti, Francesco, Riccardo Berta, Alessandro De Gloria. 2010. "Designing Effective Serious Games: Opportunities and Challenges for Research." *International Journal of Emerging Technologies in Learning* 5 (3): 22–35.

Bellotti, Francesco, Bill Kapralos, Kiju Lee, Pablo Moreno-Ger, and Riccardo Berta. 2013. "Assessment in and of Serious Games: An Overview." *Advances in Human-Computer Interaction* Volume 2013: 1–11. DOI:10.1155/2013/136864.

Bertoldi, Stefano. 2021. "C.A.P.I. Project in the Making: 3D Applications at Poggio Imperiale Between Materiality and Virtual Reality (Poggibonsi, IT)." *Open Archaeology* 7 (1): 1444–57. DOI:10.1515/opar-2020-0201.

Bertoldi, Stefano, and Samanta Mariotti (eds). 2022. *The Past as a Digital Playground. Archaeology, Virtual Reality and Video Games*. Oxford: Archaeopress.

Birchall, Danny, Martha Henson, Alexandra Burch, Daniel Evans, and Kate Haley Goldman. 2012. "Levelling up: Towards best practice in evaluating museum games." In *Museums and the Web 2012: Selected Papers from an International Conference ePub Edition*, edited by Nancy Proctor, and Rich Cherry, 11–4. Museums and the Web LLC. https://www.museumsandtheweb.com/mw2012/epub.

Bogost, Ian. 2007. *Persuasive Games. The Expressive Power of Videogames*. Cambridge, MA: The MIT Press.

Bollwerk, Elizabeth. 2015. "Co-Creation's Role in Digital Public Archaeology." *Advances in Archaeological Practice* 3 (3): 223–34. DOI:10.7183/2326-3768.3.3.223.

Bonacchi, Chiara. 2013. "The development of Public Archaeology in Italy: a review of recent efforts." *Public Archaeology* 12 (3): 211–6. DOI:10.1179/1465518714Z.00000000044.

Bonacchi, Chiara, and Gabriel Moshenska. 2015. "Critical Reflections on Digital Public Archaeology." *Internet Archaeology* 40. DOI:10.11141/ia.40.7.1.

Bonacini, Elisa. 2023. *Storytelling culturale e piattaforme digitali. Manuale pratico con case study e best practice internazionali*. Palermo: Dario Flaccovio Editore.

Bonacini, Elisa, and Sonia Caterina Giaccone 2022. "Gamification and cultural institutions in cultural heritage promotion: a successful example from Italy." *Cultural Trends* 31 (1): 3–22. DOI:10.1080/09548963.2021.1910490.

Boyan, Andy, and John L. Sherry. 2011. "The Challenge in Creating Games for Education: Aligning Mental Models With Game Models." *Child Development Perspectives* 5 (2): 82–7. DOI:10.1111/j.1750-8606.2011.00160.x.

Camera di Commercio Arezzo-Siena. 2023. "Attrattività turistica nel territorio della provincia Siena arrivi presenze tipologia struttura." https://www.as.camcom.it/attrattivita-turistica-nel-territorio-della-provincia-siena-arrivi-presenze-tipologia-struttura.

Catalano, Chiara Eva, Angelo Marco Luccini, and Michela Mortara. 2014. "Best practices for an effective design and evaluation of serious games." *International Journal of Serious Games* 1 (1): 1–13. DOI:10.17083/ijsg.v1i1.8.

Cassone, Vincenzo Idone, and Mattia Thibault. 2016. "The HGR Framework: A Semiotic Approach to the Representation of History in Digital Games." *gamevironments* 5: 156–204. http://nbn-resolving.de/urn:nbn:de:gbv:46-00105661-11.

Champion, Erik M. 2015. *Critical gaming: interactive history and virtual heritage*. Surrey: Ashgate.

Champion, Erik M. 2017. "Bringing Your A-Game to Digital Archaeology: Issues with Serious Games and Virtual Heritage and What We Can Do About It." *The SAA Archaeological Record* 17 (2): 24–7.

Champion, Erik M. (ed). 2021. *Virtual Heritage: A Guide*. London: Ubiquity Press.

Copplestone, Tara J. 2016. "But that's not accurate: the differing perceptions of accuracy in cultural-heritage videogames between creators, consumers and critics." *Rethinking History* 21(3): 415–38. DOI:10.1080/13642529.2017.1256615.

Copplestone, Tara J. 2017. "Designing and Developing a Playful Past in Video Games." In *The Interactive Past. Archaeology, Heritage, and Video Games*, edited by Angus A. Mol, Csilla E. Ariese-Vandemeulebroucke, Krijn H. J. Boom, and Aris Politopoulos, 85–97. Leiden: Sidestone Press.

Cozza, Marco, Salvatore Isabella, Paola Di Cuia, Alessandro Cozza, Raffaele Peluso, Vincenzo Cosentino, Loris Barbieri, Maurizio Muzzupappa, and Fabio Bruno. 2021. "Dive in the Past: A Serious Game to Promote the Underwater Cultural Heritage of the Mediterranean Sea." *Heritage* 4: 4001–16. DOI:10.3390/heritage4040220.

Dawson, Beata, Pauline Joseph, and Erik M. Champion. 2020. "Evaluating User Experience of a Multimedia Storyteller Panorama Tour: The Story of the Markham Car Collection." *Collections* 16 (3): 251–78. DOI:10.1177/1550190620940966.

De Felice, Giuliano. 2015. "Racconti dalla terra. L'archeologia fra linguaggi, creatività e tecnologie." In *Opening the Past 2014. Immersive Archaeology. MapPapers 1-IV*, edited by Maria Letizia Gualandi, Gabriele Gattiglia, and Francesca Anichini, 24–7. Rome: Edizioni Nuova Cultura.

De Felice, Giuliano. 2022. "Taras e i doni del mare. Una mostra virtuale fra pandemia e ritorno alla normalità." In *Taras e i doni del mare*, edited by Eva Degl'Innocenti, Danilo Leone, Maria Turchiano, and Giuliano Volpe, 123–6. Bari: Edipuglia.

Di Pietro, Giorgio. 2021. "Changes in Italy's education-related digital divide." *Economic Affairs* 41 (2): 252–70. DOI:10.1111/ecaf.12471.

Economou, Maria. 2015. "Heritage in the Digital Age." In *A Companion to Heritage Studies*, edited by William Logan, Máiréad N. Craith, and Ullrich Kockel, 215–28. Hoboken: John Wiley & Sons, Ltd. DOI:10.1002/9781118486634.ch15.

Fazio, Gioacchino, Daniele Malfitana, Stefano Fricano, Antonio Mazzaglia, and Elisa Bonacini (eds). 2022. *Il Digital Cultural Heritage e i Serious Game: l'Esperienza del Progetto Augustus*. Palermo: Palermo University Press.

Ferdani, Daniele, Bruno Fanini, Maria Claudia Piccioli, Fabiana Carboni, and Paolo Vigliarolo 2020. "3D Reconstruction and Validation of Historical Background for Immersive VR Applications and Games: The Case Study of the Forum of Augustus in Rome." *Journal of Cultural Heritage* 43:129–43. DOI:10.1016/j.culher.2019.12.004.

First Playable Found. 2021. "Ministero delle Imprese e del Made in Italy, fondo per l'intrattenimento digitale". https://www.mimit.gov.it/it/incentivi/fondo-per-l-intrattenimento-digitale.

Francovich, Riccardo, and MarcoValenti (eds). 2007. *Poggio Imperiale a Poggibonsi. Il Territorio, lo Scavo, il Parco*. Milan: Silvana Editoriale.

Fronza, Vittorio, Alessandra Nardini, Federico Salzotti, and Marco Valenti. 2001. "A GIS Solution for Excavations: Experience of the Siena University LIAAM." In *Computing Archaeology for Understanding the Past. Computer Applications and Quantitative Methods in Archaeology. Proceedings of the 28th Conference, Ljubljana, April 2000*, edited by Zoran Stančič, and Tatjana Veljanovski, 173–7. Oxford: BAR Publishing.

Giordano, Federico. 2020. "Nel mezzo del periglioso tragitto. Istituzionalizzazione e riconoscimento accademico della cultura del videogioco in Italia." In *Il videogioco e l'Italia: Storie, rappresentazioni, contesti*, edited by Marco Benoît Carbone, and Riccardo Fassone, 283–95. Milan: Mimesis Edizioni.

Giovannella, Carlo, Licia Cianfriglia, and Antonelo Giannelli. 2022. "The Italian School Ecosystems two years after the lockdown: an overview on the "digital shock" triggered by the pandemic in the perceptions of schools' principals and teachers." In *Polyphonic Construction of Smart Learning Ecosystems. SLERD 2022. Smart Innovation, Systems and Technologies, 908*, edited by Mihai Dascalu, Patrizia Marti, and Francesca Pozzi, 47–76. Singapore: Springer. DOI:10.1007/978-981-19-5240-1_4.

Goleman, Daniel. 1995. *Emotional Intelligence: Why It Can Matter More Than IQ*. London: Bloomsbury.

Hageneuer, Sebastian (ed). 2020. *Communicating the Past in the Digital Age. Proceedings of the International Conference on Digital Methods in Teaching and Learning in Archaeology (12–13 October 2018)*. London: Ubiquity Press. DOI:10.5334/bch.

Hiriart, Juan F. V. 2017. "Designing and Using Game Environments as Historical Learning Contexts." In *CAA 2017: Digital Archaeologies, Material Worlds (Past and Present). Proceedings of the 45th annual conference on computer applications and quantitative methods in archaeology*, edited by Jeffrey B. Glover, Jessica Moss, and Dominique Rissolo, 169–77. Tübingen: Tübingen University Press. DOI:10.15496/publikation-43219.

Huggett, Jeremy. 2019. "Resilient scholarship in the digital age." *Journal of Computer Applications in Archaeology* 2 (1): 105–19. DOI:10.5334/jcaa.25.

Ibrahim, Nazrita, and Nazlena Mohamad Ali. 2018. "A Conceptual Framework for Designing Virtual Heritage Environment for Cultural Learning." *Journal on Computing and Cultural Heritage* 11 (2): 1–27. DOI:10.1145/3117801.

Inklink. 2007. "Parco di Poggibonsi." https://www.inklink.it/portfolio/parco-poggibonsi.

IVIPRO. n.d. "Italian Videogame Program, Map of Games." Accessed October 2, 2023. https://ivipro.it/it/italia-in-gioco.

Kolb, David. 1984. *Experiential Learning: Experience as the Source of Learning and Development*. Englewood Cliffs, NJ: Prentice Hall.

Konstantakis, Markos, and George Caridakis. 2020. "Adding Culture to UX: UX Research Methodologies and Applications in Cultural Heritage." *Journal on Computing and Cultural Heritage* 13 (1): 1–17. DOI:10.1145/3354002.

Lozano, Jorge. 1987. *El discurso histórico*. Madrid: Alianza.

Mariotti, Samanta. 2020a. "What if "Lara Croft" Becomes a Video Game Designer? When Archaeologists "Dig" Serious Games." In *Games and Learning Alliance. GALA 2020. Lecture Notes in Computer Science 12517*, edited by Iza Marfisi-Schottman, Francesco Bellotti, Ludovic Hamon, and Roland Klemke, 395–400. Cham: Springer. DOI:10.1007/978-3-030-63464-3_37.

Mariotti, Samanta. 2020b. "Serious Games and Archaeology: Rough Notes on Crafting Archaeological Data for Heritage Enhancement." In *Advances in Cultural Heritage Studies, Year 2020. Contributions of the European Students' Association for Cultural Heritage*, edited by Alexandra de Carvalho Antunes, Grigor Angjliu, and Mariagrazia Bellanova, 217–34. Oeiras: Mazu Press.

Mariotti, Samanta. 2021. "The Use of Serious Games as an Educational and Dissemination Tool for Archaeological Heritage. Potential and Challenges for the Future." *magazén* 2 (1): 119–38. DOI:10.30687/mag/2724-3923/2021/03/005.

Mariotti, Samanta. 2025. "10 years of 'Archaeogaming': an Italian Perspective." In Next-Gen Archaeology. Innovazioni e tradizioni tecnologiche per lo studio del passato. Atti delle Giornate di Studio "Archeologia e Nuove Tecnologie: dalla teoria ai protocolli esecutivi" (Siena, 25-27 ottobre 2023). Archeologia e Calcolatori, Supplemento 13, edited by Stefano Bertoldi, and Luca Luppino, 325-342. Sesto Fiorentino: All'Insegna del Giglio.

Mariotti, Samanta, and Nina Marotta. 2020. "Gioco e storydoing: strumenti didattici per l'insegnamento della storia nella scuola primaria." *Didattica della Storia – Journal of Research and Didactics of History* 2 (1S): 608–29. DOI:10.6092/issn.2704-8217/11224.

Masi, Luciana. 1992. *La fortezza di Poggio Imperiale a Poggibonsi. Un prototipo di cantiere dell'architettura militare del Rinascimento*. Poggibonsi: Lalli Editore.

Merchán, María José, Pilar Merchán, and Emiliano Pérez. 2023. "Serious Games to Enhance Education. Play, Technology and Archaeology in a Spanish Museum." *Revista Colombiana de Educación* 89: 59–85. DOI:110.17227/rce.num88-13992.

Modena, Elisabetta. 2019. "Musei nei videogiochi | Videogiochi nei musei." *pianoB. arti e culture visive* 4 (1): 83–105. DOI:10.6092/issn.2531-9876/10251.

Mol, Angus A. A., Csilla E. Ariese, Krijn H. J. Boom, and Aris Politopoulos (eds). 2017. *The Interactive Past. Archaeology, Heritage, and Video Games*. Leiden: Sidestone Press.

Moon, Jennifer A. 2004. *A Handbook of Reflective and Experiential Learning: Theory and Practice*. Routledge: New York.

Morgan, Colleen. 2019. "Avatars, monsters, and machines: A cyborg archaeology." *European Journal of Archaeology* 22 (3): 324–37. DOI:10.1017/eaa.2019.22.

Mortara, Michela, and Chiara Eva Catalano. 2018. "3D Virtual environments as effective learning contexts for cultural heritage." *Italian Journal of Educational Technology* 26 (2): 5–21. DOI:10.17471/2499-4324/1026.

Mortara, Michela, Chiara Eva Catalano, Francesco Bellotti, Giusy Fiucci, Minica Houry-Panchetti, and Panagiotis Petridis. 2014. "Learning Cultural Heritage by Serious Games." *Journal of Cultural Heritage* 15 (3): 318–25. DOI:10.1016/j.culher.2013.04.004.

Moscati, Paola. 2019. "Informatica Archeologica e Archeologia Digitale. Le risposte della Rete." *Archeologia e Calcolatori* 30: 21–38.

Mutino, Sabrina, Lucia Colangelo, and Michele Scioscia. 2022. "Hold the Hut, il progetto di tutela e valorizzazione della capanna arcaica di San Chirico Nuovo (Potenza, Basilicata)." In *The Past as a Digital Playground. Archaeology, Virtual Reality and Video Games*, edited by Stefano Bertoldi, and Samanta Mariotti, 73–90. Oxford: Archaeopress.

Pagano, Alfonsina, Giulia Armone, and Elisabetta De Sanctis. 2015. "Virtual Museums and Audience Studies. The case of "Keys To Rome" exhibition." In *Proceedings of the 2015 Digital Heritage International Congress, volume 1, Digitization & Acquisition. Computer Graphics & Interaction*, edited by Gabriele Guidi, Roberto Scopigno, Juan Carlos Torres, Holger Graf, Fabio Remondino, Luciana Duranti, Pere Brunet, Susan Hazan, and Juan Barceló, 373–6. New York: IEEE. DOI:10.1109/DigitalHeritage.2015.7413905.

Pagano, Alfonsina, Augusto Palombini, Guido Bozzelli, Maurizio De Nino, Ivana Cerato, and Stefano Ricciardi. 2020. "ArkaeVision VR Game: User Experience Research between Real and Virtual Paestum." *Applied Sciences* 10 (9): 3182. DOI:10.3390/app10093182.

Pescarin, Sofia (ed). 2020. *Videogames, Ricerca, Patrimonio Culturale*. Milan: Edizioni Franco Angeli.

Pescarin, Sofia, Bruno Fanini, Daniele Ferdani, Keith Misfud, and Andrew Hamilton. 2020. "Optimising Environmental Educational Narrative Videogames: The Case of 'A Night in the Forum'." *Journal on Computing and Cultural Heritage* 13 (4): 1–23. DOI:10.1145/3424952.

Piano Nazionale Scuola Digitale. 2015. https://www.miur.gov.it/scuola-digitale.

Pietroni, Eva. 2020. "Ibridazione dei media nelle applicazioni interattive." In *Videogames, Ricerca, Patrimonio Culturale*, edited by Sofia Pescarin, 150–74. Milan: Franco Angeli.

Poiron, Perrine. 2021. "Assassin's Creed Origins-Discovery Tour: A Behind the Scene Experience." *Near Eastern Archaeology* 84 (1): 79–85. DOI:10.1086/712580.

Politopoulos, Aris, Angus A. A. Mol, Krijn H. J. Boom, and Csilla E. Ariese. 2019. ""History Is Our Playground": Action and Authenticity in Assassin's Creed: Odyssey." *Advances in Archaeological Practice* 7 (3): 317–23. DOI:10.1017/aap.2019.30.

Poullis, Charalambos, Marta Kersten-Oertel, J. Praveen Benjamin, Oliver Philbin-Briscoe, Bart Simon, Dimitra Perissiou, Stella Demesticha, Evangeline Markou, Elias Frentzos, Phaedon Kyriakidis, Dimitrios Skarlatos, and Selma Rizvic. 2019. "Evaluation of "The Seafarers": A serious game on seaborne trade in the Mediterranean sea during the Classical period." *Digital Applications in Archaeology and Cultural Heritage* 12: 1–14. DOI:10.1016/j.daach.2019.e00090.

Reinhard, Andrew. 2018. *Archaeogaming: An Introduction to Archaeology in and of Video Games*. New York: Berghahn Books.

Rice, Hannah E. 2014. *Exploring the Pedagogical Possibilities of applying Gaming Theory and Technologies to Historic Architectural Visualisation.* MSc diss, Digital Heritage, University of York.

Richardson, Lorna. 2013. "A Digital Public Archaeology?" *Papers from the Institute of Archaeology* 23 (1): 1–12, DOI:10.5334/pia.431.

Ripanti, Francesco. 2022. *Unforgettable Encounters. Understanding Participation in Italian Community Archaeology*. Oxford: Archaeopress.

Sanders, Donald H. 2014. "Virtual Heritage: Researching and Visualizing the Past in 3D." *Journal of Eastern Mediterranean Archaeology and Heritage Studies* 2 (1): 30–47. DOI:10.5325/jeasmedarcherstu.2.1.0030.

Shih, Ju-Ling, Shun-Cian Jheng, and Jia-Jiun Tseng. 2015. "A simulated learning environment of history games for enhancing players' cultural awareness." *Interactive Learning Environments* 23 (2): 191–211. DOI:10.1080/10494820.2014.997249.

Simon, Nina. 2010. *The Participatory Museum*. Santa Cruz, CA: Museum 2.0. https://participatorymuseum.org/read.

Solima, Ludovico. 2018. "Gaming for the Museums. The MANN Experience." *Economia della Cultura* 28 (3): 275–90. http://www.rivisteweb.it/doi/10.1446/91289.

Valenti, Marco. 2016. "'We invest in Public Archaeology'. The Poggibonsi Archaeodrome project: an alliance between people, Municipality people, Municipality and University." *European Journal of Post-Classical Archaeologies* 6: 333–46.

Valenti, Marco. 2019. *L'Archeodromo di Poggibonsi. Un Viaggio nell'Alto Medioevo*. Bari: Edipuglia.

Valenti, Marco, and Federico Salzotti. 2017. "For a participatory culture: the experience of Archeòtipo srl and the Poggibonsi Archaeodrome (Italy, prov. Siena)." In *Bridging Theories, Strategies and Practices in Valuing Cultural Heritage*, edited by Mara Cerquetti, 243–59. Macerata: Edizioni Università di Macerata.

Volpe, Giuliano. 2020. *Archeologia pubblica. Metodi, tecniche, esperienze*. Rome: Carocci.

Volpe, Giuliano, and Giuliano De Felice. 2014. "Comunicazione e progetto culturale, archeologia e società." *European Journal of Post-Classical Archaeologies* 4: 401–20.

19 Social Network Analysis, Community Detection Algorithms, and Neighbourhood Identification in Pompeii

Matthew Notarian
Hiram College,
notarianmf@hiram.edu

Abstract

The definition and identification of urban neighbourhoods in archaeological contexts remain complex and problematic, both theoretically and empirically. As constructs with both social and spatial characteristics, their detection through material culture alone remains elusive, especially within large settlements that are incompletely excavated or preserved. Thanks to its focus upon relational ties, network analysis offers a profitable path towards untangling the complexities of urban neighbourhoods, especially with respect to their often imprecise, fuzzy boundaries. Various community detection algorithms offer mathematical solutions for partitioning large graphs into communities, but these should not be applied without careful interpretation. Two of the most widely utilized community detection algorithms based on modularity optimization, Louvain and Leiden, contain a customizable resolution parameter that is often overlooked by practitioners. This controls the density of the partitioned communities, and therefore the number identified, but it is difficult to determine the optimal value for any given network. In addition, the results of community detection algorithms vary stochastically. Reliance upon a single iteration may mask potentially significant differences between runs using even a constant resolution parameter. A recently developed algorithm, the Convex Hull of Admissible Modularity Partitions (CHAMP), is designed to overcome these complications and also generates potentially useful multiscalar network community structures. Its applicability to neighbourhood archaeology is demonstrated within three networks of Pompeian housing units based on shared public fountains.

The case study examines Pompeii's public fountains as hubs of social interaction. Given their daily frequentation by nearby inhabitants, fountains represent plausible proxies for the centres of definable neighbourhoods. It expands upon a spatial network model that connected all 2000+ external doors in the city to the 40 public fountains that were likely functional in 79 CE. Three undirected, one-mode networks were constructed in which units are linked to each other by a common fountain and weighted by the number of fountains they share. The first network connects units by the closest fountain to any

In *Advances in Digital Archaeology. Proceedings of the 2023 conference Computer Applications and Quantitative Methods in Archaeology – 50 years of synergy*, edited by J.W.H.P. Verhagen, J. Waagen, A. Brandsen, A. Queffelec, R.M. Visser and D. Taelman, 249–264. Leiden: Sidestone Press.

external door. Since many properties had side doors within reach of different water sources, these represent potential interconnections between communities. The second and third networks use incrementally larger time-to-fountain thresholds (30-second and one-minute walks to any fountain, respectively) to map potential choices, also expanding social integration. The results demonstrate that innovative methods for assessing the output of community detection algorithms offer new modes of analysis that are applicable not just to neighbourhood archaeology, but any archaeological network analysis that uses graph partitioning.

Keywords: Network Analysis; Community Detection; Neighbourhoods; Urban archaeology; Roman archaeology; Pompeii

19.1 Introduction

Neighbourhood archaeology (e.g., Pacifico and Truex 2019b; Thompson et al. 2022; Haug et al. 2023) and network community detection (Shai et al. 2021) are two topics that have seen increasing interest in recent years within their respective disciplines. In general, community detection algorithms seek to identify clusters of nodes that are more densely connected to each other than others in the network, a process with many useful applications in archaeology. Studies have used them to explore the political affiliation of Maya polities (Scholnick et al. 2013), spatial scales of ceramic similarity networks (Peeples and Bischoff 2023), Neolithic household community organization (Mazzucato 2019), and dendrochronological provenance patterns (Visser 2021). Nonetheless, advances in the quality and efficiency of community detection algorithms, and innovative methods for assessing their outputs, offer new modes of analysis that have yet to be put to widespread use in archaeological network research. This paper focuses on the potential of community detection to identify urban neighbourhoods in Pompeii, but the methodologies outlined have implications for numerous applications within archaeological network analysis that use graph partitioning.

Two of the most widely utilized community detection algorithms based on modularity optimization, Louvain and Leiden, contain a customizable resolution parameter (γ) that is often overlooked by practitioners. This controls the density of the partitioned communities, and therefore the number identified, but it is difficult to determine the optimal value for any given network. In addition, the results of community detection algorithms vary stochastically. Reliance upon a single iteration may mask potentially significant differences between runs using even a constant resolution parameter. A recently developed algorithm, the Convex Hull of Admissible Modularity Partitions (CHAMP), is designed to overcome these complications and also generates potentially useful multiscalar network community structures (Weir et al. 2017). Its applicability to neighbourhood archaeology is demonstrated within three one-mode networks of Pompeian housing units based on shared public fountains.

19.2 Neighbourhoods in Pompeii based on shared public fountains

The definition and identification of urban neighbourhoods in archaeological contexts remain complex and problematic, both theoretically and empirically (Smith 2010; Pacifico and Truex 2019a). Are neighbourhoods primarily top-down administrative units, organic bottom-up household agglomerations, or something in between? Is face-to-face interaction an important prerequisite or can larger districts exist at a more dispersed level of contact? Crucially, as constructs with both social and spatial characteristics, their detection through material culture alone remains elusive, especially within large settlements that are incompletely excavated or preserved. Nonetheless, in Pompeii, many studies have noted that public fountains were centres of daily social interaction for nearby inhabitants (Laurence 2007; Notarian 2023). Therefore, they can be considered plausible proxies for definable neighbourhoods. These are often defined by simple linear distances from fountains. Yet, thanks to its focus upon relational ties, network analysis offers a more profitable path towards untangling the complexities of urban neighbourhoods, especially with respect to their often imprecise, fuzzy boundaries (Poorthuis 2018). It also generates quantitative metrics with which to explore theoretical questions regarding the nature of urban neighbourhoods.

The excellent preservation of Pompeii's streets and domestic units permits the creation of a detailed social network based on shared fountain use. This study expands upon an earlier GIS spatial network model that connected all 2000+ external doors in the city to the 40 public fountains that were likely functional in 79 CE, when the city was destroyed (Notarian 2023). Two points layers represented doors and fountains, respectively. A polyline along the street network connected these points, which was then subdivided into 3m segments. Least-cost routes to the closest fountain from every door were identified using ArcGIS' Closest Facility function, but costs were derived in units of time rather than linear distance. Elevation values from an underlying digital elevation model were imported to each network segment endpoint to calculate its average slope. Various slope-based walking functions were used to estimate speed, which was then converted to costs in minutes. The results of this analysis revealed

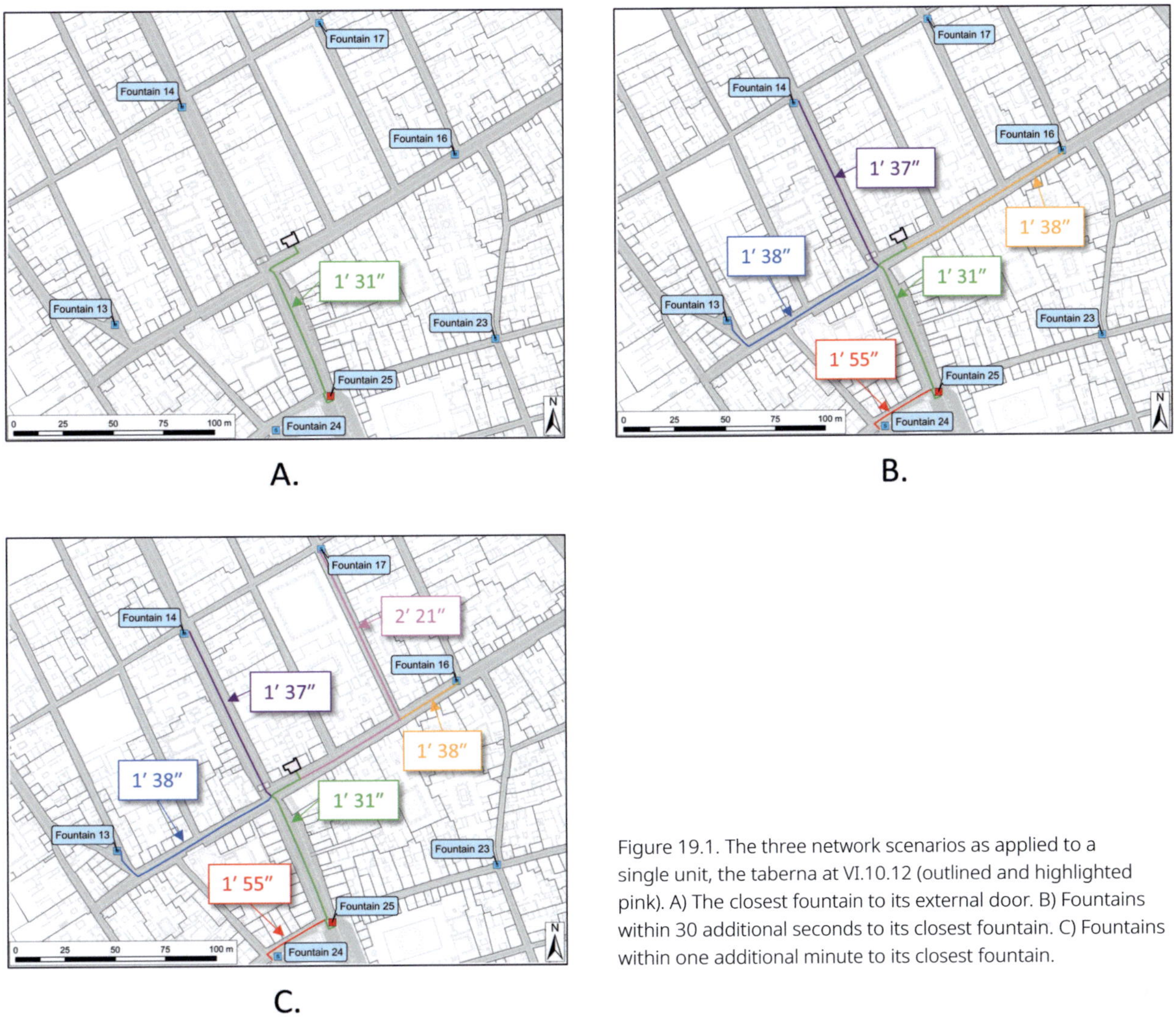

Figure 19.1. The three network scenarios as applied to a single unit, the taberna at VI.10.12 (outlined and highlighted pink). A) The closest fountain to its external door. B) Fountains within 30 additional seconds to its closest fountain. C) Fountains within one additional minute to its closest fountain.

important points that had previously been overlooked. First, many housing units with multiple exterior doors are closer to different fountains depending upon the door exited. Second, an inhabitant's choice of fountain often depended upon differences of mere seconds in walking time. In such situations it is difficult to predict which fountain a particular unit may have frequented. Individual agency must have determined the composition of the social communities tied to fountains more than previously assumed. Further, if Pompeians habitually used *multiple* fountains, the neighbourhoods formed by this activity would have been far more dynamic, fuzzy, and overlapping than a static division can represent.

19.3 Methods

To further explore these dynamics, three undirected, one-mode networks were constructed in which units are linked to each other by a common fountain and weighted by the number of fountains they share. The networks were built and analysed in Gephi (Bastian et al. 2009) and the R packages qgraph (Epskamp et al. 2012) and igraph (Csárdi et al. 2024). First, ArcGIS' Closest Facility analysis identified the 10 closest fountains to every external door. The door-to-fountain times were exported to a .csv and ranked. Ranking by door and unit identified the quickest route from any unit entrance, which formed the basis of the first network. Many properties had side doors closer to different water sources – potential interconnections between communities. Ranking by unit alone was used to construct the other two networks. Based on incrementally larger time to fountain thresholds – an additional 30 seconds and one minute of walking time beyond that to the closest fountain, respectively – these networks expand choice and also social integration. After cumulatively summing walking times to successive fountains to identify the relevant edges, each network was converted into an edge table and imported into Gephi as a bimodal network (unit to fountain), then converted to a one-mode network (unit to unit) using the multimode

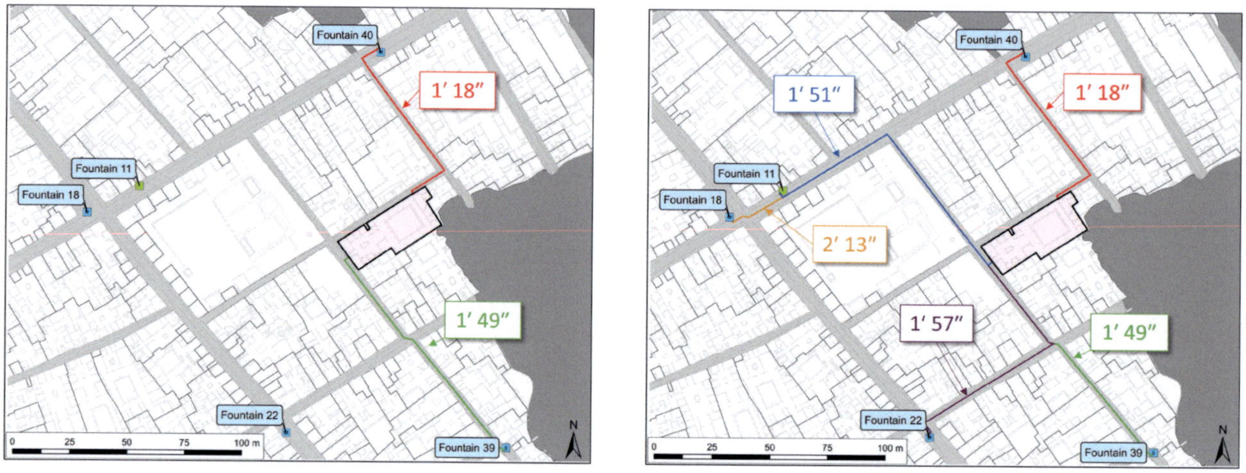

A. B.

Figure 19.2. The three network scenarios as applied to a single unit, the house at IX.6.5 (outlined and highlighted pink). A) The closest fountains to its two external doors. Also serves as its 30-second network. B) Fountains within one additional minute of the absolute closest fountain (no. 40).

Threshold	Edges	Graph Density	Network Diameter	Average Path Length	Transitivity
Closest Fountain to Door	27,267	3.5%	15	5.6	0.908
30 Second	50,240	6.4%	9	3.8	0.705
One Minute	83,411	10.7%	9	3.25	0.667

Table 19.1. Global metrics of the three Pompeian fountain social networks.

network transformation plugin. A node list imported key unit attributes, such as coordinates, so that the networks could be mapped spatially.

19.4 Defining the Three Networks

A couple of examples illustrate how the three network scenarios were formed. Taberna VI.10.12, with only one door, is closest to fountain 25, a walk of one and a half minutes (Figure 19.1a). By expanding the time threshold by 30 additional seconds, four other fountains are reached (Figure 19.1b). Extending the threshold by a full minute from the closest fountain connects one more (Figure 19.1c). In the social network, the assumption is that inhabitants of this shop frequented each option indiscriminately.

In the case of unit IX.6.5, a mid-sized house with two external doors, there is no single closest fountain as the nearest in terms of walking time varied by door (Figure 19.2a). Expanding the threshold by 30 seconds from the absolute closest (fountain 40) does not connect any additional fountains, but an additional minute of travel time would find these inhabitants visiting five other fountains (Figure 19.2b).

Following this process across all 1249 inhabited units in the city creates three different social networks with varying levels of interconnection. Although the larger project subjects these networks to a variety of global and local metrics to explore their characteristics, this paper solely focuses upon graph partitioning (Table 19.1). To obtain a sense of the location and size of the neighbourhoods formed by water collection, each network had to be partitioned into communities. With its basis in the density of the social network, this should constitute a more robust approach to Pompeii's fountain neighbourhoods than mere spatial distance alone, while also allowing for human agency with multiple fountain options for individual units.

19.4 Modularity Optimization and Stochastic Results

Many community detection methods, such as the Louvain algorithm and the newer Leiden algorithm, rely upon modularity (Q), which is a measure of the quality of cluster partitioning (Newman and Girvan 2004):

$$(1)\quad Q=\frac{1}{2m}\sum_{i,j}\left(A_{ij}-\gamma\frac{k_i k_j}{2m}\right)\delta\left(c_i,c_j\right)$$

where m is the total number of edges in the network, A_{ij} is the adjacency matrix for nodes i and j, k_i and k_j are the degree of nodes i and j, respectively, γ is a resolution parameter, and $\delta(c_i,c_j)$ is the Kronecker delta function, which checks whether nodes i and j belong to the same community (a value of 1) or not (a value of 0). Modularity compares the total weight of within-community edges (A_{ij} summed over every node in the community) to the expected weight in a random null model with the same

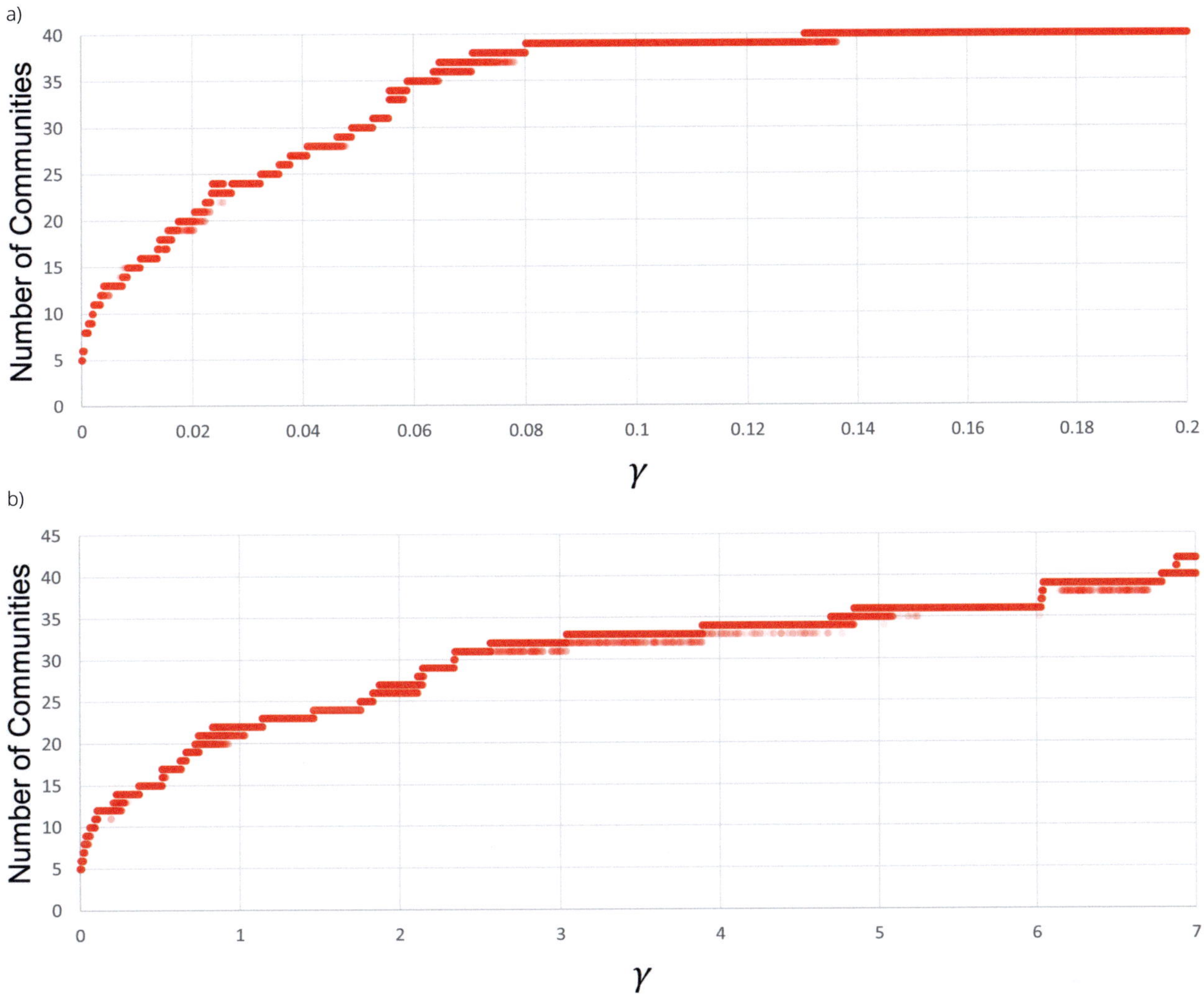

Figure 19.3. The number of communities partitioned by 125,000+ runs of the Leiden algorithm on the closest fountain by door network. 5,000 intervals between the minimum and maximum values of γ, with each value of γ run 25 times with 25 iterations per run. A) Constant Potts Model. B) Modularity.

degree distribution, the so-called configuration model $(\frac{k_i k_j}{2m})$. The configuration model rewires the network randomly while preserving each node's degree. The denser the community in comparison to the null model, the higher its modularity score, and theoretically, the better the partition. However, modularity maximization of all but the smallest networks is NP complete if done brute force by testing every possible network configuration, making it impossible to compute absolutely. As a result, several less computationally demanding heuristic algorithms have been developed, Louvain and Leiden included, to approximate optimal partitions. Nonetheless, these suffer from limitations. Most produce stochastic results when run multiple times. They output a range of near-optimal partitions that are close to the true maximum, but often vary widely in composition. Furthermore, there is no objective way to choose between varying solutions, which renders interpretation confusing. Modularity also has a resolution limit in which smaller communities are absorbed into larger ones, making it unable to detect communities smaller than a certain threshold depending on the size of the network.

The Louvain algorithm is among the most popular community detection methods used in network science (Blondel et al. 2008). It is found in many network packages such as Gephi and R and Python igraph.[1] Importantly, Louvain utilizes an adjustable resolution parameter (γ) that controls the number of returned communities. This was intended to help users work around the resolution limit. By multiplying the null model against γ, greater values lead to dense, small, and more numerous communities. Small

1 https://github.com/vtraag/louvain-igraph; https://r.igraph.org.

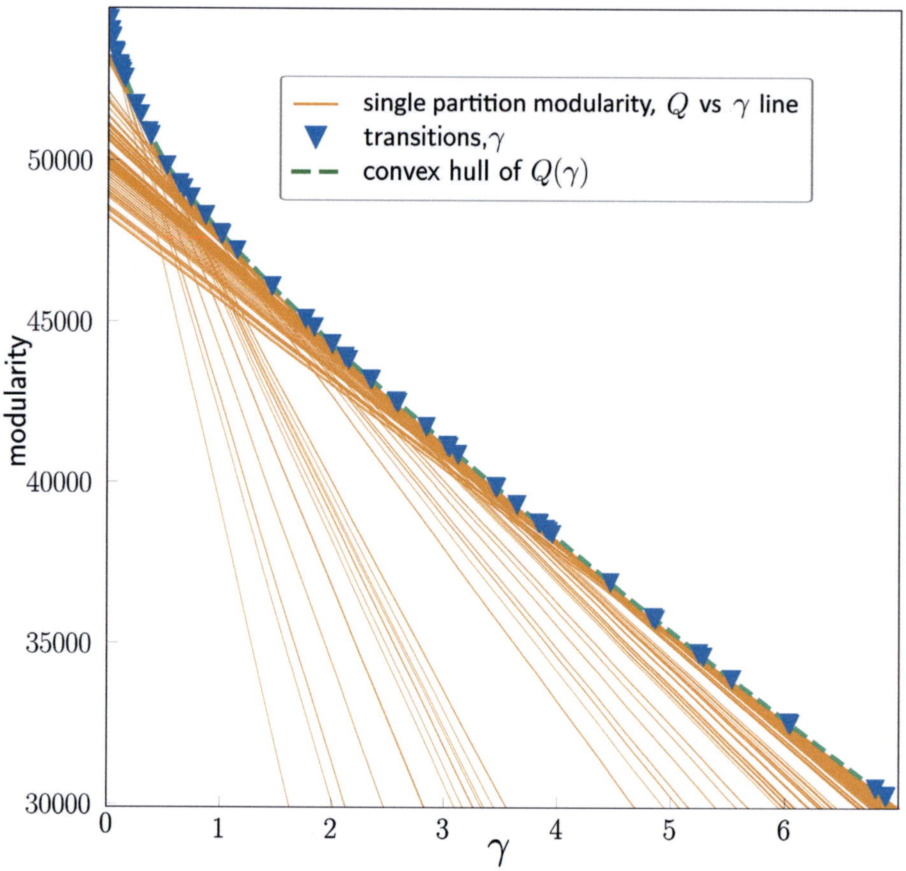

Figure 19.4. A graphical representation of the CHAMP algorithm applied to the Closest Fountain to Door network. Leiden was run with 5000 intervals between γ 0 and 7 at 25 iterations each. Each solid orange line represents a single partition identified by Leiden (here reduced to 500 for clarity), but plotted as a linear function of modularity (Q) versus γ. The convex hull of these lines (green dashed line) represents the upper envelope, that is, the partitions that produce the highest modularity score across a given range of γ. The blue triangles mark the intersection of the partition lines along the convex hull, which are the boundaries between optimal partitions, reduced to 61 from the initial 5000 results.

γ values have the opposite effect, leading to fewer loose, large communities. The resolution parameter, however, was not always available in every package, or was hidden within user guides, leading many people to use the default γ value of 1.

The Leiden algorithm improved the speed and quality of Louvain. It corrected an issue in which Louvain could create communities that were not internally connected (Traag et al. 2019). It also contains an optional alternate quality function called the Constant Potts Model (CPM) that avoids the resolution limit (Traag et al. 2011). In this version, the algorithm measures the quality of a partition not by comparing it against a null model, but by directly filtering out connections below a certain density threshold (the so-called constant, also called γ). Like Louvain, Leiden is found in many of the most popular network packages.[2]

2 https://github.com/vtraag/leidenalg; https://r.igraph.org; https://gephi.org/plugins/#/plugin/leiden-algorithm-gephi-plugin.

Due to its efficiency and accuracy, even with extremely large networks, Leiden is used exclusively in this paper as a community detection method for archaeological networks. Other community detection formulas can produce equally valid results, but these remain outside the focus of this study.

While resolution parameters were developed to give users more flexibility with which to explore their data, they lead to a bewildering set of choices. For any value of γ using either CPM or modularity, one can obtain numerous partitions. Modifying γ can produce any number of communities. But how can one determine which partition is the best representation of a particular set of data?

Partitions can be explored by iterating the algorithm at multiple values of γ and comparing the number of communities produced. As an example, Leiden was run 25 times, with 20 iterations per run, along 5000 γ intervals within the range that produces fewer than 40 communities – the number of fountains in the network (Figure 19.3). In the current case study, only communities containing one or more fountains are valid. Leiden efficiently completed these 125,000+ iterations in only a few hours. Observing a plot of the results, one might be tempted to view plateaus of a certain number of communities across a range of γ as evidence of a more robust community structure at these levels. Nonetheless, stochasticity often produces different numbers of communities even at the same γ. This method, however, does not reveal meaningful information about the actual partitions produced. Although there are multiple partitions of, for example, 36 communities, across a range of γ, it does not mean that these all represent the same 36 communities. There could be significant differences between the results, such as communities composed of vastly different units, that are not apparent without further exploration. Yet, with so many solutions, it is impossible to directly compare them.

19.5 The Convex Hull of Admissible Modularity Partitions (CHAMP)

Another algorithm, the Convex Hull of Admissible Modularity Partitions (CHAMP), available as a Python package, offers a method to significantly narrow down a subset of partitions that are potentially dominant (Weir et al. 2017).[3] After Leiden has identified hypothetically optimal partitions on a network, CHAMP calculates the modularity score for each partition using a slightly modified equation (1) across a wide range of γ, regardless of the value at which it was originally identified. The result is a linear function of γ versus modularity for each partition (Figure 19.4). A convex hull of the intersections of these lines is used to identify the upper envelope boundary. This isolates the partitions that produce the greatest modularity score across a specific range of γ, which represent the best quality partition within that span.

The pruned set of partitions can then be compared with respect to the width of the γ domain in which it is optimal and evaluated against the entire set of unique partitions using a pairwise Adjusted Mutual Information (AMI) heatmap. AMI represents the concordance of partitions to each other on scale of 0 (no alignment) to 1 (complete concordance). Using the heatmap, one can visually assess not only which partition has the widest domain of optimality, but also see how closely it relates to its neighbours in the γ space. This presents a more manageable and powerful method of directly comparing partitions than relying upon the number of communities alone. Importantly, it also eliminates from consideration the vast majority of sub-optimal partitions that result from stochasticity and improper γ selection for a given set of data.

3 https://github.com/wweir827/CHAMP.

19.6 Results and Discussion

This section presents the results of applying CHAMP across the three Pompeian fountain neighbourhoods to illustrate its utility in choosing partitions. It also offers some preliminary interpretations as they relate to defining urban neighbourhoods in Pompeii. At the time of analysis, CHAMP was unable to correctly work with CPM, so modularity alone was used. As a heuristic for exploring network data, modularity is likely more appropriate as the null model uses the network structure to identify clusters rather than an arbitrary density imposed by the user. The script was also slightly modified to correct minor errors and meet the requirements of this study.[4] CHAMP was run on each of the three networks twice – once with 1000 γ intervals and again with 5000 intervals – to test its reproducibility. The results were far more consistent than a typical Leiden run, with each iteration producing the same top partitions almost each time.

19.6.1 Closest Fountain-to-Door Network

With the network formed by the closest fountain to each unit door, CHAMP pruned 196 unique partitions down to 61, but this still represents a rather volatile community structure (Figure 19.5). The widest γ domains are mainly found in higher γ values, with 34 or more communities. This is expected since the network exhibits a modular topology with few interconnections between clusters. Many partitions, however, are remarkably similar, as indicated by the uniformity of dark blue in the AMI matrix. In fact, all the optimal partitions between γ 3.9 and 7 have AMI scores > 0.9. The widest domain in both CHAMP runs was a partition of 39 communities. This partition, however, contains three singleton communities – single housing units defined as whole neighbourhoods. For the purposes of this study, this partition must be rejected, underlining the importance of closely inspecting the output of the algorithm within the parameters of specific research questions.

The next widest γ domain is a partition into 34 neighbourhoods. Mapping this partition in topographical space and colouring each node by its community permits a visual inspection of the neighbourhoods' spatial characteristics (Figure 19.6). Dotted lines indicate the boundaries of the closest fountain in the *spatial* network, that is, the single closest fountain in terms of walking time from any external door belonging to a unit, allowing comparison between the two. The detected neighbourhoods largely mirror the closest fountain to each unit in the spatial network, except for 6 communities formed by pairs of adjoining fountain users in the spatial network (e.g., the light blue

4 Modified code and data are available online: https://zenodo.org/badge/latestdoi/686189050.

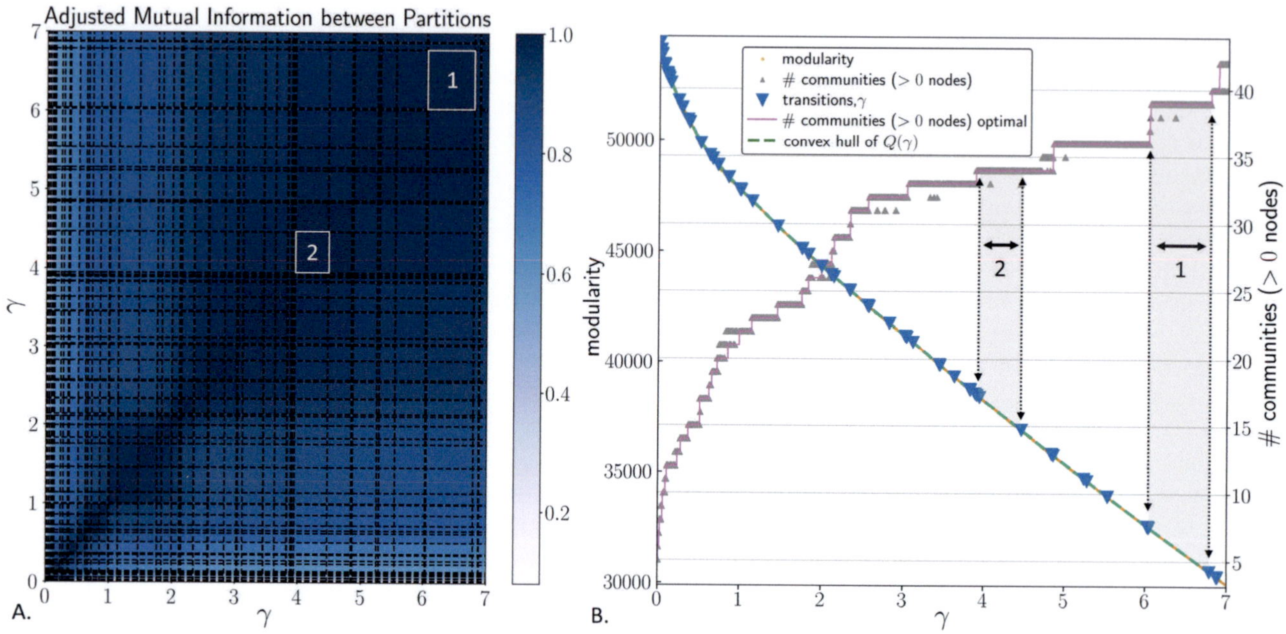

Figure 19.5. Closest Fountain-to-Door Network. Results of CHAMP using Leiden algorithm with modularity. 5000 intervals between γ 0 and 7 at 25 iterations each. A) Pairwise adjusted mutual information (AMI) of the subset of partitions identified by CHAMP. Dashed lines represent transitions between ranges of γ. The widest domain (no. 1: γ 6.04-6.79, 39 neighbourhoods) and second widest domain (no. 2: γ 3.95-4.47, 34 neighbourhoods) are outlined in white. B) Modularity versus γ. Grey upward triangles represent a random sampling of 2000 partitions plotted against their number of communities, while the solid pink stepped line shows the number of communities in the optimal partition for the range of γ. The dashed green line is the convex hull. Blue downward triangles show the transition points between various ranges of γ. The grey zones between the dotted lines identify the widest domains (no. 1: 39 neighbourhoods, no. 2: 34 neighbourhoods).

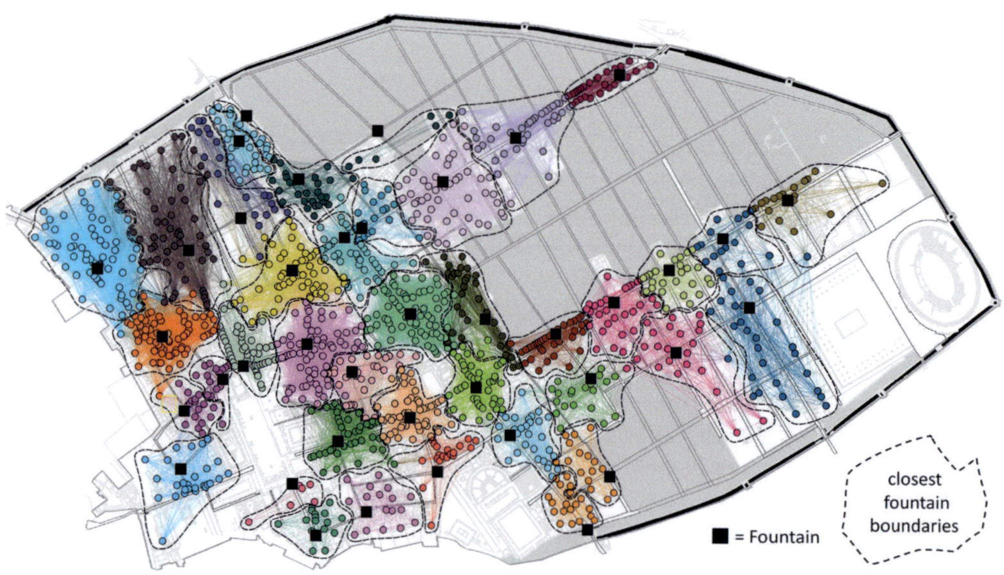

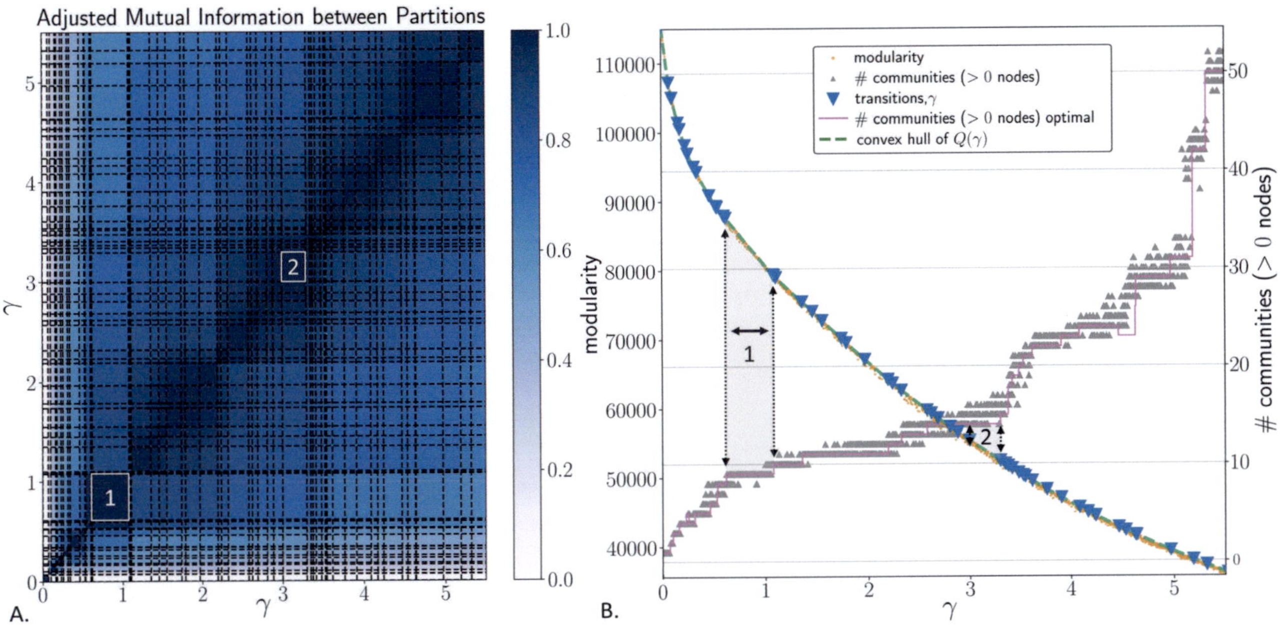

Figure 19.7. 30-Second Network. Results of CHAMP using Leiden algorithm with modularity. 5000 intervals between γ 0 and 5.5 at 25 iterations each. A) AMI of the subset of partitions identified by CHAMP. The widest domain (no. 1: γ 0.62 – 1.08, 9 neighbourhoods) and third widest domain (no. 2: γ 3.0 – 3.3, 14 neighbourhoods) are outlined in white. B) Modularity versus . Grey upward triangles represent a random sampling of 2000 partitions plotted against their number of communities, while the solid pink stepped line shows the number of communities in the optimal partition for the range of γ. The dashed green line is the convex hull. Blue downward triangles show the transition points between various ranges of . The grey zones between the dotted lines identify the widest domains (no. 1: 9 neighbourhoods, no. 2: 14 neighbourhoods).

Table 19.2. Contingency table. 30-Second Network. Widest domain (9 neighbourhoods, lettered) compared with third widest domain (14 neighbourhoods, numbered).

	1	2	3	4	5	6	7	8	9	10	11	12	13	14	All
A	0	129	0	0	0	0	81	0	5	0	0	0	0	15	230
B	0	0	0	5	0	0	0	77	0	0	69	0	0	39	190
C	0	0	125	0	0	0	0	0	4	0	0	0	59	0	188
D	134	0	0	0	0	0	0	0	0	36	0	0	0	0	170
E	0	0	0	0	106	0	0	0	0	37	0	0	0	0	143
F	0	0	0	109	0	0	0	0	0	0	0	0	0	0	109
G	0	0	0	0	0	0	0	0	66	0	0	37	0	0	103
H	0	0	0	0	0	93	0	0	0	0	0	0	0	0	93
I	0	0	0	0	0	0	0	0	0	0	0	23	0	0	23
All	134	129	125	114	106	93	81	77	75	73	69	60	59	54	1249

(Opposite page) Figure 19.6. Closest Fountain-to-Door Network. Partition into 34 neighbourhoods as identified by the second widest γ domain output by CHAMP. Colours represent neighbourhoods as partitioned by CHAMP. Dashed lines outline zones defined by the single closest fountain to each unit in the spatial network.

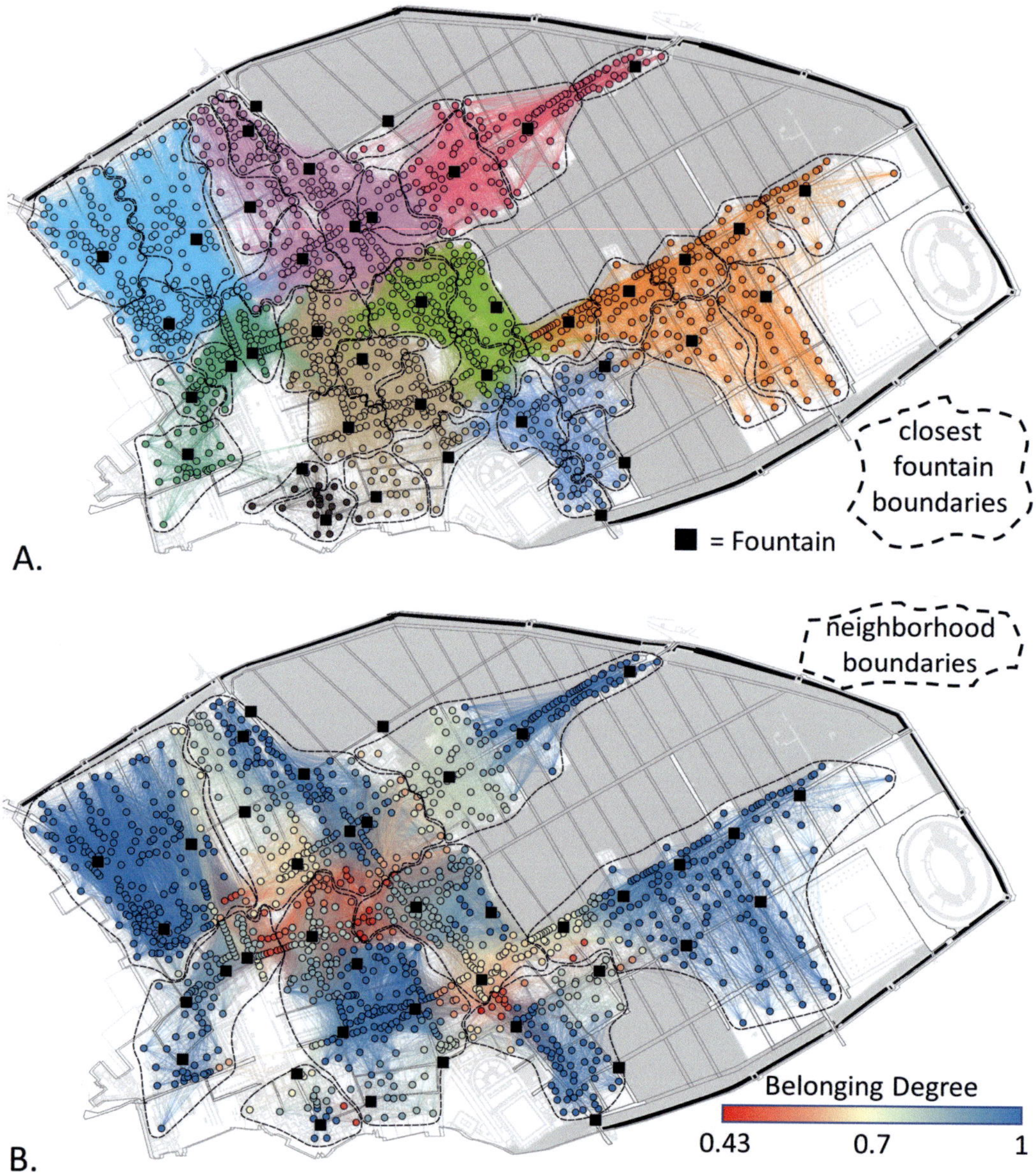

Figure 19.8. 30-Second Network. Partition into 9 neighbourhoods as identified by the widest γ domain identified by CHAMP. A) Colours represent neighbourhoods as partitioned by CHAMP. Dashed lines outline zones defined by the single closest fountain to each unit in the spatial network. B) Colour ramp represents each node's belonging degree. Dashed lines outline the neighbourhood boundaries as partitioned by CHAMP.

neighbourhood near the Vesuvian gate). Interestingly, these neighbourhoods must share enough interconnection to constitute single communities, defying the overall pattern. Nonetheless, these results affirm an insular network structure in which a tiny number of units formed vital interconnections between small, tightly clustered neighbourhoods.

19.6.2 30-Second Network

The 30-second network, with almost double the number of edges, represents a much more interconnected city, and this is reflected in the CHAMP results (Figure 19.7). The algorithm pruned more than 2400 unique partitions down to 57. A 9-neighbourhood partition, clearly delineated in the AMI heatmap, was returned as the widest domain twice. However, also visible in the matrix are at least four other "scales" of smaller communities at larger ranges of γ. These are represented by larger dark blue rectangles in the AMI plot that cross several dashed γ transitions. These might represent sub-divisions of the 9 neighbourhoods, or another kind of grouping altogether, a topic further explored below. Comparing the 9-neighbourhood map to the closest fountain divisions, we can see these communities combine users of several fountains, but near the interfaces some units are grouped with more distant fountains (Figure 19.8a). These internal community characteristics can be intuitively measured using belonging degree (Poorthuis 2018; Figure 19.8b). This is the fraction of a node's intra-community weight over its total weight. Nodes with a belonging degree of 1 only share ties with other community members, while those with lower values share ties with nodes in other neighbourhoods. Not surprisingly, nodes with the lowest belonging degree are found in the centre of the city, adjacent to neighbourhood boundaries. Nodes with low levels of belonging are likely those whose community membership might shift stochastically with each iteration of most community detection algorithms. The hearts of the neighbourhoods though are far more stable.

The second widest domain returned by CHAMP, with 29 neighbourhoods, was rejected due to singleton communities, but the third widest consists of 14 communities. A contingency table allows us to assess whether these represent smaller subdivisions of the 9-neighbourhood partition (Table 19.2).

Some of the 14 districts are equal subdivisions of larger communities. Neighbourhoods 3 and 13 in the 14-neighbourhood partition, for example, mostly bisect neighbourhood C in the 9-district partition. However, other small communities cut across larger ones, taking nodes out of two or three, often those with low belonging degrees. For instance, number 9 in the 14-neighbourhood partition draws in units from neighbourhoods A, C and G, while community 10 is evenly split between neighbourhoods D and E. In terms of Pompeian neighbourhood structures, this might suggest that at smaller scales, the composition of communities would have cut across larger neighbourhood boundaries, rather than forming clean subdivisions of these greater social districts.

19.6.3 One-Minute Network

The one-minute network is the densest and most complex of the three. This suffered from a great deal of stochasticity running Leiden independently, but CHAMP returned 73 partitions out of over 1800 unique results. The widest domain is a clearly delineated partition of 6 communities (Figure 19.9). One would anticipate a greater degree of integration across the city with the longer time threshold, and these results confirm that hypothesis. These 6 divisions largely reflect the topographical divide formed by the forum and the Via del Vesuvio / Stabiana corridor, which bisects the city north to south (Figure 19.10a). The orange neighbourhood, however, constitutes an important bridge connecting east and west. In terms of belonging degree, the lowest scoring units are as usual found near the edges, but the centre of the city again represents the area with the lowest community cohesiveness (Figure 19.10b). Nonetheless, the preponderance of blue nodes (100% belonging) indicates these are durable neighbourhoods in which individuals were unlikely to cross paths with outsiders.

The second widest domain identified by CHAMP is a partition of 10 communities, still representing rather large subdivisions of the city, but a more modular structure than the top result (Table 19.3).

Comparing this against the 6-community structure, we can again see that some smaller neighbourhoods bisect the larger divisions. Here, number 7 in the 10-neighbourhood partition is formed by large groups of units from two of the 6-neighbourhood partition communities (A and D), as well as 8 nodes from C. Numbers 3 and 4 in the 10-neighbourhood partition, on the other hand, are entirely subdivisions of the large neighbourhood A. This reminds us that some larger neighbourhoods remained internally closed, even at more individual, face-to-face, scales, while others became mixed at these smaller scales.

19.7 Conclusion

This brief discussion only touches upon the variety of analyses possible using community detection to partition archaeological neighbourhoods. By identifying multiple dominant partitions across different ranges of γ, CHAMP offers a multiscalar approach to network community detection within single networks. This case study, however, already considers different network scales using time thresholds. One could also directly compare the top partitions in each of the three networks.

Another useful measure of neighbourhood integration is the intra-cluster density, that is the total density of node ties within a community. Since ties represent units that used a common fountain, the greater the density, the higher the probability that inhabitants met face-to-face. Larger neighbourhoods have lower intra-cluster densities, meaning neighbours were far less likely to meet face-to-face at a fountain even though they shared more social connection in general compared to other regions of the city. Few neighbourhoods in the one-minute network's 6-community partition rise above 50%. In such communities, ties between neighbours must have been more dispersed, relying upon mutual contacts. Intra-cluster densities approaching 100%, however, would mean that inhabitants of almost every housing unit had an equal chance of rubbing shoulders at a fountain. These would be the most cohesive and perhaps the most bonded neighbourhoods, with almost daily direct contact

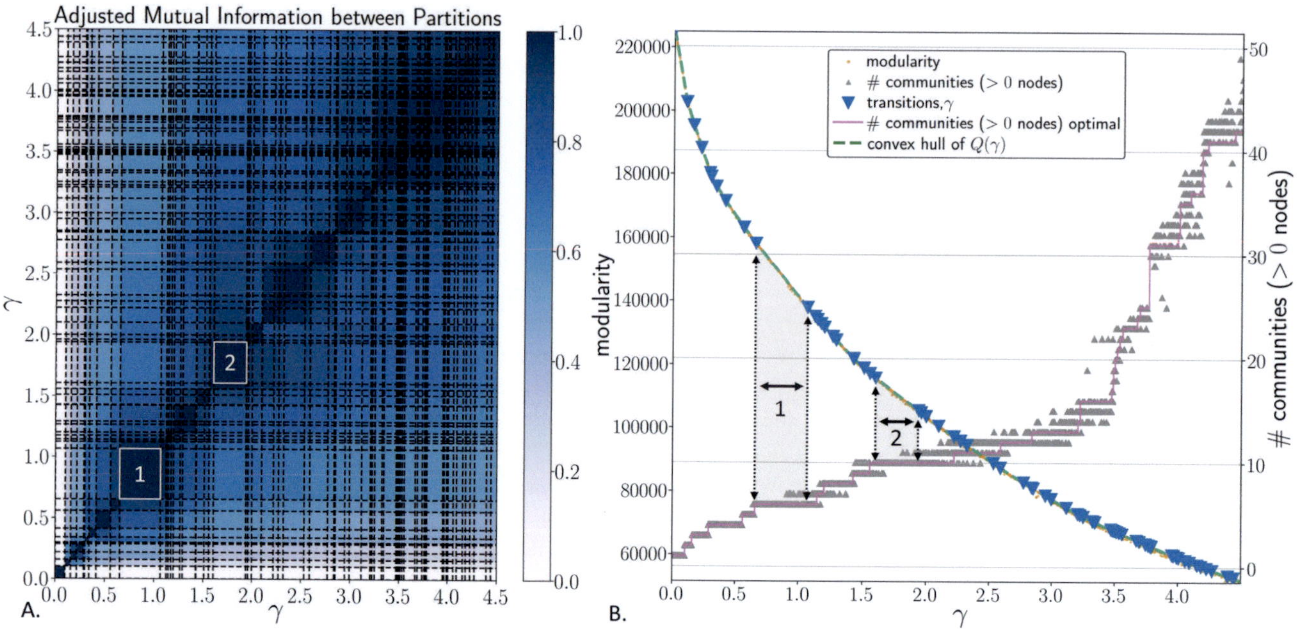

Figure 19.9. One-Minute Network. Results of CHAMP using Leiden algorithm with modularity. 5000 intervals between γ 0 and 4.5 at 25 iterations each. A) AMI of the subset of partitions identified by CHAMP. The widest domain (no. 1: γ 0.65 – 1.06, 6 neighbourhoods) and second widest domain (no. 2: γ 1.6 – 1.94, 10 neighbourhoods) are outlined in white. B) Modularity versus γ. Grey upward triangles represent a random sampling of 2000 partitions plotted against their number of communities, while the solid pink stepped line shows the number of communities in the optimal partition for the range of γ. The dashed green line is the convex hull. Blue downward triangles show the transition points between various ranges of γ. The grey zones between the dotted lines identify the widest domains (no. 1: 6 neighbourhoods, no. 2: 10 neighbourhoods).

	1	2	3	4	5	6	7	8	9	10	All
A	0	0	144	144	0	0	17	0	0	3	308
B	0	43	0	0	0	119	0	0	90	0	252
C	196	0	0	0	0	10	8	0	1	31	246
D	0	0	0	0	130	0	88	0	0	0	218
E	0	126	0	0	0	0	0	0	0	0	126
F	0	0	0	0	0	0	0	99	0	0	99
All	196	169	144	144	130	129	113	99	91	34	1249

Table 19.3. Contingency table. One-Minute Network. Widest domain (6 neighbourhoods, lettered) compared with second widest domain (10 neighbourhoods, numbered).

between households. 28 out of the 34 neighbourhoods in the closest-by-door network achieve 100%, but not all. The remaining six range from 52 to 74%.

It should be emphasized that there is no single "correct" community partition. Rather, utilizing the resolution parameter and examining its output in CHAMP offers a multiscalar method of assessing graph partitioning. The choice of scale should be determined with respect to the data and the research questions. CHAMP's utility lies in its ability to narrow down the range of potential options and identify larger patterns across a range of γ, rather than relying upon an arbitrary choice of partition returned by the default algorithm settings or a single iteration.

As a tool for identifying urban neighbourhoods, this approach holds much potential. A more complex Pompeian network that incorporates additional variables of social integration beyond fountains, such as bakeries, bars, communal shrines, and baths, would constitute a more multifaceted social network. Such dense networks would be nearly impossible to partition using topology alone. Thankfully, the algorithms outlined here can efficiently handle extremely large and convoluted networks, returning manageable but statistically solid outputs suitable for detailed analysis and interpretation.

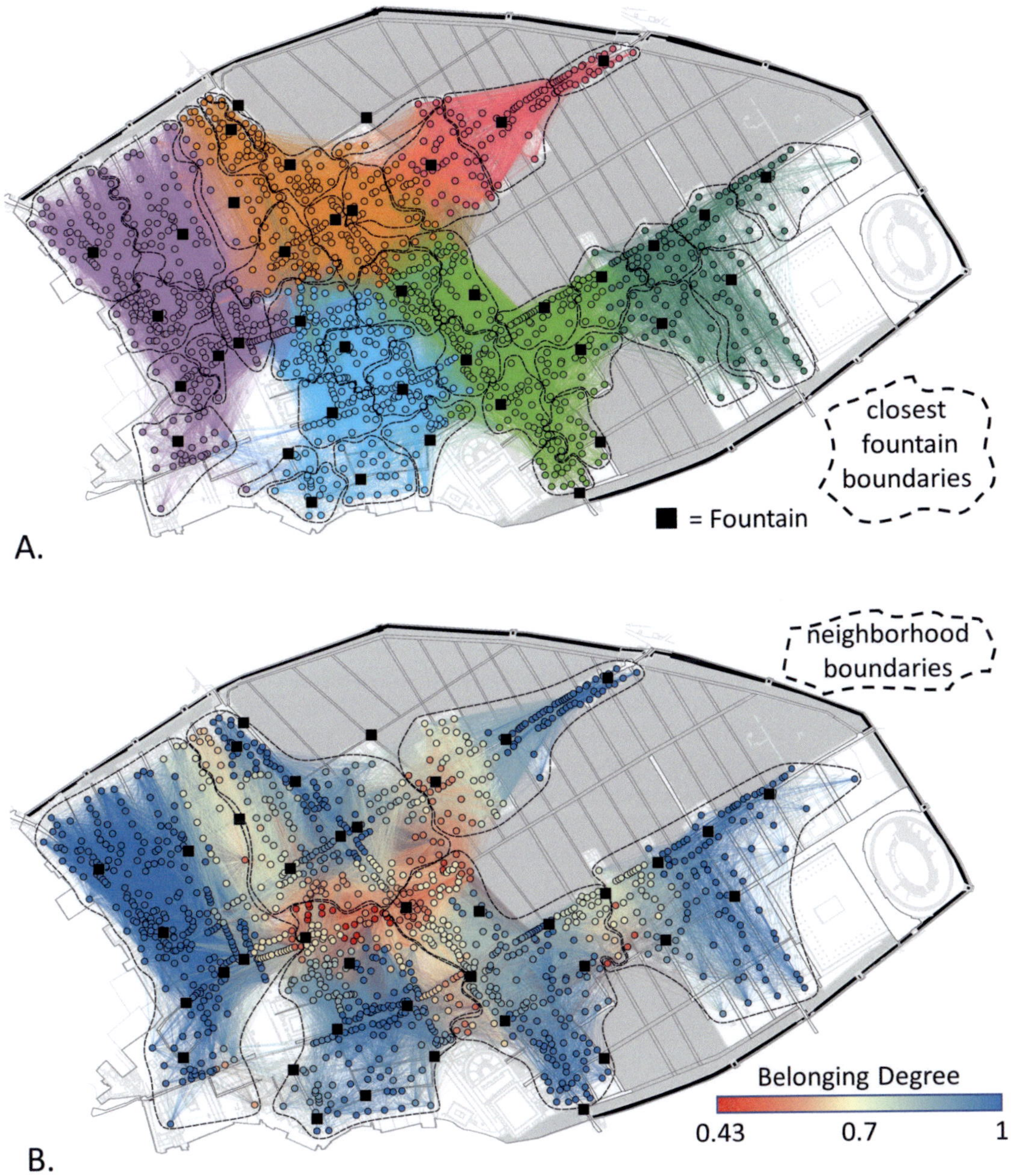

Figure 19.10. One-Minute Network. Partition into 6 neighbourhoods as identified by the widest domain identified by CHAMP. A) Colours represent neighbourhoods as partitioned by CHAMP. Dashed lines outline zones defined by the single closest fountain to each unit in the spatial network. B) Colour ramp represents each node's belonging degree. Dashed lines outline the neighbourhood boundaries as partitioned by CHAMP.

Acknowledgements
I give my sincere thanks to Peter Mucha for discussing aspects of this study, especially the applicability of CHAMP. I also thank Eric Poehler and the Pompeii Bibliography and Mapping Project for the spatial data underlying this project. The three reviewers provided helpful feedback that greatly improved the accessibility of the final draft. Any remaining errors are, of course, my own.

Funding
No additional funding sources were used for this project.

Conflict of interest disclosure
The author declares that he complies with the PCI rule of having no financial conflicts of interest in relation to the content of the article.

Data, Scripts, Code, and Supplementary Information Availability
All of the data and scripts used in this article are available online at https://zenodo.org/badge/latestdoi/686189050.

Peer review
This article has been reviewed and recommended by PCI Archaeology.

Laguna-Palma, D. 2024. "A Valuable Contribution to Archaeological Network Research: A Case Study of Pompeii." *Peer Community in Archaeology* 100403. https//doi.org/10.24072/pci.archaeo.100403.

References

Bastian, Mathieu, Sebastien Heymann, and Mathieu Jacomy. 2009. "Gephi: An Open Source Software for Exploring and Manipulating Networks." *Proceedings of the International AAAI Conference on Web and Social Media* 3 (1): 361–2. DOI:10.1609/icwsm.v3i1.13937.

Blondel, Vincent D., Jean-Loup Guillaume, Renaud Lambiotte, and Etienne Lefebvre. 2008. "Fast Unfolding of Communities in Large Networks." *Journal of Statistical Mechanics: Theory and Experiment* 2008 (10): P10008. DOI:10.1088/1742-5468/2008/10/P10008.

Csárdi, Gábor, Tamás Nepusz, Kirill Müller, Szabolcs Horvát, Vincent Traag, Fabio Zanini, and Daniel Noom. 2024. "Igraph for R: R Interface of the Igraph Library for Graph Theory and Network Analysis." Zenodo. DOI:10.5281/ZENODO.7682609.

Epskamp, Sacha, Angélique O. J. Cramer, Lourens J. Waldorp, Verena D. Schmittmann, and Denny Borsboom. 2012. "Qgraph: Network Visualizations of Relationships in Psychometric Data." *Journal of Statistical Software* 48 (4): 1–18. DOI:10.18637/jss.v048.i04.

Haug, Annette, Adrian Hielscher, and Anna-Lena Krüger (eds). 2023. *Neighbourhoods and City Quarters in Antiquity: Design and Experience. Decorative Principles in Late Republican and Early Imperial Italy.* Berlin: De Gruyter. DOI:10.1515/9783111248097.

Laurence, Ray. 2007. *Roman Pompeii: Space and Society*. London: Routledge.

Mazzucato, Camilla. 2019. "Socio-Material Archaeological Networks at Çatalhöyük a Community Detection Approach." *Frontiers in Digital Humanities* 6: 8. DOI:10.3389/fdigh.2019.00008.

Newman, Mark E. J., and Michelle Girvan. 2004. "Finding and Evaluating Community Structure in Networks." *Physical Review E* 69 (2): 026113. DOI:10.1103/PhysRevE.69.026113.

Notarian, Matthew. 2023. "A Spatial Network Analysis of Water Distribution from Public Fountains in Pompeii." *American Journal of Archaeology* 127 (1): 85–118. DOI:10.1086/722233.

Pacifico, David, and Lise A. Truex. 2019a. "Chapter 1. Why Neighborhoods? The Neighborhood in Archaeological Theory and Practice." *Archaeological Papers of the American Anthropological Association* 30 (1): 5–19. DOI:10.1111/apaa.12110.

Pacifico, David, and Lise A. Truex (eds). 2019b. "Special Issue: Excavating Neighborhoods: A Cross-Cultural Exploration." *Archaeological Papers of the American Anthropological Association* 30 (1). DOI:10.1111/apaa.12108.

Peeples, Matthew A., and Robert J. Bischoff. 2023. "Archaeological Networks, Community Detection, and Critical Scales of Interaction in the U.S. Southwest/Mexican Northwest." *Journal of Anthropological Archaeology* 70: 101511. DOI:10.1016/j.jaa.2023.101511.

Poorthuis, Ate. 2018. "How to Draw a Neighborhood? The Potential of Big Data, Regionalization, and Community Detection for Understanding the Heterogeneous Nature of Urban Neighborhoods." *Geographical Analysis* 50 (2): 182–203. DOI:10.1111/gean.12143.

Scholnick, Jonathan B., Jessica L. Munson, and Martha J. Macri. 2013. "Positioning Power in a Multi-Relational Framework: A Social Network Analysis of Classic Maya Political Rhetoric." In *Network Analysis in Archaeology: New Approaches to Regional Interaction*, edited by Carl Knappett, 95–124. Oxford: Oxford University Press. DOI:10.1093/acprof:oso/9780199697090.003.0005.

Shai, Saray, Natalie Stanley, Clara Granell, Dane Taylor, and Peter J. Mucha. 2021. "Case Studies in Network Community Detection." In *The Oxford Handbook of Social Networks*, edited by Ryan Light and James Moody, 309–33. Oxford: Oxford University Press. DOI: 10.1093/oxfordhb/9780190251765.013.16.

Smith, Michael E. 2010. "The Archaeological Study of Neighborhoods and Districts in Ancient Cities." *Journal of Anthropological Archaeology* 29 (2): 137–54. DOI: 10.1016/j.jaa.2010.01.001.

Thompson, Amy E., John P. Walden, Adrian S. Z. Chase, Scott R. Hutson, Damien B. Marken, Bernadette Cap, Eric C. Fries, M. Rodrigo Guzman Piedrasanta, Timothy S. Hare, Sherman W. Horn III, George J. Micheletti, Shane M. Montgomery, Jessica Munson, Heather Richards-Rissetto, Kyle Shaw-Müller, Traci Ardren, Jaime J. Awe, M. Kathryn Brown, Michael Callaghan, Claire E. Ebert, Anabel Ford, Rafael A. Guerra, Julie A. Hoggarth, Brigitte Kovacevich, John M. Morris, Holley Moyes, Terry G. Powis, Jason Yaeger, Brett A. Houk, Keith M. Prufer, Arlen F. Chase, and Diane Z. Chase 2022. "Ancient Lowland Maya Neighborhoods: Average Nearest Neighbor Analysis and Kernel Density Models, Environments, and Urban Scale." *PLOS ONE* 17 (11): e0275916. DOI: 10.1371/journal.pone.0275916.

Traag, V. A., P. Van Dooren, and Y. Nesterov. 2011. "Narrow Scope for Resolution-Limit-Free Community Detection." *Physical Review E* 84 (1): 016114. DOI: 10.1103/PhysRevE.84.016114.

Traag, Vincent A., Ludo Waltman, and Nees J. Van Eck. 2019. "From Louvain to Leiden: Guaranteeing Well-Connected Communities." *Scientific Reports* 9 (1): 5233. DOI: 10.1038/s41598-019-41695-z.

Visser, Ronald M. 2021. "Dendrochronological Provenance Patterns. Network Analysis of Tree-Ring Material Reveals Spatial and Economic Relations of Roman Timber in the Continental North-Western Provinces." *Journal of Computer Applications in Archaeology* 4 (1): 230-253. DOI: 10.5334/jcaa.79.

Weir, William, Scott Emmons, Ryan Gibson, Dane Taylor, and Peter Mucha. 2017. "Post-Processing Partitions to Identify Domains of Modularity Optimization." *Algorithms* 10 (3): 93. DOI: 10.3390/a10030093.

20 Rivers vs. Roads?

A route network model of transport infrastructure in Northern Italy during the Roman period

James Page
Barcelona Supercomputing Centre
james.page@bsc.es
ORCID 0000-0001-6130-0902

Abstract

Northern Italy has often been characterised as an isolated and marginal area during the Roman period, a region constricted by mountain ranges and its distance from major shipping lanes. Historians have frequently cited these obstacles, alongside the lack of a major seaport on the Po, as a barrier to the region's economic development and connectivity to the rest of the Roman world. However, how isolated was the interior of Northern Italy in reality? To answer these questions, this paper analyses the results of a route network model of Northern Italy's transport network during the Roman period. Containing over 136 nodes, it enables a significantly more detailed analysis of the region's transport network than previous modelling. The model explores which were the most cost-effective routes for imports arriving from the Adriatic and Ligurian coasts, alongside which ports were the most accessible from sites in the upper and middle valley. The chapter's results confirm the importance of the Po-Veneto water network in facilitating the cost-efficient movement of goods from the Adriatic coast to areas hundreds of kilometres inland and vice versa, suggesting that prior assumptions of its isolation have been over-estimated.

Keywords: Networks; Roman Transport; Northern Italy; Rivers; Roads

20.1 Introduction

Over the past three decades, network analyses have been increasingly used by the archaeological community to map past exchanges, interactions, and identities (Collar et al. 2015; Knappett 2013; Mills 2017). The ability of network analysis to handle and visualise large, complex datasets, alongside its compatibility with more established tools such as GIS, has helped drive its adoption amongst researchers, especially in the study of ancient transport systems (Brughmans 2010; 2013; Knappett 2013). As transport infrastructure exists within spatial networks in real space, it readily lends itself towards reproduction in network graphs, where each edge represents a section of the route (such as a road, river, or sea-lane) and each node a junction between them. Network modelling has been applied extensively to the study of Roman transport at a variety of levels, ranging from the entirety of the Roman Empire, in the case of the Stanford ORBIS model (Meeks 2015; Scheidel 2014), to that of a single city (Livarda and Orengo 2015). Modelling has been used to identify the configuration of transport networks, highlighting important routes and junctions within the network alongside mapping areas of high and

In *Advances in Digital Archaeology. Proceedings of the 2023 conference Computer Applications and Quantitative Methods in Archaeology – 50 years of synergy*, edited by J.W.H.P. Verhagen, J. Waagen, A. Brandsen, A. Queffelec, R.M. Visser and D. Taelman, 265–278. Leiden: Sidestone Press.

low connectivity. Theoretically, the lower the cost in time and money to reach one place from another, the greater the level of that region's connectivity, and the greater the scope for goods and people to access it from further afield (Brughmans 2013; Cioffi 2016; Horden and Purcell 2000). Archaeological and geomorphological investigation has helped to reconstruct the landscape and physical routes of the ancient transport networks used in these models, while extant literary and epigraphic evidence, in particular Diocletian's Edict on Maximum Prices, has been used to give estimates of the time and cost of different transport modes (De Soto 2019).

Although network modelling is increasingly applied to ancient transport networks, its coverage across the Roman world remains somewhat uneven. While ORBIS covered the extent of the Roman Empire, it did so at low resolution, with detail sacrificed to maintain the legibility of such a large-scale model. More detailed transport models exist at provincial or sub-provincial level, although their coverage of the Roman world remains patchy. In particular, the Italian peninsula, despite the extent and evolution of its Roman transport network being well-documented, has seen limited model application, with only a handful of published studies applying it to the region (Carreras and Soto 2013; Flückiger et al. 2021; Scheidel 2014). Several shortcomings of prior modelling are especially apparent in the north of the country. Here, previous studies have often been conducted at low resolution, with significant pieces of infrastructure, including many of the region's minor roads and a major para-littoral canal between Ravenna and Aquileia, missing from network graphs. Natural waterways are also underrepresented, with the Po frequently assumed to be the only navigable river in the region and, even then, only navigable as far as Piacenza. The results of prior modelling have been used to highlight the isolation of Northern Italy (and the Po valley in particular) from the rest of the Italian peninsula and Rome, something that has also been commented on by historians such as Harris (2011), Patterson (2006), and Scheidel (2014). Yet how poorly connected was the interior of Northern Italy in reality? An analysis of the available archaeological evidence suggests that Northern Italy's transport network was extensive and complex. Located far inland, the western reaches of the Po valley were hundreds of kilometres from the nearest seaport yet consumed goods from across the Roman world. A robust and extensive transport network was necessary to convey these imported goods from the coast inland and transport local exports in the opposite direction. Creating a dedicated network model provides a way to test assumptions of marginality and connectivity by mapping the cost of reaching inland areas from the coast.

This paper analyses the results of a route network model of Northern Italy's transport network during the Roman period. Containing over 136 nodes, the model enables a significantly more detailed analysis of the region's transport network than previous studies. The model answers several questions about the transport network of Northern Italy, exploring which were the most cost-effective routes for imports arriving from the Adriatic and Ligurian coasts, alongside which ports were the most accessible from sites furthest inland. The results of the analysis confirm the importance of the Po-Veneto water network in facilitating the cost-efficient movement of goods from the Adriatic coast to areas hundreds of kilometres inland and vice versa, suggesting that prior assumptions of its isolation have been over-estimated.

20.2 Materials and Methods

The network analysis is based on the methodology developed by De Soto (2019), with additions in the form of transhipment, slope, and canal costs. The network presented here encompasses the peak extent of the transport network within Northern Italy during the second century AD and tracks a hypothetical cargo of 1000 kg. The hypothetical cargo begins its journey on land. The model assumes that transport was taking place during optimum weather and hydrological conditions on the region's rivers. It also assumes that transport travelled at a constant speed, and applies the maximum cost given by the Price Edict to transport. ArcGIS was chosen as the software to analyse the network, using the program's Network Analyst suite of tools. The network model itself is comprised of a series of four vector datasets, containing the roads, navigable rivers, canals, and sea-lanes within the study area which provide the nodes and edges for the network analysis (Page 2023b).

For the road network, a relatively complete map of the region's major roads can be constructed from the archaeological record. The road vector dataset was originally imported from the Ancient World Mapping Centre's (AWMC) shapefile resource page (http://awmc.unc.edu/wordpress/map-files; accessed March 13, 2023). Although the AWMC vector data offered a useful starting point, it needed significant alterations to be usable in the model. While the main pathways of the roads were broadly accurate, they did not consider the topography of the region (some roads are mapped as traversing near-vertical surfaces in the Alps). As a result, most of the AWMC vectors were redrawn in their entirety. This involved tracing the pathway of roads over a digital elevation model (DEM) using satellite imagery, alongside georeferencing high resolution survey maps in GIS. The Copernicus EEA-10 DEM was the used to provide elevation data (DOI:10.5270/ESA-c5d3d65). This resulted in far more accurate road vectors that followed realistic paths through the region's topography and matched the surviving archaeological evidence. This was especially true in the Alpine and Apennine areas of the model, where road gradient did not exceed 13 percent after the redrawing of the vectors. Due to the sharp changes

Transport Type	Cost (kg wheat/T/km)
Maritime	0.093
Fluvial (downstream)	0.33
Fluvial (upstream)	0.66
Canal	0.66
Overland	4.92
Transhipment	10.00

Table 20.1. The values for the cost of transport used within the network model. Cost is expressed as kg of wheat, per tonne, per kilometre.

in elevation over short distances and circuitous nature of routes through the mountains, it is possible some minor errors in the path and gradient of the trans-Alpine road network remain. However, given the scale of the model, they are unlikely to significantly impact on its results. The AWMC dataset was then supplemented by other road data taken from regional publications, which were manually added to the shapefile (Calzolari 1992; Labate 2019; Marini Calvini 1999; Ortalli 1992).

The river network was created from the data for navigable rivers during the Roman period (see Page 2022a: Chapter 3, for a discussion of the evidence). The paths of the Po, Adige, and other rivers during the Roman period were taken from the AWMC river vector shapefile and corroborated with more recent geomorphological research (Bosio 1979; Calzolari 2007; Uggeri 2016). These geomorphological investigations have mainly used a combination of aerial photography and LiDAR data to highlight traces of paleochannels in the landscape. In some cases, this was coupled with coring surveys to check the validity of the aerial photography and LiDAR, as well as providing material for dating the paleochannels. In some cases, historical data from the Roman and post-Roman period has been used to establish the connections between rivers, such as Early Medieval accounts of the Reno being a tributary of the Po (Racine 2000). Additional rivers not included in the AWMC vector file, such as the Fiume Stella, were manually added to the shapefile. There is inevitably a degree of assumption on the course of these smaller, less intensively studied rivers during the Roman period, although their broad route is accurate. Only rivers known to have been navigable were included, although it is likely there were significantly more navigable waterways within the region.

The canal network vectors were manually created. Given the limited archaeological evidence for the paralittoral canals (canals running parallel to the coast) of the *Fossae Augusta*, *Claudia*, and *Flavia*, a degree of guesswork was necessary in constructing the vectors. Reconstructions of the path of the canals were taken from several sources and compared with the ancient topography (Manzelli 2000; Grazia Maioli 2018; Rousse 2013; Uggeri 1978). From this, a possible route for the canals was created between Ravenna and Aquileia. Canal vectors were also placed in areas where ports (such as those at Milan, Tortona, and Vercelli) were connected to the river network by manmade channels (Page 2022b). Finally, canal vectors were also used to model travel across the glacial pre-Alpine lakes of the region, as craft using these lakes would have incurred similar challenges and costs.

The maritime network vectors included in the model represent movement along the Adriatic and Ligurian coasts. A para-littoral route was selected, with connections to the region's major ports. Although fluvio-maritime vessels, such as the Comacchio and Parco Teodorico wrecks, had the ability to move interchangeably on inland and coastal waters, allowing near-seamless movement between maritime, para-littoral canal, and fluvial contexts, it was decided to keep a firm separation between fluvial/canal and maritime transport (Beltrame 2002; Willis and Capulli 2018). This separation removed the possibility of the network modelling river vessels that did not possess seaworthy attributes (such as flat-bottomed barges) as being able to use maritime routes.

The locations where the vector polylines join form the major nodes of the network, representing prominent sites within the region. At nodes where separate transport types intersected, network junctions were created which allowed transfer between them. These network junctions fell into the categories of Maritime to Land, Maritime to River, Maritime to Canal, River to Land, River to Canal, and Canal to Land.

With the network nodes and edges generated, it was then necessary to apply weights to them in the form of cost. The figures for transport cost in the ancient world have their basis in Diocletian's Price Edict of AD 301. The Price Edict text gives the maximum price of transport across 51 maritime routes, with costs ranging between 4 and 26 *denarii* for the transport of a single *kastrensis modius* (approximately 12.9 litres of wheat). For fluvial transport, the Edict gives a price of 1 *denarius* per *kastrensis modius* per 20 Roman miles of downstream travel and 2 *denarii* per *kastrensis modius* per 20 Roman miles of upstream travel (*Edict of Maximum Prices*, XXXVA.31-33). For terrestrial transport, the Edict gives the maximum prices of 2 *denarii* per Roman mile for a passenger in a carriage, 4 *denarii* for a fully laden donkey per Roman mile, 8 *denarii* for a camel carrying 600 Roman pounds per Roman mile, and 20 *denarii* for a wagon carrying 1,200 Roman pounds per Roman mile (*Edict of Maximum Prices*, XVII.1-5). The figures presented in the Price Edict have allowed the extrapolation of different ratios of cost between overland, upstream, downstream, and maritime transport, and from them, a base cost per mile/kilometre (see below). However, the Edict is a problematic piece of evidence, and it has been extensively critiqued as a source of pricing in the Roman era (Corcoran and DeLaine 1994; Duncan-Jones 1982). It survives in a fragmentary state, and only records maximum prices relevant to the early fourth century AD. There was probably significant variation in costs below this total, and prices may have been higher or lower in the preceding and following periods. Furthermore, the decree seems to have been principally enacted in the eastern half of the empire, giving the potential for regional price variation. These concerns aside, Russell has shown that the ratios extrapolated from transport costs given by the Price Edict are not dissimilar to cost ratios between land, river, and sea transportation from other periods (Russell 2013, 96).

The figures used to weight the model are listed in Table 20.1. These values, based on Diocletian's Price Edict, are taken from De Soto (2019), with the addition of the cost estimates for canal transport and transhipment taken from Page (2022a). Prices are expressed in their wheat equivalents, rather than *denarii* as the value of wheat is thought to have remained relatively stable throughout the Roman period, (with demand and consumption remaining constant). Expressing transport costs as a unit of wheat allows them to be used for transport in earlier periods when the *denarius* had greater value (Corbier 1985; DeLaine 1992). Within each layer, the length of each polyline in the shapefile was generated in kilometres. This figure was then multiplied by the transport cost to generate figures for the total cost to traverse each network edge. For roads, a cost penalty based on the average gradient across each polyline was added to generate new cost values. The methodology applied here was developed by Bell et al. and uses the equation tan(slope)/tan(1°) to generate an adjusted cost (Bell et al. 2002). For rivers, downstream and upstream travel were distinguished via tf (to-from) and ft (from-to) values respectively, allowing the assignment of separate values depending on the direction of travel. These figures were stored in the attribute table of each layer's shapefile. For network junctions, a transhipment cost was applied to all movement between water, maritime, and canals, and land. The only exception was movement between water and canals, which was likely seamless and utilised the same vessels. Consequently, no transhipment cost was assigned to water to canal junctions.

A multi-modal network model was created using ArcCatalog, with the steps taken outlined in detail in (Page 2023b). Four layers of connectivity were created (sea-lanes, navigable rivers, roads, and canals), with network junctions enabling transfer between them at selected points. Nodes for input sites, representing the points that goods entered the region, were selected. These were Altinum, Aquileia, Ariminum, and Ravenna on the Adriatic coast, and Genoa, Luna, Porto Maurizio, and Savona on the Ligurian coast. In addition, the inland site of Turin, in the west of the Po valley, was selected to compare how goods might move out of the region. From these, access surfaces were mapped for cost using the program's Service Area Function, creating a series of vector polygons that mapped all accessible areas within a specified impedance from a set starting point or points. For cost, bands of 100 kg wheat were mapped, covering the entirety of the study area.

20.3 Results

The results of the analysis are outlined in the following section. Figure 20.1 maps the incremental cost of transport for a hypothetical 1000 kg cargo from the four Adriatic ports. The model suggests the maximum transport cost from the Adriatic ports to reach another part of the study area was 1800 kg wheat, 80% more than the value of the 1000 kg cargo. The model suggests that the entirety of the Adriatic coast could be reached for less than 100 kg wheat, a reflection of the low-cost of maritime and para-littoral canal transport. The importance of the para-littoral canals is shown where they are absent between Ravenna and Ariminum, with transport costs increasing to 200 kg wheat. The para-littoral canal system between Aquileia, Altinum, and Ravenna allowed goods originating from these ports to seamlessly access the Po-Veneto fluvial network, a transition further streamlined by the absence of transhipment costs between canal and fluvial transport. Inland sites along the Adriatic coast were accessible for under 100 kg wheat, while cities in the middle Po valley, such as Cremona, could be reached for a cost of under 200 kg wheat. Cost continued to accumulate as transport progressed upstream. Cities at the upper limits of the river network, such as Turin, cost 400 kg wheat to reach via fluvial routes, double the cost of transport to sites in the middle river. This formed the maximum transport cost for sites situated on a river, lake, or canal, a cost equivalent to 40% of the total value of the hypothetical 1000 kg cargo. The high density of the Po-Veneto river network helped ensure that urban centres located on the valley floor that were not on navigable waterways could be accessed for under a cost of 500 kg wheat. In the Southern Alps, the glacial lakes of Garda, Como, and Maggiore were connected to the river network. This allowed lower-cost movement into mountainous areas, which otherwise would have been significantly more expensive to access.

Transport costs sharply increased in areas where a navigable river was absent, particularly in the Alps and Apennines. 100 kg wheat could pay for 151.51 km of upstream fluvial transport, as opposed to 20.32 km of overland transport over level ground. This distance would further decrease if there was a gradient. The impact of overland transport on cost is clearly seen in the upper Po valley, where the price of transporting 1000 kg of cargo from the Adriatic coast to Aosta (800 kg wheat) doubled from 400 kg wheat over a distance of 68 km overland after

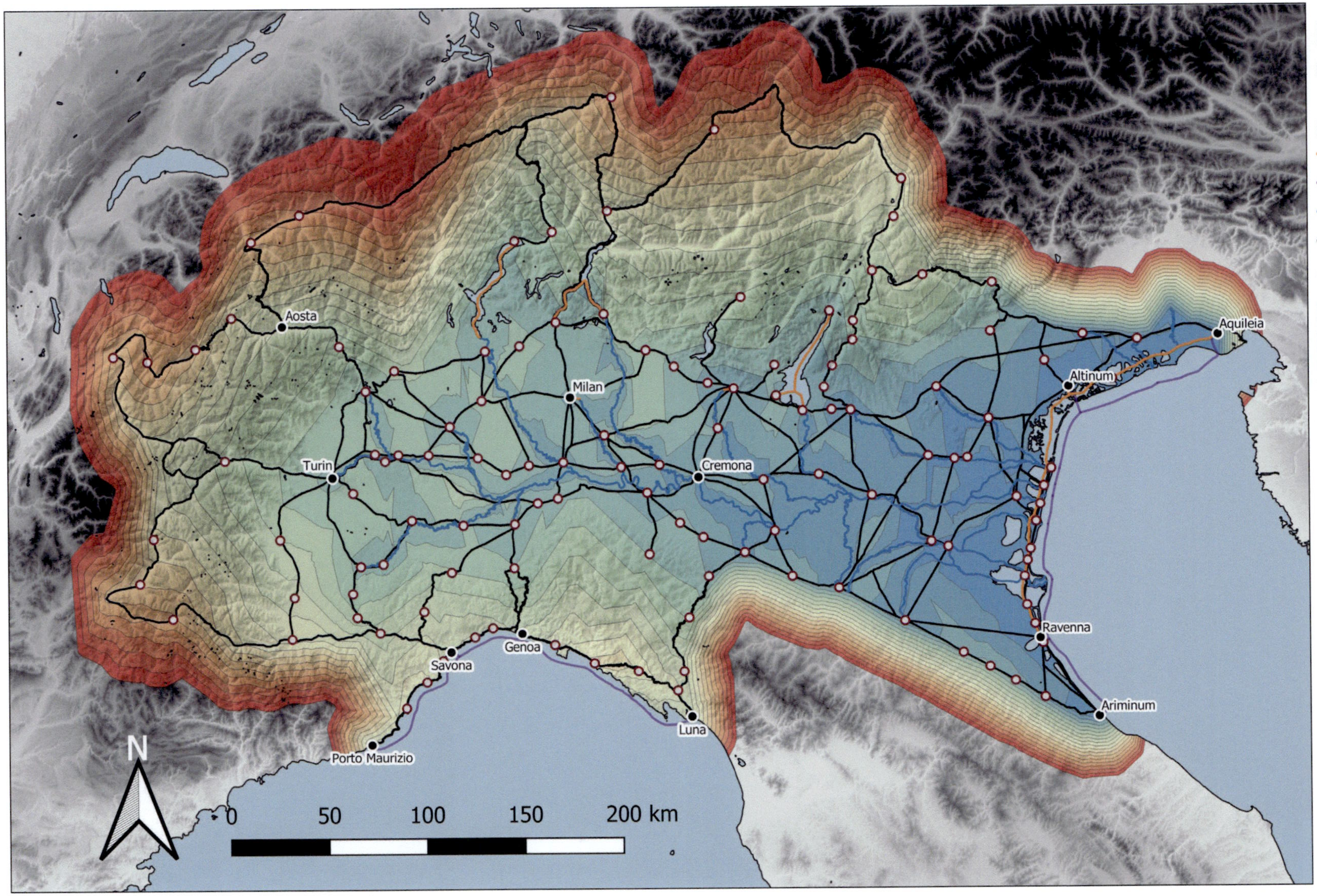

Figure 20.1. The incremental cost of transport from the Adriatic ports of Altinum, Ariminum, Aquileia, and Ravenna.

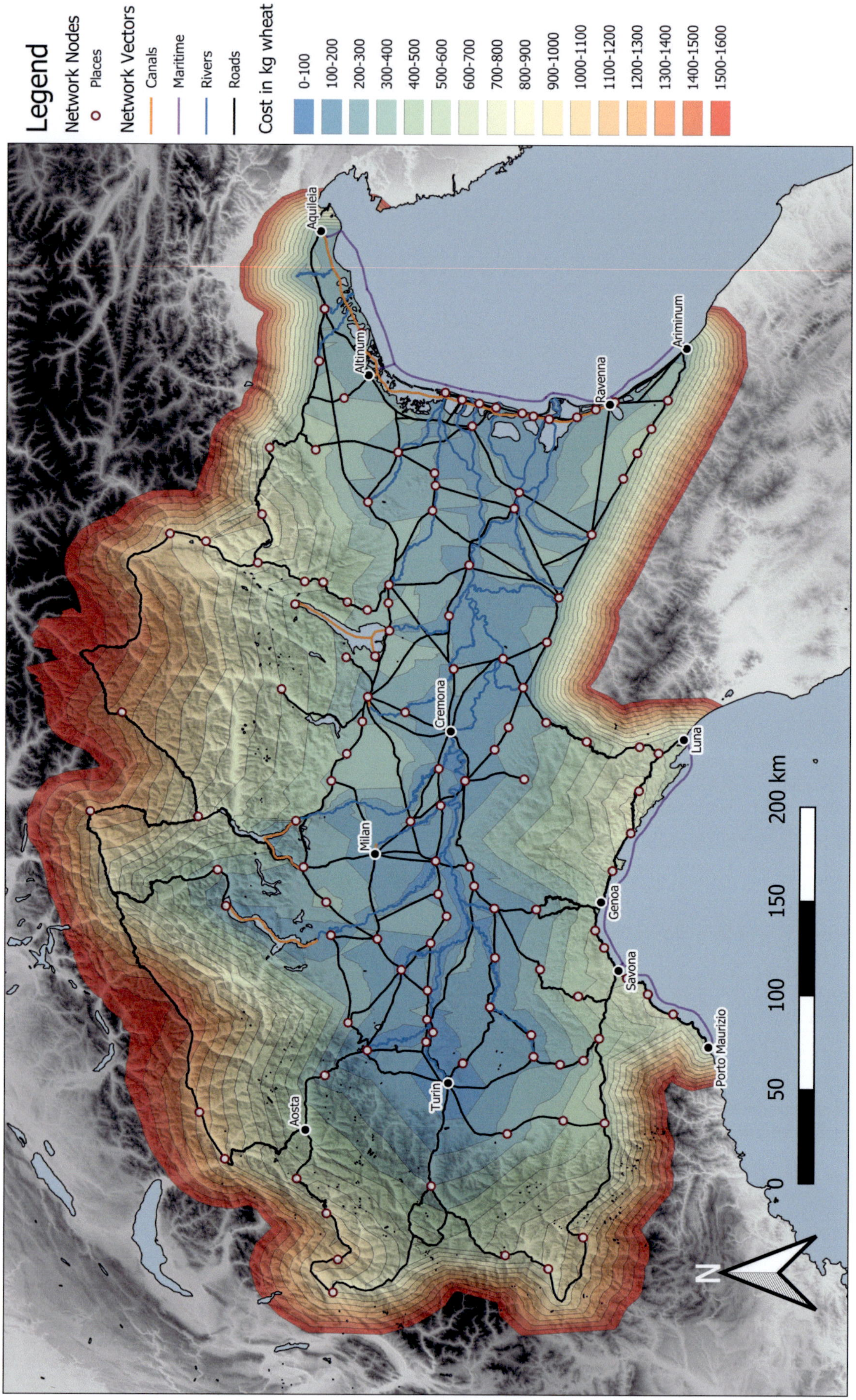

Figure 20.2. The incremental cost of transport from the Ligurian ports of Genoa, Luna, Porto Maurizio, and Savona.

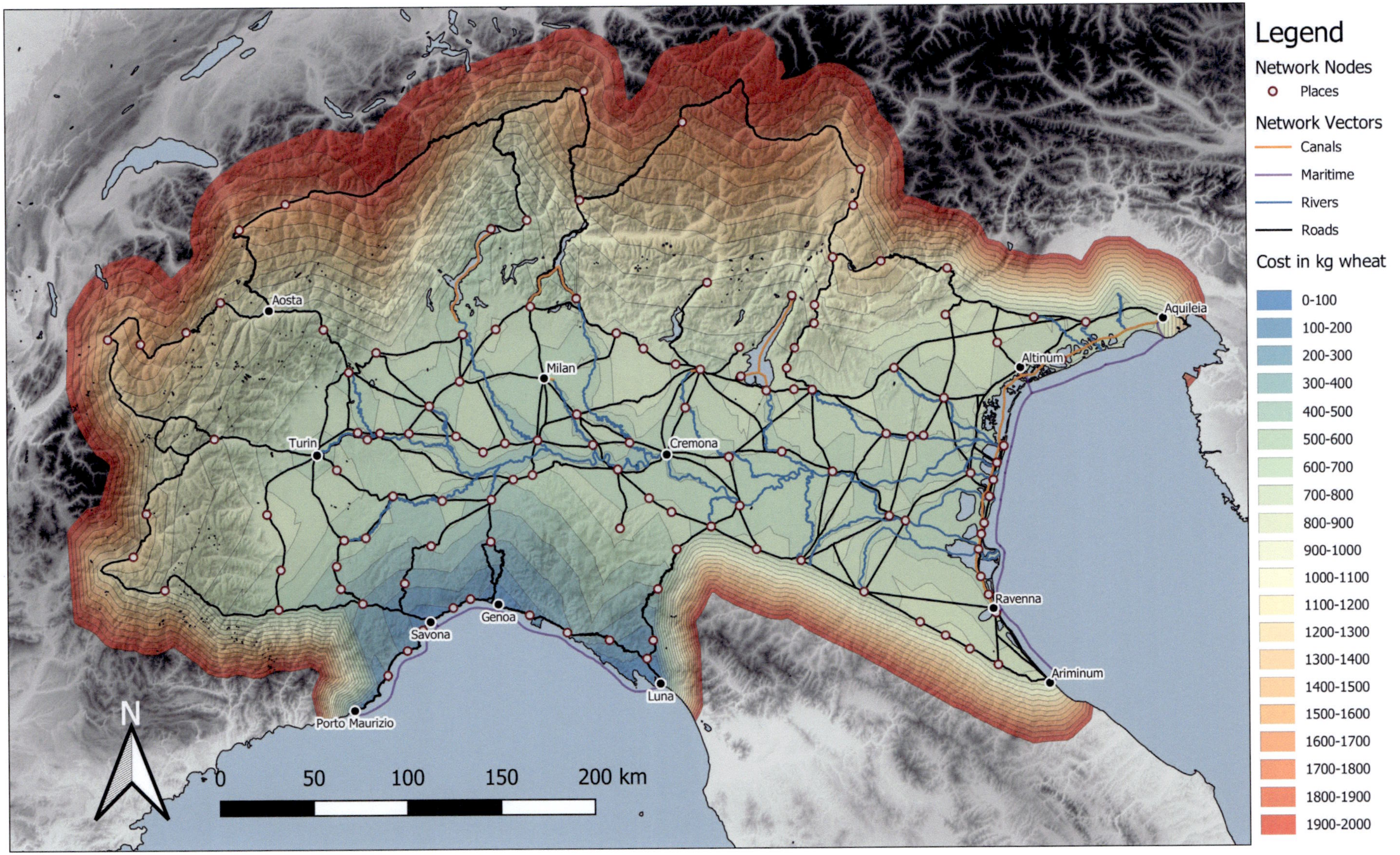

Figure 20.3. The incremental cost of transport from Turin.

it left the river network. This cost then doubled again to 1600 kg wheat in order to reach sites on the other side of the Gran San Bernado Pass in the Rhône valley. The cost of this transport exceeded the value of the 1000 kg cargo by 60%. The high prices shown here are representative of the greater cost of overland transport and especially the challenge presented by gradient in mountainous areas.

Figure 20.2 maps the incremental cost of transport for a hypothetical 1000 kg cargo from the four Ligurian ports. The model suggests the maximum transport cost from the Ligurian ports to reach another part of the study area was 2000 kg wheat, double the value of the 1000 kg cargo and 200 kg wheat more than the maximum transport cost from the Adriatic ports. Transport costs from the Ligurian coast are far more uneven than those from the Adriatic, with costs rapidly increasing as overland routes moved away from ports. It cost seven times as much to transport goods overland between Luna and Genoa as it did by sea, a result of the steep and difficult roads that follow Liguria's rugged coastline.

The Apennines presented a significant cost barrier for overland travel, with prices varying between 400 and 700 kg wheat to traverse them. Beyond the mountains, the Monferrato, Langhe and Colline del Po hills forced more circuitous routes to be taken to urban centres in the south-west of the region, adding additional cost. At a minimum, these urban centres could be reached at a cost of 500-600 kg wheat, a cost of over half the value of the goods being transported. Of the Ligurian ports, Genoa and Savona seem to have been best placed from a cost perspective to access the Po valley, lying on or close to roads that crossed the Apennines which soon intersected with a navigable river. Although Luna also sat upon a trans-Apennine road, the model suggested it was 300 kg wheat cheaper to transfer goods via boat to Genoa, cross the Apennines using the via Postumia, and send goods into the lower Po valley along the river network, rather than use the trans-Apennine road to the eastern Po valley.

At the point that cargo reached an urban centre with a navigable river, the waterways become the primary vector of travel. The lower cost of downstream transport would have allowed goods moving from the Ligurian coast to reach ports on the Adriatic for under 700 kg wheat, up to a 200 kg wheat reduction on the cost of the same journey from an Adriatic direction. Moving off the valley floor and into the Alpine valleys and passes incurred a similar penalty to that seen in transport from the Adriatic coast. Aosta could just be reached for 1000 kg wheat, equivalent to the value of the goods transported.

Finally, Figure 20.3 maps the incremental cost of transport for a hypothetical 1000 kg cargo from Turin, an inland site at the supposed navigable limit of the Po. The model suggests that the maximum transport costs from Turin to another part of the study area was 1600 kg wheat. The map of costs from Turin clearly demonstrates the advantages of being on a navigable river and the possibilities offered by the low cost of downriver transport. Free of the need to overcome the steep mountain gradients of the Apennines or battle upstream against a river's current to gain access to the interior, the model suggests cargo originating from Turin enjoyed low transport costs to reach other areas within the region. Almost all areas of the valley floor could be reached for under 300 kg wheat, less if they were on a navigable river. The model suggests it was possible to travel as far as Cremona for 100 kg wheat and reach the mouths of the Po for 200 kg wheat. The Ligurian ports were more expensive to reach than their Adriatic counterparts, with travel to Genoa and Savona costing between 500 and 600 kg wheat. It remained cheaper for cargo to tranship to maritime from overland routes in order to reach Porto Maurizio and Luna, with the steep coastal road adding significant costs.

20.4 Discussion

The network analysis outlined above reveals the separate challenges faced by those transporting goods from the Adriatic and Ligurian coasts, alongside inland sites, in reaching different areas of Northern Italy. Different transport modes offered various advantages and disadvantages, which the model threw into sharp relief.

Fluvial transport was shown to have had the biggest effect on how cargo moved within the model. The low cost of upstream transport allowed sites such as Turin, lying in the far west of the valley, to be reached for under 400 kg wheat from the Adriatic ports, significantly cheaper than the cost of an equivalent overland journey. Indeed, the availability of upstream transport meant that it was cheaper to reach many sites in the western valley from the Adriatic coast, despite them being geographically closer to Ligurian ports. However, while it is undeniable that the Po and its tributaries formed cost-efficient routes into the interior of Northern Italy from the Adriatic, it is worth pointing out that, in large areas of the south-west Po valley, there was less than 100 kg wheat difference in the cost of travel from the Adriatic and Ligurian coasts (see Figure 20.4). In this section of the valley, where the difference in transport originating from the Adriatic and Ligurian coasts was at its lowest, small changes to the price of transport or extra costs could have significantly altered the viability of one route over another. Transaction costs, such as negotiations and taxes, could significantly increase the price of cargo and transport costs would also have been accrued before goods reached ports in Northern Italy. Transport may have been charged less than the maximum, pushing back the point at which transport from one coast became cheaper or vice-versa. Goods might also be bought and sold multiple times by the time they reached their point of consumption, further complicating costs (Tchernia 2016; Terpstra 2019).

With this in mind, it is possible that transport from the Ligurian coast was more cost-efficient for a wider range of sites in the west and south-west than the network model suggests. Consequently, the dominance of the Adriatic axis of transport over the Ligurian should not be assumed across the entirety of the region. The model also demonstrated the importance of the river network in providing low-cost transport from inland sites to the coast. From Turin, every site on a river connected to the Po could be reached for under 200 kg wheat, while the major Adriatic ports fell within the cost bracket of between 200-300 kg wheat. This underpins the importance of the Po as a corridor for goods produced in the western part of the region travelling to Aquileia, and beyond that, the Danubian *Limes*. Indeed, the merchant L. Tettianus Vitalis, buried in Turin, recorded on his grave monument that the Po and the Sava (a tributary of the Danube) were the two rivers most important to his business (*CIL* V.7047; V.7127; Gabucci et al. 2000; Gabucci and Mennella 2003).

Moving away from navigable rivers, transport became more costly. This was especially true for the more mountainous areas of the region, in particular, the northern and western Alps. While the entirety of the valley floor was traversable for well below 1000 kg wheat, cost rapidly increased as soon as attempts were made to scale any of the major Alpine passes such as the San Bernadino, the Great St. Bernard, and the Little St. Bernard, where slopes frequently exceeded 10%. Indeed, for peripheral sites in the Alps, such as Aosta, there may not have been much difference in cost between transporting goods from Gaul (in particular goods originating from the Rhône valley) and transporting goods from the Adriatic and Ligurian seaboards (Gabucci 2017). Gradient significantly affected the cost of overland transport, although the path of roads tried to limit this as much as possible. In mountainous areas, roads routinely followed the path of valley floors before ascending and, where this was not possible, infrastructure such as bridges, viaducts, and buttresses helped to reduce the gradient (Mollo Mezzana 1992). Of course, when ascending an Alpine pass, there was a limit to how much could be done to reduce the impact of slope, reflected in the high cost these areas of the model incur. While some areas of the Apennines, such as the road between Luna and Po valley, were also significantly affected by gradient, the via Postumia, the main trans-Apennine road between the Po valley and Genoa, followed the valley of the Torrente Scrivia for much of its path. This reduced the route's elevation and slope, which, in turn, reduced the cost of transport using it to cross the Apennines.

Crucially, the model challenges the assumption that the Apennines made transport from the Ligurian coast into the Po valley uneconomical. Although the Apennines did form a significant obstacle in terms of cost for goods arriving from Ligurian ports, this was matched by the cost of transporting goods from the Adriatic coast into the upper reaches of the valley. This presents the question as to whether different areas of the valley may have been linked into either western (served by the Ligurian ports) or eastern (served by the Adriatic ports) Mediterranean markets. Although the model suggests that, in certain areas, it was possible for goods travelling over the Apennines to compete with those coming up from the Po in terms of transport cost, the question remains as to whether or not there was specific demand to make this journey worthwhile (Page 2023a). The proximity of Adriatic production areas to the study area and the demands from other, more accessible markets in the west for goods passing through the Ligurian ports, may have made the trans-Apennine journey unappealing to potential traders.

Although the network analysis focused on inland regions, the model suggested that maritime routes retained an important role in the movement of cargo in coastal areas. In the case of the Ligurian ports, they allowed cargo to be transported at low cost from ports such as Porto Maurizio and Luna, to harbours better placed to begin the overland journey across the Apennines. This also worked in reverse, where cargo could be transferred from overland to maritime transport to circumvent the expensive and time-consuming journey along the Ligurian coast road. The cost-efficiency of maritime transport often meant that if one port on a coastline could be reached, then other ports on that seaboard could normally be accessed within the same or adjacent cost bracket. The density of maritime, canal, and fluvial routes along the Adriatic coast contributed to the low cost of navigating this area of the network.

Transhipment penalties had a mixed effect on the cost and speed of transport. A 2% transhipment cost does not seem to have significantly impacted smaller cargoes, as the high cost of overland transport enabled waterborne goods could easily absorb the additional price. Of course, the model cannot account for quirks in human nature and non-quantifiable factors that may have influenced decision-making. For example, although high cost did not pose a barrier to transhipment in the model, the transfer of goods and materials posed significant risks, especially with large, bulky loads such as stone and marble that were difficult to handle (Russell 2013). The potential for breakage or loss of cargo increased with each transfer, and it is questionable whether shippers would have risked transhipping cargo if it could have been avoided.

The network analysis of Northern Italy's Roman transport network suggests that, far from being a difficult and prohibitively costly region to traverse, there was good accessibility for large areas of the Po valley from coastal regions and vice versa. The model largely confirms the importance of waterways in facilitating cost efficient travel within inland regions, with the Po and its tributaries forming an important axis for transport due to their extent

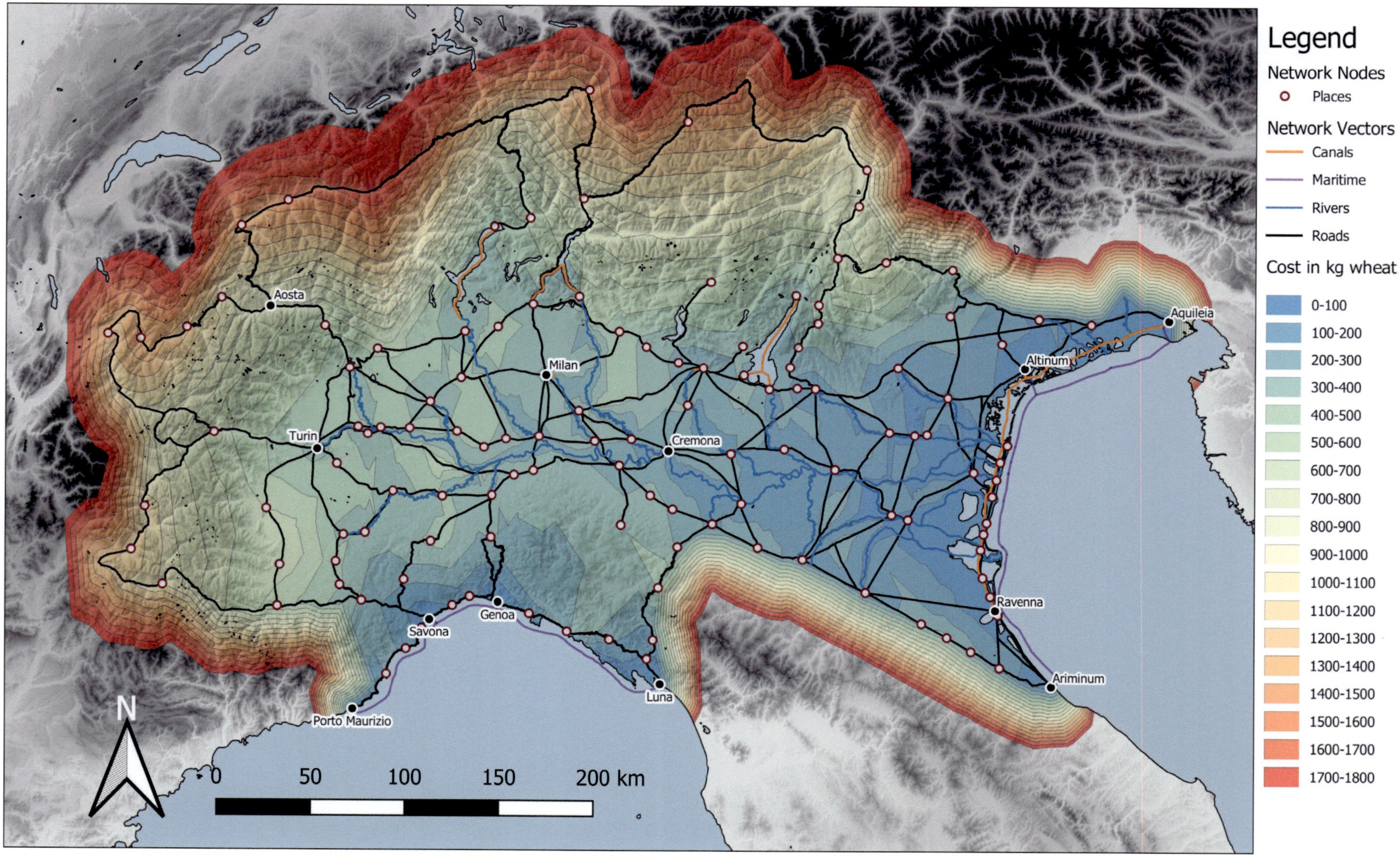

Figure 20.4. The incremental cost of transport from the Adriatic and Ligurian ports.

and density across the valley floor. However, away from fluvial and maritime routes, the expense of overland transport, compounded by gradient, rapidly increased costs. While the cost of traversing overland routes, particularly those in the mountains, likely posed a significant obstacle to trade, this was not insurmountable. The picture of the transport network that has emerged is far more complex than previous studies of Northern Italy have accounted for, and the image of an isolated and disconnected region, with minimal choice and access to imports, is no longer viable.

Acknowledgements

The author would like to thank the organisers of the CAA 2023 in Amsterdam for the opportunity to present an initial version of this paper, and the valuable feedback that was given by delegates.

Funding

The research in this paper was carried out as part of a doctorate funded by the University of Edinburgh.

Conflict of Interest Disclosure

The author declares that they comply with the PCI rule of having no financial conflicts of interest in relation to the content of the article.

Data, Script, Code, and Supplementary Information Availability

The vector files used to create the route network model explored in this paper, alongside instructions on how to create the network dataset used to generate its results, are hosted online: DOI: 10.5281/zenodo.7937731.

Peer review

This article has been reviewed and recommended by PCI Archaeology.

McLean, Andrew. 2024. "Modelling Roman Transport Infrastructure in Northern Italy." *Peer Community in Archaeology* 100336. DOI: 10.24072/pci.archaeo.100336.

References

Bell, Tyler, Andrew I. Wilson, and Andrew Wickham. 2002. "Tracking the Samnites: Landscape and Communications Routes in the Sangro Valley, Italy." *American Journal of Archaeology* 106 (2): 169–86. DOI: 10.2307/4126242.

Beltrame, Carlo. 2002. "Le sutiles naves romane del litorale alto-adriatico. Nuove testimonianze e considerazioni tecnologiche." In *Archeologia subacquea. Studi, ricerche e documenti III*, edited by P. A. Gianfrotta and P. Pelagatti, 353–79. Rome: Poligrafico dello Stato.

Bosio, L. 1979. "I Septem Maria." *Archeologia Veneta* 2: 33–44.

Brughmans, Tom. 2010. "Connecting the dots: towards archaeological network analysis." *Oxford Journal of Archaeology* 29: 277–303. DOI: 10.1111/j.1468-0092.2010.00349.x.

Brughmans, Tom. 2013. "Thinking Through Networks: A Review of Formal Network Methods in Archaeology." *Journal of Archaeological Method and Theory* 20 (4): 623–62. DOI: 10.1007/s10816-012-9133-8.

Calzolari, Mauro. 1992. "Le Strade Romane della Bassa Padania." *Atlante tematico di topografia antica* 1: 161–8.

Calzolari, Mauro. 2007. "Il Delta padano in Età romana: idrografia, viabilità, insediamenti." In *Genti nel delta da Spina a Comacchio: uomini, territorio e culto dall'antichità all'alto Medioevo*, edited by F. Berti, M. Bollini, S. Gelichi and J. Ortalli, 153–72. Ferrara: Corbo.

Carreras, Cèsar, and Pau de Soto. 2013. "The Roman transport network: a precedent for the integration of the European mobility." *Journal of Quantitative and Interdisciplinary History* 46 (3): 117–33. DOI: 10.1080/01615440.2013.803403.

Cioffi, Robert L. 2016. "Travel in the Roman World." *Oxford Handbooks in Classical Studies*, edited by Oxford Handbooks Editorial Board, 1–39. Oxford: Oxford Academic. DOI: 10.1093/oxfordhb/9780199935390.013.110.

Collar, Anna, Fiona Coward, Tom Brughmans, and Barbara J. Mills. 2015. "Networks in Archaeology: Phenomena, Abstraction, Representation." *Journal of Archaeological Method and Theory* 22 (1): 1–32. DOI: 10.1007/s10816-014-9235-6.

Corbier, Mireille. 1985. "Dévaluation et évolution des prix, Ier - IIIe siècles." *Revue Numismatique* 27: 69–106.

Corcoran, Simon, and Janet DeLaine. 1994. "The unit measurement of marble in Diocletian's Prices Edict." *Journal of Roman Archaeology* 7: 263–73. DOI: 10.1017/S1047759400012617.

De Soto, Pau. 2019. "Network Analysis to Model and Analyse Roman Transport and Mobility." In *Finding the Limits of the Limes. Modelling Demography, Economy and Transport on the Edge of the Roman Empire*, edited by Philip Verhagen, Jaimy Joyce and Mark R. Groenhuijzen, 271–90. Cham: Springer. DOI: 10.1007/978-3-030-04576-0_13.

DeLaine, Janet. 1992. "Design and construction in Roman imperial architecture: the Baths of Caracalla in Rome." PhD diss., University of Adelaide.

Duncan-Jones, Richard P. 1982. *The Economy of the Roman Empire: Quantative Studies, 2nd Ed.* Cambridge: Cambridge University Press.

Flückiger, Matthias, Erik Hornung, Mario Larch, Markus. Ludwig, and Allard Mees. 2021. "Roman Transport Network Connectivity and Economic Integration." *The Review of Economic Studies*: 1–71. DOI: 10.1093/restud/rdab036.

Gabucci, Ada. 2017. *Attraverso le Alpi e lungo il Po: importazione e distribuzione di sigillate galliche nella Cisalpina.* Rome: École française de Rome. DOI: 10.4000/books.efr.3241.

Gabucci, Ada, and Giovanni Mennella. 2003. "Tra Emona e Augusta Taurinorum. Un mercante di Aquileia." *Aquileia Nostra* 74: 318–34.

Gabucci, Ada, Giovanni Mennella, and L. Pejrani Baricco. 2000. "Un mercante di Aquileia tra 'Emona' e 'Augusta Taurinorum'." *Aquileia Nostra* 71: 522–4.

Grazia Maioli, Maria. 2018. "Antiche acque di Ravenna." In *Il genio delle acque: scavi nelle piazze di Ravenna*, edited by Chiara Guarnieri and Giovanna Montevecchi, 331–42. Ravenna: Longo Editore.

Harris, William V. 2011. "Trade and the River Po: A Problem in the Economic History of the Roman Empire." In *Rome's Imperial Economy: Twelve Essays*, edited by William V. Harris, 189–97. Oxford: Oxford University Press. DOI: 10.1093/acprof:osobl/9780199595167.001.0001.

Horden, Peregrine, and Nicholar Purcell. 2000. *The Corrupting Sea: A Study of Mediterranean History.* Oxford: Wiley.

Knappett, Carl 2013. "Introduction: Why Networks?" In *Network Analysis in Archaeology: New Approaches to Regional Interaction*, edited by Carl Knappett, 3–15. Oxford: Oxford University Press. DOI: 10.1093/acprof:oso/9780199697090.001.0001.

Labate, Donato 2019. "Archeologia di una strada consolare: la via Emilia dalla fondazione all'età contemporanea." *Atlante tematico di topografia antica* 29: 195–212. DOI: 10.1400/269868.

Livarda, Alexandra, and Hector A. Orengo. 2015. "Reconstructing the Roman London flavourscape: new insights into the exotic food plant trade using network and spatial analyses." *Journal of Archaeological Science* 55: 244–52. DOI: DOI: 10.1016/j.jas.2015.01.008.

Manzelli, V. 2000. "Documentazione Archeologia." *Atlante tematico di topografia antica* 8: 39–196.

Marini Calvini, Mirella 1999. "Strade Romane dell'Emilia Occidentale." *Atlante tematico di topografia antica* 8: 187–92.

Meeks, Elijah. 2015. "The design and implementation of ORBIS: The Stanford geospatial network model of the Roman world." *Bulletin of the Association for Information Science and Technology* 41 (2): 17–21. DOI: 10.1002/bult.2015.1720410206.

Mills, Barbara J. 2017. "Social Network Analysis in Archaeology." *Annual Review of Anthropology* 46 (1): 379–397. DOI: 10.1146/annurev-anthro-102116-041423.

Mollo Mezzana, Rosanna 1992. "La strada romana in Valle d'Aosta: procedimenti tecnici e costruttivi." *Atlante tematico di topografia antica* 1: 58–72.

Ortalli, Jacopo. 1992. "La Cispadana Orientale: Via Emilia e altre Strade." *Atlante tematico di topografia antica* 1: 147–60.

Page, James R. 2022a. "From the Adriatic to the Alps: An Examination of Inland Trade in Northern Italy Between the First Century BC and Fifth Century AD." PhD diss., University of Edinburgh.

Page, James R. 2022b. "Riverbed, banks and beyond: an examination of Roman infrastructure and interventions in response to hydrological risk in the Po–Venetian plain." *Papers of the British School at Rome* 90: 171–200. DOI: 10.1017/S0068246221000258.

Page, James R. 2023a. "'Carrying Up It All the Products of the Seas': The Po-Veneto Water Network and Trade in the Roman Period." In *Rivers and Waterways in the Roman World. Empire of Water*, edited by Andrew Tibbs and Peter B. Campbell, 85–99. London: Routledge. DOI: 10.4324/9781003277613.

Page, James R. 2023b. *Modelling Transport in Northern Italy During the Roman Period.* Zenodo. DOI: 10.5281/zenodo.7937731.

Patterson, John R. 2006. *Landscapes and Cities: Rural Settlement and Civic Transformation in Early Imperial Italy.* Oxford: Oxford University Press. DOI: 10.1093/acprof:oso/9780198140887.001.0001.

Racine, Pierre 2000. "Il vescovo di Piacenza, signore della città (997)." *Studi di storia medioevale e di diplomatica – Nuova Serie* 18: 79–96. DOI: DOI: 10.54103/2611-318X/9811.

Rousse, Corinne. 2013. "Opérations de canalisation dans les ports fluvio-maritimes de la Regio X Venetia Histria: réflexions sur l'urbanisme et les transformations du territoire à l'époque Romaine." *Antichità Altoadriatiche* 76: 123–40.

Russell, Ben 2013. *The Economics of the Roman Stone Trade.* Oxford: Oxford University Press. DOI: 10.1093/acprof:oso/9780199656394.001.0001.

Scheidel, Walter. 2014. "The shape of the Roman world: modelling imperial connectivity." *Journal of Roman Archaeology* 27: 7–32. DOI: 10.1017/S1047759414001147.

Tchernia, André. 2016. *The Romans and Trade*. Oxford: Oxford University Press. DOI: 10.1093/acprof:oso/9780198723714.001.0001.

Terpstra, Taco. 2019. *Trade in the Ancient Mediterranean: Private Order and Public Institutions*. Princeton: Princeton University Press. DOI: 10.1515/9780691189703.

Uggeri, Giovanni. 1978. "Vie di terra e vie d'acqua tra Aquileia e Ravenna in età Romana." *Antichità Altoadriatiche* 13: 46–79.

Uggeri, Giovanni. 2016. "La Romanizzazione dell'antico delta padano. 40 anni dopo: una revisione." *Atti dell'Academia delle Scienze di Ferrara* 93: 79–104.

Willis, Staci, and Massimo Capulli. 2018. "A Report on the late 1st–2nd-century-AD Venice Lido III Sewn Timber Assemblage." *The International Journal of Nautical Archaeology* 47: 343–56. DOI: 10.1111/1095-9270.12322.

21 CORPUS NUMMORUM

A Digital Research Infrastructure for Ancient Coins

Ulrike Peter
Berlin-Brandenburg Academy of Sciences and Humanities
peter@bbaw.de
ORCID 0000-0003-0954-4322

Claus Franke
Berlin-Brandenburg Academy of Sciences and Humanities
ORCID 0000-0003-3371-6163

Jan Köster
Berlin-Brandenburg Academy of Sciences and Humanities
ORCID 0000-0003-2713-5207

Karsten Tolle
Big Data Lab
Goethe-Universität Frankfurt am Main
ORCID 0000-0002-9953-7638

Sebastian Gampe
Big Data Lab
Goethe-Universität Frankfurt am Main
ORCID 0009-0002-8700-3505

Vladimir F. Stolba
Berlin-Brandenburg Academy of Sciences and Humanities
atliche Museen zu Berlin Münzkabinett
ORCID 0000-0002-7362-8646

Abstract
CORPUS NUMMORUM indexes ancient Greek coins from various landscapes and develops typologies. The coins and coin types are published on the multilingual website www.corpus-nummorum.eu utilising numismatic authority data and adhering to FAIR principles. As an integral part of the project, the CN Editor has been developed as a multifunctional web app capable of managing the project's data entry workflow. It offers extensive search functions and various evaluation options. This open-source tool has a modular structure, allowing for swift extensions with new functions or adaptation to other object types, making it appealing for projects beyond the field of numismatics.

Keywords: Numismatics; Ancient Greek coins; Typologies; Versioning system

21.1 The Corpus Nummorum Project

Corpus Nummorum (CN) is a web portal and a powerful research tool dedicated to the study of ancient coins spanning from around 600 BC to AD 300. This brief overview introduces the fundamental concept of the portal www.corpus-nummorum.eu[1] and outlines its technical strategies, which could prove valuable for projects involving various categories of mass material, particularly those combining image and text.

Corpus Nummorum is a collaborative project of the Berlin-Brandenburg Academy of Sciences and Humanities, the Münzkabinett Berlin, and the Big Data Lab of the Goethe University Frankfurt am Main.[2] The project has received funding through various grants for over a decade.[3]

CN actively participates in international collaborative efforts aimed at creating a corpus of Greek coin types within a Linked Open Data framework (https://greekcoinage.org). The first version of the overarching ARCH portal, focusing on coins from the pre-Roman period, has recently been launched (https://greekcoinage.org/arch). Additionally, CN contributes to the ongoing international initiative for the development of typologies for Roman Provincial coinage (https://rpc.ashmus.ox.ac.uk). Geographically, CN has thus far covered four historical regions, including Thrace, Moesia Inferior, Mysia, and the Troad on both sides of the Dardanelles.

1 All links were checked on May 29, 2023.
2 See also https://www.corpus-nummorum.eu/team and Peter (2017), Peter and Weisser (2017). For a recent German language presentation of the project, see Peter et al. (2025).
3 See Section "Funding" below.

In *Advances in Digital Archaeology. Proceedings of the 2023 conference Computer Applications and Quantitative Methods in Archaeology – 50 years of synergy*, edited by J.W.H.P. Verhagen, J. Waagen, A. Brandsen, A. Queffelec, R.M. Visser and D. Taelman, 279–288. Leiden: Sidestone Press.

Differing from traditional collection databases, CN operates on multiple levels – ranging from individual coins and coin dies to coin types and issues. Each coin, die, and coin type is assigned a unique and stable resource identifier (Uniform Resource Identifier – URI). The multilingual portal indexes ancient Greek coins from various collections and develops typologies using numismatic authority data, especially from nomisma.org. With the provision of a Resource Description Framework (RDF) representation, the data is not only accessible via the CN website but also through the mentioned ARCH portal, and as RDF dumps via nomisma.org (see: http://nomisma.org/datasets).[4]

CN aims at including as many existing coins of the above regions as possible from both public and private collections, as well as from commerce[5] in order to create comprehensive online catalogues of coin types. The fact that ancient coins are available in large quantities and dispersed all over the world, makes this an enormous task. Supported by a range of grants, each typically tailored to specific themes,[6] the portal provides varying levels of coverage for different regions. As an example, a comprehensive collection of coins from Thrace has been compiled since 2012, leading to the development of nearly complete typologies. Consequently, this region currently boasts the most comprehensive representation.

Regarding the adjacent regions, a three-year funding initiative, beginning in 2018, focused on digitising and documenting coins from Moesia Inferior, Mysia, and the Troad in the Berlin Coin Collection. This project also included the digitisation of plaster casts of coins from these regions held in the Berlin-Brandenburg Academy of Sciences and Humanities. Wherever possible, efforts have been made to complement this data with coins from other collections, such as the Bibliothèque nationale de France, the SHH collection (http://www.hourmo.eu/01_Sylloge_Greece/Index_01_Greece.html), etc. However, it is important to note that the collection of the material for Moesia, Mysia, and the Troad is not yet comprehensive for the respective mints. Hence, attaining a comprehensive typology will require additional time.

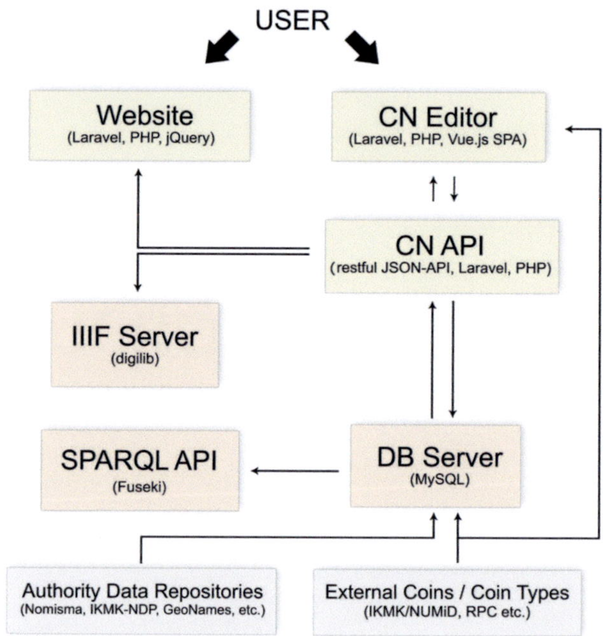

Figure 21.1. CN infrastructure.

The website https://data.corpus-nummorum.eu provides insight into the general technical structure of Corpus Nummorum (Figure 21.1). Its relationally structured dataset is stored in a MySQL database, accessible through a RESTful JSON API. Additionally, it is mapped to the RDF, the technical standard for the formal description of resources. This mapping allows for additional searchability via the graph-based query language SPARQL. All relevant fields are linked to authority data of the numismatic repository, http://nomisma.org, enabling exchange via Linked Open Data (LOD). The public website https://www.corpus-nummorum.eu offers data on coins, dies, coin types, literature, and typologies for general users. The International Image Interoperability Framework (IIIF) server facilitates access to IIIF data of images.

To adhere to the FAIR principles,[7] we employ descriptive metadata for enhanced findability, utilise Persistent Identifiers (URIs for data and DOIs for GitHub repositories) and incorporate standard vocabularies such as nomisma.org, geonames, etc. Open Access and user-friendly

4 The datasets are machine readable, and the data is published under a CC BY license–see details below. We also promote our portal through other portals, publications, conferences, and social media, aiming not only to link to other sources but also to encourage other parties to include links to our coin types and coins in their datasets. How else CN adheres to the FAIR principles, see further down.

5 Studying ancient coinages is inconceivable without material from auctions and private collections, given the significant role these collections have always played in numismatics. The most successful results consistently arise through collaboration among professional numismatists, museums, private collections, and the coin trade. The inclusion of coins from commerce not only significantly expands the datasets but also highlights often rare and unique materials that might otherwise be at risk of being lost. Simultaneously, we strongly condemn illegal excavations and violations of cultural heritage protection. See Elkins (2022) with further literature and publication guidelines, especially p. 60.

6 See Section "Funding" below.

7 For the first publication of the FAIR principles as a guide for enhancing data reusability, see Wilkinson et al. (2016; 2019). We express our gratitude to Ronald Visser for the reference to these publications.

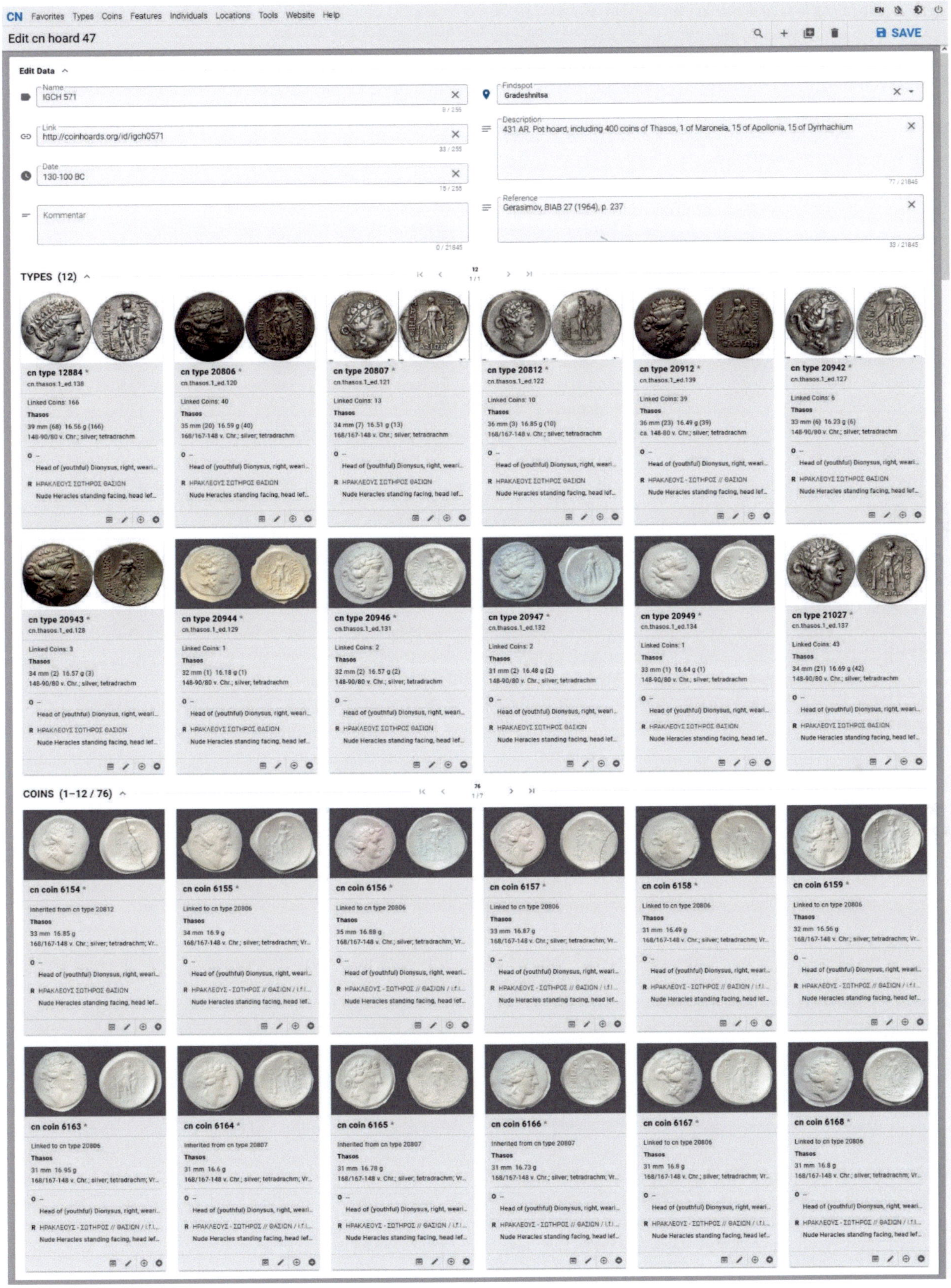

Figure 21.2. Example of an entry for a hoard with linked coin types and coins in the CN Editor.

formats facilitate accessibility, with data presented in commonly used, open, and machine-readable formats like RDF, XML, etc., ensuring compatibility with various tools and platforms. Interoperability is maintained through standardised formats and protocols, including the provision of an API enabling seamless interaction with our data for easy access by other systems. Data reuse is facilitated by a CC-BY license. Additionally, we offer comprehensive documentation detailing the structure, content, and usage of our data. Regular updates and curation guarantee accuracy and relevance over time, with any changes or versions clearly indicated (see below).

21.2 CN Editor

As part of the project, the CN Editor was developed, a multifunctional web application for creating and managing coin and coin type datasets (Köster and Franke 2024). This powerful and useful tool can also be employed for other projects dealing with serial data. Its modular structure facilitates easy adaptation and extension. The editor operates as a single-page application (SPA), built on Laravel and Vue.js, and currently supports English and German.

The CN Editor enables users to modify and edit all data associated with coins, coin types, and related entities, including mints, material, owners, persons, rulers, denominations, etc. An overview of our complex data model can be found at https://www.corpus-nummorum.eu/resources/database.[8] The editor facilitates the structured entry of comprehensive coin information, encompassing details such as monograms, symbols, and legend directions. Users can organise coins by types or create groups and issues. The multi-inherit options streamline data entry and structuring, allowing coins to inherit information from corresponding coin types. Additionally, there is a one-click data import feature from diverse sources and partners, including the IKMK family (IKMK family, https://ikmk.net), the American Numismatic Society (American Numismatic Society, https://numismatics.org/resources), and coins listed in platforms like https://www.coinarchives.com and https://www.acsearch.info. Existing export interfaces for coin collections and regex-based full-text recognition for auction coin websites are leveraged. Rapid and straightforward import of images linked to the dataset is supported. Images combining obverse and reverse views from certain portals are automatically separated into two files. This efficient system enables the swift addition of new coins to existing types, as only metrological and provenance data need to be imported, with type-specific data inherited from pre-existing types. Imported data can be customised to meet the system's requirements.

Images are organised into sets that comprise obverse and reverse pictures of a coin. A coin may have more than one image set, such as photos of an original coin and a plaster cast. Uploaded images can be modified by rotating, zooming, or moving their contents. These modifications do not affect the original file, which remains unchanged. Instead, these changes are only applied to the thumbnails. In addition, the modification parameters are stored in a separate JSON file, enabling the original to be transformed on the fly when accessed through our IIIF image service (Digilib).

Aligned with the regional focus of the portal, CN also documents coin hoards, capturing necessary parameters (composition, chronology, reference, etc.) and geographical data (Figure 21.2). Links to hoards published in relevant portals (http://coinhoards.org, https://chre.ashmus.ox.ac.uk) are provided.

As of recently, the portal also allows for indexing coin forgeries to warn users and prevent the inclusion of counterfeits (Boteva-Boyanova et al. 2025; Figure 21.3). The existence of forgeries has always been a problem in numismatics. Nowadays, distinguishing many forgeries from original coins has become increasingly difficult. Therefore, it is crucial to identify counterfeits to understand which types have been falsified and to improve the overall quality of the data.

Adding new coins to our portal is straightforward, and we encourage collectors and other interested parties to join us in sharing their coins. By publishing them on our website, material that might otherwise be lost to scholarly research becomes known.

While access to our web portal is open and unrestricted, a simple registration is necessary to access the Editor (via the "Participate" button on the website). This allows for the input and modification of data records and information to be assigned to the respective individuals. Additionally, users can be granted varying levels of rights, ranging from basic read-only access (including coins not yet released for the external site) to various write permissions. For example, collectors may be given the right to input and modify only their own coins, providing reassurance that they will not accidentally delete data belonging to others. Other authorization levels encompass modifying all entries associated with the coins. Further rights include creating and modifying authority data and typologies, as well as news and the "Coin of the Month" feature on the website. The highest level extends to user management through administrator rights.

All published data is accessible via the JSON API, covering coins, coin types, dies, designs, legends, and auxiliary tables such as mints, find spots, materials, etc.

8 Our definition of a coin type is highly detailed; see Peter (2019, 399–403).

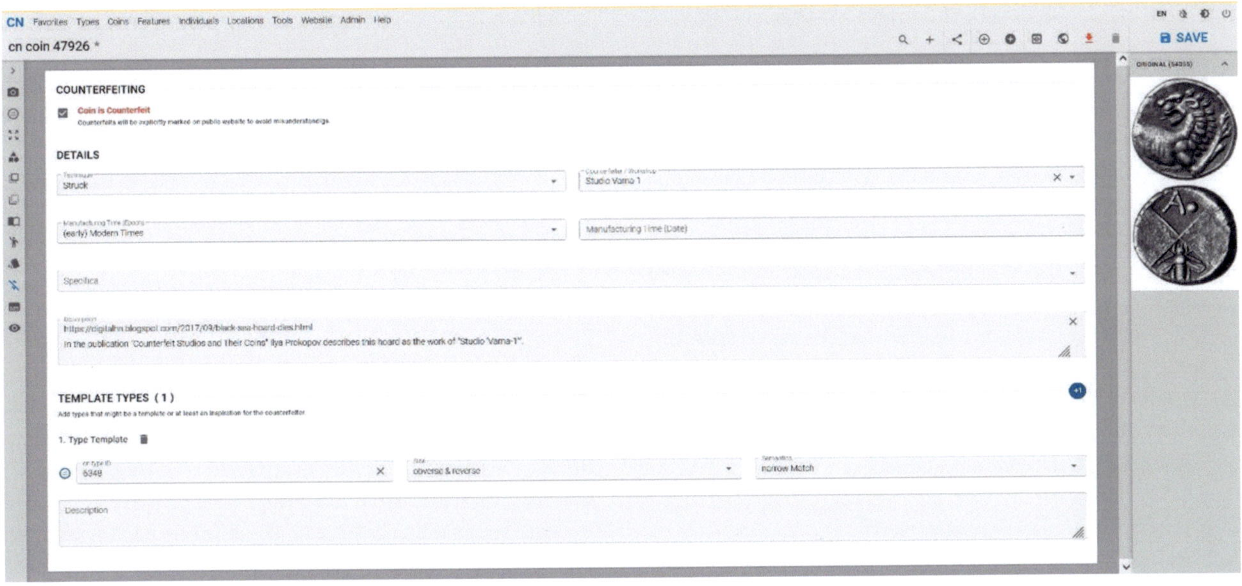

Figure 21.3. Example of an entry for a counterfeit coin in the CN Editor.

The API enables searches across all entities, offering up to 70 different search options and filtering options.

The CN portal facilitates the identification and description of relevant coins. Individual specimens can be assigned by linking to CN dies, types, and series, hierarchically structured and rigorously described. Simultaneously, the growth of the CN database allows for the identification of new types and the correction of existing ones (e.g., based on better readable monograms or legends on new specimens). As mentioned, collectors and collections have the option to publish their relevant coins directly (or via spreadsheet uploads) in the Corpus Nummorum database. A simple click on the button with their collection provides an online presentation of their data, along with a display of records linked to a map and timeline. The portal enables the creation of coin, die, and coin type corpora for specific mints, addressing various research questions through numerous search and filter options. CN functions not only as a research database with a range of options but also allows interested users to create their own database or independent instance on their computers or servers using the freely available editor, which can easily be adapted to specific needs and expanded with new functions. In line with the Open Access and Open Source policy,[9] the code and documentation of the CN Editor are available on GitHub/Zenodo for any projects related to the collection and analysis of ancient coins or other serial data.[10]

In the future, we aim to enhance and expand the export functions and interfaces so that our typologies can be utilised in collection databases to describe the coins within them.

21.3 Versioning System

For the unambiguous citation and continuous development of the typologies, we have established a versioning, or edition, system.[11] The edition number follows a specific format, composed of “cn” (Corpus Nummorum), followed by the issuer of the coin in the form of the nomismaID (nomisma-mint or nomisma-ruler_ID), the edition number (version_number_ed) and a unique number indicating the sort order (sequence_number). For instance, “cn.maroneia.1_ed.31” (https://www.corpus-nummorum.eu/types/cn.maroneia.1_ed.31) refers to the 31st coin type in the first edition of the coin typology of Maroneia. The criteria for arrangement are similar to those used in a printed catalogue, and these sort orders are available on our website at https://www.corpus-nummorum.eu/resources/typology-sortorder.
All recorded material is open source for linking to other

9 https://edoc.bbaw.de/frontdoor/index/index/docId/3366.

10 DOI: 10.5281/zenodo.10458195 – For technical reasons, the publicly available version of the CN Editor represents an older state and does not include all the functions of our productive instance. A larger release with additional functions and an optimised setup is in preparation. See https://data.corpus-nummorum.eu/wiki, for more information about the CN Editor source code and its features.

11 For the importance of versioning the scholarly data, see also Bürgermeister (2022).

digital data, visualization, and further research inquiries (also via SPARQL).

In addition to the conscious decision-based edition system, we employ an automatic versioning system that documents even small changes, such as the correction of a spelling mistake. If a published coin or type record is modified, the current state is stored as a separate JSON file, using CN ID and timestamp for the file name. All versions can be directly accessed via the API. It is also possible to input any arbitrary timestamp; in this case, the API will verify the version's validity for the given date and provide the corresponding data. The individual versions are linked to the editions, ensuring that older data states can always be reconstructed and cited independently of the constantly changing database.

21.4 Further Development

Currently, CN is undergoing further development as part of our projects, "Data Quality for Numismatics Based on Natural Language Processing and Neural Networks (D4N[4])" and "Iconography and AI-Methods in Numismatics". The goal is to establish artificial intelligence research tools for numismatics, which can be used independently or integrated into the CN Editor. Our approaches are particularly suitable for other object categories that combine images and text and are available in large quantities.

These digital tools aim to enhance data quality and facilitate the more efficient recording of coins accessible on the web. Text and image recognition are employed to expedite this process. Since July 2021, we have been testing machine-learning methods for typological coin assignments. This includes: 1) natural language processing (NLP) methods for multilingual and non-standardised coin descriptions (Figure 21.4), linking them to a hierarchical iconographic thesaurus; this combination enables more sophisticated semantic searches for specific coin and coin type data; 2) complex image recognition of entire design compositions and their individual elements using deep learning.[12]

Convolutional Neural Networks (CNNs) have been trained to add new coins to coin types and mints available in the database. In addition to coin types, the goal is to differentiate patterns and elements on coins, such as monograms, persons, objects, etc. (Luong 2022). Our high-quality training and testing datasets, essential for the successful development of machine-learning-based image recognition methods like Convolutional Neural Networks (CNN), have been published recently (Corpus_Nummorum 2023). Currently, the varying degree of preservation of coins and the similarity of different images present challenges in applying AI models. However, these models have immense potential in numismatics for automated image annotation, analysis, interpretation, and retrieval.

To get a preview of how these tools function, one can explore Google Colab. For NLP, one can click on the design description (Figure 21.5) or upload a coin description to see which named entities (NER and RE) the program can detect (link to GitHub containing the code and the link to Google Colab for testing: https://github.com/Frankfurt-BigDataLab/NLP-on-multilingual-coin-datasets). Alternatively, one can upload a photo of a coin (obverse and reverse separately) to predict the mint or coin type from the CN dataset (link to GitHub containing the code and the link to Google Colab for testing: https://github.com/Frankfurt-BigDataLab/IR-on-coin-datasets; for both links see also https://www.corpus-nummorum.eu/resources/open-source-tools).

Promising initial results have already been published, but we aim to enhance recognition by combining these methods (Klinger et al. 2018; Gampe and Tolle forthcoming). A multimodal approach should not only improve recognition but also enable monitoring of data quality. The project has successfully implemented quality controls to supervise the accuracy of the growing data.[13]

Additionally, our goal is to establish an authority data portal for ancient Greek coin iconography – a hierarchical *Thesaurus Iconographicus Nummorum Graecorum* (ThING). We have initiated a prototype of a hierarchical thesaurus in both English and German. It primarily relies on CN data with the standardised design descriptions, but integration of other coin descriptions and images is possible through data harvesting in the form of LOD. The objective is to index entire image compositions, as well as individual elements (Figure 21.6). ThING will evolve as a portal for standardised iconographic data, with each entry illustrated by corresponding coin types and coins. To facilitate more detailed identification of different images and cross-genre semantic and iconological analyses, we plan to establish links to similar representations in other object classes such as gems, pottery, sculpture, etc. Moreover, links to digital image repositories will encompass resources relevant to the reception of ancient coins (Figure 21.7).

Given the large and continuously increasing number of coins available online, manual marking is impractical.

12 For details on training the computer and its initial accuracy results, see Gampe (2021). Additionally, in the CAA proceedings of 2023, our colleagues Sebastian Gampe and Karsten Tolle presented a special paper on this machine learning method, based on our coin dataset. The paper discusses the challenges faced by image recognition models when identifying mint classes, which have significantly more images than other mints: Gampe and Tolle (2024).

13 Utilising the nomisma.org/RDF modeling of CN data, a tool has been developed that performs various quality checks (consistency checks) in the form of SPARQL queries. This tool is reusable by others. For more detail, see Peter and Tolle (2024).

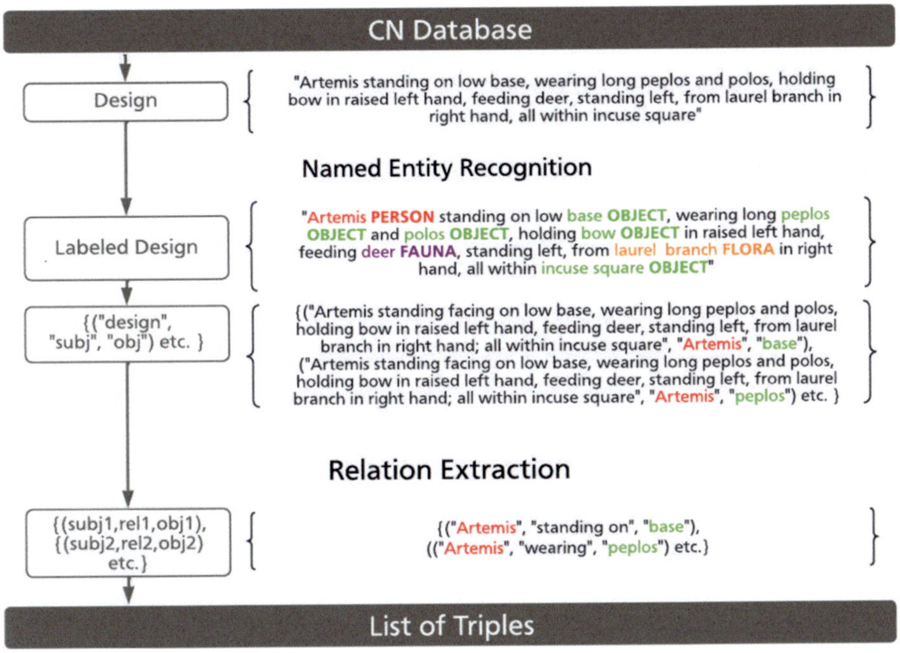

Figure 21.4. Example of a description of a coin image and the Named Entity Recognition and Relation extraction of the NLP pipeline.

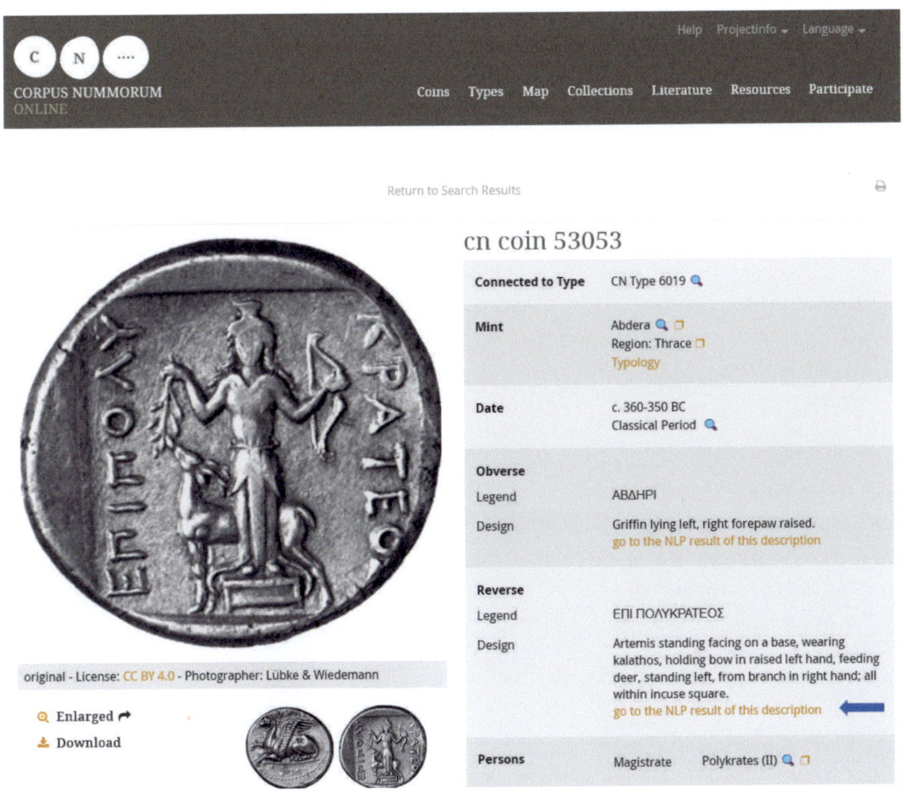

Figure 21.5. Access to the NLP pipeline is possible directly from the coin description on the web portal.

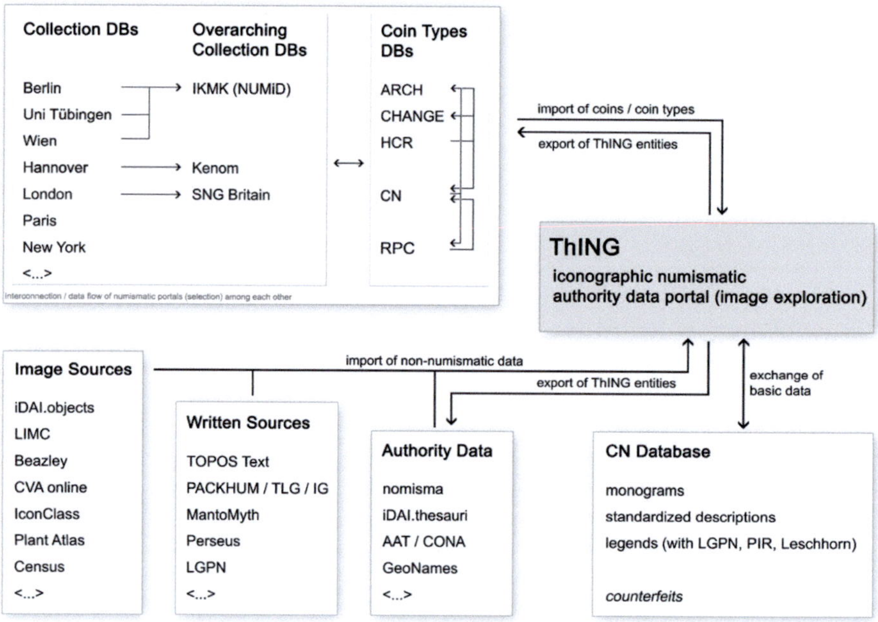

Figure 21.7. Schema for the in- and output of the *Thesaurus Iconographicus Nummorum Graecorum* (ThING).

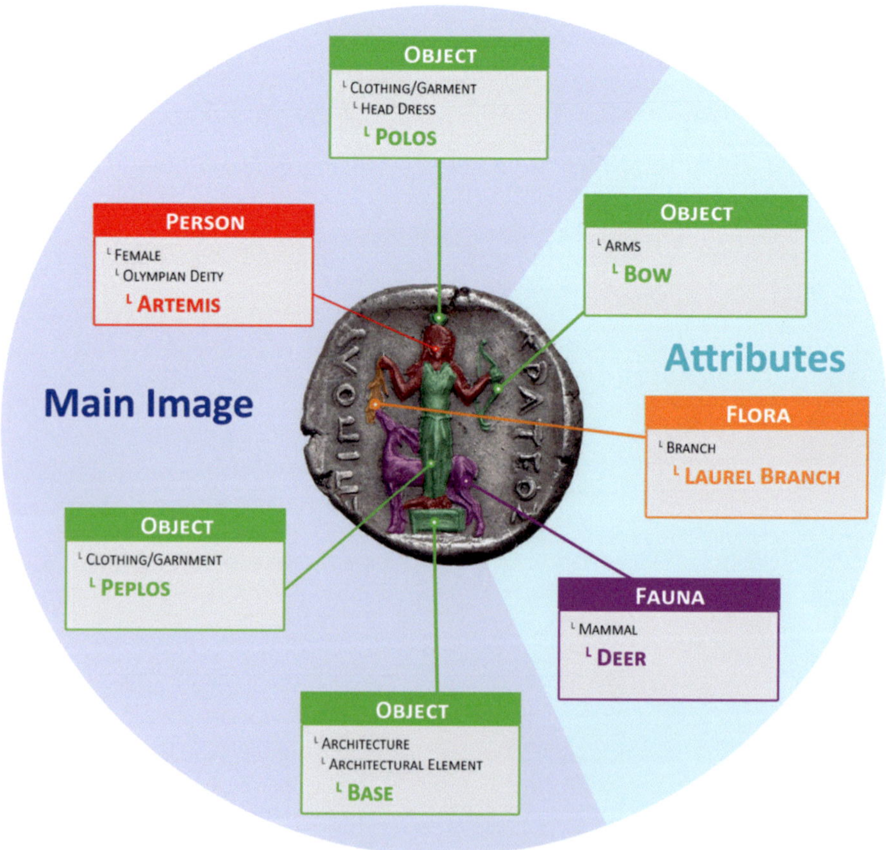

Figure 21.6. Example of a coin image with labelled entities, which should be identified through NLP and, in the future, also through object detection. These entities are linked with the hierarchical iconographical thesaurus.

Therefore, it is necessary to train the developed algorithm for semi-automatic marking. The goal is to ensure that different descriptions of the same image types, especially more complex compositions like depictions of the heroic deeds of Heracles, are recognised. This allows for the comparison of coins with each other and with similar scenes on other object categories. The combination of NLP and the iconographic thesaurus will enable new semantic searches. In addition, a new graphical user interface should make semantic searches possible, even for users without SPARQL experience (Wirth 2019).

We encourage you to utilise our website for your research. Currently, we already offer more than 37,700 coins and 12,800 coin types online. In the internal database, an additional 27,000 coins and over 7000 coin types are awaiting the final quality control before publication. Check the CN portal regularly for both new coins and coin types, as well as updates on new developments.

Acknowledgements

We thank the entire CN team (https://www.corpus-nummorum.eu/team) for their enthusiasm and support, without which this project could not have been realised. We are also grateful to Ronald Visser, Fleur Kemmers, and an anonymous reviewer who reviewed this paper and suggested a number of amendments.

Funding

The D4N[4] project "Datenqualität für Numismatik basierend auf Natural Language Processing und Neuronalen Netzen / Data Quality for Numismatics Based on Natural Language Processing and Neural Networks" is funded by the Deutsche Forschungsgemeinschaft (DFG) / German Research Council within the "e-research-technologies / Technologien" program. The IKKINUM project "Ikonographie und KI-Methoden in der Numismatik / Iconography and AI-Methods in Numismatics" has been supported by the Berlin Senate, Department for Science, Health, Care, and Equality. In its earlier phases, Corpus Nummorum has also received funding from the DFG and the Federal Ministry of Education and Research (see Peter 2020, 296–9 and https://gepris.dfg.de/gepris/projekt/203766501; https://gepris.dfg.de/gepris/projekt/317085821; https://www.tib.eu/de/suchen/id/TIBKAT:1809906555/Corpus-Nummorum-Online-die-antiken-griechischen?cHash=ee3cc81ca50e070a46ac49243f2bdb46; https://gepris.dfg.de/gepris/projekt/449148027).

Conflict of interest disclosure

The authors declare that they comply with the PCI rule of having no financial conflicts of interest in relation to the content of the article.

Data, Scripts, Code, and Supplementary Information Availability

Scripts and code are available online at https://github.com/telota/corpus-nummorum-editor and https://github.com/telota/corpus-nummorum-editor/blob/public/DOCUMENTATION.md. See also DOI:10.5281/zenodo.10458195 and https://data.corpus-nummorum.eu/wiki.

Peer Review

This article has been reviewed and recommended by PCI Archaeology.

Ronald Visser. 2024. "The valuable Corpus Nummorum: a not so Little Minion." *Peer Community in Archaeology* 100393. DOI:10.24072/pci.archaeo.100393.

References

Boteva-Boyanova, Dilyana, Ilya Prokopov, Jan Köster, Jonas E. Flueck, and Valentina Grigorova-Gencheva. 2025. "Ancient Coin Counterfeits." In *Proceedings of the XVI International Numismatic Congress, 11-16.09. 2022, Warsaw* Vol. IV: Medals, Modern and General Numismatics, 343–50. DOI:10.1484/M.WSA-EB.5.145496.

Bürgermeister, Martina 2020. "Enabling the Scholarly Discourse of the Future: Versioning RDF Data in the Digital Humanities." In *Graph Technologies in the Humanities – Proceedings 2020,* edited by T. Andrews, F. Diehr, T. Efer, A. Kuczera, and J. van Zunder, 1–17. CEUR Workshop. ceur-ws.org.https://ceur-ws.org/Vol-3110/paper1.pdf.

Corpus_Nummorum. 2023. *Corpus Nummorum – Coin Image Dataset (1.0)* [Data set]. Zenodo. DOI:10.5281/zenodo.10033993.

Elkins, Nathan T. 2022. "Provenance and Legal Issues." In *Survey of Numismatic Research, 2014–2020,* edited by Michael Alram, Jarosław Bodzek, and Aleksander Bursche, 55–64. Warsaw: International Numismatic Council.

Gampe, Sebastian 2021. "Neuronale Netze zur Bestimmung römischer Kaiser auf Bildern antiker Münzen." MA diss., Goethe-Universität Frankfurt am Main. http://www.bigdata.uni-frankfurt.de/wp-content/uploads/2022/05/Masterarbeit_Sebastian_Gampe_online.pdf.

Gampe, Sebastian, and Karsten Tolle. 2024. *Creating an Additional Class Layer with Machine Learning to Counter Overfitting in an Unbalanced Ancient Coin Dataset.* Zenodo. https://zenodo.org/records/10980380.

Gampe, Sebastian, and Karsten Tolle. forthcoming. "Combination of Machine Learning Methods of Image and Natural Language Recognition on Ancient Coin Data." In *Proceedings Computer Applications and Quantitative Methods in Archaeology (CAA) Conference in Kraków 2019.*

Klinger, Patricia, Sebastian Gampe, Karsten Tolle, and Ulrike Peter. 2018. "Semantic Search based on Natural Language Processing – a Numismatic Example." *Journal of Ancient History and Archaeology* 5 (3): 68–79. DOI:10.14795/j.v5i3.334.

Köster, Jan, and Claus Franke. 2024. *Corpus Nummorum Editor.* Zenodo. DOI:10.5281/zenodo.10458195.

Luong, Huy 2022. "Klassifizierung von Motiven auf antiken Münzen mit Mask R-CNN." MA diss., Goethe-Universität Frankfurt am Main. http://www.bigdata.uni-frankfurt.de/wp-content/uploads/2023/02/Masterthesis-Huy-Luong.pdf.

Peter, Ulrike 2017. "Corpus Nummorum Thracorum – A Research Tool for Thracology and an Example of Digital Numismatic Collaboration." In *XV International Numismatic Congress Taormina 2015. Proceedings. Volume 2,* edited by Maria Caccamo Caltabiano, 1306. Rome: Arbor Sapientiae Editore.

Peter, Ulrike 2019. "Von Mommsen zum Semantic Web: Perspektiven der vernetzten numismatischen Forschung – die Münzen der westlichen Schwarzmeerküste online." In *Advances in Ancient Black Sea Studies: Historiography, Archaeology and Religion. The Proceedings of the International Symposium, Constanța, August 20–24, 2018,* edited by V. Cojocaru, L. Ruscu, Th. Castelli, and A.-I. Pázsint, 393–418. Cluj-Napoca: Mega Publishing House.

Peter, Ulrike 2020. "Das Münzkabinett und die Berlin-Brandenburgische Akademie der Wissenschaften – Eine enge Partnerschaft." In *Münzkabinett – Menschen, Münzen, Medaillen,* edited by Bernhard Weisser, 285–300. Regenstauf: Battenberg-Gietl Verlag.

Peter, Ulrike, and Karsten Tolle. 2024. "Corpus Nummorum – Coins, Types and Data Quality Control." In *Proceedings of the 8th Joint Meeting of ECFN and nomisma.org on Coin Finds and Digital Numismatics. Università degli Studi di Messina (2-4 maggio 2019). Atti,* edited by Mariangela Puglisi and Christian Mondello, 101-106. Messina: Messina University Press. https://messinaup-pubblicazioni.unime.it/index.php/mup/catalog/book/13.

Peter, Ulrike, and Bernhard Weisser. 2017. "CNT – The Web Portal for Thracian Coins." In *XV International Numismatic Congress Taormina 2015. Proceedings. Volume 1,* edited by Maria Caccamo Caltabiano, 247. Rome: Arbor Sapientiae Editore.

Peter, Ulrike, Jan Adamik-Köster, Angela Berthold, Claus Franke, Sebastian Gampe, Andrea Gorys, Vladimir Stolba, Karsten Tolle, and Bernhard Weisser. 2025. "Eine digitale Forschungsinfrastruktur für antike Münzen: neue Entwicklungen im Projekt Corpus Nummorum." In *Proceedings of the XVI International Numismatic Congress, 11-16.09. 2022,* edited by Aleksander Bursche et al. Warsaw. Vol. I: Greek Numismatics, 63-68. DOI: 10.1484/M.WSA-EB.5.144857

Wilkinson, Mark D., Michel Dumontier, IJsbrand Jan Aalbersberg, Gabrielle Appleton, Myles Axton, Arie Baak, Niklas Blomberg, et al. 2016. "The FAIR Guiding Principles for Scientific Data Management and Stewardship." *Scientific Data* 3 (1): 160018. DOI:10.1038/sdata.2016.18.

Wilkinson, Mark D., Michel Dumontier, IJsbrand Jan Aalbersberg, Gabrielle Appleton, Myles Axton, Arie Baak, Niklas Blomberg, et al 2019. "Addendum: The FAIR Guiding Principles for Scientific Data Management and Stewardship." *Scientific Data* 6 (1): 6. DOI:10.1038/s41597-019-0009-6.

Wirth, Alicia 2019. "SPARQL-Abfrageschnittstelle ikonografischer Daten im Ressource Description Framework." BA diss., Goethe-Universität Frankfurt am Main. https://github.com/aliciawrt/IGSApplication/blob/master/SPARQL-Abfrageschnittstelle%20ikonografischer%20Daten%20im%20Resource%20Description%20Framework.pdf.

22 ARIADNEplus Visual Media Service 3D configurator

Toward full guided publication of high-resolution 3D data

Marco Potenziani
ISTI-CNR
Pisa
marco.potenziani@isti.cnr.it
ORCID 0000-0003-4644-4638

Federico Ponchio
ISTI-CNR
Pisa
federico.ponchio@isti.cnr.it
ORCID 0000-0002-2974-0577

Marco Callieri
ISTI-CNR
Pisa
marco.callieri@isti.cnr.it
ORCID 0000-0002-5832-680X

Paolo Cignoni
ISTI-CNR
Pisa
paolo.cignoni@isti.cnr.it
ORCID 0000-0002-2686-8567

Abstract

The use of digital visual media in everyday work is nowadays a common practice in many different domains, including Cultural Heritage (CH). Because of that, the presence of digital datasets in CH archives and repositories is becoming more and more relevant. However, the correct management of these assets, specialized and often complex, it is not always trivial, especially for communities of users lacking specific training. In these cases, systems enabling assisted data management during the different phases of their life cycle, can be a solution.

The Visual Media Service (VMS) is a web-based platform that enables the easy publication of complex visual media assets, specifically targeting the CH domain. It allows users to upload high-resolution images, RTI (Reflectance Transformation Imaging) images, and 3D models, transforming them into an efficient format for interactive web visualization. The VMS is an end-to-end solution able to support the entire publishing process, from data uploading to presentation customization. To expand its adoption in the CH community, the ARIADNEplus project aimed to enhance its features, providing innovative services for archaeological data publication.

This paper introduces the VMS 3D configurator, a new tool designed to improve the visual organization of 3D archaeological datasets in the VMS. The configurator guides content creators through a multi-step wizard, offering customization options for the presentation of 3D models. The configurator consists of five different configuration stages, each providing specific customization features, such as model orientation, appearance, scene navigation, viewer interface, and annotation of points of interest.

In addition to provide a detailed description of all the configuration possibilities, the paper will also discuss uses, limitations, and potential developments of the 3D configurator, and of the entire platform too, highlighting the value of the VMS as a tool for publishing, exploring, and disseminating CH data.

Keywords: Visual Media Service; Web Publishing and Visualization; 3D Models; Web3D; WebGL

22.1 Introduction

Using cutting-edge visual technologies for analysing, documenting, preserving, and sharing artifacts is a consolidated trend in the Cultural Heritage (CH) domain (Bustillo et al. 2015). As is well established that, to become valuable resources for learning, study, and research,

In *Advances in Digital Archaeology. Proceedings of the 2023 conference Computer Applications and Quantitative Methods in Archaeology – 50 years of synergy*, edited by J.W.H.P. Verhagen, J. Waagen, A. Brandsen, A. Queffelec, R.M. Visser and D. Taelman, 289–298. Leiden: Sidestone Press.

the digital datasets generated by these technologies should be FAIR – Findable, Accessible, Interoperable, and Reusable (Wilkinson et al. 2016). The Visual Media Service (VMS; Ponchio et al. 2016)[1] is a platform designed following these principles.

Developed in the context of the EC Infra ARIADNE project (Meghini et al. 2017), the VMS provides easy publication and presentation on the web of complex visual media assets. It is an automatic service aimed at people working in the CH domain, that allows content creators to upload three different types of visual media (high-resolution images, RTI – Reflectance Transformation Imaging images, and 3D models) on a server and to transform them into an efficient web format, making them ready for web-based visualization.

To boost the adoption of the service by the CH community, possibly transforming the VMS in a solution exploitable in a more systematic and structured way, the Horizon 2020 ARIADNEplus project[2] aimed at expanding the VMS features, implementing innovative services for users addressed to archaeological data publication.

In this context, one of the goals of the project was to design and develop new services for improving the visual organization of 3D archaeological datasets. Initially planned as a simple redesign of the way of linking the 3D model of an artifact or a monument to its archaeological documentation, finally the work has involved not only the 3D data enrichment stage, but also all the other configuration options already provided for customizing the VMS 3D presentation.

The result of this work is a brand-new configurator for 3D models, proposed as a complete multi-step wizard able to guide the content creator through the publication process. The current 3D configurator is composed of five different configuration steps, appropriately divided according to the type of customization they provide: Alignment, Material & Light, Navigation, Interface, and Annotation.

This paper introduces the VMS 3D configurator and the key concepts behind its design. After a brief introduction of the VMS platform, useful to contextualize the application domain, the different configuration stages of the 3D setup wizard will be presented in detail and illustrated with practical examples. The paper concludes with a discussion of uses, limitations, and possible development directions of the proposed 3D data publishing approach.

22.2 Visual Media Service

The current digital era of CH is characterized by large-scale, transnational, interdisciplinary and collaborative data-centric projects. For this reason, making digital data accessible is now imperative. The advent of web platforms (e.g., Europeana[3], ARCHE[4], Data Station Archaeology[5]) specifically addressed at hosting and disseminating CH datasets, allowed a wider audience access to CH digitized objects, enabling the possibility to appreciate them in previously unattainable ways.

Unfortunately, these platforms, usually focused at storing very different digital media, turn out to be quite poor in visualization possibilities. This issue is particularly relevant for some complex visual media assets widely used in CH, like for instance 3D data (Wachowiak and Karas 2009; Arnold and Kaminski 2014), that would need peculiar visualization features. With these platforms the publication of such data often either relies on external services, like Sketchfab[6] (a practice that implies a partial loss of control over the data), or is quite minimalist, so unable of providing those data-specific visualization functions provided only by specialized tools, like Smithsonian Voyager[7] or Potree[8] (very valuable, but requiring programming skills to be used).

Finding a quick and easy way to enable visualization of digitized artifacts is therefore essential. The VMS tries to meet these needs.

The VMS (Figure 22.1) is a web service developed in the framework of the ARIADNE and ARIADNEplus projects. It is a ready-to-use platform enabling large digital datasets to be processed and displayed seamlessly and quickly.

The VMS provides easy publication on the web of three different types of complex visual media assets:

- “reality-based” **3D models**, i.e., high-resolution unstructured geometries originating from the digitization of physical objects by means of optical scanners or photogrammetry (supported input formats: PLY, OBJ, NXS, and NXZ);
- high-resolution **2D images**, i.e., gigapixel photographs or huge planar images (supported input formats: JPG, JPEG, PNG, GIF, TIF, and TIFF);
- Reflection Transformation Imaging **(RTI) images** (also known as relightable images), i.e., 2D+ images created through computational photography where the user can interactively change the lighting at viewing time (supported input formats: PTM and RTI).

The VMS allows content creators to upload these visual media on a server that automatically transforms them into an efficient web format ready for online publication. Moreover, it also creates a web-based presentation

1 http://visual.ariadne-infrastructure.eu.
2 https://ariadne-infrastructure.eu.

3 https://www.europeana.eu.
4 https://arche.acdh.oeaw.ac.at.
5 https://dans.knaw.nl/en/archaeology.
6 https://sketchfab.com.
7 https://smithsonian.github.io/dpo-voyager.
8 https://potree.github.io.

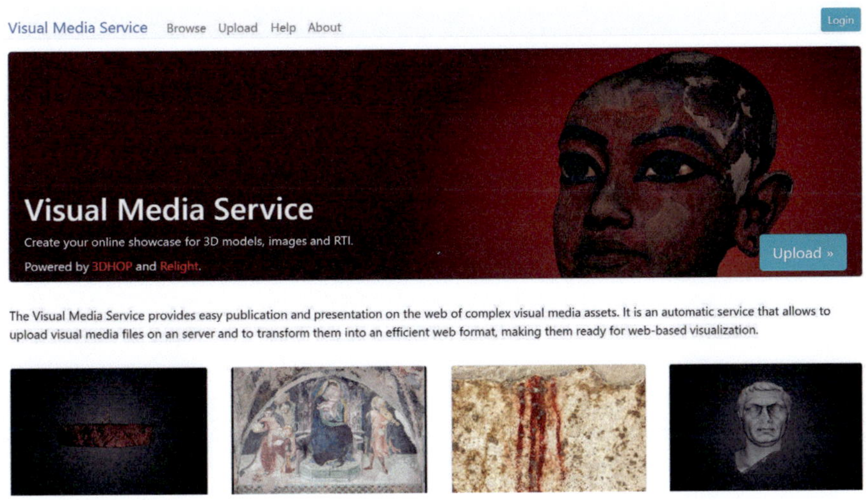

Figure 22.1. The landing page of the Visual Media Service platform website.

enabling content creators, but also end users, to access and interactively explore the published media. Finally, the VMS technology provides a full set of interactive tools for the displayed objects. As such, this service can be considered a valuable tool for the publication, exploration, and dissemination of CH.

The VMS platform also allows users to browse through the resources uploaded by other users and set as publicly accessible. However, this option must not mislead: VMS is not to be intended as an archive or a repository. It is rather a platform to allow scholars/professionals to publish on the web large visual data and to share them with colleagues, supporting cooperative work.

VMS has been designed to give people working in the CH domain the opportunity to experiment with web publishing, offering them multiple possibilities, with multiple levels of access:

- **public vs private publication:** content creators can decide to make their visual media accessible to anyone through the web platform, or whether to keep them private;
- **personal shareable link:** for sharing the uploaded media only with a selected group of end users;
- **iframe embedding:** for integrating the resulting presentation in the uploader's own web page;
- **viewer download:** after configuring the viewer on the platform, a content creator can download it with all its settings, to then further customize and deploy the created viewer on its own system, by working on the source code for self-publishing or local offline use.

Therefore, the multiple levels of access are meant not just for the end-users, but also for content creators, depending on their software development skills. This democratizes the access to cutting-edge software solutions, that is one of the primary targets of the VMS. In fact, the VMS allows content creators to exploit high-performance lower-level software exposed in a shared environment through easy-to-use interfaces.

Particularly, the VMS is based on:

- **3DHOP**[9] (Potenziani et al. 2015), an open-source framework for the creation of interactive web presentations of high-resolution 3D models;
- **Nexus**[10] (Ponchio and Dellepiane 2015), a library for the creation and visualization of large 3D models online;
- **Relight**[11]**/OpenLIME**[12] (Ponchio et al. 2018), which are libraries to create and view on the web relightable images.

These solutions, all developed by CNR-ISTI Visual Computing Lab, are low or middle-level solutions. This means that users are generally required to write source code to make them work. Conversely, using the VMS platform, even a content creator without computer programming knowledge can exploit them interacting with simple interfaces developed ad-hoc, without the need for coding.

The VMS can be considered an end-to-end solution, supporting content creators in each step of the publishing process, from login to presentation customization. For each of the three supported visual media the platform implements:

- **Multi-option login system**: to upload a visual media and create a presentation, a content creator has to log in to the platform. The VMS supports 3 different login modes. Users can log in using a Google account, a D4Science account, or simply using an email address.

9 https://3dhop.net.
10 https://vcg.isti.cnr.it/nexus.
11 https://vcg.isti.cnr.it/relight.
12 https://github.com/cnr-isti-vclab/openlime.

- **Informative data support**: when the content creator selects the visual media to upload, simple information about that media (title, description, copyright owner, and so on) can be provided. Since the VMS does not aim to be a structured archive, currently informative data support is very simple. However, it is enough to provide minimal documentation and a tag-based search system for the uploaded resources.
- **Automatic server-side data processing**: when the content creator decides to upload a resource, the VMS server processes the selected visual media creating a web-friendly multiresolution version of it, exploiting the Nexus format for 3D data, and Microsoft Deep Zoom[13] for 2D/RTI images. Since data processing could take some time, it happens in the background (i.e., the user can continue to navigate the platform). At the end of the processing the server sends a message to the content creator to notify that the processing is finished.
- **Automatic creation of web presentations**: at the end of the processing, the platform also creates a basic web presentation of the chosen visual media. By default, media is uploaded as a private resource, but this can manually be changed by the owner.
- **Assisted customization of web publication**: once the basic web presentation has been created, the content creator can configure it in a specific section. The configuration process introduces to the user all the customization possibilities.

This last point represents the core of this work. Particularly, we focused on the configuration section for 3D models, which has been completely renewed, changing from a single-page simple editor with very few functionalities aimed at customizing the viewer interface (backgrounds, skins, buttons) to a complete multi-step wizard able to thoroughly edit the 3D scene, guiding the content creator through the whole publishing process.

22.3 3D Configurator

The current 3D configurator is composed of five different configuration steps: Alignment, Material & Light, Navigation, Interface, and Annotation.

Alignment: the first step allows the content creator to fix the model orientation (Figure 22.2). One of the more common issues arising from working with 3D models is that the model is often visualized with the wrong orientation. This happens because the 3D model has not been oriented correctly at the time of creation, or because the different tools composing the 3D working pipeline (data acquisition, editing, publication) use different reference systems. In any case, if the model is not in the correct orientation, in the alignment wizard the content creator can re-orient it using different commands:

- First of all, one can correct the model orientation rotating the model along an axis; there are 3 different sliders, one for each axis, and one can use them to independently rotate your model on a selected axis;
- Then, one can define the upward side (UP) of the model; this is another issue that happens very often, since software used for creating 3D models follow different notations; so, UP vector can be defined in two different ways (Y-vertical, used mostly by Computer Graphics tools, and Z-vertical, used mostly by engineering and geographical tools), and this leads to weird behaviour in visualization; since is not possible knowing in advance what is the notation used for the given 3D model, in this panel one can switch from a notation to the other;
- Finally, one can use the "advanced straightening" function to orient the model to match predefined views while directly interacting with the model in the 3D scene using a spherical trackball.

Material & Light: the second step allows the content creator to set up the 3D model appearance (Figure 22.3). More specifically:

- the material wizard provides a set of tools to select the startup colour of the 3D model (texture or solid colour), define the solid colour used, add or remove a toolbar button for switching between texture and solid colour, and finally customize the glossiness level (dull, low, medium or shiny).
- the lighting setup provides a set of tools to define the startup lighting of the scene, add or remove a toolbar button for switching between enabled and disabled lighting, and finally add or remove a toolbar button for enabling the interactive control of light direction.

Navigation: the third step allows the content creator to define the scene navigation setup (Figure 22.4). In particular, this wizard provides a set of tools to select the trackball paradigm used in the scene for manipulating the 3D model (turntable, that just allows a two-axis manipulation, with vertical tilting and horizontal rotation of the model, preserving the vertical axis; or sphere, that enables full and free rotation on all axes), define the initial trackball position, customize the field of view angle of the virtual camera (using a slider or three different buttons with predefined values), specify the type of projection used by the camera at the startup (perspective or orthographic), and finally add or remove a toolbar button for switching between perspective and orthographic projection.

13 https://learn.microsoft.com/en-us/previous-versions/windows/silverlight/dotnet-windows-silverlight/cc645050(v=vs.95).

Figure 22.2. The Alignment setup in the 3D configurator wizard. The panel on the right contains the controls for rotating the model along an axis, recalling the original orientation, setting the UP vector, accessing the dedicated panel for enabling advanced straightening. The 3D viewer on the left is updated in real time according to the customization in the right panel.

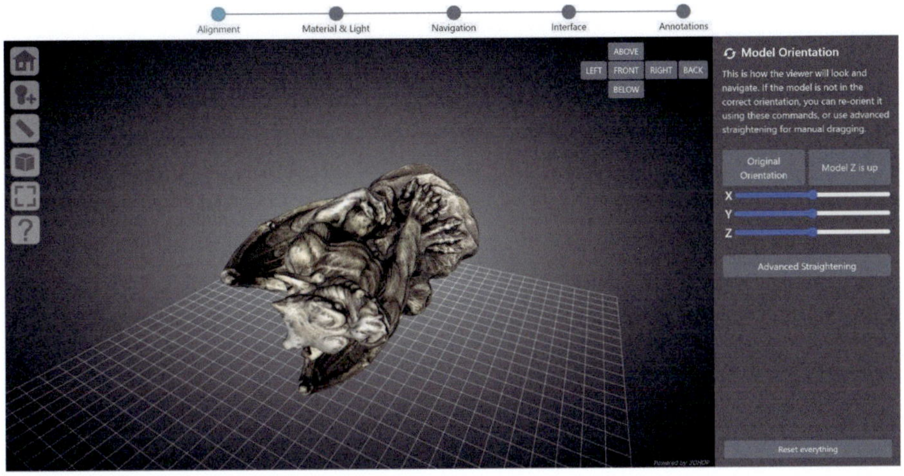

Figure 22.3. The Material & Light setup in the 3D configurator wizard. The panel on the right contains the controls to set the initial appearance of the model, modify the solid colour, add/remove the texture/solid colour toggle button in the toolbar, define the level of model's glossiness, set the initial lighting of the scene, add/remove the lighting control button in the toolbar. The 3D viewer on the left is updated in real time according to the customization in the right panel.

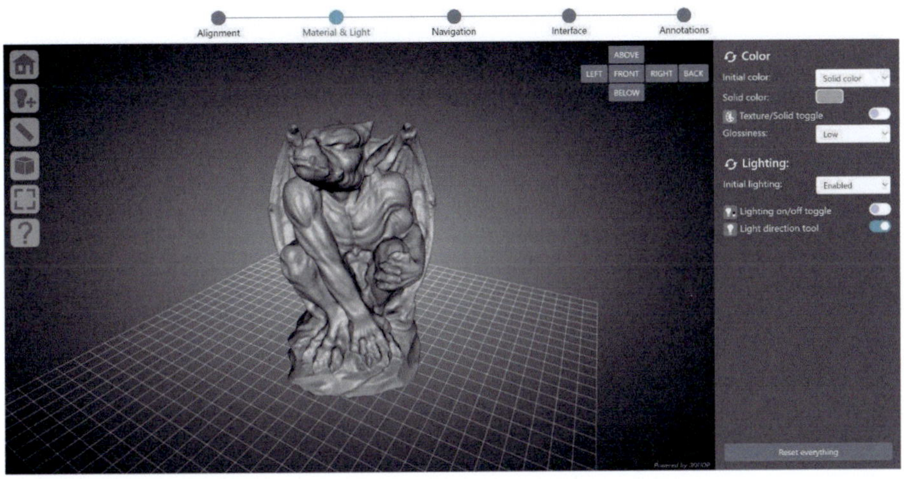

Figure 22.4. The navigation setup in the 3D configurator wizard. The panel on the right contains the controls for changing the trackball, setting the initial view, modifying the FOV, defining the type of camera projection, adding/removing the camera projection button in the toolbar. The 3D viewer on the left is updated in real time according to the customization in the right panel.

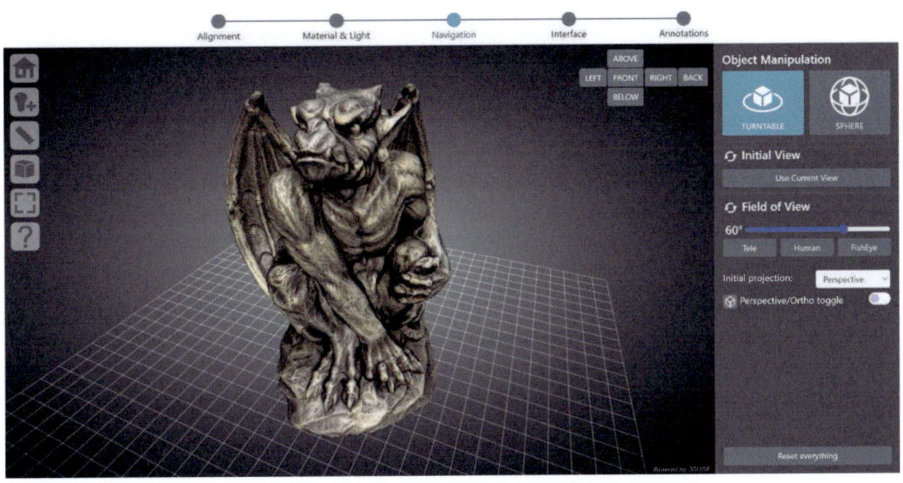

Figure 22.5. The Interface setup in the 3D configurator wizard. The panel on the right contains the controls for changing the toolbar skin, setting the viewer background, selecting the tools to enable adding/removing the related buttons in the toolbar, choosing the navigation/ orientation widget to add to the 3D scene. The 3D viewer on the left is updated in real time according to the customization in the right panel.

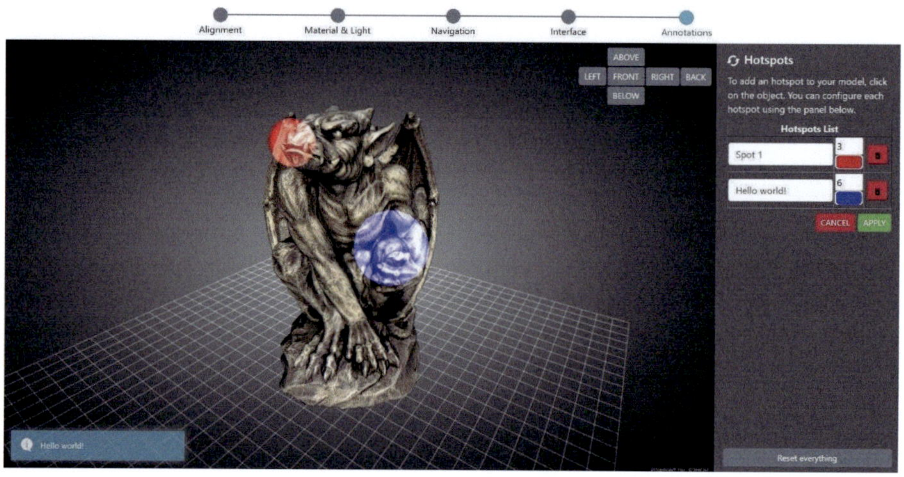

Figure 22.6. The Annotation setup in the 3D configurator wizard. The panel on the right contains the controls for adding/removing spherical hotspots (in red and blue) to the 3D model, modifying the hotspots setup (radius, colour), and editing the information linked to each hotspot. Moving the mouse cursor over one of the hotspots in the 3D scene recalls the linked information through a panel visible on the bottom left of the viewer.

Interface: the fourth step allows the content creator to customize the viewer interface (Figure 22.5). This specific wizard provides a set of tools to customize the toolbar skin (six different themes are available: light, dark, minimal light, minimal dark, transparent light, transparent dark), add or remove tool buttons from the toolbar (lighting, light direction, measurement, point picking, sections, solid colour, projection, full screen), define the viewer background (flat colour, linear gradient, radial gradient, predefined images), and finally select which widget to provide to the end user (base grid, compass, canonical views, navigation cube).

Annotation: the fifth step allows the content creator to add hotspots (points of interest highlighted by clickable geometries) to the 3D model and link them to some basic annotation (Figure 22.6). The annotation wizard provides a set of tools to add or remove custom hotspots to the 3D model, define the size and colour of each hotspot, and finally edit the text information linked to the hotspot. Once at least one hotspot is defined, the wizard automatically adds a toolbar button to enable or disable the hotspot visibility. If hotspots are visible, moving the mouse cursor over their geometry triggers a panel (in the bottom left of the viewer) showing the text associated with that specific hotspot.

22.4 Discussion

Released in early 2015 and integrated in the ARIADNE portal shortly after, to date the VMS counts around 1500 visual media resources uploaded, processed, and visualized. Among these, around 1000 are still online, while the remaining have been removed. The number of content creators exploiting the platform over the years counts 460 unique users.

As mentioned before, in the VMS data owners can select between restricted or open access, which is an important option when data of ongoing, not yet published research is being managed and processed. The usefulness of this option is visible in the fact that, currently, only a subset of the material (around 30%) is publicly accessible. A similar deduction can also be made from the difference between the total objects processed and the current number of available objects: users have exploited this service to put online, temporarily, restricted-access data, and then they removed it after having used it, or have used the VMS just to create and configure the viewer, that has then been downloaded for private, local use.

These two types of use, which are quite different from what is offered by other online services, have certainly contributed to the good results obtained so far, and to the adoption of the VMS by its target community. Indeed, currently the VMS is used by a number of cultural institutions. Among these, there are several universities (Florence, Milan, Turin, Rome, New York, Lincoln, Zacatecas, and many others) plus some research centres (INRAP, CNRS, CNR). Also, there is widespread use of the service in education, especially at the university level (from master's degree courses to Ph.D. courses). Finally, a few 3D scanning/processing companies use the VMS as a tool to test the 3DHOP library functionalities and its potential, to develop the interface, and (rarely) to preview or present 3D and RTI material to clients.

These examples of use, together with the figures mentioned above, show there is good interest in and appreciation for the VMS. Nevertheless, so far, we have not received any news about a more systematic or structured use of the platform. The new configurator system aims at filling this gap, providing content creators with a set of customization options that have never been so extensive and easy to use. These new possibilities shouldn't just impact the mere publishing of content, but they also should be able to stimulate a discussion concerning the reproducibility/applicability of the proposed data publishing approach to different media (e.g., applying the same configurator settings to other data), or even contexts (e.g., porting the configuration wizard in similar data publishing infrastructures, or even in archives and repositories where the content configurator can be exploited for media asset ingestion, or to re-configure the data already stored in these platforms).

Obviously, although the 3D configurator is 100% up and running, we are aware that, to date, for some aspects, it is still a demonstrator. And because of that, independently of the current limitations, due to its specialization, it cannot be considered a solution suitable for all eventualities.

For instance, since this 3D wizard is tailored to the specificity of 3D models, the same five configuration steps might not make sense with the other visual media supported by VMS (RTI & high-resolution 2D images). On the other hand, some specific customization features (interface, some inspection tools, and mostly annotations) would fit very well also with two-dimensional data. So, the same approach could also be replicated for these media, which would certainly benefit from the potential provided by a more structured configuration process. For this reason, moving the RTI & high-resolution 2D Images configurators from the current single-page editors (similar to the old single-page 3D configurator) to a multi-step wizard is on the road map of future developments.

Future developments that are not limited to overcoming the configurator limitations, but also aiming at increasing and diversifying the publication possibilities provided to content creators.

The first step of this process is trying to go beyond the current single object visualization, for instance allowing content creators to upload objects as a collection of items, so as to visually organize their exploration in a dedicated section, but also to apply one specific configuration setup to the whole collection. This makes sense if one is publishing a collection of similar items and could save the content creator a lot of time. A beta version of the tool for creating 3D collections has already been tested for a large set of lithic artifacts (Ardelean et al. 2022), and it is currently in the evaluation stage to be publicly released.

With collections you have multiple items grouped together, but each one will typically have its own viewer. However, one may want to have multiple objects in the same viewer. Actually, the VMS already supports this particular data organization, but currently this feature is restricted just to high-resolution 2D images. These particular collections of images are called **Image Sets** and are already online (it is possible to browse them on the platform website). Image Sets are very useful, for instance to keep all the pages of one book together, but they are a quite trivial example of multiple objects in the same viewer (because the final user can just visualize one item per time, jumping from a visualization of an item to the other).

For this reason, we are exploring the possibility to develop something more for 3D objects, designing a viewer able to load and display multiple objects together. Having more than one object in the same scene opens up various use scenarios: as a basic interaction, it would be possible to toggle the visibility of each component. However, to fully exploit the multiple objects, it will be necessary to add some more interaction with the objects. For this reason, the road map includes the release of various multi-object publication templates, each one with a specific built-in interaction, easily configurable. Examples could include a two objects comparison template, in which a content creator uploads two objects, and the viewer lets the user toggle between the two models, apply cross-transparencies, or use a slider to switch from one to the other (Figure 22.7A). Use scenarios: before/after restoration, display variants, artist's concept vs. actual statue. Another possible template is a sequence explorer, in which a content creator uploads multiple objects, each one depicting a "stage" of the same entity, and the user

Figure 22.7. Illustrative examples of possible future developments: A) two objects comparison template, in which a content creator uploads two objects, and the viewer lets the user use a slider to switch from one to the other; B) sequence template, in which a content creator uploads multiple objects, and the user can display multiple stages with transparencies/sections; C) technical viewer, providing more advanced features, such as points/polylines/areas annotations, able to help professional users.

can follow the time sequence, see an "exploded" view, or display multiple stages with transparencies/sections (Figure 22.7B). Use scenarios: archaeological excavations, evolution of a building/site.

Other development directions might aim at a more technical approach. Although usable in a technical environment, the VMS viewer is still more suitable as a tool for the general public dissemination rather than as a technical instrument. For this reason, the introduction of more advanced features, able to help professionals, is in the development road map. For instance, the current feature of hotspots authoring is useful, but still limited. Technical extensions could include points/polylines/areas annotations, groups and layers of annotations, and exporting functionality (Figure 22.7C). Also, the introduction of more technical tools would give the possibility of exploiting the metric quality of the high-resolution visual media in the VMS. Advances in this regard could include new measurement tools (e.g., angles), dimensioning, and functionalities to export annotations/measurements.

22.5 Conclusions

We presented a multi-step wizard for customizing 3D model web presentations and for guiding the content creator through the publication process.

Composed of five different configuration steps (Alignment, Material & Light, Navigation, Interface, and Annotation), this 3D configurator system represents a significant step toward the assisted integration of complex visual media assets in the context of the archaeological domain.

Initial testing started on selected datasets provided by ARIADNEplus project partners led to positive feedback, indicating the proposed publishing approach may have a substantial impact on future research practices, as well as on data reuse.

All the planned developments, together with the continuous update and maintenance of all the software components of the VMS (3DHOP, Nexus, Relight/OpenLIME), aim at improving the already good results obtained by the service so far.

Funding

The research leading to these results has received funding from the European Union Horizon 2020 Programme (H2020-INFRAIA-2018-2020) under the Grant Agreement n. 823914 (H2020-INFRAIA-2018-1 "ARIADNEplus" project) and under the COST Action n. 18128 (CA18128 "SEADDA" Saving European Archaeology from the Digital Dark Age).

Conflict of interest disclosure

The authors declare that they comply with the PCI rule of having no financial conflicts of interest in relation to the content of the article.

Data, Scripts, Code, and Supplementary Information Availability

Link to the Visual Media Service website: http://visual.ariadne-infrastructure.eu.

Link to the ARIADNEplus website: https://ariadne-infrastructure.eu.

Link to the 3DHOP website: https://3dhop.net.

Link to the Nexus website: https://vcg.isti.cnr.it/nexus.

Link to the Relight website: https://vcg.isti.cnr.it/relight.

Link to the OpenLIME website: https://github.com/cnr-isti-vclab/openlime.

Peer review

This article has been reviewed and recommended by PCI Archaeology.

Moffat, Ian. 2024. "ARIADNEplus Visual Media Service 3D configurator: a new tool for the visual organisation of 3D datasets." *Peer Community in Archaeology* 100350. DOI: 10.24072/pci.archaeo.100350

References

Ardelean, Ciprian Florin, Alejandro Mitrani, Jose Luis Ruvalcaba-Sil, Thomas J. Williams, Nancy Velchoff, Federico Ponchio, and Marco Callieri. 2022. "3D Models of Seventy-Seven Representative Stone Tools from Chiquihuite Cave, Zacatecas, Mexico." Zacatecas: Universidad Autónoma de Zacatecas. DOI: 10.48779/D2NQ-F182.

Arnold, David, and Jaime Kaminski. 2014. "3d Scanning and Presentation of Ethnographic Collections – Potentials and Challenges." *Journal of Museum Ethnography* 27: 78–97.

Bustillo, Andres, Mario Alaguero, Ines Miguel, Jose M. Saiz, and Lena S. Iglesias. 2015. "A Flexible Platform for the Creation of 3D Semi-Immersive Environments to Teach Cultural Heritage." *Digital Applications in Archaeology and Cultural Heritage* 2 (4): 248–59. DOI: 10.1016/j.daach.2015.11.002.

Meghini, Carlo, Roberto Scopigno, Julian Richards, Holly Wright, Guntram Geser, Sebastian Cuy, Johan Fihn, et al. 2017. "ARIADNE: A Research Infrastructure for Archaeology." *Journal on Computing and Cultural Heritage* 10 (3): 1–27. DOI: 10.1145/3064527.

Ponchio, Federico, Massimiliano Corsini, and Roberto Scopigno. 2018. "A Compact Representation of Relightable Images for the Web." In *Web3D '18: Proceedings of the 23rd International ACM Conference on 3D Web Technology*, 1–10. New York: ACM. DOI: 10.1145/3208806.3208820.

Ponchio, Federico, and Matteo Dellepiane. 2015. "Fast Decompression for Web-Based View-Dependent 3D Rendering." In *Web3D '15: Proceedings of the 20th International Conference on 3D Web Technology*, 199–207. New York: ACM. DOI: 10.1145/2775292.2775308.

Ponchio, Federico, Marco Potenziani, Matteo Dellepiane, Marco Callieri, and Roberto Scopigno. 2016. "ARIADNE Visual Media Service: Easy Web Publishing of Advanced Visual Media." In *CAA2015. Keep The Revolution Going. Proceedings of the 43rd Annual Conference on Computer Applications and Quantitative Methods*, edited by Stefano Campana, Roberto Scopigno, and Gabriella Carpentiero, 433–42. Oxford: Archaeopress.

Potenziani, Marco, Marco Callieri, Matteo Dellepiane, Massimiliano Corsini, Federico Ponchio, and Roberto Scopigno. 2015. "3DHOP: 3D Heritage Online Presenter." *Computers & Graphics* 52: 129–41. DOI: 10.1016/j.cag.2015.07.001.

Wachowiak, Melvin J., and Basiliki Vicky Karas. 2009. "3d Scanning and Replication for Museum and Cultural Heritage Applications." *Journal of the American Institute for Conservation* 48 (2): 141–58. DOI: 10.1179/019713609804516992.

Wilkinson, Mark D., Michel Dumontier, IJsbrand Jan Aalbersberg, Gabrielle Appleton, Myles Axton, Arie Baak, Niklas Blomberg, et al. 2016. "The FAIR Guiding Principles for Scientific Data Management and Stewardship." *Scientific Data* 3 (1): 160018. DOI: 10.1038/sdata.2016.18.

23 Percolation Package

From script sharing to package publication

Sophie C. Schmidt
Freie Universität Berlin
s.c.schmidt@fu-berlin.de
ORCID 0000-0003-4696-2101

Simon Maddison
University College London
simon.maddison@ucl.ac.uk
ORCID 0000-0001-5006-6604

Abstract

In this paper we trace the development of an R-package starting with the adaptation of code from a different field, via scripts shared between colleagues, to a published package that is being successfully used by researchers world-wide. Our aim is to encourage researchers to prepare their custom analysis code in a way that is useful and easily reusable for others. The paper starts with a short background as to the scientific aims of the software package before relating the collaboration journey and the detailed processes involved. We then move to a review of code sharing in archaeology and the lessons we have learned in publishing code for others to use and share.

Keywords: Research Software; Code Sharing; Software Reuse; Code Publication; Scripting Language R; R Package Development

23.1 Introduction

In this paper we describe the development of a suite of R scripts for use within archaeology, building on work from a different domain. This was originally undertaken for a specific university research project, but the results were sufficiently interesting to warrant dissemination at conferences. It is an example of Research Software, which is discussed in more detail later. Presentation at a CAA international event stimulated a conversation between the authors, which led to code sharing. This in turn led to collaboration on extending the code's application scope, and to the decision to prepare an R-package for publication and open use.

To set the scene, we start with a brief description of the scientific aims of the code package. We then relate the journey of collaboration and the detailed processes involved, and in particular the goals in wishing to publish it in the form of a package. We then discuss the lessons that we have learned in going through this process.

We move on to review how code is currently shared in archaeology, drawing on the list open-archaeo and articles published in the Journal of Computer Applications in Archaeology. We present and discuss the results of this analysis within the context of good practices for sharing Research Software.

In conclusion we summarise all these lessons and evangelise our view that publication of Research Software for open use and sharing is a worthwhile and effective goal for others to follow.

In *Advances in Digital Archaeology. Proceedings of the 2023 conference Computer Applications and Quantitative Methods in Archaeology – 50 years of synergy*, edited by J.W.H.P. Verhagen, J. Waagen, A. Brandsen, A. Queffelec, R.M. Visser and D. Taelman, 299–310. Leiden: Sidestone Press.

23.2 The scientific aims of the package

Percolation Analysis is a well-established process for identifying clusters amongst spatially distributed points. The percolation package (Maddison and Schmidt 2020), published as percopackage, evolved from work undertaken at UCL by Simon Maddison on the distribution of Hillforts. The aim was to find an approach to identify regional groupings, independent of geographical and political boundaries of any period. Percolation Analysis provided a conceptually simple technique and had recently been used in geography by Elsa Arcaute at UCL for identifying and classifying urban density through road junctions (Arcaute et al. 2016). This had been adopted within the Institute of Archaeology for identifying clusters of Domesday settlements in England by Stuart Brookes (Arcaute et al. forthcoming) and from that was taken up for the study of Hillfort distribution by Simon, see Figure 23.1b. This work was applied to data from the Atlas of Hillforts in Britain and Ireland (https://hillforts.arch.ox.ac.uk) which was being compiled at that time and was subsequently published online in 2017 (Lock and Ralston 2017), see Figure 23.1a.

The geographical work was undertaken using a C program to efficiently manage the very large databases involved. Elsa kindly produced a simple program in the scripting language R (R Core Team 2023) that could be readily adapted and developed for the exploratory work on other, smaller archaeological datasets. This adapted program suite was written to be readily used by others and the work was presented at CAA, where it caught Sophie Schmidt's interest for a project she was working on.

23.3 Collaboration

This personal meeting of the co-authors at the CAA 2018 conference in Tübingen spurred the next phase in the development of the package. After discussing their relevant papers and research aims, Simon shared his four scripts with Sophie, who was able to reuse the code to analyse her own data concerning features along a strip excavation in Saxony-Anhalt, Germany (see Figure 23.2).

At this point the code had some comments and a three-page description that enabled a basic understanding of the program within a couple of hours. In re-using the code on a dataset of a very different geographic scale (compare the scales of Figure 23.1 and Figure 23.2), some problems arose that needed to be addressed in order to extend the program's range of application. During the next two years Sophie successfully applied the code to her project work and a paper was prepared, in which the performance of the code applied to these rather different datasets and a comparison with different clustering methods was evaluated (Maddison and Schmidt 2020).

23.3.1 Detailed Process

The collaboration between the authors was organised rather traditionally, by emailing versions of the R scripts back and

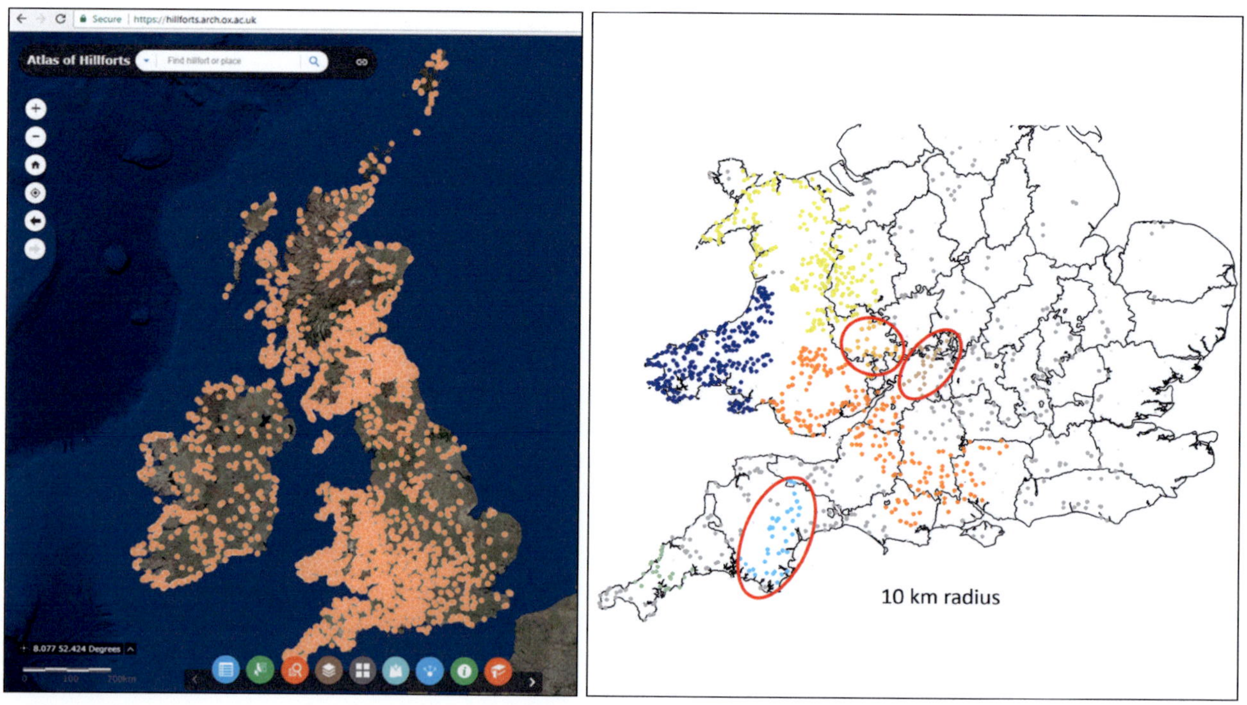

Figure 23.1. a) screenshot of the online hillforts atlas (https://hillforts.arch.ox.ac.uk/), b) percolation results of hillforts at 10km radius, taken from Maddison (2016).

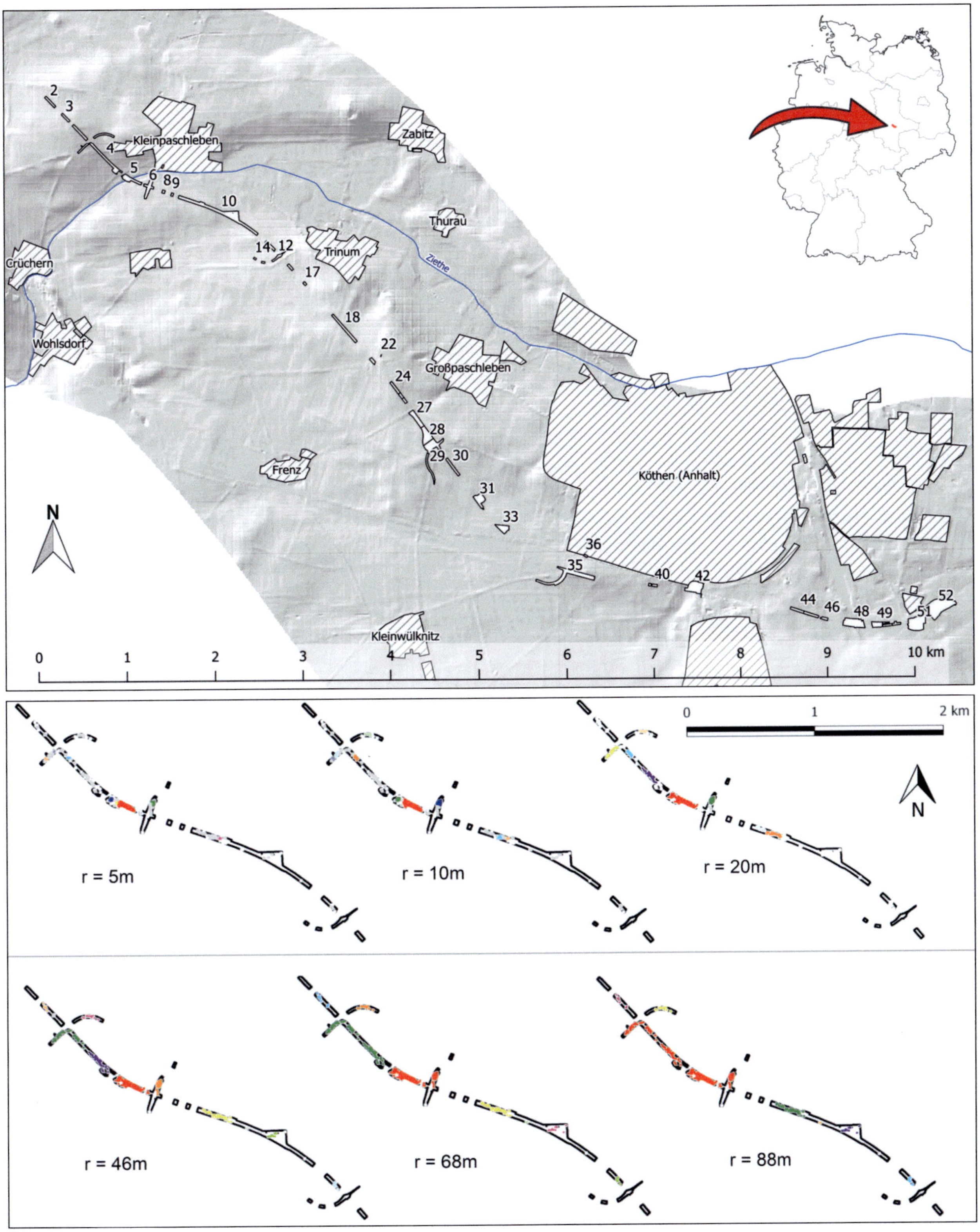

Figure 23.2. a) site of strip excavation of road B6n near Köthen (Maddison and Schmidt 2020, Fig. 11); b) overview of percolation results of features excavated along the transect at varying radii (Maddison and Schmidt 2020, Fig. 15).

forth. On one side git and a private Github repository were used for version control. The package named "percopackage" was created and the scripts converted into functions, which were documented using the package *roxygen2* (Wickham et al. 2022). *Roxygen* automatically creates manuals and organises the NAMESPACE as well as parts of the DESCRIPTION file.

The DESCRIPTION file is a txt which contains the metadata of the package. Name, description, authors and dependencies are the most important ones. It is the defining file for the package.

The NAMESPACE file defines the functions that are to be usable by the person installing the package. This file makes a package readily usable (Wickham and Bryan 2023).

A vignette, which explains the package functions in more detail, and an example dataset for users to try out the functions were added. These are not necessarily needed for an R package to run, but greatly improve usability. The dataset provided was a file of the hillfort locations used in Simon's research, derived from the Atlas database (Lock and Ralston 2017).

The paper was published in the Journal of Computer Applications in Archaeology (JCAA) in 2020. The GitHub package is now open as well (https://github.com/SCSchmidt/percopackage). However, Github is not a publishing platform and does not currently support long term stability. The package was therefore released on the Open Science Framework (OSF, https://osf.io), which offers DOIs for research output. This way the package is citable and reliably findable.

Any package that is in a tar.gz-format can be installed in R manually and packages on Github can be installed using *remotes* (Csárdi et al. 2023). For these reasons we took a simpler approach by publishing the package on Github and OSF. The package's DOI (DOI:10.17605/OSF.IO/7EXTC) was included in the paper. As it was linked to the paper, the package was also peer-reviewed as part of the publication process, which was a really effective way to have it tried and critically evaluated. The paper itself was a useful promotional vehicle and we can now see people using the package and citing our paper as well (for example: Díaz-Rodríguez and Fábregas-Valcarce 2022; Hu et al. 2022; Pajdla 2023; Verhagen 2023).

Although it has not yet been released on the Comprehensive R Archive Network (CRAN, https://cran.r-project.org/), it is our intention to do this. CRAN offers significant advantages for users and is great for easy installation and seamless integration into R but does require a further tranche of work. We have some significant enhancements to the package in planning and we intend to complete these first.

23.3.2 Lessons learned

Traditionally, script sharing needs personal contact, either at an institution, at a conference or by contacting the author of the paper who stated for example "the code of this program can be requested". Creating something new from a shared script needs either a really good understanding of it or, which we think more likely, a prolonged engagement with the original author, asking questions and proposing adaptations.

As a package, the original code was developed to have more flexible input schemas and therefore not only a broader variety of use applications, but also more comfortable handling. The code can now be adopted without contact with the original authors. As it is licenced and citable, no legal issues arise.

Other points that come out of our experiences are:

- Comment your code properly from the very beginning; it makes it much easier to adapt later. It is a very old dictum, everyone says this, and it remains true. It is also an important and very valuable part of the code creation process.
- Testing is essential from the start. The original software was rigorously tested during development, and particularly by successive versions of the source hillfort data, which was very much work in progress at the time, with many minor errors. Different sources of data, used for comparative analysis, were also useful in this process. Collaboration opened a new dimension in testing and is a valuable element in development.
- Going from script to function requires some thought about standard inputs and possible applications outside of the original research question. For both of these, a collaboration with someone working on similar (but distinct) issues is very helpful.
- It also makes the process easier, as tasks can be split. In this case, Simon remained the main author of the actual implementation of the working code, while Sophie did the restructuring to create a package, documentation and vignette.
- It is not as hard as it initially seemed. Creating a package can seem daunting, but the guidance provided by Wickham and Bryan, for example, is very helpful and detailed.

Another topic we learned more about during this project was the way code can and should be shared within a scientific community. So called Research Software is being developed for most disciplines today. It may describe anything from an elaborate program suite to a simple code script that has been developed with the aim of generating, processing or analysing research data (Hettrick et al. 2014).

23.3.3 Good practice for code sharing

Putting the software online is only one step in making it available and useful to others. The FAIR (Findable, Accessible, Interoperable and Reusable) Guiding Principles for Data by Wilkinson et al. (2016) have been adapted to the publication of Research Software (Lamprecht et al. 2020; Goedicke and Lucke 2020) creating the FAIR Principles for Research Software (FAIR4RS Principles, Barker et al. 2022). Importantly it has been considered to contribute to the quality of research software (Homburg et al. 2020). To summarise, the guidelines for FAIR Research Software (Barker et al. 2022) suggest that:

Findable and Accessible: Software should be easy to find and access. Unique and persistent identifiers (PIDs) that allow for differentiation between different versions of the same software should be assigned to the software. Only this way can any (FAIR) metadata describing the software include the identifiers of the software they describe. Access should be given via standardised, open and free protocols.

Interoperable: The software should be able to exchange data and/or metadata with other software to enable its integration into workflows or other programs (e.g., dependency management).

Reusable: Software can be executed as well as understood, modified, built upon, or incorporated into other software. This includes an up-to-date description of the software, as well as an open licence, which allows for its reuse.

The full FAIR recommendations are extensive; in our view one needs to be pragmatic depending on the scope and complexity of the Research Software in question.

We will now consider how code is being actually shared in the archaeological discipline and if and to what extent these principles are being employed.

23.4 Code Sharing in Archaeology

At the outset of writing this paper we believed that with the increase in computational approaches within archaeological research, requiring more complex programming code, the need for sharing programs intensifies in order to keep the approaches scientific and reproducible. Creating a package or plugin as described above is one possible way of distributing the code. The following aims at contextualising our approach and discovering if and to what extent other methods are being used in archaeological research.

Particularly in older publications, code is often published in a printed form. Since 2008, research software engineers have been using Github, Gitlab or similar collaborative platforms, and there are of course websites, blogs, journal supplementary materials, bespoke repositories, such as CRAN or PyPI, or general repositories such as osf.io or zenodo.org, where code is being published. However, we now consider how widespread this practice actually is. Also, as addressed before, publishing is just one step in sharing code in a reusable way, so we also need to consider what community standards there are to make other researchers aware of published code.

Free and Open Source solutions are often advertised with links to the code at talks and presentations at conferences, such as ArcheoFOSS (https://www.archeofoss.org/) or CAA. At CAA especially the "Little Minion" sessions aim at demonstrating coding solutions. A useful collection of Free and Open Source Software (FOSS) tools for archaeology is open-archaeo (https://open-archaeo.info), where short descriptions of programs, some information on the maintainers, and a link to the software are collected and tagged with keywords. This catalogue can be also used to understand code sharing practices in archaeology. A second dataset was collected from articles in JCAA and analysed with the same aims.

For the following analyses code and data are available online under https://github.com/SCSchmidt/CAA2023_code_sharing and DOI: 10.5281/zenodo.8307960. They were created in R (R Core Team) with the packages *here* (Müller 2020), *stringr* (Wickham 2022), *forcats* (Wickham 2023), *dplyr* (Wickham et al. 2023), *tidyr* (Wickham et al. 2023), *ggplot2* (Wickham 2016) and *viridis* (Garnier et al. 2021).

23.4.1 Analysis of Open-Archaeo data

Joe Roe and Zack Batist have already shown an analysis of open-archaeo data for the CAA conference in 2021 (Batist and Roe 2021). Drawing on the open-archaeo dataset and their analysis we can see that most of the resources in open-archaeo are actually packages and libraries that either extend existing software or are standalone software solutions (see Figure 23.3a). The research software is most often on GitHub and in some cases further promoted: Those tools are linked to a scientific paper, a website, a blogpost or similar, which explicitly "advertise" their program. Of 488 entries, some are on several platforms, mostly with overlap to Github (335, see Figure 23.3b). About 117 are linked to a website, nine have been linked to a paper and 18 to a DOI (with some overlap), 19 are on CRAN, two on PyPI – R and Python being the most common platforms (Batist and Roe 2021). The scientific publication and the archiving of a released version with a repository that gives a persistent identifier is most common for packages and libraries. All in all, though, the open-archaeo data suggests that there is a lot of material online which is rarely or not referenced in other publication outlets and may be hard to find for potential users. This also reveals what a valuable contribution open-archaeo constitutes to the archaeological community.

Nonetheless, open-archaeo is a collection of online resources and an online platform may not always link to a journal publication or similar. Another question that may be difficult to answer via open-archaeo data is how analysis code for research papers is being treated. Therefore, a further

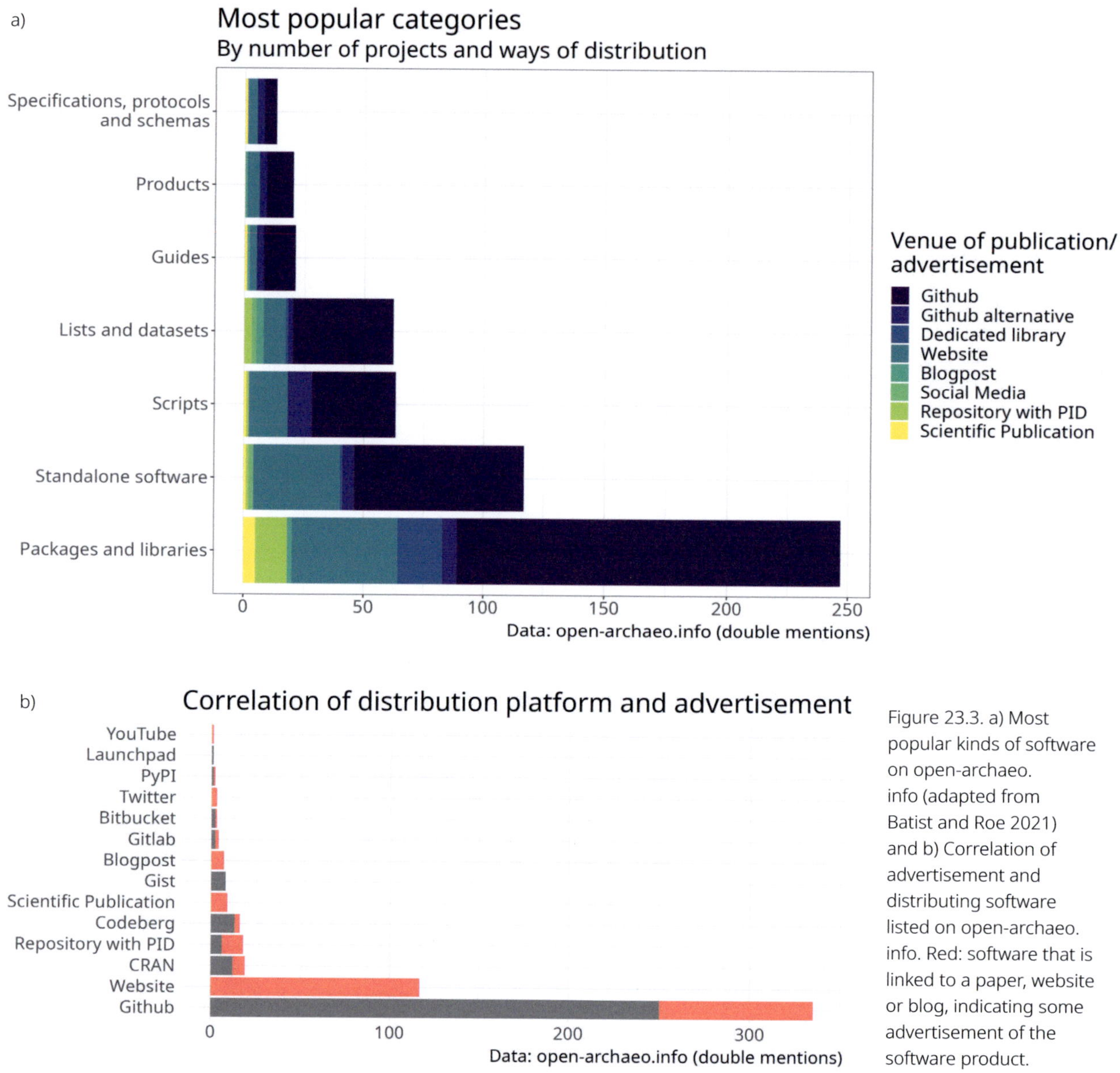

Figure 23.3. a) Most popular kinds of software on open-archaeo.info (adapted from Batist and Roe 2021) and b) Correlation of advertisement and distributing software listed on open-archaeo.info. Red: software that is linked to a paper, website or blog, indicating some advertisement of the software product.

angle was taken as well, and articles published in JCAA analysed. JCAA recommends using repositories for Open Code and Open Methods (https://journal.caa-international.org/reproducibility). It is one of the main publishing venues for computational archaeology and so particularly interesting to analyse in a CAA publication. It is not by far, though, the only journal in which relevant articles are being published (for R see Schmidt and Marwick 2020), Figure 23.4 and https://github.com/benmarwick/ctv-archaeology).

23.4.2 Analysis of JCAA articles

There are at the time of submission 68 research articles and case studies published in JCAA between 2018 and 2023. They were checked manually for references to program code used in the analysis and the way this code may have been published. The search was restricted to case studies and research articles, as it seemed more probable that programming was needed for the creation of the published analysis than for reviews, position papers or editorials. Of the 68 articles, in 32 cases it can be assumed program code was produced for the research (the database under DOI: 10.5281/zenodo.8307960 consists of 58 articles, as articles of a theoretical nature were not included). Of those, 22 articles contained links to published code, two of which did not work (though they were DOIs) and one article printed SPSS code. These publications from the last five years may capture current trends within the CAA community, but no long-term developments. The documentation of the submitted code was quickly and qualitatively checked, and the following variables noted: the format (*comments only*, *added README*, or *manuals*); the length (*good*, *some*, *little*); whether the code

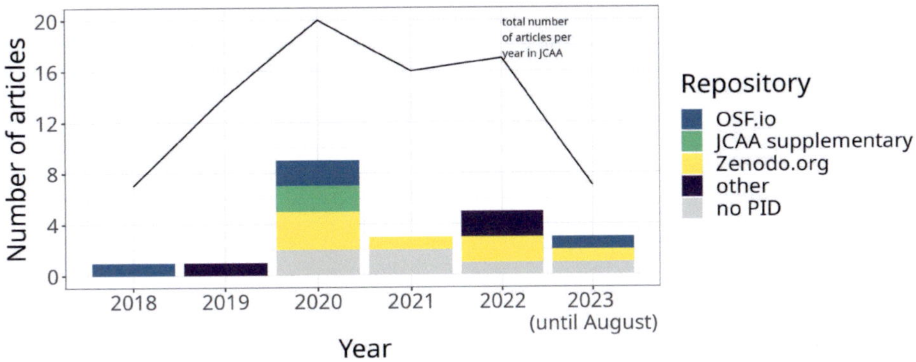

Figure 23.4. Number of articles published in JCAA (black line) and the number of times a repository was used to gain a Persistent Identifier (PID) for the publication of code. Grey indicates code publication without a PID.

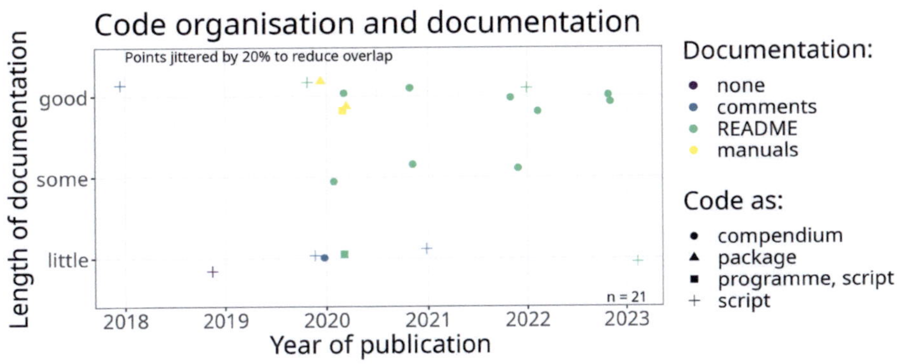

Figure 23.5. Jittered scatter plot to show the way code has been published ("Code as"), the kind of documentation available and the length of this publication.

Table 23.1. correlation of repository and metadata provided.

Repository / Metadata	none	little	some	plenty
Zenodo.org	0	0	6	1
OSF.io	0	1	3	0
JCAA supplementary	1	1	0	0
diverse	1	0	0	1
No PID giving repo	1	3	1	1

was licensed and how metadata was provided (*plenty* if a number of structured entries, *some* if some basic information was given, *little* is usually just author and publication date).

The articles for 2023 cannot yet be considered representative of the year and the peak in 2020 (see Figures 23.4 and 23.6) is most probably related to the pandemic induced reduction of publications in the years 2021 and 2022. The number and percentage of publications using persistent identifiers to link to code seems to be growing, except for 2021 (see Figure 23.4).

Zenodo has been used most often to create a persistent identifier, though OSF.io and the supplementary materials of JCAA have been employed as well. "Other" refers to a university repository, printed code and one not resolving DOI. It is noteworthy that no kind of persistent identifier other than DOI was used for code in this sample of JCAA articles.

In most cases where research software is published together with the paper, the code is organised in some way, e.g., in the form of a research compendium, package or program (package denoting any kind of extension on existing software, whereas program is a stand-alone, see Figure 23.5). Of those, most have a README as documentation, which are in some cases more elaborate than others. Manuals are available only for programs and packages. About half of the time (10 times) the code is organised in a compendium (denoting a folder structure with code, data, README or some other kind of documentation), seven times only scripts were published.

Licences were given in all but seven cases, most often MIT, GPL-3.0 or a CC-BY variant. Metadata, structured information on the published code to improve results of human and machine search, seems to be provided more in recent years (see Figure 23.6). The material published in the Zenodo repository is more often associated with providing at least some metadata than research software in other repositories (see Table 23.1). Zenodo is also quite often used in combination with Github (six times, OSF.io: two times, Github being

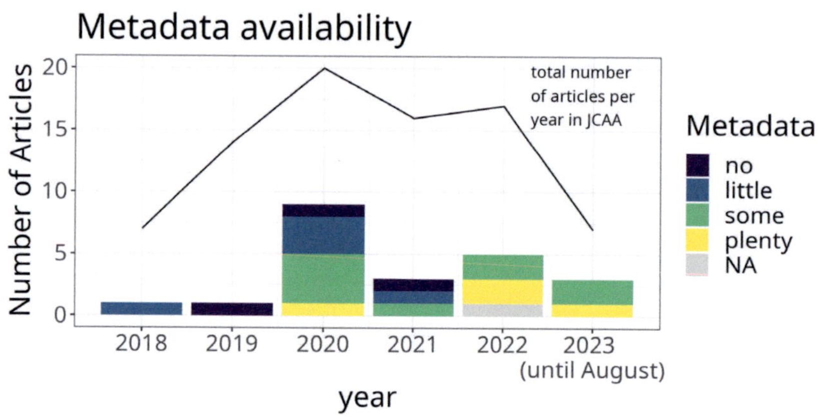

Figure 23.6. Amount of metadata provided per year (no: no additional information, little: usually author, date of publication, some: adds 2-3 more structured points of information, plenty: more than that, NA: DOI did not resolve).

used 15 times altogether). It offers an easy integration and publication of Github repositories (https://docs.github.com/en/repositories/archiving-a-github-repository/referencing-and-citing-content).

This small study of JCAA case studies and research articles shows that archaeologists are aware of methods for making research software FAIR. They utilise persistent identifiers for publishing code, though structured metadata is still rarely employed to its full potential. Documentation of code varies, especially not just the width and breadth of code comments, but rather providing additional information to make it easier for other researchers to gauge the usefulness of this software for their own project. Commendable is the use of research compendia, structuring analysis data and code. These are quite common, showing the aim of making research reproducible, which may also be linked to JCAA's reproducibility statement (https://journal.caa-international.org/reproducibility), encouraging authors to provide code and data.

Github is used for version control, collaboration and publication of code about two thirds of the time. It is good practice to archive a Github repository for accessibility and long-term stability of the code. A repository version can e. g. be released via Zenodo or OSF.io and Github used for eventual further development and version control. About half of the people using Github employed such a strategy.

The open-archaeo data shows that archaeological research software engineers use Github as much as any other professional software developers. Here however, the percentage of persistent identifiers used is much lower. Both might be due to the way the data was collected, as it was gathered manually from collaborative software development platforms (Batist and Roe 2021). There may be links missing to other resources, such as to studies, in which software was employed. No research software within the open-archaeo dataset links to a JCAA article, which also shows the limitations of this small study. Links to other online resources such as websites or bespoke repositories for software publication (CRAN, PyPI) are given more often than within the JCAA datasets.

The two datasets exemplify two different areas that come together in research software. The online list open-archaeo links to the platforms that host the software development process. This process is open-ended, as software routinely continues to be further developed, adapted and enhanced. PIDs are rare, but metadata is usually more amply added, as the findability of a software within the library is valued. In contrast, the Journal of the CAA focuses on research results. Here PIDs are more common, to ensure the exact version of the code (and data) used to generate these results can be accessed later: The reproducibility of the results is often the main reason for sharing the code. Within these publications, though, metadata provision seems less standardised, maybe because the paper itself is regarded as the main venue through which the code is supposed to be found.

23.5 Conclusions

In this article we elaborated on code sharing practices in archaeology. It was inspired by the development of an R package, which we describe in the beginning and of which we share lessons learned. The second part is an analysis of two datasets that show two different stages of scientific research software: development and use for creating research results. Here we will summarise the main points and further discuss the advantages of properly shared FAIR research software.

The process described above exemplifies how script sharing and co-creation "traditionally" works: personal contact between researchers leads to a collaboration, in which different versions are mailed back and forth. The script adaptation for own use requires communication between the script author and the person implementing. In our case this led to a discussion of flexibility of input and use cases, which inspired the creation of the package. The package creation was a time costly endeavour, especially the documentation. This reflected shortcomings in the original code writing process and illustrates the point that it should be done properly in the first place, however limited the original aims might have been.

To make a program, package or library useful to others, it is a good idea to consider standard inputs and possible applications outside of the original research question. For this, collaboration is a very valuable way of working towards publication, in terms of diversity of application, testing through unfamiliar datasets and sharing of work. With this contribution we wanted to show that it is not as hard as it might seem and that it is an important way of adding to the corpus of research tools.

As stressed throughout the paper, there are benefits to a thorough publication. The FAIR standards are on one hand a way to enable others to more easily gain from the effort put into the code creation in the first place and on the other hand give benefits to the developer as well. They create long-term stability and accessibility to the code and facilitate re-use and further development.

By making the research software citable the developer can be cited as its author. Citations are a currency of scientific research and can, in this case, showcase how research software development can be part of the skill set of modern researchers. For a sample of archaeological articles from the years 2010-2017 from the web of science, it could be shown that researchers that cite R Core are on average more often cited than those that do not (Schmidt and Marwick 2020, 24).

Just as other researchers may rely on an analysis published as a research paper, they are able to reuse code already published. Also, a researcher who continues his research on a topic does not need to re-publish his code with each paper when he can refer to his FAIR program version. The process of publication may also improve the code. Bespoke code repositories such as CRAN or PyPI have a code checking process and the publication together with a paper can lead to the code being peer reviewed as well. In general, developers may be more careful in their work when they know it will be published at some point. Reviews of published software can be a valuable source of checking for the quality of the program as well (Homburg et al. 2020).

It seems that in the CAA community there are people aware of these benefits who move towards a more formal publication of software than an upload to Github. We want to encourage others to follow their example and release the version of a software used for an article to a PID issuing repository, such as Zenodo or OSF.io.

To return to our package: Following the work to bring the package to publication, the code is now much easier to use and no contact with the authors is needed, which means time is saved by the person using the code. This supports the thesis by Schmidt and Marwick (2020), that code sharing may speed up scientific progress in archaeology. Also, the contribution is citable and there is no need to ask permission to reuse the program. This greatly improves usability, as can be seen by its application in different papers since 2020. We therefore strongly suggest, that though sharing of scripts is a valid approach that already speeds up the adoption and adaptation of new methods, once the code is developed further, it should be distributed in a structured and easy to implement format suited to the environment it is run in (e.g., R package, QGIS plugin or similar) and uploaded to the domain repository (such as CRAN, PyPI or QGIS plugin repository).

Acknowledgements
Thanks to Joe Roe and Zack Batist for sharing their analysis and data for open-archaeo.info on Github and agreeing to letting us analyse it further. Thanks also to the very constructive comments of the reviewers.

Funding
Sophie Schmidt's travel costs to Amsterdam for the CAA conference were financed by the Berlin Graduate School of Ancient Studies and CAA International.

Conflict of interest disclosure
The authors declare that they comply with the PCI rule of having no financial conflicts of interest in relation to the content of this article.

Data, Scripts, Code, and Supplementary Information Availability
Code and Data for the analysis of code sharing practices in archaeology are available on https://github.com/SCSchmidt/CAA2023_code_sharing and DOI:10.5281/zenodo.8307960.

The discussed R-package for percolation analysis, "percopackage", can be found under https://github.com/SCSchmidt/percopackage and DOI:10.17605/OSF.IO/7EXTC.

Peer review
This article has been reviewed and recommended by PCI Archaeology.

Allison, J. 2023. "Sharing Research Code in Archaeology." *Peer Community in Archaeology* 100333. DOI:10.24072/pci.archaeo.100333

Bibliography

Arcaute, Elsa, Stuart Brookes, Theo Brown, Mark Lake, and Andrew Reynolds. forthcoming. "Case studies in percolation analysis: the distribution of English settlement in the 11th and 19th centuries compared." *Journal of Archaeological Science*.

Arcaute, Elsa, Carlos Molinero, Erez Hatna, Roberto Murcio, Camilo Vargas-Ruiz, A. Paolo Masucci, and Michael Batty. 2016. "Cities and regions in Britain through hierarchical percolation." *Royal Society Open Science* 3 (4): 150691. DOI: DOI: 10.1098/rsos.150691.

Barker, Michelle, Neil P. Chue Hong, Daniel S. Katz, Anna-Lena Lamprecht, Carlos Martinez-Ortiz, Fotis Psomopoulos, Jennifer Harrow, Leyla Jael Castro, Morane Gruenpeter, Paula Andrea Martinez, and Tom Honeyman. 2022. "Introducing the FAIR Principles for research software." *Scientific Data* 9 (1): 622. DOI: 10.1038/s41597-022-01710-x.

Batist, Zacharias, and Joe Roe. 2021. "Open archaeology: a survey of collaborative software engineering in archaeological research." Presented at *Computer Applications & Quantitative Methods in Archaeology, Limassol (Virtual), 14–18 June 2021*. https://github.com/zackbatist/caa2021-openarchaeo.

Csárdi, Gábor, Jim Hester, Hadley Wickham, Winston Chang, Martin Morgan, and Dan Tenenbaum. 2023. "remotes: R Package Installation from Remote Repositories, Including 'GitHub'. R package version 2.4.2.1." CRAN. https://CRAN.R-project.org/package=remotes.

Díaz-Rodríguez, Mikel, and Ramón Fábregas-Valcarce. 2022. "Evaluating the effectiveness of three spatial cluster analysis methods on Palaeolithic site location distributions in Galicia, NW Iberian Peninsula." *Journal of Archaeological Science: Reports* 41: 103323. DOI: DOI: 10.1016/j.jasrep.2021.103323.

Garnier, Simon, Noam Ross, Bob Rudis, Antônio Pedro Camargo, Marco Sciaini, and Cédric Scherer. 2021. "Viridis – Colorblind-Friendly Color Maps for R. R package version 0.6.2." CRAN. https://cran.r-project.org/web/packages/viridis/index.html.

Goedicke, Michael, and Ulrike Lucke. 2020. "Nationale Forschungsdateninfrastruktur für und mit Computer Science (NFDIxCS)." https://www.dfg.de/download/pdf/foerderung/programme/nfdi/nfdi_konferenz_2020/nfdixcs_abstract.pdf.

Hettrick, Simon, Mario Antonioletti, Les Carr, Neil Chue Hong, Stephen Crouch, David De Roure, Iain Emsley, Carole Goble, Alexander Hay, Devasena Inupakutika, Mike Jackson, Aleksandra Nenadic, Tim Parkinson, Mark I. Parsons, Aleksandra Pawlik, Giacomo Peru, Arno Proeme, John Robinson, and Shoaib Sufi. 2014. "UK Research Software Survey 2014." Zenodo. DOI: 10.5281/zenodo.14809.

Homburg, Timo, Anne Klammt, Hubert Mara, Clemens Schmid, Sophie C. Schmidt, Florian Thiery, and Martina Trognitz. 2020. "Recommendations for the review of archaeological research software." *Archäologische Informationen 43*: 357–70. DOI: 10.11588/ai.2020.1.81423.

Hu, Xinyu, Yidian Wang, Hui Wang, and Yi Shi. 2022. "Hierarchical Structure of the Central Areas of Megacities Based on the Percolation Theory – The Example of Lujiazui, Shanghai." *Sustainability* 14 (16): 9981. https://doi.org /10.3390/su14169981.

Lamprecht, Anna-Lena, Leyla Garcia, Mateusz Kuzak, Carlos Martinez, Ricardo Arcila, Eva Martin Del Pico, Victoria Dominguez Del Angel, Stephanie van de Sandt, Jon Ison, Paula Andrea Martinez, Peter McQuilton, Alfonso Valencia, Jennifer Harrow, Fotis Psomopoulos, Josep Ll Gelpi, Neil Chue Hong, Carole Goble, and Salvador Capella-Gutierrez. 2020. "Towards FAIR principles for research software." *Data Science* 3: 37–59. DOI: 10.3233/DS-190026.

Lock, Gary, and Ian Ralston. 2017. "Atlas of Hillforts of Britain and Ireland." University of Oxford. https://hillforts.arch.ox.ac.uk/.

Maddison, Simon. 2016. "The Spatial Distribution of Iron Age Hillforts in the British Isles." MSc diss., University College London.

Maddison, Simon, and Sophie C. Schmidt. 2020. "Percolation Analysis – Archaeological Applications at Widely Different Spatial Scales." *Journal of Computer Applications in Archaeology* 3 (1): 269–87. DOI: DOI: 10.5334/jcaa.54.

Müller, Kirill 2020. "here: A Simpler Way to Find Your Files. R package version 1.0.1." CRAN. https://CRAN.R-project.org/package=here.

Pajdla, Petr 2023. "Spatial Patterns and Grave Goods Differences at the Cemetery of Vedrovice (Czech Republic): A Resampling Approach to Identity Markers in the Early Neolithic." *Journal of Computer Applications in Archaeology* 6 (1): 1–15. https://doi.org /10.5334/jcaa.85.

R Core Team. 2023. "R: A language and environment for statistical computing. R Foundation for Statistical Computing." https://www.R-project.org/.

Schmidt, Sophie C., and Ben Marwick. 2020. "Tool-Driven Revolutions in Archaeological Science." *Journal of Computer Applications in Archaeology* 3 (1): 18–32. DOI: 10.5334/jcaa.29.

Verhagen, Philip. 2023. "Centrality on the periphery: an analysis of rural settlement hierarchy in the Dutch part of the Roman limes." *Archaeological and Anthropological Sciences* 15: 45. DOI: 10.1007/s12520-023-01745-0.

Wickham, Hadley. 2016. *ggplot2: Elegant Graphics for Data Analysis.* Switzerland: Springer Nature. https://ggplot2.tidyverse.org.

Wickham, Hadley. 2022. "stringr: Simple, Consistent Wrappers for Common String Operations" https://stringr.tidyverse.org, https://github.com/tidyverse/stringr.

Wickham, Hadley. 2023. "forcats: Tools for Working with Categorical Variables (Factors)". https://forcats.tidyverse.org/, https://github.com/tidyverse/forcats.

Wickham, Hadley, and Jenny Bryan. 2023. "R Packages (2e). Learn how to create a package, the fundamental unit of shareable, reusable, and reproducible R code." https://r-pkgs.org.

Wickham, Hadley, Peter Danenberg, Gábor Csárdi, and Manuel Eugster. 2022. "roxygen2: In-Line Documentation for R. R package version 7.2.3." CRAN. https://CRAN.R-project.org/package=roxygen2.

Wickham, Hadley, Romain François, Lionel Henry, Kirill Müller, and Davis Vaughan. 2023. "dplyr: A Grammar of Data Manipulation.". https://dplyr.tidyverse.org, https://github.com/tidyverse/dplyr.

Wickham, Hadley, Davis Vaughan, and Maximilian Girlich. 2023. "tidyr: Tidy Messy Data. R package version 1.3.0." CRAN. https://CRAN.R-project.org/package=tidyr.

Wilkinson, Mark D., Michel Dumontier, IJsbrand Jan Aalbersberg, Gabrielle Appleton, Myles Axton, Arie Baak, Niklas Blomberg, et al. 2016. "The FAIR Guiding Principles for Scientific Data Management and Stewardship." *Scientific Data* 3 (1): 160018. DOI: 10.1038/sdata.2016.18.

24 Machine Learning for UAV and Ground-Captured Imagery

Toward Standard Practices

Kayeleigh Sharp
Northern Arizona University
Flagstaff
kayeleigh.sharp@nau.edu
ORCID 0000-0003-1084-6619

Brooklyn Christofis
San Diego State University

Hossein Eslamiat
Southern Illinois University
Carbondale

Upesh Nepal
Cooper Machine Company Inc.
Wadley
GA

Carlos Osores Mendives
Pontifical Catholic University
of Peru
Lima

Abstract

Our collaborative work began in 2019 with the intent to overcome obstacles that had arisen from the inability to access curated artifact collections from remote locations. It was our specific aim to not only create digital twins of excavated objects that could not be exported out of their country of origin, but also to emphasise the contextual associations of objects residing in hidden museum collections using a range of digital techniques. As part of the expanding field project, machine learning (ML) with YOLO was used to classify visual data to advance our understanding of in situ archaeological phenomena prior to destructive fieldwork. While not the sole contribution, the use of this object-based machine learning model improved quality and range of information obtained in non-destructive site surveys and improved data sharing capacity. Despite challenges encountered while training the algorithm and classifying objects, combining ML with UAV data collection continues as part of our long-term spatial data recording procedure. Despite both success and failures reported here, this work contributes to greater standardisation of ML techniques in archaeological practice.

Keywords: Machine Learning; Archaeology; UAV & Ground-based Imagery Classification; YOLOv5; Non-destructive Site Survey

24.1 Introduction

As part of our growing field project in 2022, we applied machine learning with YOLOv5 (SoftwaresAI 2020; Jocher 2020), a family of compound-scaled object detection models trained on the COCO dataset (see PyTorch 2023) to classify visual data and advance our understanding of in situ phenomena on the ground prior to conducting destructive archaeological fieldwork. Beyond what have become well-established digital field and laboratory methods in archaeology (e.g. high-resolution digital data capture, instant digital recording and transfer with tablets and other small devices) over the past few decades, the application of Machine Learning (ML) for Unmanned Aerial Vehicle (UAV) and ground-captured imagery has greatly improved our ability to select areas for intensified investigation or excavation in expedient, non-destructive ways. Expanding on what we had learned while analysing physical collections in previous field and laboratory analyses (see Sharp 2019), the

In *Advances in Digital Archaeology. Proceedings of the 2023 conference Computer Applications and Quantitative Methods in Archaeology – 50 years of synergy*, edited by J.W.H.P. Verhagen, J. Waagen, A. Brandsen, A. Queffelec, R.M. Visser and D. Taelman, 311–322. Leiden: Sidestone Press.

development of a neural network that was aimed directly at survey presented several unforeseen challenges.

Although initial difficulties while learning to train the algorithm and classify objects were time consuming and tedious, the ML strategy continues to be ever more tightly integrated into our standard data evaluation procedure. With intensifying efforts to integrate ML into various disciplines and industries, however, we still find ourselves in relatively uncharted territory with a growing list of archaeological models to follow (but see Alexakis et al. 2012; Bonhage et al. 2021; Caspari and Crespo 2019; Lambers et al. 2019; Orengo et al. 2021; Sakai et al. 2023; Verschoof-Van der Vaart 2022; Verschoof-Van der Vaart et al. 2019), and with an ever growing need to improve accuracy and precision.

Upon our return to the field in 2022 after a three-year hiatus, for example, we discovered that some areas of our study area had become dangerous and inaccessible, necessitating the incorporation of remote sensing technology in our initial surveys. The application of ML object/structure detection was expected to facilitate not only precision recording of all areas of interest but also to help determine various environmental risk factors like El Niño/La Niña climate fluctuations. Additionally, we were hopeful that our non-destructive site monitoring data would assist with heritage preservation issues that would arise in the future (e.g., Caster et al. 2022).

This paper discusses our successes and failures and future directions of our work in northern Peru, with the primary aim to contribute to the dialogue at this transformational moment in digital archaeology. Looking toward the future and aiming to foreshadow challenges that our project and others will continue to face, we urge for intensified efforts toward standardisation of practice and integration of streamlined methods in this fast-expanding branch of computational archaeology.

24.2 Implementing YOLO for UAV and Ground-based Image Classification and Analysis

In 2022, we applied UAV-remote sensing and ML in our short fieldwork season to increase the amount of terrain our small team could study over the ten-day period. In anticipation of training a dataset for automated object detection and classification, we used digital cameras and LiDAR enabled smartphones with GPS to augment the range of data that our survey teams encountered on the ground (and which were expected to be encountered in the future). As we have witnessed in other cases, we anticipated the quality and coverage of data collected to improve dramatically using these cost-effective techniques and highly portable tools. Additionally, we aimed to test the feasibility of applying UAV in our proposed long-term research; one of several non-destructive remote sensing survey techniques that we are hopeful will become standardised in our challenging topographical, environmental, and biodiverse terrain.

In this regard, the range of circumstances we confronted in regional surveys are both long-standing and recent. In northern coastal Peru, concerns that have become more prominent are the result of increased frequency of extreme climate events, as well as reduced site monitoring and protection capacity over the past several years. Given the challenging environment and sometimes perilous terrain, the ability of UAV to ensure the safety of field crews makes it an ideal choice.

Nepal and Eslamiat (2022) provided the context and justification for using UAVs as they are increasingly employed in numerous domains, including traffic monitoring, surveillance, inspection, surveys, etc. UAV use in contemporary fieldwork has transformed the way the world is viewed. ML algorithms increase both speed and accuracy of information capture. With the deployment of deep neural networks in recent years, UAVs have taken over aerial sensing research in the urban, environmental, and agricultural sectors (see Nepal and Eslamiat 2022).

ML algorithms use multiple layers to extract data features and recognise patterns. Their application has been used in a wide range of industries, from creating autonomous UAV trajectories (Li et al. 2019) to making significant strides in unified, real-time object detection (Redmon 2016). After training and verification, these methods provide real-time object detection which makes them appropriate for autonomous robotics and UAV applications in archaeology. The development of computer vision and machine learning methods has also been aided by the usage of Graphics Processing Units (GPUs) for ML algorithms (Nepal and Eslamiat 2022). This allowed us to incorporate object detection methods appropriate for real-time application in our archaeological fieldwork.

In this study, we tested the feasibility of integrating both UAVs (both DJI Mavic and DJI Phantom 4 Pro) and ground-based image capture (iPhone Pro MAX and various Android smartphones) in our archaeological fieldwork. When combined with increasingly established object detection capabilities of ML programming, we found these methods to be both economical and accessible, a clear advantage recognised in other academic and industry applications of the technique (see Nepal and Eslamiat 2022).

In the world of Artificial Intelligence (AI), ML plays a critical role in facilitating automated learning. Several ML algorithms have become more widely use over the past decade (e.g., Naïve Bayes, Decision Trees, Neural Networks, Fuzzy C-Means or Convolutional Neural Networks). YOLO (You Only Look Once) is a single stage object detection system that is extremely fast because it looks at entire images rather than pixels and uses a single convolutional network (Davies 2022). Several ML algorithms like recurrent neural networks (RNN, see Mittal 2020), or the R-CNN (Regions with CNN features)

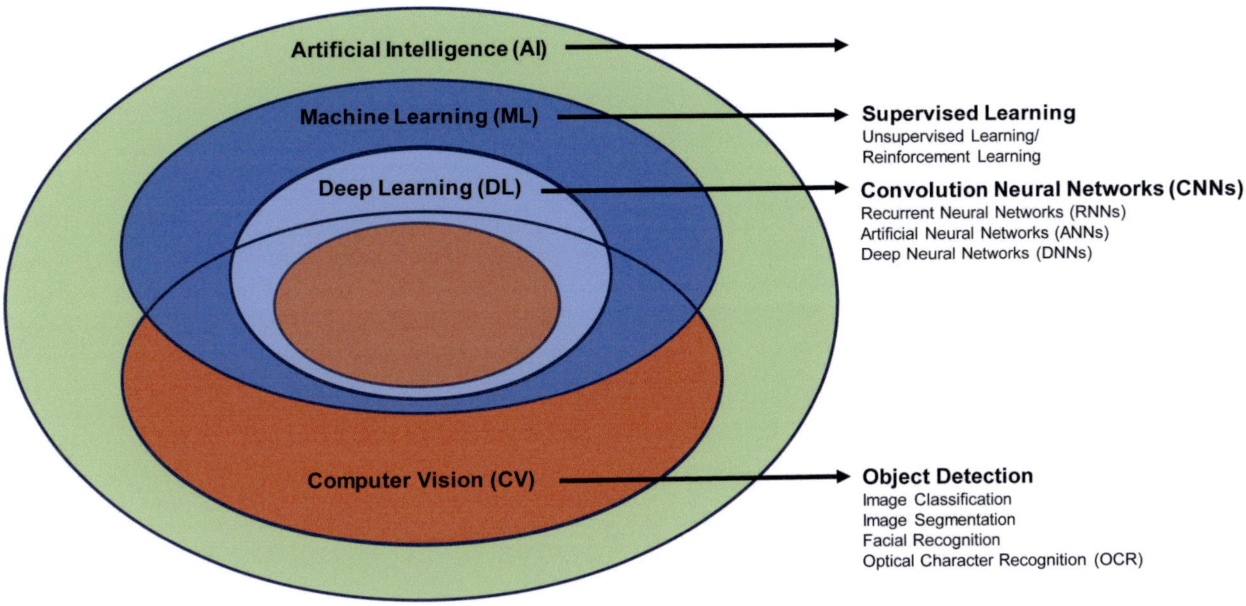

Figure 24.1. Diagram of the relationship between YOLO, ML and CV as subfields of AI.

model (see Girshick et al. 2014) use two-shot object detection which improves accuracy but is more computationally expensive (Kundu 2023) because of their structure (Baheti 2021). YOLO is an object detection algorithm that uses deep learning techniques to predict classes and bounding boxes or an entire image in a single run of the algorithm. A single-shot detection method, like YOLO, achieves the ideal balance between performance and speed/resources, whereas two-shot detection models perform better. YOLO enables the detection across a neural network in forward propagation (see Deepchecks 2024), making it appropriate for real-time application (Figure 24.1). Because of its accelerated rate of detection and our team's prior experience using it (Nepal and Eslamiat 2022), YOLO was the object detection system used in this study.

24.3 Data Set Successes and Challenges

The initial dataset selected for training the YOLOv5 algorithm consisted of aerial (100+ m above surface) and near surface terrestrial imagery (ca. 1 m) captured during 2022 fieldwork. While it was possible to distinguish various site components and concentrations of artifacts, construction materials and features including roads and walls in the UAV footage (Figure 24.2), we opted to use near surfaces imagery to explore the possibility of training the algorithm to identify smaller objects such as pottery in order to maximise the data collected during our short field season (Figure 24.3). For this reason, the images selected for training ranged from pictures of individual pottery fragments, pottery in a local workshop visited by the survey team in 2019, vessels fragments photographed in the lab during 2015 field season (Sharp 2019), and images downloaded from the internet that were representative of the range of vessel forms and decorative styles on pottery observed in the field.

Downloading and installing programs to begin training revealed many compatibility issues while offline training of the algorithm with installed programs was bulky and required several steps. Considering the limitation of offline training on a Windows PC, we trained YOLOv5 for pottery sherd detection using the online Google Colab tool which allows Python commands to be implemented and stored in the cloud and easily shared (Zeman 2023).

Once we began working in the cloud, we were able to use several computing tools like the AI engine makesense.ai, to label our datasets categorically through bounding-boxes which made the method feasible when using consumer-grade PCs. The archaeologists on our team found this technique to be easy to learn and apply successfully, requiring only basic programming skills. Conveniently, the collaboration between GitHub repository and Ultralytics (Jocher 2020) supplied a Google Colab forum prefixed with a YOLOv5 training notebook[1]. This provided the foundational base where our dataset (taken from 2022 fieldwork imagery) was input into Colab's YOLOv5 training applications, but the results were initially unsuccessful (Figures 24.4a and b).

After our YOLOv5 repository was established, a master folder containing training datasets (images) and their allocated labels was created – a compartment for each, titled "images" and "labels". Inside these two folders,

1 Helpful support from Weights and Biases' online YOLOv5 tutorial (Davies 2022), a step-by-step guide on how to download and kickstart YOLO's object detection features.

Figure 24.2. Aerial imagery initially proposed for training the algorithm.

Figure 24.3. Example of field images of pottery and other materials in physical setting that comprise original training data which include pottery fragments in association with stones and twigs.

two more spaces were created to separate "train" and "validation" images and/or labelling. We then selected subsets from our original image data to create validation datasets used to fine-tune and evaluate the performance of our model during training. For this purpose, we chose collections that replicated the natural "noise" of the landscape, where pottery sherds were scattered along rocks, found on dirt, and in association with sticks and leaves. With the master folder uniform, we began the process of bounded-box labelling for both the training and validation datasets. Makesense.ai allowed us to upload photos, set up personalised labels, and transfer our new labels into various components of our images.

During initial training, it was revealed that YOLOv5's pre-existing classes were confusing object detection, requiring re-classification. For example, in the initial training session, the YOLOv5 misidentified pottery specimens as modern objects like toilets, hammers or books (Figure 24.5). Ergo, we edited the code on this file to match the classes/labels that we had created initially. Ensuring that our project-specific constraints were now recognised, we changed the number of classes to 4, and the names (labels) to "stone", "sherd", "stick", and "leaf" which improved detection (Figures 24.6a and b) and produced meaningful results (Figure 24.7). With these adjustments in place, the data were re-imported back into Colab's YOLOv5, where we could finally test detection capabilities in our workspace[2]. After training at 150 epochs, we achieve a precision score of .28 and a recall score of .23, based on a surprisingly few 56 images used in the training of the initial model. Although statistically marginal, several important observations were made. Our results of this pilot experiment are discussed in the following section.

24.4 Preliminary Findings

Although we consider our pilot test successful, we await the ability to expand research to improve ML results. Our first attempts at training the algorithm offline with installed software were not as easy as expected. For example, predefined classification of object categories was transferable to our archaeological objects, which necessitated redefinition and a significant amount of trial and error. We also discovered that using the lab imagery from previous years, which had been processed at a lower resolution and was free of "background noise", did not work as well as (considerably more complex) field imagery.

In fact, while training the algorithm, Christofis discovered that the prepared diagnostic imagery and images of whole-vessel pottery specimens downloaded from the web worked exactly 0% of the time (see Figures 24.3a and b). Although such images are certainly useful for typological identification of pottery and other artifacts, they were unsuitable for training the algorithm alongside field-captured imagery. That YOLOv5 was never able to identify any pottery sherd images taken in a lab setting once we used images captured in the field suggests the technique must be restricted to one group of images or another[3]. We plan to retest the efficacy of using collections photos and other prepared diagnostics imagery if trained separately from the objects photographed in the field.

While we initially trained at 150 bounds, 60 was identified as the ideal constraint as we monitored YOLOv5's performance throughout iterations. As visualised in the chart shown in Figure 24.8, the model became relatively constant after 60 iterations at which point it began overfitting the data. After training at 150 epochs, we obtained a precision score of 0.28 and a recall score of 0.23 which supports the foundational proposition that YOLOv5 can correctly detect sherds against the complexities upon the natural landscape (as seen in our collation of stones, leaves, and sticks). Given that only 56 images were used for training the model used in this experiment, which normally requires that thousands of images be used (for example, see Nepal and Eslamiat 2022), we remain highly optimistic in this procedure. Although both outputs exhibit low precision and recall, we expect precision and accuracy to continue to improve when new data are added.

To analyse initial results, we used mAP 0.5 or mean Average Precision metric, which measures the performance of a model when used in object detection tasks and for information retrieval on images (Ahmed 2023). A common way to monitor a model's performance during a training session is by plotting mAP as a function of the number of iterations. The graph below provides information on the YOLOv5 model's performance during our training process. This gives us guidance on how well the model is fitting the training data. As illustrated below, during the initial stage of the training, mAP increases rapidly, and then slows down as the number of iterations increased. After 60 iterations, the model remained relatively constant, which means that the model began to overfit the data. Although we achieved a mAP value of only 0.19[4], interpretation of archaeological data remains quite complex.

The interpretation of a mAP value depends on the dataset and the specific task being evaluated, in addition, archaeological evidence can be exceptionally complex when small objects meet undergrowth and variable terrain quality. Thus, a score of 0.19 may be considered "good" or "bad" depending on the difficulty of the task assigned given different types of images and complexity of definable objects depicted in them (see an excellent overview in Verschoof-van der Vaart 2022, 123-8). In other words, archaeological object detection may be more difficult than other utilities, and therefore, what is considered a "good" mAP value for detecting scarce or small objects with irregular distributions

2 Following the exportation of our labels, our master training folder (now consisting of full datasets and labels) was ready to be uploaded for YOLOv5 training. Here, we transitioned to the next part of our research with the help of Google Colab._Google Colab's YOLOv5 workspace is conveniently set up as a functioning tutorial – much of the code needed to run, validate, detect, and train through YOLOv5 has already been provided. After cloning YOLO, we activated the first line of code. This allowed us access to all applications in an individual Colab session. After cloning finalised, we uploaded and unzipped our training data into Colab.

3 In all lab-based datasets, YOLOv5 could not detect the differences between stone and sherd. These occurrences continued through approximately 50 images and three training runs, where all sherds were incorrectly detected as stones in our output. These results continued to come back just as inconclusive, even with aid provided by comparative training of lab-based datasets against stock images of stones. This means that, given the current capabilities of YOLOv5, the algorithm cannot be utilised for legacy assemblages if training multiple datasets (like survey imagery) subsequently and/or simultaneously.

4 0.19 means that model's performance in detecting and localising objects in the images may not be ideal for non-archaeological applications, given that mAP score ranges from 0 to 1, where a score of 1 indicates perfect performance, and a score of 0 indicates that the model is not able to detect any objects correctly.

a)

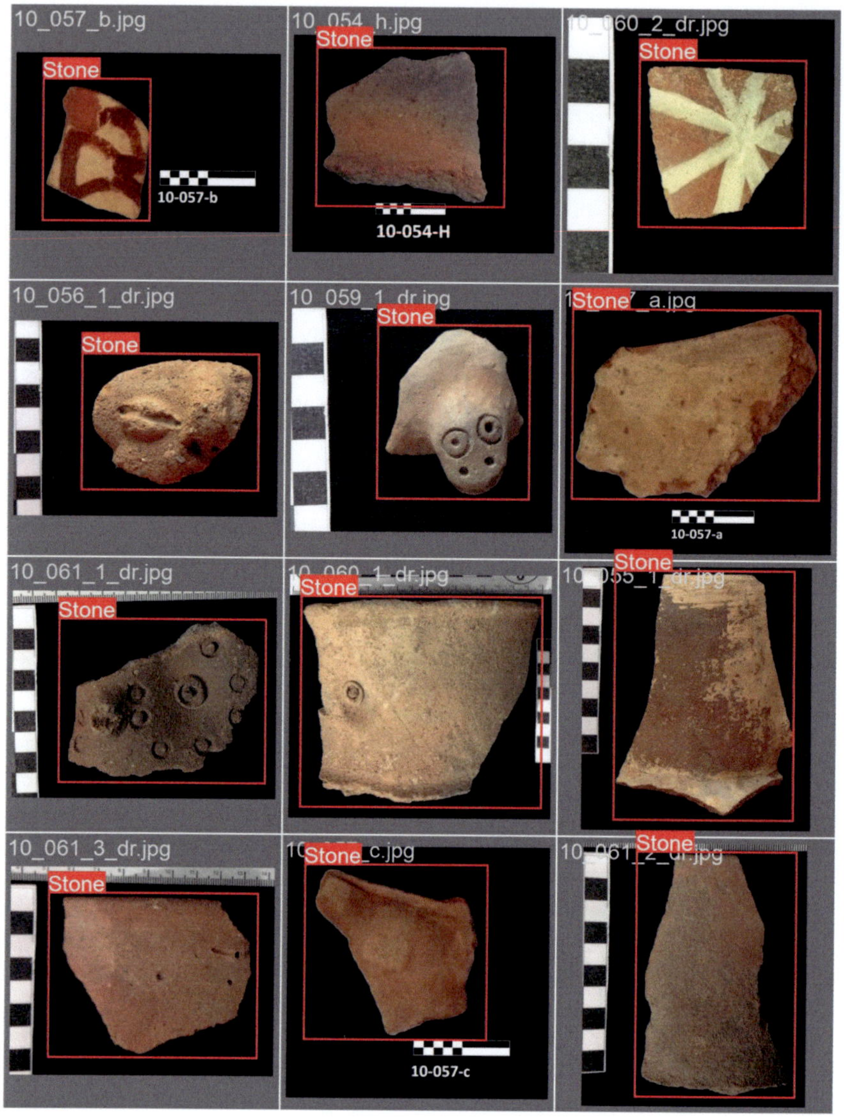

Figure 24.4. a. (left) Unsuccessful training using low-resolutions images (640 px x 592 px) processed in the lab and b. (below) results. Graphs depict results where x-axis is the number of iterations.

b)

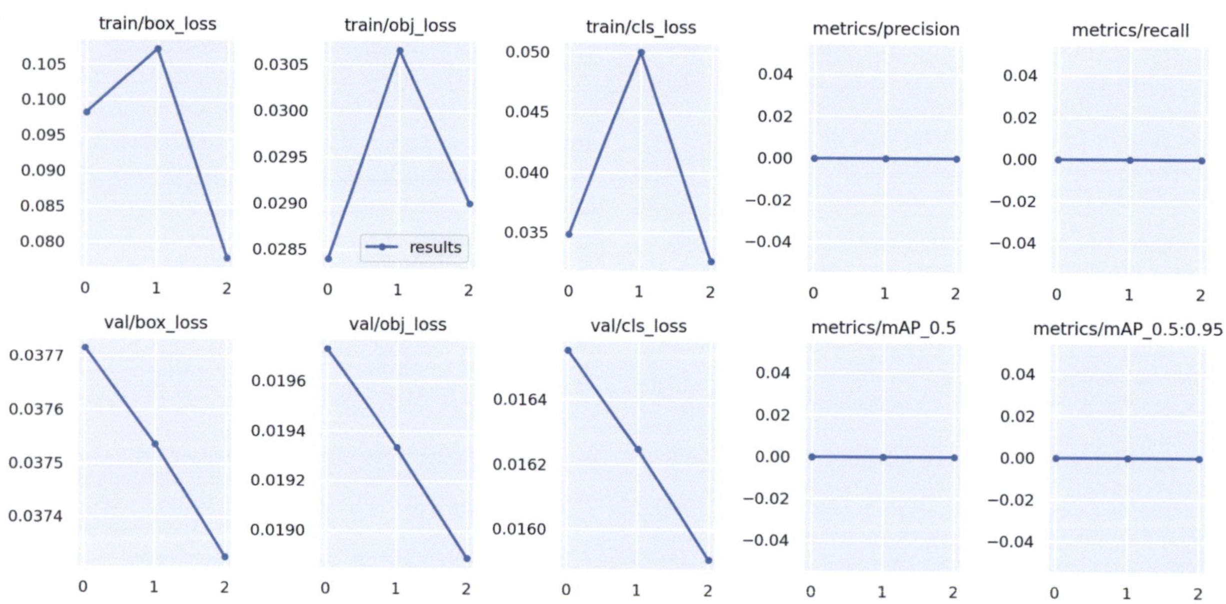

at archaeological sites may be lower than detection rates in other applications. Results we obtained suggest that the YOLOv5 model can be improved either through improved data quality, algorithm optimisation or by improving annotation process by using more images.

24.5 Discussion and Concluding Remarks

With the partly successful training of the algorithm, we hope to standardise the ML methodology and apply it in increasingly multi-scalar ways to our low altitude UAV, terrestrial LiDAR and geolocated pedestrian survey images in the future. How do the techniques applied in this pilot study fit into this picture? Certainly, several new platforms like Google Colab provided us with convenient tools when access to high-end computers was limited, purchasing new equipment was too costly, and software downloads and versioning presented critical problems. A critical question that emerged, was whether it would eventually be necessary to work independent of online tools like Google Colab when potential risks for data loss or product discontinuation[5], and when several options for off-line training exist but would require significant equipment upgrades. Such concerns, although significant, are relatively minor given the overall implications for advancement in this area of archaeological research.

The above challenges notwithstanding, the ability to conduct high-resolution analysis using semi-automated classification of objects on the ground without collecting them or using precision GPS units presents several important advantages over traditional techniques. The ability to study a complex material culture assemblage which lies in an area fraught with environmental and occasional social concerns like looting and invasive settlement, for example, has opened a new world of possibility. Application of newly accessible machine learning techniques when combined with near-surface data capture with the tools available has allowed us to enter a new era of non-destructive computational archaeology along with our peers.

For our work in northern Peru, this affordable approach is transformational. We have already produced high-resolution spatial data through UAV survey and on-the-ground image capture with LiDAR/GPS enabled smart phones that is more than sufficient to make determinations about future work. Through the application of machine learning techniques, we are now able to study material culture records off-site in ways that are highly informative, contextually situated, easily accessible (i.e., limited post-processing), and of course, non-destructive. Among others, the ability to weed out non-essential data and focus on the essential, visually navigate and detect objects and features non-destructively are proving to be key advantages (see also Mittal 2020). While fundamentally successful at detecting pottery sherds on the ground, the ability to transfer attribute data back into our GIS for spatial analysis has already transformed our approach to regional and local survey, object recording, and artifact collection.

5 Such has been the case with other Google products like Google Poly or the hosting of Arts & Culture sites.

Figure 24.5. Image depicting a shell and pottery fragment misidentified as a toilet and book.

For archaeologists working in areas where site access may be limited (i.e., culturally insensitive or physically dangerous), a critical advantage of incorporating combined remote-sensing and object-based machine learning techniques is never having to touch an artifact or damage a site, while at the same time being able to analyse sites and materials stylistically, quantitatively, and locationally. Through high-resolution in situ recording, using images captured on the ground or remotely using UAVs, the preservation of fragile and at-risk archaeological sites is significantly improved. Furthermore, through the advancement of non-destructive techniques, we gain a high-resolution view of the landscape and surrounding environment while actively working towards conservation.

In this experiment, YOLOv5 has exhibited potential for consistent detection of archaeological phenomena, although statistically marginal. In this case, it was successful at detecting and classifying the presence of pottery sherds when used with images captured on the ground rather than the UAV imagery. Presently, images captured using our UAV camera were too vague to produce the necessary detail for distinguishing pottery from rocks. During the next step of this project, we plan to re-capture drone data at lower altitudes (approximately 15-20 m) and use higher-resolution cameras to test our methodology.

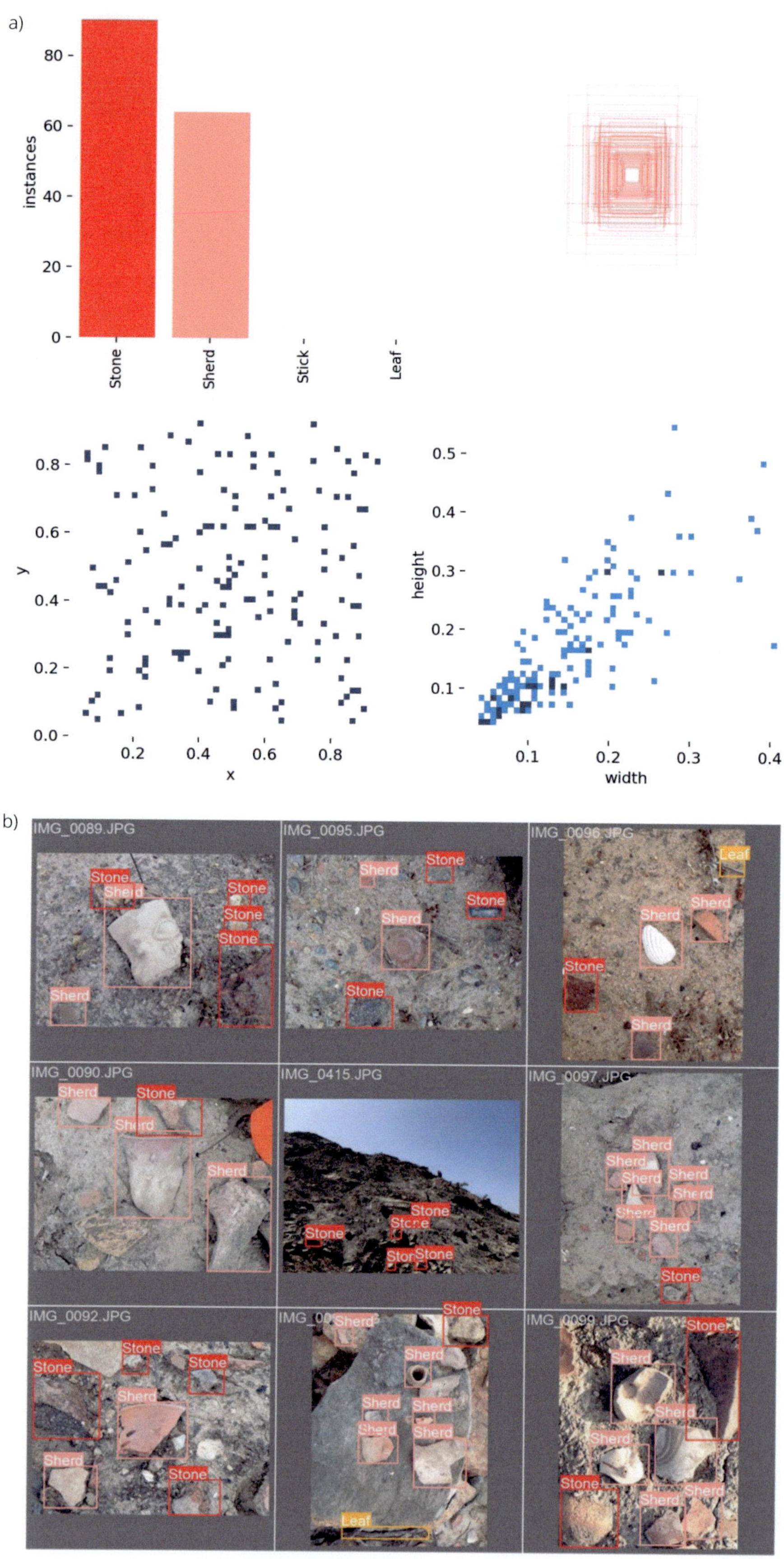

Figure 24.6. a. Improved object detection using smaller set of relevant classes, and b. successful identification of objects using a limited number of higher resolution images (4032 px x 3024 px).

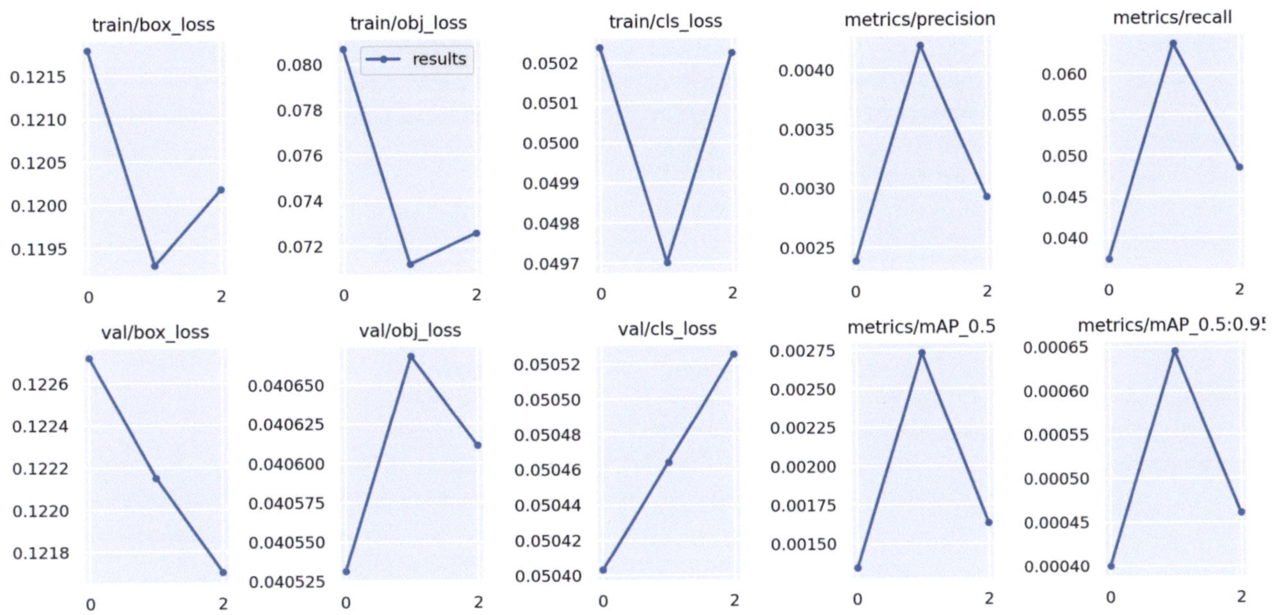

Figure 24.7: Object detection results after redefinition of classes. Graphs depict results where x-axis is the number of iterations.

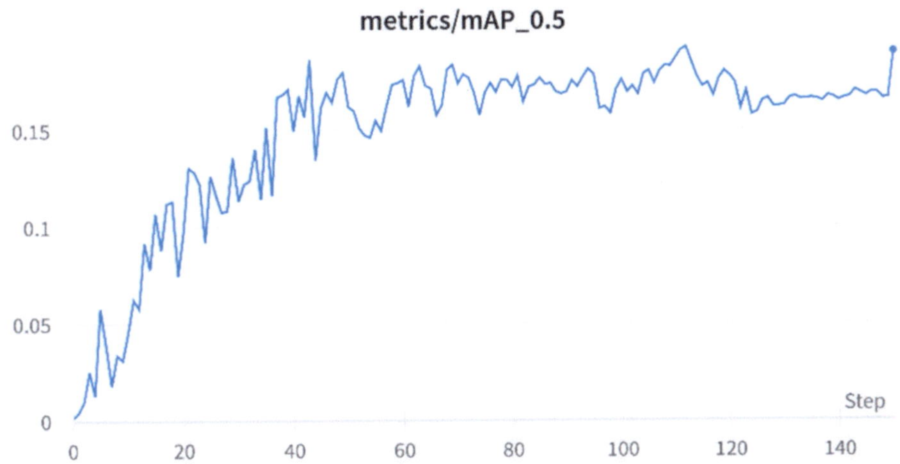

Figure 24.8: Graphical illustration of results after 150 iterations.

We also believe that, given more time to expand the dataset and retrain the model, we support integration of tools like YOLOv5 in the study of non-destructive archaeological survey data which can supplement and considerably improve the way that today's digital archaeological fieldwork and surveying is conducted. UAV-captured surveying and diagnostic evaluation with machine learning tools saves time, money and resources, while allocating more space to actively research, excavate, and connect with communities. The immense amount of data collected by drones and AI-commanded algorithms, as well as its "no-touch" approach also leaves opportunities for a better (and more ethical) digital recording of both archaeological and contemporary phenomena; thus, assisting in the current revolution to advance non-destructive methods in archaeology and emphasise preservation.

Yet with our new-found ability to detect, analyse, interpret and share, we find ourselves ever at the cross-roads of experimentation, trial, and error. Although creative and thought provoking, we aim for standardised methodologies to lend credibility, longevity, and repeatability to our approach. With this paper and our shared insights, it is our aim to contribute to the dialogue on combining such approaches, helping to further integrate this advancing technique into our trans-disciplinary community of computational archaeology practitioners.

Acknowledgements
The authors wish to thank the field crew from the 2022 field season of Proyecto de Investigación Arqueológica Gallinazo del Norte (or PIAGN) for their help in recording the data used in this research. We are grateful for the loan of the DJI Mavic 2 drone used to capture data in 2022 PIAGN survey by Aerospace Controls Research Lab (ACRL) of Dr. Hossein Eslamiat, Southern Illinois University, Carbondale.

Funding
A portion of this project was funded through NSF Award # 1519048 Doctoral Dissertation Research Award: "Social Interaction as Determined Through Spatial and Technological Analysis".

Conflict of interest disclosure
The authors declare that they comply with the PCI rule of having no financial conflicts of interest in relation to the content of the article.

Data, Script and Code, and Supplementary Information Availability
Link to repository which contains code and datasets: DOI: 10.5281/zenodo.11050465.

Peer review
This article has been reviewed and recommended by PCI Archaeology.

Brandsen, Alex. 2024. "Machine Learning for UAV and Ground-Captured Imagery: Toward Standard Practices." *Peer Community in Archaeology* 100405. DOI: 10.24072/pci.archaeo.100405

References
Ahmed, Nisha Arya. 2024. "Mean Average Precision (mAP): A Complete Guide." Kili Technology. https://kili-technology.com/data-labeling/machine-learning/mean-average-precision-map-a-complete-guide.

Alexakis, D., Athos Agapiou, D. Hadjimitsis, and Apostolos Sarris. 2012. "Remote Sensing Applications in Archaeological Research." In *Remote Sensing – Applications*, edited by Boris Escalante-Ramirez, 435–62. InTech. https:/doi.org/ 10.5772/37668.

Baheti, Pragati. 2021. "Convolutional Neural Networks: Architectures, Types & Examples." V7. https://www.v7labs.com/blog/convolutional-neural-networks-guide.

Bonhage, Alexander, Mahmoud Eltaher, Thomas Raab, Michael Breuß, Alexandra Raab, and Anna Schneider. 2021. "A Modified Mask Region-Based Convolutional Neural Network Approach for the Automated Detection of Archaeological Sites on High-Resolution Light Detection and Ranging-Derived Digital Elevation Models in the North German Lowland." *Archaeological Prospection* 28 (2): 177–86. DOI: 10.1002/arp.1806.

Caspari, Gino, and Pablo Crespo. 2019. "Convolutional Neural Networks for Archaeological Site Detection–Finding 'Princely' Tombs." *Journal of Archaeological Science* 110: 104998. DOI: 10.1016/j.jas.2019.104998.

Caster, Joshua, Joel B. Sankey, Helen Fairley, and Alan Kasprak. 2022. *Terrestrial Lidar Monitoring of the Effects of Glen Canyon Dam Operations on the Geomorphic Condition of Archaeological Sites in Grand Canyon National Park, 2010–2020.* Reston, VA: US Geological Survey. DOI: 10.3133/ofr20221097.

Davies, David. 2022. "Weights & Biases." W&B. https://wandb.ai/onlineinference/YOLO/reports/YOLOv5-Object-Detection-on-Windows-Step-By-Step-Tutorial---VmlldzoxMDQwNzk4.

Deepchecks. 2024. "What Is YOLO (Object Detection Algorithm)." https://deepchecks.com/glossary/yolo-object-detection-algorithm.

SoftwaresAI. 2020. "YOLOv5 Training with Custom Data." https://www.youtube.com/watch?v=GRtgLlwxpc4.

Girshick, Ross, Jeff Donahue, Trevor Darrell, and Jitendra Malik. 2014. "Rich Feature Hierarchies for Accurate Object Detection and Semantic Segmentation." In *2014 Proceedings of the IEEE conference on computer vision and pattern recognition, Columbus, OH, USA*, 580–7. IEEE. DOI: 10.1109/CVPR.2014.81.

Google. n.d. "Google Colab." Accessed March 26, 2024. https://research.google.com/colaboratory/faq.html.

Jocher, Glenn. 2020. "YOLOv5 by Ultralytics." Zenodo. DOI: 10.5281/zenodo.3908559.

Kundu, Rohit. 2023. "YOLO Algorithm for Object Detection Explained [+Examples]." V7. https://www.v7labs.com/blog/yolo-object-detection.

Lambers, Karsten, Wouter B. Verschoof-van der Vaart, and Quentin P. J. Bourgeois. 2019. "Integrating Remote Sensing, Machine Learning, and Citizen Science in Dutch Archaeological Prospection." *Remote Sensing* 11 (7): 794. DOI: 10.3390/rs11070794.

Li, Yilan, Hossein Eslamiat, Ningshan Wang, Ziyi Zhao, Amit K Sanyal, and Qinru Qiu. 2019. "Autonomous Waypoints Planning and Trajectory Generation for Multi-Rotor UAVs." In *DESTION '19: Proceedings of the Workshop on Design Automation for CPS and IoT*, 31–40. New York: ACM. DOI: 10.1145/3313151.3313163.

Mittal, Payal, Raman Singh, and Akashdeep Sharma. 2020. "Deep Learning-Based Object Detection in Low-Altitude UAV Datasets: A Survey." *Image and Vision Computing* 104: 104046. DOI: 10.1016/j.imavis.2020.104046.

Nepal, Upesh, and Hossein Eslamiat. 2022. "Comparing YOLOv3, YOLOv4 and YOLOv5 for Autonomous Landing Spot Detection in Faulty UAVs." *Sensors* 22 (2): 464. DOI: 10.3390/s22020464.

Orengo, Hector A., Arnau Garcia-Molsosa, Iban Berganzo-Besga, Juergen Landauer, Paloma Aliende, and Sergi Tres-Martínez. 2021. "New Developments in Drone-based Automated Surface Survey: Towards a Functional and Effective Survey System." *Archaeological Prospection* 28 (4): 519–26. https://doi-org.libproxy.nau.edu/10.1002/arp.1822.

PyTorch. 2023. "PyTorch." https://www.pytorch.org.

Redmon, Joseph, Santosh Divvala, Ross Girshick, and Ali Farhadi. 2016. "You Only Look Once: Unified, Real-Time Object Detection." In *2016 Proceedings of the IEEE conference on computer vision and pattern recognition, Las Vegas, NV, USA*, 779–88. IEEE. DOI: 10.1109/CVPR.2016.91.

Sakai, Masato, Yiru Lai, Jorge Olano Canales, Masao Hayashi, and Kohhei Nomura. 2023. "Accelerating the Discovery of New Nasca Geoglyphs Using Deep Learning." *Journal of Archaeological Science* 155: 105777. DOI: 10.1016/j.jas.2023.105777.

Sharp, Kayeleigh. 2019. "Rethinking the Gallinazo: A Northern Perspective from the Mid-Zaña Valley, Peru." PhD diss., Southern Illinois University at Carbondale.

Verschoof-van der Vaart, W. B. 2022. "Learning to Look at LiDAR: Combining CNN-Based Object Detection and GIS for Archaeological Prospection in Remotely-Sensed Data." PhD diss., Leiden University.

Verschoof-Van der Vaart, Wouter Baernd, and Karsten Lambers. 2019. "Learning to Look at LiDAR: The Use of R-CNN in the Automated Detection of Archaeological Objects in LiDAR Data from the Netherlands." *Journal of Computer Applications in Archaeology* 2 (1): 31–40. DOI: 10.5334/jcaa.32.

Zeman, Benjamin. 2023. "What Is Google Colab?" Android Police. https://www.androidpolice.com/google-colab-explainer.

25 3Duewelsteene

A website for the 3D visualisation of the megalithic passage grave Düwelsteene near Heiden in Westphalia, Germany

Louise Tharandt
Humboldt University of Berlin
louise.tharandt@hu-berlin.de
ORCID 0009-0009-5967-2809

Abstract

In 1932 the Düwelsteene, one of the southernmost megalithic tombs of the Funnel Beaker culture, were excavated and restored, which changed the appearance of the original tomb. In 2017 a digital twin of the current megalithic tomb was created through image-based modelling. Through a Citizen Science project, in which the citizens of the surrounding areas were asked to send in old photographs of the megalithic tomb, digital reconstructions of the tomb from 1932 and 3000 BCE could be created.

For a master's thesis in Digital and Computational Archaeology at the University of Cologne the author created a website to be able to show the 3D reconstructions and not have them only be shown as rendered images. The Düwelsteene or "Devil's Stones" are displayed as a digital 3D model of how the grave looks today, they are also depicted as a 3D reconstruction before their restoration in 1932 and as a reconstruction model of how the megalithic tomb could have looked like around 3000 BC. The website also gives information on the metadata, the workflow of building the models and the sources for the reconstructions.

Keywords: 3D Reconstruction; Funnel Beaker Culture; Megalithic Passage Grave; Citizen Science

25.1 Introduction

The Düwelsteene, one of the southernmost sites of a megalithic tomb of the Funnel Beaker culture in Westphalia, western Germany, have been a place of interest for archaeological research since the early modern period and are now the foundation for new digital research methods. This megalithic tomb holds special interest for a study project because of its reconstruction history. The Düwelsteene are a restored archaeological structure and the current positioning of the megaliths dates to 1932. At that time the megalithic tomb was restored and the stones that had been in situ were relocated to recreate the structure as it was believed to have been in antiquity.

As part of a master's thesis, this study compared the extensive impact that such an intrusive restoration had, in contrast to the contact-less method of virtual reconstructions. By integrating a citizen science project carried out by the Altertumskommission für Westfalen of the LWL (Landschaftsverband Westfalen-Lippe), using digital research methods and creating virtual reconstructions, the advantages and disadvantages of digital reconstructions and public outreach in archaeology were examined.

In *Advances in Digital Archaeology. Proceedings of the 2023 conference Computer Applications and Quantitative Methods in Archaeology – 50 years of synergy*, edited by J.W.H.P. Verhagen, J. Waagen, A. Brandsen, A. Queffelec, R.M. Visser and D. Taelman, 323–326. Leiden: Sidestone Press.

Figure 25.1. 3D rendered model of the Düwelsteene before 1932, on top of how the tomb looks today.

25.2 Methods

25.2.1 Image-based modelling

In 2017 a 3D model of the current tomb structure of the Düwelsteene was created by the Altertumskommission für Westfalen for their megalithic tombs in Westphalia project. The model was built by taking photos of the megalithic tomb from every possible direction and using Agisoft Metashape to create a 3D mesh from the images. The photographs, taken with a Nikon digital SLR camera, were also photogrammetrically rectified to correct any geometric distortion in the images. Since the 3D Düwelsteene mesh had been converted from over 378 million measuring points to a 3D model with 4,373,938 (triangle-)polygons, the number of polygons that form the 3D tomb used in this study has been decimated in the open-source 3D modelling software Blender with the "Decimate Modifier" for better and faster loading in the 3D viewer.

25.2.2 Citizen science

Through the citizen science project "Stein für Stein zurück in die Vergangenheit. Bürgerwissenschaft unterstützt die Rekonstruktion des Großsteingrabs Düwelsteene" of the LWL and the participation of the inhabitants of Heiden (Westphalia) and the surrounding area, the collected photographs of the tomb could be used for the reconstruction of the Düwelsteene. This virtual reconstruction also provided more informative sources for the creation of a digital reconstruction of the original Düwelsteene structure of around 3000 BC. The initiative started as a top-down citizen science project engaging the public to collect data. It resulted in a community driven, bottom-up project with the subsequent reconstructions being built with open-source programs and shared online.

25.2.3 3D reconstruction

The 3D model of the Düwelsteene, which had been created through image-based modelling, was used to "cut out" each individual stone, so that these megalithic stones could now be moved freely. The gaps on the stones, which were created by taking them out of the 3D model, were closed by the Poisson Surface Reconstruction algorithm in the software CloudCompare. The photographs were positioned in the 3D software Blender, so that the megalithic stones could be digitally "turned back". To distinguish between the original surface of the megalithic stones and the surface closed by the algorithm, a wireframe modifier was used in Blender, so that the difference between reconstruction and original can be seen clearly by looking at the different textures.

The reconstruction of the last model depicting the tomb at around 3000 BC was carried out from the current model of the tomb as well as the reconstruction of the megalithic tomb before 1932 by classifying the stones and researching other similar megalithic tombs in the surrounding area. The stones that still exist today were classified according to their position before 1932, their dimensions and their volume. They were divided into one of four categories: capstone, supporting stone, enclosing stone or wedge stone. Comparable megalithic tombs used for the reconstruction were found in Westphalia, Lower Saxony and the Netherlands. After repositioning the still existing 3D megaliths, the stones that no longer exist were modelled in Blender. These reconstructed stones were deliberately modelled and textured in such a way that they can be recognisably distinguished from the still existing megalithic stone models.

25.2.4 Online presentation

The website to display the virtual reconstructions and 3D model of the current structure was built with Bootstrap and is hosted on GitHub. The advantage of GitHub is the integrated version control and open access to the data and code used for the website. To display the virtual models, the 3D viewer 3DHOP (3D Heritage Online Presenter) was used. The basic 3DHOP viewer has several features already integrated, which are helpful for displaying cultural

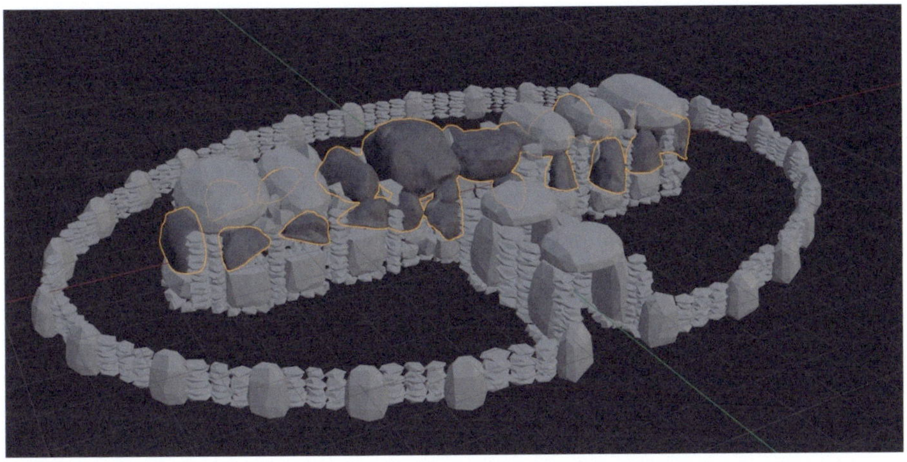

Figure 25.2. The reconstruction model of the Düwelsteene around 3000 BC.

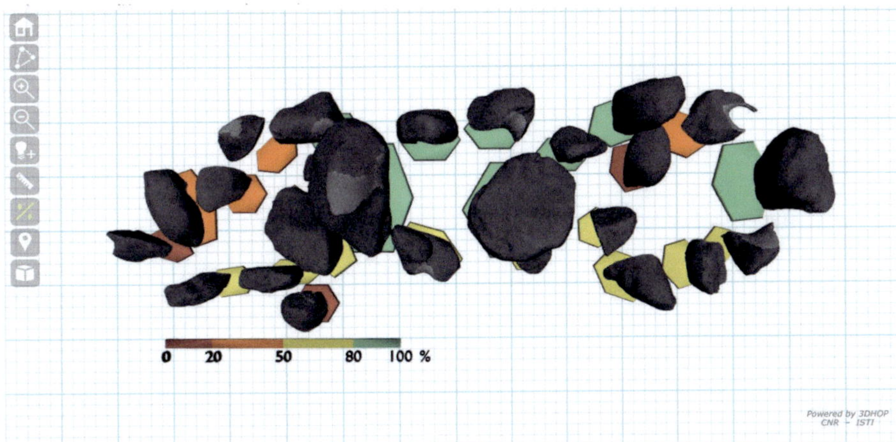

Figure 25.3. Certainty visualisation of the reconstructed positioning of the megaliths before the restoration in 1932.

heritage content. It is possible to change the lighting, zoom in and out of the model and measure the 3D models in the viewer. The 3D objects can be cut into sections to see inside and a basic code for annotations is provided. For this website even more features were built, like the visualisation of the certainty with which the reconstructed megaliths were positioned. On the website it is also possible to toggle the reconstructed hill on and off and view the metadata for each model.

25.3 Conclusion

The digital reconstruction work of the Düwelsteene would have been much harder without the photographs collected through the citizen science project. Needing to rely on data from outside of archaeology shows the impact of hands-on restoration work on tangible cultural heritage sites, especially when such work is not documented enough. This also emphasises the benefits of virtual reconstructions, where hypotheses can be tested and comparisons between structures are much easier implemented.

Using digital methods and three-dimensional models can help visualise the changes and lead to new findings. Especially with many archaeological sites presently being excavated and documented using digital methods in surveys, it is much easier to use the resulting data for further research. Even without prior excavation or documentation work, many cultural heritage sites can easily be turned into digital models due to new image-based modelling techniques, that do not require time consuming methods and expensive equipment.

For this project, digital archaeological research and virtual visualisations were combined to also benefit the general public. It was demonstrated that projects using 3D reconstruction modelling as a research environment can be published and help spread awareness and information on cultural heritage sites to the general public. Most programs and software that were used, were open source. The publication of the 3D models on the website can be tracked and downloaded, which means the workflow and features can be used and applied to other cultural heritage projects.

Data, Scripts, Code, and Supplementary Information Availability

The website: https://3duewelsteene.github.io.

English Version: https://3duewelsteene.github.io/index_en.html.

Data, scripts, code, and supplementary information can be found at the GitHub repository:
https://github.com/3Duewelsteene/3Duewelsteene.github.io.

Peer review

This article has been reviewed and recommended by PCI Archaeology.

Schmidt, S. and Allison, J. 2024. "Online presentation of the digital reconstruction process of a megalithic tomb: "3Duewelsteene"". *Peer Community in Archaeology* 100331. DOI:10.24072/pci.archaeo.100331.

References

Hageneuer, Sebastian. 2020. "The Challenges of Archaeological Reconstruction: Back Then, Now and Tomorrow" In *Communicating the Past in the Digital Age: Proceedings of the International Conference on Digital Methods in Teaching and Learning in Archaeology (12–13 October 2018)*, edited by Sebastian Hageneuer, 101–12. London: Ubiquity Press. DOI:10.5334/bch.h.

Klinke, Leo. 2018. "Virtuelle Rekonstruktion – Bürgerwissenschaft unterstützt Megalithforschung. In: Schierhold, K., Stapel, B., Die Düwelsteene bei Heiden, Kreis Borken." *Megalithgräber in Westfalen* 3: 14–7

Klinke, Leo. 2021. "Virtuelle Massen-Bewegung. Die digitale 3-D-Rekonstruktion des Megalithgrabes Große Sloopsteene bei Lotte-Wersen, Kreis Steinfurt." *Ausgrabungen und Funde in Westfalen-Lippe* 15: 257–326.

Potenziani, Marco, Callieri, Marco, Dellepiane, Matteo, Corsini, Massimiliano, Ponchio, Federico and Roberto Scopigno. 2015. "3DHOP: 3D Heritage Online Presenter." *Computers & Graphics* 52: 129–41. DOI:10.1016/j.cag.2015.07.001.

26 Mobility and the reuse of Roman Roads for the deposition of Viking Age silver hoards in North-West England

Wyatt Wilcox
School of Archaeology
University of Oxford
wyatt.wilcox@arch.ox.ac.uk
ORCID 0009-0008-5961-6981

Abstract
Discussions on Viking Age silver hoards in North-West England have been dominated by analysis of the material compositions of the hoards. Despite a multi-century research legacy concerning the material composition of the Viking Age silver hoards, the relationship of the hoards to their transport and depositional locations has been understudied. The relationship of the hoards to early medieval overland transport links is studied in this paper with an optimal pathway modelling process in a Geographic Information System (GIS). The modelling process incorporates multiple cost of vertical movement functions to simulate human agency when moving through the landscape, error inherent in the Digital Elevation Model creation process, and preferential movement on reused Romano-British roads. As a result of this analysis, it is suggested that the median travel time from early medieval period routeways to the hoard deposition points is 16 minutes. Over half of the hoards may have been placed under 25 minutes' walk from the routeways. This finding supports an interpretation that the hoards are concealed deposits intended for retrieval, rather than ritual deposits that were not intended for retrieval.

Keywords: Viking Age; Early Medieval; Least Cost Path; GIS Modelling; North-West England; Viking Silver

26.1 Introduction

There are eighteen Viking Age (*c.* AD 790-1000) silver hoards known in England's North-West (Figure 26.1), the historic counties of Cheshire, Lancashire, Cumberland, and Westmorland. These silver hoards are temporally concentrated in the tenth century, are of Viking Age Scandinavian economic character, and demonstrate material wealth accrued from a far-reaching Viking Age communication network (Kershaw 2014). The silver discovered in the North-West ranges in provenance from as near as the Scandinavian-controlled Northumbrian Kingdom in York and as far away as the Middle East (Graham-Campbell 2011; Kershaw 2014; Kershaw et al. 2021). The Scandinavian-character material

In *Advances in Digital Archaeology. Proceedings of the 2023 conference Computer Applications and Quantitative Methods in Archaeology – 50 years of synergy*, edited by J.W.H.P. Verhagen, J. Waagen, A. Brandsen, A. Queffelec, R.M. Visser and D. Taelman, 327–348. Leiden: Sidestone Press.

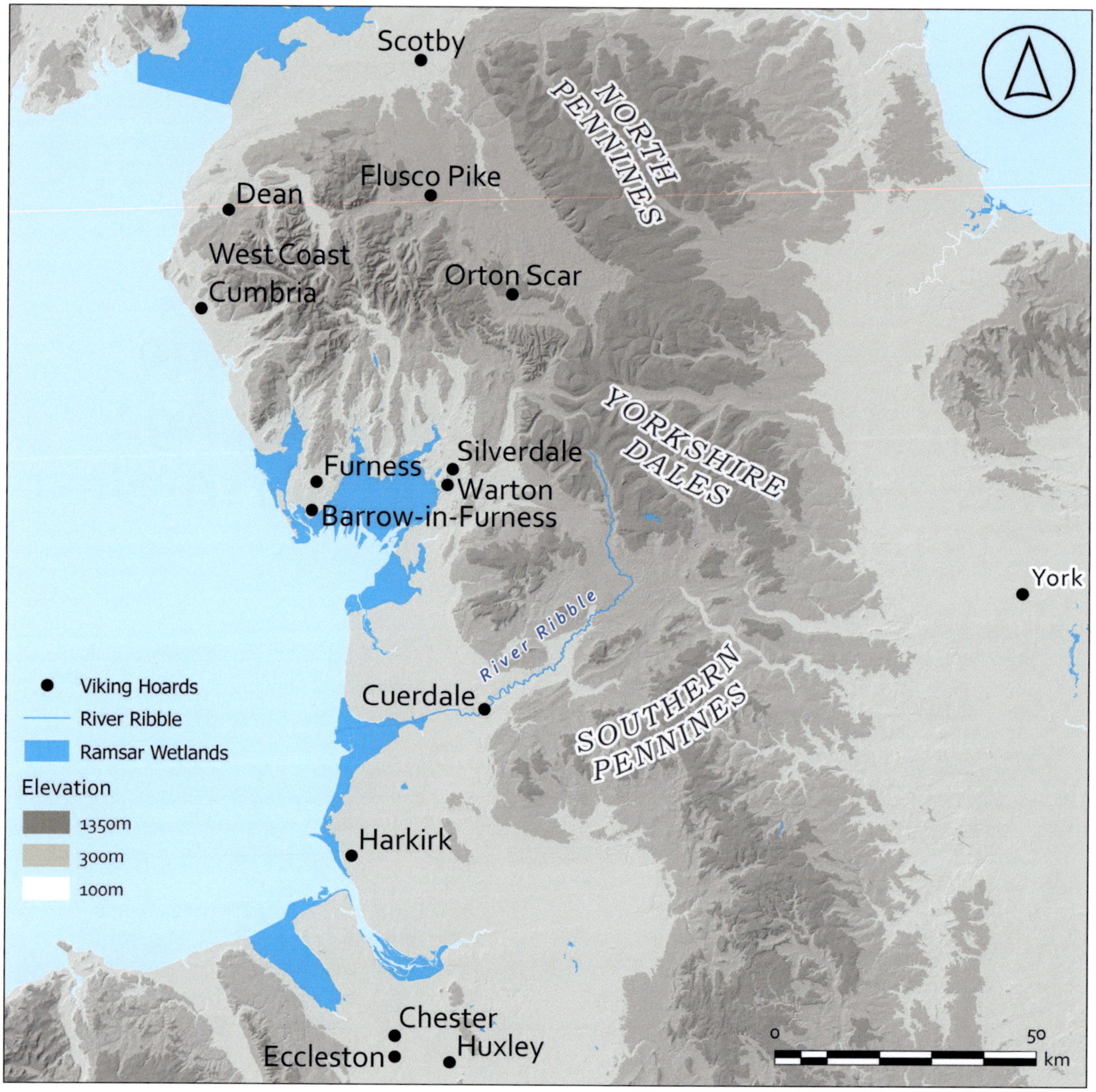

Figure 26.1. Viking Age silver hoards in North-West England. Multiple hoards are located in close proximity (under one kilometre) in Flusco Pike (2) and Chester (2). The "Lancashire Hoard", reported by antiquarian Beaupré Bell in 1734 (cf. Blunt and Stewart 1983), does not have precise coordinates due to the ambiguous reporting of its discovery in the eighteenth century, and is therefore not depicted on the map.

components of the hoards include silver bullion ("hack silver"), Anglo-Saxon and Anglo-Scandinavian coinage, ornaments of ninth century Irish Sea type, and ninth to tenth century Arabic coins, known as dirhams.

There was an apparent substantial exchange of silver across the Pennines in the Viking Age. Geographically, the North-West sits between the Pennines – the largest range of hills in England – and the Irish Sea. The North-West is historically considered the middle point between the "linked Viking kingdoms" of York and Dublin (Graham-Campbell 2011). Communication routes between the two would have traversed both the Pennines and the Irish Sea (Edmonds 2020; Horne 2021). York origin, or Anglo-Scandinavian, numismatic components are frequently found deposited in Scandinavian economic character hoards alongside metalwork of the Irish Sea, or Hiberno-Norse, region (Graham-Campbell 2011; Williams 2011; Edmonds 2020). The apparent exchange of metalwork across the Pennines coincided with the southern Scandinavian control of and alliance between the "linked" kingdoms in

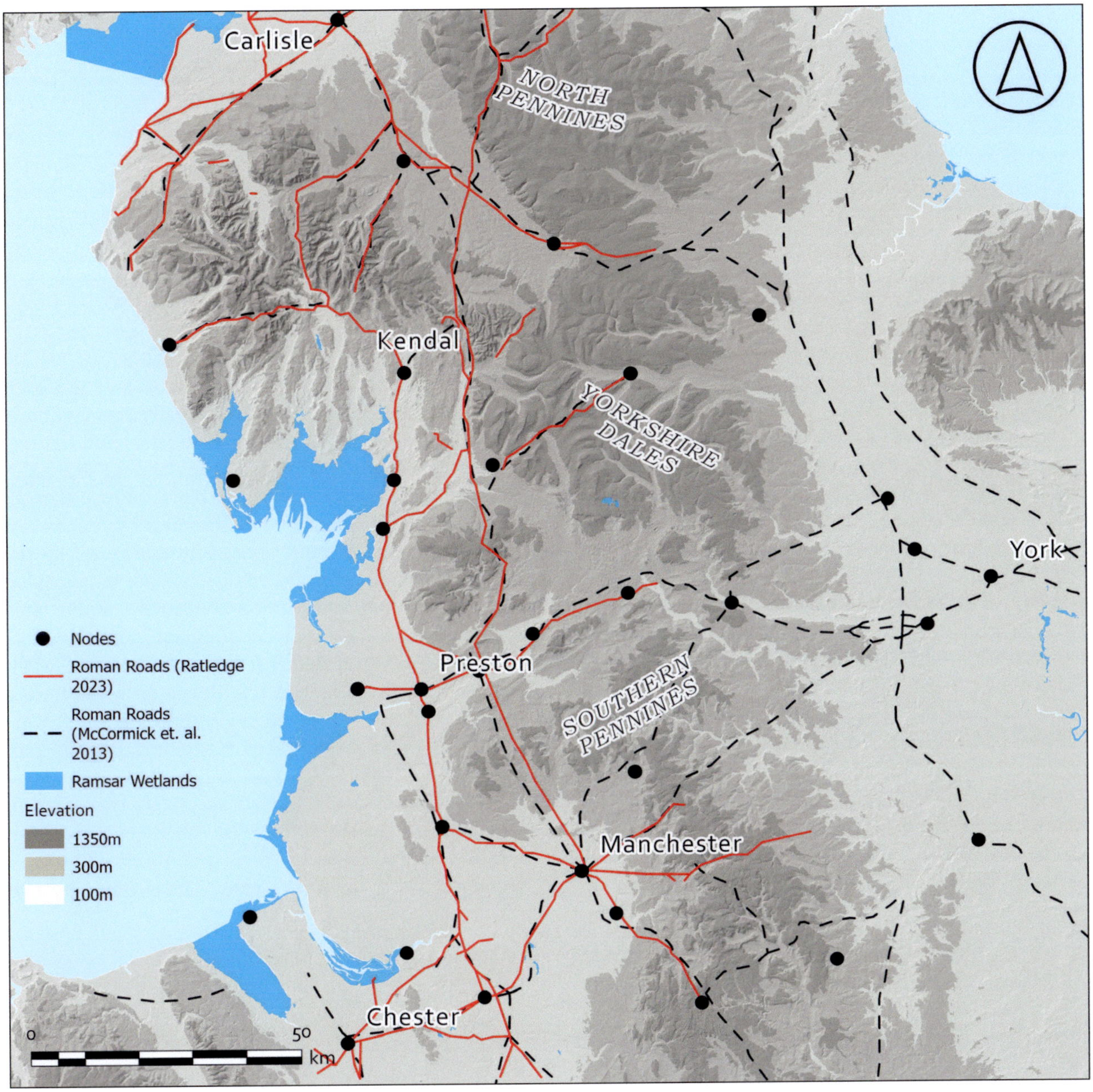

Figure 26.2. The Romano-British road network from the 1st-4th century AD, the framework of the reused medieval road network. Earlier knowledge of Roman Roads in black dash (McCormick et al. 2013) are displayed against Ratledge's (2023) newly discovered courses in solid red and Early Medieval period transport nodes (cf. Edmonds, 2020). With special thanks to David Ratledge for advice on road courses in this figure.

York and Dublin, broadly during the late ninth century to mid-tenth century, and the Scandinavian settlement in the North-West during the tenth and early eleventh centuries (cf. Higham 2004; Williams 2009).

Alongside strong implications of the flow of metalwork across the Pennines, recent investigations into the early medieval routeways and communications systems in the North-West have yielded a list of known tenth century transport nodes (Edmonds 2020) that are presumed to have been in use at a contemporary date to the deposition of the silver hoards. Specifically, communications systems formed from the framework of the remaining Romano-British road network (Figure 26.2) may have facilitated the exchange of silver across the Pennines between York and Dublin (Williams 2009; Graham-Campbell 2011; Kershaw 2014). The remnants of the Romano-British road network may have been maintained in the early medieval period for efficient overland transport across the Pennines (Edmonds 2020). Despite the knowledge that the cross-Pennine communications network existed in part on re-used Romano-British roads where available, the specific courses of early medieval period routes are not known. The uncertainty in routeway positioning is due to the fragmentary nature of current knowledge on Romano-British road courses and the possibility that previously-unmentioned transport nodes exist.

It is intended that this paper will help resolve questions as to the ritual or functional character of the hoards (Graham-Campbell 1992; 2011; Raffield 2014; Bradley 2017). Central to these debates is the relationship of the hoards to early medieval routes. If the hoards were non-ritual and intended for retrieval, they would be concealed from high-traffic areas of the landscape, but close enough to high-traffic areas to be easily recovered by those with knowledge of their location. There are two principal questions that are explored in this paper. The first of these is "how do the hoards with known locations relate to early medieval period routeways leading away from York?" The second of these questions is "can the hoards' relationships with cross-Pennine routeways be interpreted as a means for concealment away from the routeways?" To answer these questions, a bespoke Geographic Information Systems (GIS) modelling process was developed in ArcGIS Pro 3.0 (ESRI 2022) and Jupyter notebooks (Kluyver et al. 2016). This process uses a Least Cost Pathways (LCP) methodology that takes into account human agency realized with multiple cost of movement functions, random errors inherent in the Digital Elevation Model (DEM) creation process, the visualization of uncertainty in LCP modelling using rasterized line densities, and recently re-discovered fragments of Roman Road that have been observed in the last decade via Remote Sensing methods and archaeological excavation (Ratledge 2023).

26.2 Background

26.2.1 Northern England and the "Southern Scandinavian" Economy

In the mid-ninth century to eleventh century, Ireland and Central Britain were participants in a Southern Scandinavian economic sphere (Figure 26.3), part of which was driven by the exchange of silver (Horne 2021). Britain was forcibly brought into the southern Scandinavian economy in *c.* AD 866 by members of the *Uí Ímair* dynasty (Downham 2007; Nebiolini 2020; Horne 2021), who were also in control of Dublin. In the opinion of Horne (2021), Scandinavian agents were intent on establishing a "market polity" in Britain and Ireland that was able to link with the Scandinavian economic arena already in operation in Northern Europe and the Baltic during the ninth century. Various forms of silver numismatic economy existed in Anglo-Saxon England from the seventh century onward (Kershaw 2017), although the Scandinavian expansion into Britain and Ireland was likely motivated by the availability in Britain of other elements of the Scandinavian economy. Trading routes, natural resources, arable land, commodities, and slaves were all important elements of the Scandinavian economy (cf. Graham-Campbell 2011; Sindbæk 2013; Kershaw 2017; Horne 2021) that were present in Northern England in the ninth century.

Furthermore, and perhaps most importantly, Britain represented a barrier to movement between Scandinavian-controlled Dublin and the North Sea. North-West England has previously been pointed to as the midpoint between the linked kingdoms of York and Dublin (Graham-Campbell 2011). However, Horne (2021) expanded this

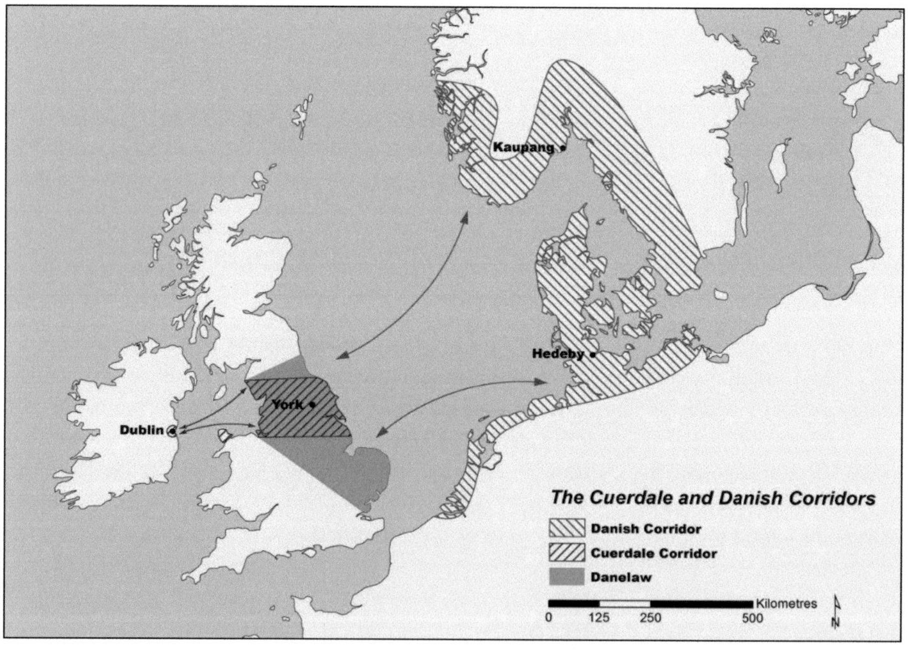

Figure 26.3. The Southern Scandinavian economic zone (Horne 2021, 13, Figure 1.2), including the "Cuerdale Corridor" across the Pennines. Image © Tom Horne 2021, reproduced with kind permission.

Figure 26.4. Vestiges of the Romano-British road at Kiln Trees Lane, near Cabus (Lancashire). The bank and agger have been worn down in centuries of usage (Ratledge 2023). Image © David Ratledge, reproduced with kind permission.

Figure 26.5. An extant bank and agger earthwork at Downham (Lancashire) associated with the Ribchester to York route. Image © David Ratledge, reproduced with kind permission.

Figure 26.6. The Silverdale Hoard. Image © The Portable Antiquities Scheme, reproduced under the CC BY-SA 4.0 license.

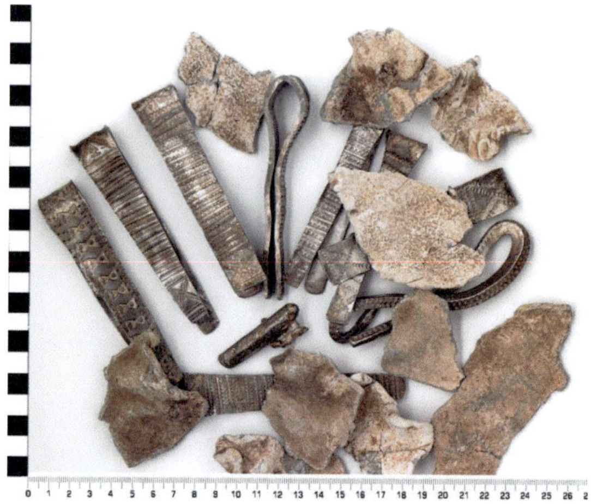

Figure 26.7. The Huxley Hoard. Image © National Museums Liverpool, reproduced under the CC BY-NC-SA 4.0 license.

thesis and stated that Northern England is the midpoint between Scandinavian-controlled Dublin and Southern Scandinavian markets around the North Sea and Baltic (see Figure 26.3). Northern England was effectively a land barrier in a maritime-based trade network and was therefore highly significant as a strategic crossing point. Horne (2021) built on Gooch's (2012) explanation that the North-West was the fastest crossing point of the Pennines, England's largest range of hills. This land crossing was the fastest link to the North Sea, compared with sailing around Scotland (Edmonds 2020; Horne 2021). Crossing was facilitated by the Romano-British road network in North-West England. These roads (Figures 26.4 and 26.5) were the "path of least resistance" between Ireland and Southern Scandinavia, a phenomenon dubbed by Horne (2021) as the "Cuerdale corridor". The capture of York in 866 therefore eliminated the barrier to the path of least geographical resistance for the distribution of economic assets between Scandinavian-controlled Ireland and markets of Southern Scandinavia and Northern Europe.

After Britain was brought into the Scandinavian economic zone, the trade of silver forms compatible with the Scandinavian economy was introduced. A silver Anglo-Scandinavian coinage was established in the mid-late ninth century (Blackburn 2004). However, vast quantities of bullion silver were imported to Southern Scandinavia from the Arabic world in the ninth and tenth centuries in the form of *dirham* coins (Graham-Campbell 2011; Kershaw 2014; 2017; Horne 2021). Additionally, many silver ornaments from Ireland were common imports into Britain and Scandinavia and were valued according to their display value or as bullion (Graham-Campbell 2011). Despite having silver Anglo-Scandinavian coinage, ornament and bullion silver was important in England in the ninth and tenth centuries as it was a mutable form of silver that could be universally traded within the Scandinavian economy based on weight. It has been shown through an analysis of single finds of silver bullion and cubo-octohedral weights used to weigh silver bullion that bullion was actively used in the Danelaw alongside numismatic silver and was traded according to set weight units (Kershaw 2017). The use of bullion alongside official coinage can be interpreted as a method of both exchange with diverse forms of economy and a retainer of southern Scandinavian identity (Kershaw 2017). These silver economic uses all play a part in the observed composition of Viking Age silver hoards found in North-West England, which will be discussed below.

26.2.2 Hoard Composition

The composition of Scandinavian-character silver hoards in North-West England (Table 26.1) illustrates different methods of exchange in the Southern Scandinavian economy and fall into three categories. These are:

1. Ornamental hoards that contain complete silver ornaments traded by display value,
2. Bullion/hack-silver hoards that contain silver (including coins) traded by weight value,
3. Mixed bullion hoards that contain both ornaments and hacksilver.

The 42.6 kg mixed-category Cuerdale Hoard (Lancashire) dates from approximately AD 905-910 and contained a broad range of silver pieces in a lead container, with many silver ornaments, bullion pieces, and a strong coin component of around 7500 coins. Many of the coins deposited in the Cuerdale Hoard were freshly minted in York preceding its deposition (Archibald 1992; Graham-Campbell 2011; Williams 2020). Debates on the assembly

	Name	County	Category	Deposition Date Range (AD)	Container
1	Cuerdale	Lancashire	Mixed	905-910	Lead
2	Huxley	Cheshire	Bullion	900-910	Lead
3	Silverdale	Lancashire	Mixed	900-910	Lead
4	Harkirk	Lancashire	Mixed	910-915	
5	Dean	Cumbria	Coin	915-925	Lead
6	Lancashire	Lancashire	Coin	910-920	
7	Chester (St. John)	Cheshire	Coin	915-920	
8	Warton/Carnforth	Lancashire	Mixed	920-929	
9	Flusco Pike (2)	Cumbria	Mixed	920-929	
10	Scotby	Cumbria	Mixed	935-940	
11	Flusco Pike (1)	Cumbria	Ornament	920-939	
12	Orton Scar	Cumbria	Ornament		
13	Eccleston	Cheshire	Bullion		
14	Barrow-in-Furness	Cumbria	Mixed	900-930	
15	Chester (Castle Esplanade)	Cheshire	Mixed	965-970	Pot
16	Halton Moor	Lancashire	Mixed	1025-1030	Silver Cup
17	West Coast Cumbria	Cumbria	Mixed	850-950	
18	Furness	Cumbria	Mixed	955-957	

Table 26.1. Viking Age silver hoards with their material composition and container types.

point of the Cuerdale Hoard have been prevalent in its historiography. It has been suggested that the hoard was assembled in Ireland (Graham-Campbell 1992; 2011), and other authors have suggested that the hoard could have been assembled in York (Williams 2011; Horne 2021). Given the freshly minted York coin and the availability of the Irish-origin components across central Britain in other Viking hoards, it is likely that the hoard was assembled in York or nearer its deposition point in Lancashire. The mixed-category Silverdale Hoard (Lancashire) (Figure 26.6) dates from around AD 910 and is largely of similar composition to the Cuerdale Hoard, although its weight is substantially smaller than Cuerdale at roughly 1 kg. The Silverdale Hoard features several particularly remarkable broad-band and pennannular arm rings, comparable to those found at Cuerdale and the Hare Island Hoard in Ireland (Boughton 2011). The Silverdale Hoard also featured numerous ingots and bullion, around 20 coins, and fragments of a lead container (ibid.). One of the coins from Silverdale is a likely Northumbrian issue and references a previously unknown Norse-Northumbrian ruler *"Iredeconvt"* or *"Harthacnut"* (ibid.). The bullion-category Huxley Hoard (Cheshire) (Figure 27.7) contained numerous bullion pieces including flattened bracelets, a piece of hacked bracelet, an ingot, and fragments of a lead box (Oakden 2014). The other hoards in North-West England did not include archaeological evidence for containers but could have feasibly included organic containers due to soil preservation conditions (cf. Gruszczynski 2019).

26.2.3 Concealed versus Ritual Deposits

Bradley (2017) alluded to two strands of thought concerning hoarded or votive deposits: one relating to the study of the artefact assemblage and another relating to the landscape environment of the deposit. Bradley claimed that hoarded artefacts had been "studied to exhaustion", whereas the study of the landscape context of hoards would yield more fruitful results, particularly at multiple spatio-temporal scales. Speaking purely of artefactual composition, assemblages are often considered ritual or votive in character if there is a physical quality of the assemblage that demonstrates it is not intended for retrieval. This may be because the deposit contains artefacts that are deliberately broken or non-functional in their normal purpose (Raffield 2014; Bradley 2017). Another indicator of votive deposition is that an assemblage is not enclosed in a container, implying that the depositor is not concerned with keeping its contents assembled for a later date (Gruszczynski 2017). On the other hand, whole or functional artefacts may be considered non-ritual and intended for retrieval (Bradley 2017) or artefacts that are deposited in containers can indicate intent for retrieval (Gruszczynski 2017). It is acknowledged that containers are often made of organic components and are prone to decomposition in certain soil conditions, rendering them archaeologically invisible (ibid.). However, the lack of a container can be inferred where artefacts of different temporal scales and type have been continually deposited at a site, such as the continual prehistoric to Scandinavian

Iron Age assemblages from Vimose, Denmark (Jensen 2007) or the Viking Age metalwork found near London Bridge (Wilson 1965).

A more granular understanding of hoarding and its relationship to votive deposition can be gained from the study of the landscape in which assemblages are deposited than from the study of artefacts alone. Context is often key to interpreting the way in which sites and assemblages relate to one another, by adding a spatio-temporal dimension to their interpretation. Bradley (2017) illustrates that watercourses and bogs have been shown to be consistent attractors for votive deposition over the *longue durée*, particularly in Scandinavia from the Bronze Age to the post-Roman Iron Age. Raffield (2014) illustrated that in Viking Age England, votive deposition of weaponry was often concentrated at bogs or watercourses, particularly in wetlands around the Thames and the vast wetlands of the Fens. An important finding of Raffield's study is that Viking Age weaponry deposited in irretrievable environments in England, such as the Fens, could be both broken or whole. In fact, whole pre-depositional alteration of weapons was only securely observed in four of 70 examples presented in Raffield's 2014 paper. This has significant implications for the understanding of Viking Age votive deposition in England – votive deposits need not be broken or non-functional to be considered votive, they simply need to be placed in an irretrievable location. Building on this thesis, Raffield (2014) postulated that the landscapes of Viking Age silver hoards in England were potentially deposited in votive locations. The Harkirk, Silverdale, and Carnforth hoards were deposited near windblown sand beaches that had potentially cosmological implications in the minds of their depositors, and the Cuerdale Hoard was deposited near a fording point on the banks of the River Ribble. However, Raffield does imply that the understanding of the landscape of votive deposition in England is hindered by the lack of understanding of Early Medieval routeways (2014) and hints that routes may also play a part in the landscape setting of hoards. Furthermore, the extent of wetland areas in Early Medieval period England is unknown and highly conjectural at the local scale (cf. Bradley 2017, 23; Stein 2014), except where large-scale post-medieval dyking has drained large historically attested former wetland basins, such as in the Fens, Holderness, or Morecambe Bay lowlands. Finally, the need for the assessment of the artefacts in conjunction with landscape is illustrated with Raffield's (2014) study, particularly where silver hoards in North-West England are concerned. The silver hoards were of considerable current economic value when they were deposited: although some objects, such as coins, brooches, and ingots were hacked with a type of chisel before deposition, this is due to the objects being actively used as bullion. The range of cultural connections, political prowess, commodity exchange, and physical force that helped assemble silver hoards in North-West England must have been considerable and contributed to their current value at the point of deposition.

Origin	Destination
York	Knaresborough, Tadcaster
Knaresborough	Broughbridge, Tadcaster
Broughbridge	Richmond, Ilkley
Tadcaster	Manchester, Doncaster,Ilkley
Ilkley	Manchester, Bainbridge, Ingleton, Elslack
Ribchester	Preston
Clitheroe	Elslack, Ribchester
Walton-le-Dale	Preston, Wigan
Manchester	Wigan, Stockport, Northwich, Carlisle
Chester	Northwich, Runcorn, Meols, Repton, Dore
Lancaster	Ribchester, Preston, Carnforth, Ingleton
Kendal	Carnforth, Ingleton, Bainbridge, Ravenglass, Barrow
Doncaster	Dore
Bainbridge	Richmond, Ingleton
Carnforth	Barrow
Brough	Richmond, Penrith
Ravenglass	Carlisle
Preston	Kirkham, Ribchester

Table 26.2. Major route pairings relevant to Early Medieval North-West England (for GIS data, reference this article's supplemental material at DOI:10.5281/zenodo.11067607).

26.3 Materials and Methodology

Two principal methodological steps are key to address the research questions that drive this paper. The first of these is the creation of a suite of probabilistic LCPs displayed as line densities to describe movement between early medieval period transport nodes derived from Edmonds (2020; Table 26.2). The second of these is the depiction of optimal paths line densities leading from the points of highest-density travel near the hoard locations to the hoard's depositional points. The GIS modelling process was implemented using ArcGIS Pro 3.0 geoprocessing tools within a Jupyter notebook (supplied in this article's supplemental material page at DOI:10.5281/zenodo.11067607).

26.3.1 Creation of Optimal Paths

A methodology was devised to create a network suite of probability-based optimal paths that depict varying densities of foot travel, with barriers to foot travel at major wetlands. The base logic of the model is the use of a Monte Carlo simulation to account for error in the creation of the Digital Elevation Model (DEM) (cf. Lewis 2021), multiple costs of movement functions to simulate human agency as slope is encountered, and the use of magnitude-per-unit area calculations to describe line density (Figure 26.8). The model was weighted to preference sections of digitized Romano-British roads derived from recent work by Bishop (2014) and Ratledge (2023), such as the re-discovered fragments of the Lancaster-Kendal route (Ratledge 2023). Five model simulations were completed to accommodate the available computing resources required to simulate random errors inherent in DEM creation. Vehicle transport was not chosen as a model parameter, as Edmonds (2020) considered foot and horse travel as the most likely trans-Pennine crossing methods. Foot travel here is estimated as a proxy for horse-bound travel between known segments of Romano-British roads. Foot travel in this model is again preferred to travel on navigable waterways, as navigable waterways did not traverse the Pennines and were considerably slower than terrestrial travel (Edmonds 2020).

26.3.1.1 Costs of horizontal and vertical movement

For foot travel on a Romano-British road course, a factor of 1.0 was applied to reflect the suggested cost factor for blacktop roads (Herzog 2014). For travel off Romano-British road courses, a factor of 1.1 was applied, the suggested factor for grass (ibid.). These factors were rasterized across the study area for application as the cost of horizontal movement in the model. Additional cost factors, such as those for heavy brush, ploughed fields, and loose sand may be appropriate in future study, but at this stage, fine-grained understanding of past land use in the study area is not known. Wetlands also play a part in defining possible areas of movement. While major wetlands would not have ultimately been a barrier for movement for maritime societies of the Viking Age, major land routes would likely have diverted around marsh bogs for ease of travel purposes. For example, the Ramsar-designated wetland near the Silverdale and Arnside Area of Outstanding Beauty (AONB) was drained in the early modern period and would likely have been a barrier to foot travel in the early medieval period. Romano-British and early medieval routeways known in this area divert around this wetland, rather than attempting a crossing by boat. To approximate past wetlands in the absence of geoarchaeologically delineated wetland evidence across the study area, Ramsar Wetlands of International Importance in England were used in the model as barriers to horizontal movement. Recent wetland prediction models, such as the Wetland

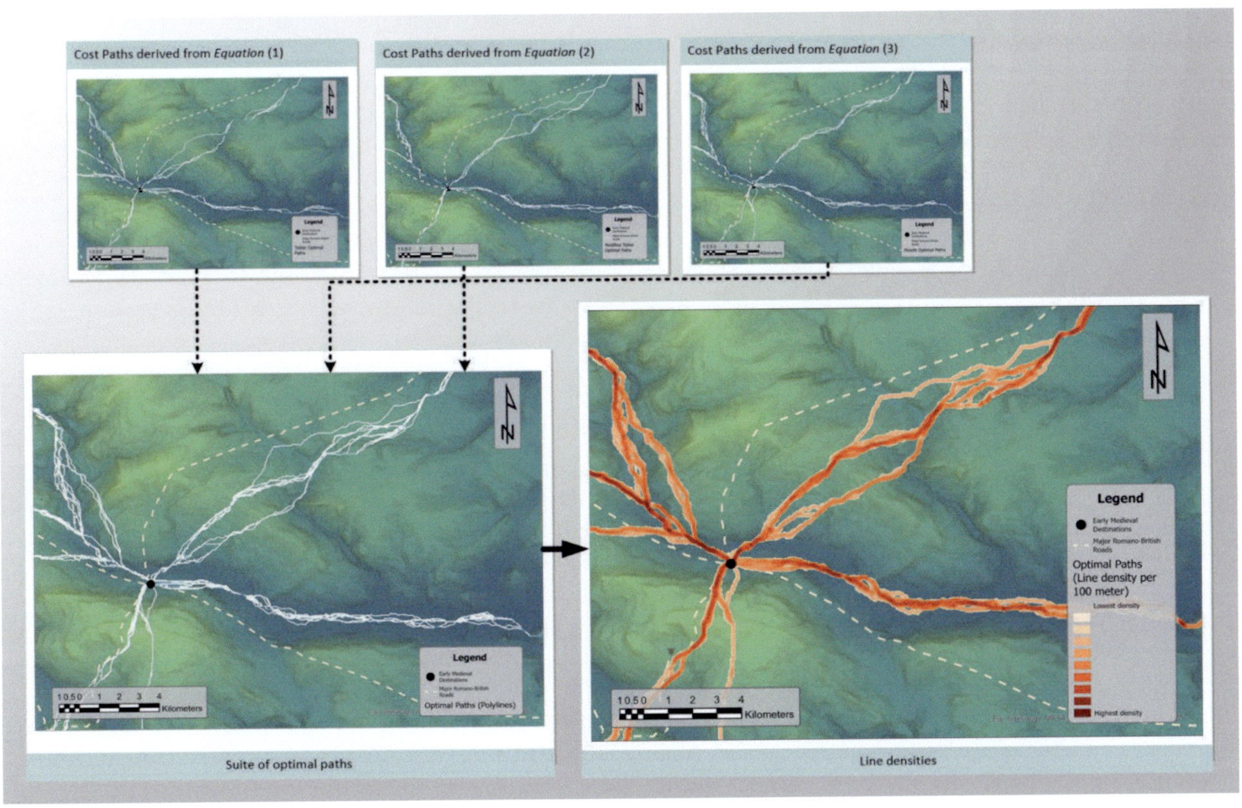

Figure 26.8. The optimal paths modelling workflow. Paths formed from the cost of vertical movement according to Equations (1), (2), and (3) across all iterations ($n = 5$) are combined into an overall suite of optimal pathways. The suite of optimal pathways is converted into a line density raster according to Equation (4).

Identification Model (O'Neil et al. 2020) hold much potential for the delineation of past wetlands but remain unproven for archaeological study. Therefore, Ramsar wetlands were applied in raster format, derived from a base dataset (Natural England 2021) in shapefile format. Other possible barriers to movement, such as a lack of maintenance on sections of road in the tenth century, are possible but at present unknown in specific locations.

Three functions that describe the costs of vertical movement with respect to slope were used in the model. These three functions are standard and common options to describe slope-dependent costs of horizontal movement (cf. Herzog 2010; 2014; Lewis 2021) and were used to create rasterized line densities describing the costs of horizontal movement. Three functions were selected because of limits on available Random Access Memory (RAM) computing capabilities within ArcGIS Pro 3.0. Future studies may implement more or all common cost functions to create rasterized optimal path line densities, such as those described in Herzog (2014) or Lewis (2021). The first equation used in this model is the classic Tobler's (1993) hiking function, given as Equation (1).

01. $V(s) = 6*\exp(-3.5*\text{abs}(s+0.05))$

The second equation used was the modified version of Tobler's hiking function described in Márquez-Pérez et al. (2017), given as Equation (2).

02. $V(s) = 4.8*\exp(-5.3*\text{abs}((s*0.7)+0.03))$

The third equation used to describe the cost of vertical movement was the sixth-degree polynomial following Minetti et al. (2002) and Herzog (2010), given below as Equation (3).

03. $\text{Cost}(s) = 1337.8\ s^6 + 278.19\ s^5 - 517.39\ s^4 - 78.199\ s^3 + 93.419\ s^2 + 19.825\ s + 1.6$

26.3.1.2 Model iteration process

To iterate multiple equally possible outcomes in the LCP creation process, a custom Monte Carlo simulation was created in a Jupyter notebook for ArcGIS Pro 3.0. It is recognized that the standard errors inherent in the DEM creation process have the potential to change modelling outcomes, particularly in the case of viewshed studies (Fisher 1993) and LCP studies (Lewis 2021). Monte Carlo simulation is a common method of describing multiple outcomes in the modelling process (Fisher 1993; Lewis 2021) and is used here to address multiple equally probable outcomes in LCP creation. The base DEM used for this model was the United Kingdom Ordinance Survey Terrain-50 DEM product, a 50 m resolution elevation raster which has a standard error of ±4 m (Ordnance Survey 2022). The model was automated in the Jupyter notebook with multiple iterations. For each iteration, the base DEM was combined with a second DEM consisting solely of random errors according to the base DEM's standard deviation (cf. Lewis 2021). One optimal path per route pairing was created for each of the three employed cost functions, using the "Distance Accumulation" (ESRI 2024a) and "Optimal Path as Line" (ESRI 2024c) tools. The Distance Accumulation tool utilizes Sethian's (1999) interpretation of the Eikonal Equation to compute geodesic paths across surfaces. Across five iterations of the Monte Carlo simulation, fifteen optimal paths were created per route pairing.

The steps performed by the iterating process to create the optimal paths are as follows:

1. A base DEM (OS Terrain-50) of ±4 m was interpolated to discrete point data and combined with random errors to yield a new DEM with incorporated random errors.
2. The Surface Parameters "Slope" tool (ESRI 2024d) was applied to the random errors DEM to calculate degrees of slope across the DEM.
3. The Surface Parameters "Aspect" tool (ESRI 2024d) was applied to the random errors DEM to calculate the direction of downslope change in the DEM as a compass angle.
4. The on-path/off-path factors raster was given as the cost of horizontal movement.
5. The cost of vertical movement from each Equation (1,2,3), respectively, was implemented in a Vertical Factor (VF table) spreadsheet and used in alternating model runs. The VF table was computed outside GIS and inserted into the GIS as a .txt file. The VF table for each Equation (1,2,3) uses the corresponding cost function to compute the cost of movement at a cell of a given slope.
6. One pathway between each set of early medieval period transport nodes was given for each cost function.

26.3.1.3 Conversion to rasterized line densities

The model outputs were stored as polyline features in a geodatabase and converted to line densities. The line densities displayed areas of highest-probability traffic flow following the Monte Carlo simulation of multiple cost of vertical movement functions. Line densities were computed as a raster with magnitude-per-unit area values using the Line Density tool (ESRI 2024b) in ArcGIS Pro 3.0. The line densities were computed according to Equation (4). The equation calculates for every cell the density of polyline features within a set neighbourhood radius (cf. Silverman 1986),

04. $\text{Density} = ((L1 * V1) + (L2 * V2)) / (\text{neighbourhood radius})$

where L1 and L2 are the lengths of portions of lines that lie within the neighbourhood radius, and V1 and V2 are

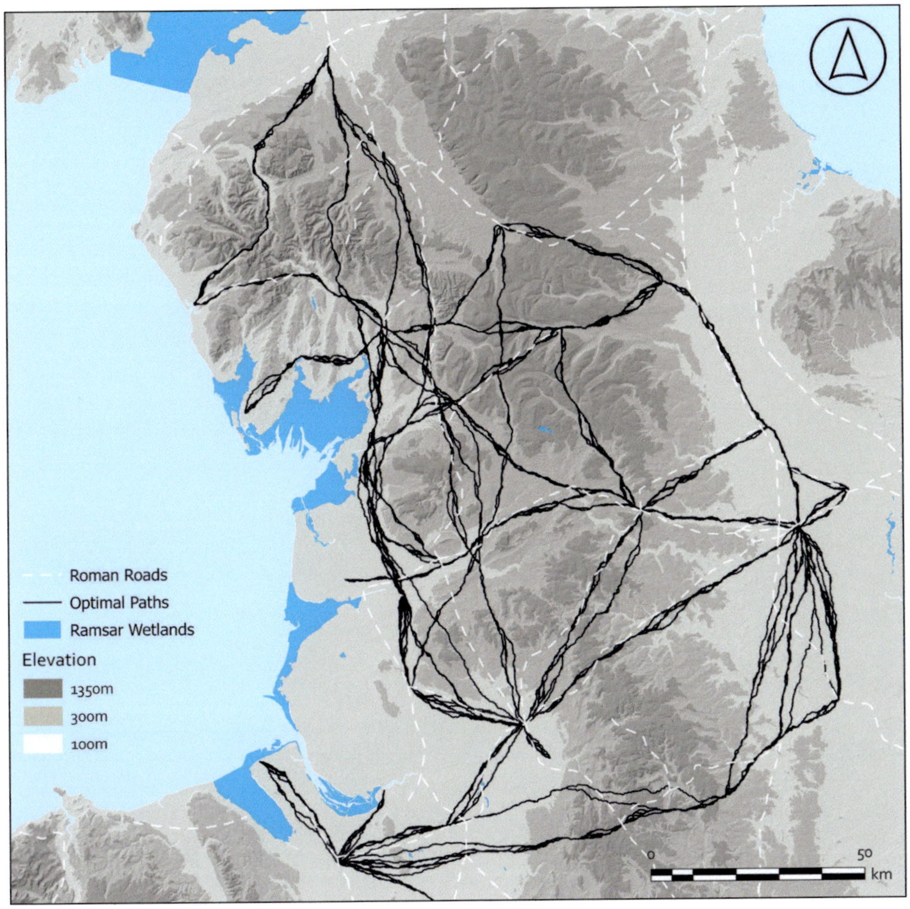

Figure 26.9. The network suite of optimal paths.

magnitude values. The neighbourhood radius is the search area for LCPs that occur around a particular point in the map. The neighbourhood radius needs to be sufficient to account for the width of possible two-dimensional variation in course of the optimal paths. Deng et al. (2014) highlight the arbitrary nature in selecting neighbourhood search radii when estimating density of GIS features and note that the neighbourhood radius needs to be appropriate to the scale of the related features in a spatial distribution. For the LCPs depicted in the current study, no special weighting was added to the magnitude values of each line and each pathway must be considered equally due to the nature of the Monte Carlo simulation. A neighbourhood radius of 100 m is considered by the author to be appropriate for this study to capture all deviations in course between parallel LCPs between the same nodes and was used to create line densities depicted in this paper.

26.3.2 Validation of Routes Between Nodes

Single finds from the PAS are typically recovered by metal detectorists and can be viewed as artefacts which have likely been accidentally lost by their owners, perhaps while travelling through the landscape (Kershaw 2014). The distribution of PAS single finds is biased towards metal detecting tendencies, the availability of permission to detect in certain areas, and Romano-British road courses (Richards et al. 2009). However, the presence of single finds in an area can be viewed as positive indicators that activity took place within a landscape. All single finds on the PAS from the eighth to eleventh centuries were downloaded to test their distribution against the generated optimal paths. The positions of single finds in the study area are presented in the results as one means of model performance assessment.

26.3.3 Departure Pathways Modelling and Validation of Routes

To analyse the relationship of the hoard depositional points to the generated optimal paths, departure paths from the main routes to the silver hoard locations were computed. The departure paths created in this process were designed to simulate off-route travel to the depositional locations, to simulate the walking time and potential pathways for a depositing or recovering agent to encounter hoard locations. Departure paths were simulated to reflect possible events where a hoard was deposited while in transit between destinations, or a previously deposited

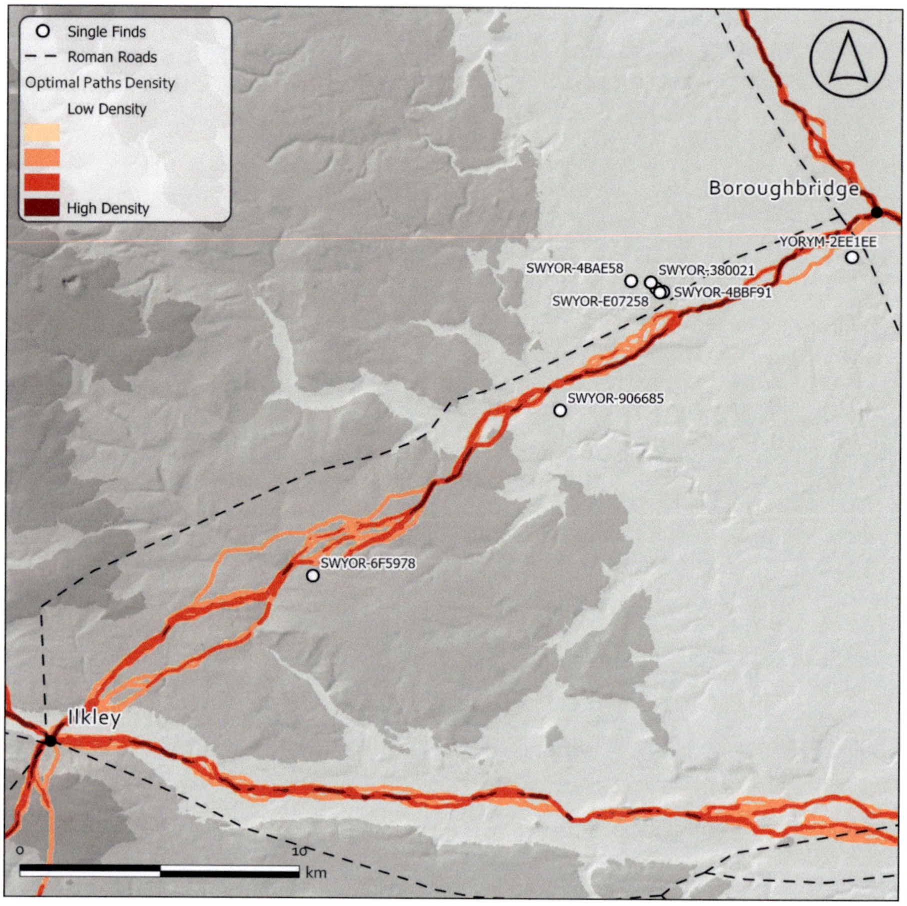

Figure 26.10. Single finds on the Broughbridge-Ilkley Pennine crossing path.

hoard was encountered by an agent moving on a major route. To test this scenario, departure points were set at regular intervals of 100 m along the highest optimal path densities at a perpendicular angle to the hoard locations. These departure points were used to calculate optimal paths using the same modelling process as above, from the areas of highest density to the hoard depositional points. Walking times in this analysis were estimated assuming an average walking speed of 1.4 m per second. It is intended that depositional locations that are located away from routeways, such as those that required several minutes' walking time away from high-traffic areas of the landscape, may be considered "concealed" deposits under this framework.

26.4 Results

26.4.1 Optimal Path Performance

The network suite of optimal paths largely mirrors the Romano-British roads on a regional scale (Figure 26.9). However, in some instances, the optimal paths deviate from the Romano-British road courses (see discussion of *waingates* below). Many of the routes showed evidence for early medieval period use. In particular, routes from Aldborough to Ilkley, Ilkley to Preston, Penrith to Ingleton, Kendal to Barrow-in-Furness, and Broughbridge to Richmond showed positive evidence for use in the early medieval period. Furthermore, this analysis finds that the silver hoard depositional locations are placed with a median walking time of 16 minutes away from the routes depicted in this model.

26.4.1.1 Relationship of routeways to single finds

The Broughbridge-Ilkley Pennine crossing contained several single finds that were used to validate model performance (Figure 26.10). This section is part of the broader York-Ribchester route, a route that may have gone out of use following the Romano-British period and been supplanted by other roughly parallel paths of medieval date (Ratledge pers. comm.). The optimal paths in this section support the assertion that the Romano-British route had gone out of use and been supplanted by a parallel route as many single finds are recorded along the optimal paths route. The first that hints at the usage of a parallel track is a cast lead weight (PAS 'Find-ID' SWYOR-6F5978) of 22 grams that is thought to date from AD 850-1000 and has been compared to Hiberno-Norse weights of the same

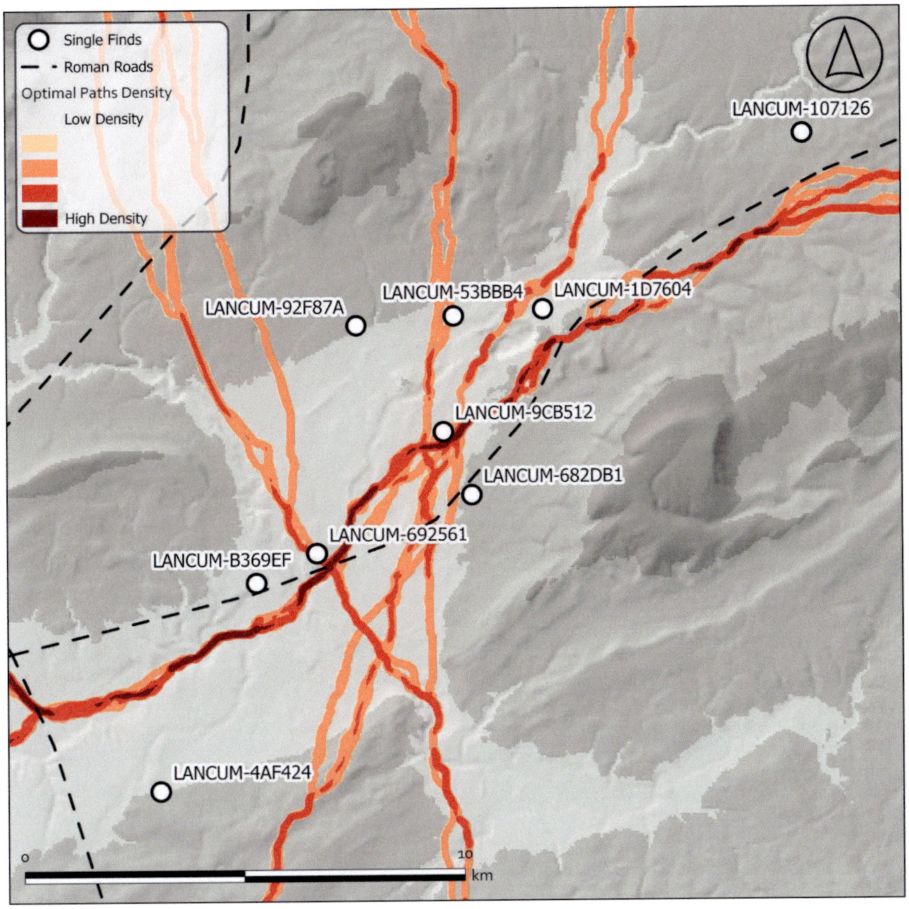

Figure 26.11. PAS Finds in the Ribble Valley. The east-west routes to Ilkley follow the same general path, but the north-south routes diverge. The distribution of single finds largely follows the distribution of optimal paths.

mass (Downes 2020). The second single find is a ninth century Carolingian copper-alloy brooch (SWYOR-906685) that may have arrived in England from Viking activity (Downes 2008). A *c.* AD 750-950 copper alloy Thomas Class A, Type 2 strap end (YORYM-2EE1EE) was recorded near the optimal paths. Interestingly, a group of single finds including early medieval gaming pieces, weights, and a fragmented *dirham* from *c.* AD 750-950 (SWYOR-E07258) were found in close proximity to the optimal paths, slightly north of the Romano-British road line and the optimal paths. Finds of this nature are often indicative of Viking Age trading sites or campsites and are observed to occur in places overlooking routeways (Hadley et al. 2016). I do not suggest here that this distribution is a Viking Age trading or camp site (as it consists of five finds) but that a precedent exists for explaining distributions of these types of finds near to, but slightly away from, tenth century routes and can be applied as a rule of thumb for understanding their overall distribution in relation to observed routes.

In the Lancashire and Cumbrian routes, single finds were also closely associated with the model outputs. The optimal paths between the Ribble Valley and Ilkley contained six Viking Age single finds distributed within *c.* 500 m from the points of highest density. These artefacts included two copper ingots (LANCUM-53BBB4, LANCUM-9CB512), a Swedish-Varangian style scabbard (LANCUM-692561), and a late tenth century Petersen Type X sword pommel (LANCUM-682DB1) (Figure 26.11). On the north-south route that runs between Penrith and Ingleton, a gold Viking-type finger ring (LANCUM-ED5E96) was found that parallels forms from Ireland in the late ninth and early tenth centuries (Boughton 2008). Routes from Kendal to Barrow-in-Furness and Lancaster demonstrated positive evidence for stray object loss with both a Viking-import Irish stick pin (LANCUM-332D63) and a tenth or eleventh century quillion (LANCUM-F7D49D) recorded in the PAS.

26.4.1.2 Comparison with documentary and placename evidence

The optimal paths in this model additionally performed well in Lancashire when compared to post-medieval documentary evidence. The antiquarian John Leland famously recorded the route taken northwards from Preston towards Lancaster (Leland, ed. Smith 1909). Leland gave particular mention to bridges and distances travelled. In *c.* 1540, Leland writes that he crossed the

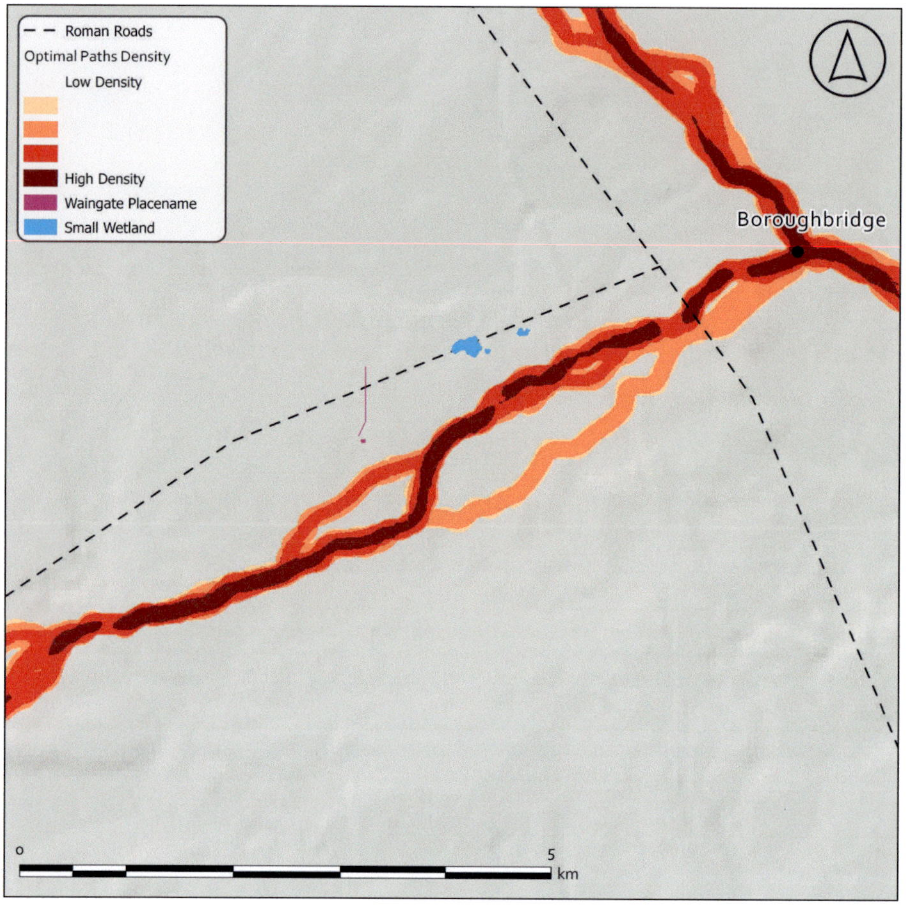

Figure 26.12. Optimal paths and the Roecliffe waingate. The optimal paths pass 200 m from Waingate Lane, Roecliffe, and a small wetland across the original road course.

Savick Brook "one mile without Preston". It is recorded by Ratledge (2023) that the Romano-British road that passes through Moor Park in Preston crosses another Romano-British road (modern Watling Street Road) near Savick Brook. This crossing point is presumably the crossing point that Leland used, as it sits nearly 0.95 miles north of the post-medieval boundary of Preston in the Moor Hall and Gallows Hill area. The optimal paths in this model performed well in this context, as the paths crossed Savick Brook at the same point as Leland in the sixteenth century.

Across the Pennines on routes from York, optimal paths across most iterations divert near the modern village of Roecliffe (Yorkshire), away from the small wetland at the River Tutt. Waingates Lane is located west of the small wetland in this location. A *waingate* is defined as a "wagon street", a placename believed to date from *c.* 1700 originating from Yorkshire's West Riding (Smith 1961). Here, the denoted "wagon street" diverts *c.* 200 m from the Romano-British road course and may be associated with poor drainage near the River Tutt. The modelled optimal paths reflect this local topography and placename by also diverting around the wetland (Figure 26.12).

26.4.2 Hoards' relationship to routeways

Areas of high-density early medieval period travel suggested by this modelling process are located up to *c.* 60 minutes' walk from the depositional points of Viking Age silver hoards in North-West England (Table 26.3, Figure 26.13). A concentration of 11 hoards in the North-West were located in the sub-25 minute travel time range. Furthermore, all hoards that are known to have been deposited with containers (n = 5) were located in the sub-25 minute travel time range.

Hoards related to cross-Pennine routes were the Cuerdale, Halton Moor, Scotby, both Chester hoards, and both Flusco Pike hoards. The Scotby Hoard is related to routes at the Tyne Gap. The Flusco Pike hoards are related to routes in the Eden Valley. The Cuerdale Hoard is related to routes in the Pennine Dales Fringe and Lancashire Valleys. The Chester hoards are related to routes through the Southern Pennines (all Table 26.3).

Hoards related to North-South travel along the west coast of Lancashire are Silverdale, Wharton/Carnforth, and Halton Moor. Hoards related to the West Cumbria Coastal Plain North-South routes are the Dean and West Coast Cumbria Hoards. The Huxley and Eccleston hoards are likely related to travel south from Cumbria (all Table 26.3).

	Name	County	Category	Deposition Date Range (AD)	Container	Off-path travel time (minutes)	Related Route
1	Cuerdale	Lancashire	Mixed	905-910	Lead	20.6	Preston-Ribchester
2	Huxley	Cheshire	Bullion	900-910	Lead	10.1	Chester-Repton
3	Silverdale	Lancashire	Mixed	900-910	Lead	5.9	Lancaster-Kendal
4	Harkirk	Lancashire	Mixed	910-915		16.0	Wigan
5	Dean	Cumbria	Coin	915-925	Lead	16.1	Ravenglass-Cockermouth
6	Lancashire	Lancashire	Coin	910-920			
7	Chester (St. John)	Cheshire	Coin	915-920		0.5	Chester
8	Warton/Carnforth	Lancashire	Mixed	920-929		10.4	Lancaster-Kendal
9	Flusco Pike (2)	Cumbria	Mixed	920-929		32.0	Penrith-Ingleton
10	Scotby	Cumbria	Mixed	935-940		60.9	
11	Flusco Pike (1)	Cumbria	Ornament	920-939		29.6	Penrith-Ingleton
12	Orton Scar	Cumbria	Ornament			37.0	Penrith-Ingleton
13	Eccleston	Cheshire	Bullion			10.5	Carlisle-Penrith
14	Barrow-in-Furness	Cumbria	Mixed	900-930		46.8	Barrow-Kendal
15	Chester (Castle Esplanade)	Cheshire	Mixed	965-970	Pot	4.0	Chester
16	Halton Moor	Lancashire	Mixed	1025-1030	Silver Cup	16.2	Lancaster-Ingleton
17	West Coast Cumbria	Cumbria	Mixed	850-950		55.2	Ravenglass-Cockermouth
18	Furness	Cumbria	Mixed	955-957		17.6	Barrow-Kendal

Table 26.3. Approximate off-path travel times from the optimal paths to the hoard locations, given in minutes.

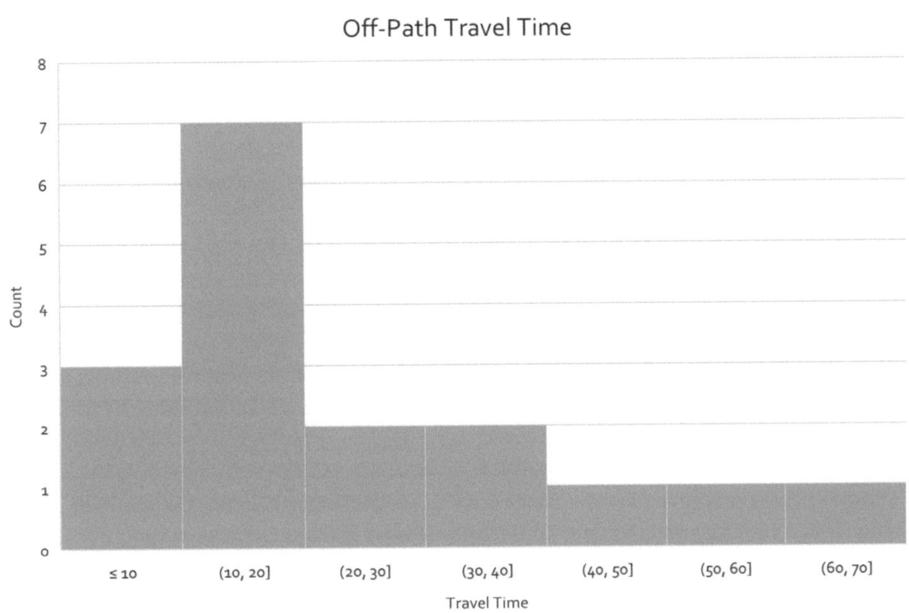

Figure 26.13. The distribution of approximate off-path travel time in minutes. The range of approximate off-path travel times was up to *c.* 60 minutes' walk from the nearest points of highest density in the optimal path network. The median off-path travel time is 16.0 minutes. There is a concentration of 11 hoards that are located in the sub-25 minute walking time zone.

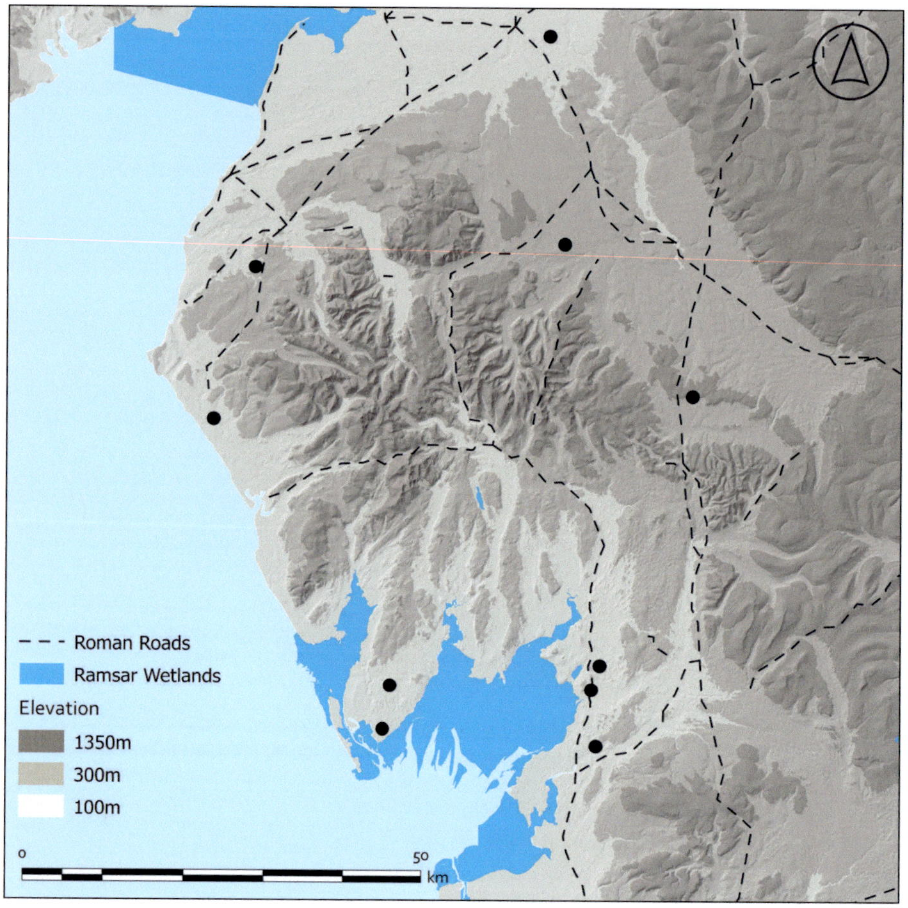

Figure 26.14. The distribution of silver hoards and Ramsar wetlands around the Morecambe Bay. The hoards lay in well-drained positions away from the large wetlands. Some hoards are located over 20 km from the nearest wetland. The roads model includes Ratledge's revised Lancaster-Kendal line (2023).

26.5 Discussion

26.5.1 Concealed Deposits

Debates have prevailed in Viking Age hoarding studies as to the ritual or non-ritual status of individual hoards. It has been suggested by Gruszczynski (2017) that Viking Age coin hoards in Scandinavia can be viewed as ritual in nature if they are deposited in areas that are impossible to retrieve, and several authors (Raffield 2014; Bradley 2017; Gruszczynski 2017) suggest that wetlands are a location frequented for ritual deposition of objects in the Viking Age. However, Bradley (2017) states that it is difficult to discern the wetland status of hoards. None of the hoards in the North-West were located in Ramsar-designated wetlands (Figure 26.14). Although further study of the relationship of the hoards to wetlands can be undertaken, preliminary indications from this study are that the hoards conform to a non-wetland depositional context.

Further clues to the non-ritual status of the hoards in this analysis are the presence of containers and economically valuable objects. Gruszczynski (2017) suggested that containers indicate that hoards are intended to be retrieved. Six of the hoards in the North-West were buried with containers, and the presence of organic containers in the other cases cannot be ruled out due to soil preservation conditions. Bradley (2017) suggests that Viking Age hoards are non-ritual in nature if they contain artefacts of whole or fragmentary nature. Bradley's implication is that the hoards are intended to be retrieved if they contain objects that will be of future economic or practical use to the owner. All of the hoards in North-West England are composed of objects that were of current economic value at the time of their deposition.

If hoards are ritually deposited if they are placed in areas that are impossible to retrieve (Gruszczynski 2017), the hoards in the North-West are by implication non-ritual deposits, as they were deposited in areas that were highly retrievable within short walking distances of major routes. Based on an analysis of its material composition, it is possible that the Cuerdale Hoard was in transit from York (Williams 2011) or assembled in the Ribble Valley, a central meeting place between York and Dublin (Graham-Campbell 2011). However, both authors imply transportation of the hoard immediately prior to deposition. The deposit location is on a dry rise near the riverbank – the hoard was only discovered when the decision was made to construct a wider river channel and bank in 1840. The depositional location

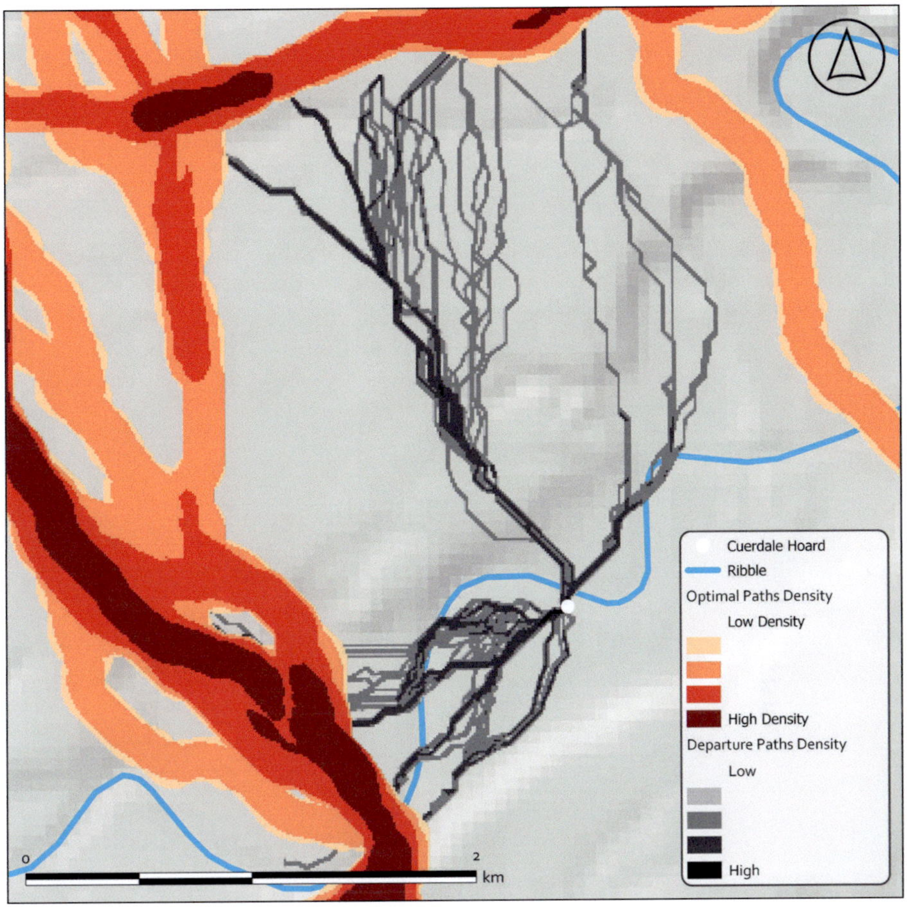

Figure 26.15. The relationship of off-path routes to the Cuerdale Hoard. The intersection of routes in the Preston area is *c.* 2.5 km away from the hoard deposit. To encounter the hoard location, the Ribble would have needed to be forded in most scenarios, as shown with the departure path densities.

was on the opposite side of the bank from the east-west Romano-British road leading away from Preston towards Pennine crossings past the Lancashire valleys. The hoard was located approximately two kilometres from the Roman bridge at Walton-le-Dale and one kilometre from the river crossings indicated by the optimal paths model (Figure 26.15). Thus, if elements of the hoard from Ireland arrived by ship, the depositors likely would have sailed between one and two kilometres past popular Ribble crossing locations before choosing a location to bury the hoard. If elements of the hoard arrived by land, the depositors may have left popular land routes for some one to two and a half kilometres. Measured in minutes' walking time, the results of this project indicate that the Cuerdale Hoard may have been deposited approximately 20 minutes' walking time from high-traffic pathways. Future work must be undertaken to analyse the visibility of the hoard findspot from major routeways and the deepest channels of the Ribble, but preliminary indications in this study are that the findspot is away from major routes.

Similarly, another case study is the second Flusco Pike hoard (Figure 26.16), buried approximately 1.5-2.5 km from the optimal paths' highest-density segments through the modern Penrith vicinity. The indicated walking times from high-density areas lends an estimate of approximately 30 minutes. The hoard, similarly to Cuerdale, was placed away from the location of the optimal pathways between major transport nodes.

In all instances, the hoards were buried up to one hour's walking time away from high-traffic areas of the landscape, with a concentration of deposits in the under-25 minute category. The hoards were likely intended to be retrieved due to economically valuable components deposited together in a container in several instances, with further non-ritual indications coming from the doubtful wetland status of the deposits addressed. The summation of the elements discussed here depicts a framework where the hoard depositors chose locations away from high-traffic routes, as the economically valuable hoard components were likely transported on those routes from their various origin points to their final depositional location. Furthermore, the depositors may have chosen locations that were peripheral to high-density traffic flow to assist in their concealment from others on the routes, and to ensure the safekeeping of the deposit in anticipation of the owners' return.

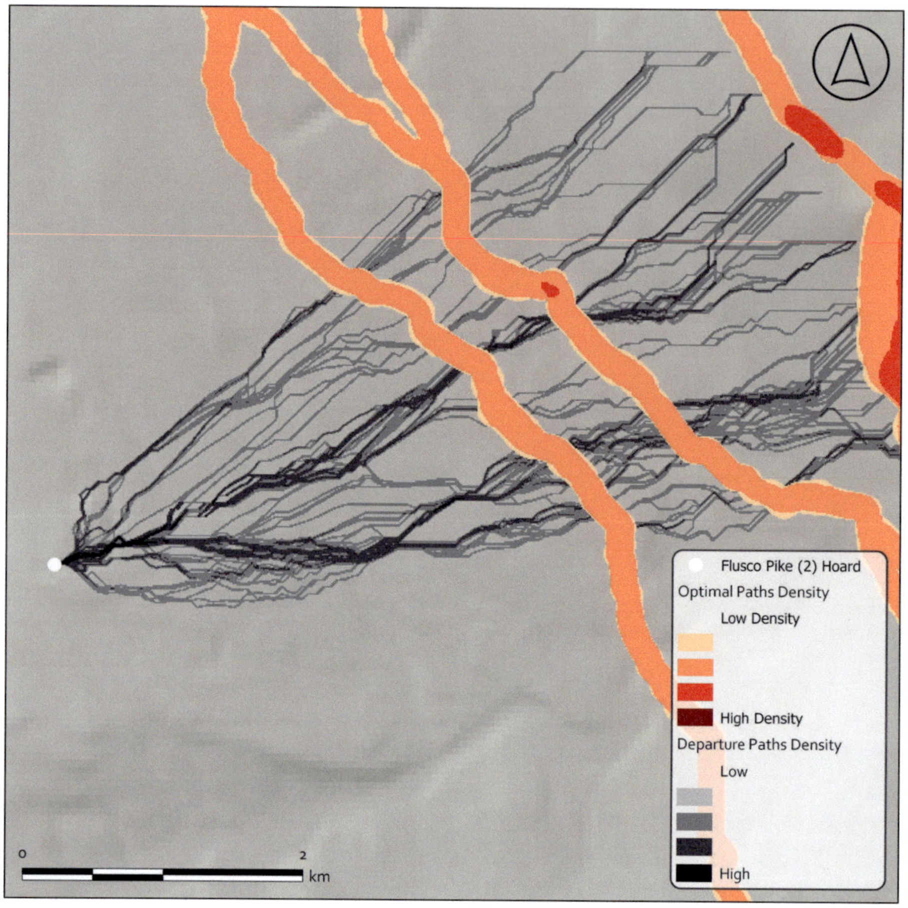

Figure 26.16. The relationship of off-path routes to the second (most recently discovered) hoard in the Flusco Pike/Penrith area.

26.6 Conclusion

Viking Age silver hoards in the North-West are often viewed as being deposited in an intermediary landscape between York and Dublin. However, the nature of the relationship between specific courses of routeways and depositional points was unclear, leaving unresolved questions in the scholarship related to why certain locations were chosen to bury Scandinavian-economic character silver hoards in the study area. Furthermore, this research gap has allowed debates to persist on the hoards' relationship to overland transit and the intent of the depositors to return for the hoards. To move towards resolving these debates, optimal pathways were implemented that took into account re-discovered Romano-British road segments, uncertainty in DEM production, and the agency of multiple walkers in the landscape via multiple cost of vertical movement equations.

This study has targeted two specific previously understudied research questions relating to the silver hoards as discussed in the introduction. Firstly, this study set out to examine the relationship of the hoards to their routeways. It was shown that the hoards' depositional points are related to early medieval communication routes between Northumbria and the Irish Sea region. The links between Northumbria and the Irish Sea are significant as they were the locations of two hubs of Scandinavian influence in the area – the "linked kingdoms" of York and Dublin, which were sources of Viking bands operating on the western shores of England in the early tenth century and the apparent influx of Scandinavian settlers in the North-West at this time. Secondly, this study set out to test if the hoards were concealed deposits intended for retrieval. It was shown that further to the hoards being related to the early medieval period routes, the hoards were buried up to one hour's walk from the routes, with a median walking time of 16 minutes. Eleven of the hoards in the study were located within a sub-25 minute walking time. Taken together with the presence of other non-ritual elements, such as containers in some instances, the hoards are viewed as a group of similar deposits that were concealed from routeways and intended by their depositors to be retrieved.

26.7 Future Research

To further this hypothesis of seclusion from routes, GIS-based visibility analysis of the routes and silver hoard locations will likely prove profitable. Visibility analysis may take the form of a traditional viewshed analysis from locations along routes, similar to the locational analysis proposed by Eve and Crema (2014) or may take the form of a seclusion or covert space analysis as proposed by Gillings (2015). Furthermore, a structuring of node importance will improve the understanding of the network's relationship to hoard locations, and a working model of node structuring can be derived from processes inspired by Brooks and Nguyen Huynh (2018). It is hoped that the summation of these analyses applied to hoard locations will continue to contribute to the understanding of depositional landscapes. The inclusion of LiDAR data in substitution for the Terrain-50 DEM may yield further granularity to the analysis presented here and may assist in wetland analysis at a large scale. Finally, the method presented in this paper will be of interest to those studying hoards of other periods and geographic regions, and it is hoped that it will be useful in contexts other than the study of Early Medieval Britain.

Acknowledgements

This paper derives from research initially undertaken for the author's master's dissertation at the University of Oxford, supervised by Dr. Jane Kershaw and Dr. John Pouncett (Wilcox 2022). The author would like to thank Dr. John Pouncett, Dr. Tom Horne, and Mr. David Ratledge for feedback on a draft of this paper. For use of images, the author would like to thank Mr. David Ratledge and Dr. Tom Horne. The author would finally like to thank those at Session 44: *Roads to Complexity* of the 2023 Computer Applications and Quantitative Methods in Archaeology, International Conference in Amsterdam, Netherlands (CAA 2023) for their comments and feedback on the presentation that preceded the publication of this paper.

Funding

The author declares that no specific funding for this study was received. The travel expenses associated with the presentation of this research at CAA 2023 were funded by the St Hugh's College, Oxford Alumni Association and the CAA concessionary travel grant.

Conflict of Interest Disclosure

The author has no conflicts of interest, financial or otherwise, in relation to the content of the article, in compliance with the rules set out by PCI Archaeology.

Data, Scripts, Code, and Supplementary Information Availability

The grid coordinates of artefacts recorded through the Portable Antiquities Scheme (PAS) are restricted to users with Research-level access, subject to Crown Copyright and the conditions, responsibilities, and stipulations of the 1996 Treasure Act of the United Kingdom of Great Britain and Northern Ireland. Therefore, the grid coordinates of specific artefacts registered with the PAS discussed in this article are not publicly available. Similarly, some silver hoards are registered with county Historic Environment Record (HER) offices in England. Permission to use these coordinates for academic study must be obtained directly from the relevant HER offices.

Python scripts used to perform the optimal pathways modelling depicted in this paper are available in .ipynb format in the Supplemental Material:

Wilcox, Wyatt. 2024. "Mobility and the reuse of Roman Roads for the deposition of Viking Age silver hoards in North-West England (Supplemental Material) (Version 1)." Zenodo. DOI: 10.5281/zenodo.11067607.

The Supplemental Material link also includes the optimal paths between nodes depicted in the paper in both line and raster format, a nodes feature class, and VF tables used in the analysis.

Peer Review

This article has been peer reviewed by PCI Archaeology.

Visser, R. 2024. "Moving away from the ritual deposition: hoards from the Viking Age, Least Cost Paths and reused Roman Roads." *Peer Community in Archaeology* 100348. DOI: 10.24072/pci.archaeo.100348.

References

Archibald, Marion. 1992. "Dating Cuerdale: The Evidence of the Coins." In *Viking Treasure from the North-West: The Cuerdale Hoard in Its Context: Selected Papers from "The Vikings of the Irish Sea" Conference, Liverpool, 18-20 May 1990*, edited by James Graham-Campbell, 15–20. Liverpool: National Museums & Galleries on Merseyside.

Bishop, Mike C. 2014. *The Secret History of the Roman Roads of Britain*. Barnsley, South Yorkshire: Pen & Sword Military.

Blackburn, Mark. 2004. "The Coinage of Scandinavian York." In *Aspects of Anglo-Scandinavian York*, edited by R. A. Hall, 325–49. York: Council for British Archaeology.

Blunt, Christopher E., and B. H. Ian H. Stewart. 1983. "The Coinage of Regnald I of York and the Bossall Hoard." *The Numismatic Chronicle* 143: 146–63.

Bradley, Richard. 2017. *A Geography of Offerings: Deposits of Valuables in the Landscapes of Ancient Europe*. Havertown: Oxbow Books.

Brookes, Stuart, and Hoai Nguyen Huynh. 2018. "Transport Networks and Towns in Roman and Early Medieval England: An Application of PageRank to Archaeological Questions." *Journal of Archaeological Science: Reports* 17: 477–90. DOI:10.1016/j.jasrep.2017.11.033.

Boughton, Dot. 2008. "LANCUM-ED5E96: An Early Medieval Finger Ring." https://finds.org.uk/database/artefacts/record/id/211836.

Boughton, Dot. 2011. "LANCUM-65C1B4: An Early Medieval Hoard." https://finds.org.uk/database/artefacts/record/id/462949.

Deng, Yongxin, Brendan Wallace, Derek Maassen, and Johnathan Werner. 2016. "A Few GIS Clarifications on Tornado Density Mapping." *Journal of Applied Meteorology and Climatology* 55 (2): 283–96. DOI:10.1175/JAMC-D-15-0141.1.

Downes, Amy 2008. "SWYOR-906685: An Early Medieval Brooch." https://finds.org.uk/database/artefacts/record/id/241530.

Downes, Amy 2020. "SWYOR-6F5978: An Early Medieval Weight." https://finds.org.uk/database/artefacts/record/id/999987.

Downham, Clare. 2007. *Viking Kings of Britain and Ireland: The Dynasty of Ívarr to AD 1014*. Edinburgh: Dunedin Academic.

Edmonds, Fiona. 2020. "Pathways Through the Past: Routes between the Gaelic World and the Northumbrian Kingdom." In *Gaelic Influence in the Northumbrian Kingdom: The Golden Age and the Viking Age, 1st Ed.* Woodbridge: The Boydell Press. DOI:10.1017/9781787445864.

ESRI. 2022. *ArcGIS Pro*. V 3.0. Redlands, CA: Environmental Systems Research Institute.

ESRI. 2024a. "Distance Accumulation (Spatial Analyst – ArcGIS Pro Documentation." https://pro.arcgis.com/en/pro-app/latest/tool-reference/spatial-analyst/distance-accumulation.htm.

ESRI. 2024b. "Line Density (Spatial Analyst) – ArcGIS Pro Documentation." https://pro.arcgis.com/en/pro-app/latest/tool-reference/spatial-analyst/line-density.htm.

ESRI. 2024c. "Optimal Path as Line (Spatial Analyst) – ArcGIS Pro Documentation." https://pro.arcgis.com/en/pro-app/latest/tool-reference/spatial-analyst/optimal-path-as-line.htm.

ESRI. 2024d. "Surface Parameters (Spatial Analyst) – ArcGIS Pro Documentation." https://pro.arcgis.com/en/pro-app/latest/tool-reference/spatial-analyst/surface-parameters.htm.

Eve, Stuart J., and Enrico R. Crema. 2014. "A House with a View? Multi-Model Inference, Visibility Fields, and Point Process Analysis of a Bronze Age Settlement on Leskernick Hill (Cornwall, UK)." *Journal of Archaeological Science* 43: 267–77. DOI:10.1016/j.jas.2013.12.019.

Fisher, Peter F. 1993. "Algorithm and Implementation Uncertainty in Viewshed Analysis." *International Journal of Geographical Information Systems* 7 (4): 331–47. DOI:10.1080/02693799308901965.

Gillings, Mark. 2015. "Mapping Invisibility: GIS Approaches to the Analysis of Hiding and Seclusion." *Journal of Archaeological Science* 62: 1–14. DOI:10.1016/j.jas.2015.06.015.

Gooch, Megan. 2012. "Money and Power in the Viking Kingdom of York, c.895 – 954." PhD diss., Durham University. http://etheses.dur.ac.uk/3495.

Graham-Campbell, James. 1992. "Northumbria, Mercia and the Irish Sea Norse, 893-926." In *Viking Treasure from the North-West: The Cuerdale Hoard in Its Context: Selected Papers from "The Vikings of the Irish Sea" Conference, Liverpool, 18-20 May 1990*, edited by James Graham-Campbell, 21–30. Liverpool: National Museums & Galleries on Merseyside.

Graham-Campbell, James. 2011. *The Cuerdale Hoard: And Related Viking-Age Silver and Gold from Britain and Ireland in the British Museum*. London: British Museum.

Gruszczynski, Jacek. 2019. "The Importance of Containers for the Deposition and Non-Retrieval of Silver Hoards: A Comparison between Gotland and Pomerania." In *Silver, Butter, Cloth: Monetary and Social Economies in the Viking Age*, edited by Jane Kershaw, Gareth Williams, Søren Sindbæk, and James Graham-Campbell, 169–88. Oxford: Oxford University Press.

Hadley, Dawn M., Julian D. Richards, and Elizabeth Craig-Atkins with contributions by Hannah Brown. 2016. "The Winter Camp of the Viking Great Army, AD 872–3, Torksey, Lincolnshire." *The Antiquaries Journal* 96: 23–67. DOI:10.1017/S0003581516000718.

Herzog, Irmela. 2010. "Theory and Practice of Cost Functions." In *Proceedings of the 38th Annual Conference of Computer Applications and Quantitative Methods in Archaeology, CAA 2010*, edited by F. Contreras, M. Farjas, and F. J. Melero, 375–82. Oxford: BAR International.

Herzog, Irmela. 2014. "Least-Cost Paths – Some Methodological Issues." *Internet Archaeology* 36. DOI:10.11141/ia.36.5.

Higham, Nicholas J. 2004. *A Frontier Landscape: The North-West in the Middle Ages*. Macclesfield: Windgather Press.

Horne, Tom. 2021. *A Viking Market Kingdom in Ireland and Britain: Trade Networks and the Importation of a Southern Scandinavian Silver Bullion Economy*. London: Routledge. DOI:10.4324/9780429341625.

Jensen, Xenia. 2007. "Preliminary Remarks on the Roman Military Equipment from the War Booty Sacrifice of Vimose, Denmark." *Analecta Romana Instituti Danici* 38: 131–6.

Kershaw, Jane. 2014. "Viking-Age Silver in North-West England: Hoards and Single Finds." In *In Search of Vikings*, edited by Stephen E. Harding, David Griffiths, and Elizabeth Royles, 162–77. Boca Raton: CRC Press. DOI:10.1201/b17946-14.

Kershaw, Jane. 2017. "An Early Medieval Dual-Currency Economy: Bullion and Coin in the Danelaw." *Antiquity* 91 (355): 173–90. DOI:10.15184/aqy.2016.249.

Kershaw, Jane, Stephen W. Merkel, Jani Oravisjärvi, Ellen Kooijman, and Melanie Kielman-Schmitt. 2021. "The Scale of Dirham Imports to the Baltic in the Ninth Century: New Evidence from Archaeometric Analyses of Early Viking-Age Silver." *Fornvännen* 116 (3): 185–204.

Kluyver, Thomas, Benjamin Ragan-Kelley, Fernando Pérez, Brian Granger, Matthias Bussonnier, Jonathan Frederic, Kyle Kelley, et al. 2016. "Jupyter Notebooks – a publishing format for reproducible computational workflows." In *Positioning and Power in Academic Publishing: Players, Agents, and Agendas*, edited by F. Loizides and B. Schmidt, 87–90. IOS Press: Amsterdam. DOI: 10.3233/978-1-61499-649-1-87

Leland, John. 1909. *The Itinerary of John Leland in or about the Years 1535-1543*. Edited by Lucy Toulmin Smith. London: G. Bell.

Lewis, Joseph. 2021. "Probabilistic Modelling for Incorporating Uncertainty in Least Cost Path Results: A Postdictive Roman Road Case Study." *Journal of Archaeological Method and Theory* 28 (3): 911–24. DOI:10.1007/s10816-021-09522-w.

Márquez-Pérez, Joaquín, Ismael Vallejo-Villalta, and José I. Álvarez-Francoso. 2017. "Estimated Travel Time for Walking Trails in Natural Areas." *Geografisk Tidsskrift-Danish Journal of Geography* 117 (1): 53–62. DOI:10.1080/00167223.2017.1316212.

McCormick, Michael, Guoping Huang, Giovanni Zambotti, and Jessica Lavash. 2013. "Roman Road Network (Version 2008)." Harvard Dataverse. DOI:10.7910/DVN/TI0KAU.

Minetti, Alberto E., Christian Moia, Giulio S. Roi, Davide Susta, and Guido Ferretti. 2002. "Energy Cost of Walking and Running at Extreme Uphill and Downhill Slopes." *Journal of Applied Physiology* 93 (3): 1039–46. DOI:10.1152/japplphysiol.01177.2001.

Natural England. 2021. "Ramsar (England)." ESRI Shapefile. https://www.data.gov.uk/dataset/67b4ef48-d0b2-4b6f-b659-4efa33469889/ramsar-england.

Nebiolini, Brittany. 2020. "Silver Hoards and the Economic Interrelationship of Viking York and Dublin (800–1000)." *The Journal of Irish Archaeology* 29: 139–58.

Oakden, Vanessa. 2014. "LVPL-C63F8A: An Early Medieval Hoard." https://finds.org.uk/database/artefacts/record/id/649929.

O'Neil, Gina L., Jonathan L. Goodall, Madhur Behl, and Linnea Saby. 2020. "Deep Learning Using Physically-Informed Input Data for Wetland Identification." *Environmental Modelling & Software* 126: 104665. DOI:10.1016/j.envsoft.2020.104665.

Ordnance Survey GB. 2022. "OS Terrain 50™ – Overview". Version 1.5. https://www.ordnancesurvey.co.uk/documents/product-support/support/os-terrain-50-overview-v1.5.pdf.

Raffield, Ben. 2014. "'A River of Knives and Swords': Ritually Deposited Weapons in English Watercourses and Wetlands during the Viking Age." *European Journal of Archaeology* 17 (4): 634–55. DOI:10.1179/1461957114Y.0000000066.

Ratledge, David. 2023. "Roman Roads in Lancashire." In *The Roads of Roman Britain: A Gazetteer*. https://www.romanroads.org/gazetteer/lancspages.html.

Richards, Julian, John Naylor, and Caroline Holas-Clark. 2009. "Anglo-Saxon Landscape and Economy: Using Portable Antiquities to Study Anglo-Saxon and Viking Age England." *Internet Archaeology* 25. https://intarch.ac.uk/journal/issue25/2/toc.html.

Sethian, James Albert. 1999. *Level Set Methods and Fast Marching Methods: Evolving Interfaces in Computational Geometry, Fluid Mechanics, Computer Vision, and Materials Science, 2nd Ed.* Cambridge: Cambridge University Press.

Silverman, Bernard W. 1986. *Density Estimation for Statistics and Data Analysis*. New York: Chapman and Hall.
Sindbæk, Søren M. 2013. "Crafting Networks in Viking Towns." *Medieval and Modern Matters* 4: 119–32. DOI: 10.1484/J.MMM.5.109773.
Smith, Albert H. 1961. *The Place-Names of the West Riding of Yorkshire, Part One: Lower & Upper Strafforth and Staincross Wappentakes*. Cambridge: Cambridge University Press.
Stein, Samantha. 2014. "Understanding Torksey, Lincolnshire: A Geoarchaeological and Landscape Approach to a Viking Overwintering Camp." PhD diss., University of Sheffield. https://etheses.whiterose.ac.uk/9616.
Tobler, Waldo. 1993. *Three Presentations of Geographical Analysis and Modelling. Technical Report 93-1*. Santa Barbara, CA: National Center for Geographic Analysis.
Wilcox, Wyatt. 2022. "The landscape contexts of Viking Age silver hoards in northwest England". MSc diss., The University of Oxford.
Williams, Gareth. 2009. "Hoards from the Danelaw from Cuerdale to the Vale of York." In *The Huxley Viking Hoard: Scandinavian Settlement in the North-West*, edited by James Graham-Campbell and Robert A. Philpott. Liverpool: National Museums Liverpool.
Williams, Gareth. 2011. "The Cuerdale Coins." In *The Cuerdale Hoard: And Related Viking-Age Silver and Gold from Britain and Ireland in the British Museum*, edited by James Graham-Campbell and Barry Ager, 151–9. London: British Museum.
Wilson, David. 1965. "Some Neglected Late Anglo-Saxon Swords." *Medieval Archaeology* 9 (1): 32–54. DOI: 10.1080/00766097.1965.11735686.

27 Establishing a workflow for recording and analysing bioarchaeological data

Kiriakos Xanthopoulos
Laboratory of Biological Anthropology
Democritus University of Thrace
Komotini
ancbiosoc@gmail.com

Aggeliki Georgiadou
Laboratory of Biological Anthropology
Democritus University of Thrace
Komotini

Christina Papageorgopoulou
1. Laboratory of Biological Anthropology
Department of Humanities
Democritus University of Thrace
Komotini
Greece

2. Institute of Applied Bioarchaeological Research
Democritus University of Thrace
Komotini
Greece

Abstract

Bioarchaeology has long focused on understanding past human life through skeletal remains, including oral pathology and stable isotope analysis. Despite advancements in statistical analysis, correlations are still largely made manually. To streamline this, we propose a tool to automatically identify correlations between dental pathologies and isotope values. Our work is part of the ongoing APOIKIA project on Corinthian colonisation in 7th century BC. We analyse osteoarchaeological material from the Western Necropolis of Amvrakia, Greece, founded around 640 BC. Our methodology integrates novel data collection approaches and FAIR principles for data longevity and accessibility, utilising R Markdown documents and cloud webware.

Keywords: Osteoarchaeology; Colonisation; Data analysis; Archaeological methodology

27.1 Introduction

Bioarchaeology has laboured for many decades to reconstruct the living conditions and socioeconomic aspects of past human experiences through the study of skeletal remains. In lack of either material or textual evidence, bioarchaeological approaches hold great value in developing a synergy effect with historical, demographic and archaeological data. Within the vastly broad area of bioarchaeological research lies oral pathology, and stable carbon and nitrogen analysis. These approaches are regarded today as powerful tools for archaeologists to monitor the shifts in the carbohydrate intake and the dietary protein consumption of past populations. Several previous studies have demonstrated the combination of stable isotopic and dental health data to shed light on the lifestyle, diet, nutrition, and subsistence economy (White 2007; Ossenberg 2013; Colleter et al. 2020; Constantinou and Nikita 2022; Caruso et al. 2023; Georgiadou et al. 2023; Caruso and Nikita 2024). Despite the significant efficiency in the correlation process of bioarchaeological data through varied statistical analyses, the estimations are still performed by the observation, interpretation and comparison of different statistical plots. To avoid time-consuming procedures, we are in the process of generating a tool that enables the researcher to automatically find if there are any correlations between dental pathologies and isotope values.

Our research is part of an ongoing project entitled "APOIKIA: Ancient DNA analysis in novel multidisciplinary approach of ancient Corinthian colonisation. Ancient Amvrakia

In *Advances in Digital Archaeology. Proceedings of the 2023 conference Computer Applications and Quantitative Methods in Archaeology – 50 years of synergy*, edited by J.W.H.P. Verhagen, J. Waagen, A. Brandsen, A. Queffelec, R.M. Visser and D. Taelman, 349–360. Leiden: Sidestone Press.

Figure 27.1. Corinth (metropolis) and Amvrakia (colony) in Greece.

and Ancient Tenea as demonstration examples". Amvrakia (Figure 27.1) was officially founded in 625 BC during various colonisation endeavours of the Corinthians in Epirus, Greece. Five research institutes have partnered to enhance the archaeological research on the phenomenon of colonisation by elaborating current lines on the scientific network or carving new ones. The study presented here focuses on the osteoarchaeological and biochemical research field of the project.

Bioarchaeologists are more and more specialising in a specific field of study as technological advances limit the researchers' ability to keep track of them. Collaboration among specialists is the only viable way to conduct research in the coming years. The obstacles that arise through such collaborations may throw whole scientific projects off balance or even lead to their termination. One of those obstacles is the complexity of merging diverse types of recorded data into a unified database. In attempts to address this challenge, bioarchaeologists have turned to utilising different web-based platforms, including Google Drive, Dropbox, Box, and GitHub. While these tools have been beneficial, they often lack a cohesive interface, making them less user-friendly. To mitigate these issues, there is a growing trend within the scientific community to develop new tools, ranging from mobile applications to cloud-based software, with varying licenses and methodological applications, spanning from historical research to forensic law enforcement (Berg and Kenyhercz 2017; Scott et al. 2018; Hunt 2019; Bartholdy et al. 2019; Klales 2020; Colleter et al. 2020).

27.2 Material and Methods

The osteoarchaeological material comes from various excavational periods of the Western Necropolis (WN) and Eastern Necropolis (EN) of Amvrakia between 1993-2022 (Figure 27.2). The WN stands out as one of Greece's largest and most intact necropolises uncovered to date. It has revealed over 600 grave sites, collectively containing more than 700 individuals. The EN of Amvrakia is more segmented than WN with approximately 200 grave sites and

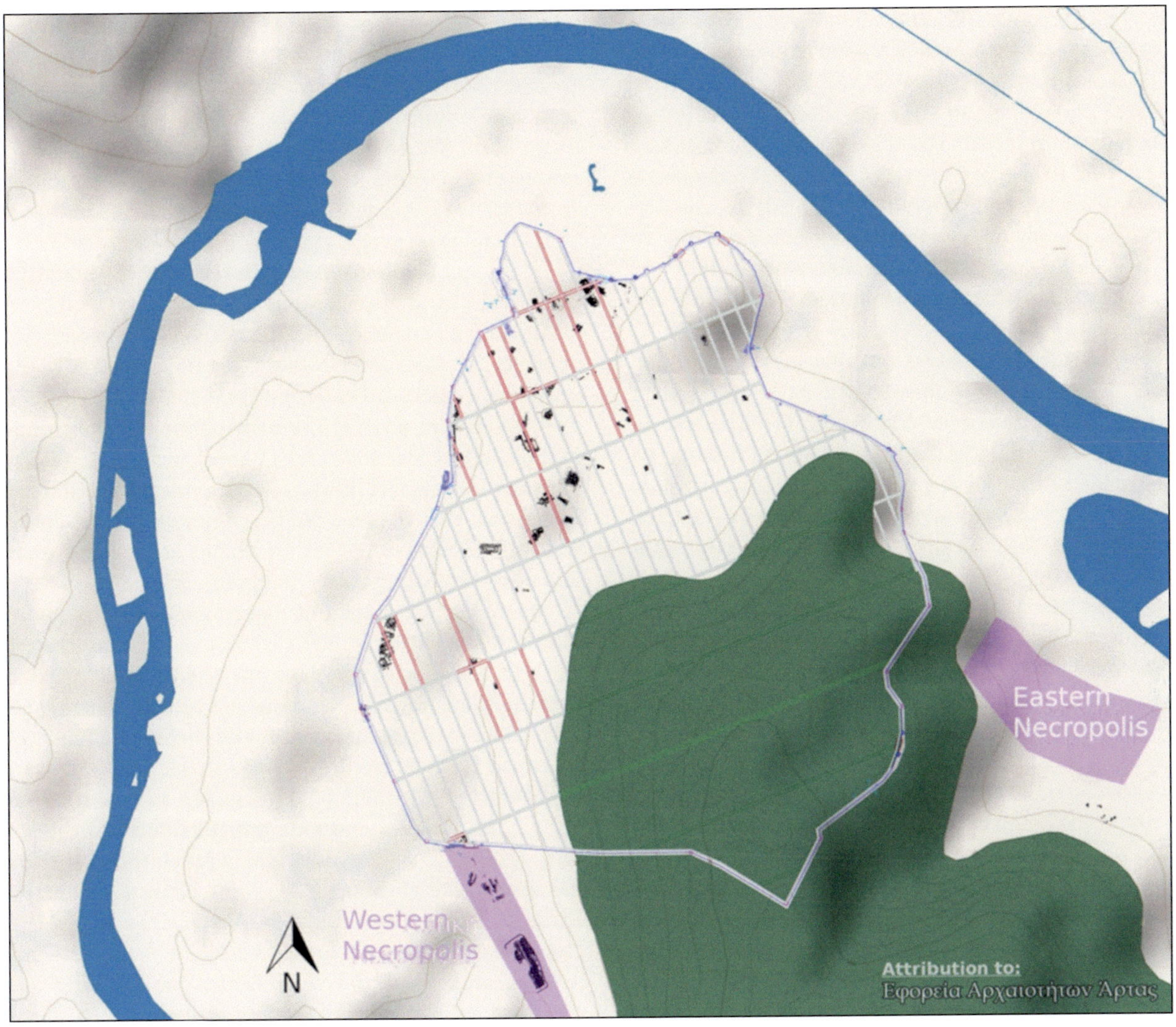

Figure 27.2. Western Necropolis and Eastern Necropolis (in purple areas), and City of Amvrakia (inside the grey perimeter; Papadopoulou et al. 2021).

around 100 individuals. The fragmented state of skeletal preservation in both Necropolises posed an interesting challenge of creating a proper database for commingled and individual burial (Adams and Konigsberg 2008) as well as establishing a convenient methodology for filtering and selecting the most appropriate samples for isotope analysis.

The methodology was designed on the basis of novel approaches to data collection and FAIR (Findable, Accessible, Interoperable, Reusable) principles (Schmidt and Marwick 2020). Proprietary software is used as minimally as possible and only for transitioning from old but established methodologies into new tools based on free and preferably open-source software. The principle behind this is to maximise the longevity of data and maintain their expediency. In particular, we create R programming language scripts that correlate paleodemographic, palaeopathological, osteometric and isotope data by following revised methodology and utilising free cloud webware.To adhere to each tenet of FAIR principles, meticulous scrutiny was applied to the processes of material management and data documentation.

First of all, findability of osteological material was facilitated through the implementation of a carefully devised file storage protocol, informed by internationally recognised guidelines (Buikstra and Ubelaker 1994; Schwartz 1995; Scheuer and Black 2000; Hillson 2005; Lewis 2007; Schaefer et al. 2009; White et al. 2012; Nikita 2017; Seguchi and Dudzik 2019; Nikita and Karligkioti 2020). All files were systematically recorded and stored locally, leveraging the cloud-based service provided by Dropbox. This approach not only ensures accessibility but also offers robust mechanisms for file integrity preservation, enabling restoration to previous versions in cases of file corruption. Additionally, the platform extends the option to share files publicly, enhancing accessibility and dissemination.

Data pertaining to storage were meticulously documented in spreadsheets, utilising file formats such as .ods or .xlsx. Demographic, pathological, and osteometric data, on the other hand, were systematically recorded in databases, employing file formats like .odb or .accdb. To facilitate statistical analyses, databases were exported to spreadsheets in the .csv format, ensuring compatibility and ease of manipulation.

The skeletal material was securely stored within the infrastructure of the archaeological museum in Arta (Greece) to facilitate accessibility for researchers. To further ensure accessibility on the aspect of data, we have proposed the use of governmental servers so that future researchers can have remote access to the data. Despite the fact that the Greek legal framework has not yet addressed the matter, there are indications that it will do so in the near future (Ελληνική Κυβέρνηση / Hellenic Republic 2015).

The selection of file types and platforms, whether local or cloud-based, facilitates interoperability. Given the swift pace of technological advancement, it is essential to employ files and platforms that ensure medium-term data usage across diverse computational systems. This approach remains crucial until novel technologies offer alternative solutions to preserve interoperability.

The utilisation of foundational file formats –such as .csv– particularly in conjunction with programming in R (Marwick 2017), facilitates the reusability of both data analysis procedures and the raw data itself. The R programming language safeguards the sustainability of data analysis processes, even amidst alterations in the file formats currently employed for statistical analysis brought about by technological advancements (RStudio Team 2020). Leveraging R programming packages capable of seamlessly converting file formats enhances the adaptability of data files for future applications.

We create databases based on international bibliography and protocols created in the Laboratory of Biological Anthropology of Democritus University of Thrace. We use naked-eye observation to record the morphoscopical traits for age calculation and sex determination and the pathological lesions for palaeopathology study. Moreover, we use endoscopy to record specific pathologic lesions – e.g., Hyperostosis Frontalis Interna – in the endocranium. Lastly, we use digital osteometric tools to record dimensions of bones that can facilitate height calculation.

We create a pipeline of procedures that begin with the recording of bioarchaeological and biochemical data and finish with their statistical analysis while valuable insights are generated alongside a webware environment. We use open-source databases and spreadsheets in digital repositories for recording and storing data and R (Marwick 2017) as the programming language for creating webware applications that process the data (RStudio Team 2020). We utilise R packages[1] to facilitate database management, data tidying, and statistical analyses in addition to the default packages provided by the R programming language.

Statistical analysis follows the standard methodology employed in bioarchaeological studies (Sokal and Rohlf 2012; Baxter and Cool 2016; Nikita 2020). Descriptive statistical analysis aims to gain a general overview of the data and explore potential patterns in its distribution. Specifically, we analyse the distribution of age groups and biological sex. Additionally, bone measurements are examined to compute measures such as mean, median, and dispersion. Furthermore, the frequency and distributions of dental lesions, osteoarthritic lesions as well as cranial and post-cranial lesions are analysed.

Based on the results of descriptive statistics, more elaborate statistical analysis is employed. Exploratory Data Analysis is conducted in order to investigate the correlation between bone measurements and age by using techniques such as scatterplots, histograms, and correlation matrices (Vark and Howells 1984).

Predictive Modelling is anticipated to be employed only if the samples and data are considered sufficient and reliable. In this case, the correlation of bone measurements for biological sex inference is examined through regression analysis (Viciano et al. 2013). Hypothesis testing, including t-tests, chi-square tests, ANOVA, and correlation tests, is also conducted to test correlations between parameters and unravel differences between groups e.g., between males and females (Nikita et al. 2013). Bayesian statistics is employed to explore age of death based on new data derived from prior knowledge. This field provides an insight into the data, enhancing the interpretation of parameters (Hens and Godde 2020). Survival Analysis is utilised to estimate the risk of disease occurrence between groups. The time to event occurrence, such as the time between disease onset and individual death, is estimated using techniques such as Kaplan-Meier estimation and Cox proportional hazards regression (Kubehl and Temple 2020). Multivariate Analysis is applied to examine correlations between morphological and metric characteristics and to identify patterns (Calce et al. 2017). Techniques to be applied include Principal Component Analysis, Factor Analysis, and Cluster Analysis.

1 A short but comprehensive list of the relevant packages includes *readxl* (Wickham and Bryan 2023), *tidyverse* (Wickham et al. 2019), *writexl* (Ooms 2024), *gtsummary* (Sjoberg et al. 2021), *ggplot2* (Wickham 2009), *shiny* ("Rstudio/Shiny" [2012] 2022).

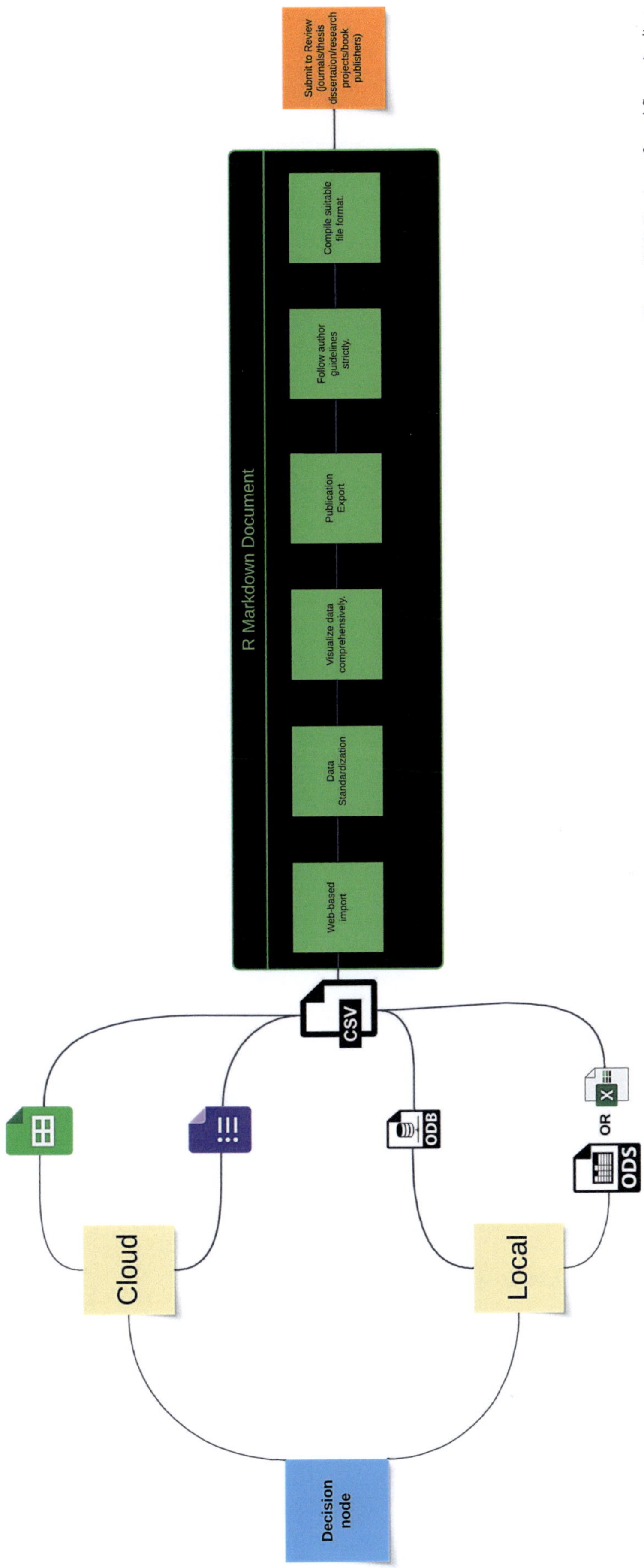

Figure 27.3. Design of workflow pipeline.

27.2.1 Workflow Pipeline

27.2.1.1 Recording Data

Prior to commencing data recording, researchers must deliberate on the approach to be undertaken. This decision, as depicted in Figure 27.3, hinges primarily on the physical proximity of collaborators, which is contingent upon the accessibility of the study material.

In one scenario, Google Cloud environment is employed due to its provision of diverse tools facilitating simultaneous collaboration. Of particular significance is the integrated chat room feature, enabling real-time communication and swift resolution of data wrangling issues, thereby optimising time efficiency. The offline functionality is invaluable in situations where researchers opt to work within a browser environment, mitigating the risk of data loss in the event of internet connectivity disruptions. Upon reconnecting to the internet, cloud files are automatically updated, ensuring seamless collaboration and synchronisation of data across collaborators' files.

Alternatively, researchers may opt for Open Office spreadsheets and/or locally saved databases on Dropbox. In this setup, researchers work with their respective local databases and subsequently import them into the web-based application.

For researchers desiring bespoke cloud services, the option exists to leverage open-source technologies underlying cloud server environments such as ~okeanos (https://okeanos.grnet.gr). These "Infrastructures as a Service" (IaaS) can facilitate the online data collection even further in cases of remote research teams and collaborators.

After the decision is made, the researchers start gathering the data including demographic information, pathological indices, osteometric measurements, stable isotope and ancDNA samples.

27.2.1.2 Importing and Tidying Datasets

Datasets are uploaded onto the web-based application via drag-and-drop or local upload mechanisms. The application facilitates data table amalgamation while allowing for specific standardisation and data cleaning techniques such as NA omission and laterality determination for bilateral indices. Parameterisation protocols adhere to standard statistical analysis methodologies derived from pertinent literature pertaining to the research domain. In our case study, parameterisation is informed by literature on age estimation, sex determination, height estimation, dental pathology, and isotope analysis.[2]

After thorough data cleaning is conducted, the data are preprocessed to identify and rectify any errors, inconsistencies, or missing values in the datasets. Quality control measures are implemented to assess the reliability and validity of the collected data, including checks for sample contamination, data outliers, and measurement errors (Sokal and Rohlf 2009; Baxter 2012; Nikita 2020).

27.2.1.3 Analyses and Publication

Following parameter definition, the application generates descriptive tables and correlation plots. Subsequently, researchers engage in result discussions and formulate conclusions that inform the formulation of new research inquiries. Relevant features and variables from both osteological and biochemical datasets are identified during this process in order to address the research questions and/or hypotheses. Statistical analyses explore the relationships among osteological and biochemical variables and the findings are further interpreted by researchers so that implicit biological or social mechanisms can be discovered (Reitsema and McIlvaine 2014; Kyle et al. 2020).

The final step offers researchers the option to export results in a suitable publication format (e.g., CSV, PDF, HTML, DOC, PNG). Researchers are required to input requisite values as stipulated in the author guidelines. Initial tool iterations incorporate typical requirements such as DPI values, table/picture dimensions, and file formats. Future iterations are planned to accommodate additional specifications as necessitated by relevant author guidelines. A preliminary draft of R Markdown document is provided at DOI:10.5281/zenodo.14013053 as a sample of the aforementioned pipeline.

27.3 Discussion

The study is still ongoing as part of the corresponding author's PhD studies and the discussed applications, codes and results are to be expected. The need to integrate archaeological data such as grave findings and burial datings in future studies ordained the study – from its initial stages already– to set an open framework for collecting data. Therefore, this methodology is considered

2 For more detailed bibliography on the relevant fields of bioarchaeological analysis see: **age calculation** (Buckberry and Chamberlain 2002; Kemkes-Grottenthaler 2002; Schaefer et al. 2009; Al Qahtani et al. 2010; Παπαγεωργοπούλου et al. 2015b), **sex determination** (Walrath et al. 2004; Walker 2008; Klales et al. 2012; Viciano et al. 2013; Passalacqua et al. 2013; Rennie and Ohman 2014; Παπαγεωργοπούλου et al. 2015b; Brůžek et al. 2017), **height estimation** (Raxter et al. 2006; Παπαγεωργοπούλου et al. 2015a; Raxter and Ruff 2018; Koukli et al. 2023), **dental pathology** (Scott 1979; Smith 1984; Šlaus et al. 2004; Boldsen 2007; Keenleyside 2008; Garcin et al. 2010; D'Anastasio et al. 2013; Rathmann et al. 2017; Rathmann et al. 2019; Primeau et al. 2018; Beck and Smith 2019), **cranial pathology** (Hershkovitz et al. 1999; Keenleyside and Panayotova 2006; Walker et al. 2009; Rinaldo et al. 2019; Godde and Hens 2021), **postcranial pathology** (Waldron 2009; DeWitte 2014; Manzon and Gualdi-Russo 2016; Calce et al. 2017; Ventades et al. 2018; Rinaldo et al. 2019; Kinkopf et al. 2021) and **isotope data** (Reitsema et al. 2022).

adaptable to further implementations of research tools and integrations with "Little Minions in Archaeology" as introduced by the CAA community in 2018.

The use of more powerful database tools – such as MySQL, PostgreSQL, SqLite, MicrosoftSQL Server and Oracle Database – is also worth bringing into discussion as it can effectively enhance the methodology of storing material and recording data. However, these tools require a more sophisticated training for anthropologists and therefore can intimidate them before even starting to build their databases. On the other hand, the use of R programming language is considered to be the most appropriate tool for this line of work as it is easier to learn and can handle the amount of data that anthropologists are usually called to deal with (Adler 2010).

In conclusion, we hail the opportunity to advance bioarchaeological studies through simulation models equivalent to the ones that have been presented in archaeological literature in the last decade (Chliaoutakis 2020). The opportunity is at hand. Human osteoarchaeological material can become a valuable source of input data for simulation models only if bioarchaeologists decide to add programming skills to their scientific quiver.

Acknowledgements

The authors express their acknowledgements to all the collaborators participating as members of the research consortium APOIKIA (https://www.apoikia.org). All of them equally created a synergistic and productive environment that is all the more needed in the Humanities. Sincere appreciation is due to the reviewing committee provided by PCI Archaeology. Recommender Christianne Fernee and two anonymous reviewers have offered valuable insights during the preprint evaluation phase.

Funding

We acknowledge support of this work by the project "ΑΠΟΙΚΙΑ: Ancient DNA analysis in novel multidisciplinary approach of ancient Corinthian colonisation. Ancient Amvrakia and Ancient Tenea as demonstration examples." (MIS 5056266) which is implemented under the Special Action "Open Innovation In Culture" funded by the Operational Programme "Competitiveness, Entrepreneurship and Innovation 2014-2020 (EPAnEK)" implemented under Regional Operational Programs of the Partnership and Cooperation Agreement (NSRF 2014-2020) and co-financed by Greece and the European Union (European Regional Development Fund).

Conflict of interest disclosure

The authors declare that they comply with the PCI rule of having no financial conflicts of interest in relation to the content of the article.

Peer review

This article has been reviewed and recommended by PCI Archaeology.

Fernee, C. 2024. "Establishing a workflow for recording and analysing bioarchaeological data." *Peer Community in Archaeology* 100396. 10.24072/pci.archaeo.100396.

References

Adams, Bradley J., and Lyle W. Konigsberg. 2008. "How Many People? Determining the Number of Individuals Represented by Commingled Human Remains." In *Recovery, Analysis, and Identification of Commingled Human Remains*, 241–55. Humana Press. DOI:10.1007/978-1-59745-316-5_12.

Adler, Joseph. 2010. *R in a Nutshell, 1st Ed.* Sebastopol, CA: O'Reilly.

AlQahtani, Sakher J., Mark P. Hector, and Helen M. Liversidge. 2010. "Brief Communication: The London Atlas of Human Tooth Development and Eruption." *American Journal of Physical Anthropology* 142 (3): 481–90. DOI:10.1002/ajpa.21258.

Bartholdy, Bjørn Peare, Menno L. P. Hoogland, and Andrea Waters-Rist. 2019. "How Old Are You Now? A New Ageing Method for Nonadults Based on Dental Wear." *International Journal of Osteoarchaeology*, April: oa.2758. DOI:10.1002/oa.2758.

Baxter, Mike. 2012. "R-Chaeology." Academia.edu. https://www.academia.edu/3380479/R-chaeology.

Baxter, Mike, and Hilary Cool. 2016. "Basic Statistical Graphics for Archaeology with R: Life Beyond Excel". Academia.edu. https://www.academia.edu/29415755/Basic_Statistical_Graphics_for_Archaeology_with_R_Life_Beyond_Excel_R_code.

Beck, Jess, and Bennett Holly Smith. 2019. "Don't Throw the Baby Teeth out with the Bathwater: Estimating Subadult Age Using Tooth Wear in Commingled Archaeological Assemblages." *International Journal of Osteoarchaeology* 29 (5): 831–42. DOI:10.1002/oa.2802.

Berg, Gregory E., and Michael W. Kenyhercz. 2017. "Introducing Human Mandible Identification [(Hu)

MANid]: A Free, Web-Based GUI to Classify Human Mandibles." *Journal of Forensic Sciences* 62 (6): 1592–98. DOI:10.1111/1556-4029.13479.

Boldsen, Jesper L. 2007. "Early Childhood Stress and Adult Age Mortality – A Study of Dental Enamel Hypoplasia in the Medieval Danish Village of Tirup." *American Journal of Physical Anthropology* 132 (1): 59–66. DOI:10.1002/ajpa.20467.

Brůžek, Jaroslav, Frédéric Santos, Bruno Dutailly, Pascal Murail, and Eugenia Cunha. 2017. "Validation and Reliability of the Sex Estimation of the Human Os Coxae Using Freely Available DSP2 Software for Bioarchaeology and Forensic Anthropology: BRŮŽEK et Al." *American Journal of Physical Anthropology* 164 (2): 440–9. DOI:10.1002/ajpa.23282.

Buckberry, Jo L., and Andrew T. Chamberlain. 2002. "Age Estimation from the Auricular Surface of the Ilium: A Revised Method." *American Journal Physical Anthropology* 119 (3): 231–9. DOI:10.1002/ajpa.10130.

Buikstra, Jane E., and Douglas H. Ubelaker (eds). 1994. *Standards for Data Collection from Human Skeletal Remains: Proceedings of a Seminar at the Field Museum of Natural History, Organized by Jonathan Haas*. Fayetteville, AR: Arkansas Archeological Survey.

Calce, Stephanie E., Helen K. Kurki, Darlene A. Weston, and Lisa Gould. 2017. "Principal Component Analysis in the Evaluation of Osteoarthritis." *American Journal of Physical Anthropology* 162 (3): 476–90. DOI:10.1002/ajpa.23130.

Caruso, Antonio, Anna Karligkioti, Gkampriella Selempa, and Efthymia Nikita. 2023. "STARC OSTEOARCH: An Open Access Resource for Recording and Sharing Human Osteoarchaeological Data." *International Journal of Osteoarchaeology* 33 (5): 973–5. DOI:10.1002/oa.3256.

Caruso, Antonio, and Efthymia Nikita. 2024. "Dental Diseases and Dental Wear as a Proxy for Dietary Patterns in Hellenistic-Early Roman Menainon, Sicily." *International Journal of Paleopathology* 44: 10–9. DOI:10.1016/j.ijpp.2023.11.002.

Colleter, Rozenn, Jean-Baptiste Romain, and Jean-Baptiste Barreau. 2020. "HumanOS: An Open Source Nomadic Software Database for Physical Anthropology and Archaeology." *Virtual Archaeology Review* 11 (23): 94. DOI:10.4995/var.2020.13422.

Constantinou, Chrysovalantis, and Efthymia Nikita. 2022. "SexEst: An Open Access Web Application for Metric Skeletal Sex Estimation." *International Journal of Osteoarchaeology* 32 (4): 832–44. DOI:10.1002/oa.3109.

D'Anastasio, Ruggero, Deneb T. Cesana, Joan Viciano, Maria Sciubba, P. Nibaruta, and Luigi Capasso. 2013. "The Possible Correlation between Dental Enamel Hypoplasia and a Historic Natural Disaster in the Roman Population of Herculaneum (79 AD? Central Italy)." *Anthropologischer Anzeiger*, December, 369–83. DOI:10.1127/0003-5548/2013/0312.

DeWitte, Sharon N. 2014. "Differential Survival among Individuals with Active and Healed Periosteal New Bone Formation." *International Journal of Paleopathology* 7: 38–44. DOI:10.1016/j.ijpp.2014.06.001.

Garcin, Virginie, Petr Velemínský, Pavel Trefný, Alduc Le Bagousse, Arnaud Lefebvre, and Jaroslav Bruzek. 2010. "Dental Health and Lifestyle in Four Early Mediaeval Juvenile Populations: Comparisons between Urban and Rural Individuals, and between Coastal and Inland Settlements." *HOMO* 61 (6): 421–39. DOI:10.1016/j.jchb.2010.06.004.

Georgiadou, Angeliki, Elissavet Ganiatsou, Kiriakos Xanthopoulos, and Christina Papageorgopoulou. 2023. "Estimating the Human Diet in the Ancient Greek Colony of Ambracia Using Stable Isotopes (δ15N, δ13C) and Bayesian Mixing Model." Paper presented at *EAA2023, Belfast, 30 August - 2 September*.

Godde, Kanya, and Samantha M. Hens. 2021. "An Epidemiological Approach to the Analysis of Cribra Orbitalia as an Indicator of Health Status and Mortality in Medieval and Post-medieval London under a Model of Parasitic Infection." *American Journal of Physical Anthropology* 174 (4): 631–45. DOI:10.1002/ajpa.24244.

Hens, Samantha M., and Kanya Godde. 2020. "New Approaches to Age Estimation Using Palatal Suture Fusion." *Journal of Forensic Sciences* 65 (5): 1406–15. DOI:10.1111/1556-4029.14485.

Hershkovitz, Israel, Charles Greenwald, Bruce M. Rothschild, Bruce Latimer, Olivier Dutour, Lyman M. Jellema, and Susanne Wish-Baratz. 1999. "Hyperostosis Frontalis Interna: An Anthropological Perspective." *American Journal of Physical Anthropology* 109 (3): 303–25. DOI:10.1002/(SICI)1096-8644(199907)109:3<303::AID-AJPA3>3.0.CO;2-I.

Hillson, Simon. 2005. *Teeth*. Cambridge: Cambridge University Press. DOI:10.1017/CBO9780511614477.

Hunt, Gill. 2019. "Skelly-Pad." United Kingdom: Hunt Lancaster Ltd.

Keenleyside, A. 2008. "Dental Pathology and Diet at Apollonia, a Greek Colony on the Black Sea." *International Journal of Osteoarchaeology* 18 (3): 262–79. DOI:10.1002/oa.934.

Keenleyside, Anne, and Kristina Panayotova. 2006. "Cribra Orbitalia and Porotic Hyperostosis in a Greek Colonial Population (5th to 3rd Centuries BC) from the Black Sea." *International Journal of Osteoarchaeology* 16 (5): 373–84. DOI:10.1002/oa.831.

Kemkes-Grottenthaler, Ariane. 2002. "Aging through the Ages: Historical Perspectives on Age Indicator Methods." In *Paleodemography: Age Distributions from Skeletal Samples*, edited by Robert D. Hoppa and James W. Vaupel, 48–72. Cambridge Studies in Biological and Evolutionary Anthropology. Cambridge: Cambridge University Press. DOI:10.1017/CBO9780511542428.004.

Kinkopf, Katherine M., Sabrina C. Agarwal, Caroline Goodson, Patrick D. Beauchesne, Trent M. Trombley, Francesca Candilio, Mauro Rubini, and Alfredo Coppa. 2021. "Economic Access Influences Degenerative Spine Disease Outcomes at Rural Late Medieval Villamagna (Lazio, IT)." *American Journal of Physical Anthropology* 174 (3): 500–518. DOI:10.1002/ajpa.24180.

Klales, Alexandra R. 2020. "MorphoPASSE: Morphological Pelvis and Skull Sex Estimation Program." In *Sex Estimation of the Human Skeleton*, 271–8. Academic Press. DOI:10.1016/B978-0-12-815767-1.00016-X.

Klales, Alexandra R., Stephen D. Ousley, and Jennifer M. Vollner. 2012. "A Revised Method of Sexing the Human Innominate Using Phenice's Nonmetric Traits and Statistical Methods." *American Journal of Physical Anthropology* 149 (1): 104–14. DOI:10.1002/ajpa.22102.

Koukli, Marianna, Frank Siegmund, and Christina Papageorgopoulou. 2023. "Stature Estimation in Ancient Greece: Population-Specific Equations and Secular Trends from 9000 BC to 900 AD." *Archaeological and Anthropological Sciences* 15 (5): 53. DOI:10.1007/s12520-023-01744-1.

Kubehl, Kayla, and Daniel H. Temple. 2020. "Reproductive Life Histories Influence Cariogenesis: Exploring Sex-Specific Variation in Dental Caries and Survivorship in the Human Past." *American Journal of Physical Anthropology* 172 (3): 376–85. DOI:10.1002/ajpa.24034.

Kyle, Britney, Eduard Shehi, Marlon Koçi, and Laurie J. Reitsema. 2020. "Bioarchaeological Reconstruction of Physiological Stress during Social Transition in Albania." *International Journal of Paleopathology* 30: 118–29. DOI:10.1016/j.ijpp.2020.06.003.

Lewis, Mary E. 2007. *The Bioarchaeology of Children: Perspectives from Biological and Forensic Anthropology*. Cambridge University Press.

Manzon, Vanessa S., and Emanuela Gualdi-Russo. 2016. "Health Patterns of the Etruscan Population (6th–3rd Centuries BC) in Northern Italy: The Case of Spina." *International Journal of Osteoarchaeology* 26 (3): 490–501. DOI:10.1002/oa.2438.

Marwick, Ben. 2017. "Computational Reproducibility in Archaeological Research: Basic Principles and a Case Study of Their Implementation." *Journal of Archaeological Method and Theory* 24 (2): 424–50. DOI:10.1007/s10816-015-9272-9.

Nikita, Efthymia. 2017. *Osteoarchaeology: A Guide to the Macroscopic Study of Human Skeletal Remains*. Amsterdam: Elsevier/Academic Press.

Nikita, Efthymia. 2020. *Introduction to Statistics Using R (for archaeologists)*. Nicosia: The Cyprus Institute. https://repository.cyi.ac.cy/handle/CyI/1170.

Nikita, Efthymia, and Anna Karligkioti. 2020. *Basic Guidelines for the Excavation and Study of Human Skeletal Remains*. Zenodo. DOI:10.5281/zenodo.4641953.

Nikita, Efthymia, David Mattingly, and Marta Mirazón Lahr. 2013. "Methodological Considerations in the Statistical Analysis of Degenerative Joint and Disc Disease." *International Journal of Paleopathology* 3 (2): 105–12. DOI:10.1016/j.ijpp.2013.03.002.

Ooms, Jeroen. 2024. "writexl: Export Data Frames to Excel 'xlsx' Format". https://docs.ropensci.org/writexl/.

Ossenberg, Nancy. 2013. "Brief Communication: Cranial Nonmetric Trait Database on the Internet." *Am. J. Phys. Anthropol.* October. DOI:10.1002/ajpa.22377.

Passalacqua, Nicholas V., Zhen Zhang, and Steven J. Pierce. 2013. "Sex Determination of Human Skeletal Populations Using Latent Profile Analysis: Sex Determination of Human Skeletal Populations." *American Journal of Physical Anthropology* 151 (4): 538–43. DOI:10.1002/ajpa.22295.

Primeau, Charlotte, Preben Homøe, and Niels Lynnerup. 2018. "Childhood Health as Reflected in Adult Urban and Rural Samples from Medieval Denmark." *HOMO* 69 (1): 6–16. DOI:10.1016/j.jchb.2018.03.004.

Rathmann, Hannes, Giulia Saltini Semerari, and Katerina Harvati. 2017. "Evidence for Migration Influx into the Ancient Greek Colony of Metaponto: A Population Genetics Approach Using Dental Nonmetric Traits." *International Journal of Osteoarchaeology* 27 (3): 453–64. DOI:10.1002/oa.2569.

Rathmann, Hannes, Britney Kyle, Efthymia Nikita, Katerina Harvati, and Giulia Saltini Semerari. 2019. "Population History of Southern Italy during Greek Colonization Inferred from Dental Remains." *American Journal of Physical Anthropology* 170 (4): 519–34. DOI:10.1002/ajpa.23937.

Raxter, Michelle H., Benjamin M. Auerbach, and Christopher B. Ruff. 2006. "Revision of the Fully Technique for Estimating Statures." *American Journal of Physical Anthropology* 130 (3): 374–84. DOI:10.1002/ajpa.20361.

Raxter, Michelle H., and Christopher B. Ruff. 2018. "Full Skeleton Stature Estimation." In *New Perspectives in Forensic Human Skeletal Identification*, edited by Krista E. Latham, Eric J. Bartelink, and Michael Finnegan, 105–13. Academic Press. DOI:10.1016/B978-0-12-805429-1.00010-7.

Reitsema, Laurie J., Britney Kyle, Marlon Koçi, Rachel N. Horton, Katherine L. Reinberger, Surja Lela, and Eduard Shehi. 2022. "Bioarchaeological Evidence for Ancient Human Diet and Migration at Epidamnus/Dyrrachion and Apollonia in Illyria, Albania."

Archaeological and Anthropological Sciences 14 (5): 87. DOI:10.1007/s12520-022-01553-y.

Reitsema, Laurie J., and Britney Kyle McIlvaine. 2014. "Reconciling "Stress" and "Health" in Physical Anthropology: What Can Bioarchaeologists Learn from the Other Subdisciplines?" *American Journal of Physical Anthropology* 155 (2): 181–5. DOI:10.1002/ajpa.22596.

Rennie, Samuel, and James C. Ohman. 2014. "Hips Don't Lie: A Multivariate Approach to Sex Determination from Complete and Fragmentary Pelves." DOI:10.13140/2.1.3760.2883.

Rinaldo, Natascia, Nicoletta Zedda, Barbara Bramanti, Irene Rosa, and Emanuela Gualdi-Russo. 2019. "How Reliable Is the Assessment of Porotic Hyperostosis and Cribra Orbitalia in Skeletal Human Remains? A Methodological Approach for Quantitative Verification by Means of a New Evaluation Form." *Archaeological and Anthropological Sciences* 11 (7): 3549–59. DOI:10.1007/s12520-019-00780-0.

RStudio Team. 2020. *RStudio: Integrated Development Environment for R*. Boston: RStudio, PBC. http://www.rstudio.com/.

"Rstudio/Shiny". (2012) 2022. R. RStudio. https://github.com/rstudio/shiny.

Schaefer, Maureen, Louise Scheuer, and Sue M. Black. 2009. *Juvenile Osteology: A Laboratory and Field Manual*. Amsterdam / Burlington, MA: Elsevier / Academic Press.

Scheuer, Louise, and Sue M. Black. 2000. *Developmental Juvenile Osteology*. San Diego: Academic Press.

Schwartz, Jeffrey H. 1995. *Skeleton Keys: An Introduction to Human Skeletal Morphology, Development, and Analysis*. New York: Oxford University Press.

Scott, E. C. 1979. "Dental Wear Scoring Technique." *American Journal of Physical Anthropology* 51 (2): 213–7. DOI:10.1002/ajpa.1330510208.

Scott, G. Richard, Marin A. Pilloud, David Navega, João d'Oliveira Coelho, Eugénia Cunha, and Joel D. Irish. 2018. "rASUDAS: A New Web-Based Application for Estimating Ancestry from Tooth Morphology." *Forensic Anthropology* 1 (1): 18–31. DOI:10.5744/fa.2018.0003.

Seguchi, Noriko, and Beatrix Dudzik (eds). 2019. *3d Data Acquisition for Bioarchaeology, Forensic Anthropology, and Archaeology*. San Diego: Elsevier.

Sjoberg, Daniel D., Karissa Whiting, Michael Curry, Jessica A. Lavery, and Joseph Larmarange. 2021. "Reproducible Summary Tables with the Gtsummary Package." *The R Journal* 13 (1): 570–580. DOI:10.32614/RJ-2021-053.

Šlaus, Mario, Nives Pećina-Šlaus, and Hrvoje Brkić. 2004. "Life Stress on the Roman Limes in Continental Croatia." *HOMO* 54 (3): 240–63. DOI:10.1078/0018-442X-00072.

Smith, B. Holly. 1984. "Patterns of Molar Wear in Hunter–Gatherers and Agriculturalists." *American Journal of Physical Anthropology* 63 (1): 39–56. DOI:10.1002/ajpa.1330630107.

Sokal, Robert R., and F. James Rohlf. 2009. *Introduction to Biostatistics, 2nd Ed.* Mineola, NY: Dover Publications.

Sokal, Robert R., and F. James Rohlf. 2012. *Biometry: The Principles and Practice of Statistics in Biological Research, 4th Ed.* New York: W.H. Freeman and Company

Van Vark, Gerrit. N., and William W. Howells. 1984. *Multivariate Statistical Methods in Physical Anthropology: A Review of Recent Advances and Current Developments*. Dordrecht: Springer. DOI:10.1007/978-94-009-6357-3.

Ventades, Nerea G., Imanol M. Laza, Montserrat Hervella, and Concepción de-la-Rúa. 2018. "A Recording Form for Differential Diagnosis of Arthropathies." *International Journal of Paleopathology* 20: 45–9. DOI:10.1016/j.ijpp.2018.01.004.

Viciano, Joan, Sandra López-Lázaro, and Inmaculada Alemán. 2013. "Sex Estimation Based on Deciduous and Permanent Dentition in a Contemporary Spanish Population." *American Journal of Physical Anthropology* 152 (1): 31–43. DOI:10.1002/ajpa.22324.

Waldron, Tony. 2009. *Palaeopathology*. Cambridge: Cambridge University Press. DOI:10.1017/CBO9780511812569.

Walker, Phillip L. 2008. "Sexing Skulls Using Discriminant Function Analysis of Visually Assessed Traits." *Am. J. Phys. Anthropol.* 136 (1): 39–50. DOI:10.1002/ajpa.20776.

Walker, Phillip L., Rhonda R. Bathurst, Rebecca Richman, Thor Gjerdrum, and Valerie A. Andrushko. 2009. "The Causes of Porotic Hyperostosis and Cribra Orbitalia: A Reappraisal of the Iron-Deficiency-Anemia Hypothesis." *American Journal of Physical Anthropology* 139 (2): 109–25. DOI:10.1002/ajpa.21031.

Walrath, Dana E., Paul Turner, and Jaroslav Bruzek. 2004. "Reliability Test of the Visual Assessment of Cranial Traits for Sex Determination." *American Journal of Physical Anthropology* 125 (2): 132–7. DOI:10.1002/ajpa.10373.

White, Tim D., Michael T. Black, and Pieter A. Folkens. 2012. *Human Osteology, 3rd Ed.* San Diego: Academic Press.

White, William. 2007. "Databases." In *Advances in Human Palaeopathology, 1st Ed.*, edited by Ron Pinhasi and Simon Mays, 177–88. Chichester: John Wiley and Sons. DOI:10.1002/9780470724187.ch9.

Wickham, Hadley. 2009. *Ggplot2*. New York: Springer. DOI:10.1007/978-0-387-98141-3.

Wickham, Hadley and Jennifer Bryan. 2023. readxl: Read Excel Files. https://CRAN.R-project.org/package=readxl.

Wickham, Hadley, Mara Averick, Jennifer Bryan, Winston Chang, Lucy McGowan, Romain François, Garrett Grolemund, Alex Hayes, Lionel Henry, Jim Hester,

Max Kuhn, Thomas Lin Pedersen, Evan Miller, Stephan Milton Bache, Kirill Müller, Jeroen Ooms, David Robinson, Dana Paige Seidel, Vitalie Spinu, Kohske Takahashi, Davis Vaughan, Claus Wilke, Kara Woo, and Hiroaki Yutani. 2019. "Welcome to the Tidyverse." *Journal of Open Source Software* 4 (43): 1686. DOI:10.21105/joss.01686.

Ελληνική Κυβέρνηση / Hellenic Republic. 2015. *Εθνική Στρατηγική Έξυπνης Εξειδικευσης*. http://www.gsrt.gr//central.aspx?sId=110I458I1163I646I453967&olID=402&neID=589&neTa=1_1034&ncID=0&neHC=0&tbid=0&lrID=2&oldUIID=aI402I0I100I271I941I0I1&actionID=load.

Παπαγεωργοπούλου, Χριστίνα, Κωνσταντίνος Μωραΐτης, Ευθυμία Νικήτα, Κωνσταντίνος Ηλιόπουλος, και Ευφροσύνη Βήκα. 2015a. "Προσδιορισμός του αναστήματος και του βάρους σώματος: μεθοδολογικά ζητήματα και διαχρονικές τάσεις." In *Ειδικά Θέματα Σκελετικής Ανθρωπολογίας, Ταφονομίας και Βιοαρχαιολογίας*. ΚΑΛΛΙΠΟΣ. https://repository.kallipos.gr/handle/11419/4763.

Παπαγεωργοπούλου, Χριστίνα, Κωνσταντίνος Μωραΐτης, Ευθυμία Νικήτα, Κωνσταντίνος Ηλιόπουλος, και Ευφροσύνη Βήκα. 2015b. "Προσδιορισμός του φύλου και εκτίμηση ηλικίας θανάτου στον ανθρώπινο σκελετό." In *Ειδικά Θέματα Σκελετικής Ανθρωπολογίας, Ταφονομίας και Βιοαρχαιολογίας*. https://repository.kallipos.gr/handle/11419/4762.

Παπαδοπούλου, Βαρβάρα, Αριστείδης Βάσιος, Δήμητρα Παπακώστα, and Κυριάκος Ξανθόπουλος. 2021. "ΑΠΟΙΚΙΑ Ένα Ερευνητικό Πρόγραμμα Ανασύστασης Της Πληθυσμιακής Εικόνας Της Αμβρακίας Την Εποχή Του Κορινθιακού Αποικισμού." *Θέματα Αρχαιολογίας* 5 (1): 112–23.

Editor biographies

Philip Verhagen is associate professor at the Faculty of Social Sciences and Humanities, Vrije Universiteit Amsterdam, specialized in computer applications and quantitative methods in archaeology, with an emphasis on GIS, spatial analysis and modelling. Dr. Verhagen's research focuses on the methodological and theoretical aspects of spatial analysis and modelling in landscape archaeology. He has published widely on archaeological predictive modelling and settlement pattern analysis, as well as on the application of agent-based modelling of ancient land use and demography and network analysis, focusing primarily on Roman archaeology in the Netherlands.

He has been Publication Officer of Computer Applications and Quantitative Methods (CAA) from 2011-2016 and is currently Managing Editor of the Journal of Computer Applications in Archaeology (JCAA). He is also Scientific Director of ARCHON, the Dutch Research School for Archaeology.

Main publications:

Verhagen, P., 2023. 'Centrality on the periphery: an analysis of rural settlement hierarchy in the Dutch part of the Roman limes'. Archaeological and Anthropological Sciences 15. DOI: 10.1007/s12520-023-01745-0

Verhagen, P., M. de Kleijn and J. Joyce. 2021. 'Different models, different outcomes? A comparison of approaches to land use modeling in the Dutch limes'. Heritage 4(3): 2081-2104. DOI: 10.3390/heritage4030118

Verhagen, P., S.A. Crabtree, H. Peeters and D. Raemaekers. 2021. 'Reconstructing human-centered interaction networks of the Swifterbant culture in the Dutch wetlands: An example from the ArchaeoEcology project'. Applied Sciences 11(11):4860. DOI: 10.3390/app11114860

Verhagen, P., J. Joyce and M.R. Groenhuijzen (eds). 2019. Finding the Limits of the Limes. Modelling Demography, Economy and Transport on the Edge of the Roman Empire. Cham: Springer. DOI: 10.1007/978-3-030-04576-0

Verhagen, P. and T.G. Whitley. 2012. 'Integrating Archaeological Theory and Predictive Modeling. A Live Report from the Scene'. Journal of Archaeological Method and Theory 19, 49-100. DOI: 10.1007/s10816-011-9102-7

Jitte Waagen's research engages with landscape archaeology, archaeological prospection, (UAS) remote sensing, imaging, Geo-ICT, statistics, 3D modeling, eXtended Reality and Blended Learning, with a focus on methodological development, reflection on processes of knowledge production and communication, as well as the adoption of technical methods in the general field of heritage studies. His fieldwork is spread throughout Europe, Asia and the Caribbean.

Recent publications:

Waagen, J., & Stek, T. D. (2025). Run to the Hills: A Stratified Sampling Approach to Site Clustering on High Grounds in Ancient Samnium (Molise, Italy). *Journal of Field Archaeology 50*(5), 397–407.

Waagen, J., & van Hilst, A. (2025). Drones over excavations – Enhancing the archaeologist's eyes. An empirical case study into the deployment of UAS remote sensing as a research tool for archaeological excavation, in Veldhoven, the Netherlands. *Journal of Archaeological Science: Reports, 62,* Article 105043.

Waagen, J., Scholte, L. M., Verhagen, J. W. H. P., Verschoof-van der Vaart, W. B., Visser, R., & Rensink, E. (2025). ARCfieldLAB: Stimulating Networks, Knowledge Exchange, and Experimentation in Applied Sensor Archaeology for Dutch Field Research. *Advances in Archaeological Practice* 13(4):599-612.

Waagen, J., & van Wijngaarden, G. J. (2024). Understanding Archaeological Site Topography: 3D Archaeology of Archaeology. Journal of Computer Applications in Archaeology, 7(1), 237-243.

Waagen, J., Lanjouw, T., & Huurdeman, H. (2024). Virtual Past Places: Reinventing the Classroom using Virtual Reality in Humanities Education. In I. Saloul, S. Berrebi, N. Munawar, & M. Panico (Eds.), AHM Conference 2024: 'Heritage, Memory and Material Culture' (pp. 85-91). (History, Culture, and Heritage; Vol. 3). Amsterdam University Press.

Ronald Visser is a senior lecturer in Archaeology and researcher for the lectorate Sustainable Areas and Soil Transitions at Saxion University of Applied Sciences. He is an interdisciplinary researcher focussing on archaeology, data science, dendrochronology, Roman period, conflict archaeology and education.

Main publications:

Fischer, A. D., H. van Londen, A. L. Blonk-van den Bercken, R. M. Visser, and J. Renes. 2021. Urban Farming and Ruralisation in the Netherlands (1250 up Tot the Nineteenth Century), Unravelling Farming Practice and the Use of (Open) Space by Synthesising Archaeological Reports Using Text Mining. Nederlandse Archeologische Rapporten 68. Rijksdienst voor het Cultureel Erfgoed. https://www.cultureelerfgoed.nl/publicaties/publicaties/2021/01/01/urban-farming-and-ruralisation-in-the-netherlands.

Marter, Phil, Ronald Visser, Pim Alders, et al. 2018. 'The Excavation of WWII RAF Bomber, Halifax LV881-ZA-V'. Journal of Conflict Archaeology 12 (1): 29–45. https://doi.org/10.1080/15740773.2017.1414423.

Visser, Ronald M. 2021. 'On the Similarity of Tree-Ring Patterns: Assessing the Influence of Semi-Synchronous Growth Changes on the Gleichläufigkeitskoeffizient for Big Tree-Ring Data Sets'. Archaeometry 63 (1): 204–15. https://doi.org/10.1111/arcm.12600.

Visser, Ronald M. 2025. 'Relating Roman Rings. An Interdisciplinary Study Using Archaeology, Data Science and Tree Rings to Understand Timber Provision in the German Provinces of the Roman Empire'. PhD Thesis, Vrije Universiteit. https://doi.org/10.5463/thesis.1062.

Visser, Ronald M., Karsten Lambers, Kenneth Aitchison, et al. 2025. 'Lessons Learned: Creating Tutorials to Teach Agent-Based Modelling to Archaeologists'. Journal of Computer Applications in Archaeology 8 (1): 354–67. https://doi.org/10.5334/jcaa.241.

Alex Brandsen worked as a PhD and postdoc at Leiden University, where he created an intelligent search engine for archaeological texts and worked extensively with text mining methods and large language models. He has been an organiser of the Digital Archaeology Group for 8 years, and is the Communications Officer of the CAA-NL-FL local chapter. He is currently working as Interoperability Project Lead at the Thematic Digital Competency Centre - Social Sciences and Humanities.

Recent publications:

Van den Dikkenberg, L., & Brandsen, A. (2025). Using Text Mining to Search for Neolithic Vlaardingen Culture Sites in the Rhine-Meuse-Scheldt Delta. Journal of Computer Applications in Archaeology, 8(1).

Tenzer, M., Pistilli, G., Brandsen, A., & Shenfield, A. (2024). Debating AI in Archaeology: applications, implications, and ethical considerations. Internet Archaeology, (67).

Brandsen, A. (2023). Information extraction and machine learning for archaeological texts. In Discourse and Argumentation in Archaeology: Conceptual and Computational Approaches (pp. 229-261). Cham: Springer International Publishing.

Brandsen, A., Verberne, S., Lambers, K., & Wansleeben, M. (2022). Can BERT dig it? Named entity recognition for information retrieval in the archaeology domain. Journal on Computing and Cultural Heritage (JOCCH), 15(3), 1-18.

Alain Queffelec is a specialist of archaeometry of lithic materials at the CNRS, based at the UMR5199 PACEA laboratory at the University of Bordeaux. He employs different techniques of spectroscopy and microscopy to characterize raw materials and archaeological artifacts from various periods and contexts, including the Ceramic Age of the Caribbean islands. Additionally, he devotes part of his time to Open Science initiatives, notably as the founder of PCI Archaeology.

Main publications:

Leck, A., Bellot-Gurlet, L., Carazzo, G., Gratuze, B., Langlade, J., Le Bourdonnec, F.-X., Leandri, C., Shearn, I., Stouvenot, C., and Queffelec, A., 2024, Obsidian in the Caribbean islands? Mysterious Ceramic Age glass artefacts in the Lesser Antilles, Archaeometry, 66(6), 1255–79. DOI: 10.1111/arcm.12980

Queffelec, A., 2023, Diversity and similarity in the Ceramic Age lapidary production in the Caribbean islands, Revista de Arqueología Americana(41), 191–244. DOI: 10.35424/rearam.v0i41.4308

Queffelec, A., Maureille, B., Arzarello, M., Blasco, R., Crandell, O., Doyon, L., Halcrow, S., Karoune, E., Ruiz-Redondo, A., and Van Peer, P., 2023, Peer Community In Archaeology: a community-driven free and transparent system for preprints peer-reviewing, Archeologia e Calcolatori, 34(1), 125–34. DOI: 10.19282/ac.34.1.2023.14

Queffelec, A., Bellot-Gurlet, L., Foy, E., Lefrais, Y., and Fritsch, E., 2021, First identification of sudoite in the Caribbean Ceramic Age lapidary craftsmanship, Gems and Gemology, 57(3), 206–26. DOI: 10.5741/GEMS.57.3.206

Queffelec, A., Fouéré, P., Bellot-Gurlet, L., and Bérard, B., 2020, Stone ornaments from Guadeloupe and Martinique Early Ceramic period sites (200 BC – AD 400), detailed analysis and comparison with a Late Ceramic period site (AD 750 – 1000), Journal of Caribbean Archaeology, 20, 1–44.

Devi Taelman is a postdoctoral researcher in Archaeology at the Vrije Universiteit Brussel (Belgium), affiliated with the research groups Interdisciplinary Historical Food Studies (FOST) and Archaeology, Environmental Changes & Geo-Chemistry (AMGC). His research focuses on human–environment interactions and economic networks in the Roman Mediterranean through an integrated approach combining material culture studies, archaeometry, landscape archaeology, and computational approaches.

Main publications:

Taelman, D., Erdkamp, P., Keenan-Jones, D., Heinrich, F.B.J., Hansen, A.M., Corona, C., Drysdale, R.N., Stoffel, M., Verdon-Kidd, D.C., Zanchetta, G. (in press). Climate and societal change in Central Italy, from Late Republic to Late Antiquity, in: Huebner, S.R., McDonald, B.T. (Eds.), The Roman Climate Optimum. Cham: Springer International Publishing.

Taelman, D. (2025). Mapping Architectural White Marble Use in Roman Italy: A Quantitative Study of Archaeometric Provenance Data. Rendiconti Lincei. Scienze Fisiche e Naturali 36, pp. 23–38.

Taelman, D. (2022). Marble trade in the Roman Mediterranean: a quantitative and diachronic study. Journal of Roman Archaeology 35, 848–875.

Taelman, D., Elburg, M., Smet, I., De Paepe, P., Lopes, L., Vanhaecke, F., & Vermeulen, F., (2013). Roman Marble from Lusitania: Petrographic and Geochemical Characterisation. Journal of Archaeological Science 40, 2227–2236.

Verhoeven, G., Taelman, D., & Vermeulen, F. (2012). Computer vision-based orthophoto mapping of complex archaeological sites: the ancient quarry of pitaranha (portugal-spain). Archaeometry 54, 1114–1129.